THE ART OF
TEACHING RUSSIAN

THE ART OF TEACHING RUSSIAN

EVGENY DENGUB, IRINA DUBININA,
and JASON MERRILL, *Editors*

Georgetown University Press / Washington, DC

Library of Congress Cataloging-in-Publication Data

Names: Dengub, Evgeny, editor. | Dubinina, Irina, editor. | Merrill, Jason, editor.
Title: The art of teaching Russian / Evgeny Dengub, Irina Dubinina, Jason Merrill, editors.
Description: Washington, DC : Georgetown University Press, 2020. | Includes bibliographical references and index.
Identifiers: LCCN 2019054590 (print) | LCCN 2019054591 (ebook) | ISBN 9781647120016 (hardcover) | ISBN 9781647120023 (paperback) | ISBN 9781647120030 (ebook)
Subjects: LCSH: Russian language—Study and teaching—United States. | Russian philology—Study and teaching—United States. | Russia—Civilization—Study and teaching—United States.
Classification: LCC PG2068.U5 A78 2020 (print) | LCC PG2068.U5 (ebook) | DDC 491.780071—dc23
LC record available at https://lccn.loc.gov/2019054590
LC ebook record available at https://lccn.loc.gov/2019054591

21 20 9 8 7 6 5 4 3 2 First printing

Cover design by Jeremy John Parker

To our mentors and students,
from whom we have learned so much

CONTENTS

ILLUSTRATIONS

FIGURES

TABLES

ACKNOWLEDGMENTS

The editors wish to express their sincere gratitude to all who contributed to *The Art of Teaching Russian: Research, Pedagogy, and Practice.* We greatly enjoyed the process of working with our colleagues in all the stages of the creation of this volume, from initial idea to final publication. We appreciate our authors' enthusiasm, responsiveness, patience, and openness to suggestions and feedback from their peers. This book is a collective effort that highlights each author's expertise, experience, and creativity.

This collection could not have been possible without the professional, expert insights of colleagues who were willing to review submissions and provide feedback on manuscript versions of the articles presented here. The following colleagues served as reviewers for this volume: Maria Alley, Thomas Beyer, Jennifer Bown, William Comer, Karen Evans-Romaine, Thomas Garza, Susan Gass, Victoria Hasko, Olga Kagan, Betty Lou Leaver, Maria Lekic, Cynthia Martin, Julia Mikhailova, Dianna Murphy, Maria Polinsky, Charlene Polio, David Prestel, Beckie Bray Rankin, Benjamin Rifkin, William Rivers, Richard Robin, Shannon Spasova, and Patti Spinner.

Our special gratitude goes to Karen Evans-Romaine and Benjamin Rifkin for their invaluable advice in the initial stages of this work. George Fowler has been an enthusiastic proponent of our project from the beginning, for which we are very grateful. We also would like to thank our editor, Hope LeGro, at Georgetown University Press.

Three universities provided financial support for this project: Amherst College, Brandeis University (through the Theodore and Jane Norman Fund for Faculty Research and Creative Projects in Arts and Sciences), and Middlebury College (through the Kathryn Wasserman Davis School of Russian and the Middlebury College Language Schools). We also thank Alex Gurvets (Amherst College) for helping prepare chapter manuscripts for review and Polina Potochevska (Brandeis University) for assisting with the formatting of the completed manuscripts.

Finally, we thank our families, friends, and colleagues who supported us as we were working on this volume.

INTRODUCTION

Evgeny Dengub, Irina Dubinina, and Jason Merrill

In the introduction to their 2000 volume *The Learning and Teaching of Slavic Languages and Cultures*, Olga Kagan and Benjamin Rifkin express the hope that "our future colleagues—our current students—will publish another volume on issues of critical importance" (p. 6). While the present collection is late in arriving—Kagan and Rifkin anticipated the next volume "by 2015"—we hope that it can be considered a next step in the development of research and best practices in teaching the Russian language. Kagan and Rifkin included other Slavic languages in their book, but given the scope of the volume and the number of topics, the editors of this volume decided to return to the precedent set by previous volumes and focus solely on the teaching and learning of Russian, although we hope that the ideas and suggestions presented in these chapters will be useful for our colleagues who teach other languages.

Several edited collections that have been published in the United States provide a snapshot of the field and the issues that were dominating it at the time of publication. These works set an excellent example for us throughout this project and demonstrate how Russian language pedagogy has developed over the last 40 years. Brecht and Davidson (1977) bring together Soviet and North American research on a variety of topics, all of which touch on "the appropriateness of the 'rationalist' or 'structural' approach for the presentation of grammar" (p. i). In 1983 Brecht et al. gathered groups of papers on "communicative competence," "the role of the native language," "the role of literature within the language curriculum," and linguistic accuracy (pp. 1–2). Lubensky and Jarvis (1984) organized their book into overviews of pedagogical materials, "suggestions for teaching the four language skills," "ideas on pedagogical games and language camps," and "the verb" (p. vii). Kagan and Rifkin (2000) report that the two largest "methodological developments" that influence their volume's contributions are "the proficiency movement," which was just beginning when Lubensky and Jarvis published their collection in 1984, and "the maturation of the discipline of second language acquisition," which they see in the several research projects focused on the acquisition of Russian (p. 1). Kagan and Rifkin's volume is the first to have articles that present work informed by the American Council on the Teaching of Foreign Languages (ACTFL) Proficiency Guidelines.

The current volume continues some of these important trends and highlights new developments in the field. Since Kagan and Rifkin's volume, the ACTFL Proficiency

Guidelines have been significantly revised. They form the basis of much of today's teaching and classroom-based research and have become the standard of measurement of programs across the country. Another important development for the Russian field is the revision of the World-Readiness Standards for Learning Languages, which were expanded to include learning scenarios for postsecondary students, and the creation of Russian-specific standards (Garza, Merrill, & Shuffelton, 2015). *The Art of Teaching Russian* benefits from two related chapters: one specifically dedicated to the Russian version of the Standards (Garza, chap. 5) and the other to the relevance of the Standards for the teaching and learning of Russian at the postsecondary level in the United States (Murphy, Sahakyan, & Sieloff Magnan, chap. 6). Together, the ACTFL Proficiency Guidelines and the World-Readiness Standards have become the principle framework for guiding Russian language instruction in the 21st century, particularly regarding material and curriculum development (Kagan & Kudyma; Jens, Lucey, & Rifkin; and Evans-Romaine, Goldberg, Kresin, & Galloway, chaps. 12, 10, and 11, respectively) and task design (Anderson & Walsh, chap. 19).

Significant work also is being done on pedagogical innovations in Russian that are based on new developments in second language acquisition (SLA) and pedagogy along with the revised guidelines and standards, as evidenced by several chapters in this collection (Comer, chap. 8; deBenedette, chap. 9; and Anderson & Walsh, chap. 19).

Certainly one of the greatest changes in the field of teaching foreign language has to do with the technological revolution of the 21st century, which affects language teaching and learning in unprecedented ways. Although Russian, a less-commonly taught language (LCTL), lags behind Spanish and French in technology-mediated teaching methods, important innovations in our field make the teaching and learning of Russian more dynamic, more flexible, and more effective. We invite readers to explore this volume's chapters that examine the possibilities for the use of technology in the classroom (Anderson, chap. 19; Spasova & Welsh, chap. 18). The volume also offers a chapter on the use of language corpora in teaching Russian, with specific recommendations for instructors and a list of resources (Kisselev & Furniss, chap. 14).

Students also have changed since the publication of Kagan and Rifkin's volume. Those who study Russian today have diverse interests that reach beyond the traditional subjects of language and literature (Martin, chap. 2; Germain-Rutherford, chap. 1). The field responded to this diversification of interests and motivations by finding new approaches to teaching language, and this volume highlights some of these approaches, from using songs to teach language and culture (chap. 11) to conducting oral history fieldwork (chap. 10). At the same time, as Russian culture became more accessible to students in the post–Cold War era, the field responded with more systematic and innovative approaches to incorporating culture into the language classroom. This collection presents several chapters that focus on teaching culture alongside and through language, in the classroom and outside of it, or as part of extracurricular or cocurricular activities (chaps. 10 and 11; Nemtchinova, chap. 15; Smorodinska, chap. 16; and Epsteyn & Solovieva, chap. 17). It also includes a chapter on teaching Russian in specific intensive environments, such as at the Defense Language Institute (Leaver & Campbell, chap. 7).

Language students also are more diverse in their ethnic, racial, and gender identities, something that the field has noted but not yet addressed fully, and this collection is glad to feature a chapter that addresses the question of diversity and inclusion in Russian language textbooks (Stauffer, chap. 13).

This volume captures a moment in time but also looks to the future and addresses some of the challenges undergraduate and graduate Russian programs face in the 21st century, among them under-enrollment, the diminishment of the humanities, and graduate student language preparedness (Kraemer, Merrill, & Prestel, chap. 3; Anderson, Mikhailova, & Tumarkin, chap. 4).

We hope this volume will encourage ongoing conversations about teaching and learning Russian and engage educators and researchers in further exploration and dialogue. As editors and colleagues we advocate for deeper conversations about the very important issues of assessment, K–12 language education, and school-to-college curriculum articulation. We see a great need in classroom-based research that bridges the gap between SLA studies and classroom practices.

We hope that the next generation of colleagues will undertake the creation of another volume dedicated to the teaching and learning of the Russian language. We expect that many of the issues presented here will be explored further and new issues will be addressed in response to changes in our field.

REFERENCES

Brecht, R. D., & Davidson, D. E. (Eds.). (1977). *Soviet-American Russian language contributions.* Urbana, IL: G&G.

Brecht, R. D., Davidson, D. E., & Sendich, M. (Eds.). (1983). *Soviet-American contributions to the study and teaching of Russian: Theory, strategy, and tools.* East Lansing, MI: Russian Language Journal.

Garza, T. J., Merrill, P., & Shuffelton, J. (2015). *The World-readiness standards for Russian language instruction*, revised and expanded edition to include K–12 and postsecondary programs. Yonkers, NY: American Council on the Teaching of Foreign Languages. CD and online versions, 2018.

Kagan, O., & Rifkin, B. (2000). "Editors' introduction." In O. Kagan & B. Rifkin (Eds.), *The learning and teaching of Slavic languages and cultures* (pp. 1–7). Bloomington, IN: Slavica.

Kagan, O., & Rifkin, B. (Eds.). (2000). *The learning and teaching of Slavic languages and cultures.* Bloomington, IN: Slavica.

Lubensky, S., & Jarvis, D. K. (Eds.). (1984). *Teaching, learning, acquiring Russian.* Columbus, OH: Slavica.

Makarova, V. (Ed.). (2012). *Russian language studies in North America: New perspectives from theoretical and applied linguistics.* New York: Anthem.

PART I

◇◇◇◇

THE STATE OF THE PROFESSION

1
LANGUAGE EDUCATION IN THE UNITED STATES
Yesterday, Today, and Tomorrow

Aline Germain-Rutherford

Language learning is not isolated, but totally enmeshed with all important issues for the future of humanity. (Fischer, 2012, p. 23)

Perhaps the best way to start this chapter on language education in the United States is to quote an elementary school student who, in a video produced in 2014 by the Baltimore County Board of Education to promote the teaching of Spanish in elementary schools, explained why learning Spanish as a second language was special to her: "I think it is a good idea for kids to learn about Spanish because it's important and you can learn more about the world and you can speak with more people" (BCPS-TV, 2014). This little girl is right. In today's globalized world, learning languages and developing cross-cultural understanding can change our lives. These essential activities have important political and economic impact, and proficiency in world languages and intercultural awareness can have a transformative effect on our contemporary societies (della Chiesa et al., 2012). Numerous studies show, for instance, that sharing a common language increases the number of trade opportunities and that, conversely, communication barriers caused by a lack of cultural knowledge and language skills have a negative effect on business (della Chiesa et al., 2012; Helliwell, 1999; Hutchinson, 2002).

Paradoxically, in a country that throughout its immigration history has absorbed millions of speakers of languages other than English, "the American experience is remarkable for its near mass extinction of non-English languages" (Rumbaut, 2009, pp. 36–37). In his study analyzing immigrants' native-language retention rates from 1980, 1990, and 2000 U.S. Census data, Rumbaut (2009) identifies a pattern of language loss in which third-generation immigrants use English as their dominant and preferred language and retain very little of their mother tongues: "To the extent that language fluency is an asset and that knowledge of a foreign language represents a scarce resource in a global economy, immigrants' efforts to maintain that part of their cultural heritage and to pass it on to their children certainly seem worth supporting" (p. 55).

Unfortunately, language education in the United States is often overlooked when national and state education budget priorities are determined (Aujla, 2009; Friedman, 2015; Pufahl & Rhodes, 2011; Rivers & Robinson, 2012; Stein-Smith, 2016). And although more than 60 million people over the age of four in the United States today speak a language other than English at home, this number represents only 20.7% of the total population of that age. This number contrasts markedly with the 231 million people who speak only English at home (US Census Bureau, 2015; American Academy of Arts and Sciences [AAAS], 2017):

> Most Americans do not speak another language, and the percentage of college students who are enrolled in a course in a language other than English has decreased from 16% in 1960 to 8% at the present time, this at a time when globalization has made knowledge of other languages and cultures exponentially more important to our economic and national security, as well as to our own ability as individuals to effectively navigate our multicultural communities and to enjoy to the fullest the experience of and interaction with other cultures. (Stein-Smith, 2014, p. 42)

This chapter presents a historical look at foreign language education in the United States and discusses why there is hope for better prospects in the future teaching and learning of languages other than English.

LANGUAGE EDUCATION AND NATIONAL IDENTITY IN THE UNITED STATES

The history of language policies and education in the United States is complex and checkered, and it has been largely influenced and shaped by the fluctuating feelings of national identity American citizens felt at different times in their history. In its early days the United States did not legislate language issues, and immigrant communities settling in the country were quite free to establish bilingual schools where both the language of the community and English were taught and used because "although the authors of the Constitution ultimately decided not to endow English with a special legal status, they assumed that English would develop as a common language in the United States" (Schmid, 2001, p. 15).

In fact, until an open immigration policy in the 1830s and 1840s encouraged large numbers of newcomers to settle in the United States, bilingual instruction was not unusual and was even legislated in several states, in both private and public schools (Macías, 2014; Schmid, 2001). Germans formed the largest immigration group throughout the first half of the 19th century, and despite the fact that they settled in largely unpopulated areas of the country, they were able to influence local governments to establish bilingual schools and even entirely German schools (Leibowitz, 1971). Involuntary linguistic assimilation processes, however, were also important forces shaping the linguistic landscape of the country. African languages, spoken by enslaved Black

Africans brought to North America, were forcefully repressed with the compulsory ignorance laws that prohibited the Black population from learning how to read and write any languages; they were taught a circumscribed version of English that was just adequate enough to understand commands (Macías, 2014). Similarly, Native Americans were prevented from speaking their mother tongues, and government schools for Native American children were conducted exclusively in English (Leibowitz, 1971). In the off-reservation residential schools begun in 1879, "English-language instruction and abandonment of the native language became complementary means to the end" (Leibowitz, 1971, p. 70). Notably, all these language policies were driven by localized political, social, and economic factors and not by a systematic ideology about language itself (Macías, 2014; Nieto, 2009; Ovando, 2003; Schmid, 2001; Simon, 1980).

From the late 19th to the early 20th century large numbers of immigrants from southern and eastern Europe came to the United States and were able to fill the many unskilled positions the expanding economy was creating. They were, however, perceived as less educated and thus less able to be integrated easily into American society than previous immigrant groups from northwestern European countries such as Great Britain, Germany, the Netherlands, and Sweden. This negative perception contributed to a strong sense of national identity that included the desire to restrict entrance of others into the United States. This resentment resulted in the 1906 revision of the Naturalization Act to declare "the first English-language requirement for naturalization" (Schmid, 2001, p. 34), which contributed to a profound reduction of bilingual instruction in the United States (Nieto, 2009).

World War I amplified this resistance to linguistic and ethnic diversity and in 1917 led to an amendment to the Espionage Act, which required all foreign-language newspapers to provide English translations of articles about the war, and in 1919 led 15 states to legislate English as the sole language of instruction (Schmid, 2001). This number quickly grew to 34 states by 1923 (Leibowitz, 1971). Americanization classes, which presented a glorified and ethnocentric image of American society, were introduced in numerous urban schools to help integrate recent immigrants (Macías, 2014; Ovando, 2003).

Adding to the anti-immigrant xenophobia of the 1920s, the scientific community of the time, relying on new psychometric tools based on standardized IQ tests and research methodologies that did not control for socioeconomic status as a variable (Barac & Bialystok, 2010), published reports and studies about the negative effect of bilingualism on first language acquisition and cognitive development. The results of these studies had a strong negative impact on language education and led to a significant reduction of bilingual and foreign language instruction in schools.

With the outbreak of World War II, monolingual Americans found themselves disadvantaged and unprepared for war. This shortage of speakers of other languages prompted the federal government to fund the Army Specialized Training Program (ASTP), a large US wartime program for foreign language teaching, in order to address the need for American soldiers to become orally proficient in the languages of their allies and enemies. The ASTP was based on a new approach to language training developed in 1941 by the American Council of Learned Society (ACLS), which had anticipated the need for efficient language training. Funded by the Rockefeller Foundation, this new approach focused on learning to speak a language, contrary to the long-established norm in language education of putting an emphasis on reading and writing (Moulton, 1963). In 1942 a small group of linguists headed by J. Milton Cowan developed the Intensive Language Program, which included "no less than 56 courses in 26 languages at 18 universities, involving a total number of some 700 students" (Moulton, p. 85). Even after ASTP was terminated in 1944, linguists and language teachers saw how intensive method focusing on speaking skills could significantly benefit language instruction in schools and colleges. In 1946 Cowan adapted the ASTP approach to college language teaching at Cornell University, with the additional inclusion of reading instruction. In the late 1950s, during the Cold War and the Sputnik era, the National Defense Education Act contributed funds to help high schools and colleges implement adapted versions of the ASTP, with a primary emphasis on listening and speaking to be followed later by instruction in reading and writing (Moulton, 1963). Larger numbers of students were able to learn foreign languages in schools using newly installed language laboratories funded by Title III-A of the National Defense Education Act and Title VI-A of the Higher Education Act: "Unquestionably, the 1960s were the golden years of the language laboratory. There was an explosion in the number of facilities, thanks to generous federal support. [. . .] Keck and Smith claimed: 'By mid-decade an estimated 10,000 language laboratories had been installed in secondary schools; 4,000 more could be found in institutions of higher learning (1972, p. 5)'" (Roby, 2004, p. 525).

Nonetheless, this increase in foreign language enrollments in schools and colleges was short-lived. In the 1970s and 1980s, "increased immigration and concentration of newcomers in a few states and metropolitan areas [fostered] the perception that immigrants [were] no longer learning English" (Schmid, 2001, p. 41), which reignited a strong sense of national identity and a rejection of languages other than English.

Some hoped that the Bilingual Education Act of 1968 would help to promote linguistic diversity in the United States. Indeed, while recognizing the unique education needs of children in US schools with limited English-speaking ability (LESA), the act, also called Title VII of the Elementary and Secondary Education Act, stipulated that government funding would be provided to school districts through competitive federal grants for bilingual education program development and research, staff training, and educational resources. However, the ambiguity of the goals of the program and the lack of guidelines for the instruction of LESA students instead reinforced a perception that students who had been educated for a few years in both their mother tongues and English should assimilate quickly and transition into the English stream as soon as possible (Crawford, 2007; Nieto, 2009; Ovando, 2003; Schmid, 2001; Stewner-Manzanares, 1988): "The goal of a bilingual program was to prepare LESA students to participate effectively in the regular classroom as quickly as possible" (Stewner-Manzanares, 1988, p. 3).

The 1979 publication of the report "Strength through Wisdom: A Critique of U.S. Capability" by the President's Commission on Foreign Language and International Studies revived the debate on the language skills deficit in the United States and proposed important recommendations "to extend the knowledge of other civilizations to the broadest population base possible and to build these topics into the general curricula for students of all ages at all levels of study throughout the nation" (Bullard, 1979, p. 1).

In an attempt to compare language education in the United States with language education elsewhere in the world, Rep. Paul Simon contacted all the nations that had an embassy in Washington and asked them to describe the language requirements in their school systems. After 77 nations responded, Simon (1980) commented that "none can compare with the United States in neglect of foreign languages" (p. 77). In 1991, 10 years after the publication of his book *The Tongue-Tied American: Confronting the Foreign Language Crisis*, now-senator Simon looked back at the previous decade and could only observe that the United States still needed to address a foreign language deficit compared to other nations in the world and that although some recommendations of the President's Commission on Foreign Languages and International Studies had been implemented, many challenges still remained (Simon, 1991).

Political movements such as US English, English Only, and English First, all advocating for making English the official language of the United States by lobbying the government to restrict state and federal funding for bilingual and foreign language programs, grew rapidly in the 1980s and 1990s. Although scientists in several countries had already begun to report on the positive impact of bilingualism on cognitive development, in 1998 California passed Proposition 227, which eliminated bilingual education throughout the state. It was soon followed by similar measures passed in Arizona in 2000, Colorado in 2001, and Massachusetts in 2002 (Crawford, 2007; Nieto, 2009). The year 1998 was also when Rep. Gerald Salomon, speaking against Puerto Rico's proposal to become a bilingual state, declared: "We are the melting pot of the world, of every ethnic background in the entire world, and we are proud of that. But had we let these various languages become part of our American culture, this democracy would not be here" (Schmid, 2001, p. 167). His view illustrates the resentment that many Americans in the late 20th century felt toward massive immigration from developing countries and of the need to promote a strong sense of national identity that had English as the unifying language for all (Macías, 2014; Schmid, 2001).

As seen in this brief review, historical circumstances and shifting political, social, and economic influences have shaped, some might say doomed, language education in the United States in the absence of a consistent national language policy (Ovando, 2003). "With the exception of brief periods in American history, [it seems that] languages other than English in the United States have been tolerated rather than embraced" (Schmid, 2001, p. 31). Will this past impede the future of foreign language programs in American schools?

US FOREIGN LANGUAGE EDUCATION IN THE 21ST CENTURY

At the dawn of the 21st century something changed. The September 11 attacks and the consequent awareness of national security considerations once again exposed the language deficit in the United States, and restarted the argument in favor of developing and offering more language learning programs across the country. Several language initiatives flourished in the years immediately after 9/11. One was the creation in 2002 of the Language Flagship, a federally funded National Security Education Program (NSEP), to help students gain professional proficiency in the less-commonly taught languages (LCTLs) that had been identified by the US government as critical to national security. This initiative was followed in 2006 by the STARTALK program, launched by the Office of the Director of National Intelligence, to offer K–16 students and language teachers summer opportunities to learn critical foreign languages or innovative, effective ways of teaching those languages. That same year the US Department of State, in cooperation with the American Councils for International Education (ACIE), established the National Security Language Initiative for Youth (NSLI-Y) program for high school students and the Critical Language Scholarship (CLS) program for undergraduate and graduate university students. The goal of these two programs is to promote critical language learning among American youth by sending students to countries where these languages are spoken. Students learn the language while being immersed in the culture of the host country. Targeted critical languages for all these programs include Arabic, Azerbaijani, Bengali, Chinese, Hindi, Indonesian, Japanese, Korean, Persian, Punjabi, Russian, Swahili, Turkish, and Urdu, although the list can change over time as economic and political situations shift and develop.

For a while these initiatives helped to revive student interest in learning both critical languages and traditional European languages, as shown in Tables 1.1 and 1.2, which present 1998 to 2016 data gathered by the Language Map Data Center of the Modern Language Association (MLA). Enrollments for LCTLs remain comparatively low. The data also indicate how fragile and unstable offerings for LCTLs can be, and how program cutbacks or closures for reasons such as the 2008 economic recession in the United States have reversed the growth in enrollments for most languages. MLA data for 2016 indicate a decrease in enrollments for most languages (except Japanese and Korean, the only two to show some growth), and the 2018 MLA preliminary report, which includes data up to 2016, reveals an overall drop of 15.3% in enrollments since 2009, with a 9.2% decline between 2013 and 2016, the second-largest decline in the history of the census. Among higher education institutions the ratio of language course enrollments to total students registered fell from 8:1 in 2013 to 7:5 in 2016 (Looney & Lusin, 2018). Furthermore, in 2009–10 only 50.7% of higher education

TABLE 1.1. Critical Language Undergraduate and Graduate Course Enrollments for Entire United States

	2016	2013	2009	2006	2002	1998
Arabic	30,296	32,286	34,908	23,987	10,584	5,505
Azerbaijani	0	0	2	0	0	0
Bengali	113	64	98	92	54	35
Chinese	53,069	61,084	59,876	51,381	34,153	28,456
Hindi	1,426	1,813	2,173	1,962	1,430	831
Indonesian	375	289	296	301	225	223
Japanese	68,810	66,771	72,357	65,403	52,238	43,141
Korean	13,936	12,256	8,449	7,146	5,211	4,479
Persian/Farsi	2,330	2,700	2,559	2,282	1,202	614
Punjabi	124	124	465	105	99	32
Russian	20,353	21,979	26,740	24,770	23,921	23,791
Swahili	1842	2,259	2,555	2,166	1,593	1,241
Turkish	628	730	648	624	314	218
Urdu	315	351	330	349	152	35

Source: Data from the 2018 Language Map Data Center of the Modern Language Association. All census figures reflect the fall semester only.

TABLE 1.2. Traditional European Language Undergraduate and Graduate Course Enrollments for Entire United States

	2016	2013	2009	2006	2002	1998
French	175,667	197,679	215,244	206,014	201,985	199,064
German	80, 594	86,782	95,613	94,147	91,1900	89,013
Italian	56,743	70,982	80,322	78,176	63,899	49,287
Spanish	712,608	789,888	861,015	822,094	745,215	649,245

Source: Data from the 2018 Language Map Data Center of the Modern Language Association. All census figures are taken from the fall semester only.

institutions required study of a language other than English for a baccalaureate degree, down from 67.5% in 1994–95 (Goldberg et al., 2015).

Pufahl and Rhodes (2011) examined language education in K–12 programs in 2008 by surveying more than 5,000 public and private elementary and secondary schools. When comparing language instruction in elementary schools in 2008 with the data from previous surveys (Rhodes & Branaman, 1999; Rhodes & Oxford, 1988), Pufahl and Rhodes observed an increase in elementary school language instruction from 22% to 31% from 1987 to 1997 but a decrease from 31% to 25% from 1997 to 2008. Notably, 88% of these language programs in 2008 offered Spanish instruction. This decrease was even more pronounced when looking solely at public elementary schools: the number of language programs decreased from 24% in 1997 to 15% in 2008. The decline of language programs in middle schools was more dramatic, going from 75% in 1997 to 58% in 2008, but high school programs were stable over the same period, changing from 90% to 91%, with an overwhelming majority of these high schools offering Spanish instruction. The authors explain the overall regression of K–12 language programs as being partly due to the adverse effect created by the 2002 No Child Left Behind (NCLB) legislation, which mandated the creation of adequate annual targets and forced schools to spend more time and resources on teaching and testing for reading, math, and science to the detriment of adequate funding for second or foreign language classes.

When we consider that 53% of European citizens self-describe as speaking more than one language (Eurostat, 2016), it seems that US language education in the 21st century is once again considered to be a low priority and that a US language deficit is a continuing reality. According to Eurostat data, 80% of European primary school students were studying a foreign language in 2013, and 51% of those were studying two foreign languages (English being the language a majority of students chose to learn across the member states) (Eurostat, 2015; 2016). For several decades learning at least one foreign language during their education has been a mandatory requirement of most European children, and resolutions passed in 2002 and 2008 by the European Commission recommended teaching at least two foreign languages to all pupils from a very early age (Baidak et al., 2010).

In a comparative study of language policies of twenty-nine industrialized countries, only three—the United States, Australia, and New Zealand—do not have a national requirement for students to learn a foreign language. As for the typical age when students start learning a language, the United States has the oldest, with students on average starting to learn a language at age 14 (Wang et al., 2010). This late start explains one of the biggest challenges for US language education, that is, the limited number of long-sequence K–16 language programs ensuring foreign language proficiency and fluency for students: "Less than 1 percent of American adults today are proficient in a foreign language that they studied in a U.S. classroom. That's noteworthy considering that in 2008 almost all high schools in the country—93 percent—offered foreign languages, according to a national survey" (Friedman, 2015, n.p.).

For a Brighter Future

Long-sequence language education from kindergarten to college can benefit today from new forces that all conflate in a more positive outlook for language education in the United States. In 2013 Richard D. Brecht led the Language Enterprise project and the Language for ALL? initiative (Abbott et al., 2013), both of which used empirical evidence to inform educators, school administrators, decision-makers, and the nation's leaders of the advantages of long-term language education and proposed a concrete plan of action to implement a "common vision of universal and equal access to language education in the United States" (p. 4). This common vision proposes a progression of proficiency levels linked to specific linguistic and cultural purposes and learning contexts inside and outside the classroom throughout the academic curriculum, going from "second language exposure and global awareness" at the elementary level to "usable occupational and personal language skills" at the middle- and high-school levels, and then to "global professional practice" and "expertise" at the undergraduate and graduate levels (Abbott et al., 2013, p. 5). What makes this vision a tangible possibility is that the first decade of the 21st century has seen a large consensus developing around the benefits of learning foreign languages, supported by a growing demand for language education by parents and employers: "For perhaps the first time in the history of the United States, there is now broad agreement that multilingualism is important, if not critical, to our nation's well-being, as well as to the personal success of its residents. This agreement is reflected in the general and growing acceptance among the population of this country that learning a second language should be part of K–12 education" (Brecht et al., 2013, p. 8).

The "growing acceptance" that Brecht mentions was already noticeable in Rumbaut's analysis (2009) of the findings from the General Social Survey conducted in 2000. The study shows that a large majority of Americans (75%) want their children to learn a foreign language before they leave high school and that they (78%) fully support bilingual education programs in public schools; moreover, the growing parental support for language education is forcefully demonstrated by California voters, who in November 2016 overwhelmingly (73.5%) passed Proposition 58, which reversed Proposition 227 and the requirement that the state's English Language Learners (ELLs) receive English-only instruction in special classes before being moved into the regular stream. Under Proposition 58 school districts are once again allowed to provide bilingual education programs to ELLs, an important step toward closing the achievement gap that has been undermining the academic experience and career prospects of non-English-speaking students (Cummins, 2009).

Multiple other factors, including important research in cognitive development and neuroscience, accumulated evidence and awareness of the importance of developing global and intercultural competencies in order to thrive in our globalized world, and new access possibilities and learning experiences provided by the Internet and today's technologies, have reenergized the debate about language education in the United States and presented new opportunities to rethink its place in the American educational system.

Language Learning and Neuroscience

Research in neuroscience has convincingly demonstrated the positive benefits of learning multiple languages on academic progress in subjects other than language and on overall cognitive development, often resulting in greater cognitive flexibility, better problem-solving and higher-order thinking skills, and creative thinking (Armstrong & Rogers, 1997; Barac & Bialystok, 2010; Bialystok et al., 2012; Curtain & Dahlberg, 2004; Prior & MacWhinney, 2010).

By the mid-1980s one group of researchers (Guttentag et al., 1984) had demonstrated that among bilinguals both languages remain active during language processing, which led them to hypothesize that the constant management of two competing languages enhances the brain's executive functions (Bialystok, 2001). Today's advances in neuroscience point to significant evidence that bilingualism is associated with more effective and controlled processing among children speaking two or more languages. Several studies in neurolinguistics show, for instance, that bilingual children are better able to focus their attention on relevant information and ignore distractions because their executive control function has been trained to sort through two systems and quickly attend to what is relevant (Bialystok et al., 2004; Bialystok & Martin, 2004; Carlson & Meltzoff, 2008). Research now shows that the benefits of being bilingual seem to last throughout one's lifetime. Bialystok's research clearly indicates that "the bilingual advantages in controlled processing observed for children [are] sustained into adulthood" and that these advantages "provide a defense against the decline of these executive processes that occurs with normal cognitive aging" (Bialystok et al., 2004, p. 301).

Bilingual advantages have also been observed across a variety of domains, such as the development of sociocognitive skills to enhance effective communication. One study (Fan et al., 2015) tested a social communication task with three groups of young children: one group bilingual, one group with regular but limited exposure to another language, and one group monolingual. To succeed at the task the children had to take into consideration the perspective of the person with whom they were interacting. Both the bilingual and the exposure groups performed better at the task than the monolingual group. However, when tested on executive function tasks, the exposure group had lower scores than the bilingual group. The authors conclude that the communicative advantages demonstrated by the bilinguals and the exposure group may be social in origin and not due to enhanced executive control, and that, "if multilingual exposure indeed benefits effective communication, then miscommunication might be reduced through active exposure of young children to varied linguistic environments" (Fan et al., 2015, p. 1095). Awareness, understanding, and tolerance of other cultures are essential skills to live and succeed in the globalized context of the 21st century, and early exposure to foreign languages and cultures as part of a child's education will help him or her develop these critically important intercultural skills.

Global Competence, Intercultural Awareness, and Plurilingual Education

In his *Seven Complex Lessons in Education for the Future* French sociologist and philosopher Edgar Morin (1999) suggests that the education of the future has to get past a compartmentalized vision of learning that "is deeply, drastically inadequate to grasp realities and problems which are ever more global, transnational, multidimensional, transversal, polydisciplinary and planetary" (p. 13). For knowledge to be "pertinent," Morin believes that we must learn "about the world as world" (p. 13) in its contextual, global, multidimensional, and complex reality.

To better frame the concept of *global competence* that Morin refers to, and to identify specific strategies to make it integral to academic programs, Boix-Mansilla and Jackson (2011) have developed a global competence matrix, which outlines skills and knowledge that apply across disciplines and beyond the students' immediate environment. The matrix consists of four core capacities that are associated with global competence: (1) investigating the world, (2) recognizing perspectives, (3) communicating ideas, and (4) taking action. For each capacity, specific can-do statements help the teacher and the students define learning objectives and tasks to assess performance. World languages and area studies are included in these four core capacities, along with the development of intercultural abilities for successful interactions in multicultural environments.[1]

The 2013 UNESCO report *Intercultural Competences: Conceptual and Operational Framework* defines intercultural competence as having "adequate relevant knowledge about particular cultures, as well as general knowledge about the sorts of issues arising when members of different cultures interact, holding receptive attitudes that encourage establishing and maintaining contact with diverse others, as well as having the skills required to draw upon both knowledge and attitudes when interacting with others from different cultures" (p. 16).

The knowledge, skills, and attitudes defined here need to be considered not only for preparing students for cross-cultural interactions when they travel and work internationally, but also, and perhaps just as or even more important, locally, especially considering that more than 350 languages are spoken across the United States and that large cities usually count more than 150 different languages spoken in their neighborhood communities (US Census Bureau, 2015). US Census officials, citing increasing diversity, report that as the country grows more diverse, it is becoming a *plurality nation*. "The next half century marks key points in continuing trends—the United States will become a plurality nation, where the non-Hispanic white population remains the largest single group, but no group is in the majority" (Cooper, 2012, n.p., quoting Thomas L. Mesenbourg, the Census Bureau's acting director). This diversity represents a wealth of cross-cultural experiences and perspectives that may have a significant impact on peoples' attitudes and thought processes. A body of research investigating how diversity influences subjects' behaviors and creative thinking in problem-solving situations reports that being around people from different ethnic backgrounds makes us more creative, more diligent, and more hardworking. The studies demonstrate that diversity forces participants to question their worldviews and beliefs, provokes divergent thinking, and enhances one's power of anticipation; all of these are important, essential skills for developing the ability to propose creative and innovative solutions to a problem (Phillips, 2014).

Furthermore, the growing consideration of crosslinguistic and intercultural mediation in the last 15 years has led in Europe, in Canada, and more recently in the United States to an interest in the ability to exploit students' plurilingual and pluricultural repertoires within the language classroom. At the core of the Council of

Europe's policies lies the concept of a plurilingual education, with the goal of "developing every individual's language repertoire and highlighting the social value of linguistic diversity. [. . .] Plurilingual education challenges monolingual attitudes and embraces all language learning, e.g., mothertongue/s, language/s of schooling, foreign languages, [and] regional and minority languages" (European Center for Modern Languages website, n.d.). From a plurilingual perspective, languages are not seen as mentally coexisting as separate entities; rather, they are entwined and interrelated to form a composite competence, which allows students to develop more effective learning strategies using all the linguistic and cultural tools at their disposal (Coste, 2014; Coste et al., 2009; Council of Europe, 2001). More important, students' daily at-home languages and cultures are acknowledged and seen to be valued in the learning activities, which is essential for easing the integration of migrant students into schools and society (Boix-Mansilla & Jackson, 2011; Cummins, 2007). In this context Cummins' Literacy Engagement Framework for ELL, which highlights cultural identity as one of the four pillars for literacy and language attainment, is a powerful example of the plurilingual and pluricultural approach in language education that supports literacy development in both English as a second language and the student's mother tongue (Cummins & Early, 2011; Cummins et al., 2013). Asked to collaboratively write texts in English that relate to their personal experiences, students are encouraged to use their mother tongue, or any languages they know, to share ideas and experiences, to research visual or audio illustrations, and to discuss their drafts in order to complete the task. A home language becomes the tool for learning English as a second language (ESL), as the student compares language structures, lexical similarities and differences, cultural values and beliefs in the target language and the different mother tongue spoken by other students of the group. The end product is a multimodal creative text in both English and the different mother tongues of the students who have participated. These multilingual *identity texts* (Cummins & Early, 2011), in which students have invested their linguistic and cultural identities in the writing process, enable students to develop cross-language pattern recognition skills and validate their home languages and cultures, a powerful force for engaging students and accelerating the development of their capabilities in English. Cummins et al. (2013) describe, for instance, the experience of one little girl from Pakistan who had recently arrived in Canada and was having difficulty learning in a traditional ESL class. She was placed in a class that used a plurilingual approach and thrived, even though she had at first only a limited knowledge of English:

> Her home language, in which all her experience prior to immigration was encoded, became once again a tool for learning. She contributed her ideas and experiences to the [writing of the] story, participated in discussions about how to translate vocabulary and expressions from Urdu to English and from English to Urdu. [. . .] The fact that instruction was conducted in English and the teacher did not know Urdu or the other home languages of students in

her multilingual classroom was not an impediment to the implementation of bilingual instructional strategies. (p. 34)

Changes in Language Education Driven by New Technology Trends

Social media technology already plays an important role in enabling language teachers and students across the world to interact with others, working on collaborative and interdisciplinary projects, developing knowledge and understanding of other ways of viewing the world, and acquiring linguistic and global competencies. Connect All Schools, for instance, a consortium of organizations linking US schools with other schools around the world, currently involves more than 15,000 educators from 153 different countries. The association offers a lengthy list of resources for collaborative projects and involved schools. Connect All Schools follows in the steps of iEARN (International Education and Resource Network), a nonprofit organization started in 1988 when the Copen Family Foundation pioneered the use of telecommunication technology for educational purposes. Pairing 12 schools in Moscow with 12 schools in New York State, the organization offered American and Russian students the opportunity to interact in English and in Russian while working collaboratively on curriculum-based projects designed by their teachers. The project was so successful that the organization replicated the partnership with schools in additional countries, and today iEARN works with over 30,000 schools and youth organizations in more than 140 countries, allowing students to develop linguistic and cultural skills while working collaboratively with their peers from across the world in a safe and structured online environment.

Social media and Web 2.0 technology have opened language classrooms to the world and can truly help students develop stronger linguistic and intercultural skills via online interactions with native speakers, thereby achieving deeper global competence. Asked to identify future directions in educational technologies that will support and enhance learning in the 21st century, a panel of 56 technology experts from across the world identified several trends of particular importance in the shaping of new models of teaching and learning for the future (Johnson et al., 2016). The proliferation of open-source educational resources, for instance, allows teachers to enrich their courses with freely available content, exposes students to a larger diversity of authentic materials, and exposes students to other means of gaining language skills. The ways in which people learn have been expanding as more and more interactive content has been made freely available on the Internet. Opportunities for informal learning have increased, and "many experts believe that a blending of formal and informal methods of teaching and learning can create an environment that fosters experimentation, curiosity, and above all, creativity" (Johnson et al., 2016, p. 22).

Measuring and adapting learning and learning experiences through data-driven practice and assessment is another important trend identified by the panel. Individualized learning driven by data analytics leads to more sophisticated ways to create adaptive learning. A decade ago the Carnegie Mellon University's Open Learning Initiative used the Cognitive Tutor program to demonstrate that the intelligent tutoring characteristic of adaptive learning environments proved almost as effective as one-on-one human tutors (Koedinger & Corbett, 2006). In the future the growing field of learning analytics and educational data mining will foster the creation of even more intelligent, effective, and engaging e-learning environments that can adapt to the individual skills and learning strategies of students (Koedinger et al., 2014).

Two other trends identified by the panel are augmented or virtual reality and makerspace environments. These two directions bring to the forefront important pedagogical concepts that already are part of language education's project-based and problem-solving approaches and are rooted in a content and language integrated learning (CLIL) perspective: active learning, interdisciplinary approach, critical thinking, and creativity. Developing virtual reality environments that simulate intercultural situations where students are able to communicate and interact in a target language (the 3-D virtual world Second Life and the open-source virtual reality environment High Fidelity have already given us a taste of the possibilities) and designing interdisciplinary projects where students collaboratively create products and prototypes while interacting in a target language have the potential to enhance learning experiences and ensure language proficiency and fluency, as well as greater global competence.

CONCLUSION

This journey through the history of language education in the United States illustrates how fluctuating feelings of national identity due to specific events and circumstances in American history, combined with the absence of a consistent national language policy, have fed and maintained the continuing, controversial political debate over the relevance of foreign language education in school curricula.

The US foreign language deficit, convincingly chronicled by language educators and informed advocates of multilingual education, is startlingly evident. Yet today there is also unprecedented opportunity. Advances in neuroscience, the widening acceptance of the need to develop linguistic and intercultural skills in order to thrive in a globalized world, and the increasing ease of access to educational technologies and virtual interactive environments all fuse to offer unique opportunities to all US students and teachers in learning, teaching, and experiencing world languages and cultures.

In their white paper "Languages for ALL?: The Anglophone Challenge" Brecht et al. (2013) speak of a *generational shift* among the population across the United States "toward a more diverse and cosmopolitan populace that increasingly supports the teaching and learning of foreign languages at all levels and that demands ever-expanding language services" (p. 12). While acknowledging the difficulty to establish common policies for language education at the federal level, these authors urge all sectors of American society to maintain momentum by mobilizing and joining efforts to bring long-sequence multilingual education to the schools and colleges in their communities. Notably, Robinson et al. (2011), Rivers and Robinson (2012), and Rivers et al. (2013) acknowledge that previous arguments for national security needs and in favor of world-class education to justify expanding language education might not be persuasive enough; more is needed to encourage language professionals to explore opportunities in the language "industry" of translation and interpretation, human language technology, and language-testing services. Furthermore, in a recent report published by the American Academy of Arts and Sciences (2017) in response to a request from members of the US Congress regarding the economic impact of language learning and the actions needed to advance efficient language education, five combined strategies were recommended that put an emphasis on more teaching staff; long-sequence language education enhanced by public-private partnerships among schools, government, business, and local communities; support for heritage languages spoken in the United States to preserve language diversity; experiential and immersive language opportunities; and targeted support for Native American languages as languages of schooling.

Finally, it is noteworthy to see that Martha G. Abbott, executive director of the American Council on the Teaching of Foreign Languages (ACTFL) and ardent advocate for language education, was appointed in 2016 by Pres. Barack Obama to the National Security Education Board (White House, 2016). May this appointment lead world languages and cultures to find, at last, their undeniably rightful, necessary, and deserved place in the education system of the United States.

NOTE

1. In the early years of the 21st century a number of language departments in the United States decided to rename their foreign language departments to world language departments to acknowledge that languages such as Spanish are widely spoken in the United States and to reduce the divisive connotation of the word "foreign" (Jaschik, 2011). I use "world languages" when the referenced author(s) use this term; otherwise, I use "foreign languages," which is still widely used in the field inside and outside the United States.

REFERENCES

Abbott, G. M., Brecht, R., Davidson, D. E., Rivers, W. P., Slater, R., Weinberg, A., Wiley, T., Fenstermacher, H., & Fisher, D. (2013). *Languages for ALL?: Final report.* Retrieved from https://www.americancouncils.org/sites/default/files/LFA2013_Final Report.pdf

American Academy of Arts and Sciences (AAAS). (2017). *America's languages: Investing in language education for the 21st century.* Commission on Language Learning.

Armstrong, P. W., & Rogers, J. D. (1997). Basic skills revisited: The effects of foreign language instruction on reading, math, and language arts. *Learning Languages, 2*(3), 20–31.

Aujla, S. (2009). At Texas flagship, budget cut may translate into shrinking language requirements. *The Chronicle of Higher Education.* Retrieved from http://chronicle.com/article/At-Texas-Flag ship-Budget-Cut/48658/

Baidak, N., Borodankova, O., Kocanova, D., & Motiejunaite, A. (2012). *Key data on teaching languages at school in Europe.* Brussels: Eurydice.

Baltimore County Public Schools TV (BCPS-TV). (2014). *Passport 11-06-14.* Retrieved from https://www.bcps.org/bcpstv/video.html?Program=PP&VideoID=340

Barac, R., & Bialystok, E. (2010). Cognitive development of bilingual children. *Language Teaching, 44*(1), 36–54.

Bialystok, E. (2001). *Bilingualism in development: Language, literacy, and cognition.* New York: Cambridge UP.

Bialystok, E., Craik, F. I., Klein, R., & Viswanathan, M. (2004). Bilingualism, aging, and cognitive control: Evidence from the Simon task. *Psychology and Aging, 19*(2), 290–303.

Bialystok, E., Craik, F. I., & Luk, G. (2012). Bilingualism: Consequences for mind and brain. *Trends in Cognitive Sciences, 16*(4), 240–50.

Bialystok, E., & Martin, M. M. (2004). Attention and inhibition in bilingual children: Evidence from the dimensional change card sort task. *Developmental Science, 7*(3), 325–39.

Boix-Mansilla, V., & Jackson, A. (2011). *Educating for global competence: Preparing our youth to engage the world.* New York: Asia Society and Council of Chief State School Officers.

Brecht, R., Abbott, G. M., Davidson, D. E., Rivers, W. P., Slater, R., Weinberg, A., & Yoganathan, A. (2013). Languages for all?: The Anglophone challenge. White Paper, University of Maryland.

Bullard, B. (1979). Personal statement to the president's commission on foreign language and international studies. In J. Perkins (Ed.), *President's commission on foreign language and international studies: Background papers and studies* (pp. 1–8). Washington, DC: Government Printing Office.

Carlson, S. M., & Meltzoff, A. N. (2008). Bilingual experience and executive functioning in young children. *Developmental Science, 11*(2), 282–98.

Connect All Schools. Retrieved from https://us.iearn.org/programs/connect-all-schools

Cooper, M. (2012). Census officials, citing increasing diversity, say U.S. will be a "plurality nation." *The New York Times.* Retrieved from http://www.nytimes.com/2012/12/13/us/us-will-have-no-ethnic-majority-census-finds.html?_r=0

Coste, D. (2014). Plurilingualism and the challenges of education. In P. Grommed & A. Hu (Eds.), *Plurilingual education* (pp. 15–32). Amsterdam: John Benjamins.

Coste, D., Moore, D., & Zarate, G. (2009). *Plurilingual and pluricultural competence.* Strasbourg, France: Council of Europe.

Council of Europe. (2001). *Common European framework of reference for languages: Learning, teaching, assessment.* Cambridge, UK: Cambridge UP.

Crawford, J. (2007). The decline of bilingual education: How to reverse a troubling trend? *International Multilingual Research Journal, 1*(1), 33–37.

Cummins, J. (2007). *Promoting literacy in multilingual contexts: What works? Research into practice.* Ontario Ministry of Education or Literacy and Numeracy Secretariat Research Monograph #5. Retrieved from http://www.edu.gov.on.ca/eng/literacynumeracy/inspire/research/cummins.pdf

Cummins, J. (2009). Transformative multiliteracies pedagogy: School-based strategies for closing the achievement gap. *Multiple voices for ethnically diverse exceptional learners, 11*(2), 38–56.

Cummins, J., Brown, K., & Sayers, D. (2007). *Literacy, technology, and diversity: Teaching for success in changing times.* Boston: Allyn & Bacon.

Cummins, J., & Early, M. (2011). *Identity texts: The collaborative creation of power in multilingual schools.* Stoke-on-Trent, UK: Trentham.

Cummins, J., Mirza, R., & Stille, S. (2013). English language learners in Canadian schools: Emerging directions for school-based policies. *TESL Canada Journal, 29*(6), 25–48.

Curtain, H., & Dahlberg, C. A. (2004). *Languages and children: Making the match: New languages for young learners, grades K–8* (3rd ed.). New York: Longman.

Dahlberg, C. A. (2002). Foreign language education. *Encyclopedia of education.* Retrieved from https://www.encyclopedia.com/education/encyclopedias-almanacs-transcripts-and-maps/foreign-language-education

della Chiesa, B., Scott, J., & Hinton, C. (Eds.). (2012). *Languages in a global world: Learning for better cultural understanding.* OECD Publishing.

eTwinning. Retrieved from https://www.etwinning.net/en/pub/index.htm

European Center for Modern Languages. (n.d.). Plurilingual education. Retrieved from http://www.ecml.at/Thematicareas/PlurilingualEducation/tabid/1631/language/en-GB/Default.aspx

Eurostat. (2015). News release. *European day of languages: More than 80% of primary school pupils in the EU were studying a foreign language in 2013.* Retrieved from http://ec.europa.eu/eurostat/documents/2995521/7008563/3-24092015-AP-EN.pdf/bf8be07c-ff9d-406b-88f9-f98f5199fe5a

Eurostat. (2016). Foreign language learning statistics. Retrieved from http://ec.europa.eu/eurostat/statistics-explained/index.php/Foreign_language_learning_statistics

Fan, S. P., Liberman, Z., Keysar, B., & Kinzler, K. D. (2015). The exposure advantage: Early exposure to a multilingual environment promotes effective communication. *Psychological Science, 26*(7), 1090–97.

Fischer, W. K. (2012). Preface: Language learning and culture in a time of globalization In B. della Chiesa, J. Scott, & C. Hinton (Eds.), *Languages in a global world: Learning for better cultural understanding* (pp. 23–24). OECD Publishing.

Friedman, A. (2015). America's lacking language skills. *The Atlantic.* Retrieved from http://www.theatlantic.com/education/archive/2015/05/filling-americas-language-education-potholes/392876/

Goldberg, D., Looney, D., & Lusin, N. (2015). *Enrollments in languages other than English in United States institutions of higher education.* New York: Modern Language Association of America.

Guttentag, R. E., Haith, M. M., Goodman, G. S., & Hauch, J. (1984). Semantic processing of unattended words by bilinguals: A test of the input switch mechanism. *Journal of Verbal Learning and Verbal Behavior, 23*(2), 178–88.

Helliwell, J. (1999). Language and trade. In A. Breton (Ed.), *Exploring the economics of language* (pp. 5–30). Ottawa, ON: Department of Heritage.

High Fidelity [software]. Retrieved from https://www.highfidelity.com

Hutchinson, W. K. (2002). Does ease of communication increase trade? Commonality of language and bilateral trade. *Scottish Journal of Political Economy, 49*(5), 544–56.

International Education and Resource Network (iEARN). Retrieved from https://iearn.org

Jaschik, S. (2011, October 5). Not so foreign languages. *Inside Higher Ed.* Retrieved from https://www.insidehighered.com/news/2011/10/05/not-so-foreign-languages

Johnson, L., Adams Becker, S., Cummins, M., Estrada, V., Freeman, A., & Hall, C. (2016). *NMC horizon report: 2016 Higher education edition.* Austin, TX: New Media Consortium.

Keck, M. E. B., & Smith, W. F. (1972). *A selective, annotated bibliography for the language laboratory, 1959–1971.* New York: ERIC Clearinghouse on Languages and Linguistics.

Koedinger, K. R., Brunskill, E., Baker, R., S.J.d., McLaughlin, E. A., & Stamper, J. (2014). New potentials for data-driven intelligent tutoring system development and optimization. *AI Magazine, 34*(3), 27–41.

Koedinger, K. R., & Corbett, A. (2006). Cognitive tutors: Technology bringing learning science to the classroom. In K. Sawyer (Ed.), *The Cambridge handbook of the learning sciences* (pp. 61–78). New York: Cambridge UP.

Leibowitz, A. H. (1971). *Educational policy and political acceptance: The imposition of English as the language of instruction in American schools.* ERIC document no. ED047321 (March). Washington, DC: ERIC Clearinghouse for Linguistics, Center for Applied Linguistics.

Looney, D., & Lusin, N. (2018). *Enrollments in languages other than English in United States institutions of higher education, summer 2016 and fall 2016: Preliminary report.* Retrieved from https://www.mla.org/content/download/83540/2197676/2016-Enrollments-Short-Report.pdf

Macías, R. F. (2014). Benefits of bilingualism: In the eye of the beholder? In R. M. Callahan & P. C. Gándara (Eds.), *The bilingual advantage: Language, literacy and the U.S. labor market* (pp. 16–44). Toronto, ON: Multilingual Matters.

Modern Language Association (MLA). (n.d.). *Language map data center.* Retrieved from https://apps.mla.org/map_main

Morin, E. (1999). *Seven complex lessons in education for the future.* UNESCO Publishing. Retrieved from http://unesdoc.unesco.org/images/0011/001177/117740eo.pdf

Moulton, W. G. (1963). Linguistics and language teaching in the United States, 1940–1960. In C. Mohrmann, A. Sommerfelt, and J. Whatmough (Eds.), *Trends in European and American Linguistics, 1930–1960* (pp. 82–109). Utrecht: Spectrum.

Nieto, S. (2009). *Language, culture, and teaching: Critical perspectives.* (2nd ed.). Language, Culture, and Teaching Series. Abingdon, UK: Taylor & Francis.

Ovando, C. J. (2003). Bilingual education in the United States: Historical development and current issues. *Bilingual Research Journal, 27*(1), 1–24.

Phillips, K. W. (2014). How diversity makes us smarter. *Scientific American*, *311*(4). Retrieved from http://www.scientificamerican.com/article/how-diversity-makes-us-smarter

Poulin-Dubois, D., Blaye, A., Coutya, J., & Bialystok, E. (2011). The effects of bilingualism on toddlers' executive functioning. *Journal of Experimental Child Psychology, 108*(3), 567–79.

Prior, A., & MacWhinney, B. (2010). A bilingual advantage in task switching. *Bilingualism: Language and Cognition, 13*(2), 253–62.

Pufahl, I., & Rhodes, N. C. (2011). Foreign language instruction in U.S. schools: Results of a national survey of elementary and secondary schools. *Foreign Language Annals*, *44*(2), 258–88.

Rhodes, N. C., & Branaman, L. E. (1999). *Foreign language instruction in the United States: A national survey of elementary and secondary schools.* McHenry, IL: Delta Systems and Center for Applied Linguistics.

Rhodes, N. C., & Oxford, R. (1988). Foreign languages in elementary and secondary schools: Results of a national survey. *Foreign Language Annals*, *21*, 51–69.

Rivers, W., & Robinson, J. P. (2012). The unchanging American capacity in LOEs: Speaking and learning languages other than English, 2000–2008. *Modern Language Journal*, *96*(iii), 369–79.

Rivers, W., Robinson, J. P., Brecht, R., & Harwood, P. (2013). Language votes: Attitudes toward foreign language policies. *Foreign Language Annals, 46*(3), 329–38.

Robinson, J. P., Rivers, W., & Harwood, P. G. (2011). Stability and change in Americans' foreign language policy attitudes: 2000–2008. *Journal of the National Council of Less Commonly Taught Languages, 11*, 1–20.

Roby, W. B. (2004). Technology in the service of language learning: The case of the language laboratory. In D. H. Jonassen (Ed.), *Handbook of research on educational communications and technology* (2nd ed.). Mahwah, NJ: Lawrence Erlbaum. 523–41.

Rumbaut, R. (2009). A language graveyard? The evolution of language competencies, preferences and use among young adult children of immigrants. In T. G. Wiley, J. S. Lee, & R. Rumberger (Eds.), *The education of language minority immigrants in the United States* (pp. 35–71). Bristol, UK: Multilingual Matters.

Schmid, C. L. (2001). *The politics of language: Conflict, identity, and cultural pluralism in comparative perspective.* New York: Oxford UP.

Second Life [software]. Retrieved from http://secondlife.com/

Simon, P. (1980). *The tongue-tied American: Confronting the foreign language crisis.* New York: Continuum.

Simon, P. (1991). Priority: Public relations: A decade of change to a decade of challenge. *Foreign Language Annals*, *24*(1), 13–18.

Stein-Smith, K. (2014). The U.S. foreign language deficit and language for specific purposes. *Journal of Languages for Specific Purposes (JLSP), 1,* 41–53.

Stein-Smith, K. (2016). *The U.S. foreign language deficit: Strategies for maintaining a competitive edge in a globalized world.* New York: Palgrave Macmillan.

Stewner-Manzanares, G. (1988). The Bilingual Education Act: Twenty years later. *National Clearinghouse for Bilingual Education (NCBE)*, *6*, 1–10. Retrieved from https://ncela.ed.gov/files/rcd/BE021037/Fall88_6.pdf

UNESCO. (2013). *Intercultural competences: Conceptual and operational framework*. Paris: UNESCO Publications.

US Census Bureau. (2015). *Census bureau reports at least 350 languages spoken in U.S. homes.* Retrieved from https://www.census.gov/newsroom/press-releases/2015/cb15-185.html

Van Damme, D. (2012). Prospects for language policies in an age of globalization. In B. della Chiesa, J. Scott, & C. Hinton (Eds.), *Languages in a global world: Learning for better cultural understanding* (pp. 463–69). OECD.

Wang, S. C., Jackson, F. H., Mana, M., Liau, R., & Evans, B. (2010). *Resource guide to developing linguistic and cultural competency in the United States.* College Park, MD: National Foreign Language Center at the University of Maryland. Retrieved from http://docplayer.net/11286460-Resource-guide-to-developing-linguistic-and-cultural-competency-in-the-united-states.html

White House, Office of the Press Secretary. (2016). *President Obama announces more key administration posts.* Retrieved from https://www.whitehouse.gov/the-press-office/2016/09/07/president-obama-announces-more-key-administration-posts

2

LOOKING BACK, MOVING FORWARD

Teaching and Learning Russian in the United States in the Post-Soviet Era

Cynthia L. Martin

Since the publication of *Teaching, Learning, Acquiring Russian* (Jarvis & Lubensky, 1984), a remarkable evolution has taken place in the teaching and learning of Russian at all levels in the United States. Kagan and Rifkin captured some of those changes in their book in 2000, and the current volume aims to outline the present state of affairs. This retrospective essay discusses several salient changes in the profession. Opportunities for learners, language instructors, and scholars in the early post-Soviet period increased, but since then the Russian language field has contracted considerably. During the post-Soviet period the field of language teaching shifted toward real-world proficiency and communicative competence; learners' and scholars' interests expanded beyond the traditional language and literature focus; there have been major changes in curriculum design and instructional materials; the Internet has given unprecedented access to authentic language in all modalities; and we have experienced a downward trend in undergraduate and graduate enrollments, degrees awarded, and faculty positions (as advertised by the Modern Language Association since 1984). I discuss each of these below in an attempt to tell the story of our evolving field.

POST-SOVIET CHANGES IN LANGUAGE AND CULTURE

The most obvious change from 30 years ago is that the country that many of us visited, studied, and were intrigued by has ceased to exist.[1] In 1985 very few specialists predicted the collapse of the Soviet system that occurred just six years later; that event naturally led to profound and ongoing changes in Russian culture (both small "c" everyday culture and Big "C" culture that is manifested in art, music, film, theater, and so on), and inevitably, to changes in the language itself. Keeping up with these changes poses a perpetual challenge.

With the collapse of the USSR, many words fell out of use as they no longer reflected reality. For example, it is hard to imagine teaching the word товарищ [comrade] as anything other than a historical relic, and if used today it would have a subtext most of our students would miss. As Ryazanova-Clarke and Wade (2002) document, many words saw their meanings shift in the post-Soviet period: some words with previously positive connotations now have negative ones, such as великая стройка коммунизма [the great building of communism] and пролетарское правосудие [proletarian justice]; some that were clearly used with negative connotations now are mostly positive or at least neutral, such as бизнес [business], коммерческий [commercial], частная собственность [private property], диссидент [dissident], многопартийная система [multiparty system], and рыночная экономика [market economy]; and the connotations of many words depend entirely on the user, such as моральность [morality], патриот [patriot], and патриотизм [patriotism]. Today's learners and teachers of Russian also must address the enormous quantity of borrowings into Russian, largely from English and many related to free-market enterprise, modern digital technologies, and Western popular culture. The Russian language is voraciously incorporating new words, making it hard to stay current.[2]

Another language change resulting from the collapse of the Soviet centralized political and social system has been the gradual shift away from the normative rules previously maintained and imposed by the Academy of Sciences, such as word choice, position of word stress, or gender assignment for borrowed nouns.[3] During the Soviet period those with public roles in mass media and publishing were expected to conform to prescribed standards. Post-Soviet sociopolitical changes have led to the relaxation of Soviet-era rules requiring the use of formal registers in public discourse. Lowered stylistic registers, profanity, and vulgarity have become so widespread throughout the public sphere that, starting in the late 1990s, the government took measures to protect the Russian language from нецензурная брань [obscenities].[4] The federal law «О государственном языке Российской Федерации» [On the state language of the Russian Federation] was passed in 2005 and amended in 2014 despite protestations that such legislation represents an assault on free speech. The law prohibits the use of obscenities in television broadcasts and plays, bans films with swear words from widespread distribution, and requires books to carry an obscenity warning.[5] Media watchdog Роскомнадзор [Roskomnadzor] uses a search program to root out offenders in online sources.[6] Whatever the outcomes of the law for Russian society, students today encounter the overuse of informal registers, nonstandard pronunciation, and profanities in authentic sources. Keeping up with language change is more challenging than it was 30 years ago, when the pace of language change was much slower.

Russians themselves may have a hard time keeping up with the changes, as evidenced by numerous programs focused on the Russian language, such as the radio programs «Грамотей» [*A literate person*] hosted by Elena Shmeleva, «Как правильно?» [*What is correct?*], «Говорим по-русски» [*We speak Russian*], and «Ликбез» [*Likbez, eradication of illiteracy*] or the television program «На каком языке мы говорим?» [*What language do we speak?*] (Ryazanova-Clarke, 2009).

As the Russian language itself experiences major changes, its status in the post-Soviet era has also shifted. When the former Soviet republics declared independence, all 14 of them reclaimed their national languages and Russian lost its status as the primary state language and, in some cases, as a state language altogether (Aref'ev, 2012).

The most obvious effect of these new official language policies has been the reduction in the number of Russian speakers, mostly along generational lines. Since Russian is no longer the only official language of education, knowledge of Russian can no longer be assumed for those born after the late 1980s.

Many of the former republics represent areas of strategic interest, and US-based scholars and policymakers can no longer rely on the use of Russian to study and interact in these regions. American Russianists are increasingly pursuing study of the languages of the former republics, especially those in Central Asia and the Caucasus. This trend has been reflected in national organizations that traditionally were dominated by the study of Russian.

NATIONAL PROFESSIONAL ORGANIZATIONS

A number of national organizations have supported the field for many decades. The most visible of these are briefly discussed in this section.

AAASS and ASEEES

In an effort to reflect post-Soviet geopolitical realities, in 2010 the American Association for the Advancement of Slavic Studies (AAASS), founded in 1948, changed its name to the Association for Slavic, East European, and Eurasian Studies (ASEEES). Today the association has approximately 3,000 individual members and 60 institutional members and tends to focus on political and social sciences, history, literature, and interdisciplinary studies, with a lesser focus on language, linguistics, and pedagogy.

AATSEEL

The oldest national organization for Slavists, the American Association of Teachers of Slavic and East European Languages (AATSEEL), was established in 1941. Its focus remains on Slavic languages, linguistics, literature, and pedagogy.

ACTR and ACIE

The youngest of our national organizations, the American Council of Teachers of Russian (ACTR), was founded in 1974 and became a pioneering example for how to organize and implement successful educational, cultural, and professional development programs in areas not well represented in the United States. In 1976 ACTR launched its first study abroad program for graduate students at the Pushkin Institute in Moscow, subsequently expanding to include undergraduate students. Numerous scholars and teachers in the field benefited directly from ACTR's programs: as of 2014 there were more than 4,000 alumni of the ACTR's Russian Language and Area Studies Program (ACIE, 2014). ACTR has supported the development of teachers and learners, new technologies, instructional materials, curriculum design, and standardized assessments.[7] In 2005 ACTR became the host institution for the *Russian Language Journal*, the annual founded over 60 years ago. Today ACTR provides regular webinars for teachers, it recognizes outstanding student achievement (National Secondary and Post-Secondary Russian Essay Contests, and the Secondary and Post-Secondary Russian Scholar Laureate Awards), and it sponsors the annual Olympiada of Spoken Russian, to name a few of the ways it continues to support the field.

Today's American Councils for International Education (ACIE, or AC) grew out of ACTR. AC currently works in 70 countries, in 37 languages, and has more than 30 offices and 55,000 alumni worldwide (ACIE, 2014). AC works at all levels of educational and public policy, from K–16 to exchanges of professionals in fields as diverse as education, public service, technology, international media, and human rights. In March 2014 the American Councils Research Center (ARC) was launched, with a primary goal being to "address central issues in US language policy with a global perspective to research policy formation by providing data and new analyses related to language learning" (American Councils Research Center, 2014).

ACTFL

Founded in 1967, the American Council on the Teaching of Foreign Languages (ACTFL) is the largest national advocacy organization for language educators, with current membership of approximately 12,500. In ACTFL's early years the organization did not focus on less commonly taught languages (LCTLs), but that has changed over the past two decades. The Russian field has seen increased exposure and collaboration with teachers of other languages through both the individual memberships of Slavists in ACTFL and collaboration between ACTR and ACTFL on projects such as the World-Readiness Standards for Learning Languages (NSCB, 2015). Perhaps ACTFL's most significant impact, however, is a direct result of its enduring commitment to teaching and learning languages for real-world communication. The ACTFL Proficiency Guidelines, first published in 1982 and last updated in 2012, helped move us toward proficiency-based curricula. Next I present some of the major changes in student and faculty profiles over the last 30 years, since the shift to real-world proficiency and the changing composition of learners and faculty are closely related.

UNDERGRADUATE STUDIES

In terms of undergraduate studies, the field has seen many changes in enrollments and student profiles. This section describes these changing enrollments, as well as the most salient changes in the student population as observed by the author.

Enrollments

Included in this section are data collected since 1958 by the Modern Language Association (MLA) on undergraduate course enrollments and degrees awarded. Also offered are some reflections on changing student profiles that are not captured by enrollment data.

According to the College Board, there are currently 159 universities in the United States that offer a Russian major (College Board, n.d.). I was unable to find historical data on the number of universities that offered a Russian major 30 years ago, but anecdotal evidence suggests that a number of small programs that experienced a significant drop in enrollments in the post-Soviet era have been discontinued.

Table 2.1 shows MLA data on Russian two- and four-year university enrollments from 1958 to 2013 (fall semester). Total enrollment does not equal the number of students studying Russian, since a student may be enrolled in more than one course. For reference, total enrollments in languages other than English are indicated for those same years when data are available.

There was a 157.3% spike in enrollments in Russian between 1958 and 1959, the largest jump for a single year. The increase usually is attributed to the Soviet launch of *Sputnik 1* in 1957. A robust growth in Russian language enrollments occurred from 1958 to 1968: 16,042 in 1958 to 41,280 in 1968 (257.3% increase). By 1980 there was a decline of 41.8% to 23,987, the lowest number since 1959. The 1980s saw a rise in enrollments of 85.4%, to an all-time high of 44,476 by 1990, just as the USSR was collapsing. Enrollments then declined 50.6% between 1990 and 2013, with only a modest increase (8%) between 2006 and 2009. In 2013, the final year for which

TABLE 2.1. Enrollment in Russian Courses at Two- and Four-Year Institutions (Fall Semesters Only)

Year	Enrollments in Russian	Total enrollments in languages other than English	Enrollments in Russian as % of total enrollments
1958	16,042	—	—
1959	26,675	—	—
1960	31,122	—	—
1961	32,703	—	—
1963	33,663	—	—
1965	33,818	1,059,258	3.1%
1968	41,280	—	—
1970	36,369	1,153,747	3.1%
1972	37,374	—	—
1974	32,522	946,389	3.4%
1977	27,960	—	—
1980	23,987	942,352	2.5%
1983	30,167	—	—
1986	33,945	1,003,548	3.3%
1990	44,476	—	—
1995	24,729	1,138,772	2.1%
2002	23,921	1,397,253	1.7%
2006	24,770	1,577,810	1.6%
2009	26,753	1,682,627	1.6%
2013	21,962	1,562,179	1.4%

Source: Adapted from "Enrollments in languages other than English in United States institutions of higher education" (MLA, 2013).

data were available, enrollment was the lowest it has ever been, with the exception of 1958.

Although the main focus of this article is higher education, it is also important to consider precollege enrollments. According to a report in April 2016 by the Committee on College and Pre-College Russian, since 1998 more than 230 precollege programs have been terminated across the United States, and by 2016 it appears that more than 20 states had no high school programs in Russian (Committee on College and Pre-College Russian, 2016).

Our common hope is that enrollments have stabilized and will begin to climb as a result of a number of factors, including the increased attention being paid to Russia and its geopolitical role. Perhaps in the coming decades Russia and the United States will find more common interests and provide expanded opportunities for collaboration and cooperation rather than conflict, both in the US government and the private sector, and our language enrollments will improve accordingly.

Degrees Awarded

Table 2.2 shows the available data for degrees awarded for Russian and Slavic for 1992–93, 2011–12 and 2013–14 and for Russian, Central European, East European, and Eurasian studies for 2011–12 and 2013–14.

The data for degrees awarded in 1992–93 and 2013–14 follow the same trajectory as Russian language enrollments, at least for the bachelor's degree in Russian language and literature, which dropped from 612 in 1992–93 to 371 in 2013–14. This 39.4% decrease is 10% less than the drop in enrollments (50.6%) over the same period. Since enrollment figures are not the same as number of students, it is difficult to draw any direct conclusions.

Students

The past 30 years have seen our student population change in significant ways, which are not captured by enrollment or degree data. It is difficult to describe a "typical"

TABLE 2.2. Bachelor's Degrees Awarded in Russian-Related Fields

	Year		
	1992-93	**2011-12**	**2013-14**
Russian language, literature	612	392 (−36%)	371 (−5%)
Russian studies	—	93	81 (−13%)
Slavic languages	77	63 (−18%)	66 (+5%)
Slavic studies	—	4	4 (+/−0%)
Russian, Central European, East European, and Eurasian studies	—	27	20 (−26%)

Source: Adapted from "Digest of education statistics" (National Center for Education Statistics, 1995, 2013, 2014).

undergraduate, as students today have diverse profiles. But one commonality is that they have grown up in the digital world, unlike many of their instructors. Anyone educated in the predigital age experienced learning quite differently than current students. One change is the immediate availability of information, a phenomenon that seems to create an expectation that much learning can be accomplished relatively quickly and negatively affects student expectations regarding the pace of language acquisition. Data from a major survey of over 2,000 students (of various languages) conducted at the University of Maryland in 2005–6 included a section on students' expectations for the pace of language acquisition. The results clearly indicate that expectations are unrealistic and students tend to underestimate the time required to reach various levels of proficiency (Martin, 2009). The data confirm that students' expectations do not align well with those of their instructors, most of whom are more realistic about the time required to gain proficiency. The genuine acquisition of new language forms essentially means repatterning one's brain. Current research in the fields of neuroscience, cognitive neuroscience, and neurolinguistics is illuminating just what happens to the brain when we are producing and learning languages (Morgan-Short et al., 2012). What we can learn from neuroscience about brain activity may help to explain the language "difficulty" categories that are well-known in our field. There is evidence to suggest that patterning the complex morphology of a language such as Russian takes more time for a learner whose dominant language is English, for example, than it would for learners who speak a Romance language (McGinnis, 1994). While Russian teachers have moved away from purely mechanical drills to communicative activities, acquisition of complex morphology still requires a lot of time. The time-on-task principle has endured and repetition does not appear to be relinquishing any ground as the mother of learning.

Over three decades of teaching in the United States I have seen many students who are high achievers in general and have a positive self-perception; they see themselves as having gone off the beaten path to study an "exotic" language such as Russian, usually arriving in an elementary course with the common perception that Russian is a "hard" language but one for which they are capable of rising to the challenge. Now, more than ever, faculty must help students understand how to set realistic expectations and coach them through the moments or even prolonged phases when their self-esteem is wounded because the (unrealistic) expectations they have set for themselves are not met. Most often these engaged students make reasonable and predictable progress but then sometimes conclude that they are not succeeding because of the slow pace of acquisition. Those who stick with the language often manage to achieve high levels of proficiency but not without periods of turbulence and frustration. I have observed a growing resistance among students for tolerating the inevitable discomfort that comes with learning a language.

The notion that our best learning happens only when we are comfortable is misleading. When you give students an opportunity to reflect on their experiences with other types of skills they have acquired, such as in music or sports, they recognize that growing their proficiency means tackling periodic discomfort, especially at critical junctures of moving to the next-higher level. The notion that acquiring a new language necessarily requires tolerating discomfort is not new (Ely, 1986; Liskin-Gasparro, 1998; Spielman & Radnofsky, 2001). What is new is having to make the case to students that discomfort is *normal* and is a result of the complexity of the endeavor, not that they are bad language learners or the materials, teacher, or course is subpar. Effective language learners learn to tolerate discomfort and even use it to their advantage: they develop skills to recognize, analyze, and even embrace discomfort as an important sign of growth. This is particularly true in the immersion and study abroad contexts, when students experience various types of discomfort: linguistic, cultural, social, psychological, and even physical. Students who run toward their comfort zone when confronted with discomfort usually end up interacting in English with other students from their group. As a result, progress is often not as great for them as for those who tolerate the discomfort and seek opportunities to engage in Russian. Strategies for coping with discomfort and using it to one's advantage are critical, but students today are not in an academic or cultural environment that fosters the development of skills to deal with discomfort as a normal part of the learning process. Today's language educators must help students become better learners by providing them with strategies for embracing discomfort and risk-taking as necessary components of the acquisition process, all the while learning to resist internalizing their frustration as personal failure.

Another change is the significant presence in today's classrooms of a heritage population, a group that was virtually nonexistent prior to the mid-1980s. There is a growing body of scholarship on heritage learners and several organizations dedicated to heritage learner pedagogy, such as the National Heritage Language Resource Center (NHLRC) at UCLA. According to US Census Bureau data for 2011, the number of Russian speakers in the United States between 1980 and 2011 rose from 173,226 to 905,843, an increase of 423%. Prior to the dissolution of the Soviet Union, however, emigrants lost their Soviet citizenship and had no expectation of being able to return in the future. Russian often remained a "home language" for children in these families and was rarely seen as potentially useful in their adult professional lives. Perceptions of the "homeland" and opportunities for using their Russian are now quite different than in prior decades, increasing the motivation for some heritage speakers to improve their proficiency for professional use in the future. Many heritage learners also enroll in Russian courses to improve their language in order to stay in touch with families and friends who live in the United States, Russia, the former Soviet Republics, Europe, Israel, or elsewhere, and to preserve Russian as a language of self-identity. Russian language instructors are challenged to address the varying needs of these students with appropriate instructional approaches (Polinsky & Kagan, 2007; Dubinina & Polinsky, 2013; Swender et al., 2014).

Another major change is the diversity of interests and goals that bring students to Russian programs. Thirty years ago students studying Russian were predominantly considering one of two career tracks: academia or government service. Since the collapse of the USSR students have sought ways to combine their interest in the Russian

TABLE 2.3. First and Second Majors in Russian, 2001–13

Year	Total number of bachelor's degrees in Russian conferred	Number of Russian first majors	Number of Russian second majors	Russian second majors as % of total
2001	441	335	106	24%
2013	564	392	172	30%

Source: Adapted from "Enrollments in languages other than English in the United States institutions of higher education" (MLA, 2013).

language and culture with a wider range of fields, including regional studies, international relations, global security studies, terrorism studies, cybersecurity, journalism, medicine, law, business, economics, computer science, sports management, criminology, law enforcement, public health, law, and theater and film studies. The MLA report on second majors in the fields of foreign languages (MLA, 2013) shows that in 2001 the number of second majors in all foreign languages was 28% of first majors, and by 2013 that number had risen to 38.6%; this more than 10% increase represented the largest percentage of second majors for any field. Table 2.3 shows the 6% increase in second majors for Russian between 2001 and 2013.

Over the years 2001 to 2013, 6,050 undergraduate degrees in Russian were awarded, with a total of 4,171 first majors and 1,879 second majors (31% of the total). The number of students who combine Russian with another major has hovered at 24–30% since 2001. It is difficult to determine from the data whether students are prioritizing a first or second major, since in many cases a second major is simply added chronologically, but this does not always indicate it is a lesser priority.

Undergraduate students' varied interests continue to challenge faculty to design programs that can address both general interests and more specific ones. A first step in rethinking curricular design is to understand student motivation. Merrill (2013) surveyed students attending the Middlebury Russian School between 1991 and 2011; although the purpose of the survey was not necessarily to determine how interests have changed over that decade, the data reveal that student interests are indeed diverse, extending well beyond literature and language alone.

GRADUATE STUDIES

Graduate programs in Russian have evolved to include more areas of specialization than the traditional literature or linguistic tracks offered in the mid-1980s. A review of US doctoral programs listed on the AATSEEL website shows that today there are few offerings in theoretical and historical linguistics, medieval literature, and even pre-19th-century literature, but there has been an expansion in specializations such as interdisciplinary studies, cultural studies, film studies, and second language acquisition (SLA). The AATSEEL website lists 38 graduate programs in North America, 25 of which offer a PhD degree. As Table 2.4 shows, all 25 programs feature a literature

TABLE 2.4. Slavic/Russian PhD Programs in the United States and Canada

University	Literature	Linguistics	Indication of interdisciplinary work as part of PhD
Brown University	✔		Students work with departmental faculty as well as with faculty in related fields such as comparative literature, theater and performance studies, history, political science, and international relations.
Columbia University	✔		Doctoral students in the Slavic Department are required to develop a strong minor in a second Slavic literature or a related field in the humanities, arts, or social sciences, or complete the concentration in comparative literature and society.
Harvard University	✔	✔	
Indiana University	✔	✔	
McGill University	✔		
New York University	✔		Interdisciplinary specialization in Russian (ISR), a new field of doctoral study in history or in comparative literature, encompassing literature, history, and culture.
Northwestern University	✔		Students are encouraged to participate in the Graduate School's Interdisciplinary Initiative program, including "clusters" in critical theory, poetry and poetics, theater and performance, gender and sexuality studies, and other fields.
Ohio State University	✔	✔	Slavic literature, film, and cultural studies and Slavic linguistics.
Princeton University	✔		
Stanford University	✔		
University of Alberta	✔		PhD.in comparative literature, not specifically Russian.

University of California, Berkeley	✔	✔	Students may pursue designated emphases in film; folklore; women, gender and sexuality studies; critical theory; Renaissance and early modern studies; etc., or individually designed areas of specialization. Slavic Department collaborates with the departments of Comparative Literature, Linguistics, Anthropology, History, Theater, Music, and Art History, and with the Institute of Slavic, East European, and Eurasian Studies, which houses the Berkeley Program in Soviet and Post-Soviet Studies and the Caucasus and Central Asia Program.
UCLA	✔	✔	Department of Slavic, East European, and Eurasian Languages and Cultures offers courses covering all periods of Slavic culture, from medieval to 21st century, as well as training in pedagogy and a range of East European languages and cultures. Cooperation with other programs offers the possibility of interdisciplinary research in media, digital studies, theory, translation, history, and religion.
University of Chicago	✔		Opportunities for cross-disciplinary inquiry in graduate workshops and the Franke Institute for the Humanities; many students in the Slavic Department forge innovative programs of study that cut across traditional boundaries.
University of Illinois at Chicago	✔		
University of Illinois at Urbana-Champaign	✔		Slavic languages and literatures, with emphasis on cultural and interdisciplinary studies and study in more than one Slavic language and literature.
University of Kansas	✔	✔	Students interested in Russian culture, intellectual history, Slavic folklore, or interdisciplinary themes pursue studies through the Russian literature PhD concentration. PhD students interested in the field of Slavic language pedagogy pursue studies through the Slavic linguistics PhD concentration.
University of Michigan	✔		In addition to existing PhD curriculum, which focuses on a single national language and literature, another track was launched that allows for comparative study and research in two East European literatures as well as interdisciplinary work. The primary Slavic literature may be Bosnian-Croatian-Serbian, Czech, Polish, Russian, or Ukrainian. The second literature may be one of the above or another East or Central European literature taught within the university (e.g., Yiddish or German). The third component of a student's program will comprise relevant work in another discipline, e.g., history of art or architecture, cinema, comparative literature, philosophy, anthropology, history, or sociology.

(*continued*)

TABLE 2.4. *(Continued)*

University	Literature	Linguistics	Indication of interdisciplinary work as part of PhD
University of Pittsburgh	✔		Also offers PhD in film studies with a concentration in Slavic as the associated department.
University of Southern California	✔		The doctorate in Slavic languages and literatures . . . provides a thorough grounding in Russian literary and cultural history as well as in the theoretical perspectives current in the field. Elective coursework, particularly at the upper level, allows students to take advantage of the department's expertise in such additional areas as Russian art, Russian theater, and eastern European cinema. . . . Depending on departmental offerings, further study in a second Slavic language and culture may also be possible.
University of Toronto	✔	✔	Slavic and Baltic languages
University of Virginia	✔		
University of Washington	✔		
University of Wisconsin–Madison	✔		Slavic languages and literature PhD in comparative Slavic culture is under development. Graduate students may also complete a PhD in SLA.
Yale University	✔		The department offers the PhD in Russian literature and culture and, by special arrangement, in medieval Slavic literature and philology. The department also offers, in conjunction with the program in film studies, a combined PhD degree in Slavic languages and literatures and film studies.

Note: The University of Chicago Slavic Department is not currently accepting applications to the PhD program. Students must apply to PhD programs in related fields such as comparative literature, cinema and media studies, or linguistics.

TABLE 2.5. Graduate Degrees Awarded in Russian and Slavic, 1992-93, 2011-12, 2013-14

	Years		
	1992-93	2011-12	2013-14
MA Russian language, literature	68	49 (-28%)	14 (-71%)
MA Russian studies	—	17	48 (+182%)
PhD Russian	4	2 (-50%)	1 (-50%)
MA Slavic languages	93	55 (-40%)	46 (-16%)
MA Slavic studies	—	3	1 (-67%)
PhD Slavic languages	24	25 (+4%)	34 (+36%)
PhD Slavic studies	—	—	1
MA Russian, Central European, East European, and Eurasian studies	—	30	33 (+10%)

Source: Adapted from "Digest of education statistics" (National Center for Education Statistics, 2014).

specialization, only seven (28%) have a track in linguistics, and only two (8%) offer the possibility of studying medieval Slavic literature and philology (UCLA and Yale), while 16 (67%) specifically indicate offering interdisciplinary study in areas such as film, cultural studies, history, or political science.[8]

A variety of factors may be driving the move toward interdisciplinarity, including: (1) developments in a variety of fields beyond Russian language and literature that intersect with North American Slavists' scholarly interests, (2) a response to student interest in a variety of other fields, and (3) a response to the demands of the academic market that have changed over time and a need to hire academics who can teach courses to new generations of students.[9]

Table 2.5 shows the available data on graduate degrees awarded from 1992 to 2014. Note that a specialization in literature or linguistics is not reported separately, and the categories that are used in the database are provided.

The data indicate a downward trend in language and literature master's degree programs since 1992, but a significant increase in Russian studies master's degree programs since 2011. Furthermore, almost as many degrees were awarded in Russian, Central European, East European, and Eurasian studies (63) as were awarded in Russian studies (65), with a combined total of 128. These trends are reflected in the academic job market.

FACULTY POSITIONS IN RUSSIAN AND SLAVIC

A review of the MLA's Job Information List (a well-known source of job openings) confirms two major trends in Russian and Slavic Studies over the last 30 years: a significant contraction of the field and the evolution of the field away from the traditional literature and linguistics tracks toward interdisciplinarity. Table 2.6 shows

TABLE 2.6. Russian and Slavic Positions Advertised in the MLA Job Information List (Tenure-Track and Non-Tenure-Track)

Time period	Total positions advertised	Tenure-track positions (% of total)	Non-tenure-track positions (% of total)
1984-89	424	268 (63.2%)	156 (36.8%)
1989-94	334	221 (66.2%)	113 (33.8%)
1994-99	162	94 (58%)	68 (42%)
1999-2004	128	80 (62.5%)	48 (37.5%)
2004-9	99	61 (61.6%)	38 (38.4%)
2009-14	85	39 (45.9%)	46 (54.1%)
2014-15	23	14 (60.9%)	9 (39.1%)
2015-16	24	14 (58.3%)	10 (41.7%)
2016-17	14	11 (78.6%)	3 (21.4%)
Total 2014-17	61	39 (63.9%)	22 (36.1%)

Source: Modern Language Association job information list (n.d), retrieved from https://www.mla.org/Resources/Career/Job-Information-List.

the total number of tenure- and non-tenure-track positions in Russian and Slavic advertised in five-year periods beginning in 1984. Tables 2.7 and 2.8 break down these categories (tenured and non-tenure-track) by area of specialization.

The number of tenure-track positions advertised by the MLA decreased in every five-year period from 1984 to 2014, with an 80% overall decrease over these 30 years. During 2014–17 there was the same number of tenure-track advertisements as during 2009–14, so, assuming there is at least one opening over the next two years, 2014–19 will be the first five-year period since 1984 that has witnessed an increase from the previous five-year period. The majority of advertised positions were tenure-track for each five-year period from 1984 through 2009, but 2009–14 was the first for which the advertisements for non-tenure-track jobs comprised the majority (54.1%). A significant drop in total numbers of non-tenure-track advertisements each five-year period occurred from 1984 to 2009, with the first increase (by eight jobs total) coming during the 2009–14 period. It is notable that from 1984 to 2009 the percentage of non-tenure-track positions in relation to total positions remained consistent—in the 30% range—but increased to 42% from 1994–99 and exceeded 50% for the first time during 2009–14. It is not clear whether the trend toward non-tenure-track positions will continue, but there is considerable discussion across the humanities of the overall reduction in tenure-track positions and the increase in non-tenure-track positions (Bousquet, 2008; Garcia Mathewson, 2016; Gerber, 2014; Gittleman, 2015). Humanities fields are swimming against two powerful interrelated national currents: (1) a shift toward the STEM fields of science, technology, engineering, mathematics, and (2) the narrowing vision of higher education as a place for vocational and professional training without a commitment to humanistic ideas as the foundation of all higher education. Humanities scholars continue to advocate for a solid humanities grounding for professionals in all fields, including STEM, but national policymakers, parents, and students do not appear to be heeding the call.

Advertised Positions for Tenured and Tenure-Track Positions in Russian and Slavic

Table 2.7 shows the breakdown of tenured and tenure-track positions between the traditional categories of language and linguistics versus language and literature. Additionally, advertisements specifying an advantage to the applicant with an interdisciplinary profile are indicated in the far-right column.

Openings for specialists in Slavic linguistics have always been fewer than those for Slavic language and literature teachers. The number of job openings for Slavic linguists dropped in each five-year period since 1984, with the exception of 2004–9, and only one position (2.5%) was advertised from 2014–17. Total openings for linguists did not exceed 19% of positions advertised in any given period, and this number has fallen sharply since 2009. Conversely, the number of positions that explicitly advertise for individuals with an interdisciplinary focus has increased from 3.3% (1984–89) to 46.1% (2009–14), and over 50% of the positions advertised for each year of the current three-year period (2014–17) seek candidates with interests in areas beyond traditional language and literature.

TABLE 2.7. Advertised Positions by Specialization

	Tenured and tenure-track			
Time period	**Number of positions**	**Language and linguistics (% of total)**	**Language and literature (% of total)**	**Number that indicate interdisciplinary focus a plus (% of total)**
1984–89	268	47 (17.5%)	221 (82.6%)	9 (Soviet interdisciplinary, 3.3%)
1989–94	221	42 (19%)	179 (80.1%)	14 (6.3%)
1994–99	94	16 (17%)	78 (83%)	10 (10.6%)
1999–2004	80	7 (8.8%)	73 (92%)	27 (33.8%)
2004–9	61	8 (13.1%)	53 (86.9%)	26 (42.6%)
2009–14	39	3 (7.7%)	36 (92.3%)	18 (46.1%)
2014–15	14	1 (7.1%)	13 (92.9%)	9 (64.2%)
2015–16	14	—	14 (100%)	8 (57.1%)
2016–17	11	—	11 (100%)	6 (54.5%)
2014–17	39	1 (2.5%)	38 (97.5%)	23 (58.9%)

Source: Modern Language Association job information list (n.d.), retrieved from https://www.mla.org/Resources/Career/Job-Information-List.

TABLE 2.8. Advertised Positions in the MLA Job Information List (Non-Tenure-Track)

Time period	Total number of positions	Visiting or temporary professor rank (% of total)	Lecturer or instructor rank (% of total)
1984-89	156	85 (54.5%)	71 (45.5%)
1989-94	113	52 (46%)	61 (54%)
1994-99	68	30 (44%)	38 (56%)
1999-2004	48	30 (62.5%)	18 (37.5%)
2004-9	38	17 (44.7%)	21 (55.3%)
2009-14	46	24 (52.2%)	22 (47.8%)
2014-15	9	5 (55.5%)	4 (44.5%)
2015-16	10	2 (20%)	8 (80%)
2016-17	3	2 (66.7%)	1 (33.3%)
2014-17	22	9 (40.9%)	13 (59.1%)

Source: Modern Language Association job information list (n.d.), retrieved from https://www.mla.org/Resources/Career/Job-Information-List.

Advertised Positions for Non-Tenure-Track Positions in Russian and Slavic

Table 2.8 shows the MLA data on non-tenure-track openings, divided by those for a visiting/temporary professorial rank (assuming a PhD) and those for a lecturer or instructor (which are usually open to those holding at least an MA).

Table 2.8 shows that the proportion of non-tenure-track positions for a visiting professor versus a lecturer or instructor was fairly evenly split, hovering around 50% (44% to 52.2%), except for a spike in the period of 1999–2004, when openings for a visiting assistant professor rose to 62.5% of all non-tenure-track positions. The most recent three-year period (2014–17) has seen a decrease in visiting professor positions (40.9%) and an increase in lecturer or instructor positions (59.1%).

FACULTY COMPOSITION

A clear change from the mid-1980s to today is the increase in the number of US-based faculty who are native speakers of Russian holding degrees from Russian and/or US institutions. Prior to the collapse of the Soviet Union it was difficult for Russianists from the USSR to study or work in an American university, even temporarily. ACTR sponsored a program that invited curriculum consultants from the Soviet Union for temporary teaching and consulting positions in the United States, but there were few such positions. Not until after the collapse of USSR were both faculty and students in any significant numbers able to travel to the United States to work and study. There was, to be sure, a small number of faculty who taught in American universities in the early years of the American Slavic field (late 1940s to 1960s) who had been educated in Russia or Eastern Europe. Perhaps the most famous and influential was Roman Jakobson, who taught at Harvard from 1949–67 and influenced a generation of scholars, including Dell Hymes, Horace Lunt, Charles Townsend, Dan E. Davidson, and Richard D. Brecht. Davidson and Brecht went on to chart the course of a relatively new field of study for Russianists, namely SLA with a focus on Russian, by launching the Bryn Mawr graduate program. Today's research, with its focus on the acquisition of Russian, can in some ways can be traced back to interaction between American scholars and émigré scholars from Russia and Eastern Europe. The collapse of the USSR brought previously unprecedented opportunities for interaction among scholars of Russian, irrespective of national origin or citizenship, which clearly strengthened the field.[10]

THE PROFICIENCY REVOLUTION AND NATIONAL STANDARDIZED ASSESSMENTS

The evolution of proficiency assessment and the increasing use of standardized instruments within it has changed our profession. Thirty years ago there were very few such instruments and students were not assessed for grants, study abroad, graduate entrance or exit exams, or even jobs to the degree that they are today. Previously one's credentials were often limited to a degree and a transcript, neither of which attests to real-world, current skills. Reading, listening, and grammar tests offered by the Educational Testing Service occasionally were used to gauge progress in study abroad programs, but few validated external assessments were in widespread use. Today the most widely administered tests in the higher educational context are official ACTFL assessments based on the ACTFL Proficiency Guidelines (delivered by Language Testing International): the Oral Proficiency Interview (OPI) and the Oral Proficiency Interview by Computer (OPIc); the Writing Proficiency Test (WPT); and the newest, the Reading Proficiency Test (RPT) and the Listening Proficiency Test (LPT). For K–12 learners, ACTFL has developed and is currently administering its Assessment of Performance toward Proficiency in Language (AAPPL). ACTFL circulated the first draft of its Proficiency Guidelines in 1982, and soon thereafter held the first training workshops for conducting and rating OPIs. Since then ACTFL's proficiency assessments have been used in widespread academic, governmental, and commercial contexts. As of 2017 LTI had administered over one million official assessments since its founding in 1992. The LTI website lists over 120 schools and universities, 95 government clients (including many state departments of education), and 95 commercial entities that regularly use ACTFL assessments.

Another innovative model that uses the ACTFL Proficiency Guidelines as a framework for assessing proficiency is the Advanced Placement (AP) prototype for Russian developed by ACTR to promote better articulation between high school and college programs. As of summer 2017 the National Examination in World Languages (NEWL) for high school students was under development by American Councils for Arabic, Chinese, Korean, Portuguese, and Russian (ACIE, n.d.).

It should be noted that the US government proficiency scale, known as the Interagency Language Roundtable scale (ILR), the precursor to the ACTFL Guidelines, has also found increased applications in the field, especially as it relates to US government job opportunities and financial support for language study (ILR, n.d.).

The ACTFL Proficiency Guidelines continue to have a transformative impact on the way we teach, research, and learn languages in general, and Russian in particular (Comer, 2012).[11] They have changed our pedagogies and methodologies, affected the way goals are set and learning outcomes are articulated, the design of curriculums, the selection of instructional materials, the method for developing and using existing assessments, and the way students are guided on their path to becoming independent learners.

THE TECHNOLOGY REVOLUTION AND LANGUAGE LEARNING

Innovations in the area of technology have greatly influenced our profession. Although today's Internet can trace its origins to the early 1960s, and the personal computing revolution was well under way by the mid-1980s, it was not until around 1995 that the web became a significant factor in teaching in the United States (Leiner et al., n.d.). Prior to the mid-1990s, access to authentic foreign language and culture required much more than turning on a mobile device. One had to travel to a place where that language and culture actually existed, or depend on someone else to travel there, and try to capture tangible artifacts through a variety of more traditional media. Access to authentic sources *in real time* is relatively new to our language learning and teaching efforts. Students now can access any language register, style, or genre on their own, including language inputs that may not lend themselves to being efficiently or appropriately integrated or that might, in fact, even work against instructional goals. Integrating authentic material requires a great deal of imagination, time, and planning and must take into consideration the level of the learners, the complexity of the material in relation to that level, the appropriateness for the specific instructional context, and the method for integrating it into broad curricular goals. Our challenge is how to harness our virtually limitless access to authentic material, since greater access does not necessarily translate into more efficient language acquisition.

New technologies are also transforming how we think about what should and perhaps what should no longer be done in the physical classroom (Garza, 2013). Teachers should ask, "What do students need *me* and the *classroom space* for; what can I do for them that they cannot do on their own?" Answers of 30 years ago would have been very different than the answers we would give today. Motivated students can do a great deal of learning independently. There are web-based resources for much of what we used to do in the classroom, including sites for learning to write the alphabet, going through pronunciation drills, and learning grammar and meaning. Today we no longer have traditional language labs with reel-to-reel recordings, and we do not need to take up valuable contact hours watching something together or spending class time teaching something like handwriting, when we have Internet-based resources that allow such activities to occur outside the classroom. Digitally recorded independent work that can be done from virtually anywhere can now supplement traditional written assignments. US universities are using learning management systems that, among other things, allow students to submit work and interact with instructors in text, audio, or video formats, transforming traditional "homework" into what I would call "independent learning," as well as facilitating more effective individualized feedback. The role of the teacher is changing, from one who used to be in control of the collective learning process in an institutional setting to one who facilitates individualized and independent learning within the context of an institution (Garza, 2013).

STUDY ABROAD

In the mid-1980s there existed four major organizations that provided to students the opportunity to study in the USSR: the International Research and Exchanges Board and the Fulbright Program (which primarily supported graduate study) and ACTR and the Council on International Education Exchange (which offered programs to both undergraduates and graduate students). Space in these programs was limited and admission was highly competitive. All four organizations remain leaders in academic study abroad; however, opportunities have expanded with the creation of regional programs and direct institutional partnerships. Many of the newer programs focus on combining Russian language study with other fields, and there are increasing opportunities to study Russian in the former Soviet republics. Furthermore, today students have the opportunity to pursue direct enrollment in many Russian institutions of higher education.

One of the most important changes impacting language acquisition is the widespread availability of homestays. Of course, much depends on student motivation and attitude, but a homestay provides essential interactions with native speakers in an authentic situation. Prior to 1991 students studying in Russia were housed in dormitories or sections of dormitories designated for foreign students. Foreigners visiting the country were permitted little freedom of movement without explicit permission from the Ministry of Internal Affairs. While strict visa requirements for studying in Russia still exist, those requirements are vastly different and much less restrictive than they were 30 years ago. Greater access to the country and people in ways that were unimaginable in the Soviet era has great advantages for language acquisition, though we know that just being in a country is not enough; language gains are greatly dependent of how students actually spend their time and how intentional they are in managing their learning. Rivers (2008) was one of the first to investigate the impact of homestays and students' purposeful engagement with the language, suggesting that students participating in homestay programs may benefit from predeparture training in how to maximize gains by managing linguistic inputs and interactions. He and subsequent scholars argue that students must take more responsibility for their language learning; they must engage in purposeful, effortful attention to language gains, both in terms of the explicit instruction they receive from professional language educators and in terms of their implicit exposure through total immersion (Davidson et al., 2017; Pellegrino Aveni, 2005).

GOVERNMENT SUPPORT FOR CRITICAL LANGUAGES

The US government established the National Security Education Program (NSEP) in 1991 "to develop a much-needed strategic partnership between the national security community and higher education to address national needs for expertise in critical languages and regions" (NSEP, n.d.). Since the inception of NSEP, Russian has continually remained on the list of over 60 critical languages. One major program supported by US government funding for the study of 10 critical languages is the Language Flagship; there are now 27 Flagship Centers at US universities supporting 10 languages (Language Flagship, n.d.). The goal is for students to reach ACTFL Superior/ILR 3 proficiency by time of graduation. The NSEP annual reports document the proficiency levels in speaking, reading, and listening reached by Language Flagship students. The results are quite impressive and challenge the notion that it is impossible to reach Advanced or Superior proficiency prior to graduation. The Flagship program has inspired curricular reforms in both content and proficiency goals in order to meet the needs of the US government by helping students achieve professional proficiency (Brown & Bown, 2015; Murphy & Evans-Romaine, 2016).

Three other initiatives support the study of Russian: (1) the Critical Languages Scholarship Program, which is open to graduating high school seniors, undergraduates, and graduate students, supports summer study at all levels but focuses particularly on the Intermediate-Advanced threshold (Critical Languages Scholarship Program, n.d.); (2) the National Security Language Initiative for Youth (NSLI-Y) administered by the US Department of State, open to US high school students aged 15 to 18 (National Security Language Initiative for Youth, n.d.); and (3) STARTALK, launched in 2006 and overseen by the US National Security Agency, which aims to expose learners as young as five to critical languages (STARTALK, n.d.). The infusion of significant government funding for critical languages has highlighted the need to give learners an opportunity to start earlier and to take them as far as possible during their K–16 experience. Unquestionably, the Russian field in particular has benefited from trends in government support for critical languages.

LOOKING FORWARD: CONTEMPORARY CHALLENGES AND TRENDS IN THE TEACHING AND LEARNING OF RUSSIAN

Reflecting on the landscape of today's teaching and learning of Russian, I see many challenges and exciting initiatives. There is growing support to design better-integrated and well-articulated curricula along the entire K–16 continuum, such as STARTALK, NSLI-Y, the AP Russian Prototype exam, and the NEWL. These efforts mean that we are likely to see more students enter postsecondary education armed with previous

Russian study. One resulting challenge is to find ways to place those students appropriately within university programs.

The presence of heritage learners in Russian language classrooms continues to pose a challenge for us, since these learners usually come with varied oral and literacy skills and few programs offer dedicated heritage tracks. As the demographics of Russian-speaking immigrant communities change, so do the heritage populations in our classrooms. Research on heritage language acquisition is an important direction for our field and can inform curriculum design, materials, and course development for this unique group of learners.

We are doing more, but not yet enough, to integrate study abroad into our curricula at home. We need to give students strategies to manage their learning abroad so as to maximize their language gains. To integrate the students' overseas experiences into our domestic curricula we might devise ways to engage students from their home campuses during their time abroad, perhaps as one- or two-credit courses that require regular interactions with an instructor.

The proficiency revolution in the mid-1980s and into the 1990s helped us to redesign our approaches so that we now can get learners to the Intermediate proficiency level in most of our university programs, even if they do not participate in an immersion experience. In recent years, however, the focus has understandably shifted to how we can move our learners toward reaching the Advanced and Superior levels, which were once thought of as virtually impossible to attain by the time of completion of a bachelor's degree. It remains difficult to reach these levels within the curricula of most traditional university programs. The National Flagship Program is changing this traditional framework by requiring program enhancements that substantially increase contact hours, that focus on language development targeted to higher levels, and that require academic and cultural immersion in country. Such programmatic changes force the learner to take greater responsibility for purposeful learning. The field will continue to benefit from the innovations, scholarship, and practices produced by the Russian Flagship Centers.

Advances in technologies will continue to challenge us to explore new possibilities to make the language learning process ever more efficient, effective, and engaging. As a result, the relationship between teacher and learner will continue to evolve.

There is an increasing global demand for speakers of Russian in a wide range of fields and our academic programs must either address the changes in student interests or risk becoming obsolete. The MLA report "Foreign Languages and Higher Education: New Structures for a Changed World" (2007) argues that "foreign language departments, if they are to be meaningful players in higher education—or, indeed, if they are to thrive as autonomous units—must transform their programs and structure" (MLA, 2007). Ten years later researchers Lara Lomicka Anderson and Gillian Lord conducted a national survey to see whether the advice of the MLA has been heeded. They found that while more than half of their respondents reported having read the report, only 39% reported having embarked on curricular changes as a result

(Redden, 2017). Rethinking our curricula is urgent if we are to stay relevant in the future.

In the mid-1980s it was impossible to foresee the changes that awaited our field as a result of shifting geopolitical realities and truly transformative technological advances. We couldn't have imagined how these changes would affect our world and what the implications would be for language learning and teaching 30 years hence. Impossible as it may be to predict, we can nonetheless contemplate: What changes are in store for our field in the next 30 years?

NOTES

1. I hold a bachelor's degree in Russian and political science (double major) from a mid-sized state university (1980) and a PhD in Slavic languages and literatures from an Ivy League institution (1990). My first visit to the USSR was in 1977; then I spent every summer between 1979 and 1983 there; then a graduate year at the Pushkin Institute (Moscow, ACTR); followed by two years working as a translator and editor in a major Soviet publishing house. I have been faculty at my current Research I state university since 1990.
2. For a discussion of English borrowings and an assertion that approximately 75% of borrowings at the end of the 20th century came from English, see http://festival.1september.ru/articles/410377/. For a discussion of English as the main source for borrowings into youth slang, see http://nauchforum.ru/node/1569.
3. When the euro was introduced in the 1990s, the academy determined that the gender of the noun евро [euro] is masculine, not the predictable neuter, since it really is an abbreviation of евродоллар [eurodollar].
4. There is a perception among many cultural elites that the Russian language has deteriorated and the culture has coarsened in the post-Soviet period, as evidenced by discussions in many TV programs, articles, blogs, etc.
5. See http://www.consultant.ru/document/cons_doc_LAW_162558/. For the official statement about this law and its amendments, see http://kremlin.ru/acts/news/20931.
6. Роскомнадзор: Федеральная служба по надзору в сфере связи, информационных технологий и массовых коммуникаций [The federal service for supervision of communications, information technologies, and mass media].
7. In 1997 ACTR launched Russnet, the first Internet-based resource for teachers and learners, which provides free language-learning support modules, virtual classroom space, useful databases, and forums for exchanging information. Russnet was originally supported by ACTR and a grant from the Ford Foundation, with additional support provided over the years from other sponsors, including the US Department of Education, the National Endowment for the Humanities, and the Fund for the Improvement of Post-Secondary Education.
8. Information on each program comes from its individual website.
9. Bryn Mawr College offered a graduate program in Russian and SLA from 1992 to 2008, awarding 37 PhD degrees (Bryn Mawr College, n.d.). Today only the University

of Wisconsin offers a PhD in SLA that collaborates specifically with the Slavic Department.

10. I am not aware of any demographic study documenting country of origin, country of highest degree earned, or languages spoken by faculty in our field.
11. In 2015 ACTFL conducted 167 workshops with over 2,000 participants and certified its 1,000th OPI tester in 2016, including 54 certified testers of Russian. (Data provided via email dated September 6, 2016, from ACTFL's Department of Professional Programs in response to a direct inquiry.)

REFERENCES

American Association of Teachers of Slavic and East European Languages (AATSEEL). (n.d.). Graduate program listings. Retrieved from http://www.aatseel.org/graduate_programs

American Council on the Teaching of Foreign Languages (ACTFL). (2012). *ACTFL Proficiency Guidelines 2012*. Retrieved from http://www.actfl.org/publications/guidelines-and-manuals/actfl-proficiency-guidelines-2012

American Councils for International Education (ACIE). (n.d.). National examination in world languages. Retrieved from https://www.americancouncils.org/newl

American Councils for International Education (ACIE). (2014). Annual report. Retrieved from https://www.americancouncils.org/sites/default/files/Annual_Report_2014_FULL_web.pdf

American Councils for International Education (ACIE). (2014). *New ARC research center examines the role of language in education and the workplace*. Retrieved from https://www.americancouncils.org/news/new-arc-research-center-examines-role-language-education-and-workplace

Aref'ev, A. L. (2012). Русский язык на рубеже XX–XXI веков [The Russian language at the border of the 20th and 21st centuries]. Retrieved from http://www.isras.ru/files/File/Publication/russkij_yazyk.pdf

Bousquet, M. (2008). *How the university works: Higher education and the low-wage nation*. New York: New York UP.

Brown, A., & Bown, J. (Eds.). (2015). *To advanced proficiency and beyond: Theory and methods for developing superior second-language ability*. Washington, DC: Georgetown UP.

Bryn Mawr College. (n.d.). Graduate program in Russian description. Retrieved from https://www.brynmawr.edu/russian/graduate-program-0

College Board. (n.d.). Retrieved from https://bigfuture.collegeboard.org/college-search?navId=www-cs

Comer, W. (2012). Communicative language teaching and Russian: The current state of the field. In V. Makarova (Ed.), *Russian language studies in North America: New perspectives from theoretical and applied linguistics* (pp. 133–60). London: Anthem.

Committee on College and Pre-College Russian. (2016). Report. Retrieved from http://fs2.american.edu/jschill/www/

Critical Languages Scholarship Program. (n.d.). Retrieved from http://clscholarship.org/

Davidson, D. E., Garas, N., & Lekic, M. (2016). Assessing language proficiency and intercultural development in the overseas immersion context. In D. Murphy & K. Evans-Romaine (Eds.), *Exploring the US Language Flagship Program: Professional competence in a second language by graduation* (pp. 156–76). Bristol, UK: Multilingual Matters.

Dubinina, I., & Polinsky, M. (2013). Russian in the USA. In M. Moser & M. Polinsky (Eds.), *Slavic languages in migration* (pp. 1–28). Vienna, Austria: University of Vienna.

Ely, C. M. (1986). An analysis of discomfort, risktaking, sociability, and motivation in the L2 classroom. *Language Learning*, *36*(1), 1–25.

Garcia Mathewson, T. (2016, August 13). Tenure is disappearing, much to the detriment of higher ed. *EducationDive.* Retrieved from http://www.educationdive.com/news/tenure-is-disappearing-much-to-the-detriment-of-higher-ed/417296/

Garza, T. (2013). Keeping it real: Intensive instruction and the future of Russian language and culture in U.S. universities. *Russian Language Journal*, *63*, 7–24.

Gerber, L. G. (2014). *The rise and decline of faculty governance: Professionalization and the modern American university.* Baltimore, MD: Johns Hopkins UP.

Gittleman, S. (2015, October 29). Tenure is disappearing, but it's what made American universities the best in the world. *The Washington Post.* Retrieved from https://www.washingtonpost.com

Gorham, M., Lunde, I., & Paulsen, M. (Eds.). (2014). *Digital Russia: The language, culture, and politics of new media communication.* New York: Routledge.

Interagency Language Roundtable (ILR). (n.d.). Skill level descriptions. Retrieved from http://www.govtilr.org/

Jarvis, D., & Lubensky, S. (Eds.). (1984). *Teaching, learning, acquiring Russian.* Bloomington, IN: Slavica.

Kagan, O., & Martin, C. (2016). Heritage language learners in flagship programs: Motivation, language proficiency, and intercultural communicative competence. In D. Murphy & K. Evans-Romaine (Eds.), *The US Language Flagship Program: Professional competence in a second language by graduation* (pp. 137–55). Bristol, UK: Multilingual Matters.

Kagan, O., & Rifkin, B. (Eds.). (2000). *The learning and teaching of Slavic languages and cultures.* Bloomington, IN: Slavica.

The Language Flagship Program. (2015). Annual report. Retrieved from https://www.thelanguageflagship.org/media/docs/reports/2015-Annual-Report-the-Language-Flagship.pdf

Leiner, B., Cerf, V. G., Clark, D. D., Kahn, R. E., Kleinrock, L., Lynch, D. C., Postel, J., Roberts, L. G., & Wolff, S. (n.d.). Brief history of the Internet. Retrieved from http://www.internetsociety.org/internet/what-internet/history-internet/brief-history-internet

Liskin-Gasparro, J. (1998). Linguistic development in an immersion context: How advanced learners of Spanish perceive SLA. *Modern Language Journal*, *82*(2), 159–75.

Martin, C. (2009). Achieving Level 2/Advanced or Level 3/Superior proficiency in Russian in a university setting: The case of curricular reform via the Language Flagship (Russian Domestic) at the University of Maryland. In R. D. Brecht & D. E. Davidson

(Eds.), *Mnemosynon: Studies on language and culture in the Russophone world. Presented to Dan E. Davidson by his students and colleagues* (pp. 369–86). Moscow: Azbukovnik.

Martin, C. (2015). Introduction: Past context, present focus, future directions: Shifting focus from Intermediate skills in classroom training to Advanced/Superior and beyond. In A. Brown & J. Bown (Eds.), *To Advanced proficiency and beyond: Theory and methods for developing Superior second-language ability* (pp. xiii–xxiv). Washington, DC: Georgetown UP.

McGinnis, S. (1994). The less common alternative: A report from the task force for teacher training in the less commonly taught languages. *ADFL Bulletin*, *25*(2), 17–22.

Merrill, J. (2013). Our Russian classrooms and students: Who is choosing Russian, why, and what cultural content should we offer them? *Russian Language Journal*, *63*, 51–78.

Modern Language Association (MLA). (n.d.). Data on second majors in language and literature, 2001–2013. Retrieved from https://www.mla.org/Resources/Research/Surveys-Reports-and-Other-Documents/Teaching-Enrollments-and-Programs/Data-on-Second-Majors-in Language-and-Literature-2001-13

Modern Language Association (MLA). (n.d.). Job information list. Retrieved from https://www.mla.org/Resources/Career/Job-Information-List

Modern Language Association (MLA). (2007). Foreign languages and higher education: New structures for a changed world. Retrieved from https://www.mla.org/Resources/Research/Surveys-Reports-and-Other-Documents/Teaching-Enrollments-and-Programs/Foreign-Languages-and-Higher-Education-New-Structures-for-a-Changed-World

Modern Language Association (MLA). (2013). Enrollments in languages other than English in United States institutions of higher education. Retrieved from https://www.mla.org/Resources/Research/Surveys-Reports-and-Other-Documents/Teaching-Enrollments-and-Programs/Enrollments-in-Languages-Other-Than-English-in-United-States-Institutions-of-Higher-Education

Morgan-Short, K., Steinhauer, K., Sanz, C., & Ullman, M. (2012). Explicit and implicit second language training differentially affect the achievement of native-like brain activation patterns. *Journal of Cognitive Neuroscience*, *24*(4), 933–47.

Murphy, D., & Evans-Romaine, K. (Eds.). (2016). *Exploring the US Language Flagship Program: Professional competence in a second language by graduation*. Bristol, UK: Multilingual Matters.

National Center for Education Statistics. (1995, 2013, 2014, 2015). Digest of education statistics. Retrieved from https://nces.ed.gov/programs/digest/d95/dtab241.asp; https://nces.ed.gov/programs/digest/d13/tables/dt13_318.30.asp; https://nces.ed.gov/programs/digest/d14/tables/dt14_311.70.asp; and https://nces.ed.gov/programs/digest/d15/tables/dt15_318.30.asp

National Heritage Language Resource Center (NHLRC). (n.d.). Retrieved from http://www.nhlrc.ucla.edu/nhlrc

National Security Education Program (NSEP). (n.d.). Retrieved from https://www.nsep.gov/content/critical-languages

National Security Language Initiative for Youth. (n.d.). Retrieved from http://www.nsliforyouth.org/

National Standards Collaborative Board (NSCB). (2015). *World-readiness standards for learning languages* (4th ed.). Alexandria, VA: Author. Retrieved from http://www.actfl.org/publications/all/world-readiness-standards-learning-languages.

Pelligrino Aveni, V. (2005). *Study abroad and second language use: Constructing the self.* New York: Cambridge UP.

Polinsky, M., & Kagan, O. (2007). Heritage languages: In the wild and in the classroom. *Language and Linguistics Compass*, *1*(5), 368–95.

Redden, E. (2017). Call to action on languages, 10 years later. *Inside Higher Education.* Retrieved from https://www.insidehighered.com/news/2017/01/06/survey-looks-foreign-language-programs-response-decade-old-call-transform-teaching

Rivers, W. (2008). Is being there enough? The effects of homestay placement on language gain during study abroad. *Foreign Language Annals*, *31*(4), 492–500.

Ryazanova-Clarke, L. (2009). What's in a foreign word: Negotiating linguistic culture on Russian radio programmes about language. In B. Beumers et al. (Eds.), *The post-Soviet Russian media: Conflicting signals* (pp. 105–22). New York: Routledge.

Ryazanova-Clarke, L., & Wade, T. (2002). *The Russian language today.* New York: Routledge.

Spielmann, G., & Radnofsky, M. L. (2001). Learning language under tension: New directions from a qualitative study. *Modern Language Journal*, *85*(2), 259–78.

STARTALK. (n.d). STARTALK's mission. Retrieved from https://startalk.umd.edu/public/

Swender, E., Martin, C., Rivera-Martinez, M., & Kagan, O. (2014). Exploring oral proficiency profiles of heritage speakers of Russian and Spanish. *Foreign Language Annals*, *47*(3), 423–46.

US Census Bureau. (2011). Appendix Table 2: Languages spoken at home, 1980, 1990, 2000 and 2007. Retrieved from https://www.census.gov/library/publications/2010/acs/acs-12.html

3

RUSSIAN PROGRAMS IN THE 21ST-CENTURY UNIVERSITY

Preparing for the Future

Angelika Kraemer, Jason Merrill, and David Prestel

The humanities remind us where we have been and help us envision where we are going. Emphasizing critical perspective and imaginative response, the humanities—including the study of languages, literature, history, film, civics, philosophy, religion, and the arts—foster creativity, appreciation of our commonalities and our differences, and knowledge of all kinds. (AAAS, 2013, p. 9)

Russian language instructors are familiar with the notion of a "crisis of the humanities." Descriptions are usually accompanied by statistics showing rapidly decreasing enrollments in humanities disciplines (e.g., Lewin, 2013). While the nature and validity of these numbers has been debated (e.g., Bérubé, 2013; Hirsch, 2013), they provide fuel for administrators and politicians searching for areas to cut in the face of declining funding for education and can be used to justify the elimination or attempted elimination of entire programs.[1] Popular opinion is often on their side; for example, in May 2012 *Forbes* published an article bluntly titled "To Boost Post-College Prospects, Cut Humanities Departments" (Cohan, 2012). The author, citing high levels of student debt and the "waste produced by the mis-match between the educational system and the demand for labor" (para. 2), insists that we must "cut out the departments offering majors that make students unemployable" (para. 1). A quick glance at the reader comments to any article on this topic reveals that many agree with these sentiments (e.g., Hutner & Mohamed, 2013; Levitz & Belkin, 2013).

The fact that Russian language departments are small compared to other humanities disciplines means that our programs can be particularly vulnerable, and instructors of Russian can find themselves in the center of the so-called crisis of the humanities. Colleagues in Russian and other languages use their websites to propagate and explain the many benefits of studying languages, Russian in particular (e.g., AATSEEL & ACTR, n.d.; Florida State University, 2013; for general benefits of language learning see ACTFL, n.d.). Many Russian colleagues have taken steps toward making their programs more innovative, with the goals of increasing enrollments, improving outcomes, and advancing collaboration.[2] In this chapter we address trends and developments under discussion or that have already been implemented and that are likely to affect Russian programs in the near future. Our goal is to increase awareness of how Russian programs might prepare and respond to potential changes in ways that are appropriate for their particular institutional contexts.

A 2013 article published in *The New York Times* titled "As Interest in the Humanities Fades, Colleges Worry" (Lewin, 2013) identifies serious causes for concern, such as the decrease in humanities enrollments and majors and the primacy of science and technology fields on many campuses. We remain confident, however, that Russian programs can proactively prepare themselves for coming developments. As we hope to show, despite the concerns there are still significant reasons for humanists, and specifically those of us in Russian studies, to choose to be invigorated.

TRENDS IN RUSSIAN ENROLLMENTS

In 2009 Russian enrollments were described as a "mixed bag" (SRAS, 2010), and that same phrase could be applied to Russian student numbers in the Modern Language Association's (MLA's) 2013 enrollment report (Goldberg et al., 2015) and its 2016 preliminary enrollment report (Looney & Lusin, 2018). The 2013 MLA report notes that overall enrollments in languages other than English have decreased by 6.7% since 2009, whereas from 2013–16 they fell another 9.2%, the "second-largest decline in the history of the survey" (Looney & Lusin, 2018, p. 2).[3] Most languages saw enrollment declines from 2009 to 2013 (Goldberg et al., 2015), and from 2013–16 only Japanese and Korean showed gains in enrollment (Looney & Lusin, 2018). At first glance the situation with Russian looks particularly dire: Russian is one of four languages—along with Ancient Greek, Modern Hebrew, and Latin—that experienced what the MLA terms "radical decreases" in student numbers over the years 2009–13 (Goldberg et al., 2015, p. 2). Russian enrollments decreased by 17.9% over these same four years. From 2013–16 Russian fared better than most languages, with a "less radical" decrease of 7.4% (Looney & Lusin, 2018, p. 3). These declines came after modest increases in the previous two MLA reports: from 2002 to 2006 Russian enrollments went up 3.5%, and from 2006 to 2009 they increased by 8.0% (Goldberg et al., 2015). Since 2009 Russian enrollments are down 25.2% at two-year colleges and 17.6% at four-year institutions.[4] Russian, the report asserts, has seen a "serious decline" since the MLA began keeping numbers in 1960 (p. 4), and—along with French and German—Russian "fell precipitously" in 1995 and has "yet to recover" (p. 6).[5] In 1990 Russian accounted for 3.8% of language courses, but in the last four MLA full surveys it has been under 2%. As of 2013 Russian accounts for only 1.4% of all language course enrollments other than English.[6]

The 2013 MLA report contains two points that should be considered alongside the grim enrollment numbers. First it cautions that overall enrollments in higher education have decreased since the 2009 report (Goldberg et al., 2015), although the report unfortunately does not describe the scope of this decrease nor attempt to link it further with the loss of language students.[7] The report notes that "declines in overall enrollments for French, Ancient Greek, Biblical Hebrew, and Russian coincide with drops in the number of institutions reporting enrollments in those languages in 2013" (p. 14). By 2013, 17 fewer institutions (436) reported having Russian enrollments than those that did in 2009 (453). This decline looks even more drastic over a longer period of time: in 1990, 626 institutions reported Russian enrollments, meaning that the 436 institutions reporting Russian enrollments was a decrease of 30.4% over 23 years. The decrease was felt slightly more at two-year institutions: in 2013, 36.1% fewer two-year institutions (119 in 1990 down to 76 in 2013) and 28.3% fewer four-year colleges and universities (502 down to 360) reported Russian enrollments.[8] The MLA offers only the explanation that "one may conclude that some programs in these languages have been suspended or shuttered" (p. 14).[9]

The second point is that there may be a silver lining to the MLA numbers. The 2013 report draws special attention to the question of advanced-level students and notes that in only four languages did advanced students (defined by the MLA as third- and fourth-year) comprise 20% or more of the total undergraduate enrollment in that language; these were Chinese (21.9%), Portuguese (22.7%), Russian (25.5%), and Biblical Hebrew (57.0%) (Goldberg et al., 2015). For enrollments through 2016 the MLA reports similar numbers: after Biblical Hebrew (with a ratio of 2:1), Russian, Portuguese, and Chinese are the only languages with a 3:1 ratio of introductory-to-advanced undergraduate enrollments (Looney & Lusin, 2018). For other popular modern languages this ratio is typically 5:1 (Spanish, French, German, Japanese, Korean) or as high as 7:1 (Arabic, Modern Hebrew). Russian numbers at the advanced level have been strong since the MLA started tracking students by level in 2006; except for Biblical Hebrew (29.7%), Russian had the highest percentage of advanced students overall (27.1%) (Goldberg et al., 2015). In 2009 Russian (24.7%) was tied with Korean (after Biblical Hebrew at 51.5%), while Portuguese (at 25.3%) had a slightly higher percentage of enrollments at the advanced level. In 2013, 25.5% of Russian enrollments were at the advanced level (5,444 of 21,353 students), meaning that, except for Biblical Hebrew, Russian had the highest percentage of students at the advanced level of the languages reported. As of 2016 Russian continues to be a leader in upper-level enrollments.

The MLA has provided the percentage of students studying a language at the advanced level in only the last four reports, but Russian's larger percentage of upper-level undergraduate students means that while overall enrollments are down, students who sign up for Russian stay in our programs longer than in other languages. This conclusion is supported by the fact that despite fewer programs reporting data on Russian enrollments, the number of bachelor's degrees awarded in Russian increased by 20.6% from 2008–9 to 2012–13 (Goldberg et al., 2015).[10]

The MLA also found that since 2009, and "despite the large decline in Russian enrollments in 2013 (17.9%), 16.6% of all Russian programs reported stability, and 32.1% reported growth" (p. 14). This means that close to half (48.7%) have not seen a decline in the number of students and one of three programs has actually grown since the 2009 MLA report. The latest MLA reports, therefore, are indeed a "mixed bag" but contain information that should give us cause for optimism.

RELEVANCE OF LANGUAGE STUDY

The anti-humanities sentiment expressed in the *Forbes* article mentioned earlier (Cohan, 2012) is widespread in the media and has been taken up by politicians who make funding decisions. The rapidly increasing costs of undergraduate education make for compelling political theater despite the fact that little of this increase ends up supporting humanities programs but rather goes toward infrastructure, technology, and administrative and support staff (Jesse, 2015; Newfield, 2015). North Carolina's governor Patrick McCrory, for example, stated in January 2013 that he planned to change his state's higher education funding model so that "it's not based on butts in seats but on how many of those butts can get jobs" (Kiley, 2013, para. 3). In January 2016 Kentucky's governor Matt Bevin announced a funding model that would "produce more electrical engineers and less [*sic*] French literature scholars" because his state's universities are not graduating enough students with degrees in areas that "people want" (Beam, 2016, para. 2). The National Conference of State Legislatures notes that this is a growing trend, as "at least 15 states offer some type of bonus or premium for certain high-demand degrees" (Cohen, 2016, para. 3). This increasing emphasis on "practical" majors and degrees comes in the face of already declining overall state funding for higher education. At Michigan State University (MSU), for example, in 1960 state support accounted for 77% of MSU's General Fund budget, whereas by FY 2010–11 it accounted for only 27% of the General Fund budget (MSU, 2011), and by FY 2013–14 it had dropped further, to 21.7% (MSU, 2014). It is inevitable that these financial pressures will continue to affect perceptions of the relevance of language study: in a 2014 article in the *Financial Times*, for instance, Simon Kuper opines, "Learning another language? Don't bother."

The media spends significantly less time reporting the fact that businesspeople value the skills that students acquire in language classes and other humanities courses. Although public officials who advocate radical changes in the manner in which states fund higher education often target the humanities and liberal arts majors, a negative view of these majors is not supported by those who actually hire recent graduates. In a *Forbes* article that cites data from the National Association of Colleges and Employers, Adams (2014) lists the 10 skills most desired by employers. The first five are being able to "work in a team structure," "make decisions and solve problems," "communicate verbally with people inside and outside an organization," "plan, organize, and prioritize work," and "obtain and process information," all of which certainly can be addressed meaningfully in a language classroom. Another survey, by Hart Research Associates (2013), found that most employers (93%) agree that "a candidate's demonstrated capacity to think critically, communicate clearly, and solve complex problems is more important than their undergraduate major" (p. 1). Even more encouraging for humanities majors, including those in foreign languages, is that more than 90% of employers agreed that "it is important that those they hire demonstrate ethical judgment and integrity; intercultural skills; and the capacity for continued new learning" (p. 1). The Hart survey shows that 43% of employers would like to see more emphasis by universities and colleges on proficiency in foreign languages, while an additional 39% would like the emphasis on foreign languages to remain the same. A similarly high number of employers believe that all students should learn about societies and cultures outside the United States (78%) as well as global issues and developments (85%).

Although the humanities impart skills vital to the world beyond the university, the threat of cuts to language programs is not likely to cease anytime soon. There is plenty of evidence that language education does not hinder but in fact help students prepare for employment in an increasingly global world. How we present ourselves is of utmost importance and it is urgent that language professionals be prepared to react to initiatives and issues that are already being discussed by administrators and faculty and that have the potential to become more relevant in the coming years.

LANGUAGE REQUIREMENTS

Many institutions require the study of a second language.[11] The University of Pennsylvania, for example, has a four-semester requirement because "competence in a foreign language is essential for an educated person" (College of Arts & Sciences, n.d.). Not all educators, however, agree with the argument that language study is an essential part of education, and many institutions have begun questioning language requirements. The percentage of universities requiring language study has dropped over the last 20 years; according to the MLA, "in 2009–10, 50.7% of institutions had a language requirement for the baccalaureate, a decline of almost 17 percentage points from 1994–95, when 67.5% of institutions had a requirement" (Lusin, 2012, p. 1). There are two main reasons that could be cited in favor of the elimination of a language requirement. The first is time required to complete a degree: over the last three decades over 60% of undergraduates have taken more than four years to graduate, a number that has "increased markedly" (Bound et al., 2010). Universities have been encouraged, often with funding strings attached, to reduce time to degree, and language requirements, at least in the eyes of many administrators, are a major impediment to completion of degrees in a timely manner, particularly in the STEM disciplines (Blumenthal & Grothus, 2009). The second reason is declining enrollments, especially in the humanities. As other humanities fields, which have traditionally maintained language requirements, lose enrollments and majors, we should expect a corresponding decrease in the number of students taking languages to fulfill these requirements. Colleagues in these same fields may wonder if the language requirement is causing students to choose majors with no such requirement.

In addition, some humanities fields may be placing less emphasis on training future scholars in languages other than English. The MLA report of the Ad Hoc Committee on Foreign Languages (MLA, 2007) notes that the "lack of foreign language competence is as much a fact within academic disciplines as in the society at large" (p. 242). One MLA survey found that only half of the 118 existing English doctoral programs require reading knowledge of two additional languages (Steward, 2006). Perhaps even more concerning is that "citation indexes reveal a steady decrease in the use of non-English sources in research across the humanities and social sciences, a deficiency that impoverishes intellectual debate" (MLA, 2007, p. 242). This means that scholars who disseminate their research in English are consulting non-English sources less frequently, and a reduction in required language study in graduate programs could further affect students' ability to conduct research on a global scale.

Opposition to language requirements has also come from students. A 2012 article in the *Yale Daily News* titled "Kill the language requirement" describes this point of view:

> The conventional wisdom, stated on the Center for Language Study's website, is that knowledge of a foreign language has become "increasingly important" in our increasingly globalized world. That sounds nice—like Yale values diversity—but is it actually true? Is knowledge of Zulu or Dutch—two languages one can study to fulfill the language requirement—really "increasingly important" to succeed in the world? Ask yourself: Of all the successful people you know, how many of them speak those, or any foreign language, regularly? Either the administration actually believes what it says and only mainstream, "increasingly important" languages—such as Mandarin, Hindi or Arabic—should count toward the language requirement, or it tacitly admits not all students need to know another tongue in order to succeed. (Schiffers)

The author of this comment, while not explicitly arguing against a language requirement, raises an important point for language supporters, namely, that the rationale for requiring language study must be clearly and convincingly stated.[12] Students need to be shown how this required language study can help them professionally and how it complements their other areas of interest.[13]

If we do not continue to explain and promote the benefits of language study, in students' minds the language requirement could become lumped together with all other required courses and be seen as an onerous task that is yet another hurdle to graduation instead of a skill that can greatly benefit them in their future careers and lives. The small amount of research on this question suggests that college faculty also do not unanimously support a language requirement. Those opposed often feel that required language study takes time away from other (more important) subjects and scares potential students away from majors or universities that have a language requirement (Wilkerson, 2006). It is essential that colleagues in the humanities and other disciplines do not allow the language requirement to become a divisive issue; we must communicate, work cooperatively, and focus on the valuable contribution that language learning plays in the education of undergraduate students.

Given the various challenges faced by language programs, it is no surprise that the language requirement has found itself under pressure at some institutions. In 2015 Mount Holyoke College reduced its language requirement from two semesters to one, and the College of Arts and Sciences at Texas Tech also reduced the requirement by one semester, from two semesters of a second-year language to one semester for students entering in 2017. The College of the Holy Cross reduced its requirement from four to two semesters, and in 2011 George Washington University's Columbian College of Arts and Sciences eliminated its language requirement altogether.

A question that needs to be asked is how the elimination or modification of a language requirement might impact Russian. Should Russian instructors fear or welcome changes to the language requirement? Language enrollments likely would decrease in the short term, but it is unlikely that all languages would be affected equally. Every institution has its own complex variety of factors that go into a student's choice to study language, so it is unlikely that weakening or eliminating language requirements would have the same effect on all Russian programs. Colleagues at Mount Holyoke and Holy Cross report being unable to see any direct connection between enrollments and the reduction of the language requirement, whereas George Washington saw a significant drop in Russian numbers immediately after the elimination of the language requirement. Despite strengthening the language requirement, Drew University has also seen a decrease in Russian enrollments (J. Merrill, personal communication, October 11, 2016).

It is important to recall that in the last four MLA enrollment reports, Russian has had one of the highest percentages of students studying at the advanced level because more of them are staying beyond second-year classes compared to most other languages. Even while Russian enrollments decreased between 2009 and 2013, the number of Russian majors increased significantly over this same time period, by 20.6% (Goldberg et al., 2015). These numbers suggest that fewer students take Russian to satisfy a language requirement and more do so because of an interest in the subject that keeps them in our classrooms beyond the completion of a language requirement.

A language requirement introduces an interesting dynamic into introductory language classrooms, where students who are motivated by sincere interest in the language study alongside students whose primary goal is only to satisfy a graduation requirement. Our classrooms would certainly look different with only students who truly want to be there. Elimination of a requirement might alter perceptions of language courses from a requirement that one must fulfill to something one has the choice to take.

The position of the MLA regarding a language requirement is clear. In the section of the 2007 Ad Hoc Report titled "Strengthening the Demand for Language Competence within the University," three of the seven recommendations explicitly involve creating or strengthening a language requirement. The MLA recommends that universities establish language requirement guidelines for relevant fields, that they encourage doctoral programs to maintain and enforce the requirement, and that they work with colleagues in social science and policy-oriented departments to strengthen the requirement within their majors (MLA, 2007).

It is likely that at some point most institutions will face some questioning of their language requirement and encounter efforts to modify or eliminate it. Regardless of the position that Russian programs and individual faculty members ultimately take on the question of a language requirement, faculty must be aware of the many sides of this issue in order to be able to make the best decisions for their programs and their students.

GLOBAL COMPETENCE

The Spellings Commission Report (US Department of Education, 2006) raises questions about the United States' ability to compete globally. The report asserts that while "other nations rapidly improve their higher education systems, we are disturbed by evidence that the quality of student learning at U.S. colleges and universities is inadequate and, in some cases, declining" (p. 3). The report cites numerous employer complaints that employees lack the critical skills required in 21st-century workplaces. To remedy the situation the commission advocates for greater accountability and innovation, for example, through "new pedagogies, curricula, and technologies to improve student learning" (p. 4; see also Wurst, 2008b). The report encourages new pedagogical approaches as a means of staying globally competitive.[14]

In the United States, the National Education Association (NEA) argues that "global competence is a 21st century imperative" (NEA, 2010, p. 1). The NEA's authors share the Spellings Report's concern that "most American students, low-income and minority groups in particular, lag behind their peers in other countries in their knowledge of world geography, foreign languages, and cultures" (p. 1). They bolster their argument by citing four reasons for the urgent need for global competence: the increasing diversity of our society, the increasing complexity of global challenges, the interdependence of world economies (one in five jobs in the United States is tied to international trade), and the fact that global competence enhances overall academic achievement. The NEA authors agree with the American Council on Education and the Coalition for International Education that "global competence must become part of the core mission of education—from K–12 through graduate school" (p. 2).

Global competence, according to the NEA policy brief, includes "extensive knowledge of international issues" (p. 1). Added to this are "international awareness" and "appreciation of cultural diversity." The fourth part of the definition is "proficiency in foreign languages" (p. 1). It is important to emphasize that although language programs play a central role in this vision of building global competence and are well positioned to provide leadership, they cannot accomplish this challenging task alone; they must work in concert with other humanities disciplines (see also MLA, 2007).

A significant step in developing a framework for restructuring language curricula with a goal of developing global competence was taken by the American Council on the Teaching of Foreign Languages (ACTFL) in developing its Standards for

Foreign Language Learning (NSFLEP, 1996). The Standards took into account the viewpoints of educators, business leaders, and government officials regarding the role of foreign language instruction in American education. The ACTFL task force identified five goal areas for the Standards: Communication, Cultures, Connections, Comparisons, and Communities. *Communication* is at the heart of second-language studies, and through it we should be able to lead students to an understanding of other *cultures*. This in turn provides *connections* to other bodies of knowledge such as history, economics, and political science, through which *comparisons* with other cultures can enable students to recognize the multiple ways in which the world is perceived and therefore participate in multilingual *communities* at home and abroad in ways that are culturally appropriate. In the latest version, called the World-Readiness Standards for Learning Languages (NSCB, 2015), the Standards have been revised based on 15 years of data on their use. Although the five goal areas have been retained, in the revised version a concerted effort is made to identify more clearly what language learners should be expected to do to demonstrate progress in each area. Given the expectations of employers, government, and our own professional associations, it seems prudent for language programs, including Russian, to consider the way curricula have been structured. The main focus of traditional Russian programs has been on developing language skills, with cultural content often understood as literature, usually in translation (Merrill, 2013). Programs should ask if this approach achieves the objective of preparing globally competent students who can meet the challenges of the 21st-century job market. If they decide the answer is no, one solution is to move toward a model that emphasizes global competence as defined in the World-Readiness Standards, that is, developing students' ability to "use the language to investigate, explain, and reflect on the relationship between the products and perspectives of the cultures studied" (NSCB, 2015).

Unfortunately, culture is still often taught in English, and there is still no consensus in many programs as to how to integrate language with culture instruction. As the MLA document states, the goals and approaches of language instruction are hotly debated, which we believe is still the case these many years later (MLA, 2007; see also Wurst, 2008b). The report identifies the two divergent approaches—instrumentalist and constitutive—to language and its functions: "At one end, language is considered to be principally instrumental, a skill to use for communicating thought and information. At the opposite end, language is understood as an essential element of a human being's thought processes, perceptions, and self-expressions and as such it is considered to be at the core of translingual and transcultural competence" (MLA, 2007, p. 235).

Wurst (2008b) notes that emphasizing the instrumentalist approach might lead to increased calls for proficiency testing, and, we could add, a singular focus on language (see VanPatten, 2015). On the constitutive side the emphasis would be on "cultural and literary traditions, cognitive structures, and historical knowledge" (MLA, 2007, p. 236). Stryker and Leaver (1997) point out that within language majors, cultural content "is frequently decided arbitrarily by the teacher and is usually based on academic tradition" (p. 5). In many cases "academic tradition" refers to the study of literature and the fact that language departments frequently are divided into language instructors (often non-tenure-track) and literature professors (often tenure-track), the latter of whom are more empowered to make curricular decisions. Thus "the study of culture equates to the study of literature" (p. 7).

If our goal is to overcome the split between language and literature/culture, a split that makes articulation through all levels of language instruction virtually impossible, we must work together as language and culture experts in developing a constitutive approach that transforms the traditional paradigm of two to three years of language courses followed by literature/culture courses (the latter of which are often taught in English). Such a change, which has already been undertaken in some institutions (see Wurst, 2008a), would likely include the introduction of authentic cultural material as early as first year and would seek to "situate language study in cultural, historical, geographic, and cross-cultural frames within the context of humanistic learning" (MLA, 2007, p. 238; see also Peters, 2003). While the creation of a curriculum that provides translingual and transcultural competence is not an easy task (Byram & Kramsch, 2008), it must be pursued collaboratively throughout the curriculum. Kramsch (1993) points out the "profound pleasure that comes from understanding and being understood, from discovering multiple layers of meaning and having the ability and power to manipulate these meanings" and asserts that foreign language instructors "would do well to be on the look-out for the potential occurrence of dialogic experiences" between the languages and cultures at play (p. 30). Similarly, Byrnes (2008) advocates fostering explicit discussions concerning the nature of culture as well as the interlingual and intercultural milieu that emerges in the classroom.

The goal of translingual and transcultural competence as defined in a broad sense in the MLA report has retained its relevance long after the report's publication. Students should acquire the kind of transcultural understanding that will enable them "to comprehend and analyze the cultural narratives" that appear in a wide range of media, from belles lettres, drama, journalism, political rhetoric, legal documents, and advertising to performative—including music—as well as visual forms (MLA, 2007, p. 238). The report provides a general model for achieving the goal of translingual and transcultural competence. In the remainder of this chapter we describe more specifically some curricular innovations and high-impact practices that reflect developments in higher education and address our own institution's needs and priorities as we seek to proactively engage in preparing students for living and working effectively in an increasingly global world.

CURRICULAR INNOVATION

Any curricular innovation or, for that matter, any program's curriculum must be developed in the context of institutional priorities. In order to address the requirements of the workplace and develop lifelong learners who are effective leaders, MSU created Undergraduate Learning Goals that emphasize the skills that every graduate should demonstrate. We must develop language programs within the parameters of individual institutions' learning goals that will integrate the proficiency goals and transcultural competencies outlined in the previous section. According to the Undergraduate Learning Goals, the MSU graduate

- uses ways of knowing from mathematics, natural sciences, social sciences, humanities, and arts to access information and critically analyzes complex material in order to evaluate evidence, construct reasoned arguments, and communicate inferences and conclusions. [. . .]
- comprehends global and cultural diversity within historical, artistic, and societal contexts. [. . .]
- participates as a member of local, national, and global communities and has the capacity to lead in an increasingly interdependent world. [. . .]
- uses a variety of media to communicate effectively with diverse audiences. [. . .]
- integrates discipline-based knowledge to make informed decisions that reflect humane social, ethical, and aesthetic values. (MSU, n.d.)

All MSU departments and programs are expected to integrate these goals into their curricula and assess outcomes accordingly. Given the concerns of some politicians and, no doubt, many parents regarding the prospects for employment of students majoring in the humanities, and the needs and preferences of potential employers, it is essential that all language programs take their institution's learning goals seriously and strive to make certain their students meet them. The Russian program at MSU is in a large department named Linguistics and Germanic, Slavic, Asian and African Languages. The department includes PhD programs in linguistics, German, and second language studies. Although in terms of structure and advocacy there are certainly disadvantages inherent in not being a part of an autonomous Russian or Slavic department, there are potential advantages to be gained in being closely associated with linguists and applied linguists.

All language units within the department plus those in the department of Romance and Classical Studies are connected by the Center for Language Teaching Advancement (CeLTA), which was formed in August 2008 to advance language teaching through the dissemination of innovative practices and collaboration across units on campus and in local and regional communities.[15] CeLTA provides holistic support in the areas of curricular innovation, technology, media resources, assessment and proficiency, cocurricular activities, mentoring, and professional development. Although language resource centers have had a tendency to be instrumentalist in their practices in the past, CeLTA has attempted to take the constitutive approach and seeks to assist language programs in developing a broader approach to the curricula, where language and culture are taught not as separate parts of the curriculum but as a whole.

Innovative Technologies

Increasingly language departments are relying on innovative technologies to support learning and teaching. Technology assists students to coconstruct knowledge, meaning, and content (Dooly, 2008; Sykes et al., 2008), gain language awareness (Dooly et al., 2008), build a language learning community (Rasulo, 2009), be better prepared for cross-cultural interactions (Warschauer, 2000), and enhance language skills in a variety of skill areas (Dodd, 2001; Belz, 2007).

In 2013 CeLTA established a faculty technology cluster in order to promote best practices in language pedagogy through the use of technology. The languages involved in the project were Chinese, German, and Russian. The primary goal of the cluster is to develop blended and online courses in order to improve the quality of instruction and increase flexibility for students in time, space, and pace. On a broader scale the cluster aims to encourage best practices in blended and online environments across all language programs and create a pool of expertise that can be shared across the College of Arts & Letters. In Russian the work of the technology cluster has so far resulted in the blending of second-year Russian (see Spasova & Welsh in this volume) and first-year Russian. The Russian faculty member who led the blending efforts won an MSU AT&T Instructional Technology award for online study abroad modules related to the blending of second-year Russian.

HIGH-IMPACT EDUCATIONAL PRACTICES

Kuh (2008) identifies a number of "high-impact practices" that require significant time and effort from students, provide meaningful learning opportunities outside the classroom, and include rich intellectual interaction with faculty members and collaboration with diverse groups of fellow students. Among these activities are first-year seminars and experiences, learning communities, writing-intensive courses, collaborative assignments and projects, undergraduate research, service or community-based learning, and internships. Most institutions already engage in cocurricular activities within their language programs; while many focus on more traditional ones like clubs, teas, and film series, we do not believe these practices will be sufficient if language faculty are to build and maintain vibrant 21st-century programs. In the following sections we suggest some ways in which language programs can use high-impact activities to enhance the experiences of their students and better prepare them for leadership roles in the global workplace they will soon be entering.

Badges and Certifications

Digital badges and microcredentials have increased in popularity in education over the past decade, in part due to the support of entities such as the MacArthur Foundation, the US Department of Education, and Mozilla. The concept of a "badge" in itself is not new. A badge represents achievement of a certain skill level in a certain area. A digital badge, however, offers increased versatility since it can be displayed in an online portfolio, on a personal website or network, and on a résumé to help document lifelong learning. While digital badges have received much attention in higher education in general, the use of badges for language learning is still in an early stage.[16] The Title VI National Foreign Language Resource Center at The University of Texas at Austin, the Center for Open Educational Resources and Language Learning, offers resources for open badges for foreign language education (https://openbadges.coerll.utexas.edu/). ACTFL has developed a suite of badges related to language learning and teaching (http://badges.actfl.org/), and the University of Hawai'i at Mānoa's Center for Language and Technology also offers badges for their faculty and graduate students (https://clt.manoa.hawaii.edu/projects/clt-badges/).

Service Learning and Outreach

In order to provide real-life experiences for language learners where they can apply their knowledge, CeLTA offers service learning and outreach opportunities for students through its Community Language School (CLS), a community language program that is also a revenue source for CeLTA activities. MSU undergraduate volunteers are placed as teacher assistants in weekly language classes for children and summer camps held on MSU's campus; they help with group activities and the teaching of basic language and culture concepts. They shadow the native and near-native speaker instructors and learn from and interact with them as well as team teach in enrichment programs at area elementary schools.[17]

CLS also collaborates with K–12 schools in underserved areas such as Detroit, Flint, and Lansing. These outreach programs aim to open doors to participating K–12 students. One particular program, BEYOND Insights (https://celta.msu.edu/projects/), is a collaborative project between various College of Arts & Letters units and Lansing Public Schools. The program engages sixth-graders in a wide range of activities focused on creativity, global culture, and the arts and humanities. Weekly workshops follow a centralized theme such as "My City," which evolves into a combination of skills and lessons that showcase the connections of creativity, culture, and the humanities in the students' lives. In the language and culture sessions, participating students learn basic phrases in various languages, discuss the meaning of cultural representation of buildings and flags, and engage in creative activities related to the cultures they are learning about.

Outreach programs like BEYOND Insights and the Community Language School provide valuable connections within the K–12 community. They are important for undergraduate students, who are able to both use their studied language in various contexts and pass their enthusiasm onto others. They are also important for community participants because these events expose them to different language and cultures, increasing their global competence and creating enthusiasm for language learning.

PROFESSIONAL DEVELOPMENT

In order to build strong language programs, support services should extend beyond the students and involve faculty as well. Most institutions have some kind of faculty or organizational development office that provides general training and resources to assist with teaching innovations, mentoring, student engagement, community building, and similar areas. Most of these services are broad in nature and address the needs of faculty from a variety of fields. Support services specific to language learning and language teaching offer valuable supplements to more generic offerings. At MSU, CeLTA provides resources and also partners with the College Educational Technology Office to offer professional development opportunities, especially those focused on the development of online courses and materials.

Faculty Learning Communities

Faculty Learning Communities (FLCs) are focused on "a continuous process of learning and reflection, supported by colleagues, with an intention of getting things done" (McGill & Beaty, 2001, p. 11). FLCs have the potential to transform institutions into learning organizations through their holistic approach to professional development.

College of Arts & Letters FLCs typically meet once a month over the course of an academic year, and activities range from discussions around projects or readings to more hands-on building, creating, and doing. Some learning communities have specific products (e.g., grant proposals, courses, collaboratively constructed conference presentations, manuscripts), while others are devoted to discussions on topics important to the profession.

FLCs hosted by CeLTA have focused on language learning in online environments with the goal of expanding and enhancing blended and online course offerings across the college's language programs. During the monthly meetings faculty and academic staff discuss relevant topics related to online learning, language learning, and the connection between the two. They also engage in hands-on activities creating blended or online course models. Another FLC focused on building bridges between language, language acquisition, and teaching. It engaged participants, including language teachers and second-language studies researchers, via discussions about language acquisition research and how it informs classroom practice. Educators from various language programs and levels of instruction discuss research findings, teaching approaches and techniques, and their connections. Meetings are recorded and archived to allow for flexible participation and to integrate graduate students from CeLTA's online master's degree in foreign language teaching program, many of whom are K–12 educators who live elsewhere in the United States and abroad and are unable to attend in person.

Fellowships

CeLTA also offers academic-year fellowships for language teaching faculty and graduate students who wish to pursue a project that is beyond the scope of their regular teaching, research, or curriculum development duties. The fellowships provide funding for ideas that lead to innovative, high-impact practices, materials, or research. The projects contribute to advancing language instruction at MSU. Projects have included the hybridization of courses, investigation of learning analytics, integration of film and storytelling, community outreach programs, and the development of visual teaching materials.

The reality is that most Russian programs are too small to establish programs like MSU's on their own. Therefore, if Russian programs want to stay abreast of developments in language pedagogy and participate in innovations, it is imperative that they actively seek out colleagues in other languages and exchange ideas with them.

CONCLUSION

In the 2007 MLA report Daniel Yankelovich identifies "the need to understand other cultures and languages" as one of the five critical needs that higher education must address if it is to stay relevant (MLA, 2007, p. 235). If anything Yankelovich's words are even more pertinent today: "Our whole culture [. . .] must become less ethnocentric, less patronizing, less ignorant of others, less Manichaean in judging other cultures, and more at home with the rest of the world. Higher education can do a lot to meet that important challenge" (p. 235).

Berman (2011) identifies the cause of the problem cited by Yankelovich as the exceptionally low level of language skills displayed by Americans born into English-speaking families and, citing the National Foreign Language Center, notes that "eighty-two percent of US residents are monolingual, and the United States is the only industrialized country where language study is, for the most part, optional rather than mandatory" (Berman, 2011). Berman proposes a specific tactic for confronting this crisis: we should challenge the argument that language enrollments are too small and for this reason should be cut. He suggests that reductions should be made in administrative costs rather than in language programs and that we as language professionals "must do a better job of explaining the importance of languages" (Berman, 2011). While not discounting Berman's advice, the approach we have taken in this chapter does not anticipate rapid major changes in the American educational system such as making language study mandatory or significantly increasing funding for language programs.

Instead we are suggesting that individual language departments be more proactive and collaborative in seeking to create programs that are innovative and directly address student needs within the context of the criticisms expressed by state governors and others regarding the humanities in general and language programs in particular. Perhaps even more threatening and worthy of concern is the news reported by the American Academy of Arts and Sciences and cited in *Inside Higher Education* that the number of bachelor's degrees conferred in humanities fields fell 8.7% from 2012 to 2014. As a percentage of all bachelor degrees at 6.1%, humanities degrees awarded were at their lowest level for all years back to 1948, beyond which no reliable data exist (AAAS, 2016; Jaschik, 2016). The concern here is that the attacks on the humanities, at least to some degree, are influencing students and their academic choices. What we suggest in response does not compromise our core values of proficiency-based instruction and an emphasis on communication and cultural literacy but also does not neglect what Wurst calls "the liberal learning goals (the dispositions the successful graduate should possess)" (Wurst, 2008b, p. 5). Returning to *The Heart of the Matter* (AAAS, 2013), we see that working together the humanities and social sciences "provide an intellectual framework and context for understanding and thriving in a changing world, and they connect us with our global community. When we study these subjects, we learn not only *what*, but *how* and *why*" (p. 17). Working toward creating this type of global competence brings both the humanities and the social sciences together and aligns them more explicitly with the desires expressed by many employers.

We have mentioned a wide variety of curricular, cocurricular, and professional activities that language programs and departments can undertake to prepare their students more effectively for life after graduation, which, of course, includes employment. Peter Stokes (2015), in his book *Higher Education and Employability: New Models for Integrating Study and Work*, points out that at the start of the 2008 recession, many people in higher education were concerned with how long it would take for things to return to normal. But it was not too much later that the discussion turned to the "new normal." By this Stokes means that the global focus on economic development and job creation made it imperative for higher education to address "the task of preparing work-ready graduates who can thrive amid these new economic realities" (p. 168). As we hope we have shown, there is no need for humanities programs to despair in this environment. The critical thinking, writing, language, and analytical skills humanities graduates possess are in demand, especially when combined with technical skills. One of Stokes's examples of institutions that have moved to provide this type of technical training is Middlebury College, whose MiddCORE bridge program was designed to assist liberal arts students develop business skills that will help position them well for employment after graduation. Institutions will approach these issues in a variety of ways, and each will be tailored to local resources and the needs of their students. What we want to emphasize, however, is that Russian language programs have a wide range of options and opportunities to better serve students. We choose to be invigorated about the future.

NOTES

1. Bérubé (2013) argues that the numbers that "prove" the humanities are in crisis are wrong and the crisis has become a universally accepted truth that nobody bothers to question. Bérubé says a drop in humanities enrollments did in fact take place, but it happened entirely during the 1970s, meaning it is not a "recent" trend and there is no "steady downward spiral" (Bérubé). In fact, he argues, the humanities have seen some growth since the mid-1980s, which suggests that overall humanities enrollments have only dropped 0.1% from their highpoint in 1970 (17.1%) to 2010 (17%). While Bérubé is only talking about enrollment numbers, more recent statistics indicate that the number of bachelor's degrees in the humanities has "declined 8.7% from 2012 to 2014, falling to the smallest number of degrees conferred since 2003" (Jaschik, 2016, para. 2).

2. *Russian Language Journal* published two issues that highlight opportunities for innovation in Russian programs. In volume 63 (2013) Thomas Garza describes a successful model for an intensive undergraduate Russian program, Alla Kourova advocates connecting English as a Foreign Language and Russian language classrooms, and Jason Merrill presents research designed to better understand students' motivation for taking Russian. Volume 64 (2014), a special issue dedicated to "Humanities+," includes several articles that discuss innovative Russian programs and ways Russian connects with the professional world. For example, Sigrid Berka and John Grandin describe a collaboration between Russian and engineering departments, and Anthony Brown discusses professional opportunities for those studying languages. In addition, Jason Merrill (2007) shares details of a study abroad collaboration between Russian and engineering programs.
3. The MLA news about declining enrollments in foreign languages caused *The Washington Post* to declare that "Americans are beginning to lose their love for foreign languages" (Ferdman, 2015), but of course one could question the notion that at any point in their history Americans have "loved" foreign languages.
4. The 2016 MLA preliminary report does not describe enrollments in individual languages at two-year colleges. As of the last available numbers, two-year colleges account for less than 10% of overall Russian enrollments, and this number is declining (9.67% in 2009 down to 8.89% by 2013) (Goldberg et al., 2015).
5. One could argue that the MLA's starting point of 1960 is unfortunate for Russian because that year saw high enrollments that started in 1958 due to the launch of *Sputnik 1* in October 1957, which was followed by increased government funding for the study of Russian (Shane, 1984).
6. For the sake of comparison, in 2013 Spanish accounted for 50.6% of language enrollments (other than English), followed by French (12.7%), American Sign Language (7%), German (5.5%), Italian (4.6%), Japanese (4.3%), Chinese (3.9%), Arabic (2.1%), Latin (1.7%), Russian (1.4%), Hebrew (1.2%), Ancient Greek, Portuguese, and Korean (all 0.8%), and other languages (2.6%). The total number of language enrollments in 2013 was 1,562,179 (Goldberg et al., 2015).
7. Enrollment reports provide examples of conflicting numbers or ways of reporting. While the 2013 MLA report (Goldberg et al., 2015) states that the decline in language enrollments parallels an overall drop in undergraduate enrollments, Ferdman's *Washington Post* article contradicts the MLA report and asserts that "the number of students enrolled in college rose by well over 150,000" over this same period (Ferdman, 2015, para. 3).
8. We were unable to reconcile a small discrepancy in the MLA numbers for 1990: Table 12a reports 626 institutions submitting Russian enrollments, but Table 12b gives 119 two-year institutions and 502 four-year schools, which add up to only 621.
9. The MLA (Goldberg et al., 2015) reports that 30% fewer institutions submitted Russian data and speculates that some of that difference may be due to closed or suspended programs; Ferdman (2015) uses these numbers to assert that the number of programs offering Russian has decreased by 30%. Because the MLA relies on

self-reporting by individual programs, it is not clear to what extent not reporting enrollments can be considered the same as not having enrollments.

10. In addition, Russian graduate program enrollments grew 0.8% from 2009 to 2013 (Goldberg et al., 2015, p. 6).
11. Language requirements almost always involve the study of language for a certain amount of time. An alternative approach is a proficiency-based requirement (see Schulz, 1988). In the 1980s several institutions implemented proficiency-based language requirements, including, for example, the University of Minnesota (Arendt et al., 1986), the University of Pennsylvania (Freed, 1987), and the University of Southern California (Smith, 1984). Today none of these institutions have a proficiency-based requirement.
12. A failure to expose students to languages might result in more students agreeing with, as the author states, the "fact" that the only use students have for language is communication, and that "the only language most students will need is English" (Schiffers, 2012). Lawrence H. Summers (2012) expressed a similar point of view in *The New York Times*: "English's emergence as the global language, along with the rapid progress in machine translation and the fragmentation of languages spoken around the world, make it less clear that the substantial investment necessary to speak a foreign tongue is universally worthwhile." Many colleagues, such as Michael Geisler (2012), offered spirited rebuttals to Summers's ideas. It is worth pointing out that *The Economist* criticized the proposal that the European Union (EU) should switch to an English-only policy (Greene, 2013). Robert Lane Greene argues that doing so would ask all other countries to accept "second-class linguistic citizenship," and the value of operating in multiple languages is vital to the EU's mission of diversity and maintaining identities within the whole.
13. Perhaps one model for this type of rationalized and integrated language requirement is found at Indiana State University (see Calvin & Rider, 2004).
14. For additional perspective on this topic, see American Academy of Arts and Sciences (2013), particularly pp. 58–59.
15. CeLTA is entrepreneurial in generating funds to support its operations. Parts of its programming (like the Community Language School and the online master's program in foreign language teaching) are designed to be self-sustaining. Grant activities and revenue earned from online courses help fund the center, in addition to some institutional support.
16. Penn State University is among the leaders in digital badging (see http://badges.psu.edu/).
17. For more information on community language programs and the role of the language center, see Schenker and Kraemer (2018), Shanker and Kraemer (2014), and Kraemer and Schenker (2012).

REFERENCES

Adams, S. (2014, November 12). The 10 skills employers most want in 2015 graduates. *Forbes*. Retrieved from https://www.forbes.com/sites/susanadams/2014/11/12/the-10-skills-employers-most-want-in-2015-graduates

American Academy of Arts and Sciences (AAAS). (2013). *The heart of the matter: The humanities and social sciences for a vibrant, competitive, and secure nation*. Cambridge, MA: American Academy of Arts and Sciences. Retrieved from https://www.humanitiescommission.org/_pdf/hss_report.pdf

American Academy of Arts and Sciences (AAAS). (2016). Humanities indicators: Bachelor's degrees in the humanities. Retrieved from https://humanitiesindicators.org/content/indicatordoc.aspx?i=34

American Association for the Advancement of Slavic Studies & American Council of Teachers of Russian (AATSEEL & ACTR). (n.d.). Why study Russian? Retrieved from http://modules.russnet.org/why/

American Council of Teachers of Foreign Language (ACTFL). (n.d.). What the research shows. Retrieved from https://www.actfl.org/advocacy/what-the-research-shows

Arendt, J. D., Lange, D. L., & Wakefield, R. (1986). Strengthening the language requirement at the University of Minnesota: An initial report. *Foreign Language Annals, 19*(2), 149–57.

Beam, A. (2016, January 29). Kentucky Gov. Matt Bevin wants state colleges and universities to produce more electrical engineers and less French literature scholars. Retrieved from https://www.usnews.com/news/us/articles/2016-01-29/in-kentucky-a-push-for-engineers-over-french-lit-scholars

Belz, J. A. (2007). The role of computer mediation in the instruction and development of L2 pragmatic competence. *Annual Review of Applied Linguistics*, *27*, 45–75.

Berka, S., & Grandin, J. (2014). The University of Rhode Island International Engineering Program: Merging technology with the humanities. *Russian Language Journal*, *64*, 25–52.

Berman, R. (2011). The real language crisis. *Academe*, *97*(5). Retrieved from https://www.aaup.org/article/real-language-crisis

Bérubé, M. (2013, July 1). The humanities, declining? Not according to the numbers. *The Chronicle of Higher Education*. Retrieved from https://www.chronicle.com/article/The-Humanities-Declining-Not/140093/

Blumenthal, P., & Grothus, U. (2009). Expanding study abroad in the STEM fields: A case study of U.S. and German programs. In *Institute of International Education* (Ed.), *IIE Study Abroad White Paper Series 5: Promoting study abroad in science and technology fields* (pp. 10–25). New York: IIE.

Bound, J., Lovenheim, M. F., & Turner, S. (2010). Increasing time to baccalaureate degree in the United States. *NBER Working Paper No. 15892*. Retrieved from https://www.nber.org/papers/w15892

Brown, N. A. (2014). Unlocking professional opportunities through foreign language study. *Russian Language Journal*, *64*, 71–82.

Byram, K., & Kramsch, C. (2008). Why is it so difficult to teach language as culture? *The German Quarterly*, *81*(1), 20–34.

Byrnes, H. (2008). Articulating a foreign language sequence through content: A look at the culture standards. *Language Teaching*, *41*(1), 103–18.

Calvin, L., & Rider, N. (2004). Not your parents' language class: Curriculum revision to support university language requirements. *Foreign Language Annals*, *37*(1), 11–25.

Cohan, P. (2012, May 29). To boost post-college prospects, cut humanities departments. *Forbes*. Retrieved from https://www.forbes.com/sites/petercohan/2012/05/29/to-boost-post-college-prospects-cut-humanities-departments

Cohen, P. (2016, February 21). A rising call to promote STEM education and cut liberal arts funding. *The New York Times*. Retrieved from https://www.nytimes.com/2016/02/22/business/a-rising-call-to-promote-stem-education-and-cut-liberal-arts-funding.html

Dodd, C. (2001). Working in tandem: An Anglo-French project. In M. Byram, A. Nichols, & D. Stevens (Eds.), *Developing intercultural competence in practice* (pp. 162–76). Clevedon, UK: Multilingual Matters.

Dooly, M. (2008). Understanding the many steps for effective collaborative language projects. *Language Learning Journal*, *36*(1), 65–78.

Dooly, M., Masats, D., Müller-Hartmann, A., & De Rodas, B. C. (2008). Building effective, dynamic online partnerships. In M. Dooly (Ed.), *Telecollaborative language learning: A guidebook to moderating intercultural collaboration online* (pp. 45–77). Bern, Switzerland: Peter Lang.

Ferdman, R. (2015, February 19). Americans are beginning to lose their love for foreign languages. *The Washington Post*. Retrieved from https://www.washingtonpost.com/news/wonk/wp/2015/02/19/americans-are-beginning-to-lose-their-love-for-foreign-languages/

Florida State University. (2013). Top 10 reasons to study Russian. Retrieved from https://modlang.fsu.edu/programs/slavic-russian/top-10-reasons-study-russian

Freed, B. F. (1987). Preliminary impressions on the effects of a proficiency-based language requirement. *Foreign Language Annals*, *20*(2), 139–46.

Garza, T. (2013). Keeping it real: Intensive instruction and the future of Russian language and culture in U.S. universities. *Russian Language Journal*, *63*, 7–24.

Geisler, M. (2012, March 6). Larry Summers is wrong about languages. *Inside Higher Ed*. Retrieved from https://www.insidehighered.com/views/2012/03/06/geisler-essay-why-larry-summers-wrong-about-languages

Goldberg, D., Looney, D., & Lusin, N. (2015). *Enrollments in languages other than English in United States institutions of higher education, Fall 2013*. Retrieved from https://www.mla.org/content/download/31180/1452509/2013_enrollment_survey.pdf

Greene, R. L. (2013, September 17). Johnson: Just speak English? *The Economist*. Retrieved from https://www.economist.com/prospero/2013/09/17/johnson-just-speak-english

Hart Research Associates. (2013). *It takes more than a major: Employer priorities for college learning and student success*. Washington, DC: Hart Research Associates.

Hirsch, M. (2013). Vulnerable times at the Chicago convention. *MLA Newsletter*, *45*(3), 2–3. Retrieved from https://president.commons.mla.org/2013/09/18/vulnerable-times-at-the-chicago-convention/

Hutner, G., & Mohamed, F. G. (2013, September 6). The real humanities crisis is happening at public universities. *The New Republic.* Retrieved from https://newrepublic.com/article/114616/public-universities-hurt-humanities-crisis

Jaschik, S. (2016, March 14). The shrinking humanities major. *Inside Higher Ed.* Retrieved from https://www.insidehighered.com/news/2016/03/14/study-shows-87-decline-humanities-bachelors-degrees-2-years

Jesse, D. (2015, July 13). Universities say funding system broke, lawmakers disagree. *Detroit Free Press.* Retrieved from https://www.freep.com/story/news/local/michigan/2015/07/13/michigan-university-tuition-increases/30053397/

Kiley, K. (2013, January 30). Another liberal arts critic. *Inside Higher Ed.* Retrieved from https://www.insidehighered.com/news/2013/01/30/north-carolina-governor-joins-chorus-republicans-critical-liberal-arts

Kourova, A. (2013). Connecting classrooms: Russian language teaching project at UCF. *Russian Language Journal, 63,* 79–90.

Kraemer, A., & Schenker, T. (2012). Reaching all learners through community-based language programs. In T. Sildus (Ed.), *Touch the World* (pp. 1–19). Milwaukee, WI: CSCTFL.

Kramsch, C. (1993). *Context and culture in language teaching.* Oxford: Oxford UP.

Kuh, G. (2008). *High-impact educational practices: What they are, who has access to them, and why they matter.* Washington, DC: Association of American Colleges & Universities.

Kuper, S. (2014, September 5). Learning another language? Don't bother. *Financial Times.* Retrieved from https://www.ft.com/content/3da3335c-330d-11e4-93c6-00144feabdc0

Levitz, J., & Belkin, D. (2013, June 6). Humanities fall from favor: Far fewer Harvard students express interest in field with weak job prospects. *The Wall Street Journal.* Retrieved from https://www.wsj.com/articles/SB10001424127887324069104578527642373232184

Lewin, T. (2013, October 30). As interest in the humanities fades, colleges worry. *The New York Times.* Retrieved from https://www.nytimes.com/2013/10/31/education/as-interest-fades-in-the-humanities-colleges-worry.html

Looney, D., & Lusin, N. (2018). *Enrollments in languages other than English in United States institutions of higher education, summer 2016 and fall 2016: Preliminary report.* Retrieved from https://www.mla.org/content/download/83540/2197676/2016-Enrollments-Short-Report.pdf

Lusin, N. (2012). *The MLA survey of postsecondary entrance and degree requirements for languages other than English, 2009–10.* Retrieved from https://www.mla.org/content/download/3316/81618/requirements_survey_200910.pdf

McGill, I., & Beaty, L. (2001). *Action learning* (2nd ed., rev.). Sterling, VA: Stylus.

Merrill, J. (2007). Meeting the challenges of the global university through study abroad: Developing a multi-disciplinary study experience in Russia for all college students. *NewsNet: News of the American Association for the Advancement of Slavic Studies, 47*(3), 9–13.

Merrill, J. (2013). Our Russian classrooms and students: Who is choosing Russian, why, and what cultural content should we offer them? *Russian Language Journal, 63,* 51–78.

Michigan State University (MSU). (n.d.). Undergraduate learning goals. Retrieved from https://undergrad.msu.edu/programs/learninggoals

Michigan State University (MSU). (2011). Michigan State University budgets 2010–2011. Retrieved from https://opb.msu.edu/functions/budget/documents/2010-11Budgets.pdf

Michigan State University (MSU). (2014). Michigan State University budgets 2013–2014. Retrieved from https://opb.msu.edu/functions/budget/documents/2013-14Budgets.pdf

Modern Language Association (MLA). (2007). Foreign languages and higher education: New structures for a changed world. *Profession*, 234–45. Retrieved from https://www.mlajournals.org/doi/pdf/10.1632/prof.2007.2007.1.234

National Endowment for the Arts (NEA). (2010). *Global competence is a 21st century imperative.* NEA Policy Brief No. PB28A.Washington, DC: NEA Education Policy and Practice Department.

National Standards Collaborative Board (NSCB). (2015). *World-readiness standards for learning languages* (4th ed.). Alexandria, VA: Author.

National Standards in Foreign Language Education Project (NSFLEP). (1996). *Standards for foreign language learning: Preparing for the 21st century (SFFLL).* Lawrence, KS: Allen.

Newfield, C. (2015). The humanities as service departments: Facing the budget logic. *Profession.* Retrieved from https://profession.mla.org/the-humanities-as-service-departments-facing-the-budget-logic/

Peters, G. F. (2003). Kulturexkurse: A model for teaching deeper German culture in a proficiency-based curriculum. *Die Unterrichtspraxis/Teaching German, 36*(2), 121–34.

Rasulo, M. (2009). The role of community formation in learning processes. In M. Thomas (Ed.), *Handbook of research on Web 2.0 and second language learning* (pp. 80–100). Hershey, PA: Information Science Reference.

Schenker, T., & Kraemer, A. (2018). The role of the language center in community outreach: Developing language enrichment programs for children. In E. Lavolette & E. Simon (Eds.), *Language center handbook* (pp. 71–88). Auburn, AL: International Association for Language Learning Technology.

Schiffers, G. (2012, February 3). Kill the language requirement. *Yale Daily News.* Retrieved from https://yaledailynews.com/blog/2012/02/03/schiffres-kill-the-language-requirement/

School of Russian and Asian Studies (SRAS). (2010). Russian enrollment trend report. Retrieved from http://www.old.sras.org/ccpcr_fall_2009_precollege_and_college_russian_enrollment_trend_report

Schulz, R. A. (1988). Proficiency-based foreign language requirements: A plan for action. *ADFL Bulletin, 19*(2), 24–28.

Shane, A. M. (1984). The Ph.D. in Slavic languages and literatures: Should the product fit the market? In S. Lubensky & D. K. Jarvis (Eds.), *Teaching, learning, acquiring Russian* (pp. 1–10). Columbus, OH: Slavica.

Shanker, S., & Kraemer, A. (2014). The role of higher education in raising global children. *Learning Languages, 20*(1), 6–10.

Smith, K. L. (1984). The USC proficiency-based program in foreign language instruction: Methods and their effects on achievement and motivation. *Die Unterrichtspraxis / Teaching German, 17*(2), 240–54.

Steward, D. (2006). The foreign language requirement in English doctoral programs. *Profession*, 203–18. Retrieved from https://www.jstor.org/stable/25595842

Stokes, P. J. (2015). *Higher education and employability: New models for integrating study and work*. Cambridge: Harvard Education Press.

Stryker, S. B., & Leaver, B. L. (1997). Content-based instruction: From theory to practice. In S. B. Stryker & B. L. Leaver (Eds.), *Content-based instruction in foreign language education: Models and methods* (pp. 3–28). Washington, DC: Georgetown UP.

Summers, L. H. (2012, January 20). What you (really) need to know. *The New York Times*. Retrieved from https://www.nytimes.com/2012/01/22/education/edlife/the-21st-century-education.html

Sykes, J. M., Oskoz, A., & Thorne, S. L. (2008). Web 2.0, synthetic immersive environments, and mobile resources for language education. *CALICO Journal, 25*(3), 528–46.

University of Pennsylvania College of Arts & Sciences. (n.d.). Foreign language requirement. Retrieved from https://www.college.upenn.edu/language-policy

US Department of Education. (2006). *A test of leadership: Charting the future of U.S. higher education. A report of the commission appointed by Secretary of Education Margaret Spellings*. Retrieved from https://www2.ed.gov/about/bdscomm/list/hiedfuture/reports/pre-pub-report.pdf

VanPatten, B. (2015). Where are the experts? *Hispania, 98*(1), 2–13. Retrieved from https://c.ymcdn.com/sites/www.aatsp.org/resource/resmgr/Hispania_Open_Access/Hispania_98.1_VanPatten.pdf

Warschauer, M. (2000). On-line learning in second language classrooms: An ethnographic study. In M. Warschauer & R. Kern (Eds.), *Network-based language teaching: Concepts and practice* (pp. 41–59). Cambridge: Cambridge UP.

Wilkerson, C. (2006). College faculty perceptions about foreign language. *Foreign Language Annals, 39*(2), 310–19.

Wurst, K. (2008a). How do we teach language, literature, and culture in a collegiate environment and what are the implications for graduate education? *Die Unterrichtspraxis/ Teaching German, 41*(1), 57–60.

Wurst, K. (2008b). Winds of change? How do we teach literature in a collegiate environment? *The German Quarterly, 81*(1), 4–7.

4

RUSSIAN LANGUAGE READINESS IN GRADUATE TEACHING ASSISTANTS

Implications for Teaching and Learning

Cori Anderson, Julia Mikhailova, and Anna Tumarkin

Research shows that students' Russian language proficiency levels at the end of an undergraduate program is on average in the Intermediate range in all skills (Brecht et al., 1993; Thompson, 1996; Comer, 2000; Rifkin, 2005). These low proficiency levels create difficulties for students who enter graduate programs in Russian language, literature, and linguistics, where they serve as graduate teaching assistants (TAs). In this chapter we examine the causes and implications of the problem of language readiness among the majority of graduate student TAs who are not native speakers of any Slavic language and for whom Russian is a foreign language (FL), and we propose solutions for its remediation.

Language readiness among newly accepted non-heritage and non-native speaker graduate students is not a new concern but it is well known to be a problematic aspect of graduate student recruitment in North America. As far back as 2000 Comer commented on the problem of low language proficiency:

> With years of testing data from Russian, we know that most students completing a BA program in Russian have speaking skills somewhere in the Intermediate range. With a semester or a year of study abroad some students may reach the Advanced level of speaking proficiency, although study abroad is no automatic guarantee of this. Thus, we can expect that most students entering US graduate programs in Slavic from their undergraduate study of the language will still be in the Intermediate range. (Comer, 2000, p. 543)

Unfortunately, despite the acknowledgment of this issue by leading figures in the field (Comer, 2000; Rifkin, 2005), little has changed in the past two decades. Graduate programs frequently face difficult admission decisions, having to weigh prospective graduate students' qualifications as literary scholars against the likelihood of their success as future teachers of Russian. It is a fact that in order to be viable, Russian programs must admit some students with Intermediate proficiency, which presents significant curricular and programmatic challenges. Since TA positions constitute the main source of graduate student funding in many North American institutions, programs have to carry the burden of (1) delaying the appointment of graduate students with inadequate language skills to teaching positions until those students' proficiency improves, and (2) funding such students through other types of appointments, such as project assistantships, teaching assistantships in literature or culture courses, or grading positions for introductory Russian language courses.

Inadequate language proficiency has equally significant implications for the TAs themselves. Graduate students with Intermediate-level proficiency often struggle to provide level-appropriate teaching inputs (even for the Novice level learner) and to design meaningful activities that enable students to move successfully through the language acquisition process. These limitations affect TAs' ability to deliver effective and engaging instruction and harm their self-perceptions and teaching attitudes. Our personal classroom observations of TAs who are not native speakers of a Slavic language and for whom Russia is an FL reveal that they often develop self-doubt and anxiety in teaching due to gaps in their own language knowledge. The realization that their dream of becoming a teacher of Russian may be crushed due to inadequate language skills can lead them to quit graduate studies and search for other professional opportunities, such as teaching or editing English or pursuing an entirely new career.

As we analyze the roots and implications of inadequate language readiness among graduate students, we discuss proficiency requirements for language instructors, review proficiency outcomes among typical undergraduate Russian language majors, and highlight the gap between these outcomes and the recommended proficiency levels for FL college instructors. We then present a case study that illustrates proficiency in all skills among incoming Russian language graduate students using data from one North American institution and analyze its approaches to language readiness remediation. We conclude with a discussion of the implications of inadequate language proficiency and teaching experience for the job market and suggest means of language maintenance and improvement, so graduate students can be not only more effective language instructors but also better professionals and scholars overall.

LANGUAGE PROFICIENCY REQUIREMENTS FOR TEACHERS

The minimum oral proficiency required to teach a foreign language at any level has been under discussion since ACTFL's 1996 publication, *Standards for Foreign Language Learning in the 21st Century*, particularly in light of the shift from the grammar-translation model to the communicative approach.[1] Within the grammar-translation model, as Huhn (2012) notes, there was never a debate about teachers' minimum language proficiency because the focus of the class was on reading texts, not on communication. As Schick and Nelson (2001) observe, the shift to the communicative approach meant that FL teachers needed to have Advanced proficiency in all four skills—reading, writing, listening, and speaking—with special emphasis placed on the area of oral communication:

> In the past . . . the goal for foreign language education was that students [would] learn grammar and ultimately study the literature of the target language, [so] most foreign language teachers were prepared in the reading and writing but not necessarily in the oral comprehension and speaking of the foreign language. In the past forty to fifty years, however, the field of foreign language education has shifted to an aural / oral proficiency-based model, in large part due to the challenging needs of the United States and global societies. (p. 301)

As a part of the move to the communicative approach in FL instruction, ACTFL's Proficiency Guidelines (2012) and World-Readiness Standards for Learning Languages (2015) established a framework and goals for the FL classroom. Standards-based language instruction in the global language classroom should incorporate five areas of learning: Communication, Cultures, Connections, Communities, and Comparisons (2015). Students are expected to communicate in real-life situations, show cultural understanding, be able to connect language learning with other subject areas, be able to compare similarities and differences between their native language and culture and the target language and culture, and be able to apply classroom language experience to real-life situations in multicultural and multilingual communities. More specifically, learners "are expected to be problem solvers equipped with the necessary strategies for interpreting authentic texts, to explain cultural perspectives that undergird products and practices, and to acquire new knowledge in content-based courses" (Huhn, 2012, p. s164). Consequently, demands on the FL instructor have increased and now require strong language proficiency in order to create effective meaningful communicative and interactive classroom learning. In two additional documents, "ACTFL Position Statements" (2010) and "ACTFL/CAEP Program Standards for the Preparation of Foreign Language Teachers" (2015), ACTFL has advocated for establishing Advanced Low proficiency as a requirement for K–16 teachers of FL: "Advanced Low is the minimum level at which teachers can speak spontaneously in the classroom (i.e., without a script), provide the language input that is necessary for language acquisition to occur, and interact with their students in the foreign language" (ACTFL/CAEP Program Standards, 2015, p. 26). The ACTFL/CAEP Program Standards, however, stipulate that for teachers of a language that does not use the Roman alphabet (for example, Arabic, Chinese, Korean, Japanese, or Russian), and which requires "increased amount of time necessary to acquire proficiency," the minimum level of oral proficiency should be set at Intermediate High (p. 26).

Using Advanced Low as the minimum required level of oral proficiency among FL teachers to provide quality input in the language classroom (based on the ACTFL standards), has been supported by Pearson et al., 2006; Chambless, 2012; Huhn, 2012;

Burke, 2013; Tedick, 2013; and Glisan, 2013. For example, Pearson et al. (2006) emphasize that teachers "must provide sufficient target language input to learners (e.g., using the target language to the maximum extent possible at all levels of instruction, including in spontaneous interaction) and create a supportive classroom (e.g., meaningful interaction and negotiation of meaning through personalized, open-ended responses which allow for risk-taking in the language)" (p. 509). Tedick (2013) argues that Intermediate proficiency is not sufficient for the kind of language teaching that can promote high-quality learning. She writes: "Advanced proficiency is a necessary *prerequisite* for effective language teaching and, ultimately, quality student learning" (p. 535, emphasis in original). Tedick also states that although there are no data that show the impact of a FL teacher's proficiency on students' learning, there is indirect support from research on both first and second language acquisition demonstrating that a better quality and quantity language input environment correlates with the development of child's language, and the effect of input on students' learning. Tedick concludes that Advanced proficiency in the target language is "an essential prerequisite for effective language teaching because it is not feasible to implement communicative pedagogy or other approaches, such as content-based instruction (CBI), without Advanced level proficiency and the confidence that it brings" (p. 536).

ACTFL recommends that instructors use the target language "as exclusively as possible (90% plus) at all levels of instruction during instructional time and, when feasible, beyond the classroom" and employ "a variety of strategies to facilitate comprehension and support meaning making" (ACTFL Position Statements, 2010). According to the ACTFL framework, instructors must:

1. Provide comprehensible input that is directed toward communicative goals;
2. Make meaning clear through body language, gestures, and visual support;
3. Conduct comprehension checks to ensure understanding;
4. Negotiate meaning with students and encourage negotiation among students;
5. Elicit talk that increases in fluency, accuracy, and complexity over time;
6. Encourage self-expression and spontaneous use of language;
7. Teach students strategies for requesting clarification and assistance when faced with comprehension difficulties; and
8. Offer feedback to assist and improve students' ability to interact orally in the target language. (ACTFL Position Statements, 2010)

Based on these ACTFL frameworks, we propose that in order to effectively conduct communicatively oriented language classes, TAs must have at least Intermediate High oral proficiency to teach first-year Russian but exhibit at least Advanced Low to teach second-year Russian. Our assumption is that Intermediate High is sufficient to teach introductory language courses in the target language and to provide meaningful and comprehensible inputs because speakers with this level of oral proficiency can "handle successfully uncomplicated tasks and social situations requiring an exchange of basic information related to work, school, recreation, particular interests, and areas of competence" (ACTFL Proficiency Guidelines, 2012). Nonetheless, as we will show, even the Intermediate High level of proficiency is rare among non-native and non-heritage incoming graduate students (Rifkin, 2005).

UNDERGRADUATE STUDENT PROFICIENCY OUTCOMES: DATA FROM RUSSIAN

Data on undergraduate student proficiency outcomes have been addressed in several publications (Thompson, 1996; Rifkin, 2005; Davidson, 2010). Outcomes across the studies show similar results: a correlation between Russian language competency of undergraduates and the number of years spent learning a language in a classroom setting.

Thompson (1996) studied the proficiency levels of 56 American students of Russian in all four skills (speaking, reading, listening, and writing) at different points in their studies "based on the ACTFL proficiency scale[,] in order to gather empirical data on proficiency levels currently attainable within the context of academic Russian language programs" (p. 47). Thompson's findings, summarized in Table 4.1, indicate that after four years of language study all students successfully reached Advanced proficiency in reading, but only 43% reached Advanced proficiency in speaking.[2] Her results suggest that solid Advanced proficiency in speaking was achieved after more than four years of studying Russian. However, today many undergraduate programs require only three years of language study for majors. Three years is also the minimum requirement for applicants to many graduate programs.

TABLE 4.1. Proficiency Outcomes by Year of Study and Skill (Median Scores)

Years of study	Speaking	Reading	Listening	Writing
1 year	Novice Mid	Novice Low	Novice Low	Novice High
2 years	Novice High/ Intermediate Low	Novice Mid	Novice High	Intermediate Mid
3 years	Intermediate Mid/ Intermediate High	Novice High	Intermediate Low/ Intermediate Mid	Intermediate Mid/ Intermediate High
4 years	Intermediate High/Advanced	Advanced	Intermediate High	Intermediate High
5 years	Advanced/ Advanced High	Advanced	Intermediate High	Intermediate High/ Advanced

Source: "Assessing Foreign Language Skills: Data from Russian" (Thompson, 1996).
Note: While Novice High reading proficiency after three years of study seems lower than expected, this is the median score of the range at this level according to Thompson (1996, p. 53).

Rifkin (2005) analyzes language gains in listening, reading, writing, and speaking among 352 students of Russian after a summer intensive program at the Kathryn Wasserman Davis School of Russian at Middlebury College. His preprogram data indicate that after three years of classroom instruction, students attained Intermediate Low proficiency in listening, Intermediate Mid in speaking and reading, and Intermediate Low to Intermediate Mid in writing. Davidson's findings (2010) are similar to those of Thompson and Rifkin. Davidson examines preprogram scores in tests of speaking, reading, and listening of 1,881 Russian students (with a median of three years of study) who were applying to a study abroad program in Russia. (Writing was not tested in this study.) His data show that in speaking and listening, the majority of students tested at Intermediate Low and Intermediate Mid, while in reading the mean proficiency score was Intermediate High. Davidson attributes higher scores in reading proficiency to the "emphasis on reading Russian literature in many programs" (p. 14). Table 4.2 summarizes the mean proficiency outcomes as reported by Thompson, Rifkin, and Davidson. These studies demonstrate that after three years of instruction (with no study abroad or immersive component) students rarely reach a proficiency level above Intermediate, and specifically in speaking, rarely above Intermediate Mid. Therefore, it is reasonable to assume that incoming graduate students will be in the Intermediate range.

While students do reach higher levels of proficiency with continued language learning, it is important to consider the time necessary for attaining Intermediate High and Advanced proficiency. According to the US Defense Language Institute (DLI), as reported by Language Testing International (LTI, n.d.), languages can be categorized into four groups in terms of difficulty for learners whose native language is English. According to the DLI data, in order to reach Advanced Low proficiency in one or more modalities, students of Spanish or Italian (Group I languages) need

TABLE 4.2. Median Proficiency Outcomes after Three Years of Study

	Speaking	Reading	Listening	Writing
Thompson, "Assessing Foreign Language Skills" (1996)	Intermediate Mid / Intermediate High	Novice High	Intermediate Low / Intermediate Mid	Intermediate Mid / Intermediate High
Rifkin, "A Ceiling Effect" (2005)	Intermediate Mid	Intermediate Mid	Intermediate Low	Intermediate Low / Intermediate Mid
Davidson, "Study Abroad" (2010)	Intermediate Low / Intermediate Mid	Intermediate High	Intermediate Low / Intermediate Mid	Not elicited

TABLE 4.3. Time to Aptitude in Group I Languages

Length of Training	Minimal Aptitude	Average Aptitude	Superior Aptitude
8 weeks (240 hours)	Intermediate Low	Intermediate Mid	Intermediate Mid
16 weeks (480 hours)	Intermediate High	Advanced Low	Advanced Mid
24 weeks (720 hours)	Advanced Mid	Advanced High	Superior

Source: See http://www.languagetesting.com/how-long-does-it-take.
Note: Group I languages are Afrikaans, Danish, Dutch, French, Haitian Creole, Italian, Norwegian, Portuguese, Romanian, Spanish, Swahili, and Swedish.

TABLE 4.4. Time to Aptitude in Group III Languages

Length of Training	Minimal aptitude	Average aptitude	Superior aptitude
16 weeks (480 hours)	Novice High	Intermediate Low / Intermediate Mid	Intermediate Mid / Intermediate High
24 weeks (720 hours)	Intermediate High	Advanced Low	Advanced Mid / Advanced High
44 weeks (1320 hours)	Advanced Mid	Advanced High	Superior

Source: See http://www.languagetesting.com/how-long-does-it-take.
Note: Group III languages are Amharic, Bengali, Burmese, Czech, Finnish, Hebrew, Hungarian, Khmer, Lao, Nepali, Pilipino, Polish, Russian, Serbo-Croatian, Sinhala, Thai, Tamil, Turkish, and Vietnamese.

480 instructional hours, while students of Russian (a Group III language) need at least 720 hours. This is significantly more than five years of traditional classroom instruction, or longer than the typical length of an undergraduate course of study.

Rifkin (2005) demonstrates that students of Russian need a minimum of 600 hours of instruction to reach Advanced proficiency. He proposes that programs must offer at least four to five hours of classroom instruction per week over a four-year period in order for students to reach Advanced proficiency in at least one modality without studying abroad (p. 12). However, Rifkin's survey of more than 80 institutions offering Russian language show that the average number of classroom instructional hours in four-year programs of Russian is between 408 and 453 hours, and not a single program offered 600 or more hours.

Little has changed since Rifkin's 2005 survey, as demonstrated by the data presented in Table 4.5, which show the number of contact hours for each year of study at the institutions of the authors. While these three institutions constitute only a small sampling of programs among North American colleges and universities, they are representative of a larger trend.

These numbers reflect only our standard four-skills language courses and do not include any supplemental labs or extracurricular opportunities for language study

TABLE 4.5. Contact Hours per Year of Study at Authors' Institutions

Institution	First-year Russian	Second-year Russian	Third-year Russian	Fourth-year Russian	Total hours in 4 years
University of Wisconsin-Madison: 30 weeks per year	150 (5 hours per week)	150 (5 hours per week)	150 (5 hours per week)	90 (3 hours per week)	540
University of Toronto: 24 weeks per year	120 (5 hours per week)	120 (5 hours per week)	120 (5 hours per week)	120 (5 hours per week)	480
Rutgers University: 28 weeks per year	126 (4.5 hours per week)	126 (4.5 hours per week)	84 (3 hours per week)	84 (3 hours per week)	420

(i.e., Russian conversation tables). At the University of Toronto and the University of Wisconsin–Madison students have the option to take Conversational Russian, Mass Media, Advanced Writing Skills, or Russian culture and literature courses taught in Russian in addition to the third- and fourth-year regular courses. The data in Table 4.5 also do not reflect any undergraduate study abroad or domestic immersive language learning experiences,[3] both of which increase a student's total number of contact hours.[4] It is also important to note that the differences between Russian language programs across the continent is significant. While some departments provide four or more years of Russian, many offer only three years of language study and some of these shorter programs provide only three contact hours per week in each year of instruction, yielding roughly 216 total contact hours. This number is equivalent to less than two years of study at the authors' institutions listed in Table 4.5.

The data presented above make it clear why non-native and non-heritage incoming graduate students often do not have the required proficiency level to begin teaching. It appears that the typical undergraduate language curriculum is not designed to provide appropriate opportunities for the development of language skills to match the level necessary to work as a graduate TA, nor does it help students become scholars of Russian literature or linguistics. Even though not many undergraduate students who major or minor in Russian continue their studies at the graduate level, we as language professionals should address the challenge that students face at the beginning of graduate school. Unless our undergraduate language curricula offer more contact hours or our applicants find ways to improve their language skills to the required minimum standard for teaching in graduate school, the issue of the inadequate language proficiency of incoming TAs will remain unresolved.

The task of addressing these challenges is complex and requires substantial effort on the part of both academic programs and individual students. Programs must be flexible and adaptable in order to address the needs of students with deficits in proficiency and provide alternative funding options as well as opportunities for students to improve their language skills and grow professionally as teachers.

The following section offers a closer look at how a program may approach the problem of TAs' language readiness through a case study at the University of Wisconsin–Madison.

CHALLENGES FOR NEW GRADUATE STUDENTS

In finding ways to improve graduate students' inadequate language preparation, the focus cannot be placed solely on admitting only linguistically qualified students who have reached Advanced proficiency. This approach is unrealistic, considering the state of today's undergraduate Russian instruction outcomes. Instead, the focus should be on identifying candidates with strong potential for achieving Advanced levels of proficiency across all four modalities based on undergraduate academic performance in Russian and structural command of the language.[5] The programs should also provide students with training opportunities that would allow them to attain both the language skills and the pedagogical expertise necessary for future success as professors and scholars of Russian (see Comer, 2000).

Language proficiency is an important element of graduate students' professional competence, as it is essential for both research and teaching. Despite Rifkin's (2000) call for change, many graduate programs still do not view language and pedagogy training as the top priorities of graduate students' comprehensive professional development. The low status of language and pedagogy training vis-à-vis literary research and analysis is evidenced by the fact that most language program directors and coordinators do not hold tenure-track positions. If these challenges stay in place, graduate programs must find ways to ensure that beginning- and intermediate-level Russian courses taught by graduate TAs meet basic quality standards (e.g., 90% of classroom instruction in the target language and error-free presentation of material) to fulfill their departmental missions.

Another factor that should be taken into consideration in the discussion of graduate student readiness is the fact that non-native-speaker TAs often have to teach alongside their native- or heritage-speaker peers which, inevitably, leads to comparisons, contrasts, and sometimes low morale within the program. It is often difficult for faculty and undergraduate students in large programs to avoid categorizing their language TAs into native and non-native groups. Our personal experience shows that native speakers are often viewed as more qualified even if their pedagogical skills are weaker than those of non-native instructors.[6] Such stereotyping may lead to native speaker TAs being more likely to be selected to teach higher-level or more popular courses, which only further limits the professional development opportunities for non-native speakers. Therefore, attaining a high level of language proficiency is a crucially important step in assuring that non-native TAs are prepared to teach elementary-level courses as well as intermediate and advanced courses.

ASSESSMENT AND DEVELOPMENT OF GRADUATE STUDENT LANGUAGE SKILLS: A CASE STUDY

In order to illustrate the current trends in proficiency levels of newly admitted graduate students and to discuss strategies that have been showing positive results in graduate TA training, we present here a case study of graduate student assessment and training practices at the University of Wisconsin–Madison.

Since the early 1990s the Department of German, Nordic, and Slavic Languages and Literature at UW–Madison has had in place rigorous language proficiency requirements for all admitted students seeking an advanced degree in Russian. All incoming non-native speaker graduate students are required to take five Russian competency exams that measure their competence in reading, listening, writing, speaking, and grammar. These exams include a computerized fill-in-the-blank test on grammar and syntax, computerized multiple-choice reading and listening comprehension tests, a pen-and-paper essay exam, and an unofficial (internal) Oral Proficiency Interview (OPI) conducted by an ACTFL-certified tester. The reading and listening tests measure understanding of spoken and written discourse using the ACTFL rating scale. In the writing exam students are asked to produce responses to two writing prompts, one in the formal and one in the informal mode of communication. These writing samples are also assessed according to the ACTFL Proficiency Guidelines. The passing score for proficiency-based exams (reading, listening, writing, and speaking) is Advanced Low; the passing score for the grammar exam is 80% (performance at this level demonstrates a solid command of the main concepts of Russian grammar). Every student is required to take all five tests before his or her first semester of graduate studies and every semester can retake any failed test. All graduate students must pass three of the five exams before receiving a master's degree (usually this happens after three semesters in residence). A student must pass all five exams by the end of the fifth semester in the program in order to be eligible for a doctoral degree.

Passing the competency exams is challenging for most students and the vast majority take each of the tests more than once before passing. The difficulty of the exams can be attributed to several factors, including students' insufficient levels of language proficiency in some or all modalities, test anxiety, or unfamiliarity with the test format. Figure 4.1 below presents the results of initial assessments of incoming graduate students over the course of seven years, from 2008 to 2014.

These data show that only 28% of newly admitted students entered the program with Advanced proficiency in speaking, only 23% possessed Advanced proficiency in writing, and only 21% began their graduate careers with Advanced proficiency in listening. Reading is the strongest area for most incoming students, with 60% demonstrating Advanced-level skills.

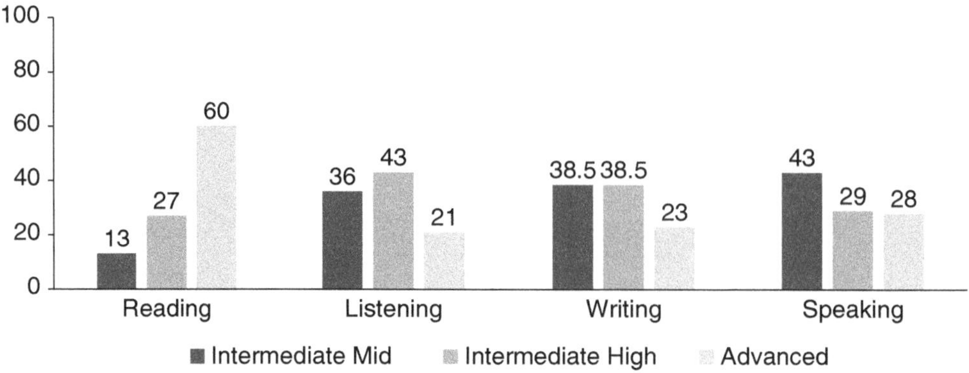

FIGURE 4.1. Proficiency Levels of Incoming Graduate Students

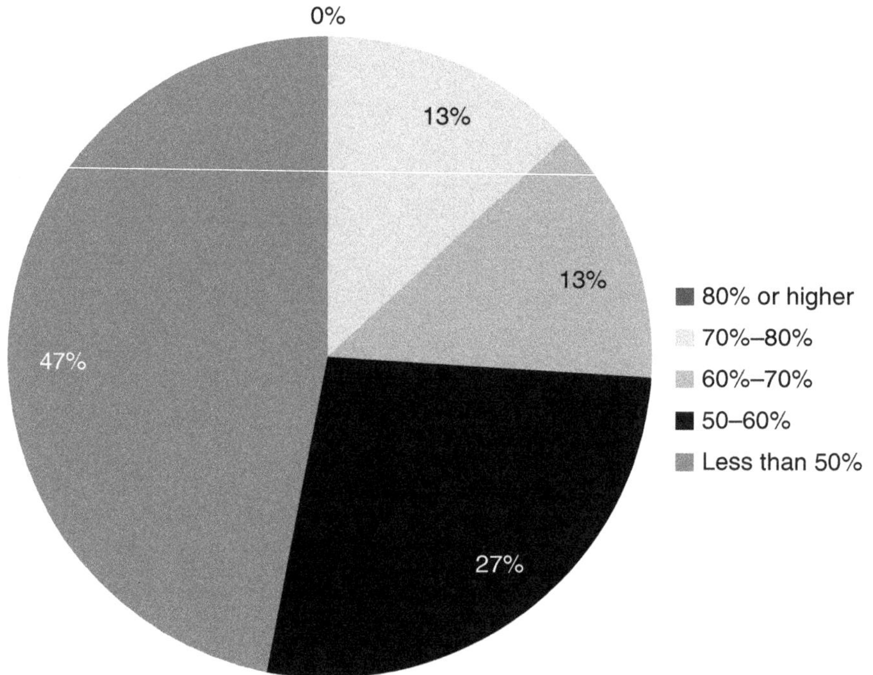

FIGURE 4.2. Grammar Exam Scores of Incoming Graduate Students

The most serious deficiencies were observed in the area of grammar, with the majority of students needing more than three attempts before achieving the required score of 80%.[7] The grammar exam consists of a long text in Russian with English cues for 70 blanks. Students are instructed to fill in each blank based on the context and the English cue provided. In addition to demonstrating control of grammatical and syntactic structures, students must also spell each item correctly to receive credit. The test is scored as the sum of correct responses out of a possible 70. Figure 4.2 presents grammar exam scores of incoming UW–Madison non-native speaker graduate

TABLE 4.6. Comparison of OPI Ratings and Grammar Exam Scores

OPI Rating	Mean grammar score	Minimum grammar score	Maximum grammar score
Intermediate Mid	37	20	51
Intermediate High	59.2	30	69
Advanced Low and Advanced Mid	61	52	70

Note: The Intermediate High maximum grammar score of 69% was an outlier. All other students with Intermediate High oral proficiency scored in the 30%–64% range.

students from 2008 to 2014. None of the non-native speakers who entered the program in the last seven years were able to reach the passing score of 80% on their initial attempt; 13% of students scored between 70% and 80%; another 13% scored between 60% and 70%; 27% of students reached the score of 50%; and 47% scored under the 50% mark.

Based on available data from testing of all skills, an inference can be made that stronger grammatical competence translates into higher levels of proficiency in other modalities and that lack of grammatical training leads to deficiencies in the other skills, particularly speaking. Table 4.6 shows the distribution of grammar exam results in comparison to students' OPI ratings and demonstrates that students with lower oral proficiency also score lower on the grammar exam.[8]

The Slavic graduate program at the University of Wisconsin–Madison recognizes the existence of this link between grammatical competence and proficiency growth in other modalities and provides graduate students with detailed feedback after each grammar exam attempt, including a list of error types and suggestions for practice exercises. This feedback allows students to target their areas of weakness as they continue to work to improve their grammar skills. Graduate students are encouraged to enroll in advanced content-based courses offered as part of the Russian Flagship Program Curriculum. These courses are designed to enable students to reach Advanced proficiency, which includes the ability to produce paragraph-level discourse in a variety of genres, to use complex syntax and devices of cohesion to form paragraphs, to control all time frames and aspects, and to employ extended vocabulary to speak about topics beyond straightforward "routine tasks and social situations" (ACTFL, 2012). In addition to addressing grammar and structural deficiencies, the language program director meets with each student individually to discuss his or her strengths and weaknesses in other modalities (reading, listening, and writing) in order to develop specific strategies for remediation. The department frequently recommends that graduate students spend a summer studying in Russia or at a domestic immersion program such as at Middlebury's Wasserman Davis School of Russian. If a student shows linguistic deficits serious enough to impede his or her eligibility for a TA position or to hamper academic work (i.e., proficiency below Intermediate High in one or more modalities), the department strongly encourages a leave of absence to study in Russia. Such students often elect to take this leave of absence for a semester, or in some cases an academic year, before the fifth semester of graduate study in order to be able to meet the requirement of passing all five exams by the end of their fifth semester in residence.

The passing of language competency exams does not necessarily determine a graduate student's eligibility to teach in the program but it factors prominently in graduate funding decisions. To be eligible for a TA position a UW–Madison Slavic graduate student must satisfy the following requirements:

- Demonstrated proficiency in all modalities (Intermediate High to teach first- and second- semester Russian; Advanced Low for third- and fourth-semester Russian);
- Completion of the course Methods of Teaching Russian;
- A three-day preservice workshop for language TAs conducted by the UW–Madison Language institute to give beginning language instructors a basic understanding of the principles and methods of communicative language teaching and general best practices for lesson design;
- A one-day preservice training workshop for all university TAs conducted by the Graduate School wherein selected teaching Fellows from across disciplines cover a host of topics that TAs will find useful as they begin their teaching appointments;[9]
- A one-day orientation workshop conducted in English by the Russian Language Program director to provide a detailed overview of the Slavic Program's policies for language instruction and introduce all TAs to the curriculum and policies of the courses they will teach; and
- A weekly TA practicum dedicated to the discussion of issues related to teaching and testing (a one-credit course that TAs are required to take every semester when they hold a teaching position).

Graduate students typically receive their first assistantship in their third semester. It is not desirable to appoint graduate students to TA positions even for beginning Russian before they pass their Russian competency exams (i.e., attain Advanced Low proficiency in all four skills) but, given the language proficiency (or lack of proficiency) of the majority of incoming graduate students, it is sometimes necessary to appoint TAs who are underqualified. However, such appointments should not lead to a decline in the quality of undergraduate instruction. If graduate students receive a teaching position before achieving Advanced proficiency, the programs must provide close oversight as well as pedagogical and linguistic support to enable these teachers to succeed. Mentoring, frequent class observations, and assistance from faculty members or more experienced TAs in lesson planning and curriculum development (e.g., helping to ensure that instructional materials and tests are error-free) are some of the steps that can be taken to ensure that programs continue to offer the highest possible quality instruction to their undergraduate students while providing linguistic and pedagogical training to graduate TAs.

Because the move from Intermediate High to Advanced Low proficiency can be difficult to make, it can be challenging for many of our TAs to achieve this growth by the end of their fifth semester of graduate study.[10] But the need to meet proficiency requirements is a strong motivating factor that pushes students to work continually on their language skills and to attribute the same importance to their proficiency development as they do to their literature coursework. The proficiency requirement also serves the function of making sure that students are prepared to teach Russian courses above the beginning level. While in the short term this requirement presents a significant challenge to many graduate students, in the long term they are better able to complete the program as well-rounded scholars and teachers who are qualified to conduct complex research in Russian and teach Russian language courses at all levels.

LANGUAGE PROFICIENCY AND THE ACADEMIC JOB MARKET

The majority of postings for university positions in Russian over the past few years specifically mention language skills in Russian (and English), and many positions also require experience in teaching language at all levels and in working with heritage speakers. Only one of the advertised jobs identified a particular ACTFL proficiency level ("advanced-level proficiency" [Academic Jobs Wiki, 2015–16]); the majority instead used vague terms such as "near-native proficiency," "near-native fluency," or "strong command." Based on the records on the Academic Jobs wiki, Table 4.7 shows the number of advertised tenure-track (TT) and visiting or non-tenure-track (NTT) positions in Russian that explicitly mention desired language competency in Russian

TABLE 4.7. Job Advertisements Requiring Both Language Skills and Teaching Experience

	Years					
	2013-14		2014-15		2015-16	
	TT	NTT	TT	NTT	TT	NTT
Total ads by position	7	20	18	10	9	10
Ads requiring language skills	7	19	17	9	7	10
Ads requiring language teaching	4	18	10	8	5	8
Ads mentioning advanced language courses	1	13	5	7	4	4
Ads not requiring either language skills or teaching	0	1	1	1	1	0

Source: Compiled by authors.
Note: TT = tenure-track; NTT = non-tenure-track

and the responsibility of teaching Russian.[11] The majority of ads mentioned experience in language teaching of some kind, although a smaller percentage specifically mentioned Russian language courses at upper levels (i.e., beyond second year). Only one or two ads per year did not mention a language proficiency requirement for applicants or language teaching among the duties of the position.

The descriptions of language proficiency in job ads, such as "near-native" and "excellent," are vague; listing specific ACTFL proficiency levels would be an improvement. Our best guess is that search committees are looking for Advanced High or Superior proficiency, which entails the ability to communicate on abstract topics in extended discourse and being understood by any native speaker, both of which require accuracy and fluency. There is not enough time during an initial job interview to adequately assess a speaker's language proficiency because a typical oral proficiency interview of Advanced or Superior level takes 25–30 minutes, according to the ACTFL OPI protocol. During first-round job interviews, language proficiency is generally assessed through one predictable question: "Tell us about your dissertation." Interviewers typically pay close attention to pronunciation, grammatical accuracy, and range of vocabulary. As discussed earlier, Advanced High or Superior proficiency is time consuming to achieve (requiring extended time in an immersive setting; cf. Rifkin, 2005, p. 11) and is not a requirement for entrance to or graduation from any graduate program we know.

Although the Russian language section of an employment interview is brief and cannot produce an accurate assessment of a candidate's language skills, we have nonetheless observed instances of candidates who had all the necessary qualifications and a successful interview with regard to questions of research but were ultimately not offered a position due to insufficient language skills. In lieu of a single question in the interview, an ACTFL OPI score as a component of a candidate's teaching portfolio or application materials would be a much better indication of proficiency. Obtaining an official OPI score can be a financial burden to graduate students who are already expected to travel at their own expense to conferences for interviews, but advisory OPI ratings can be provided at no cost if a faculty member is a certified tester.

As Table 4.7 shows, the majority of positions involve teaching language, particularly at small liberal arts colleges or as visiting faculty. Thus appropriate language proficiency is critical. Many job postings also indicate that a successful candidate should be able to teach Russian language at advanced levels. As noted earlier, graduate students do not always have the proficiency level necessary to teach even a second-year course, let alone a more advanced course. Even with adequate language proficiency, in many programs full-time lecturers teach the upper-level courses, which further prevents a graduate student from gaining the valuable experience of teaching such a course.

There are a few potential solutions to the lack of opportunities for TAs to teach advanced language courses. One is to allow for variety in teaching assignments: giving one section of a lower-level course to a full-time lecturer in order to free up an upper-level course for a TA. Such changes to the staffing of courses can add to the cohesiveness of the language program, with lecturers gaining a better understanding of the content of lower-level courses. Students in a lower-level language course can also become better acquainted with faculty members, which potentially can lead to greater retention overall. Students may enjoy the chance to continue with the same instructor in upper-level courses. Such a change in staffing may not be implementable at institutions that have positions reserved solely for TAs. A second solution is to provide TAs with opportunities to "guest teach" several lessons in an upper-level language course. Presuming that the primary instructor of the course will be available to observe, the TA can receive beneficial feedback that recreates the scenario of a sample class that is common among many campus interviews.

Similarly, graduate programs can offer an apprenticeship in language instruction. There are two possible models of such an apprenticeship in an upper-level language course: designing and implementing an entire unit or module, from materials development to implementation of activities to assessment; or team-teaching with the primary instructor, including collaboration on course and materials design, delivery of instruction, and assessment. The primary instructor and apprentice can alternate days or weeks as best suits their needs. In both models the instructor provides feedback and mentorship, approves all materials and assessments, and conducts multiple classroom observations. Both apprenticeship models provide TAs with experience in designing materials for more advanced language students and allows them to indicate on their CV or other job application materials that they do in fact have experience teaching Russian at all levels. Furthermore, this experience can be specifically commented upon in a letter of recommendation provided by the language instructor or coordinator of the apprenticeship.

In order for guest teaching or an apprenticeship to be valuable, the TA must possess adequate language proficiency to provide meaningful input in the target language. Therefore we strongly recommend that departments offer courses that will provide graduate students with adequate language preparation to successfully obtain a full-time position and effectively prepare them for teaching the next generation of undergraduate language students.

STRATEGIES FOR IMPROVING GRADUATE STUDENT LANGUAGE READINESS

As detailed earlier, the average proficiency level of incoming graduate students is not sufficient for completing the requirements of their programs, including teaching language courses. Language proficiency should be seen as a "vital part of today's foreign language classroom" (Huhn, 2012, p. s173). Therefore, graduate programs ought to provide pre- and in-service opportunities to TAs to further develop their proficiency. Admission committees should consider the language proficiency of applicants through a Russian-language interview with the language coordinator and a member of the graduate admissions committee. In some instances inadequate proficiency may mean an otherwise strong applicant will not be admitted. In other instances the faculty may suggest methods for necessary improvements to admitted students before enrollment. This practice is currently implemented in some German and Romance languages departments, where admitted students are encouraged to attend a domestic or overseas immersive program before beginning their coursework. Continued measures must be taken to improve or maintain language proficiency to ensure that these individuals are prepared for their teaching responsibilities. Recommendations for assisting graduate students in improving their language proficiency are offered later. These suggestions fall into three categories: coursework, extracurricular programming, and opportunities for study in an immersion environment. Not every department will be able to implement all of these proposals, but we present options that have the potential to make an impact on the language readiness of Russian TAs.

First, providing graduate students with appropriate language courses will allow them to continue regular practice with more active skills, such as speaking and writing as well as listening. A Russian language course for graduate students should be based on the Proficiency Guidelines, with tasks designed to maintain and improve Advanced-level performance in all four skills and at the same time strengthening grammatical accuracy. In order to ensure that enrollment is sufficient to regularly offer such a course, the topics discussed should serve to attract students from outside Slavic literature departments, for example, social scientists who plan to conduct interviews or read archival materials in Russian-speaking countries. The focus of the course could be on academic Russian in general and not limited to literary analysis. One successful model of a graduate-level language course at the University of Illinois at Urbana-Champaign, taken by first- and second-year students in the Slavic PhD program, introduces students to Russian academic prose, engages students in discussion of primary and secondary sources in their fields, reviews advanced grammar and syntax (such as participles, verbal adverbs, and connecting devices), and ends with a miniconference at which students present short papers related to their current research. This one-year course prepares students to discuss their research and a variety of other topics in Russian. Students have the option to repeat the course if desired or deemed necessary.

If a course designed specifically for graduate students is not possible, a content-based course for advanced undergraduates can also meet the needs of graduate students seeking to maintain Advanced or achieve Superior proficiency. Some Slavic programs offer such courses, but graduate students are often discouraged from enrolling by their advisors or the director of graduate studies because they want students to focus on their graduate coursework. However, as we have argued here, language proficiency is a critical part of professional development in any PhD program, and thus such coursework should be encouraged. Another alternative could be to add a one-hour discussion section in Russian to an existing literature course taught in English, and open to students who are not enrolled in the base course but who wish to work on their language skills.

Given sufficient demand, departments can also offer regular Russian conversation hours. Ideally a native or Superior-level speaker will lead the discussion and offer feedback on grammar and vocabulary as needed or requested. Many departments already offer this additional practice for undergraduates; to ensure that the level of conversation is appropriate for graduate students (who are Advanced learners or higher), programs can base conversation hours on materials from symposia, guest lectures, or film screenings organized at the university. At UW–Madison such discussions are offered through the Flagship program, but this practice can be implemented at other institutions as well, with the discussion leader serving as a volunteer or for a small remuneration.

We recognize that not all Russian language departments are able to provide their graduate students with adequate opportunities for improving their language proficiency in the limited amount of time they have before they begin teaching, but our experience at UW–Madison shows that it is possible. Students must be willing to invest additional time and, frequently, money in language and pedagogical training during their graduate careers in order to ensure their preparedness for teaching and research. It may be necessary for some students to study in an immersive setting, whether in Russia or a Russian-speaking country, or at an intensive domestic summer program. While some institutions are able to provide funding for foreign language and area studies (FLAS) to allow their graduate students the chance to engage in language study over a summer or during an academic year, others may struggle with providing appropriate levels of support. However, funding for language work should be viewed as a critical component of professional development, similar to department-funded conference attendance. Finally, mentoring and advising throughout the graduate program will raise awareness of the expectations for the job market, including the importance of language proficiency. The data from jobs ads presented in Table 4.7 highlight that near-native proficiency is a requirement for finding employment in the field.

CONCLUSION

We have discussed the fact that many graduate students in Russian enter doctoral programs with inadequate language proficiency for language teaching. We have demonstrated a connection between deficits in undergraduate instruction and the ability of graduate students to serve as TAs who teach language. We discussed how inadequate language skills can negatively affect TA performance in the classroom because they are unable to provide sufficient meaningful input in the target language. We also presented ways in which these issues translate into difficulties when entering the job market, as the majority of job announcements require native or near-native fluency in Russian. Finally, we examined possible solutions that graduate programs can implement in order to provide their students with adequate opportunities to reach the required levels of proficiency in all four skills.

In order for programs to better serve their graduate students, we suggest that greater attention be paid to language and pedagogical training, as these aspects of professional development are just as critical to finding employment as a strong research profile. Making space in the graduate curriculum for language courses will allow students to continue improving their proficiency alongside their literature coursework. Graduate programs that cannot provide adequate language training for their students should identify other means for their students to reach Advanced proficiency, such as summer immersive programs, regular tutoring with a native speaker, or extended time off to study abroad. Departments should work toward identifying funding for such language training to enable graduate students to pursue increased levels of proficiency without taking on any further expenses. While making funds available is a challenge, it is important to set expectations for achieving Advanced proficiency in all four skills; graduate programs that do so will send a signal that proficiency is crucial to success in the field and highlight that the language and teacher training programs are as valuable to the department as the literature curriculum. Finally, establishing language training as a top priority will improve graduate students' readiness for language teaching and enhance their qualifications for future professional opportunities.

NOTES

1. This document is now called World-Readiness Standards for Language Learning (2015).
2. Note that the revision of the ACTFL Oral Proficiency Guidelines of 1999 introduced the distinction between Advanced Low and Advanced Mid as part of what previously just the Advanced level; and Advanced Plus was renamed Advanced High to conform to the pattern of Novice High and Intermediate High (see Mikhailova, 2005). In 2012 the Advanced level for reading and listening was split into Advanced Low and Advanced Mid.
3. Davidson (2010) states that students of Russian who entered a study abroad program with Intermediate Mid proficiency in speaking achieved Intermediate High after one semester and Advanced Mid after one year of studying abroad.
4. At this time the data on the percentage of Russian majors who study abroad and the length of their study has not been collected.
5. Rifkin notes that "the acquisition of grammatical competence correlates with the acquisition of the four skills" (2005, p. 12).
6. Although the issue of students' and supervisors' perceptions of native vs. non-native instructors has not been studied in regard to teachers of Russian, research on native vs. non-native Spanish, ESL, and EFL teachers shows that non-native teachers tend to be perceived more negatively by students in such areas of teaching as speaking, pronunciation, and culture (Callahan, 2006). While many TA supervisors recognize that non-native-speaker instructors can be effective teachers of lexicon and grammar who are equal to their native peers (and may even have a higher level of language awareness), there still exists a significant tendency among language program

directors to appoint non-native-speaker instructors primarily to elementary-level courses (Llurda, 2005).

7. Data were not collected on the exact number of attempts taken by each student before passing the exam.
8. This conclusion corresponds to Rifkin's (2005) findings, which show that language gains in all modalities correlate with grammatical competence (p. 12).
9. Though this workshop is not focused specifically on language teaching, it does offer new TAs an opportunity to become integrated into the university TA community and better able to understand the issues relevant to TAs.
10. Rifkin (2005) hypothesizes that "attaining the advanced level . . . requires double the effort for attaining the intermediate level" (p. 12). However, we are unaware of any data that demonstrate this specifically as it relates to Russian.
11. Only graduate positions for Russian in North America were examined. Senior positions were excluded, as were positions for history, political science, and other related fields.

REFERENCES

Academic Jobs Wiki. (2013–14). Russian and Slavic. Retrieved from http://academicjobs.wikia.com/wiki/Russian_%26_Slavic_2013-2014

Academic Jobs Wiki. (2014–15). Russian and Slavic. Retrieved from http://academicjobs.wikia.com/wiki/Russian/Slavic_2014-2015

Academic Jobs Wiki. (2015–16). Russian and Slavic. Retrieved from http://academicjobs.wikia.com/wiki/Russian/Slavic_2015-2016

American Council on the Teaching of Foreign Languages (ACTFL). (2010). Position statements: Use of the target language in the classroom. Retrieved from http://www.actfl.org/news/position-statements/use-the-target-language-the-classroom

American Council on the Teaching of Foreign Languages (ACTFL). (2012). ACTFL Proficiency Guidelines 2012. Retrieved from http://www.actfl.org/publications/guidelines-and-manuals/actfl-proficiency-guidelines-2012

American Council on the Teaching of Foreign Languages/Council for Accreditation of Educator Preparation (ACTFL/CAEP) (2015). Program Standards for the Preparation of Foreign Language Teachers. Retrieved from https://www.actfl.org/sites/default/files/CAEP/ACTFLCAEPStandards2013_v2015.pdf

Brecht, R., Davidson, D., & Ginsberg, R. (1993). Predictors of foreign language gain during study abroad: ACTR/NFLC Project. Washington, DC: Occasional Papers of the National Foreign Language Center.

Callahan, L. (2006). Student perceptions of native and non-native speaker language instructors: A comparison of ESL and Spanish. *Sintagma. Revista de Lingüística*, *18*, 19–49.

Chambless, K. S. (2012). Teachers' oral proficiency in the target language: Research and its role in language teaching and learning. *Foreign Language Annals, 45* (Supplemental Issue), s141–s162.

Comer, W. (2000). Making our way toward teacher education programs in Slavic languages. In O. Kagan & B. Rifkin (Eds.), *The learning and teaching of Slavic languages and cultures* (pp. 539–48). Bloomington, IN: Slavica.

Davidson, D. (2010). Study abroad: When, how long, and with what results? New data from the Russian front. *Foreign Language Annals, 4*(1), 6–26.

Glisan, E. W. (2013). On keeping the target language in language teaching: A bottom-up effort to protect the public and students. *Modern Language Journal, 97*(2), 540–44.

Huhn, C. (2012). In search of innovation: Research on effective models of foreign language teacher preparation. *Foreign Language Annals, 45* (Supplemental Issue), s163–83.

Language Testing International. (n.d.) How long does it take to become proficient? Retrieved from http://www.languagetesting.com/how-long-does-it-take

Llurda, E. (2005). Non-native TESOL students as seen by practicum supervisors. In E. Llurda (Ed.), *Non-native language teachers: Perceptions, challenges, and contributions to the profession* (pp. 131–54). New York: Springer.

Mikhailova, J. (2005). *Comparison of interpersonal and presentational description in Russian oral proficiency testing* (Doctoral dissertation). Ohio State University, Columbus, Ohio.

National Standards Collaborative Board (NSCB). (2015). *World-readiness standards for learning languages* (4th ed.). Alexandria, VA: Author. Retrieved from http://www.actfl.org/publications/all/world-readiness-standards-learning-languages

Pearson, L., Fonseca-Greber, B., & Foell, K. (2006). Advanced proficiency for foreign language teacher candidates: What can we do to help them achieve this goal? *Foreign Language Annals, 39*(3), 507–19.

Rifkin, B. (2000). A model for teacher training and education for the Slavic languages. In O. Kagan & B. Rifkin (Eds.), *The learning and teaching of Slavic languages and cultures* (pp. 520–37). Bloomington, IN: Slavica.

Rifkin, B. (2005). A ceiling effect in traditional classroom foreign language instruction: Data from Russian. *Modern Language Journal, 89*(1), 3–18.

Schick, J., & Nelson, P. (2001). Language teacher education: The challenge for the 21st century. *The Clearing House: A Journal of Educational Strategies, Issues and Ideas, 74*(6), 301–4.

Tedick, D. (2013). Embracing proficiency and program standards and rising to the challenge: A response to Burke. *Modern Language Journal, 97*(2), 535–38.

Thompson, I. (1996). Assessing foreign language skills: Data from Russian. *Modern Language Journal, 80*(1), 47–65.

PART II

THE TEACHING OF RUSSIAN AND THE WORLD-READINESS STANDARDS FOR LEARNING LANGUAGES

5

MAKING THE STANDARDS THE STANDARD

The World-Readiness Standards and the Teaching of Russian Language and Culture

Thomas J. Garza

Foreign language educators, from the elementary to postsecondary levels (K–16), face increasing demands from legislators, institutional administrators, and taxpayers for more accountability and assessment of measurable outcomes of their programs. The substantially revised and retitled fourth edition of the World-Readiness Standards for Learning Languages (NSCB, 2015a) provides a welcome addition to the Russian language educator's repertoire of materials to help shape and maintain effective programs for students seeking to attain functional to professional proficiency in the language and culture. The current iteration of the Standards updates and extends the pedagogical reach of the "Five Cs" of foreign language education (Communication, Cultures, Connections, Comparisons, and Communities), the 11 Standards, the Sample Performance Indicators (SPIs), and the language-specific Learning Scenarios (LS) that were offered in the previous three editions of Standards for Foreign Language Learning in the 21st Century. This new document will potentially have a much greater impact on the teaching, learning, and assessment of Russian.

A number of changes in content (e.g., the inclusion of postsecondary standards, a reflection of Common Core State Standards, a consideration of heritage learners throughout), the presentation of the material (e.g., elimination of the hierarchical numeric system for presenting the five goal areas of language), and the nomenclature used (e.g., the use of "learner" instead of "student" to embrace the spectrum of types of individuals engaged in language study) are evident throughout the revised standards as they apply to the study of fourteen languages, including the addition of American Sign Language (NSCB, 2015b). In addition to these changes two major differences lie at the core of the innovation and improvement of the revised document for Russian: (1) the inclusion of postsecondary language programs and age-appropriate content in the SPIs and the LSs, and (2) a much more overt proficiency orientation of the Performance Indicators in conjunction with the relevant grade level. In order to understand more fully how the fourth edition of the Standards came to be and how it better reflects the current state of Russian language and culture instruction in the United States, here I provide a critical history of the various iterations of the Standards in the United States, with particular emphasis on the impact the Russian-specific Standards have had on the profession. Additional attention is devoted to the development of the 2015 revised Standards for Russian and how these new language-specific materials might contribute to curricular and pedagogical developments in Russian language and culture instruction.

A Brief History of the Standards

As the language teaching profession moved toward a proficiency orientation following the publication of the American Council for the Teaching of Foreign Languages (ACTFL) Proficiency Guidelines (1986), a growing number of states grappled with the need for goal-oriented, attestable standards in K–12 education in a variety of academic subjects and prompted a group of language educators, under the leadership of ACTFL, to undertake the creation of a set of generic standards common to the learning of all non-native languages. The development of such standards was seen as "intricately interrelated" to and "the natural extension" of the proficiency framework (Byrnes, 2012, p. 4). Indeed, the various editions of the ACTFL Proficiency Guidelines published from 1986 to 2012 provide parameters from measuring functional abilities in a given language that aid in assessing a learner's progress. These level-specific descriptors (Novice to Superior) have assisted curriculum developers and teachers in understanding the kinds of performance-based activities and instruction that might best enable learners to attain higher proficiency levels in the various modalities of a language. The 2013 publication of "Can-Do" Statements, through the collaboration of ACTFL and the National Council of State Supervisors of Foreign Languages (NCSSFL), further underscores the relationship between proficiency and task-based performance. By providing examples of learner performance in the form of statements, such as "I can ask for and give simple directions," can-do statements help learners and instructors better understand performance goals throughout the process of language learning. The creation of a set of standards that provide language-specific examples of a learner's functional ability at each stage of instruction followed naturally as an integral part of the creation of materials and curricula geared ultimately to attaining Advanced and Superior proficiency levels (ACTFL), or what the Interagency Language Roundtable (ILR) terms "professional proficiency" (Interagency, 2016).

Initiated in 1993, the original three-year Standards project was funded by the America 2000 (1991) initiative of the George H.W. Bush administration and continued into Bill Clinton's Goals 2000: Educate America Act (1994), both of which supported the development of national standards in most curricular areas, including foreign languages. The original intention of the project's 11-member team, which included language educators from all levels of instruction, was to create a document that would have broad application in the definition and description of content standards, be able to measure student knowledge and functional abilities in a given language in line with ACTFL proficiency descriptors, and assist individual states and school districts in creating and implementing language standards for their own programs. The product of these efforts was the first edition of Standards for Foreign Language Learning: Preparing for the 21st Century (1996).

Among the most significant and compelling features of the original volume was the representation, using interlinking multicolored circles, of the Five Cs of Foreign Language Study. This chart showed the five goal areas essential for encompassing the diverse purposes and uses of languages, from understanding printed text to communicating intentions to interacting appropriately with native speakers. The now-iconic image depicted in Figure 5.1 shows the interdependence of each of the five areas as well as the intrinsic unity and equal value among the different goal areas when viewed as a symmetrical coherent whole.

The utility of this graphic representation of the five goal areas for language learning and teaching quickly permeated the professional and public discussion of the Standards and of language and culture teaching in general. As the authors of the original Standards indicated, "Regardless of educational or career aspirations, foreign language instruction committed to providing experiences in all five goal areas will be beneficial to all students. Even if students never speak the language after leaving school, they will for a lifetime retain the cross-cultural skills and knowledge, the insight, and the access to a world beyond traditional borders" (NSFLEP, 1996, p. 31).

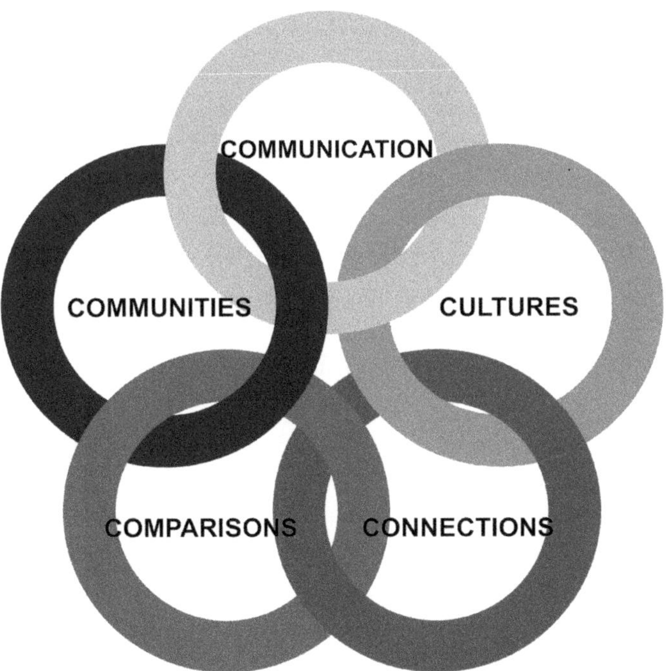

FIGURE 5.1. The Five Cs of Foreign Language Study

However, the interdependent, interlocking relationship among the five goal areas of the 1996 Standards was, to a certain extent, undermined by the hierarchical arrangement and presentation of the 11 subgoals. Each of the five goal areas was designated numerically 1 through 5 and each subgoal was given a secondary decimal numerical designation, creating the perception—if not the reality—that "using the language beyond the school setting" (Standard 5.1), for example, is of less importance in the language-learning process than "engaging in conversation" (Standard 1.1), based on their relative position and numeration:

Goal 1: Communication

Standard 1.1 Interpersonal Communication: Students engage in conversation, provide and obtain information, express feeling and emotion, and exchange opinions.

Standard 1.2 Interpretive Communication: Students understand and interpret written and spoken language on a variety of topics.

Standard 1.3 Presentational Communication: Students present information, concepts, and ideas to an audience of listeners or readers on a variety of topics.

Goal 2: Cultures

Standard 2.1 Practices and Perspective: Students demonstrate an understanding of the relationship between the practices and perspectives of the culture studied.

Standard 2.2 Products and Perspectives: Students demonstrate an understanding of the relationship between the products and perspectives of the culture studied.

Goal 3: Connections

Standard 3.1 Knowledge of Other Disciplines: Students reinforce and further their knowledge of other disciplines through the foreign language.

Standard 3.2 Distinctive Viewpoints: Students acquire information and recognize the distinctive viewpoints that are only available through the foreign language and its cultures.

Goal 4: Comparisons

Standard 4.1 Nature of Language: Students demonstrate understanding of the nature of language through comparisons of the language studied and their own.

Standard 4.2 Culture: Students demonstrate understanding of the concept of culture through comparisons of the cultures studied and their own.

Goal 5: Community

Standard 5.1 Beyond the School Setting: Students use the language both within and beyond the school setting.

Standard 5.2 Lifelong Learners: Students show evidence of becoming lifelong learners by using the language for personal enjoyment and enrichment. (National Standards for Foreign Language Learning, 1996, p. 9)

This decimal enumeration presented the Five Cs in a specific descending order that placed primary importance on communication above the other goals of language learning. This learning gives practitioners an implicit numeric hierarchy of the individual areas that belies the interdependence and integration of the goals depicted by the equal, interlocking rings of the Five Cs. Some agreed with such a ranking of the goals; Phillips and Lafayette (1996), citing Fox, affirm the basis for the hierarchy, stating "that since Goal 1 (communication) of the standards is central to all subsequent goals, it is imperative that teachers clearly understand how an individual develops communicative competence" (p. 202). Ultimately the question of whether the Five Cs should be understood as equal and interconnected or as a hierarchy is answered in the format of the 2015 World-Readiness Standards for Learning Languages. The current volume eliminates entirely the numeric designation of the learning goals, choosing instead to present the Five Cs and the 11 subgoals as being of equal value and relevance in language learning. Even though the five goal areas must necessarily be presented in some particular order, the elimination of the numeric order aligns more closely with the design of the five equal interlocking rings and, consequently, equal pedagogical weight in the process of language instruction.

Each of the 11 non-language-specific standards enumerated in 1996 was also elucidated by means of the specific learner SPIs; these practical examples demonstrate the achievement of a given standard during language learning. With their overt performance-based orientation they also serve to demonstrate the inherent connection between the Standards and the earlier ACTFL Proficiency Guidelines. In all three of the earlier editions of the Standards (1996, 1999, 2006), SPIs were assigned a grade-level designation, which suggests appropriate tasks, activities, and assessments for K–12 foreign language and culture education. For example:

<table>
<tr><td colspan="3">COMMUNICATION
1.1 Students engage in conversations, provide and obtain information, express feelings and emotions, and exchange opinions.
This standard focuses on interpersonal communication, that is, direct oral or written communication between individuals who are in personal contact. In most modern languages, students can quite quickly learn a number of phrases that will permit them to interact with each other. In the course of their study, they will grow in their ability to converse in a culturally appropriate manner.</td></tr>
<tr><td colspan="3">Sample Progress Indicators</td></tr>
<tr><td>Grade 4: Students ask and answer questions about such things as family, school events, and celebrations in person or letters, e-mail, or audio and video tapes.</td><td>Grade 8: Students exchange information about personal events, memorable experiences, and other school subjects with peers and/or members of the target cultures</td><td>Grade 12: Students exchange, support, and discuss their opinions and individual perspectives with peers and/or speakers of the target language on a variety of topics dealing with contemporary and historical issues</td></tr>
</table>

FIGURE 5.2. Sample Performance Indicators with Grade-Level Designation

TABLE 5.1. Languages Used in Four Editions of the National Standards Collaborative Board Standards

1996	1999	2006	2015
Standards for Foreign Language Learning: Preparing for the 21st Century	Standards for Foreign Language Learning in the 21st Century, 2nd ed.	Standards for Foreign Language Learning in the 21st Century, 3rd ed.	World-Readiness Standards for Learning Languages, 4th ed.
Generic standards with sporadic examples provided in French, German, and Spanish	Language-specific standards for Chinese, Classical languages, French, German, Italian, Japanese, Portuguese, Russian, and Spanish	Language-specific standards for Arabic, Chinese, Classical languages, French, German, Italian, Japanese, Portuguese, Russian, and Spanish	Language-specific standards plus postsecondary materials for American Sign Language, Arabic, Chinese, Classical languages, French, German, Hindi, Italian, Japanese, Korean, Portuguese, Russian, Scandinavian languages, and Spanish

Following the original publication of the generic Standards in 1996, each subsequent edition brought the volume closer to representing the breadth of national foreign language programs. The second edition (1999) offered language educators a much expanded and more inclusive set of materials for a number of languages: Chinese, Classical languages (Latin and Greek), French, German, Italian, Japanese, Portuguese, Russian, and Spanish. The third edition (2006) added Arabic standards and, like the earlier editions, contained SPIs and LSs for each of the 10 languages and cultures represented, in addition to language-specific references in the standards (e.g., meaningful use of tone in Chinese, use of polite forms of address in Russian, differences in written and spoken communication in Arabic, etc.). The fourth edition (2015) represents the most ambitious Standards project to date, thanks to the inclusion of postsecondary SPIs and scenarios and the incorporation of proficiency-oriented, as well as age-appropriate SPIs for each of the descriptors in the Five Cs. Table 5.1 shows the evolution of the four editions of ACTFL's Standards between 1996 and 2015 over the four editions:

RECEPTION OF THE STANDARDS BY K–12 LANGUAGE PROGRAMS

The positive impact of the Standards on K–12 language and culture instruction has been both well documented (Scott, 2009; Phillips & Terry, 1999) and attestable in diverse forms in the field, ranging from revised curricula and syllabi to new teaching and learning materials and textbooks (Blaz, 2002; Terry, 2009; Alemi & Mesbah, 2013). Most of the successes are laid out in *A decade of foreign language standards: Impact, influence, and future direction* (Phillips & Abbott, 2011), in which the substantial citation of the Standards in scholarly and professional literature is documented, including those in Russian. This report enumerates the impact of the Standards on educational institutions generally, especially in the creation and implementation of curricular frameworks and other models used in school districts and postsecondary language departments nationally. The report summarizes the Standards' influence on curricula, teaching materials, and the creation of assessment goals and instruments, and also provides several specific examples of "greatest successes in districts" (Phillips & Abbott, p. 8).

A number of scholars (Moore et al. 1998; Garza, 1999; Lange, 2003; Phillips, 2003) note particular success in applying the tenets of the Standards to existing or revised curricula in the area of integrating culture into the language classroom—both the established, overt manifestations of "Big C" culture (literature, art, history, etc.) and the ephemeral, local iterations of "small c" culture (popular culture, mores, current realia, etc.). Most of these studies praise the inclusion of "Culture" as one of the Five Cs goal areas and as a culture-specific standard under the "Connections" heading. Further, most also speak to the importance of integration of culture into the language curriculum in such a way that cultural information is conveyed *in* the target language. As Lange (1999) points out, one can make a case that culture study actually permeates the entire document: "With the new national standards for foreign language learning, there is excitement about new possibilities for the inclusion of culture in language learning. In fact, the new standards put culture at the core of foreign language learning as a major content" (p. 60).

Arens (2009) presents a compelling case for application of the Standards to "show how 'translinguistic and transcultural' language learning might be staged and practiced" (p. 179). She asserts that the Standards suggest a view of culture different from the conventional set of names, dates, places, and artifacts, offering instead the position that "culture may be profitably defined as a field of cultural practices, signifiers, and knowledge (with language in the narrower sense serving as only one set of elements in it) and that learning a culture means not only acquiring its knowledge base, but also the strategic competencies needed to function within it" (p. 160). This view, which understands culture as encompassing not only knowledge of cultural products and practices within a given environment but also the ability of the learner to operate comfortably within it, is a skill that some have called "cultural competence" (Kern, 2000; Swaffer & Ahrens, 2005; Kramsch & Nolden, 1994), complements the integrated view of culture expressed in the Standards. Thus, implementation of the culture-imbued Standards, whether in school or university programs, may be of significant benefit to educational programs in general, especially in developing the knowledge- and performance-based skills required of students who take a foreign language, skills that require learners to demonstrate both linguistic and cultural competence in world languages.

In spite of ACTFL's efforts to publicize the pedagogical benefits of incorporating the Standards into curricula and instruction, there were also reports of difficulties or even failures when it tried to implement the Standards in some language programs. For example, Allen (2002) surveyed teachers of commonly taught languages in three Midwestern states to determine their beliefs and familiarity with the Standards for Foreign Language Learning. The study indicates at least two significant disconnects between language instructors and acceptance of the Standards. First, many teachers still adhere to the "coverage model," which requires them to follow a single textbook as the sole source of input during language instruction. She contends:

> Standards-based instruction, however, is not tied to a textbook. Rather, teachers use a variety of sources (e.g., authentic materials, information from the Web, community resources, other academic content areas) from which students can obtain information. As students engage in tasks that allow them to use the language for real communication, they develop an understanding of the process by which target language speakers exchange, interpret, and present information. Their achievement is measured by authentic assessments that model real-world language use. (p. 524)

Second, the surveyed language teachers are "only somewhat familiar" with the Standards. Allen concludes that "there are important components in standards-based instruction that represent innovations with which teachers must be familiar if the standards are to achieve their potential impact" (p. 525).

In addition to some difficulties related to the reception of the Standards in schools, the framework itself faced questions concerning the relevance and acceptance of the Standards in postsecondary language programs since its first publication. The original 1996 document certainly had K–12 programs and teachers as its primary audience; after all, the individual standards and the SPIs described were addressed to specific grade levels and school-aged learners. Some ACTFL publications, commenting on the overt orientation of the Standards toward grades K–12, attempted to address the exclusion of postsecondary content in the document. Phillips, for example, states in an ACTFL-sponsored publication in 1999, "While the national *Standards* were developed under a federal program for K–12, all but two of the language-specific collaborating organizations have subsequently adopted them as guidelines for K–16" (p. 6). But she later concedes, "Dissemination efforts into college and university departments of languages and literatures must be increased so that the seamless curriculum called for in the *Standards* becomes a reality for learners" (p. 6). Still, as recently as 2011 Phillips and Abbott admit that "it is often believed that the *Standards* have had a greater impact on the K–12 level than on the postsecondary level" (p. 4). But they go on to present publication data from scholarly professional journals with a primarily university-level readership that reveal a significant number of references to the Standards in articles from these publications. Echoing Phillips (1999), they conclude that "this finding is encouraging and demonstrates that while the *Standards* project was funded as a K–12 initiative, it was adopted by professional organizations to reach into postsecondary" (p. 6). Such a conclusion supports the effort of the 2015 version of the Standards to address explicitly postsecondary programs and learners.

Following the 1999 expansion of the Standards to include language-specific guidelines, including for Russian and other less commonly taught languages, there was an expectation among language educators that, since several of these languages were taught primarily in postsecondary programs, the document would also include language and materials that were directed to young adult learners at the college or university level. However, the K–12 emphasis continued unchanged, even though many of their organizing principles were applicable for most learning environments and levels of instruction. In the introduction to the 2009 volume of the American Association of University Supervisors and Coordinators and Directors of Language Programs (AAUSC), *Principles and practices of the* Standards *in college foreign language education* Scott and colleagues describe the effect of the Standards on postsecondary education as "haphazard at best" due to both a lack of interlevel articulation of curricula, goals, and assessment, from K–12 programs and in colleges and universities, as well as failing to address the diversity in types of programs and institutions at the postsecondary level (pp. xiii–xiv). In the same volume, however, Terry (2009) offers a much more positive perspective on the impact of the Standards in postsecondary language programs: "Indeed, some colleges and universities have re-created their curricula using the national *Standards* as a framework, especially for lower-level courses. Goals and objectives for lower-level courses are based on the national *Standards*. New textbooks that are modeled on the *Standards* are being written and adopted. Assessment of learning is changing and is based on actual, realistic student performance and not simply on mastery of a given corpus of grammar" (p. 25).

In 1999 the Association of Departments of Foreign Languages (ADFL) published the results of a forum held on the Standards in the form of nine essays on a variety of topics related to foreign language programs at the postsecondary level. Brager and Rice (1999), for example, describe the Standards as "serving as the guiding principles and the innovators providing the leadership" for a "true and consistent Standards education" from K–12 through college (p. 70). Other essays note that although the Standards do not directly reference postsecondary language instruction, the research, practices, and principles that inform them have important implications for university curricula and instruction (Glisan, 1999; Long, 1999; Siskin, 1999).

This same ADFL volume contains one essay specifically related to the teaching of Russian at the university level. Diment (1999), while acknowledging that "there are plenty of excellent ideas, targets, and techniques in the *Standards*" (p. 73), only marginally engages with the Standards' actual content and principles of application to Russian. Instead, she focuses on the general state of foreign language education and her own approaches to teaching graduate students. She admits that such courses involve instruction "whose pedagogical purposes are very different from the ones discussed in the *Standards*" (p. 73). But after discussing the benefits of proficiency-based instruction, she admits that "the *Standards* materials are thoughtful, helpful, and often fun" (p. 73), although she expresses concern about the willingness and ability of individual programs to implement them successfully into curricula.

Perhaps Sharpley-Whiting (1999) best expressed the ADFL volume's position regarding postsecondary applications of the Standards in his discussion of the collaboration between K–12 teachers and faculty from postsecondary institutions as "an opportunity to improve and make invaluable foreign language education nationally and as an effective pedagogical mechanism for articulation between and within elementary, secondary, and postsecondary educational levels" (p. 85). However, Sharpley-Whiting's notion, that this collaborative opportunity between schools and universities would come to fruition with the inclusion of standards for postsecondary language and culture programs, was not realized until the 2015 iteration of the Standards. Indeed, the potential for interlevel articulation of language programs for grades K–12 to the postsecondary level, as well as for implementation of the Standards in redesigned curricula and syllabi in college courses, is greater than it has ever been in anticipation of the new postsecondary materials in the revised edition.

REACHING COLLEGES AND UNIVERSITIES: CHALLENGES AND SUCCESSES

As the Standards entered the 2010s, the extent of their reach was examined and assessed both by ACTFL and by individual language professionals. The Phillips and Abbott (2011) report on the impact of the Standards on the professional field of foreign language education and instruction outlines several areas already mentioned but further comments on the acceptance of the integrated nature of the Five Cs by the language teaching profession, noting that 40 states have either accepted fully or integrated partially the five goal areas into their own state language standards (p. 7).

The extent to which the Standards had not succeeded in reaching an audience among educators and administrators of college- and university-level language programs was well documented by James (1998) in an ACTFL white paper. In discussing the adoption of the Standards by university language departments, James cites Paul Sandrock, who at a conference of the Modern Language Association (MLA) stated, "The University curriculum has not changed" (p. 14), which suggests that the Standards had not yet influenced postsecondary programs. James then concludes: "The national *Standards* provide a vision of long coordinated sequences of language study, of interactive, interdisciplinary language programs, of programs to take heritage learners as well as learners of second languages to a high level of literacy. Such a vision, if realized, will finally raise foreign language teaching at the colleges to a genuine 'college-level'" (p. 14).

A decade later Terry (2009) is even more sanguine about the imperative for reform in the postsecondary language teaching arena and goes even further to emphasize the need to embrace the recommendations of the 2007 MLA Ad Hoc Committee report, "Foreign languages and higher education: New structures for a changed world." The MLA report recommends restructuring programs in higher education and creating majors that produce graduates with "deep translingual and transcultural competence" (p. 3). Terry concludes: "The *Standards* can give us a refreshing new perspective on foreign language study in the most inclusive sense of the discipline: language, literature, culture and the knowledge, skills, and abilities that come with such study" (p. 25). The fourth edition of the Standards picks up this thread in its statement on language learning in the United States: "The emphasis in the World-Readiness Standards on levels of performance rather than content specific to grade levels provides guidance to lead to a seamless continuity, student-centered articulation, and higher levels of performance for postsecondary learners" (p. 22). The authors conclude the section on program models with five general recommendations for faculty development of new postsecondary program models, including offering basic language instruction through affiliated centers; expanding traditional language and literature courses to include relevant area studies topics; offering bridge courses and content-based instruction in the language; and instituting dual degree programs that combine language study with another major to prepare students to work in a global economy. Such recommendations reinforce the revised 2015 Standards' connection to the 2007 MLA report on foreign languages (MLA Ad Hoc Committee on Foreign Languages).

Prior to the publication of the revised Russian Standards, Kagan and Dillon (2001) suggest that the interpersonal, interpretive, and presentational communicative modes or domains may be better suited to assessing heritage speakers of Russian than the ACTFL Proficiency Guidelines, and that these domains might better serve Russian language curricula overall (p. 510). As language programs nationally strive to address the needs of heritage speakers, whether of commonly taught languages like Spanish or less commonly taught ones like Russian and Arabic, guidance for curricula and assessment of learners is of particular importance to instructors and administrators alike (Kagan, 2010).

The 2015 edition of the Standards also recognizes the important and growing constituency of heritage students in K–16 US language programs. By providing characteristics of heritage students, from newly arrived immigrants to second- and third-generation functional bilinguals schooled in the United States, the authors contend: "Students with varying needs all require access to language instruction that will allow them to: (1) maintain existing strengths in the language, (2) develop strengths in areas in which the home background has not provided support, and (3) use the language for reading and writing to communicate interpersonally or for a variety of published pieces" (p. 24). Thus, the revised Standards further strive toward inclusivity and representation of diverse populations and languages. In that connection the language-specific Standards, including Russian, now represent an even greater resource for language instructors at all levels and address language learning for the wide variety of learners that populate our classes.

LANGUAGE-SPECIFIC STANDARDS FOR RUSSIAN

The American Council of Teachers of Russian (ACTR), which participated in the creation of the language-specific Standards in 1999, took the leading role in drafting and approving the latest iteration of the Standards for Russian. ACTR executive director Dan Davidson assembled the writing team for the 2015 revised Russian Standards. Jane Shuffelton (Brighton High School, Rochester, NY, retired) led the team, which included Peter Merrill (Whittle School and Studios, New York, NY), all members of the ACTR board of directors, and writers and contributors to the first version (1999) of the K–12 Russian Standards. In addition to the three-person writing team, a number of secondary and postsecondary instructors of Russian participated in the editing and revision of the Russian Standards (see Appendix). This expanded collective represented both the range of grade levels (K–16) as well as the varying types of public and private institutions that offer Russian language and culture courses nationally.

As writing began on the revised and updated set of standards for Russian, certain changes, such as replacing "student" with "learner," reflected the volume's commitment to inclusion of different types of learning environments and learners. The writing team also saw the need to alter the way that the SPIs were presented. The 1999 Standards had used grade-level designations (K, elementary, middle, high) to categorize age-appropriate descriptors and activities for learners. The addition of postsecondary-level materials to the Standards not only changed their breadth and reach in terms of age; it also expanded the cognitive, social, and experiential baseline for the tasks and materials recommended at the university level. A nineteen-year-old learner is, for example, emotionally and cognitively prepared to work with some materials, such as Internet social media sites or live-streaming news media, that might be inappropriate for a twelve-year-old learner. The team also acknowledged the need to consider the learner's ACTFL proficiency level (Novice, Intermediate, Advanced, Superior) for all grade levels. The resulting paradigm for describing models of activity for learners at any given stage could be viewed as a simple matrix (Figure 5.3).

Any learner, at any age and at any level of proficiency, can be "plotted" within this matrix in order to determine the kind of classroom activities or materials that may be most appropriate and of optimal utility. The writing team decided to organize materials for the Russian Standards not only by grade level but also by proficiency level for each of the Five Cs—an innovation incorporated throughout the revised Standards volume for all language-specific materials.

The Russian writing team's decision to include ACTFL proficiency levels as one of the organizing principles of the Russian Standards added substantial clarity and utility to the Five Cs and SPIs by specifying for the instructor how certain types of exercises or materials might benefit different learners even in the same class. Given

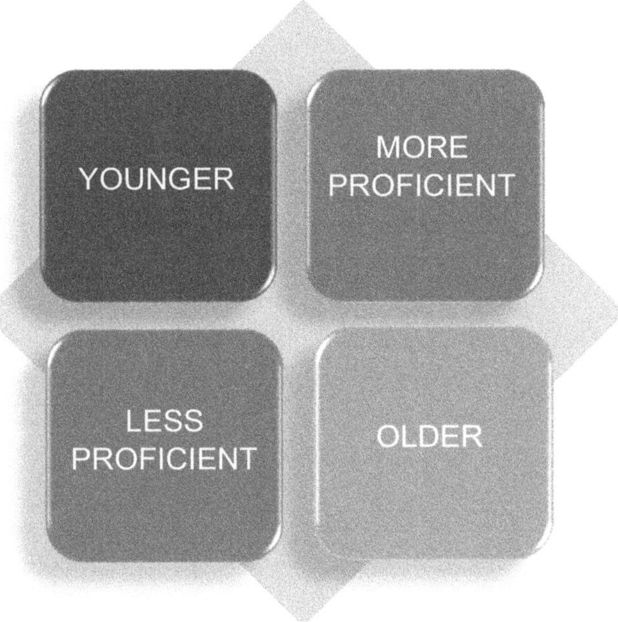

FIGURE 5.3. Matrix of Level of Instruction and Proficiency Level

that an instructor is more likely than not to have students at different proficiency levels in the same class (whether at the K–12 or postsecondary level), the identification of SPIs at different proficiency levels will help instructors attend to more students and provide more effective Standards-based instruction. Using proficiency designations the new SPIs can, for example, provide suggestions for using the same video clip or text in a given class for students who are at various levels of proficiency. By changing the specific task attached to the text, teachers can provide level-appropriate instruction and feedback for the range of students in their classes. This consideration is especially relevant when heritage learners comprise part of a given class, as their proficiency levels may have little or no correlation with their age or years of exposure to the language.

Beyond changing the organization of the Russian Standards, the writing team also undertook a systematic revision of the existing K–12 materials to reflect the changes in the delivery of instruction and in learners' interests since the publication of the original Standards in 1996. Among the most visible differences in classroom practices in the 2000s is the integration and use of technology, especially the Internet, in the delivery, practice, and assessment of language and culture materials. By the end of the 1990s educators were well aware of the potential for using Internet resources for integrating the Standards into language instruction. Gonglewski (2008) concludes that the Internet is an excellent medium for language learning, one that provides access to authentic and diverse materials that can contribute significantly to cross-cultural awareness (p. 360). Similarly, learner use of personal technology (notebooks, handheld devices, laptops, etc.), web-based instruction, and social media—especially among postsecondary students—has increased exponentially in the past decade. The authors, therefore, respond to the imperative to incorporate activities and SPIs that address the use of technology and social media, by both instructors and learners, in the teaching and learning of Russian.

To this end, the new SPIs now feature the use of technology-based communication such as e-mail, Skype, blog sites, and chat rooms. They also include familiar social media such as Facebook, Twitter, Instagram, Snapchat, and Livejournal, as well as their Russian counterparts, Одноклассники [Classmates], Вконтакте [InTouch], Чик-чирик [Tweet tweet], and Живой журнал [Live journal], in order to bring the realities of the contemporary learner's daily life to the language classroom and to the kinds of activities associated with language learning. The writing team also hopes that by using new media to incorporate alternative forms of communication into the Standards, more instructors might be positively inclined to introduce them into their own syllabi and curricula.

The addition of these crucial postsecondary materials into the latest iteration of the Standards will undoubtedly increase their appeal and demonstrate more concretely their applicability to curricula and learning environments at the college and university level.

BRINGING THE STANDARDS TO K–12 TEACHERS OF RUSSIAN

As discussed earlier, acceptance of the original Standards across K–12 schools nationally was not immediate, due in part to unfamiliarity with the content of the Standards and in part to lack of information on how best to incorporate and implement them into language and culture instruction. Since in many cases such incorporation would necessarily involve substantial revision and reworking of existing course curricula and syllabi, many instructors were daunted by the scope of the task facing them. This situation was further exacerbated by the disconnect between school-level language programs and university-level teacher education programs. Early in the discussion about the incorporation of the Standards into national language programs, Glisan (1996) commented extensively on how to reform the professional development of pre- and in-service teachers, and especially on the participation of university-level education departments and teacher preparation programs in bringing the Standards into the nation's classrooms. She cites in particular the lack of collaboration between universities and school districts as an impediment to implementing reform in teacher education necessary for successfully integrating the Standards.

One of the most effective avenues for the dissemination of the Standards to language teachers nationally, especially to languages designated as "critical" by the National Security Language Initiative—Arabic, Chinese, Dari, Hindi, Persian, Portuguese, Russian, Swahili, Turkish, and Urdu—has been the STARTALK program. In 2006 Pres. George W. Bush created the National Security Language Program

(NSLP) to improve the skills of students of languages of "critical national need," particularly in regard to security and commerce. The STARTALK program began as part of the NSLP's original charge for K–16 students and teachers. Administered by the National Security Education Program (NSEP), STARTALK's mission is "to increase the number of U.S. citizens learning, speaking, and teaching critical need foreign languages" (NFLC, 2015).

STARTALK offers a variety of programs nationally each summer for students and teachers of critical languages to be exposed to best practices in language teaching. Over the past decade a number of STARTALK programs have focused on the professional development of teachers of Russian, including recently at Columbia University, Holmes Middle School, Concordia Language Villages, Glastonbury High School, Middlebury College, University of Iowa, and Northern Virginia Community College. These programs include the Standards as part of their instructional curricula in order to inform and prepare teachers of Russian to implement Standards-based instruction at their own institutions. Teachers of Russian have benefited from STARTALK by gaining a better understanding of the content and application of the Standards in their classes. They are instructed in the systematic integration of the Five Cs and the Russian-specific Standards. Russian students have also benefited from STARTALK because it provides instruction in the language and culture using Standards-inspired curricula and materials.

THE REVISED RUSSIAN STANDARDS

In addition to the reorganized and updated descriptors under each of the Five Cs for Russian, the 2015 Russian Standards feature completely new LS, replacing the original scenarios written for the 1999 edition, for all proficiency levels, Novice to Superior, and for all levels of Russian instruction K–16. Learning scenarios have been an integral part of the published Standards since the 1999 edition by providing proficiency level- and age-appropriate models for instruction during a single class session (e.g., a daily lesson, a single topic, etc.) or may be spread across a unit of instruction (e.g., six weeks, one semester, a summer session, etc.). Typically an LS describes a multistage project or topic worked on by learners over a period of time. Instructors can choose to implement all or part of a given scenario to fit the particular learning environment and the time and frequency of instruction allocated in each program. Figure 5.4 is an example of a learning scenario for Grade 7 from the 2006 edition of the Russian-specific Standards:

In the 2015 Russian Standards the scenarios are grouped by proficiency level, then divided into grade level to indicate age-appropriate tasks, as follows:

Novice Level

"The Russian Firebird"	Grades K–6
"Urban and Rural"	Grades K–6
"Counting in Our School"	Grades 6–8

"I Am a Walrus"	Grades 6–8
"The Russian Family, the Family in Russia"	Grades 7–8
Intermediate Level	
"New York or Moscow"	Grades 9–12
"Peer Teaching Russian Fairy Tales"	Grades 10–12
"An American Intern in Russia"	Grades 13–16
"Comparing Teenagers"	Pre-College and Heritage Learners
Advanced Level	
"My Perestroika"	Grade 12
"Investigative Analysis"	Grades 13–16
"Reading Akhmatova"	Grades 13–16
Superior Level	
"Vladimir Vysotsky in 1979"	Grades 13–16

The topical breadth of these samples is exceeded only by the diversity of classroom activities that is described within them. As in earlier editions, the new Russian LSs indicate the specific standards that are reflected in each activity for each level. Now they also demonstrate the appropriateness of the scenario for the indicated ACTFL proficiency level.

Among the many constituent parts of the language-specific Standards in the 2015 edition, the SPIs have undergone the most significant change in relation to Russian

TARGETED STANDARDS

1.1 Interpersonal Communication
1.2 Interpretive Communication
1.3 Presentational Communication
2.2 Products of Culture
4.2 Cultural Comparisons
5.1 School and Community

SKITS

In the Tenafly, NJ, school system, the Tenafly Middle School and High School Russian classes, levels 1-5, organize a Russian evening for the Russian students and their parents. The event consists of catered Russian food and entertainment by the students themselves.

As part of this, the 7th grade first-year Russian class worked on and performed a Russian skit based on the story "The Turnip." A teacher from Russia, who was working at the Tenafly Middle School at that time, adapted the story into a play. Each student was assigned a role with lines to learn. In class, both the classroom teacher and the teacher from Russia rehearsed with the students, helping them to understand the story and memorize their parts.

As Russian evening approached, the skit was staged and costumes and props were added. On the night of Russian evening, before performing the skit, one of the students gave a brief description of the story in English to help the parents who did not understand Russian. Afterwards, the class discussed their performance and other ideas that could be added in the future.

FIGURE 5.4. Learning Scenario for Grade 7 from Russian-Specific Standards (2006)

language education. The authors of the Russian Standards paid particular attention to ensuring the relevance of the SPIs to teachers and learners of Russian in contemporary learning environments. Thus, age- and level-appropriate references to personal technology, such as laptops, smartphones, and other handheld mobile devices, are incorporated in many of the new SPIs used in all three modalities: Interpersonal, Interpretive, and Presentational. In addition, innovations were made in the use of social media, such as Facebook, Twitter, Instagram, and Snapchat, and for popular modes for electronic communication, such as e-mail, blogs, chat rooms, instant messaging, FaceTime, and Skype; all were added to the teaching and learning repertoire for in-class and extracurricular activities with Russians, in Russian, and in the greater Russian-speaking world. Use of most of these technologies is appropriate primarily at the high school and postsecondary levels, so they are most evident in those SPIs. Note, for example, the limited use of media other than print in the 2006 version of the Russian Standards, as shown in one of the SPIs provided for the first Communication standard:

Sample Performance Indicators: Grade 12

- Students discuss, orally or in writing, their reactions to material they have read on Russian culture, history, or significant events (e.g., the October Revolution, Stalinism, holidays, the life and poetry of Akhmatova).
- Students exchange commentary on issues that are of concern to them and to Russians (e.g., future plans, economy, violence, roles of women and men).
- Students share their reactions with classmates, with heritage learners in the Russian program, with pen pals or electronic pen pals in Russia. They compare reactions to films such as *Kolya,* current popular music, painters of the Russian avant-garde.

Source: National Standards in Foreign Language Education Project (2006, p. 443).

In contrast, the revised Russian SPIs for the same standard, modified to reflect proficiency level and to include postsecondary learners and updated to include current technology in contemporary communication, now read:

Sample Performance Indicators: Intermediate

High School and Postsecondary

- Learners discuss, orally or in writing, their reactions to material they have gathered from print or online sources on Russian history, culture, or significant events (e.g., the October Revolution, Glasnost, Russian holidays, the life and works of Akhmatova, Putin's 2012 reelection).
- Learners exchange commentary on issues and problems that are of concern to them and to their Russian peers (future plans, the economy, roles of men and women, etc.) in class and/or via e-mail.

Source: National Standards Collaborative Board (2015a).

Some new SPIs, due to the increased cognitive abilities of older learners as well as to the subject matter covered, are designated entirely as postsecondary:

Sample Performance Indicators: Intermediate

Postsecondary

- Learners request and exchange biographical and educational information via e-mail or social networking site with Russian learners enrolled at a peer institution in Russia.
- Learners work in groups to discuss and write a short review of a recent Russian film or television show about the lives of university-aged peer group (e.g., «Питер FM,» «Студенты»), expressing what they liked and did not like in the program.
- Learners use one of the Russian social media sites, such as Одноклассники or Вконтакте, to view basic profiles of some of its members. Using the information on the site, they report back to the class, providing a description of one of the profiles, including physical description from the cover photo, interests, and short biography.

Source: National Standards Collaborative Board (2015a).

The revised Russian Standards reflect not only the changes that have occurred in Russian culture and civilization—which are themselves substantial—but also the simultaneous startling technology-led transformation of human interaction and communication. The new Russian SPIs align with 21st-century capabilities to enhance exposure to and interaction with the cultural products and practices of people living in the Russian Federation. The revised Russian Standards also address the capacity for heritage learners to acquire native competence in their language and culture.

In all, the new SPIs now address the notion of the learner as *global citizen* that permeates the entire Standards document; the Russophone world is now much more easily accessed by many learners in a wide variety of learning environments. The 2015 Russian Standards are designed to "act as that beacon" to help make our K–16 programs better prepared to bring our students to full functional proficiency, cultural literacy—and beyond.

NEXT STEPS FOR THE STANDARDS

The last decade has seen the impact that instructional innovations, such as the expansion of the Standards and the establishment of the federally funded national Language Flagship programs, have had on foreign language education in US universities. Prior to the Flagship programs few teachers of Russian or other less-commonly taught languages (LCTLs) would have considered the feasibility of our students attaining Advanced- or even Superior-level proficiency during a typical undergraduate college experience. The 2015 Standards, like the ACTFL Proficiency Guidelines, can be a powerful source for language program developers trying to create Flagship-like programs at their institutions by providing language-specific recommendations for informing curricula, materials development, and classroom methods with the intent of increasing learners' proficiency. Activities suggested by the goals provided in the

SPIs and lesson plans informed by the learning scenarios can be incorporated into intensive learning environments of the Flagship-inspired classroom.

At the University of Texas at Austin, for example, the Arabic Flagship Program incorporates the Arabic Standards into both its curricula and its daily classroom practices. As learners gain proficiency and facility with the language and culture, they are exposed to increasingly complex and challenging tasks and activities aimed, like the SPIs, at focusing on what they can do in the language. In a similar fashion, several other language programs that do not have Flagship support—including Russian—use the Standards to inform the creation of online activities and out-of-class tasks that can be required in learners' portfolios. Such materials provide the kinds of meaningful practices and creative tasks that supplement traditional textbook instruction and produce a more engaging, instructional curriculum. The Russian Standards are at the heart of a modular "activity bank" housed on the university's Canvas classroom management system. Activities that require learners to interact with authentic content on various Russian-language websites and other resources are based heavily on the SPIs from the Russian Standards. Each activity or task is geared toward a particular proficiency level, which allows students who are in the same class but at various levels to find appropriate tasks to complete. As more instructors become familiar with the Standards and their applicability and utility in creating innovative and productive materials and courses, there will follow more programs for learners wanting to attain Advanced or higher proficiency.

What might be the future of the Russian Standards in the next decade? As learner expectations for higher levels of functional proficiency in Russian increase, the Standards must rise to meet this need. The next iteration of the Russian Standards for the coming decade will have to increase substantially the attention paid to Advanced-level proficiency and higher to address the needs of a market demanding global professionals capable of doing their jobs effectively and efficiently. Authors of these future Standards will want to pay particular attention to developing SPIs and LSs that will require learners to attain and maintain high levels of functional proficiency. These materials will necessarily need to provide not a single activity or a model project but rather a sequence of articulated tasks and situations that will permit the learner to be engaged in language use for an extended period of time and in several modalities (e.g., reading a report, writing a summary of it, then reporting the synopsis orally over the phone).

Finally, in most cases educating global professionals requires multiple years of training in the target language. Articulation of secondary school language courses with postsecondary programs can be greatly facilitated by the language-specific standards. Such articulation better serves both the programs and the learners, providing a seamless continuation of curricula with much better established expectations of learner outcomes and assessment at each level of instruction. Future Standards should certainly continue to provide language-specific materials for any world languages taught in secondary and postsecondary programs. As the need grows for programs that are designed and equipped to train future proficient professionals to match the increasing global demand for such specialists in the private and public realms, the role of the language-specific Standards—like Russian—will also increase. The onus is now on us as a profession to embrace the potential of the Russian Standards in all K–16 programs and to strive to incorporate them into our curricula. Thinking of the current World-Readiness Standards as "beacons" for language program planning, the time is right to allow these beacons to lead us to improved instruction, performance, and assessment in Russian language and culture programs across the nation.

APPENDIX: AMERICAN COUNCIL OF TEACHERS OF RUSSIAN, 2016 RUSSIAN STANDARDS TEAM

Task Force

Jane W. Shuffelton, Chair
Brighton High School (Ret.)
Rochester, New York

Thomas J. Garza
University of Texas
Austin, Texas

Peter T. Merrill
Whittle School and Studios
New York, New York

Learning Scenario Contributors

Mary Bordes
World Languages Magnet School
Brackenridge High School
San Antonio, Texas

Bonny Einstein
North Colonie Central Schools
Latham, New York

Thomas J. Garza
University of Texas at Austin
Austin, Texas

Paavo Husen
Illinois Mathematics and Science Academy
Aurora, Illinois

Shannon Johnson
Friends School of Maryland, Middle School
Baltimore, Maryland

Cynthia Martin
University of Maryland
College Park, Maryland

Benjamin Rifkin
Hofstra University (Scenario based on UW–Madison class)
Hempstead, NY

Richard Robin
George Washington University
Washington, DC

Elizabeth Lee Roby
Friends School of Maryland, Upper School
Baltimore, Maryland

John Rook
Glastonbury Public Schools
Glastonbury, Connecticut

Antonina Sergieff
University of California, Los Angeles
Los Angeles, California

Nataliya Ushakova
Staten Island Technical High School
Staten Island, New York

Anna Walker
Turnagain Elementary School
Anchorage, Alaska

Learning Scenario Reviewers

Ruth P. Edelman
Tenafly High School
Tenafly, New Jersey

Karen Evans-Romaine
University of Wisconsin
Madison, Wisconsin

Jonathan Z. Ludwig
Oklahoma State University
Stillwater, Oklahoma

Diane Nemec Ignashev
Carleton College
Northfield, Minnesota

REFERENCES

Alemi, M., & Mesbah, Z. (2013). Textbook evaluation based on the ACTFL standards: The case of the *Top Notch* Series. *Iranian EFL Journal*, *9*(1), 162–71.

Allen, L. Q. (2002). Teachers' pedagogical beliefs and the standards for foreign language learning. *Foreign Language Annals*, *35*(5), 518–29.

American Council on the Teaching of Foreign Languages (ACTFL). (n.d.). National Standards in Foreign Language Education. Retrieved from http://www.actfl.org/sites/default/files/pdfs/public/StandardsforFLLexecsumm_rev.pdf

American Council on the Teaching of Foreign Languages (ACTFL). (1986). *ACTFL Proficiency Guidelines*. Yonkers, NY: American Council on the Teaching of Foreign Languages.

American Council on the Teaching of Foreign Languages (ACTFL). (2013). Can-Do Statements: Performance indicators for language learners. Yonkers, NY. Retrieved from http://www.actfl.org/sites/default/files/pdfs/Can-Do_Statements_2015.pdf

Arens, K. (2009). Teaching culture: The standards as an optic on curriculum development. In V. M. Scott (Ed.), *Principles and practices of the Standards in college foreign language education* (pp. 160–80). American Association of University Supervisors, Coordinators, and Directors of Foreign Language Programs. Boston: Heinle Cengage Learning.

Association of Departments of Foreign Languages (ADFL). (1999). Forum on the Standards for foreign language learning: Preparing for the twenty-first century. *ADFL Bulletin*, *31*(1), 70–87.

Blaz, D. (2002). *Bringing the Standards for foreign language learning to life*. Poughkeepsie, NY: Eye on Education.

Brager, J. D., & Rice, D. B. (1999). Implications for the Standards for higher education: Forum on the Standards for foreign language learning. *ADFL Bulletin*, *31*(1), 70–72.

Byrnes, H. (2012). Of frameworks and the goals of collegiate foreign language education: Critical reflections. *Applied Linguistics Review*, *3*(1), 1–24.

Byrnes, K. (Ed.). (2005). Perspectives: National language educational policy. *Modern Language Journal*, *91*(3), 247–83.

Diment, G. (1999). From the perspective of Russian. In Forum on the Standards for foreign language learning: Preparing for the twenty-first century. *ADFL Bulletin*, *31*(1), 73.

Garza, T. J. (1999). The standards and the state of teaching Russian culture. *ACTR Letter*, *25*(3), 6–7.

Glisan, E. W. (1996). A collaborative approach to professional development. In R. C. Lafayette (Ed.), *National Standards: A catalyst for reform* (pp. 57–95). Lincolnwood, IL: National Textbook.

Glisan, E. W. (1999). The impact of standards on higher education: For more than just the sake of "continuity." In "Forum on the Standards for foreign language learning: Preparing for the twenty-first century." *ADFL Bulletin*, *31*(1), 75–78.

Gonglewski, M. R. (2008). Linking the Internet to the national Standards for foreign language learning. *Foreign Language Annals*, *32*(3), 348–62.

Interagency Language Roundtable (ILR). (2016). ILR speaking skill scale. Retrieved from http://www.govtilr.org/Skills/ILRscale2.htm

James, D. (1998). The impact on higher education of Standards for foreign language learning: Preparing for the twenty-first century. *ACTFL Newsletter* (Fall), 11–14.

Kagan, O. (2010). Russian heritage speakers in the U.S.: A profile. *Russian Language Journal, 60*, 215–30.

Kagan, O., & Dillon, K. (2001). A new perspective on teaching Russian: Focus on the heritage learner. *Slavic and East European Journal, 45*(3), 507–18.

Kern, R. (2000). *Literacy and language teaching.* Oxford Applied Linguistics series. New York: Oxford UP.

Kramsch, C., & Nolden, T. (1994). Redefining literacy in a foreign language. *Der Unterrichtspraxis, 27*(1), 28–35.

Lafayette, R. C. (Ed.). (1996). *National Standards: A catalyst for reform.* Lincolnwood, IL: National Textbook.

Lange, D. L. (1999). Planning for and using the new national culture standards. In J. K. Phillips & R. M. Terry (Eds.), *Foreign language standards: Linking research, theories, and practice* (pp. 57–135). Lincolnwood: National Textbook.

Lange, D. L. (2003). Future directions for culture teaching and learning: Implications of the new culture standards and theoretical frameworks for curriculum, assessment, instruction, and research. In D. L. Lange & R. M. Paige (Eds.), *Culture as the core: Perspectives on culture in second language education* (pp. 337–54). Greenwich, CT: Information Age.

Long, D. R. (1999). Breaking down the barriers: Implications of standards for foreign language learning for United States universities. "Forum on the Standards for foreign language learning: Preparing for the twenty-first century." *ADFL Bulletin, 31*(1), 78–79.

Modern Language Association Ad Hoc Committee on Foreign Languages. (2007). Foreign languages and higher education: New structures for a changed world. Retrieved from https://www.mla.org/Resources/Research/Surveys-Reports-and-Other-Documents/Teaching-Enrollments-and-Programs/Foreign-Languages-and-Higher-Education-New-Structures-for-a-Changed-World

Moore, Z., Morales, B., & Carel, S. (1998). Technology and teaching culture: Results of a state survey of foreign language teachers. *CALICO Journal, 15*(3), 109–28.

National Foreign Language Center (NFLC). (2015). STARTALK Conference, University of Maryland, College Park, MD. Retrieved from: https://STARTALK.umd.edu/public/about

National Standards Collaborative Board (NSCB). (2015a). *World-readiness standards for learning languages* (4th ed.). Alexandria, VA: Author.

National Standards Collaborative Board (NSCB). (2015b). Two-page summary of ACTFL'S World-readiness standards for learning languages. Retrieved from http://www.actfl.org/sites/default/files/pdfs/World-ReadinessStandardsforLearningLanguages.pdf

National Standards in Foreign Language Education Project (NSFLEP). (1996). *Standards for foreign language learning: Preparing for the twenty-first century.* Lawrence, KS: Allen.

National Standards in Foreign Language Education Project (NSFLEP). (1999, 2006). *Standards for foreign language learning in the twenty-first century* (2nd ed. & 3rd ed.). Lawrence, KS: Allen.

Phillips, J. K. (1999). Standards for world languages: On a firm foundation. In J. K. Phillips (Ed.), *Foreign language standards: Linking research, theories, and practices* (pp. 1–14). Lincolnwood, IL: National Textbook.

Phillips, J. K. (2003). National Standards for foreign language learning: Culture, the driving force. In D. L. Lange & R. M. Paige (Eds.), *Culture as the core: Perspective on culture in second language education* (pp. 167–72). Greenwich, CT: Information Age.

Phillips, J. K., & Abbott, M. (Eds.). (2011). A decade of foreign language standards: Impact, influence, and future directions. Report of Title VII Grant Project #P017A080037, US Department of Education.

Phillips, J. K., & Lafayette, R. C. (1996). Reactions to the catalyst: Implications for our new professional structure. In R. C. Lafayette (Ed.), *National standards: A catalyst for reform* (pp. 197–210). Lincolnwood, IL: National Textbook.

Phillips, J. K., & Terry, R. M. (Eds.). (1999). *Foreign language standards: Linking research, theories, and practices.* Lincolnwood, IL: National Textbook.

Scott, V. M. (Ed.). (2009). *Principles and practices of the standards in college foreign language education.* Boston: Heinle Cengage Learning.

Sharpley-Whiting, T. D. (1999). Postsecondary education and implications and uses of standards for foreign language education. In "Forum on the Standards for foreign language learning: Preparing for the twenty-first century." *ADFL Bulletin*, *31*(1), 84–85.

Siskin, H. J. (1999). The national standards and the discourse of innovation. In "Forum on the Standards for foreign language learning: Preparing for the twenty-first century." *ADFL Bulletin*, *31*(1), 85–87.

Swaffar, J. (1998). Major changes: The standards project and the new foreign language curriculum. *ADFL Bulletin*, *30*(1), 34–37.

Swaffar, J., & Ahrens, K. (2006). *Remapping the foreign language curriculum: An approach through multiple literacies.* New York: Modern Language Association.

Terry, R. M. (2009). The National Standards at the postsecondary level: A blueprint and framework for change. In V. M. Scott (Ed.), *Principles and practices of the standards in college foreign language education* (pp. 17–28). Boston: Heinle.

6

THE GOALS OF COLLEGIATE LEARNERS OF RUSSIAN AND THE US STANDARDS FOR LEARNING LANGUAGES

Dianna Murphy, Narek Sahakyan, and Sally Sieloff Magnan

According to their authors, the World-Readiness Standards for Learning Languages (NSFLEP, 1996, 1999, 2006; NSCB, 2015) have "galvanized the field of language education" and represent an "unprecedented degree of involvement, and of consensus, among educators at all levels" (NSCB, 2015, p. 15). The impact of the Standards to date has, however, been far greater at the K–12 levels than in postsecondary education, where Russian is most commonly taught. With the revision of the Russian-specific version of the Standards in *Standards for Russian Language Learning* (Garza et al., 2015), which includes sample learning scenarios for postsecondary students, the profession has a new opportunity to consider the fit of the Standards with the goals of postsecondary Russian programs. This chapter discusses the relevance of the Standards for the teaching and learning of Russian at the postsecondary level in the United States by presenting findings from a study that explored the alignment of the goals of the national Standards with the goals of students enrolled in first- and second-year Russian courses at US universities.

The research presented here draws on data from a large-scale, mixed-methods study conducted by the authors, who surveyed over 16,000 students enrolled in first- and second-year courses in 31 languages at 11 universities and interviewed 200 students at two universities to explore the fit between the goals of those students and the goals of the Standards (Magnan et al., 2014; Magnan et al., 2012).[1] The findings presented are based on an analysis of the responses of students of Russian in that sample ($n = 706$) and a comparison of those responses to the responses of students of the 30 other languages.

We begin with a brief discussion of the Standards and their reception to date at the postsecondary level in the United States, followed by a summary of select findings from Magnan et al. (2014) that reveal that the Standards do seem to align well with the goals of US language students, at least during the first two years of instruction at the postsecondary level. The remainder of the chapter presents the other elements of the study and explores whether the findings that were obtained by Magnan et al., based on the survey of students of 31 languages, also pertain to students of Russian, a small subset of the larger sample.[2] The study addresses two sets of research questions: (1) Do the goals of collegiate students of Russian at the first- and second-year levels of instruction correspond to the goals of the Standards? and (2) Is there a difference between students of Russian and students of other languages in their goals, in terms of the Standards?

THE NATIONAL STANDARDS

The Standards, first published over 20 years ago, attempt to describe "a vision of what learners should know and be able to do in another language" (NSCB, 2015, p. 11) for languages other than English taught in the United States, at all levels of instruction, kindergarten through college (K–16). This vision is articulated through 11 content standards that are grouped into five goal areas (the "Five Cs"): Communication, Cultures, Connections, Comparisons, and Communities (see Appendix A). The framework of the Standards was intended to represent an "expanded view of language learning" (NSCB, 2015, p. 27) that would encompass and address the many reasons that US students state for learning languages other than English, including, but not limited to, communication. In the words of the chair of the Standards task force, the aim of the Standards was to "expand the definition of foreign language education from one that addressed only communication to one that embraced other areas of the humanities, in other words, culture, literatures, [and] cross-disciplinary studies" (Phillips, 2007, p. 268).

The Five Cs goal areas and the 11 content standards (1996, 1999, 2006) are:

- *Communication:* Students communicate in languages other than English via the interpersonal (Standard 1.1), interpretive (Standard 1.2), and presentational (Standard 1.3) modes of communication.[3]
- *Cultures:* Students gain knowledge and understanding of another culture by demonstrating an understanding of the relationship between the culture's perspectives and practices (Standard 2.1) and between its perspectives and products (Standard 2.2).
- *Connections:* Students connect with and further their knowledge of other disciplines through the language of study (Standard 3.1) and by acquiring information and recognizing the distinctive viewpoints available through the language of study and its cultures (Standard 3.2).
- *Comparisons:* Students develop insights into the nature of language and culture by comparing the language of study to their own language(s) (Standard 4.1) and by comparing the cultures studied to their own (Standard 4.2).
- *Communities:* Students participate in multilingual communities at home and around the world by using the language of study both within and beyond the

> school setting (Standard 5.1) and they become lifelong learners by using the language for personal enjoyment and enrichment (Standard 5.2).[4]

This broad framework of five goal areas and 11 content standards, sometimes referred to as the "generic" Standards (NSCB, 2015, p. 14), which are applicable to any language, was supplemented by "language-specific" standards that were based on the general framework and developed for individual languages, including Russian. The Standards for Russian Language Learning, published with the 1999 and subsequent editions of the Standards, include sample progress indicators for K–12 students of Russian in grades 4, 8, and 12 as well as sample learning scenarios (examples of learning activities for students of Russian that target different content standards) from K–12 Russian programs. Both the generic and the language-specific standards are intentionally broad; they do not describe a specific curriculum. Instead, they intend to "set the broadest parameters, here called goals and standards, within which curriculum development can proceed" (Garza et al., 2015, p. 13).

Especially in the first edition (published in 1996), but also in the Russian-specific standards in the two subsequent editions (published in 1999 and 2006), the primary focus of the Standards was on K–12 education. This K–12 focus is natural, given the genesis of the initiative: the Standards were initially drafted and disseminated with federal funding that supported the development of national K–12 standards in several subject areas. The language Standards were developed by a group of national professional organizations: initially those were the American Council on the Teaching of Foreign Languages (ACTFL) and three professional organizations representing French, German, and Spanish, the languages most commonly taught at the K–12 level in the United States. After publication of the first edition of the Standards, the collaboration expanded to formally include professional organizations representing other languages (NSCB, 2015), including the American Council of Teachers of Russian (ACTR).

Despite the initial focus on K–12, advocates of the Standards have attempted from the beginning to make the case that the framework can apply to all instructional levels, including postsecondary. The most recent edition of the Standards (2015) makes the strongest case to date for the applicability of the Standards to postsecondary L2 education by offering explicit statements to that effect (NSCB, 2015); sample performance indicators for learners from the ACTFL Novice to Superior levels of proficiency, regardless of level of instruction; language-specific standards in languages that are taught almost exclusively at the postsecondary level in the United States; and example learning scenarios for postsecondary instruction. In addition, a Standards task force for Russian has revised the Standards for Russian Language Learning to include examples of learning scenarios from postsecondary instruction. Those revisions are currently pending approval by the National Standards Collaborative Board.

THE NATIONAL STANDARDS AT THE POSTSECONDARY LEVEL

The professional literature is mixed on the potential applicability of the Standards to postsecondary contexts. On the one hand, an extensive review of the professional literature from 1998 to 2009, conducted by an ACTFL (2011) task force, revealed 27 references to the Standards in the *ADFL Bulletin* and 60 references in the *Modern Language Journal*, both publications with a postsecondary audience, which suggests "considerable impact, or at least interest in the Standards, from postsecondary colleagues" (p. 4). Further interest in the Standards at the postsecondary level can be seen, for example, in the publication of the American Association of University Supervisors, Coordinators, and Directors of Language Programs (AAUSC) volume devoted solely to the topic, *Principles and Practices of the Standards in College Foreign Language Education* (Scott, 2009). On the other hand, as described by one contributor to that volume, the Standards continue to "search for relevance" (Allen, 2009) in the college-level curriculum (also see Dhonau & McAlpine, 2011), a view echoed by Byrnes (2012), who stated that the "spill-over effect" (p. 13) of the Standards from K–12 to postsecondary L2 education has been limited. Swaffar (2014) characterizes this limited impact of the Standards in higher education as resistance to a framework that would challenge long-standing divisions in curricular structures characterized by the "wide gap . . . between teaching language acquisition at elementary and intermediate levels and . . . the literacies that characterize upper division work" (p. 41) and would require a change in current practices in which "the material takes the center stage, not the learners" (p. 42).

Magnan et al. (2014), discussing the history of the reception of the Standards, suggest several reasons for their lukewarm reception in postsecondary L2 education, including suspicion that the Standards might apply pressure to standardize practices or curricula; the belief that models for learning originating at K–12 levels may not be appropriate for college-level learners; possible negative associations of the Standards with communicative language teaching and the proficiency movement; wariness on the part of college faculty of what might be perceived as another "bandwagon movement" (p. 16); concern about the lack of an empirical basis for the Standards;[5] and a general resistance to change. Additional critiques of the Standards from postsecondary perspectives cited by Magnan et al. include concerns that literary studies are not adequately addressed and that the representations of culture and culture learning are not sufficiently developed.

This general ambivalence about the applicability of the Standards to postsecondary foreign language education seems to characterize the reception of the Standards in Russian as well. Beyer (2000), for example, acknowledges that "the national consensus on standards at the K–12 level still needs to be embraced by our colleagues in higher education" and questions whether future editions of the Standards will address the "advanced goals" of collegiate students of Russian (p. 293).[6] Likewise, Diment (1999) voices skepticism about the benefits of the framework and her concerns about dogmatism and attempts to standardize teaching practices.

In contrast to these skeptical views, Rifkin (2006) argues that the Standards, along with the ACTFL Proficiency Guidelines, should be used to inform the design of postsecondary curricula in Slavic languages, seeing a close alignment of the Standards with the Essential Learning Outcomes of the Liberal Education and America's Promise (LEAP) initiative of the Association of American Colleges and Universities (Rifkin, 2012). Valdés (2000) sees promise for the Standards in higher education, particularly in describing the goals and needs of heritage language learners, including those in Slavic languages.

Perhaps not surprisingly, given that the Standards were initially developed through national professional associations, some language associations have remained an important venue for the Standards' dissemination. Davidson et al. (2006), for example, state that "the 'standards movement' has had significant impact on the teaching of foreign languages in the United States for those practitioners connected to professional organizations in which it has been discussed (especially, in the Russian context, ACTR and ACTFL)" (p. 680). In the literature on the teaching of Russian at the postsecondary level in the United States, this impact is seen primarily in providing a framework to describe curricular innovation: examples include Garn (2012), who references the Five Cs of the Standards to describe the development of new courses on Russian cinema, and Gettys (2003), who finds validation in the Standards for learning tasks that require students to make first- and second-language comparisons.[7]

POSTSECONDARY STUDENT GOALS AND THE STANDARDS

Unlike the Common European Framework of Reference for Languages (CEFR), which has put forward "can-do" statements and other tools that are intended to help language learners reflect upon, better understand, and document their developing abilities in an L2, the Standards were written by educators, for educators. Although some scholars may believe that "a standards-based curriculum is guided by students' needs and interests" (Allen, 2002, p. 37), educators should question this assumption. What is the evidence that the Standards themselves reflect students' own goals for their learning? In considering the Standards for postsecondary instruction, it is important to understand how well the goals of the Standards might align with students' own goals. This kind of inquiry is supported by Merrill (2013), who states that "the more we know about our students, the better we can prepare our language classes and keep them relevant for the realities of today's students and the challenges they face" (p. 53).

The large study on which the present research is based (Magnan et al., 2014; Magnan et al., 2012) is the first to explore the fit of the goals of language students at any level to the goals of the Standards. This study found that 89% of college-level students enrolled in first- and second-year courses had goals corresponding to the goals of the

Standards (p. 64). Perhaps surprisingly, given the large body of research that shows how important developing communicative abilities in a second language (L2) is to US students (Magnan et al., 2014, p. 5), the Five-Cs goal that was highest in terms of importance to students was Communities, not Communication; Communication was second in importance to students, followed by Cultures, Comparisons, and Connections (p. 66). The relatively low priority that students place on the presentational mode of communication (Standard 1.3, pp. 68–69) and the close connection that students seemed to make between the Communities and Communication goals in relating them to L2 use and to their desire to connect with others through their study of the L2, explains the higher ranking of Communities relative to Communication. The authors explain the middle ranking of the Cultures Standards in the hierarchy of student goals as possibly related to students' lower prioritization of culture learning in relation to their goals for language use overall; or as related to a belief, expressed by some students, that culture learning is not an integral part of learning that takes place in a language classroom; or as related to the problematic way in which culture is depicted in the two content standards in the Cultures goal area (Magnan et al., 2014).[8]

Magnan et al. (2014) looked at differences between two groups of students: the first group was comprised of students enrolled in first- and second-year courses; the second group was of students enrolled in courses in commonly taught languages (CTLs) and less-commonly taught languages (LCTLs).[9] The CTL/LCTL comparison shows that despite the fact that LCTL professional organizations were not as closely involved as CTL organizations in the initial formulation of the Standards, overall the Standards were an even better fit for LCTL college-level students than for CTL students, both in terms of the students' goals and in terms of the students' expectations for reaching those goals. Although they compare students of CTLs and LCTLs, Magnan et al. (2014, 2012) did not analyze the responses of students of individual languages or examine differences among the responses of the students based on their language of study.[10] We attempt to do just that for students of Russian. With the revision of the Standards for Russian Language Learning at both the secondary and postsecondary levels, the profession has a new opportunity to consider the fit of the Standards for the teaching of Russian at the college level. It is in the spirit of informing those discussions that we share data on the fit of the Standards with the goals of college-level students of Russian.

RESEARCH QUESTIONS

Our study was guided by two sets of research questions (RQs). The first set asked: Do the goals of collegiate students of Russian at the first- and second-year levels of instruction correspond to the goals of the Standards? How are the Five Cs of the Standards represented in a hierarchy of students' goals? How are the individual content standards represented in such a hierarchy? Are there differences between the goals of students of Russian at the beginning of the first and the end of the second year of instruction? The second set of RQs asked about differences between students of Russian and students of the other 30 languages in the sample: Is there a difference between the goals of students of Russian versus students of other languages, and are these reflected in the Standards? Are certain content standards more or less important to students of Russian, in terms of their goals, compared to students of other languages?

METHODS

This section describes the participants and the mixed-method design of the study.

Participants

Survey. Participants in the study were 706 students enrolled in first-year (n = 532) or second-year (n = 174) Russian courses at 11 US universities in the spring (second-year courses) or fall (first-year courses) of 2010 (see Table 6.1).[11]

The full study included 16,529 students enrolled in first-year (n = 11,209) or second-year (n = 5,320) courses in 31 languages.[12] The 706 students of Russian who participated in the study represent 4.3% of the full sample. Demographic data for the full sample are reported in Magnan et al. (2014); the demographic information provided here is just for the students of Russian.

Of the students of Russian who participated in the study, 53% were female; 47% were male. The average age of participants was 20.7 years. Roughly three-fourths of the participants were either first-year (28%), second-year (29%), or third-year (21%) undergraduates; the rest (22%) were fourth- or fifth-year undergraduates, graduate students, or other types of students (e.g., non-degree). A small portion of the respondents (5%) were international students. Eleven percent of the students in the Russian sample could be considered heritage learners: they were students who indicated that Russian was spoken at home sometimes (4%), often (3%), or always (4%).

TABLE 6.1. Distribution of Survey Participants, by Institution

Institution	Number	Percentage
University of Washington	111	15.7
Michigan State University	89	12.6
University of Wisconsin-Madison	85	12.0
University of Texas at Austin	76	10.8
University of Florida	72	10.2
University of California, Berkeley	53	7.5
University of Arizona	51	7.2
Georgetown University	51	7.2
Yale University	45	6.4
UCLA	40	5.7
University of Utah	33	4.7
Total	706	100.0

Note: The distribution of students of Russian among the 11 universities is similar to the distribution of students of all languages in the sample.

TABLE 6.2. Reasons for Enrolling in the Russian Course, by Importance

Reason for Enrolling	Mean
Personal interest, enjoyment, curiosity	4.46
Future travel or study abroad	3.89
Future career or graduate school	3.52
Degree requirement	2.47
Communicate with acquaintances/friends	2.43
Help learning another language	2.09
Small classes and making friends	1.89
Family background	1.85
Personal schedule	1.69

Note: Scale: 1 = Not at all important, 2 = Slightly important, 3 = Somewhat important, 4 = Very important, 5 = Extremely important.

The Russian students in the sample had a range of disciplinary interests: their current or intended majors were in the social sciences (27%), humanities (20%), natural sciences (13%), business (6%), engineering (5%), the arts (3%), or education (1%). However, close to one fourth of the sample (23%) indicated that their current or intended major was *other* than any of the options given in the questionnaire; an additional 5% indicated that they were *uncertain* about their major.[13] A little over one fourth of the respondents, 29% (n = 204), indicated that they expected to major or minor in Russian.

As shown in Table 6.2, students reported many different reasons for enrolling in the Russian course. By far the most important reason was *personal interest, enjoyment, and curiosity*, followed by the desire for *future travel or study abroad*, or plans related to the student's *future career or graduate school.*

Interviews. A subset of 200 participants—students of 27 languages at the University of California, Berkeley, and the University of Wisconsin–Madison—participated in semistructured follow-up interviews with the researchers. Of those 200 interview subjects, nine were students of Russian: four from first-year Russian courses and five from second-year courses. The proportion of students of Russian who participated in the interviews, 4.5% of the 200 interviewed students, is roughly the same as the proportion of students of Russian, 4.3%, who participated in the survey.

Survey Instrument

The study was based on a written questionnaire titled *My Language Learning Goals* (Magnan et al., 2014), which was developed by the authors in consultation with the University of Wisconsin (UW) Survey Center and the universities that participated in the study. The questionnaire centered on two main questions related to the 11 content standards, which were presented in random order as goals: *How important is this goal to you?* The wordings of the 11 content standards were modified slightly, based on the pilot study, to make the statements clear to students (Magnan et al., 2014). Finally, the questionnaire included items that gathered demographic and profile data.

Procedures

This section describes the study's data collection and data analysis procedures.

Data Collection

The four-page paper survey was administered in class at two different points in time in 2010: during the first two weeks of class at the beginning of the fall semester for students enrolled in first-year courses, and during the last two weeks of classes for students enrolled in second-year courses. The study did not survey the same cohort of students as they progressed from first to second year: students in second-year courses were surveyed in spring 2010; students in first-year course in the fall 2010. The survey was administered by the UW Survey Center with the help of local on-campus coordinators and class instructors at each participating university.

The structured interviews were administered both during and following the two waves of survey administration. The interviews began with an open-ended question about students' goals for the language of study. Then students were asked to retake the survey and explain their responses.

Data Analysis

To answer the first set of RQs, response rates for participants who indicated that they were enrolled in a Russian course were calculated for each response category and used to create charts and figures for the responses overall according to the Five C goal areas and for each of the 11 content standards individually. The mean was calculated as well, to facilitate comparisons and to show hierarchies. A two-sample Wilcoxon rank-sum (Mann-Whitney) test was performed to evaluate differences between students' goals at the first and second years of instruction. The second set of RQs, which asked about differences between students of Russian and students of other languages, was approached through a statistical model (bioprobit) that allowed for comparisons of the responses of students of Russian with students of all other languages in the sample and to control for potential differences in student characteristics, such as reason for studying the language, language used at home, self-perceived ability for learning languages, gender, and intent to major or minor in the language.[14] The bioprobit model also controlled for level of instruction (i.e., first- vs. second-year Russian) and whether the participant was a US domestic or international student. (See Magnan et al., 2014 for a discussion of these variables.)

The examination of the qualitative interview data was based on a content analysis for themes. Given the small number of interviews with students of Russian (n = 9), a full analysis of just those interviews is not included here. However, select quotes from the interviews with Russian students are provided where appropriate to illustrate possible interpretations of the survey data.

RESULTS AND DISCUSSION

The following section presents the study's findings, organized by research question.

The Goals of Students of Russian and the Standards

Overall. The first set of research questions asked about the goals of students of Russian at the first- and second-year levels and the Standards: Do the students' goals correspond to the Standards? How are the Five Cs of the Standards represented in the hierarchy of students' goals? How are the individual content standards represented in this hierarchy?

Figure 6.1 shows how students of Russian responded to the question, *How important is this goal for you?*; for all the 11 content standards taken together it shows that overall, 89% of students of Russian indicated that the Standards were *extremely* (36%), *very* (32%), or *somewhat* (21%) important to them as personal goals. These results, which are remarkably similar to those obtained in the full study, suggest that there may indeed be an affinity between the goals of postsecondary students of Russian and the Standards, at least when all of the Standards are considered together.[15]

The Five Cs. Looking at student goals in terms of the Standards' Five Cs goal areas, Magnan et al. (2014) found that the goal area that was most highly valued by the students in the full study was Communities, followed by Communication, and then by Cultures, Comparisons, and Connections (p. 66). Figure 6.2 shows how the Five Cs goal areas were prioritized by students of Russian: the Communities goal area was also the most important, followed by Communication and then Cultures. Connections and Comparisons, at the bottom of the hierarchy, were almost identical to each other in terms of their importance to students of Russian.

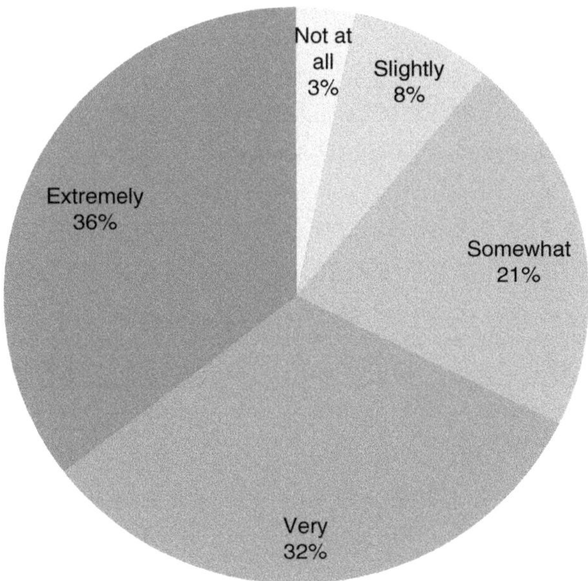

FIGURE 6.1. Importance of Goals to Students of Russian, across the Content Standards

A different way of viewing the relative importance of the Five Cs goal areas to students of Russian is provided in Table 6.3, which presents means of the responses shown in Figure 6.2. With the exception of the connections and comparisons goal areas, there is a clear hierarchy of the Five Cs goal areas in terms of their importance to students. It also shows that *all five* of the goal areas are important to students: on a scale of 1–5, with 5 corresponding to *extremely important* and 1 corresponding to *not at all important*, the lowest mean, associated with Comparisons and Connections, is 3.66, that is, between *somewhat important* and *very important*. The two highest means, for Communities and Communications, are above 4, which corresponds to *very important* on the response scale.

Content Standards. Why was Communities the most highly valued goal area to students of Russian? To better understand students' hierarchy of the Five Cs goal areas and

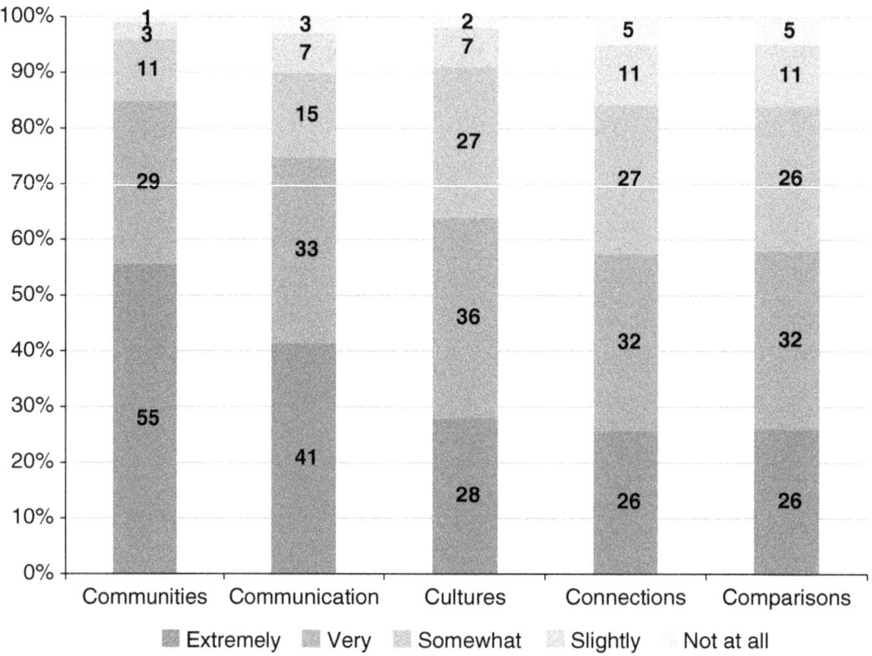

FIGURE 6.2. Importance of Goals to Students of Russian, by the Five Cs

TABLE 6.3. Importance of the Standards to Students of Russian, by the Five Cs (Average Responses, n ≈ 700)

Goal Area	Mean
Communities	4.34
Communication	4.03
Culture	3.79
Comparisons	3.66
Connections	3.66

Note: Scale: 1 = Not at all important, 2 = Slightly important, 3 = Somewhat important, 4 = Very important, 5 = Extremely important.

to explore which individual content standards are more or less important to students, we looked at students' responses to the question about their goals in relation to each of the 11 content standards. Figure 6.3 presents the 11 content standards in order of importance to students, from left to right. It shows that Communities Standard 5.1, *Use the language both within and beyond the school setting*, is more important than any other standard to students of Russian. This high prioritization of Standard 5.1 explains why the Communities goal area was so important to students: Students see Standard 5.1 as the *sine qua non* for language learning and express a strong desire to use the language outside the classroom environment. As one student of Russian commented in the structured interview, "If I'm learning a language, like I said, I want to be able to *use* it and that doesn't mean I'm just going to use it within my classroom." The second Communities Standard, Standard 5.2, *Become a lifelong learner by using the language for personal enjoyment and enrichment*, is also fairly high in the hierarchy. The analysis of the interviews in the full study suggest that students focus on enjoyment in using the L2 in responding to this standard. We can speculate that this finding might hold for students of Russian as well. As one second-year student of Russian commented, "I want to continue to learn, study my whole life, on my own or in whatever way I can. Just for my own. I just really like it and am interested in it."

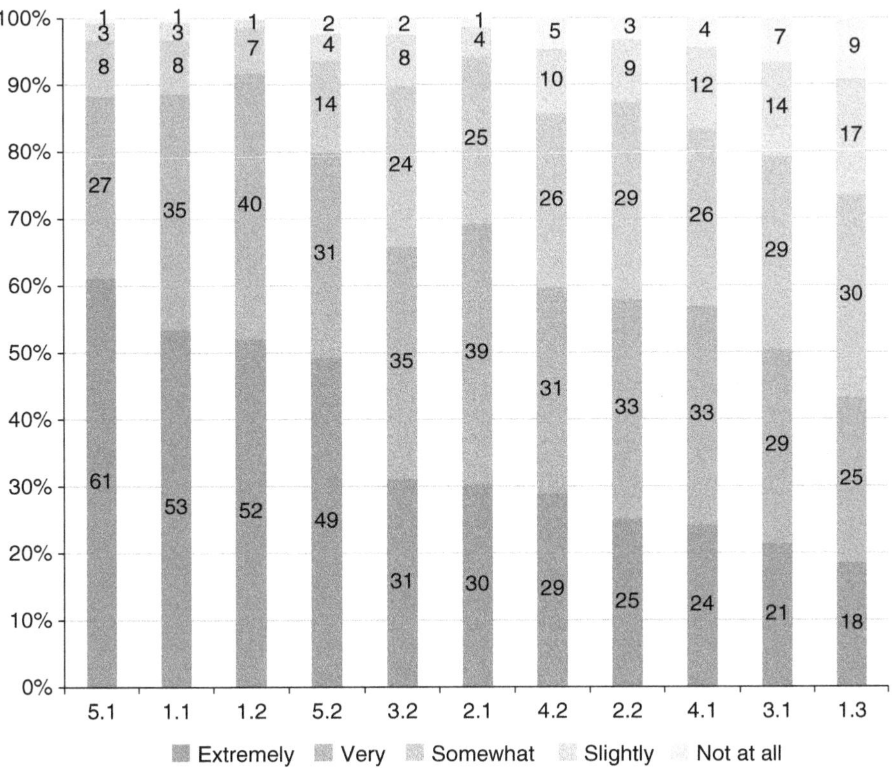

FIGURE 6.3. Importance of Standards to Students of Russian, by the 11 Content Standards

After 5.1, two Communication Standards that are of the highest importance to students of Russian are 1.1, which addresses the interpersonal mode, and 1.2, which focuses on the interpretive mode (*Understand and interpret written and spoken language on a variety of topics*). The importance of Communication Standard 1.1 to students is to be expected, given research that shows how important developing interpersonal communicative abilities is to students (see Murphy et al. 2009 for a review). The high prioritization of Communication Standard 1.2 might reflect the conceptual connection that many students seem to make between Standards 1.1 and 1.2. It also might reflect the high value that some students of Russian place on literary studies (Merrill, 2013, p. 54). As one second-year student of Russian said, in relation to Communication Standard 1.2, "I'd like to be able to be conversant on a variety of topics but, again, literature is what I'm focusing on right now." Similarly, another second-year student of Russian said, "The one thing I would like is . . . to do more reading. You know, sometimes we are given selections from *Anna Karenina* and as for that, I'd like to see more of those personally: bigger sections, more focus on that."[16] In fact, if we look at the mean responses by individual content standard (Table 6.4) instead of the percentage of students who selected each response option (Figure 6.3), Standard 1.2 (interpretive mode) was even higher in overall importance to students of Russian (mean 4.45) than was Standard 1.1 (interpersonal mode, mean 4.38).

The third Communication Standard, 1.3, the presentational mode (*Present information, concepts, and ideas to an audience of listeners or readers on a variety of topics*), is much lower in importance to students of Russian than are Communication Standards 1.1 and 1.2. In fact, it comes in last of all of the content standards in its importance to students (Figure 6.3 and Table 6.4). Such low prioritization of Standard 1.3 relative to the other two Communication Standards was found for students of all languages by Magnan et al. (2014, 2012) as well. The analysis of the interview data in Magnan et al. (2014) suggests that anxiety about public speaking (p. 81) and the belief that "I'm not someone who does that" may be behind the students' low prioritization of Communication Standard 1.3 as a personal goal. This perspective is echoed in the comments of a second-year student of Russian in the present study who remarked, "I'd say it's only slightly important for me to be able to convey ideas to an audience of listeners or readers because I don't really foresee myself doing anything like that, like giving a presentation or writing a paper. I can't see myself applying it in that way."

In a hierarchy of student goals the two Cultures Standards come after Communication Standards 1.1 and 1.2 and both Communities Standards, 5.1 and 5.2. They are fairly distant from each other in the hierarchy as well, with students valuing more highly Cultures Standard 2.1 (Demonstrate an understanding of the practices and perspectives of the other culture) than Cultures Standard 2.2 (Demonstrate an understanding of the products and perspectives of the other culture).[17] The analysis of the 200 interviews in Magnan et al. (2014) shows that not a single student said culture learning was the main point of language learning (p. 84). Moreover, although students in the study overall highly valued culture learning, with many expressing

TABLE 6.4. Importance of the Standards to Students of Russian, Ranked (Average responses, n ≈ 700)

Goal Area	Standard	Mean, ranked in importance
Standard 5.1	Use the language I am studying both within and beyond the school setting	4.48
Standard 1.2	Understand and interpret written and spoken language on a variety of topics	4.45
Standard 1.1	Engage in conversations, provide and obtain information, express feelings and emotions, and exchange opinions	4.38
Standard 5.2	Become a lifelong learner by using the language for personal enjoyment and enrichment	4.21
Standard 2.1	Understand the relationship between the practices (patterns of social interactions) and perspectives (meanings, attitudes, values, ideas) of the culture I am studying	3.94
Standard 3.2	Acquire information and recognize the distinctive viewpoints that are only available through the foreign language and its culture	3.88
Standard 4.2	Understand the concept of culture through comparisons of the cultures I am studying and my own	3.68
Standard 2.2	Understand the relationship between the products (books, tools, foods, laws, music, games) and perspectives (meanings, attitudes, values, ideas) of the culture I am studying	3.63
Standard 4.1	Understand the nature of language through comparisons of the language I am studying and my own	3.63
Standard 3.1	Reinforce and further my knowledge of other disciplines through the foreign language	3.44
Standard 1.3	Present information, concepts, and ideas to an audience of listeners or readers on a variety of topics	3.26

Note: The wording of the 11 standards matches the modified wording used in the survey. Scale: 1 = not at all important, 2 = slightly important, 3 = somewhat important, 4 = very important, 5 = extremely important.

nuanced views about the interrelationship of language and culture, some students seem to have views in line with the first-year Russian student who said, "I don't think in the language class it's as important to learn about the culture as just grammar and speaking." Referring to experiences in Russian class and responding to Cultures Standard 2.1, one second-year student of Russian said, "They [my instructors] do a lot to explain why, what the broader meanings of certain things are, like why they do toasts or why they become acquainted in a certain pattern or whatever, like rituals of culture. So they do a good job of teaching us and that's interesting. It's just not super important to me."

The concept of culture is woven throughout a number of the Standards outside of the Cultures goal area, including Connections Standard 3.2 and Comparisons 4.2. The hierarchy presented in Table 6.4 shows that Connections 3.2 and Comparisons 4.2 fall in between Cultures Standard 2.1 and Cultures Standard 2.2, suggesting that, as for the full sample, students of Russian see these four goals as being closely related.[18] Comparisons 4.1 and Connections 3.1 followed in the hierarchy. Magnan et al. (2014) found that, unlike goals in the Communities and Communication goal areas, with very few exceptions students do not consider goals related to Connections or Comparisons to be the main point of language learning. Students see value in the Connections and Comparisons Standards but their main priorities are elsewhere. This perspective is reflected in a quote from a second-year student of Russian regarding Connections Standard 3.2: "I guess that's just not my particular reason for taking the language, but I do appreciate it."

Despite students' relatively low prioritization of content standards in the Connections and Comparisons goal areas, it should be emphasized that, as shown in Table 6.4, *all* of the content standards were at least *somewhat important* to students of Russian, as well as to students in the full sample.

The Goals of Students of Russian at Different Levels of Instruction

A comparison of the goals of students of Russian at the first and at the second years of instruction reveal no statistically significant difference between the two groups for any of the 11 content standards. This finding is different from that of Magnan et al. (2014), who did find statistically significant differences between students at the first- and second-year levels, with those at the end of the second year indicating that Communication and Communities, the two goal areas most highly valued by students overall, are more important than they are for students at the beginning of the first year of instruction.[19]

The Goals of Students of Russian and Students of Other Languages

The second set of RQs asked: Is there a difference between students of Russian and students of other languages in their goals, in terms of the Standards? Are certain content standards more or less important to students of Russian in terms of their goals, compared to students of other languages? The bioprobit model was applied to control for several different variables in making the comparison: the reasons the student enrolled in the course, the perception of the difficulty of learning other languages, the intent to major or minor in the L2, the level of instruction, the student's gender, and whether the student was a domestic or international student.

TABLE 6.5. Statistical Differences between Goals, Students of Russian vs. Students of All Other Languages

	Communication			Cultures		Connections		Comparisons		Communities	
	1.1	1.2	1.3	2.1	2.2	3.1	3.2	4.1	4.2	5.1	5.2
Importance	–		–				+	+	+		–

Note: + = The importance of the standard as a goal to students of Russian is statistically significantly higher than to students of all other languages.
– = The importance of the standard as a goal to students of Russian is statistically significantly lower than to students of all other languages.
Blank = There is no statistically significant difference between students of Russian and students of all other languages.

Table 6.5 shows that statistically significant differences exist between the goals of students of Russian and students of the other 30 languages in the study for six of the 11 content standards: students of Russian attach significantly less importance to Communication Standards 1.1 and 1.3 and Communities Standard 5.2. Students of Russian attach significantly more importance to Connections Standard 3.2 and Comparisons Standards 4.1 and 4.2. No significant difference exists between the two groups for either of the Cultures Standards, 2.1 or 2.1, or for Connections Standard 3.1 or Communities Standard 5.1.

How might these findings be interpreted? We wondered if Communication Standard 1.2 (interpretive mode) is more important to students of Russian than Communication Standard 1.1 (interpersonal mode) because the students are particularly interested in literary studies. Comparing students of Russian to students of other languages, however, we see that there is no difference between students of Russian and students of other languages in the importance of understanding and interpreting written and spoken language. Students of Russian do, however, value conversational ability significantly less than do students of the 30 other languages. The higher importance that students of Russian place on Standard 1.2 relative to 1.1 might be explained by a lower prioritization of conversational ability by students of Russian, not by Russian students' relatively greater interest in literary studies.[20]

The comparison of students of commonly and less-commonly taught languages in Magnan et al. (2014) also found that students of LCTLs value Communication Standard 1.1 less than do CTL students (p. 168). In this respect, at least, the responses of students of Russian are similar to the responses of students of LCTLs as a group. Students of Russian are also similar to the group of students of LCTLs in their responses regarding the Connections and Comparisons Standards related to culture (Connections Standard 3.2 and Comparisons Standard 4.2), both of which are more important to LCTL students than to CTL students, and Communities Standard 5.2, using the L2 for enjoyment, which is less important to LCTL students than to CTL students. For all other content standards, however, students of Russian are different than the group of students of all LCTLs. For example, Communication

Standard 1.3 (presentational mode) is less important to them than to students of all other languages. The LCTL/CTL comparison shows that for LCTL students as a group, Standard 1.3 is more important than it is for CTL students.

Looking just at content standards that are more highly valued by students of Russian compared to the students of the other 30 languages in the sample (Table 6.5), we see that students of Russian more highly value the two Comparisons Standards (4.1 and 4.2) than do students of other languages. The interest in language comparisons (4.1) among students of Russian—as illustrated by one second-year student of Russian, who said that linguistic comparisons were extremely important "because that sounds like comparative linguistics and that is awesome"—should be encouraging to Gettys (2003), who advocates for the place of L1/L2 comparisons in language classes.

LIMITATIONS

There are several limitations to this study. First, the 11 universities where the survey data was collected are not representative of the range of colleges and universities in which Russian is taught in the United States: no small liberal arts colleges were included in the study, and the majority of the institutions are large public universities. Another limitation of the study is that it only included students during the first two years of their instruction. Especially given the "standard configuration" (Modern Language Association Ad Hoc Committee on Foreign Languages, 2007, p. 2) of US postsecondary foreign language curricula in which upper-level courses focus on literary studies and lower-level courses focus on the development of communicative abilities, it might be expected that students in upper-level courses would have very different goals than students in lower levels. The first two years of language study are, however, of crucial importance: not only do students in upper-level Russian courses typically come to those courses after completing lower-level ones, the first two years of instruction have the largest numbers of students. Finally, the interview data for students of Russian is very limited, so they were not analyzed for this chapter (although example quotes are provided). A larger sample of interview participants, that is, from more than just two universities, would likely yield valuable perspectives. For future research in this area it would be of particular interest to look more closely at students' interests beyond linguistics and literary studies. The students in Merrill's 2013 study, for example, indicate that, in addition to prose literature, information about everyday life, as well as history, popular culture, poetry, news media, film, and politics, should be taught in Russian language courses.

CONCLUSION

In their seminal work on L2 student motivation, Dörnyei and Ushioda (2011) argue that "many, if not most, students do not really understand (or accept) why they are involved in a learning activity" (p. 146) and that learning goals set by outsiders may not, in "extreme cases" (p. 147), be aligned with students' own goals. When this situation occurs, it is understandable that student motivation for learning is low. This study shows that despite the Standards' orientation to K–12 education and the lack of student input into the Standards' development, the goals are in fact valued by the first- and second-year students of Russian who participated in the research. This is an encouraging finding for fostering an environment where motivation for language learning is strong.

The Communities goal area is most highly valued by students in this study, due to the students' desire to use Russian outside of the classroom (Standard 5.1) and to use the language for enjoyment (Standard 5.2). In the Communication goal area, students of Russian highly valued Standards 1.1 (interpersonal communication) and 1.2 (interpretive communication), although Standard 1.1 is valued less by students of Russian than it is by students of the 30 other languages in the sample. Standard 1.3 (presentational communication) is not only the least-prioritized standard for students of Russian, it is even less important to Russian students than it is to students of other languages. The Cultures Standards are important to Russian students, but they are not students' main goals for language study. The Standards in the Comparisons and Connections goal areas are also important, but not as important to students as goals in other areas. Connections Standard 3.2 and both of the Comparisons Standards are more important to students of Russian than to students of other languages, possibly reflecting an interest among Russian students in literary studies and linguistics, among other fields.

The data obtained from this study should be encouraging for educators who are interested applying the Standards to the teaching of Russian at the postsecondary level in the United States. The high value that students in this study place on the goals of the Standards overall should encourage postsecondary Russian educators such as Rifkin (2012), who sees the expansive vision of foreign language education embodied in the Standards as closely aligned with the broader goals of the liberal arts education articulated in the LEAP Initiative of the American Association of Colleges and Universities.

Rifkin (2012) argues that the alignment of postsecondary world language curricula with the Standards and LEAP can "strengthen the place of world language education in America's colleges and universities" (p. 57) by emphasizing students' developing communicative abilities, cultural knowledge, and intercultural competencies and by focusing on the potential for language education to integrate humanistic enquiry with the study of other disciplines. Kramsch (2014) laments that "the disciplinary connections envisaged by the Standards did not get realized at the college level as could have been hoped for" (p. 302). This study suggests that lower-level postsecondary students of Russian are in fact making these disciplinary connections themselves, between their study of Russian and their other interests. Russian programs that may not explicitly promote ways for lower-level students to explore their additional interests through Russian might look to the Standards to help students make those connections. Such efforts would support the call in most recent edition of the Standards (NSCB, 2015), for colleges and universities to redesign programs for students who "want to use world languages in fields ranging from history, philosophy, business, art history, and journalism to nursing, engineering, and the sciences" (p. 22).

Scholars such as Arens (2008) have argued that the Standards can offer a "bridge between literature, culture, and language teaching in a post-secondary curriculum . . . [and] point the way to advanced literacies, beyond conversational language and past the marginalization of everyday culture often instantiated in traditional literary studies" (p. 35). Swaffar (2014) likewise sees the potential for the Standards to serve as a bridge: from lower-level to upper-level courses, to ensure that "language and other contents, set in particular contexts that require active negotiation, are interrelated from the outset of instruction" (p. 41). This study's positive findings of alignment between lower-level Russian students' own learning goals and the Standards' statements should stimulate research on curricular innovation that responds to the Standards in postsecondary Russian programs. May such innovation strengthen ongoing program-design efforts and foster new ones.

APPENDIX A: NSFLEP STANDARDS FOR FOREIGN LANGUAGE LEARNING (2006)

Communication: *Communicate in Languages Other than English*

Standard 1.1: Students engage in conversations, provide and obtain information, express feelings and emotions, and exchange opinions.

Standard 1.2: Students understand and interpret written and spoken language on a variety of topics.

Standard 1.3: Students present information, concepts, and ideas to an audience of listeners or readers on a variety of topics.

Cultures: *Gain Knowledge and Understanding of Other Cultures*

Standard 2.1: Students demonstrate an understanding of the relationship between the practices and perspectives of the culture studied.

Standard 2.2: Students demonstrate an understanding of the relationship between the products and perspectives of the culture studied.

Connections: *Connect with Other Disciplines and Acquire Information*

Standard 3.1: Students reinforce and further their knowledge of other disciplines through the foreign language.

Standard 3.2: Students acquire information and recognize the distinctive viewpoints that are only available through the foreign language and its cultures.

Comparisons: *Develop Insight Into the Nature of Language and Culture*

Standard 4.1: Students demonstrate an understanding of the nature of language through comparisons of the language studied and their own.

Standard 4.2: Students demonstrate an understanding of the concept of culture through comparisons of the cultures studied and their own.

Communities: *Participate in Multilingual Communities at Home and Around the World*

Standard 5.1: Students use the language both within and beyond the school setting.

Standard 5.2: Students show evidence of becoming lifelong learners by using the language for personal enjoyment and enrichment.

NOTES

1. The study was funded by a grant from the US Department of Education, grant # P017A090365.
2. Although Magnan et al. (2014) also looks at students' expectations for achieving goals, this chapter focuses just on students' goals, not on their expectations for achieving them.
3. The numbering of the 11 content standards is taken from the 1996, 1999, and 2006 editions. Beginning with the 2015 edition the Standards are presented in the same order as in previous editions but are not numbered, in response to concerns that the numbering implied a hierarchy of importance and did not convey the intention of presenting the Standards as interconnected and inseparable sets of goals (NSCB, 2015, pp. 272–78). In addition to this change, the 2015 edition slightly altered the summary wording of each of the Five Cs. The wording from the 2006 edition of the Standards is used here because that is the version on which the present study was based.
4. Modified from NSFLEP, 2006, p. 9.
5. Kramsch (2014) states that the Standards are viewed by those with a social science perspective as representing "at best an educational policy statement, not a scientific research study" (p. 306).
6. Among the advanced goals that Beyer (2000) describes are the ability to "read Russian texts in the original, or to develop spoken and listening skills sufficient to permit study and communication with native speakers in the foreign country . . . [as well as] . . . to understand authentic Russian in a variety of contexts. . . . There may also be some emphasis in the Standards on an appreciation of Russian or other Slavic languages as a system for expression of human thought" (p. 293).
7. References to the Standards in the literature on the teaching of Russian at the K–12 level include Sildus and Selzer (1999) and, somewhat cursorily, in a discussion of the Prototype AP® Russian Language and Culture Examination, in Marshall (2010).
8. Culture is explicitly represented outside the Cultures goal area in Connections Standard 3.2 and Comparisons Standard 4.2. An analysis by Magnan et al. (2014) finds that Standards 3.2 and 4.2 were strongly correlated with Standards 2.1 and 2.2 in terms of students' goals (pp. 194–96), suggesting that culture is indeed incorporated in goals areas beyond just Cultures.
9. The commonly taught languages are French, German, and Spanish. Less commonly taught languages are all other languages in the sample, including Russian.
10. White (2016), in a small-scale, exploratory, mixed-methods study, looks at the alignment of the Standards with the goals of first-year students of German. In contrast to Magnan et al. (2014, 2012), White finds that first-year students of German do not highly value the Communities goal area.
11. The universities chosen as sites for this study received significant funding through the US Department of Education to support instruction in less-commonly taught languages, they had faculty and staff who agreed to serve as local coordinators for

the data collection, and they represented, to the greatest extent possible, a broad geographic distribution across the United States.

12. The languages are Arabic, Armenian, Chinese, Czech, Dutch, French, German, Greek, Hebrew, Hindi, Hmong, Indonesian, Italian, Japanese, Korean, Norwegian, Ojibwe, Persian/Farsi, Polish, Portuguese, Russian, Serbo-Croatian, Spanish, Swahili, Swedish, Tagalog, Thai, Turkish, Urdu, Vietnamese, and Yoruba (Magnan et al., 2014, p. 47).
13. Given that the proclaimed majors of so many students are not captured by the response options on the questionnaire for "major of study," this variable is not used for the analysis.
14. The full term for the model is *seemingly unrelated bivariate ordered probit* (Sajaia, 2008).
15. In fact exactly 89% of the 16,529 participants in the full study indicate that the Standards are *extremely* important (32%), *very* important (35%), or *somewhat* important (22%) (Magnan et al., 2014, pp. 64–65).
16. Students of Russian are interested in many different kinds of texts, of course, not just literary ones. As one first-year student remarked, "I want to be able to read stuff in that language and understand what it's saying. That would include reading the newspaper or the magazine or maybe just a phrase off some book."
17. The parenthetical explications for the two Cultures Standards were added in the questionnaire by the researchers to make those two standards more understandable to students.
18. A correlation analysis reported in Magnan et al. (2014) shows that in terms of the goals of students in the full sample, Connections Standard 3.2 correlates more strongly with Cultures Standards 2.1 and 2.2 than it does with the other Connections standard, 3.1. Likewise, Comparisons Standard 4.2 correlates more strongly with Cultures Standard 2.1 than it does with Comparisons Standard 4.1. The strength of the correlation between Comparisons Standard 2.1 and Comparisons Standard 4.1 is identical (p. 196).
19. The absence of statistical significance in the difference between the goals of students enrolled in first- and second-year Russian courses could be due to the small sample size available for the statistical tests (530 vs. 170 students of Russian, respectively, in the first and second years of instruction).
20. As one reviewer to this article rightly points out, we should be careful not to overstate the importance of literary studies to Russian students given the diversity of interests of our students.

REFERENCES

Allen, H. W. (2009). In search of relevance: The Standards and the undergraduate foreign language curriculum. In V. Scott (Ed.), *Principles and practices of the Standards in college foreign language education* (pp. 38–52). Boston: Heinle Cengage Learning.

Allen, L. (2002). Standards-based foreign language learning and teaching pedagogical beliefs. In A. Garfinkel & L. Oukada (Eds.), *Teamwork in foreign languages* (pp. 33–46).

Columbus, OH: Central States Conference on the Teaching of Foreign Languages/ National Textbook.

American Council on the Teaching of Foreign Languages (ACTFL). (2011). *A decade of foreign language standards: Influence, impact, and future directions*. Alexandria, VA: Task Force on Decade of Standards Project. Retrieved from www.actfl.org/sites/default /files/pdfs/public/national-standards-https://www.actfl.org/sites/default/files/pdfs /StandardsImpactSurvey_FINAL.pdf

Arens, K. (2008). Genres and the Standards: Teaching the 5 C's through texts. *German Quarterly*, *81*(1), 35–48.

Beyer, T. (2000). From testing to assessment, from teaching to learning. In O. Kagan & B. Rifkin (Eds.), *The learning and teaching of Slavic languages and cultures* (pp. 285–94). Bloomington, IN: Slavica.

Byrnes, H. (2012). Of frameworks and the goals of collegiate foreign language education: Critical reflections. *Applied Linguistics Review*, *3*(1), 1–24.

Davidson, D., Rifkin, B., & Shuffelton, J. (2006). The state of the Russian field 20 years after the Report on the National Committee for Russian Language Study: A response to Rachel Stauffer. *Slavic and East European Journal*, *50*(4), 679–84.

Dhonau, S., & McAlpine, D. (2011). Weaving the national student standards into higher education foreign language programs. *ADFL Bulletin*, *41*(3), 53–63.

Diment, G. (1999). From the perspective of Russian. In Forum on the Standards for foreign language learning: Preparing for the twenty-first century. *ADFL Bulletin*, *31*(1), 73.

Dörnyei, Z., & Ushioda, E. (2011). Teaching and researching motivation (2nd ed.). New York: Longman Pearson.

Garn, R. (2012). Teaching the Five Cs with cinema. *Journal of the National Council of Less Commonly Taught Languages*, *12*, 36–71.

Garza, T., Merrill, P., & Shuffelton, J. (2015). *Standards for Russian Language Learning* (iBooks ed.). Retrieved from www.actfl.org/publications/all/world-readiness-standards -learning-languages

Gettys, S. (2003). Incorporating Comparisons Standard 4.1 into foreign language teaching. *Foreign Language Annals*, *36*(2), 188–97.

Kramsch, C. (2014). Teaching foreign languages in an era of globalization: Introduction. *Modern Language Journal*, *98*(1), 296–311.

Magnan, S. S., Murphy, D., & Sahakyan, N. (2014). Goals of collegiate learners and the Standards for foreign language learning. *Modern Language Journal*, *98*, Supplement.

Magnan, S. S., Murphy, D., Sahakyan, N., & Kim, S. (2012). Student goals, expectations, and the Standards for foreign language learning. *Foreign Language Annals*, *45*, 170–92.

Marshall, C. (2010). Examining the validity of the 2010 Prototype AP Russian Exam through a college comparability study. *Russian Language Journal*, *60*, 319–31.

Merrill, J. (2013). Our Russian classrooms and students: Who is choosing Russian, why, and what cultural content should we offer them? *Russian Language Journal*, *63*, 51–78.

Modern Language Association Ad Hoc Committee on Foreign Languages. (2007). Foreign Languages and Higher Education: New Structures for a Changed World. *Profession, 12*, 234-245.

Murphy, D., Magnan, S., Back, M., & Garrett-Rucks, P. (2009). Reasons students take courses in less commonly taught languages. *Journal of the National Council of Less Commonly Taught Languages, 7*, 45–80.

National Standards Collaborative Board (NSCB). (2015). *World-readiness standards for learning languages* (4th ed.). Alexandria, VA: Author.

National Standards in Foreign Language Education Project (NSFLEP). (1996). *Standards for foreign language learning: Preparing for the 21st century.* Yonkers, NY: Author.

National Standards in Foreign Language Education Project (NSFLEP). (1999). *Standards for foreign language learning: Preparing for the 21st century.* Yonkers, NY: Author.

National Standards in Foreign Language Education Project (NSFLEP). (2006). *Standards for foreign language learning in the 21st century.* Yonkers, NY: Author.

Phillips, J. (2007). Foreign language education: Whose definition? *Modern Language Journal, 91,* 266–68.

Rifkin, B. (2006). Fifty years of pedagogy in SEEJ: The learning and teaching of Slavic languages past, present and future. *Slavic and East European Journal, 50*(1), 29–44.

Rifkin, B. (2012). The world language curriculum at the center of postsecondary education. *Liberal Education, 98*(3), 54–57.

Sajaia, Z. (2008). Maximum likelihood estimation of a bivariate ordered probit model: Implementation and Monte Carlo Simulations, *Stata Journal, 3*(2), 311–28.

Scott, V. (Ed.). (2009). *Principles and practices of the* Standards *in collegiate foreign language education*. Boston: Heinle Cengage Learning.

Sildus, T., & Selzer, D. (1999). Video projects in the foreign language classroom. In A. Nerenz (Ed.), *Standards for a new century* (pp. 143–55). Lincolnwood, IL: National Textbook.

Swaffar, J. (2014). From language to literacy: The evolving concepts of foreign language teaching at American colleges and universities since 1945. In J. Swaffar & P. Urlaub (Eds.), *Transforming postsecondary foreign language teaching in the United States* (pp. 19–54). Dordrecht: Springer.

Valdés, G. (2000). The teaching of heritage languages: An introduction for Slavic-teaching professionals. In O. Kagan & B. Rifkin (Eds.), *The learning and teaching of Slavic languages and cultures* (pp. 375–403). Bloomington, IN: Slavica.

White, K. (2016). Student perspectives on communities-oriented goals. *Foreign Language Annals, 49*(1), 124–45.

PART III

◇◇◇◇

APPROACHES TO TEACHING RUSSIAN

7

THE SHIFTING PARADIGM IN RUSSIAN LANGUAGE PEDAGOGY

From Communicative Language Teaching to Transformative Language Learning and Teaching

Betty Lou Leaver and Christine Campbell

Directors and teachers of language courses within the US government, in Flagship programs (Davidson, 2015; Murphy & Evans-Romaine, 2016), and at some universities are encountering the need to explore new pedagogical models as they seek to help learners achieve near-native levels of proficiency (Coalition of Distinguished Language Centers, 2006).[1] Communicative language teaching (CLT) has successfully moved learners and teachers from classroom activities based on memorization of words, rules, and dialogues to those based on tasks, projects, role-plays, and the use of authentic materials (Savignon, 1983). However, language professionals striving for the highest levels of output—and in a growing number of cases, achieving it—posit that the field must now look beyond CLT to facilitate more effective and meaningful learning, one that requires a new philosophy of education. The educational philosophy proposed in this chapter—transformative language learning and teaching (TLLT)—places personal transformation into a linguistically and biculturally competent language user and learner autonomy at the center of the language learning experience. TLLT encourages learners to "transcend the linguistic and sociolinguistic aspects of language . . . and puts them in control of information flow, of idea exchange, of negotiation, and of any other communicative function . . . [allowing the subordination of] linguistic performance to social performance and sociolinguistic knowledge to psycholinguistic [skill]" (Leaver, cited in Shekhtman, 2016a, p. iv).

Research and experience in language learning, especially in learning Russian, have informed TLLT. Bringing learners to near-native proficiency in Russian has been of interest to government agencies and some universities for decades. Materials for teaching at this level, for example, appeared as early as the mid-1980s, earlier than for other languages. In commonly taught languages such as Spanish and French, achieving near-native proficiency has become an area of research only more recently because of the growing number of learners who, due to in-country immersion experiences and improved teaching, are moving beyond proficiency levels ILR Level 3 or ACTFL Superior. The Language Flagship Program incorporates into its courses in-country immersion internships lasting up to one year, which have evolved from an early emphasis on ILR Level 3 to an understanding of the need to educate for ILR Level 4 in order to achieve professional levels of competence for US national security and economic competitiveness (Murphy & Evans-Romaine, 2016).

During the last decade of the Cold War two facts combined to make the development of courses at high levels of Russian proficiency possible: (1) fewer study abroad opportunities (and a complete lack of them for US government students) pushed learners with high-level proficiency needs into US classrooms for language learning, which compelled their teachers to develop more challenging courses, and (2) the large immigration of well-educated, highly articulate native speakers (WEHANS) from the USSR to the United States, who made possible the establishment of high-level proficiency programs in government organizations and academic institutions. The WEHANS also established the need for American graduate students who aspired to become professors of Russian to develop near-native proficiency in order to compete with the WEHANS for the relatively few academic jobs available.

For the past decade the Defense Language Institute Foreign Language Center (DLIFLC) has produced graduates at ILR Level 4 in Russian and other languages in increasing numbers in its Intermediate and Advanced Courses. Undoubtedly the use of TLLT, with its focus on personal transformation into a linguistically and biculturally competent language user and learner autonomy, has contributed to this increase in proficiency scores. Here we examine TLLT within the context of higher-level language courses at the DLIFLC. First we examine the philosophical roots of TLLT in general education and then the development of TLLT. Finally, we review TLLT as it is practiced in the Intermediate and Advanced courses at the DLIFLC.

THE PHILOSOPHICAL ROOTS OF TRANSFORMATIVE LANGUAGE LEARNING AND TEACHING

The roots of TLLT lie in the general education dialogue of the past 50 years over humanistic approaches to pedagogy, wherein the teacher is viewed as a facilitator of learning (Rogers, 1986; Rogers et al., 2013). Rogers (1986) views learning as a self-regulated, self-motivated adventure that can and should be facilitated by a mentor (teacher). Learner autonomy, a term coined by language educator Henry Holec (1991) to mean a learner taking responsibility for his or her own learning, is a requirement for Rogerian programs such as the Intermediate and Advanced courses at the DLIFLC. The teacher's role shifts from that of facilitator, who, as the principal purveyor of content, retains a considerable amount of control over the learner in the learning space, to mentor/coach/advisor, who consistently develops and supports learner autonomy by encouraging learner research about and delivery of content (Leaver & Granoein, 2000). In addition to Rogerian philosophy, TLLT also draws from: the concept of andragogy based on principles of adult learning (Knowles, 1986); experimentalism/

instrumentalism centered on human change (Dewey, 1997); critical pedagogy (Ellsworth, 1989; Freire, [1968] 1998); socioconstructivist learning philosophies (Vygotsky, [1978] 2013; in L2 specifically, Byrnes, 2009);[2] distributed cognition (Hutchins, 1991); and integrative models of learning (Engeström, 1987; Nonaka & Takeuchi, 1995; Wenger, 1998; Wenger et al., 2002; Bereiter, 2002).

Learning contracts described by Knowles incorporate an important feature of Rogers' philosophy of personal development (Knowles, 1986). In Knowles's proposal an andragogic way of organizing a course directs learners to sign (and fulfill) contracts for the work they will be doing, creating a classroom and program that is self-directed. The contracts require that learners, with teacher coaching, diagnose their learning needs, specify their learning objectives, indicate learning resources and strategies, posit evidence of accomplishment, explain how the evidence will be validated, review the contract with others (e.g., peers), and evaluate their own learning to fulfill the contract.

In the 1930s Dewey (1997), a social and educational reformer, focused on experimentalism (or instrumentalism) in human experience and applied it to learning. He asserted that learning is most quickly and most deeply acquired and internalized through personal change—a notion that Knowles might contend is readily replicated through learning contracts—and he set up the conditions for such change in his classrooms. Similarly, Freire ([1986] 1998) focused on the individual nature of learning and the role of personal experience in it. Successful learning results from constructing learning activities that include the learner's personal experiences, which become learning opportunities when they are carefully chosen and supported by reflection, critical analysis, and synthesis. When using TLLT the teacher assists in the selection of the appropriate experiences and guides the reflection and analysis through questioning and suggesting. For both Freire and Dewey, learning is ultimately empowerment.

Vygotsky ([1978] 2013) also viewed learning as idiosyncratic but occurring within a social framework. In "Interaction between Learning and Development" Vygotsky explored how cognition can develop through social interaction, affirming that learners can acquire skills and strategies through cooperative learning activities that allow the less skilled to learn from the more skilled. He describes the zone of proximal development (ZPD), or "the distance between the actual developmental level as determined by independent problem solving and the level of potential development as determined through problem solving under adult guidance, or in collaboration with more capable peers" (p. 86). Learners, then, learn most easily when they are ready socially and psychologically, i.e., when they are in the ZPD.

Teachers or knowledgeable peers can help learners further develop their abilities through scaffolding, a concept dating from the 1980s by which teachers provide support during the learning process that is tailored to meet the specific needs of the learner's goals, whether they have been set by the program or through a learning contract (Sawyer, 2006). The types of support that teachers provide include resources, compelling tasks (although learners can also pose tasks), templates, and guidance in the development of cognitive and social skills. The support can take the form of task modeling or coaching. While teachers initially provide support, their role lessens as learners gain the strategies and skills to become completely autonomous (Beed et al., 1991).

As learners gain greater proficiency in a subject such as a language, scaffolding also takes into account the growing development of increasingly larger bodies of schemata, a term originally used in the field of philosophy and introduced by Immanuel Kant in 1781 (1999 ed.) to refer to bodies of knowledge organized into conceptual categories and relationships. Schema theory (Head, 1920; expanded by Piaget, 1960) asks teachers to build on the learner's current schemata when introducing new concepts and knowledge. To activate learners' schemata, teachers can either provide carefully chosen, level-appropriate authentic materials or guide learners in the selection of such materials.

When working with authentic materials, teachers should keep in mind the interplay of three categories of schema: content-based, cultural, and linguistic (morphological, lexical, and suprasegmental). When reading a text or listening to a passage, learners should be able to handle the text with some prereading or prelistening work that focuses on the missing schemata, if they have at their disposal schemata belonging to two of the three categories. If two or more categories have not yet been acquired, the reading text or listening passage is likely to be frustrating for learners and not result in effective, or at least efficient, learning.

Hutchins (1991) examines the notion of distributed cognition, and Lave and Wenger (1991) investigate the social construction of knowledge through negotiation of meaning in communities of practice. Distributed cognition proposes that reasoning, knowledge, and expertise are not only the property of individual minds; they are distributed among individuals and across environments as external symbolic representations, tools, and artifacts (Pea, 1993). A community of practice provides learners with the opportunity to be or to become transformed into cultural-historical participants in the world (Lave & Wenger, 1991).

Informed by the research above, Gunawardena et al. (2006) propose an instructional design model for building online wisdom communities (WisCom) that are rooted in socioconstructivist and sociocultural learning philosophies and distance education principles. Describing the application and evaluation of the model in an online graduate course in the United States, they state that "the WisCom model aims to facilitate transformational learning by fostering the development of a wisdom community, knowledge innovation, and mentoring and learner support in an online learning environment, based on a 'Cycle of Inquiry' module design, and a 'Spiral of Inquiry' program design" (p. 217). The wisdom community is a learning community engaged in the collaborative construction of knowledge.

Integrative models of learning such as Engeström's expansive learning model (1987), Nonaka and Takeuchi's model of knowledge creation (1995), Wenger's communities of practice (1998; see also Wenger et al., 2002), and Bereiter's theory of knowledge building (2002) share a common premise: learning must be integrated with a systemic reconstruction of the social context(s) in which the learners operate and must be applied to solve problems in the local, regional, national, and global contexts, i.e., the community in which learners find themselves.

THE DEVELOPMENT OF TRANSFORMATIVE LANGUAGE LEARNING AND TEACHING

In today's postmethod era, first announced by Kumaravadivelu (2003), teachers create their own theories of practice, typically based on their knowledge and experience and guided by principles, or macrostrategies, such as maximizing learning opportunities, facilitating negotiated interaction, promoting learner autonomy, contextualizing linguistic input, and integrating language skills. Theorists and practitioners continue to recognize the critical importance of promoting learner autonomy, a concept that emerged in the 1980s as part of the dialogue on learner-centered instruction (Nunan, 1988, 1997a, 1997b, 2004, 2006) and individual learner differences (Oxford, 1990; Ehrman et al., 2003; Dörnyei, 2005). More recently Nunan and Richards (2015) have further explored learner autonomy through a series of language learning case studies beyond the classroom, or "out-of-class learning" (p. xi). Below are some of the themes they detect across the case studies:

- Out-of-class activities provide opportunity to address some of the limitations of classroom-based learning.
- The wide-ranging benefits out-of-class opportunities provide encompass the development of language and communication skills, improvements in confidence and motivation, personal growth, and intercultural awareness.
- Out-of-class learning provides authentic language experiences and opportunities for real communication.
- There is a need to integrate classroom-based learning with out-of-classroom learning since they support each other. (p. xv)

The international dialogue around learner autonomy, a deeper understanding of Freire's and Dewey's assertions that learning is, ultimately, empowerment, and a review of the literature on transformative education have led to the conceptualization of TLLT. Instruction is understood as an immersion experience in the learning space, whether face-to-face, blended, or entirely online, where learners use unadapted authentic materials and communicate in authentic language from the first day of class. Instruction includes elements of a variety of instructional approaches—task-based (Nunan, 2006), content-based (Leaver & Bilstein, 2000; Stryker & Leaver, 1997), and learner-centered (Nunan, 2004)—but expands on them in a context informed by the World-Readiness Standards (2019): the teacher plays the role of mentor, coach, and advisor; contracts are established between individual learners and teacher and/or among individual learners, teacher, and peers that delineate objectives, materials, performance expectations, and means of assessing performance; and emphasis is on teaching and learning versus testing.

The negotiated curriculum (Nunan, 1988, 1997a, 2004, 2006) is a flexible framework, unlike a static, dense textbook. The curricular framework, which includes a syllabus, is based on an open architecture design where components (i.e., materials, activities, tasks) are easily added, upgraded, or swapped in and out. The design promotes flexibility and creativity. While textbooks are used at the lowest levels (0+ and 1) to build a solid foundation in grammatical structures and lexicon, they are generally discarded in favor of a negotiated framework once learners function at level 1+.

Assessments are both formative and summative, but all are diagnostic and educative because they provide key information on learner strengths and weaknesses for both learner and teacher to incorporate into their work. The teacher uses assessment information for lesson planning; learners apply assessment information to their individual learning plans (Leaver, 2003). Diagnostic assessments conducted by a knowledgeable teacher contain information about skill level, learning profile (cognitive style, personality type, sensory preference), areas of excellence, and areas for improvement (Cohen, 2003). Equipped with this information, learners can adjust their learning styles and apply appropriate language learning strategies to improve their performance. Some examples of the assessments used are portfolios, with multiple samples of learner performance over time such as short- and long-term projects; learner delivery of both course content and presentations on select topics, debates, skits, etc.; diagnostic assessment; and recall protocol.

The generally accepted features of TLLT (Leaver, Davidson, & Campbell, in press) incorporate

- ◇ Materials and daily communications that are authentic and not adapted;
- ◇ A classroom environment, both local and in-country (study abroad), that is a total immersion experience, where the target language is used exclusively;
- ◇ Communicative competence and intercultural competence that are acquired more effectively as a result of personal change—as language and culture are acquired at increasingly higher levels of proficiency, an accompanying progressive internal transformation occurs that blends the two cultures and the language as reflective of the culture;
- ◇ Open architecture curricular design (Leaver, 2008) that is supported by syllabi and lesson plans at the Intermediate and Advanced levels and generally does not include textbooks; rather it is guided by textbooks at the lowest levels. The open architecture allows for inclusion of current events, topics, and national and international subjects and is adapted to learner needs, styles, strategies, levels of fossilization, interests, and ZPDs;
- ◇ A grading system that focuses on formative and summative assessments such as portfolios, short- and long-term projects, presentations, and contracts that integrate outcome and process (rather than treating them as separate and distinct);

- Teachers, activities, and program goals that empower learners to take charge of their own learning; and
- A program design that empowers teachers to take charge of their own classrooms as mentors/coaches/advisors, planners, and strategists (Leaver & Campbell, 2015).

TLLT moves teachers and learners beyond the transmissive or transactive educational philosophies depicted in Table 7.1. In the transmissive classroom (Bloom, 1968, 1981), learning goes in one direction: from teacher to learner or from learning materials to learner. The learner's job is to take in what is given and to give it back when required. Teachers and programs emphasize rote memorization and exercises are intended to develop habituated responses regardless of whether or not the learner fully understands those responses. An example would be the use of translation, when the learner does not understand the meaning of a particular word (because it is not part of the student's L1 literacy) but is nonetheless able to translate it correctly. One illustration of this problem could be the Russian word тягач [prime mover], which puzzled DLIFLC learners in the 1970s courses; many never understood the meaning of either the Russian word or the English equivalent but always got the answer right. The grammar-translation method of teaching and learning at that time had its flaws.

In the transactive classroom the emphasis is on action, reaction, and interaction (Dewey, 1997; Freire, [1968] 1998). Typically, the transactive classroom offers or

TABLE 7.1. Comparison of Educational Philosophies

Educational Philosophy	Transmission	Transaction	Transformation
Theory	Mastery learning (Bloom)	Experiential learning (Dewey; Freire)	Humanistic learning (Rogers)
Classwork	exercises, memorization	tasks, projects	self-directed study, contracts
Homework	written work	projects	research
Teacher	knower	facilitator	advisor/mentor/coach
Assessment	achievement	summative (proficiency and performance)	formative, occasional summative (proficiency and performance)
Syllabus	form-based	task-based, content-based, notional-functional	contracts, open architecture, learner-centered forms of content- and task-based instruction

Source: Adapted from Leaver & Granoein (2000).

features task-based instruction, but other kinds of approaches also can be classified as at least informed by the transactive philosophy. Content-based courses, for example, which are increasingly popular in programs aiming for higher levels of proficiency, can have a syllabus format that is transmissive, transactive, or transformative, depending upon how content-based instruction is implemented in the classroom. In today's language classrooms, content-based instruction is most typically combined with task-based instruction.

Transformative classrooms build upon the work of Rogers (1968; Rogers et al., 2013) and the humanistic movement in general education, both of which seek to transform the learner, in this case a speaker of English with a background in American culture, into an autonomous language user who displays growing bilingual and bicultural competence and who coconstructs knowledge as the result of working in communities of practice that draw from his or her own experiences. TLLT involves classroom activities that differ from precommunicative transmission exercises, such as substitution drills, and expands on transactional tasks, such as role-playing, that are typical of CLT. Some aspects of TLLT used by teachers of the Intermediate, Advanced, and Defense Threat Reduction Agency (DTRA) courses at DLIFLC include

- scenario-based learning;
- learner responsibility for design and delivery of content;
- promotion of higher-order thinking skills through the flipped classroom design;
- use of authentic materials;
- use of formative and summative assessments that are diagnostic and educative (e.g., portfolios, diagnostic assessment, and recall protocols);
- promotion of collaborative learning through group presentations and projects based on learners' research;
- use of a wider variety of listening and reading genres across the full spectrum of social media platforms (e.g., wikis, blogs, etc.) (Millar, 2011);
- systematic defossilization activities;
- focus on stylistics;
- focus on discourse analysis;
- use of colloquial language;
- integration of nonstandard language; and
- top-down and bottom-up processing of high-level presentations by guest speakers on topics such as politics, economics, and history.

Activities are individualized to maximize learners' strengths, target their ZPD, and, at more advanced levels, defossilize bad habits, including teacher dependence, comfort zone affinity, and inaccurate use of grammar and vocabulary. Learners of all levels, but especially ILR Level 1+ and above, participate in the design, development, and execution of the curriculum through projects, presentations, tutoring, contract learning, and learner-fronted teaching.

However, learner autonomy and learner participation in the shaping of the language program does not relieve teachers of their responsibility to ensure the continued, rapid, accurate, and comprehensive development of communication skills. The teacher can supplement content to help learners with recall and remembering, internalization of communicative structures, and development of the skills needed to engage in naturally occurring sociolinguistically and culturally appropriate interactions. Through dynamic practice in real-life contexts, teachers continually promote automatization of language use so that learners do not fixate on how they are going to say something; rather, they focus on what they are going to say and to whom, manipulating both content and register.

TRANSFORMATIVE LANGUAGE LEARNING AND TEACHING IN SPECIALIZED RUSSIAN PROGRAMS AT THE DLIFLC

The DLIFLC conducts rigorous full-time resident language and continuing education programs in 65 languages. About one-third of the programs are held at the Presidio of Monterey and the remainder at about 25 other sites, such as at language training detachments in the United States and some other countries or at DLI-Washington; these courses are for learners at both the beginning and higher levels of proficiency. The DLIFLC also provides nonresident, postbasic course instruction at the Intermediate and Advanced levels of language proficiency, which include courses taught at language training detachments. Enrollment is rolling and classes start weekly to meet mission needs.

In 2011 the DLIFLC earned the Council for Higher Education Accreditation Award for excellence in learning outcomes, and in 2016 received the Nikolai N. Khaladjan International Award for Innovation in Higher Education from the American Association of University Administrators. Its innovative work has wide potential for application or impact on the international dimensions of postsecondary education, in this case, TLLT.

DLIFLC learners have continuous access to learning through online tools and the learning management system Sakai. Teachers use TLLT, expanding on task-based, content-based, and learner-centered approaches. Instruction is provided through teams of four to six teachers: one is a team leader, whose main tasks are to develop the weekly schedule and mentor other team members. All team members share responsibility for creating materials and adapting them according to learners' needs. The team-teaching model provides learners with exposure to a variety of teaching styles and dialects and pronunciation differences in the target language.

Accountability within the team-teaching model is ensured through several means. The capstone test is the standardized Defense Language Proficiency Test (DLPT), an exit assessment all learners take in order to graduate. In addition, teachers conduct weekly 20- to 30-minute sensing sessions during which learners are asked to comment on which aspects of the course are facilitating their learning and which are not. Monthly sensing sessions with department chairs, interim student questionnaires, and end-of-course student questionnaires allow learners to evaluate the program, the materials, and the teachers.

Specialized Russian Programs

To help learners reach the higher levels of language proficiency required to ensure the future geopolitical security of the United States, the DLIFLC has embarked on a seven-year curricular restructuring that, with the help of TLLT features, is designed to significantly improve learner outcomes. The goal of the restructuring is to increase by 30% to 80% the number of graduating students reaching Level 2+ in reading comprehension (RC) and Level 2+ in listening comprehension (LC). Although the DLIFLC is officially using TLLT, a small number of teachers still focus on transmission and a considerable number practice transaction. To assist teachers with the transition to TLLT, the DLIFLC, with the support of the Defense Language National Security Education Office, has developed Advanced Language Academies. The academies, which are open to other US government language schools and Foreign Language Flagship Programs, allow academic leaders, academic specialists, faculty trainers, and faculty to have the opportunity to discuss the theory and practice of TLLT. To further support less experienced teachers, seasoned faculty share best practices through demonstration classes, presentations, and consulting sessions following the collaborative approach to faculty development promoted by Leaver and Oxford (2005).

Learners, too, are developing a new approach to language study. One aid they receive at the time of this writing is a weekly missive from the provost, "Tips for Tuesday," that sets forth suggestions for improving their learning performance, including information about how to enhance memory; how to apply language learning strategies like risk-taking, circumlocution, and the use of context clues; how to monitor their own performance; and how to address their personality and learning style needs. Learners are also regularly encouraged to be mindful of their physiological needs, such as exercise, sleep, and healthy eating.

There are three specialized Russian programs at the DLIFLC, taught by 17 native or near-native speakers: Intermediate Course; Advanced Course; and the Defense Threat Reduction Agency (DTRA) Interpreting Course, for learners who will be responsible for weapons control work in Russia. The graduation requirements for the Intermediate Course are Level 2+ in LC and Level 2+ in RC, with a goal, not a requirement, of Level 2 in speaking. The graduation requirements for the Advanced Course and DTRA are Level 3 in LC and Level 3 in RC, with a goal, not a requirement, of Level 2 in speaking.

The American Council on Education (ACE) reviewed the courses and awarded 18 upper-division college credit hours for the Intermediate Course and 15 upper-division college credit hours for the Advanced Course. The DLIFLC has petitioned ACE to examine the DTRA courses to determine whether they merit college credit hours. Below is the credit breakdown by course:

Intermediate Courses (3 credit hours):

- Listening Comprehension Skills
- Reading Comprehension Skills
- Communicative Skills
- Intermediate-Level Grammar and Discourse Analysis
- History and Area Studies
- Military, Science, and Technology

Advanced Courses (3 credit hours):

- Russian Conversation
- Russian Civilization
- Advanced Russian
- Russian Media Language
- Russian Current Events

A grammar course taught at either the Intermediate or the Advanced level earns 2 credit hours.

When creating the curriculum, teachers use an open architecture curricular design that includes theme-based syllabi covering 24 general topic areas such as history, economics, political science, technology, and health, and specific topic areas such as trends in foreign policy. Teachers create daily assignments based on the latest authentic materials for learners to preview before class, following the flipped classroom approach. During class teachers challenge learners to engage in activities that encourage higher-order thinking skills, such as weekly roundtable discussions on a topic chosen by learners. One of the learners acts as moderator and organizes the discussion by preparing three to four thought-provoking questions. Before the discussion learners research the topic so they can actively participate. Aside from the roundtable discussions, learners also make frequent 10 to 15-minute presentations on topics they have researched. The presentations are followed by elaboration activities such as debates. Teachers direct learners to relevant websites, provide higher-level, register-appropriate expressions and connectors, and review learners' work before it is presented. To develop greater accuracy in the target language, learners attend required grammar sessions and individualized speaking sessions with teachers, where they review the fossilized errors detected by teachers during the activities.

In the DTRA course learners take interpreting excursions to local sites, such as the Naval Postgraduate School Laboratories, Monterey Bay Aquarium, Monterey airport, and other locations, where they engage in simultaneous interpreting activities. One learner gives a detailed briefing to classmates in Russian while another interprets into English (and vice versa). Both briefers and the audience are expected to ask questions so the experience is interactive. Due to the positive feedback from learners and notable improvement in learner performance, in 2015 the DTRA program doubled the number of interpreting excursions from eight to 16.

In addition to these tours, the DTRA learners engage in negotiation scenarios, where they spend two hours immersed in a variety of contexts; for example, the purchase of commercial real estate in Russia. Learners receive critiques on their performance from both teachers and peers. Learners also listen to guest speakers on a weekly basis, interpreting the guests' speeches for a large audience, gradually moving from shorter excerpts to longer ones.

To help learners develop greater register range, DTRA teachers are continually designing and preparing materials for new courses such as stylistics, which focuses on the study of the distinctive styles found in various literary and nonliterary genres and in the works of individual writers.

Through all of these activities the Russian faculty at the DLIFLC, in their role of language mentor/coach/advisor, support learners as they strive for ILR Level 3+ and Level 4 in the target language.

CONCLUSION

The teacher in today's global, fast-paced, information-rich, technology-based society is called to be both a "learning counselor/concierge and curator of content" (Bonk & Koo, 2014, p. 283) and, ultimately, a catalyst of transformations, whether individual, institutional, or social. As active participants in the construction of knowledge, teachers mediate the creation of learning, or "wisdom" (Gunawardena et al., 2006, p. 217), in both online and traditional face-to-face learning spaces. TLLT, with its emphasis on personal transformation into a linguistically and biculturally competent language user and learner autonomy, challenges teachers to move beyond transmissive and transactive educational philosophies and related pedagogies and requires learners take more responsibility for their learning as they engage in opportunities to construct knowledge.

TLLT serves the beginning language learner well in a postmodern era that emphasizes the personal nature of language. At the higher levels of language study, particularly programs that want to achieve near-native proficiency, TLLT as an educational philosophy is proving itself to spawn models that can take learners to proficiency levels where few have gone before.

NOTES

1. Here near-native proficiency is defined as Interagency Language Roundtable (ILR) Level 4 or American Council on the Teaching of Foreign Languages (ACTFL) Distinguished level (Brecht et al., 2005; Leaver & Shekhtman, 2002; Shekhtman, 2016b). The ILR Language Skill Level Descriptions, which delineate levels of proficiency using a scale of 0 through 5, informed the development of the ACTFL Proficiency Guidelines scale from Novice Low through Distinguished. See www.govtilr.org and www.actfl.org/publications/guidelines-and-manuals/actfl for more information.
2. While Byrnes (2002) combines the work of Halliday (1994) (systemic functional linguistics) and Vygotsky ([1978] 2013) and makes the development of advanced levels of foreign

language proficiency a central tenet, Leaver and Shekhtman (2002) do not agree that Halliday's propositions make a measurable difference in the acquisition of the highest levels of proficiency. In Leaver's experience with routine graduation of students at ILR Levels 3, 3+, and 4 (ACTFL Superior and Distinguished), the acquisition of grammatical accuracy, just like many other features of L2, is dependent upon meeting individual learning needs and not upon conceptualizations of grammar or lexica.

REFERENCES

American Council on the Teaching of Foreign Languages (ACFTL). (2012). ACTFL Proficiency Guidelines 2012. Retrieved from http://www.actfl.org/publications/guidelines-and-manuals/actfl-proficiency-guidelines-2012

Beed, P., Hawkins, M., & Roller, C. (1991). Moving learners towards independence: The power of scaffolded instruction. *The Reading Teacher, 44*(9), 648–55.

Bereiter, C. (2002). *Education and mind in the knowledge age.* Mahwah, NJ: Lawrence Erlbaum.

Bloom, B. S. (1968). Learning for mastery. *Evaluation comment* 1(2). Retrieved from http://programs.honolulu.hawaii.edu/intranet/sites/programs.honolulu.hawaii.edu.intranet/files/upstf-student-success-bloom-1968.pdf

Bloom, B. S. (1981). *All our children learning: A primer for parents, teachers, and other educators.* New York: McGraw-Hill.

Bonk, C. J., & Koo. E. (2014). *Adding some TEC-VARIETY: 100 activities for motivating and retaining learners online.* Bloomington, IN: Open World.

Brecht, R. D., Leaver, B. L., Lekic, M. D., & Shekhtman, B. S. (2005). Essays about high-level language learning and teaching. *Journal for Distinguished Language Studies, 3*, 63–78.

Byrnes, H. (2002). Toward academic level foreign language abilities: Reconsidering foundational assumptions, expanding pedagogical options. In B. L. Leaver & B. S. Shekhtman (Eds.), *Developing professional-level language proficiency* (pp. 34–58). Cambridge: Cambridge UP.

Byrnes, H. (2009). *Advanced language learning: The contribution of Halliday and Vygotsky.* New York: Bloomsbury Academic.

Coalition of Distinguished Language Centers. (2006). *What works: Helping students reach native-like second language competence.* Salinas, CA: MSI.

Cohen, B. (2003). *Diagnostic assessment at the Superior/Distinguished threshold.* Salinas, CA: MSI.

Davidson, D. E. (2015). The development of L2 proficiency and literacy within the context of the federally supported overseas language training programs for Americans. In T. Brown & J. Bown (Eds.), *To advanced proficiency and beyond* (pp. 117–50). Washington, DC: Georgetown UP.

Dewey, J. (1997). *Experience and education.* New York: Free Press.

Dörnyei, Z. (2005). *The psychology of the language learner: Individual differences in second language acquisition.* Mahwah, NJ: Lawrence Erlbaum.

Ehrman, M., Leaver, B. L., & Oxford, R. (2003). A brief overview of individual differences in second language learning. *System, 31*(3), 314–42.

Ellsworth, E. (1989). Why doesn't this feel empowering? Working through the repressive myths of critical pedagogy. *Harvard Educational Review, 59*(3), 297–324.

Engeström, Y. (1987). *Learning by expanding.* Helsinki: Orienta-Konsultit.

Freire, P. ([1968] 1998). *The pedagogy of the oppressed.* (M. B. Ramos, Trans.). New York: Continuum.

Gunawardena, C., Ortegano-Layne, L., Carabajal, K., Frechette, C., Lindemann, K., & Jennings, B. (2006). New model, new strategies: Instructional design for building online wisdom communities. *Distance Education, 27*(2), 217–32.

Halliday, M. A. K. (1994). *Introduction to functional grammar* (2nd ed.). London: Edward Arnold.

Head, H. (1920). *Studies in neurology.* London: Hodder & Stoughton.

Holec, H. (1991). *Autonomy and foreign language learning.* Oxford, UK: Pergamon.

Hutchins, E. (1991). The social organization of distributed cognition. In L. B. Resnick, J. M. Levine, & S. D. Teasley (Eds.), *Perspectives on socially shared cognition* (pp. 283–306). Pittsburgh: American Psychological Association.

Interagency Language Roundtable Level Descriptions. (2016). *History of the ILR Scale: Introduction.* Retrieved from http://www.govtilr.org/

Kant, I. ([1781] 1999). *Critique of Pure Reason* (P. Guyer & A. W. Wood, Trans. and Eds.). Cambridge UP.

Knowles, M. S. (1986). *Using learning contracts.* San Francisco: Jossey-Bass.

Kumaravadivelu, B. (2003). *Beyond methods: Macrostrategies for language teaching.* New Haven, CT: Yale UP.

The Language Flagship. (2016). Languages and programs. Retrieved from https://www.thelanguageflagship.org/languagesandprograms

Lave, J., & Wenger, E. (Eds.). (1991). *Situated learning: Legitimate peripheral participation.* Cambridge: Cambridge UP.

Leaver, B. L. (2003). *Individualized study plans for very advanced students of foreign languages.* Salinas, CA: MSI.

Leaver, B. L. (2008). Dismantling classroom walls for increased foreign language proficiency. *Foreign Language Annals, 22*(1), 67–74.

Leaver, B. L., & Bilstein, P. (2000). Content, language, and task in content-based instruction. In R. Kecht & K. von Hammerstein (Eds.), *Languages across the curriculum: Interdisciplinary structures, intersections of knowledge, and internationalized education* (pp. 79–118). Columbus, OH: Ohio State UP.

Leaver, B. L., & Campbell, C. (2015). Experience with higher levels of proficiency. In T. Brown & J. Bown (Eds.), *To advanced proficiency and beyond* (pp. 3–22). Washington, DC: Georgetown UP.

Leaver, B. L., Davidson, Dan E., & Campbell, C. (In press). *Transformative language learning and teaching.* Cambridge, UK: Cambridge University Press.

Leaver, B. L., & Granoein, N. (2000). Философия образования: Почему мы преподаем определенными путями [Philosophy of education: Why we teach the way we do]. *Filosofiia obrazovaniia*, *1*(1), 3–9.

Leaver, B. L., & Oxford, R. (2005). Individual difference theory in faculty development: What faculty developers should know about style. *Russian Language Journal*, *55*, 73–127.

Leaver, B. L., & Shekhtman, B. (Eds.). (2002). *Developing professional-level language proficiency*. Cambridge: Cambridge UP.

Millar, D. (2011). Promoting genre awareness in the EFL classroom. *English Teaching Forum*, *2*, 1–14.

Murphy, D., & Evans-Romaine, K. (Eds.). (2016). *The U.S. Language Flagship Program: Professional competence in a second language by graduation*. Bristol, UK: Multilingual Matters.

National Standards Collaborative Board (NSCB). (2019). *World-readiness standards for learning languages* (4th ed.). Alexandria, VA: Author. Retrieved from https://www.actfl.org/sites/default/files/publications/standards/World-ReadinessStandardsforLearningLanguages.pdf

Nonaka, I., & Takeuchi, H. (1995). *The knowledge-creating company*. New York: Oxford UP.

Nunan, D. (1988). *The learner-centered curriculum: A study in second language teaching*. Cambridge: Cambridge UP.

Nunan, D. (1997a). Designing and adapting materials to encourage learner autonomy. In P. Benson & P. Voller (Eds.), *Autonomy and independence in language learning* (pp. 192–203). London: Longman.

Nunan, D. (1997b). Does learner strategy training make a difference? *Language Modernas*, *24*, 123–42.

Nunan, D. (2004). *Go for It! Level 1*. Boston: Thomson Heinle.

Nunan, D. (2006). *Task-based language teaching*. Cambridge: Cambridge UP.

Nunan, D., & Richards, J. (Eds.). (2015). *Language learning beyond the classroom*. New York: Routledge.

Oxford, R. (1990). Language learning strategies: What every teacher should know. New York: Newbury House.

Pea, R. D. (1993). Practices of distributed intelligence and design for education. In G. Salomon (Ed.), *Distributed cognition: Psychological and educational considerations* (pp. 47–86). Cambridge: Cambridge UP.

Piaget, J. (1960). *The psychology of intelligence*. Totowa, NJ: Littlefield Adams.

Rogers, C. (1986). *Freedom to learn: A view of what education might become* (2nd ed.). Indianapolis, IN: Merrill.

Rogers, C., Lyon, H., Jr., & Tausch, R. (2013). *On becoming an effective teacher: Person-centered teaching, psychology, philosophy, and dialogues with Carl R. Rogers and Harold Lyon*. London: Routledge.

Savignon, S. (1983). *Communicative competence: Theory and classroom practice*. Reading, MA: Addison-Wesley.

Sawyer, R. K. (2006). *The Cambridge handbook of the learning sciences*. Cambridge: Cambridge UP.

Shekhtman, B. S. (Ed.). (2016a). *How to use your Russian in communication effectively*. CreateSpace.

Shekhtman, B. S. (2016b). *Working with advanced foreign language students* (2nd ed.). Virginia Beach, VA: Villa Magna.

Stryker, S. B., & Leaver, B. L. (1997). *Content-based instruction: Models and methods*. Washington, DC: Georgetown UP.

Vygotsky, L. ([1978] 2013). Interaction between learning and development. In M. Cole, V. John-Steiner, S. Scribner, & E. Souberman (Eds.), *Mind and society: The development of higher psychological processes* (79–91). Cambridge, MA: Harvard UP.

Wenger, E. (1998). *Communities of practice: Learning, meaning, and identity*. Cambridge: Cambridge UP.

Wenger, E., McDermott, R., & Snyder, W. (2002). *Cultivating communities of practice*. Cambridge, MA: Harvard Business Review Press.

8
RECONCEPTUALIZING GRAMMAR INSTRUCTION
Making It Meaningful and Communicative

William J. Comer

The 1984 volume *Teaching, Learning, Acquiring Russian* (Lubensky & Jarvis, 1984) featured nine contributions that dealt specifically with teaching language structure in the classroom. Engaging a field whose classroom practice and textbooks were dominated by the grammar-translation and audiolingual methods, Jarvis (1984), Nakhimovsky (1984), Chvany (1984), and Chaput (1984) all argue for expanding classroom practices to embrace the development of learners' communicative competence. All four recommend models of grammar instruction that start with mechanical pattern drills and then move to communicative drills as a way to give learners an opportunity to use new grammatical structures to communicate meaningful personal information. With 30 years of hindsight, one can see in these four chapters the kernels of principles that have become part of the mainstream in second language acquisition (SLA) and methodology.

In contrast, the 2000 volume *The Learning and Teaching of Slavic Languages and Cultures* (Rifkin & Kagan, 2000) includes an array of interesting pedagogical topics but not a single chapter deals with grammar instruction. This, perhaps, is not so surprising. The proficiency revolution of the 1980s–1990s asked the field to measure and teach usable language skills in reading, listening, speaking, and writing. The microlevel questions of how language structure fits into teaching those skills and how to teach language structures overall took a back seat to those broader discussions.[1]

However, the change of instructional orientation toward proficiency did not simultaneously trigger a reconceptualization of grammar instruction, and the grammar practice activities of beginning-level, communicatively oriented textbooks published in the 1990s remained primarily mechanical and separated from meaning (Comer, 2012).[2] Since 2000 the discussions of grammar instruction for Russian that have appeared in professional journals (e.g., Leaver et al., 2004; Swan, 2014a, 2014b) emphasize the importance of formal accuracy for learners of Russian but have added little to either the theoretical or practical issues of how to organize grammar instruction.

My goal here is to review the models of grammar instruction offered by current SLA theories, to articulate a conceptual framework for the teaching and learning of Russian grammar, and to demonstrate an implementation of the framework by offering examples from a beginning-level communicative textbook.[3] Before undertaking those tasks, it is worth noting that a useful conceptual framework needs to accommodate the ecology of the American university classroom in the 21st century, which is characterized by active learning and learner-centeredness and prioritizes engaging learners in higher-order thinking skills (Anderson & Krathwohl, 2001). These attributes are often connected with the "flipped" classroom approach, which favors inductive learning and classroom activities that engage students in understanding and applying the material, in analyzing and evaluating the material for patterns, and in creating rules based on exemplars (Hung, 2015; Moffett, 2015; O'Flaherty & Phillips, 2015; Sahin et al., 2015).

PREVALENT THEORIES AND MODELS OF GRAMMAR INSTRUCTION

The past 40 years have witnessed wide-ranging discussions about the role and nature of grammar instruction. On the one hand, in the early 1980s Krashen (1982) and Terrell (1982) advocated a strong meaning-based pedagogy that both minimized the need for classroom-based instruction on language structure and questioned its effectiveness. On the other hand, some researchers countered with claims that instruction needed to balance attention to meaning *and* to form in order to help learners attain high levels of proficiency in a second language (Swain, 1985; Long, 1985; Doughty & Williams, 1998). Norris and Ortega (2000), in a meta-analysis of experimental and quasi-experimental studies of instructed second language learning conducted from 1980 to 1998, found an advantage for instructed language learning, noting specifically that explicit types of L2 instruction were more effective than implicit types and that the effectiveness of L2 instruction was durable.

Ortega (2007a) provides a useful overview of nine representative SLA theories and their relationship to L2 instruction. She characterizes seven of these theories as recognizing a beneficial effect of instruction on language acquisition (although in two of those theories these effects are limited). Of those seven theories, she finds that just three—skill theory, interactionist theory, and input-processing theory—give specific recommendations for instructional design.

The skill theory approach to second language learning draws on a large body of psychological research on learning that has spanned many decades and different conceptual approaches (DeKeyser, 2007a). Skill theory posits that learners take explicit knowledge of a language phenomenon and, through guided practice, convert it into procedural knowledge, which can then be practiced further so that the particular rule or form can be automatized (i.e., produced faster, more correctly, and with less effort). Skill theory has explicit recommendations for organizing instruction around cycles of explanation, deliberate practice, and feedback, although particular classroom procedures are unspecified (Ortega, 2007a).

Interactionist theory (Gass & Mackey, 2007; Pica, 2013) suggests organizing instruction around tasks and task-based language teaching (Long, 1985, 2015; Pica, 2005, 2009) that employ "focus-on-form" activities (Doughty & Williams, 1998). Ortega (2007a) notes that the interactionist approach "conceives of instruction as externally orchestrated opportunities to attend to relevant features of the target language in context, precisely when they are embedded unobtrusively in the task at hand, during meaningful comprehension and production activities" (p. 243). The approach embraces an array of implicit and explicit instructional techniques, such as recasts, prompts, notice-the-gap activities, and the like.

Input-processing theory (VanPatten & Cadierno, 1993; VanPatten, 2004, 2007) posits that learners are likely to use certain strategies (such as assigning the first noun of the sentence the role of agent, or relying on lexical cues rather than on grammatical forms) when trying to understand the meaning of a message in the target language. The theory states that when such strategies cause learners to misinterpret target language messages, learners can benefit from processing instruction in the classroom consisting of explicit information that seeks to change their strategies for processing the target structures. Explicit information and strategy instruction are followed by structured-input tasks that push learners to use new processing strategies while interpreting L2 messages and communicating in the L2. These are followed by meaning-based output (i.e., production) activities (Lee & VanPatten, 2003). The goal of instruction in input-processing theory is to alter how learners process or parse the input during meaning-based instruction by having them notice and correctly interpret how grammatical forms in the input contribute to meaning.

One additional influential construct for L2 grammar instruction is the presentation-attention-coconstruction-extension (PACE) model developed by Adair-Hauck and Donato (2010).[4] Extracting the best of inductive and deductive approaches, they emphasize a dialogic approach to grammar instruction that starts with the presentation of language input in the form of meaningful stories. After comprehension checks (accomplished through a variety of means), learners focus their attention on some aspect of language use present in the story. By exploring this language feature, learners, with the teacher's guidance, coconstruct a grammatical explanation for the language observed. In the extension phase learners have "the chance to use the target form in ways that they see as useful, meaningful, and connected to the overarching theme of the lesson" (p. 259). The relationship between teacher and learners in the PACE model is strongly influenced by Vygotskian sociocultural theory by which specific language forms for instruction rest in the teacher's estimate of the learners' zone of proximal development.

Despite the differences in these models of grammar instruction, one can still identify three common emphases: a focus on meaning, learner engagement, and the integration of grammar with other language skills. All the approaches described recognize that the language input needs to be meaningful, that is, purposeful for accomplishing some communicative task that is of relevance to the learner. They also all recognize that instruction needs to guide learners' comprehension of the input and to verify that learners do comprehend its meaning. Comprehension work encompasses a wide range of practices, from verifying referential meaning, implications, inferences, and cultural assumptions of reading and listening texts at the macro level to checking the connections of grammar forms with their meanings at the micro level.[5] Pedagogical practices across all these theoretical approaches actively engage learners in interacting with the target language input and in expressing personalized reactions and thoughts in the target language. Work on language forms is integrated with other language modalities (speaking, reading, writing, and listening) and is built into activities connected with them. Since grammatical form is understood as contributing to meaning in target language texts, form occupies a continuous place in language learning.

Some of the differences in these theoretical models concerning how learning takes place can be accounted for by the dual-mode model of language processing proposed by Skehan (1996). According to Skehan's model, learners have dual modes for processing the target language: one is rule-based and follows the model of explicit information, proceduralization, and growing automaticity; the other is exemplar-based, where exemplars can be words or much longer units of the target language that the learner can deploy fluently in accomplishing communicative tasks. The learner can move between the two processing modes depending on the demands of the communicative context. When fluency and speed are required, the exemplar-based processing is preferred; when precision is needed, the rule-based system can be accessed. Skehan goes on to note that items that learners produce via rule-based practice can be "relexicalized," that is, turned back into exemplars that are available for fluent deployment under the exemplar-based mode.

MULTIPLICITY OF FORM-MEANING MAPPINGS

Before sketching out some essential principles that Russian grammar instruction will need to address, it is worthwhile to consider what kinds of form-meaning mappings learners may need to make as they process input in the target language. Let us take as an example the sentence "У вас есть сонеты Шекспира?" [Do you have Shakespeare's sonnets?], pronounced with rising intonation on the word есть [there is]. At least six different kinds of form-meaning connections can be made here (see Table 8.1). There is a lexical level, where learners map the words or phrases to a basic semantic meaning; there is a grammar level, where learners map the inflectional morphology to its meaning (i.e., the ы of сонеты [sonnets] to plurality; the a of Шекспира [Shakespeare] to possession); there is a phonological level where the intonation contour needs to be mapped to the notion of question; there is a functional/notional level where learners map the sentence type to the idea of making an inquiry about an object; there is a socio-linguistic mapping of вас [you] to the generalized, plural, or polite "you"; and there is a contextual level, where learners need to map the sentence to the appropriate situation where it may be used.

While I have delineated six possible levels of form-meaning mappings in this example, I do not claim that these are the *only* mappings to consider, nor that learners

TABLE 8.1. Types of Form-Meaning Mapping for the Sentence: У вас есть сонеты Шекспира?

Lexical	• map words/phrases to basic referential meanings (у вас = by you; есть = there is; сонет = sonnet; Шекспир = Shakespeare)
Grammatical	• map the ы of сонеты to the idea of plural • map the a of Шекспира to the notion of genitive of possession (= 's)
Phonological	• map the rising intonation to a yes-no question
Functional/notional	• map the sentence type to the notion of inquiring whether someone has an item
Sociolinguistic	• map вас to a generalized, polite, or plural "you"
Contextual	• map question to a context where it can be used, i.e., in a library, in a discussion of literature, in an inquiry to a bookstore sales clerk

Note: The contextual interpretation is especially likely if the sentence is rendered graphically, as "У вас есть «Сонеты» Шекспира?"

need to map all six form-meanings at once, nor that there is a specific order in which learners need to make the mappings (although lexical form-meaning mapping would appear to be the most essential for extracting the message in any utterance). The point here is to recognize that these levels of form-meaning mappings will need to be made bit by bit as learners interact with language material over time.

In planning instruction teachers should be aware of the kinds of form-meaning mappings an activity will require of learners. While mechanical exercises do little to promote learners' work in making form-meaning connections on multiple levels, certain kinds of nonmechanical exercises, such as role-plays, personalized questions, and partner interviews with personalized questions, are problematic as well. For example, a typical activity in an elementary Russian class might be for students to ask each other personalized questions, such as, "У тебя есть брат или сестра?" [Do you have a brother or sister?]. While an instructor might choose this activity to practice a range of form-meaning mappings, a learner may need to make only a lexical mapping of form to meaning in order to comprehend and respond to this question. There is nothing in the activity format that seems likely to push learners to make the *grammatical* form-meaning connections involved in case morphology (i.e., nominative = presence; genitive = absence). Furthermore, when learners are tasked to ask each other personalized questions about objects they have (say, from among a list of items, including учебник [textbook], тетрадь [notebook], ручка [pen], etc.), instructors should not take for granted that learners are making the correct form-meaning connections even at the lexical level since, without visual cues, there is almost no way to verify that the learners understand the semantic meaning of the items in the questions they are voicing. Finally, in activities such as personalized questions there is little guarantee that a respondent's answer is accurate for his or her personal situation (e.g., is the initial question in the exchange "У тебя есть учебник?" about a specific textbook or about any textbook at all, or is it about the immediate presence of the textbook [i.e., "Do you have it with you?"]). There is no guarantee that the person posing the question needs to listen to the answer for its communicative value or its grammatical form. Open-ended personalized questions as an activity type are not reliable for helping learners establish multiple form-meaning mappings.[6]

The multiplicity of form-meaning mappings has further implications for instructional design: a single exercise is too small a unit of instruction to help learners make useful mappings. Long (1985) notes this problem and proposes the notion of "task" as a more convenient unit of instruction. A task, in pedagogical terms, is a piece of work that a learner produces that meets a specific communicative goal. A task may be narrowly constructed or it can be an extensive piece of work that might conclude a large unit of instruction. Tasks can be comprehension-focused or output-oriented, that is, designed to push language learners to produce in the target language. A large output-oriented task (e.g., writing an email to an online friend to describe campus living arrangements) might be the culminating activity to a series of smaller tasks by which learners build form-meaning mappings while also learning the names of furnishings, room/apartment/house features, the grammatical means of talking about possessions, how to describe the locations of items in space, and so on. Such a series of tasks might start with model texts (in written or oral format) that demonstrate how someone accomplishes the culminating task. These model texts can serve as language input for learners.

Comprehension activities can verify in a deliberate fashion whether learners are mapping lexical, grammatical, and other features of form in the input to their meanings. Noticing activities can draw learners' attention to the form-meaning connections inherent to specific grammar features and be accompanied by explanations (e.g., explicit descriptions of the language feature, explicit correction, or other feedback, like prompts). Structured-input activities can guide learners through communicative exchanges while at the same time building up their comprehension and control of multiple exemplars of sentences that might be used in accomplishing the culminating task (Farley, 2004). Information, opinion, and reasoning gap activities can help learners deploy these multiple exemplars in contextualized exchanges that have verifiable outcomes (Comer, 2007). Working through all of these subtasks prepares learners for the large concluding task; in the course of this work there are opportunities for negotiation of meaning between teacher and learners and among learners, and learners receive feedback in various forms (recasts, prompts, etc.).

PRINCIPLES FOR A NEW FRAMEWORK

In the remaining part of this chapter I outline six principles that can form an effective conceptual framework for teaching language structure and illustrate each of those points with sample activities in Russian (see Table 8.2). The new model prioritizes the

TABLE 8.2. Six Principles of a Conceptual Framework for Teaching Language Structure

1. The prerequisite for language learning is for learners to encounter input in the target language.
2. Learners need ample opportunities to demonstrate their comprehension of the input.
3. Lexicon and grammar are tightly interconnected; a continuum exists between learning words and learning word forms.
4. Grammar learning begins with comprehension-based activities wherein learners work on mapping grammatical forms to meanings.
5. Grammar learning continues as learners perform output-based communicative activities.
6. Explicit instruction may help learners map form to meaning more effectively and efficiently, particularly when it replaces learners' faulty strategies in mapping L2 forms to meanings.

importance of providing learners with multiple opportunities to: (1) work with language input, (2) complete comprehension-based activities related to the input, (3) learn new words and word forms featured in the input, (4) map grammatical forms to their meanings, (5) express themselves in meaningful output-based activities, and (6) access explicit information about language features. These opportunities allow learners to use both rule-based and exemplar-based processing modes in the context of task-based learning. To see how these priorities and principles can be implemented, examples are drawn from the initial presentation of the "have/have not" construction found in the elementary Russian language program *Mezhdu nami* (deBenedette et al., 2015).

Inputs: The Prerequisite for Language Learning

Broad consensus exists among SLA professionals that input plays a fundamental role in language learning. Without ample opportunity to encounter message-bearing discourse in the second language (at any level of organization, whether word, phrase, sentence, or paragraph), learners will not have the opportunity to learn how the target language communicates ideas and how to communicate ideas in the target language.

Input has been defined as "message-bearing," that is, expressing the totality of the speaker's intention, in contrast to "meaning-bearing," in order to distinguish the former from language forms arranged in traditional grammar tables. While the words in a traditional table that shows the forms of the genitive singular all have meaning (at both the lexical and grammatical levels) and they may be a useful reference, such forms do not bear a message and therefore do not fit the definition of language input.

Russian language textbooks published in the United States in the 1990s show a vast improvement over earlier texts in the amount and variety of language input they provide (Comer, 2012), and *Mezhdu nami* continues that practice. Learners encounter Russian through the ongoing story of four students studying in Russia (approximately

16,000 words in total). In the micro context of the "have/not have" construction, one dose of the language input consists of a 172-word dialogue provided to the students in written form, accompanied by audio recordings and visuals (see http://www.mezhdunami.org/unit04/4_2/index.shtml).

Opportunities to Demonstrate Comprehension of the Input

If learners need message-bearing discourse as the fuel for their language learning, then they also need to have opportunities to demonstrate that they have understood the message correctly and must receive feedback that corrects misinterpretations or guides them to the sense of the message.

As learners work on comprehending the message, they also start to process the input, building form-meaning mappings of various types (i.e., at the lexical level, grammatical level, etc.). For the 172-word dialogue that provides language input on the "have/not have" construction, *Mezhdu nami* provides seven comprehension activities that cover a first stage of comprehension, verifying the referential meaning of the text (http://www.mezhdunami.org/unit04/4_2/comprehension.shtml). The comprehension activities include written, visual, and audio stimuli; some are given in English, others are in Russian; some are completed online, others using print materials.

After these factual comprehension activities, learners move to the next stage of text comprehension activities that foreground the process of form-meaning mappings. Figure 8.1 gives a sample of this kind of activity. Learners restate the propositional content of the dialogue by replacing statements that include pronouns with the full name of the person(s) referenced by the pronoun. The sentences activate learners' knowledge of the text (i.e., there is only one correct answer in terms of statement content) and at the same time provide a context for learners to map the third-person pronoun forms in the genitive case to noun forms in the genitive case. It is precisely this counterbalancing of referential meaning (i.e., recalling from the story the specific person who has the item) and the focus on form (matching pronouns and nouns) that makes the activity not a mechanical drill but a task that engages form and meaning—of multiple kinds—at the same time.

By providing the names in the genitive case after the preposition у [by], the activity eliminates the need for students to produce new genitive noun endings in new syntactic contexts and instead helps them to concentrate on making form-meaning connections between pronoun and noun forms in the have/have not statements. By reading the sentences aloud while completing the activity, students are not "producing" these forms but they are building up their skills at assimilating the phonological contours of the words and the sentence pattern. Reading aloud provides something of a rehearsal space for learners as they process the language input. The sentences in this activity provide additional language input for learners, and in Skehan's dual-mode model of processing the sentences serve as exemplars that students can incorporate into their L2 repertoire.

4.2 Зада́ние 2. У кого́?

a. Working with a partner read the sentences below and decide to whom each sentence refers. Use the phrase bank to replace the **у** + pronoun construction in each sentence with a construction that uses a specific person's name. Pay attention to the gender and number of the pronouns as you make substitutions.

У Ама́нды	**У Ма́ши и Йры**	**У Ка́ти**
У Ле́ны	**У Оле́га**	**У Ама́нды и Мони́к**

1. У неё нет ча́йника.
   ____
2. У него́ есть стол.
   ____
3. У них есть ла́мпа.
   ____
4. У него́ нет ла́мпы.
   ____
5. У него́ нет холоди́льника.
   ____
6. У неё есть микроволно́вка.
   ____
7. У них есть микроволно́вка.
   ____
8. У них почти́ ничего́ нет.
   ____
9. У него́ есть крова́ть.
   ____
10. У неё есть холоди́льник.
   ____
11. У неё есть ча́йник.
   ____

FIGURE 8.1. Comprehension Activity with a Form-Mapping Element

After the initial focus on meaning, a brief follow-up activity draws learners' attention to forms that appear in the exercise (Figure 8.2). Learners are asked to spot the differences between the inflectional forms of items when they appear in "have" and "have not" sentences and then to fill in missing endings drawn from the sentences that they have just worked through. This noticing activity provides a moment in the lesson where a teacher may opt for an explicit discussion of the grammar of case usage (nominative for existence; genitive for absence) or of case morphology. This discussion can be teacher-fronted or an interactive coconstruction between the teacher and the learners to explain the forms. The discussion might provide an introduction of explicit information on this grammar topic or it might recap the explicit explanation that the students had previously read on the *Mezhdu nami* website pages called Немного о языке [A bit about the language].

If the teacher opts for minimal or no explicit discussion of grammar at this point, the exercise requires learners to notice that the forms in the have/have not sentences are different, making them aware that their English L1 assumption (that the direct object forms in have/have not sentences will be the same) is faulty. Second, the activity also drives home for learners that words belong to different gender/declension groups

6. The activity above featured both "**есть** forms" (i.e., the dictionary form, used to express "having") and "**нет** forms" (the genitive case form, used to express absence or "not having"). Use that information, fill in the missing endings, using ø if no additional ending is needed.

Есть	ча́йник____.	Нет	ча́йник____.
Есть	холоди́льник____.	Нет	холоди́льник____.
Есть	ла́мп____.	Нет	ла́мп____.

FIGURE 8.2. Activity to Draw Attention to Form

based on their nominative case forms. It allows students to map the form **чайник** [kettle—nom.s.] to the nominative case of the word rather than to think that the noun is feminine ***чайника** [kettle—gen.s.] whose genitive singular is ***чайники** [kettle—nom.pl.]. Finally, the activity helps learners accumulate exemplars of words and word forms and attend to the relationships between them.

Interconnectedness of Lexicon and Grammar

The previous example raises several important points about the interconnectedness of lexicon and grammar. First, to understand the have/have not construction, learners need to build up a repertoire of nouns for objects that might be among their possessions. Many recent textbooks for Russian (e.g., Robin et al., 2012; Kudyma et al., 2012), in concert with the additional language input, have expanded the number of thematic vocabulary items that learners encounter. In many texts, however, too few opportunities exist for learners to attend to the semantic meaning(s) of new words while encountering them in various inflectional forms.

A second significant but difficult question is how learners store in their mental lexicon words and word forms like **чайник, чайника, чайники** [kettle—nom.s., gen.s., nom.pl.]. Do **чайник, чайника, чайники** represent three words in the learner's mental lexicon that overlap in their core semantic value, or are they versions of a single base word? And is the same storage system used for a trio of forms like **дом-до́ма-домой** [home—at home—to home] (e.g., nouns with nonproductive endings) or for the homonyms **нет** [no] and **нет** [there is not]?

Vasileva (2014) surveys the large body of research on the organization of morphological forms in the mental lexicon and concludes that native speakers seem to be able to access words and word forms both as individually stored items and as decomposed forms (e.g., a base form to which derivational and inflectional endings are added). If this is true for native speakers, who have had considerable language input to build up their knowledge of acceptable words and word bases with acceptable endings to put on those bases, then one may hypothesize that learners at the very beginning of L2 study are likely to store each word/word form they encounter as separate entries in

4.2 Упражнéние B. Есть или нет?

Vera and Anton are forever contradicting each other, even when they talk about small matters. Sometimes Vera asserts that a friend of theirs has an item, while Anton is certain that the friend does not. At other times Vera is positive that their friend does not have the item they are discussing, but Anton is certain that the friend does.

1. Read the remarks below carefully. Then decide whether you need to put **есть** or **нет** in each blank. Pay careful attention to the endings on the nouns because genitive case endings indicate absence, while the nominative case endings (**словáрная фóрма**) indicate the existence of the object. That is the only way that you can tell whether the given sentence is about "having" or about "not having." You should assume that all nouns used are singular.

Вéра говори́т, что ...	**Антóн говори́т, что ...**
у Петрá Степáновича ________ смартфóн.	у Петрá Степáновича ________ смартфóна.
у Геóргия Влади́мировича ________ гаражá.	у Геóргия Влади́мировича ________ гарáж.
у Мари́ны Алексéевны ________ пылесóса.	у Мари́ны Алексéевны ________ пылесóс.
у Ли́дии Мáрковны ________ крéсло.	у Ли́дии Мáрковны ________ крéсла.

FIGURE 8.3. Activity to Draw Attention to the Meaningfulness of Grammatical Form

their mental lexicons. Only later may learners be able to abstract out the notion of a decomposed word base and the set of acceptable endings.[7]

One implication of these studies of the organization of the mental lexicon is that for teaching grammar in a foreign language context, beginners need much greater exposure to exemplars of the word forms of a lexical item in order to become proficient at using those forms. If beginners tend to hold чайник, чайника, and чайники as separate entries, then they need enough exposure to the forms to make sure that they have made three entries in their mental lexicon and they need activities to help them associate each entry with its grammatical meaning(s).

Developing activities where comprehension depends on mapping a grammatical form to its meaning is not always easy, since grammatical forms often create meaning in combination with lexical items that appear in a sentence. For example, in the construction "У Аманды нет чайника," learners can map the lexical items to their meanings (у Аманды = Amanda; нет = doesn't have; чайника = kettle), and access its message. In this sentence the lexical item нет [there is not] and the grammatical form чайника [kettle—gen.s.] cocontribute to the "doesn't have kettle" part of the message. It is difficult to get learners to notice or attend to the meaning contributed by the cooccurring grammatical form (i.e., -a at the end of чайника), since the lexical item [нет] is easier for learners to process while extracting the message of the sentence. Thus to draw attention to the meaningfulness of this grammatical form a teacher may need to set up contexts where the grammatical form makes a unique contribution to the message.

4.2 Зада́ние 3. Что у них есть? Чего́ у них нет?

a. You overhear Ol'ga and Igor' talking about their rooms, comparing what they have or do not have. Read the statements below and place a check mark in the appropriate column to indicate whether the speaker is Igor' (whose room is shown in карти́нка А), or Ol'ga (whose room is shown in карти́нка Б).

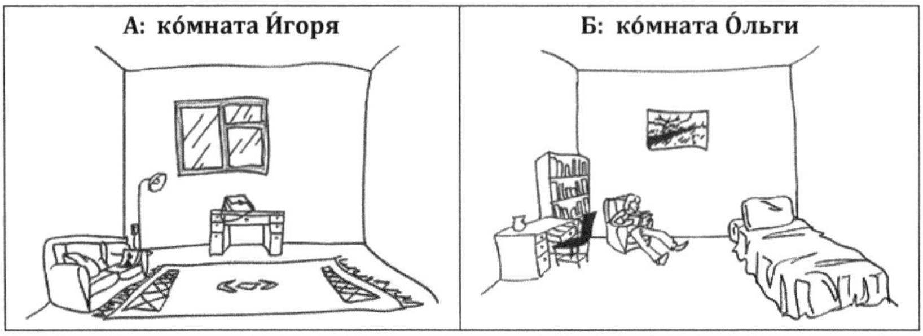

А: ко́мната И́горя	Б: ко́мната О́льги

	Э́то говори́т И́горь.	Э́то говори́т О́льга.
1. У меня́ есть стул.	___	___
2. У меня́ нет сту́ла.	___	___
3. У меня́ есть карти́на.	___	___
4. У меня́ нет карти́ны.	___	___
5. У меня́ есть окно́.	___	___
6. У меня́ нет окна́.	___	___

FIGURE 8.4. Structure-Input

This is one of the core principles in developing items for structured-input activities (Lee & VanPatten, 2003; Farley, 2004).

With the have/have not construction, isolating the genitive form is difficult to do, since the genitive of negation never occurs without a negative lexical item like нет [there is not]. Nevertheless, the teacher can craft an activity where the forms есть/нет [there is/there is not] are left out of the sentences and learners have to decide which belongs in the blank based on the grammatical forms of other words in the sentence (see Figure 8.3). This omission isolates the target grammatical feature and pushes learners to process the case endings so they can make an appropriate choice of lexical items and determine the sentence's message.

Initiating the Learning of Grammar in Comprehension-Based Activities

As seen in the previous section, structured-input activities can be designed to draw learners' attention to the meaning conveyed by grammatical forms. Structured-input activities can also be designed to initiate the process by which learners map specific forms to meaning. When introducing the difference between "have" and "have not"

4.2 Задáние 5. Что там есть? А чегó там нет?

a. Choose one of the pictures below and place a check mark in the appropriate column to indicate whether the **есть** or **нет** sentence applies to that picture.

б. Without revealing your choice, read a partner a minimum of three sentences about your picture. Your partner must wait to listen to all three sentences, and then try to guess the picture. Continue to read sentences until your partner guesses correctly. Remember to listen carefully as the pictures are very similar.

№ 1 | № 2 | № 3

Кóмната № ______

1.	____ Там есть дивáн.	____ Там нет дивáн**а**.
2.	____ Там есть лáмпа.	____ Там нет лáмп**ы**.
3.	____ Там есть кровáть.	____ Там нет кровáт**и**.
4.	____ Там есть кóшка.	____ Там нет кóшк**и**.
5.	____ Там есть телеви́зор.	____ Там нет телеви́зор**а**.
6.	____ Там есть календáрь.	____ Там нет календар**я́**.
7.	____ Там есть настóльная (table) лáмпа.	____ Там нет настóльн**ой** лáмп**ы**.

FIGURE 8.5. Information Gap Activity

constructions, it is possible to use pictures to assist students in mapping the meaning of positive sentences and negative ones, such as in Figure 8.4.

The activity demonstrated in Figure 8.4 continues with another 10 sentences so that by the conclusion learners have encountered eight pairs of sentences, with one positive, the other negative. By matching whole sentences to one of two pictures, the students build a set of exemplars of how to express the notion of having/not having these objects. This form-meaning matching activity is immediately followed by a personalizing activity in which students are asked to compare the rooms they live in with the ones described in part A, selecting all the sentences from part A that are true for them. They then share the selected sentences with a partner and read them aloud. Thus the first part of the activity verifies the students' comprehension of the referential meaning of the sentences while the follow-up allows for the selection of personally relevant information for sharing with a partner.

This structured-input activity can be slightly repackaged into an "information gap" activity, part of which is presented in Figure 8.5. In total the exercise in Figure 8.5 provides learners with another 26 exemplars of positive and negative sentences, which

4.1 ЗАДА́НИЕ 8. У ТЕБЯ́ ЕСТЬ..?

a. Prepare a set of at least 6 questions that you can ask to find out what household items your classmates own.

У тебя́ есть ________________?

У тебя́ есть ________________?

У тебя́ есть ________________?

У тебя́ есть ________________?

У тебя́ есть ________________?

У тебя́ есть ________________?

б. Now ask a partner your questions, remembering that when you ask the question **У тебя́ есть**..? the key word in the Russian sentence will be **есть** and your intonation will rise sharply on it.

Record your classmate's answers finishing the sentence:

У него́ есть...

У неё есть...

If you have something in common you can say:

У нас есть...

У него́ есть... / У неё есть...	У нас есть...

FIGURE 8.6. Information Exchange Activity

they have to process for meaning by matching statements to the relevant picture(s). In the activity in Figure 8.5 participants must attend to their partners' statements or they will not be able to complete the task successfully.

Grammar in Output-Based Communication Activities

While a person cannot learn a language without input, input is not sufficient for learners to develop a target-like L2 grammar (Swain, 1985). The comprehension-based structured-input activities described earlier require learners to *show* their comprehension of the input, to *make* form-meaning mappings, and to *notice* specific features of grammatical form. While such activities have been shown to help learners make productive use of language features, Shintani et al. (2013) find that output-based practice has more durable effects in delayed post-tests. They hypothesize that comprehension-based instruction works better for new structures, while production-based instruction (i.e., output) works better on partially acquired language features. Thus work on comprehending the input and building form-meaning mappings is a first step (i.e., it allows learners to gain partial control over language features); production-based activities help learners gain further control over the

4.2 Задáние 7. Что такóе «хорóшая кóмната» или «хорóшая квартúра»?
Work with a partner to share your views on either dorm living or apartment living. Try to find as much agreement with your partner as you can. Use the following model:

В хорóшей кóмнате (квартúре)... / В плохóй кóмнате (квартúре)...

По-мóему, в хорóшей кóмнате / в хорóшей квартúре всегдá есть...

Кóмната / Квартúра, по-мóему, плохáя, éсли (if) там нет...

Be ready to share your answers with the class.

FIGURE 8.7. Open-Ended Opinion Gap Activity

features and builds fluency in using them. Output-based activities need to be meaningful and communicative and engage the learner in oral- or written-text creation.

The output-based activity portrayed in Figure 8.6 comes at the end of a set of comprehension-based activities that work on the positive form of the "have" construction (i.e., learners have worked with у меня есть [I have] sentences but not yet with у меня нет [I don't have] sentences). This activity takes the form of a personalized information-exchange activity accomplished in several steps.

In the planning stage learners develop a set of questions; in the interaction stage they ask and answer the questions, recording the information they receive from the partner; in the final stage they must evaluate the information to see if it fits into the category "we (both) have." While these are similar to the "ask your partner" types of activities found in early communicative language textbooks, this activity has two important differences: students must record information they learn (and thereby attend to the answers that the partner gives) and they must evaluate the information collected. Both steps require learners to focus more deeply on the information shared during the communicative exchange.

After continued work with the have/have not construction in comprehension-based structured-input activities, learners have the opportunity to engage in a relatively open-ended opinion gap activity (Figure 8.7), where pairs express what features an apartment must have in order to be considered a good or bad living space.

4.3 Упражнéние Е. Сочинéние: Сейчáс я живý...
Imagine that you have set up an account on ВКонтакте (vk.com), the Russian equivalent of Facebook. Write a post in Russian of approximately 50 words talking about where you are currently living, what kind of place it is, and what kinds of items you have there. You might also note a couple of things that you are lacking and need to buy. Begin by stating whether you live in an apartment or a dorm.

FIGURE 8.8. Written Output Activity

This output-based activity allows learners to deploy a selection of the many exemplars of these constructions that they have seen, while formulating their own opinions. The activity provides for discussion between students in each pair and among pairs of students so that there is every likelihood that some exemplars will be recycled multiple times. With the teacher's guidance in managing the whole group sharing, students can comment on each pair's set of opinions, expressing agreement, disagreement, or surprise.

Output activities, while contextualized, can also be constructed to draw out production of more than one specific grammatical form. A concluding task for the instructional sequence of the have/not have construction can be a composition (Figure 8.8), where learners write a paragraph about their own living spaces and what they have or don't have. The prompt directs learners to the audience, who will read their writing, and gives several suggestions of what to include in their paragraph. The prompts highlight the immediate grammatical constructions and suggest previous exemplars that can be recycled from earlier language input. As a writing task without a time constraint performed by learners who are able to access outside resources, it seems likely that, as Skehan (1996) suggests, learners will avail themselves of rule-based processing and of exemplars from the language-input and structured-input activities. The rule-based processing may help learners produce grammatically accurate output for novel lexical items that they have looked up to describe their particular living situations.

Explicit Instruction for Effective and Efficient Form-Meaning Mapping

Norris and Ortega (2000) show an advantage for instructed second language learning, and much of the research record shows some advantage for processing instruction (understood as explicit explanation of grammar combined with structured-input activities) (VanPatten & Cadierno, 1993; VanPatten, 2004; Fernández, 2008; Henry et al., 2009; VanPatten & Borst, 2012; Comer & deBenedette, 2011). The structure to be explained, the amount of explicit information given, the timing of instruction (i.e., whether instruction needs to accompany the learner's first encounter with the feature in language input), the context for instruction (in class or in a guided online tutorial) are all considerations that instructional designers and instructors must take into account when fashioning an explanation. Some recent research (VanPatten et al., 2012;

VanPatten et al., 2013; Van de Guchte et al., 2015) suggests that for certain grammar features, structured-input activities alone may provide to learners enough exemplars of the language phenomenon so as to reduce (or eliminate) the need for explicit information about a particular form. For other constructions, explicit information seems to speed up the rate at which learners make the correct connections between form and meaning (Henry et al., 2009; VanPatten & Borst, 2012). There are no easy answers to the questions "how much do explicit learning and explicit instruction influence implicit learning, and how can their symbiosis be optimized?" (Ellis, 2011, p. 36).

When using the have/not have construction, explicit instruction and explanation seem warranted since the structures in English and Russian work so differently, with possessors and possessions mapping to different cases. Word order adds a further complication when comparing the English and Russian have/have not structures. In neutral word order in both languages, the possessor tends to appear at the start of the sentence and the possession at the end. This leads some L1 English learners of L2 Russian to make faulty assumptions. Some will mistakenly map the three words у меня есть as a single unit to the English verb "have": to express the possessor they add an unwarranted subject pronoun (e.g., *я у меня есть книга, parsed as: я [I] у меня есть [have] книга [book]). Others mistake the similarity of element order, which leads them to put the possession into the accusative case (e.g., *у меня есть книгу [I have a book—acc.s.]) to reflect the direct object status of the possession in the English sentence and the tendency for both English and Russian to have subject-verb-object (SVO) sentences. Given the possibility for multiple mismappings, explicit comparisons of how the languages express possession seem useful. In *Mezhdu nami* the explanations of this construction are built up slowly, first working primarily with the positive construction and pointing out the mismatch between the Russian construction and the English, then adding information on the use of the genitive in "have not" sentences, and finally summarizing the relationship between forms and functions in a computer animation activity where learners can test out their assumptions on form and meaning by accessing color-coded comparative sentences (see: http://www.mezhdunami.org/unit04/4_2/language.shtml). The authors assume that students will read these grammar explanations on their own and will complete small self-correcting online questions to check their comprehension of the explanations. However, instructors might want to use a portion of the explanations to address a specific question in class, and the instructions for many activities for both classroom use and homework contain reminders about relevant grammar rules before students attempt the work.

In the conceptual framework elaborated here the goal of grammar instruction is to help learners make better and more complete form-meaning mappings in their comprehension and production work. If activities by themselves can help learners make specific form-meaning mappings on their own and can provide enough exemplars of a grammatical feature of the language to reach that goal, then perhaps that particular grammar point does not need explicit treatment in class (particularly if learners have read about the rule[s] already). Some grammar features of Russian that fit this category are the lack of articles and the verb "to be" in the present tense; the formation of the regular past tense; and the agreement of possessive pronouns forms мой, моя [my] with the gender of the possession not the sex of the possessor.

In deciding when to introduce an explicit explanation of specific grammar points, instructional designers will need to weigh issues including the saliency and frequency of a given form in the input, the likelihood of learners' mismatching of forms and meanings, and the learners' developmental readiness. For example, learners might know the phrase домашнее задание [homework assignment] and even use it in several cases (nominative/accusative singular and plural) long before they notice (or are tasked to notice) that домашний [home, adj. with a stem in soft -н-] declines differently from other adjectives like интересный [interesting, adj. with a stem in hard -н-]. Explicit instruction about this class of soft adjectives will be effective only when learners have encountered more lexical items belonging to this class and have a topic and task that requires them to use those lexical items. This can be difficult to manage for grammatical categories that are not semantically linked; for soft adjectives a discussion of seasonal weather, typical weather-related activities, and needed clothing items might provide a broad enough context so that learners encounter soft adjectives like весенний [spring, adj.], летний [summer, adj.], осенний [autumn, adj.], зимний [winter, adj.] with enough frequency to notice their declensional differences from hard-stem adjectives. The grammar work on the declension of soft adjectives might also be an occasion to draw learners' attention to the important phonological distinction between hard and soft н (or hard and soft consonants, in general) and to practice the pronunciation of hard and soft -н- in select activities.

It is worth recalling that instructors should not have unreasonable expectations about the power of explicit grammar instruction. It is unreasonable to assume that instruction can lead learners to error-free automatic processing of forms even though learners' surface accuracy in morphology is likely to increase over time. As Ortega notes, "There is no evidence to support the misconception that errors should be avoided or that they stem from (much less cause) a failure to learn" (2007b, p. 189). Ortega places a priority on creating practice activities that have cognitive and linguistic complexity because they engage learners, even if learners' formal accuracy seems compromised. Learners' errors may provide evidence of growth in their language skills since they reveal learners' attempts to express notions beyond their current language ability. Negotiating the meaning of learners' faulty expressions may make them more aware of the gap in their performance and push them to fill the gap.

IMPLICATIONS FOR INSTRUCTION AT HIGHER LEVELS

While the series of principles for teaching beginning-level Russian can be applied to later stages of grammar learning, it is important to recognize that at those later stages the grammar topics will be highly dependent on the content of the language input that learners are using and the grammatical forms it contains. Any attempt to yoke a comprehensive grammar review, organized by form, to a course that uses thematically clustered authentic (or semiauthentic) language input is likely to fail because the topics and the content of the input may not match the predetermined grammatical organization. Learners may feel intensely the tension between the thematic topics and the grammar points. If instruction includes having learners discuss a thematic topic or work (e.g., a film, a story, a song), then the grammar they will need most is the grammar connected with the lexical items in the input. Grammar instruction should help learners build up their morphological control of those words and word forms as well as their usage(s) in order to talk successfully about the themes raised in the input. It seems unlikely, however, that any one text or group of texts on one theme can furnish the occasion to review all the uses of a specific case.

This is not to say that certain broad topics in Russian grammar cannot be paired with authentic language input. For example, a course that selects an action film as its main form of language input will find multiple opportunities to work on prefixed and unprefixed verbs of motion in talking *about* the actions of the film's characters. Those forms may or may not appear in the film's dialogue but a teacher can supply structured-input activities that let students match sentences containing these verbs with scenes showing the characters' actions. Similarly, a course that includes authentic nonfiction texts will have multiple opportunities for leaners to map participial forms to their grammatical meanings.

At those higher levels of language study a theme and its related input are likely to allow teachers to make learners aware of and focused on only a subset of the related meanings or uses of a particular case or form. At that level it might be quite useful and efficient to engage learners in coconstructing certain semantic blocks that a case or a feature regularly conveys. Liamkina (2008) has explored the idea of using such cognitive-semantic blocks to teach German grammar with learners at the advanced level. She looked at the semantic blocks of experiencer, possessor, and beneficiary that require the dative case in German and finds that training students to notice these semantic blocks helps them use clausal dative forms more frequently and more accurately over the course of one semester of college instruction. For Russian instruction one could imagine using that approach with certain semantic blocks expressed by the genitive, such as expressions of separation (genitive objects of the prepositions из, с, and от [from]), of quantity (genitives with два [two], пять [five], много [a lot], нет [there is no], не хватает [there is not enough], я не читаю никаких [I read no . . .]), or proximate location in space (genitive objects of the prepositions у [by], около [around], возле [nearby], вдоль [along], etc.).

CONCLUSION

While my focus here has been on grammar instruction at the beginning level, readers should not mistakenly conclude that grammar is the only thing that should occupy

Novice learners' attention or class time. Grammar tasks and activities will be only one component of a beginning language course, albeit one that can be integrated into work on other skill areas (interpretative reading and listening, interpersonal and presentational oral communication) and other content/cognitive engagement (learning about L2 culture, recognizing cross-cultural differences, etc.).

The theoretical outline here draws on existing research that has been conducted primarily with the more commonly taught languages, and its assumptions and hypotheses will need to be verified by future empirical studies of learners of Russian and Russian L2 classrooms. My hope is that the outlined principles will engage our field in a critical and empirically based conversation about the shape of grammar instruction in future Russian language textbooks.

NOTES

1. In her highly influential methods textbook Omaggio (1986, 1993) included no chapter or subchapter specifically devoted to teaching grammar. Her sparse advice about grammar instruction appears in the chapters on accuracy and error correction and on organizing classroom practice ("nearly all language practice activities, grammar explanations, readings, and cultural commentaries in a given chapter relate to that theme" and "all the exercises would be greatly improved if they consisted of sentences that were connected to one another in a logical sequence or relationship"; 1986, p. 94). The third edition of Omaggio's book (2001) reports on "focus on form" in communicative teaching (pp. 100–101) and addresses the role of explicit instruction but does not actually turn that discussion into concrete advice for guiding classroom work.
2. Similar problems have been noted in introductory textbooks of the more commonly taught languages (Aski, 2003; Paesani et al., 2016). Wong and VanPatten (2003) lay out the problems and inefficiencies of using only mechanical drills; DeKeyser (2007b), a strong proponent of practice for language learning, notes that "mechanical drills can only serve a very limited purpose, because they do not make the learner engage in what is the essence of language processing, i.e., establishing form-meaning connections" (p. 11). Comer (2012) found that the majority of nonmechanical activities found in Russian textbooks from the 1990s are role-plays and teacher-student or student-student interviews with personalized questions. The limitations of such activities are addressed later in this chapter.
3. Since the context for this volume is instruction of Russian as a foreign language, I look primarily at models of grammar instruction suggested by SLA theories that hold sway in North America. A critical examination of Russian theoretical models of grammar instruction and their practical implementations in the teaching of Russian as a foreign language is beyond the scope of this chapter.
4. The PACE model has considerable reach in US language teaching, particularly at the precollege level, because it is incorporated into Shrum and Glisan (2010), one of the few methods textbooks that specifically addresses the teaching of languages at the K–12 level.

5. The term "referential meaning" refers to the surface-level propositions expressed by an utterance. For example, if a class is sorting photographs of politicians and a teacher asks "Где фотография Путина?" [Where is the photograph of Putin?], and a learner holds up a picture of Gorbachev and declares, "Вот она" [Here it is] then the learner has made an error in referential meaning.
6. This is not to suggest that they cannot be useful as production activities, once it is clear that learners have forged the correct form-meaning connections. But even then teachers should introduce some way to hold students accountable for attending to the information exchanged.
7. This is speculative on my part, and some researchers like Gor and Jackson (2013), based on their experimental data with Russian verbal morphology, argue strongly for the notion that instructed L2 learners use decomposition for storing lexical items. That is, learners store a verb like читать [to read] as a single entry in their mental lexicon and they apply rules to produce forms they need (i.e., читаю [I read (present)], читали [they read (past)]).

REFERENCES

Adair-Hauck, B., & Donato, R. (2010). Using a story-based approach to teach grammar. In J. Shrum & E. W. Glisan (Eds.), *Teacher's handbook: Contextualized language instruction* (4th ed.) (pp. 216–44). Boston: Heinle, Cengage Learning.

Anderson, L.W., & Krathwohl, D. R. (Eds.). (2001). *A taxonomy for learning, teaching and assessing: A revision of Bloom's taxonomy of educational objectives.* New York: Longman.

Aski, J. (2003). Foreign language textbook activities: Keeping pace with second language acquisition research. *Foreign Language Annals, 36*(1), 57–65.

Chaput, P. (1984). Conversation-based drills for beginning Russian. In S. Lubensky & D. K. Jarvis (Eds.), *Teaching, learning, acquiring Russian* (pp. 95–112). Columbus, OH: Slavica.

Chvany, C. (1984). Strategies for review. In S. Lubensky & D. K. Jarvis (Eds.), *Teaching, learning, acquiring Russian* (pp. 54–80). Columbus, OH: Slavica.

Comer, W. (2007). Implementing task-based teaching from the ground up: Considerations for lesson planning and classroom practice. *Russian Language Journal, 57,* 181–203.

Comer, W. (2012). Communicative language teaching and Russian: The current state of the field. In V. Makarova (Ed.), *Russian language studies in North America: New perspectives from theoretical and applied linguistics* (pp. 133–59). London: Anthem.

Comer, W. (2015). *Homework activities for Mezhdu nami: Units 1–5.* Lawrence, KS: Jayhawk Ink.

Comer, W., & deBenedette, L. (2011). Processing instruction and Russian: Further evidence is IN. *Foreign Language Annals, 44*(4), 646–73.

deBenedette, L. (2015). *Classroom activities for Mezhdu nami: Units 1–5.* Lawrence, KS: Jayhawk Ink.

deBenedette, L., Comer, W. J., Smyslova, A., & Perkins, J. (2015). *Mezhdu nami.* Retrieved from: www.mezhdunami.org

DeKeyser, R. M. (2007a). Skill acquisition theory. In B. VanPatten & J. Williams (Eds.), *Theories in second language acquisition: An introduction* (pp. 97–114). New York: Routledge.

DeKeyser, R. M. (2007b). Introduction: Situating the concept of practice. In R. M. DeKeyser (Ed.), *Practice in a second language: Perspectives from applied linguistics and cognitive psychology* (pp. 1–18). New York: Cambridge UP.

Doughty, C., & Williams, J. (Eds.). (1998). *Focus on form in classroom second language acquisition*. Cambridge: Cambridge UP.

Ellis, N. C. (2011). Implicit and explicit SLA and their interface. In C. Sanz & R. P. Leow (Eds.), *Implicit and explicit language learning: Conditions, processes, and knowledge in SLA and bilingualism* (pp. 35–47). Washington, DC: Georgetown UP.

Farley, A. P. (2004). *Structured input: Grammar instruction for the acquisition oriented classroom*. Boston: McGraw-Hill Humanities/Social Sciences/Languages.

Fernández, C. (2008). Reexamining the role of explicit information in processing instruction. *Studies in Second Language Acquisition, 30*(3), 277–305.

Gass, S., & Mackey, A. (2007). Input, interaction, and output in second language acquisition. In B. VanPatten & J. Williams (Eds.), *Theories in second language acquisition: An introduction* (pp. 175–200). New York: Routledge.

Gor, K., & Jackson, S. (2013). Morphological decomposition and lexical access in a native and second language: A nesting doll effect. *Language and Cognitive Processes, 28* (7), 1065–91.

Henry, N., Culman, H., & VanPatten, B. (2009). More on the effects of explicit information in instructed SLA: A partial replication and a response to Fernández (2008). *Studies in Second Language Acquisition, 31*(4), 559–75.

Hung, H. (2015). Flipping the classroom for English language learners to foster active learning. *Computer Assisted Language Learning, 28*(1), 81–96.

Jarvis, D. K. (1984). Communicative competence: An overview of the research and some practical suggestions for the classroom. In S. Lubensky & D. K. Jarvis (Eds.), *Teaching, learning, acquiring Russian* (pp. 33–44). Columbus, OH: Slavica.

Krashen, S. (1982). *Principles and practice in second language acquisition*. Englewood Cliffs, NJ: Prentice-Hall.

Kudyma, A., Miller, F. J., & Kagan, O. (2012). *Beginner's Russian: A basic Russian course*. New York: Hippocrene.

Leaver, B. L., Rifkin, B., & Shekhtman, B. (2004). Apples and oranges are both fruit, but they don't taste the same: A response to Wynne Wong and Bill VanPatten. *Foreign Language Annals, 37*(1), 125–32.

Lee, J., & VanPatten, B. (2003). *Making communicative language teaching happen* (2nd ed.). New York: McGraw-Hill.

Liamkina, O. (2008). Teaching grammatical meaning to advanced learners: A cognitive-semantic perspective. In L. Ortega & H. Byrnes (Eds.), *The longitudinal study of advanced L2 capacities* (pp. 163–81). New York: Routledge.

Long, M. H. (1985). The role for instruction in second language acquisition: Task based teaching. In K. Hyltenstam & M. Pienemann (Eds.), *Modeling and assessing second language development* (pp. 77–99). Clevedon, UK: Multilingual Matters.

Long, M. H. (2015). *Second language acquisition and task-based language teaching*. Malden, MA: John Wiley and Sons.

Lubensky, S., & Jarvis, D. K. (Eds.). (1984). *Teaching, learning, acquiring Russian*. Columbus, OH: Slavica.

Moffett, J. (2015). Twelve tips for "flipping" the classroom. *Medical Teacher*, *3*(4), 331–36.

Nakhimovsky, A. (1984). Principles for a beginning Russian text. In S. Lubensky & D. K. Jarvis (Eds.), *Teaching, learning, acquiring Russian* (pp. 45–53). Columbus, OH: Slavica.

Norris, J. M., & Ortega, L. (2000). Effectiveness of L2 instruction: A research synthesis and quantitative meta-analysis. *Language Learning*, *50*(3), 417–528.

O'Flaherty, J., & Phillips, C. (2015). The use of flipped classrooms in higher education: A scoping review. *Internet & Higher Education*, *25*, 85–95.

Omaggio, A. (1986). *Teaching language in context: Proficiency-oriented instruction*. Boston: Heinle & Heinle.

Omaggio, A. (1993). *Teaching language in context: Proficiency-oriented instruction* (2nd ed.). Boston: Heinle & Heinle.

Omaggio, A. (2001). *Teaching language in context: Proficiency-oriented instruction* (3rd ed.). Boston: Heinle & Heinle.

Ortega, L. (2007a). Second language learning explained? SLA across nine contemporary theories. In B. VanPatten & J. Williams (Eds.), *Theories in second language acquisition: An introduction* (pp. 225–50). New York: Routledge.

Ortega, L. (2007b). Meaningful L2 practice in foreign language classrooms: A cognitive-interactionist SLA perspective. In R. M. DeKeyser (Ed.), *Practice in a second language: Perspectives from applied linguistics and cognitive psychology* (pp. 1–18). New York: Cambridge UP.

Paesani, K., Allen, H. A., & Dupuy, B. (2016). *A multiliteracies framework for collegiate foreign language teaching*. Boston: Pearson.

Pica, T. (2005). Classroom learning, teaching, and research: A task-based perspective. *Modern Language Journal*, *89*, 339–52.

Pica, T. (2009). Task-based approaches for teaching, learning and research. *Contemporary Applied Linguistics, Volume 1: Language Teaching and Learning*, *1*, 75–98.

Pica, T. (2013). From input, output, and comprehension to negotiation, evidence, and attention: An overview of theory and research on learner interaction and SLA. In M. D. P. G. Mayo, M. J. G. Mangado, & M. M. Adrián (Eds.), *Contemporary approaches to second language acquisition* (vol. 9, pp. 49–69). Amsterdam: John Benjamins.

Rifkin, B., & Kagan, O. (Eds.). (2000). *Learning and teaching of Slavic languages and cultures*. Indianapolis, IN: Slavica.

Robin, R., Evans-Romaine, K., & Shatalina, G. (2012). *Golosa: A basic course in Russian, Book 1* (5th ed.). New York: Pearson.

Sahin, A., Cavlazoglu, B., & Zeytuncu, Y. E. (2015). Flipping a college calculus course: A case study. *Journal of Educational Technology & Society, 18*(3), 142–52.

Shintani, N., Li, S., & Ellis, R. (2013). Comprehension-based versus production-based grammar instruction: A meta-analysis of comparative studies. *Language Learning, 63*(2), 296–329.

Shrum, J., & Glisan, E. W. (2010). *Teacher's handbook: Contextualized language instruction* (4th ed.). Boston: Heinle, Cengage Learning.

Skehan, P. (1996). A framework for the implementation of task-based instruction. *Applied Linguistics, 17*, 38–62.

Swain, M. (1985). Communicative competence: Some roles of comprehensible input and comprehensible output in its development. In S. Gass & C. G. Madden (Eds.), *Input in Second Language Acquisition* (pp. 235–53). Rowley, MA: Newbury House.

Swan, O. (2014a). Sarah Palin był duży błąd [Sarah Palin was a big mistake]: AA and the in situ learning of Polish. *Slavic and East European Journal, 58*(1), 113–31.

Swan, O. (2014b). Just how important is explanation: A response. *Slavic and East European Journal, 58*(2), 307–21.

Terrell, T. D. (1982). The natural approach to language teaching: An update. *Modern Language Journal, 66*(2), 121–32.

Van de Guchte, M., Braaksma, M., Rijlaarsdam, G., & Bimmel, P. (2015). Learning new grammatical structures in task-based language learning: The effects of recasts and prompts. *Modern Language Journal, 99*(2), 246–62.

VanPatten, B. (Ed.). (2004). *Processing instruction: Theory, research, and commentary.* Mahwah, NJ: Lawrence Erlbaum.

VanPatten, B. (2007). Input processing in adult second language acquisition. In B. VanPatten & J. Williams (Eds.), *Theories in second language acquisition: An introduction* (pp. 115–36). New York: Routledge.

VanPatten, B., & Borst, S. (2012). The roles of explicit information and grammatical sensitivity in processing instruction: Nominative-accusative case marking and word order in German L2. *Foreign Language Annals, 45*(1), 92–109.

VanPatten, B., & Cadierno, T. (1993). Explicit instruction and input processing. *Studies in Second Language Acquisition, 15*(2), 225–43.

VanPatten, B., Collopy, E., Price, J. E., Borst, S., & Qualin, A. (2013). Explicit information, grammatical sensitivity, and the first-noun principle: A cross-linguistic study in processing instruction. *Modern Language Journal, 97*(2), 506–27.

VanPatten, B., Collopy, E., & Qualin, T. (2012). Explicit information and processing instruction with nominative and accusative case in Russian as a second language: Just how important is explanation? *Slavic & East European Journal, 56*(2), 256–76.

Vasileva, M. (2014). Ментальный лексикон: где же место морфологии? [Mental lexicon: Where is the place for morphology?]. *Rossiiskii zhurnal kognitivnoi nauki, 1*(4), 31–57.

Wong, W., & VanPatten, B. (2003). The evidence is IN: Drills are OUT. *Foreign Language Annals, 36*(3), 403–23.

9

CONTENT, LANGUAGE, AND TASK IN ADVANCED RUSSIAN

Lynne deBenedette

In most language education programs, students at some point transition from lower-level courses organized around a textbook (or other form of largely semiauthentic language input) to upper-level courses involving work with authentic target language text(s) or film(s). This transition is challenging for learners and instructors alike; as the length and types of encountered texts increase, the time for addressing discrete language forms decreases. Other challenges include dealing with the quantity of new words and concepts, teaching language forms related to new expressions, and eliciting culturally aware responses to texts. Instructors must decide how much material is ideal or practical, how to assess learning of chosen content, what language forms need emphasis, and how to integrate new forms into the content material.

This chapter describes a balanced content- and language-driven course that can help learners transition from the textbook-based work of first- and second-year courses to upper level (fourth- and fifth-year) primarily content-driven courses in the target language (TL). After surveying relevant literature, I will consider the structure of a content-driven third-year Russian course and describe the audience and content and language goals. I offer examples of classroom materials that allow learners to reach these goals and consider the issue of assessment. Having had the experience of implementing such a course, I conclude with a list of principles for implementing the proposed approach with other content topics.

CONTENT-DRIVEN INSTRUCTION: AN INTRODUCTION

Language courses at any level of instruction can contain varying amounts of material related to cultural practices, historical or biographical information, or other content. The interrelationship of language-driven and content-driven work in TL courses has received some attention in second language (L2) pedagogy research. A useful framework developed by Met (1999) places TL courses that incorporate different types of content on a continuum that stretches from "primarily language-driven"—where content learning may be considered incidental or unimportant—to "primarily content-driven"—where content learning outcomes are "a driving force of instruction, and student mastery of content is held to be of paramount importance" (p. 4).

At the language-driven end of the continuum we can locate courses organized solely by grammar topics, although most introductory and intermediate textbooks organize language material around lexical themes (e.g., free time, family), with grammatical forms paralleling those themes. Learners are expected to comprehend and produce language about the themes, but they may not be expected to demonstrate specific factual content knowledge related to the themes in the target culture.[1]

At the other end of Met's continuum is a heavily content-driven form of content-based instruction (CBI), an early description of which called language "the vehicle through which the subject matter is learned rather than the immediate object of study" (Brinton et al., 1989, p. 5). CBI often involves teaching age- or grade-appropriate subject matter in the L2. A CBI course is likely to be given at the advanced level and may involve studying historical periods or cultural phenomena, with reading assignments and discussion of authentic literary or nonfiction texts or films in the TL. These texts are primarily authentic and are designed for and by native speakers, and students use the TL to learn new information (Stryker & Leaver, 1997).

Early articulations of CBI suggest that language acquisition occurs more or less naturally because of learners' focus on the content and engagement with comprehensible input (Krashen, 1982; Lightbown & Spada, 2013). Swain (1985), however, finds that in a TL content-based course, learners' L2 did not improve across all skills. She posits that some attention to language development in content-based courses is necessary for students to improve speaking and writing in the TL. The practice of providing focus on language (focus-on-form) within a content-driven course is now recognized as an important component of CBI (Doughty & Williams, 1998; Byrnes, 2000, 2005). Byrnes (2006) addresses the integration of content and language work in curricular planning, and Paesani and Willis (2012) note that there has been further work on integrating authentic texts into advanced language-focused courses at the university level as well as on integrating language-focused teaching strategies into advanced literary-cultural classes (p. s60).

We can posit a hypothetical third-year college Russian language course that aims to ease the transition to a content-based course resting somewhere on Met's continuum. Such a course would be largely content-driven but not entirely content-based and would aim for a balance of content- and language-driven work. Students in such a course would be given content-learning goals and held accountable for the outcomes. However, it also would include language-learning goals, attainment of which is would be assessed along with content learning. The course could be organized around a topic (for example, the Soviet *stiljagi* [hipsters]), which students explore in the TL via discussions of films or fiction or nonfiction reading. The course could feature considerable work on language form but would situate that work entirely in the context of the content material. We can think of this kind of content-driven course as a hybrid that balances content-driven and language-driven work.

CONTENT-DRIVEN INSTRUCTION AT LOWER LEVELS: ONE MODEL

Musumeci (1996), one of the few to document content-driven work in lower-level university courses, describes a CBI course covering Italy's social geography and culture that was implemented at the second-year level. Following Musumeci's work, Rodgers (2006) provides observations on how this content-driven course integrated a focus on language form with content-learning objectives. The course's focus-on-form activities dealt only with the course content topics, and students were involved in working with information about that content. For example, learners worked on using the comparative via an activity in which they compared life in Italy's city centers to life in the suburbs; another activity asked students to notice the usage differences between the Italian prepositions *in* and *a* (both meaning "in/at") with geographical locations such as cities, states, regions, and countries. Students' coursework was evaluated primarily for evidence of content learning. Measuring learners' content knowledge and language development at the semester's weeks 2 and 12, Rodgers showed that learners improved in both content knowledge and linguistic accuracy (2006). Rodgers notes also that requiring learners to use new expressions in meaningful contexts may have made vocabulary acquisition easier than "with more conventional approaches to language instruction" (p. 385).

Finally, it is useful to consider how content learning and linguistic development in this course were weighted in assessment. Both testing and daily work prioritized evaluation of content learning, though evaluation of language form was less emphasized in scoring. Week 12 measures in the study, however, showed significant improvement in linguistic accuracy. Rodgers concludes that a course that used a CBI format "in which grammar was not the main emphasis of learning but was studied when it arose, and always in the context of the subject matter, contributed . . . not only to the participants' knowledge of subject matter but also [to] their control of form-function relationships" (p. 384).

There are, of course, challenges inherent in this approach. The Italian course situated language-driven work fully within content learning. However, a similar proportion of content-driven and language-driven work would be challenging to accomplish in a Russian language class; third-year learners of Russian have difficulties with morphology and syntax that require a more equal balance of work on content learning and on linguistic forms. Russian students need greater focus-on-form attention to lexicon; verbs in particular require a lot of work because they trigger specific prepositions and cases. Indeed, the quantity and type of authentic reading assigned in the Italian course (using a middle-school geography text) would likely be too challenging for students in third-year Russian. Content learning that involves cultural and historical topics requires more sophisticated and detailed forms of description ways of describing those phenomena. A Russian equivalent of the geography textbook—even one written for early adolescents—would be beyond L2 learners' reading level in terms of quantity of text, amount of unfamiliar vocabulary, and the syntactic complexity of the Russian academic prose. Therefore, in applying this model to Russian, an instructor will need to narrow the range of content in order to allow for balanced work on content and language. To address the difficulties that learners at this level have with reading Russian academic prose, the teacher may need to adjust chosen content material and opt for sources that offer visual support for learning, such as a subtitled film. To provide information about historical and cultural topics related to the course, the teacher may need to adapt or abridge authentic materials, making the content more accessible to language learners.

MODELS FOR LANGUAGE-FOCUSED ACTIVITIES

Before turning to a proposed structure of a third-year content-driven course in Russian, it is useful to understand the techniques for implementing focus-on-form work that uses language input from or related to a course's texts and films. The work focuses on particular lexical and grammatical issues but situates learners' language-focused activities within the content topic of the course. The structured input (SI) model (Lee & VanPatten, 2003; VanPatten, 2004) provides a method for sequencing language-focused work, from the first encounter with new language input to eventual learner output. A typical activity sequence of SI presents input in both aural and written form, with follow-up activities that check a learner's comprehension of the input. There follows a set of cognitively engaging meaning-based activities, all of which at first are input-based. These are heavily scaffolded to allow students to use new vocabulary and forms in communication with other students (in paired or small group activities) without having to immediately *produce* new forms on their own. At the start the activities focus largely on new vocabulary, which gives learners a chance to use the new expressions in meaningful contexts before turning their attention to targeted grammatical forms. In this input phase learners can exchange information related to the input (often using a checklist of possibilities). They may match sentence openings to logical endings or evaluate statements using different kinds of binary options (true-false, logical-illogical). They may rank or order phrases or sentences, for example, properly sequencing a character's actions in a film scene, or selecting the best option from a set of alternatives to answer a question about or describe a scene in a text or film. They may also agree or disagree with a description of a character they heard or read about. While some SI activities are likely to be *affective* in nature (requiring a learner's opinion or personal response), Lee and VanPatten (2003) recommend that the initial input-based work consists primarily of *referentially oriented activities* that "use an immediate concrete reference to ascertain the truth-value of a sentence" (p. 159). These activities are particularly useful in content-driven courses as they can reinforce the course's content-learning goals.

Because of the extensive scaffolding in SI activities, the instructor can employ activities that focus on acquisition of new vocabulary before guiding learners toward noticing new language forms. New vocabulary can refer to the lexicon present in the content input (words spoken by characters in a film, for example) and to any language, including culturally important terms that students will need in order to be able to discuss the content. Forms can be understood broadly to include a range of possible lexico-grammatical, grammatical, and syntactic features.

SI activities that focus on language form may precede or follow explicit grammar explanations; indeed, these activities may themselves become the basis for inductive grammar instruction. They present learners with many exemplars of a given language form, and the teacher can create them with a targeted structure in mind. As learners work through SI activities they use the targeted structure repeatedly in meaningful interactions. The instructor then can use the SI to guide students to notice targeted structures by having learners identify and organize instances of the structure's occurrence, such as in a chart or by sorting forms into categories. Learners can then construct (or coconstruct, with the teacher's assistance) the grammatical principle behind the structure(s) they have encountered and have been using. This kind of coconstruction of grammatical rules based on extensive engagement with language input is a key part of the PACE model of grammar instruction (Adair-Hauck & Donato, 2016).[2]

STRUCTURING A RUSSIAN LANGUAGE CONTENT-DRIVEN COURSE

The third-year course described here evolved over a number of years. Previously the course was entirely language-driven. With each new iteration it became more content-driven, although language-focused work was not consistently tied to content learning. The original language-driven course did use authentic input, but the input served primarily to demonstrate particular structures or provide a contextualized basis for TL work.[3] It was the language-focused work—conveyed via vocabulary lists, activities, and grammar exercises—rather than cultural or historical content that both instructor and students regarded as the actual course focus. Learning objectives prioritized vocabulary development and language functions (e.g., description or coherent past-tense narration). Materials used scenes from films for work on grammar and syntax (e.g., comparison, indefinite constructions, indirect speech), and language-focused activities were sometimes but not always connected with the films' content. In addition to glossed vocabulary and discussion questions, students were given cultural content information about the films. The information included the names of the director and cast, the year the film was released, and English explanations of important cultural terms and phenomena referenced in the film. But learners' knowledge of this content was not assessed. Films were chosen partly because they were recognized classics or currently popular ones but also because they provided opportunities to use targeted vocabulary (e.g., verbs expressing emotional state) and lent themselves to character descriptions and narration.

The instructor realized that this version of the third-year course was not an effective bridge between the second-year textbook-based course and the fourth-year course, which requires students to discuss multiple films, readings, or works of art in the TL. The third-year course was revised to be more content-driven by addressing a single topic, usually related to important Soviet or post-Soviet events or cultural phenomena. One version of the course, "Depicting Children's World," included two films and a short story, but the focus-on-form work was not consistently tied to the content of the films or the story.[4] Course evaluations indicated that students enjoyed the content but wanted more language-focused work. The instructor noted that the quantity of content material in the course did not allow sufficient time to do close readings or viewings of particular scenes, which would have permitted a deeper focus on cultural phenomena. Individual students' familiarity with relevant Soviet and Russian history varied substantially, and gaps in learners' cultural knowledge sometimes precipitated serious misreadings of the meaning of the scenes or behaviors of the characters. The instructor decided to make further changes: first, to choose only one film as the main text; second, to use short nonfiction readings related to cultural information evoked by the film to enrich the learners' understanding. The teacher then identified specific content material, knowledge of which could be assessed on tests and in essays and presentations.

Learner Profile and Content Selection

At the author's institution students complete 260 hours of instruction (or the equivalent, as demonstrated by placement test) before beginning the third-year course, since nearly all students enter the class with four semesters of instruction consisting of five 50-minute meetings per week. The first four semesters of language study acquaint students with certain kinds of texts and narratives, particularly biographies and life stories. Students experience these mostly in two contexts: either talking about the self or through reading short biographies of famous Russians. In terms of language proficiency, learners tend to be no higher than the American Council on the Teaching of Foreign Languages' Intermediate Mid level, which is a typical outcome for students with this number of contact hours (Thompson, 2000). Course materials that learners use in their first four semesters are textbook-based.[5] The fourth-semester course also includes six hours of language-driven work on the feature film «Питер-FM» [*Piter FM*] (Glikman et al., 2006) and 15 hours working on the story «День без вранья» [*A day without lying*] (Tokareva & Comer, 2008), along with comparing Tokareva's hero to the main character in the film «Осенний марафон» [*Autumn marathon*] (Krivonoshchenko & Daneliia, 1979), which students watch as well.

Given the students' work in the first and second years, the third-year course is designed to build on learners' previous work with narratives centered on life stories and relationships. Learners' familiarity with materials of that type served as a stepping stone for working on life stories embedded in broader sociocultural topics that reach beyond the self. Linguistically the course aims to develop students' ability to comprehend and produce longer, more organized, and more complex discourse in oral and written speech.

The instructor chose film rather than print because the learners' level of proficiency limits their ability to deal with written texts. Authentic nonfiction informational texts bear little stylistic resemblance to the largely conversational language students have encountered in their language work to that point, so using them as the primary source for the course content is problematic. Literary texts may be similarly hard for students to interpret, whereas processing of the basic propositional content of an artistic film is supported visually, and subtitles can ease comprehension of dialogue during initial viewing.

Using Film as a Primary Text: Advantages and Challenges

In language teaching, feature films offer the advantage of visually supported narrative and present the learner with a world of people, places, and occurrences that contextualize the language (Altman, 1989; Stempleski & Tomalin, 1995).[6] A film set in a particular period links the viewer to a world of referential cultural information about the Soviet Union or Russia, knowledge of which can be assessed, including in the TL. Strong emotional interactions among the characters can ground learners' work on language forms and constructions that express emotional states and relationships. Characters' actions and behaviors may elicit strong reactions from the viewers, offering an additional opportunity for language work on expressing and supporting one's opinions.

Using film in a language classroom presents other challenges, many of which are similar to those an instructor would face using any artistic text. The instructor must decide which scenes to select for detailed analysis and identify each scene's intersections with points of linguistic focus and cultural information. When focusing students' work on particular historical or cultural background knowledge, the instructor must choose the language (Russian or English) for conveying that information and decide the ways that knowledge will be assessed. The content learning of the cultural and historical phenomena depicted in the film will need corresponding language-driven work, and the instructor must budget time for that to occur. Finally, as Kern (2003) notes, there is the relationship of language-driven work to the idea of the film as a text that must be read—and interpreted—in particular sociocultural contexts. Thus, helping student viewers "read" a film, in other words, become literate about it, also means helping them situate the film within the broader context of the target culture. This includes plot points and character behaviors but also extends to references to other culturally situated phenomena: historical events, cultural realia, and the circumstances of everyday life. Student viewers' reactions to a film can be fundamentally affected by the filmmaker's choices about genre, editing, and juxtaposition of images. Kern sums up the issues learners face, noting that literacy involves problem solving, "figuring out relationships between words, between larger units of meaning, and between texts and real or imagined worlds" (2003, p. 49).

Working with films as texts creates specific challenges for language-driven work as well. The language used by the characters in the film may not overlap with the language a viewer needs to use to talk about the film. Because the medium of film *shows* actions rather than *describes* them, the instructor must provide model narration as oral and written language input. To talk about a film's plot and characters, learners need vocabulary describing actions and emotional states. Language-driven work must include connectors and time expressions to place events in chronological relationship to each other. Learners need both reporting verbs (ask, tell, explain, etc.) and the syntax necessary for expressing indirect speech in order to summarize conversations between characters.

Content- and Language-Learning Goals

Taking all these challenges into consideration, the author created a third-year course that focuses on the Soviet-era stiljaga using the film «Стиляги» [*Hipsters*] (Lebedev et al., 2008) as primary text. The film (a musical) became a hit upon release in Russia in 2008. The cultural significance of the title in the lives of Soviet citizens, and the film's nostalgic and highly stylized depiction of the 1950s, and its genre all create an opportunity for students to engage the phenomenon of post-Soviet Russians making sense of their Soviet past. Another content area is the film's soundtrack itself which, rather than featuring the "decadent" Western music that stiljagi listen to, uses Russian popular music from the late Soviet and early post-Soviet years. These intentional anachronisms complicate students' ability to understand what they see and hear. Analyzing a fiction film based on a particular historical period challenges students to identify the film's depiction of Soviet realities on the one hand, and the filmmaker's choices for artistic expression on the other.

Once the theme and primary text (film) had been selected, it was easier to set out the content- and language-learning goals of the course. Content learning focuses largely on historical and cultural information relevant to the film, including events such as the death of Josef Stalin and Nikita Khrushchev's address to the 20th Communist Party Congress. Cultural topics include the use of X-ray film to record and disseminate banned Western music ("music on bones"), the prevalence of communal apartments, the Moscow высотка [elite high-rise], the Soviet campaign against so-called cosmopolitanism in the late 1940s, and the Doctors' plot of 1952–53. Students must demonstrate an understanding of this historical and cultural information by incorporating it into written and oral work about the film's plot and characters.

In terms of language goals, students need to understand and use expressions related to the film's plot and develop their ability to narrate in past and present tense using appropriate verbs and time expressions. Students are expected to compare and contrast people and things (apartments, clothes) by describing characters and their actions, appearance, and dress. Students also need to show they can read and understand informational texts about some of the film-related content topics, which contain features of formal writing, including participles.

IMPLEMENTING A BALANCED CONTENT- AND LANGUAGE-DRIVEN COURSE

To demonstrate how content and language learning intersect and can be combined, let us turn to the course's logistics and materials. I will illustrate how content learning was structured with sample activities, including a lesson plan for working on one scene, then discuss building students' vocabulary knowledge and examine some of the course's focus-on-form activities.

The fifth-semester course met five days a week in 50-minute sessions for a total 65 contact hours; students were expected to do an average of an additional 60 to 90 minutes of written homework or other preparation outside of class per day. The 65 hours include the students' in-class oral presentations about Soviet musical groups and five hours total for testing (15- to 30-minute quizzes every other week and two 60-minute tests). There was a written final exam at the end of the semester. Work on the content topic began in the second week of the semester after several days of introductory review activities dealing with personal biography and expressions related to clothing. Homework activities during the semester included: viewing assigned scenes of the film; completing comprehension checks that featured new or targeted vocabulary; preparing oral or written summaries; making comparisons or opinions about characters and scenes; and studying for vocabulary and grammar quizzes or tests. For the most part students' initial viewing of subtitled film scenes occurred outside of class time.

Work on Content Learning

Some historical and cultural information was provided to students in English, while other concepts came in readings in Russian. The English cultural information was largely given early in the semester via an initial handout that explained phenomena that student viewers will encounter and must understand; this introduction comes at a point when they are not equipped linguistically to process detailed explanations quickly in Russian. The English handout first presents the words describing the film's two groups of young people: стиляги [hipsters] and комсомольцы [Komsomol members]. The handout also explains other phenomena, all of which provide needed context for the first 30 minutes of the film: золотая молодежь [golden youth]; чувак and чувиха [a hipster guy, a hipster girl]; and Бродвей [Broadway], which refers to Gorky Street, Moscow's main avenue where the stiljagi in the film congregate. Vocabulary explanations include a small amount of additional cultural information in English.[7]

The instructor also selects short readings in Russian (300–1,000 words) outfitted with activities on topics like музыка на костях [music on bones] and космополитизм [cosmopolitanism]. Students *have* to read the Russian materials to find out cultural and historical information. Activities for learning dates and Russian names for key events can fill in gaps in students' background knowledge. Students learn about the Soviet and Russian bands whose songs serve as the soundtrack and give oral presentations about them to the class. Finally, work on the different kinds of apartments the characters inhabit creates opportunities for content learning about Soviet types of housing (the communal apartment and the elite high-rise).

Guiding Content Learning with Readings

In a series of steps the learners are guided from the first encounter with the text, through the process of comprehension, to acquiring and beginning to use the text's language.[8] Through these activities readers gain a more nuanced understanding of the text's language and can accurately map vocabulary and grammar forms to meanings. Before students are pushed to talk about the text's content in their own words (i.e., produce output), they have a chance to begin using the text's language in scaffolded input-based work, eventually using key phrases from the text to reconstitute the ideas from the text and react to them. These steps build the learners' ability to communicate using the language and ideas from the text independently.

The "music on bones" text illustrates this process. Students had already begun watching *Hipsters* by this point and had talked about the characters. But the class had not yet discussed the initial scene of a patient getting an X-ray nor made the connection between that scene and the one where one of the stiljagi uses the X-ray film to make a record containing forbidden music. Students began work on the text with prereading vocabulary activities in which they matched English and Russian equivalents and analyzed sentences to identify the meanings of individual words. For example, they were asked to make an educated guess about the meaning of the verb издавать-издать [to publish] by interpreting and analyzing the following sentence: "Э́та кни́га была́ и́здана то́лько по́сле девяно́сто пе́рвого го́да—до распа́да СССР её не публикова́ли" [The book was published only after 1991—before the collapse of the USSR it was not published]. In pairs they translated targeted words, thus constructing their own vocabulary list. After this prereading work, students were given a fixed amount of time to read the text, looking for key vocabulary and ideas. The assignment for the next class meeting was to read the text in detail, take an online comprehension quiz (10 true-false sentences in English), and fill out a reading matrix (excerpted in Table 9.1) in order to start working toward connecting textual language with referential meaning(s).

The reading matrix served as the basis for the next day's classroom activities. Students work in pairs or small groups to share their answers. As students work they compare what they have written, which provides an opportunity to correct any potential misreadings and verify that they have copied down the correct and full Russian phrase(s) requested. Students often correctly identify the location in the text containing the information but write an incomplete Russian equivalent of the English, leaving out necessary elements of the syntax. The online comprehension quiz and in-class activity allows the instructor to assess how much of the content the students had understood and whether they were beginning to map the Russian phrases to English meanings.

The lesson plan then moves to input-based comprehension activities that use selected language from the text to reconstitute the text's ideas. Activity types include true-false sentences (in Russian) about the content and matching beginnings and endings of sentences that restate text content more simply. Time is allotted to work on syntactically difficult passages, several of which are highlighted so that students can engage in parsing and ask questions of the instructor. Next students are given images that refer to the text (e.g., an image of a record made on an X-ray). The images are taped to the board with plenty of space around each one, and students work in groups

TABLE 9.1. Reading Matrix Instructions and Excerpt

Read each English phrase and decide if the information in it is present in the text or not. Cross out any English statement on the left that is not present in the Russian text. Check the remaining English sentences to make sure they render the Russian information accurately. On the right side of the table write in how the English information is conveyed in the Russian version of the text. Be careful to copy out whole phrases.	
Абза́ц № 1 [Paragraph 1]	**фразы из текста** [Phrases from the text]
jazz was officially forbidden	______________________
there was discussion of what jazz is	______________________
to mention jazz was not allowed	______________________
it was impossible to get Western records	______________________
people brought records to the USSR	______________________
rock was recognized before the 1970s	______________________
rock groups worked entirely underground	______________________

Note: The translations in brackets are not provided in the actual class handout.

to write as many pertinent words or phrases around their assigned image as they can before time is called. Students compare results and suggest additions or corrections to what their classmates have written. The next day students work on a cloze activity that consists of a connected paragraph about events that occur in the first 15 minutes of the film and combine language from the text with language from the film plot. Learners thus demonstrate they have learned language from the text, have mapped language forms to meanings, and have shown some ability to remember what they had read. They are able to produce language from and about the text on their own and incorporate the text language into their discussion of the film's narrative. The two 50-minute class periods spent on working with the text result in better-informed student reactions to the film, both during class discussion and in homework assignments where they have to describe film scenes or characters.

Work on Vocabulary in the Context of Focus on Form

The film and supplementary readings present challenges in organizing and focusing student work on vocabulary. The difficulty is not just that the dialogue of a feature film includes a large amount of input; rather, it is that students need vocabulary to describe the settings, situations, and characters' actions and emotional states that they observe on screen. From that extremely broad set the instructor must make choices

TABLE 9.2. Sample Activity: Glossing Vocabulary

ждать–подождать (когó?) imperf. present: жду, ждёшь, . . . ждут perf. future: подождý, подождёшь, . . . подождýт —Когó ты ждёшь? [Who are you waiting for?] —Я жду свою́ подрýгу и её мýжа. [I'm waiting for my girlfriend and her husband.]	to wait for (Remember that this verb does NOT need a preposition; it is like слýшать in this sense.) Notice the forms of подрýга and муж.

Note: The translations in brackets are not provided in the actual class handout.

about which vocabulary items students will need to comprehend and what they will be expected to produce in assignments. The instructor's choice of vocabulary may depend on the students' language level, the instructor's goals, and the amount of time available for discussion. Another decision is how to present lexical items that are meant to become part of students' active vocabulary. On the one hand students need a vocabulary reference that contains both lexical and grammatical information, especially for verbs describing actions and states. For students at this level the instructor should provide verb infinitives in both aspects, in conjugated forms, and in examples of verb government and usage, as in Table 9.2.

On the other hand, detailed reference material will not on its own lead learners to incorporate new language into what they say or write. In order for the lexicon on a word list to become input that learners have a reason to notice, there must be meaning-based, cognitively engaging activities that activate and situate new vocabulary. This vocabulary work is an essential first step before students attend to the detail of issues related to grammar and syntax.

Input-based vocabulary activities focus on ascertaining whether the learner has understood the messages (the meanings or propositional content) conveyed in various utterances. Dialogue from a film provides one source of input that can become fodder for vocabulary activities. However, students also need other sources of input in audio and written form that contain targeted vocabulary items for film action and characters' emotional states. Instructors will need to generate most of that input themselves—although sometimes detailed plot summaries of films found online can serve as a source.

Activities should follow SI guidelines described earlier. They should include both audio and written input, they should not require that students have to manipulate or produce language forms on their own at the start, and they must engage learners in using targeted lexicon in a meaningful context. By making initial activities referentially oriented the instructor requires learners to comprehend the input—and thus the new vocabulary—to successfully complete the activity. Learners use the input in these activities to interact with one another and, since all morphological information has been embedded in the input, students can do the activities with few grammatical mistakes.

TABLE 9.3. Sample Activity: Paired Referential Vocabulary

Кто что де́лает? [Who does what?] Ве́рсия А [Version A]	Поли́на [Polina]	Поли́нина мать [Polina's mother]
1. Она́ просыпа́ется. [She wakes up]		
2. Она́ сиди́т за столо́м. [She is sitting at the table]		
3. Она́ броса́ет оде́жду на́ пол. [She throws clothes onto the floor]		

Кто что де́лает? [Who does what?] Ве́рсия Б [Version B]	Поли́на [Polina]	Поли́нина мать [Polina's mother]
1. Она́ меша́ет чай в стака́не. [She stirs tea in a glass]		
2. Она́ вста́ла ра́ньше. [She got up earlier]		
3. Она́ кричи́т, что сожжёт америка́нскую оде́жду. [She screams that she will burn the American clothes.]		

Note: The translations in brackets are not provided in the actual class handout.

As an example, one activity is designed to help students work on a short scene near the beginning of the film in which the viewer sees Polina, the female protagonist, at home. She wakes up in the apartment she shares with her single mother, who sees herself as one who adheres strictly to Soviet-sanctioned norms of behavior. The scene establishes the conflict between mother and daughter, revealing the nature of Polina's home life. The activities help learners understand and use vocabulary for describing action, dialogue, and the characters' emotional states.[9] The learners' first task is to work in pairs and take turns reading sentences describing actions that occur in the scene; they indicate which character does the action (Polina, her mother, or both). Each student in the pair is given half of the sentences to read and cannot see the other student's' sentences, so learners must listen to one another carefully.[10] The two sets of sentences are shown in Table 9.3. Both students then look at all the sentences and arrange the events in chronological order.

Another activity involves matching the beginnings of sentences that describe the scene with their appropriate endings (Table 9.4). These sentences are written so that students must understand the targeted vocabulary in order to connect them accurately.

Because the activities described so far are referential, i.e., there is a verifiably correct answer to each question, and because students must read sentences aloud and

TABLE 9.4. Sample Activity: Match Sentence Openings and Endings

а. Поли́на, наве́рное, . . . [Polina most likely . . .]	____ сиди́т за столо́м. [is sitting at the table.]
б. Мать у́тром . . . [In the morning the mother . . .]	____ а де́вушка молчи́т. [but the girl does not speak.]
в. Мать кричи́т на Поли́ну, . . . [The mother screams at Polina]	____ ремешко́м. [with a belt.]
г. Мать хо́чет бить Поли́ну [The mother wants to beat Polina]	____ вчера́ ве́чером гуля́ла с друзья́ми. [last night was out with her friends.]

Note: Translations are not provided in the actual class handout.

TABLE 9.5. Sample Activity: Identifying Synonyms

бьёт [beats] врёт [lies] вы́растила [raised] дежу́рство [duty] молчи́т [is silent]
1. У меня́ была́ **рабо́та**. [I had **work**.] 2. Я шпио́нку **воспита́ла**. [I've **raised** a spy.] 3. Поли́на **ничего́ не говори́т**. [Polina **says nothing**.] 4. Поли́на **говори́т непра́вду**. [Polina **doesn't tell the truth**.]

Note: Translations are not provided in the actual class handout.

give an answer that is based on their understanding of the statements' propositional content, each student has multiple opportunities to use the new vocabulary items and demonstrate an understanding of the meanings of the phrases.

Identifying synonymous expressions is another way for learners to demonstrate they understand meanings of particular lexical items. Students read sentences featuring synonyms of the targeted vocabulary (marked in bold in Table 9.5) and match those items to items in a word bank. In these exercises students read sentences aloud in pairs and create similar statements using synonyms from the input (the word bank), which contains at least one extra item that serves as a distractor.

The final vocabulary-focused activity—a cloze passage based on a paragraph-length retelling of the scene—requires that students not only know the vocabulary in the word bank but also are able to get clues from surrounding context about the words omitted. Cloze activities can be given in two versions: one in which the vocabulary in the word bank is presented in the form students need (see an example in Table 9.6) and the other in which the word bank is presented in dictionary forms of the missing items.

TABLE 9.6. Sample Cloze Activity: Vocabulary in Needed Form

врёт [lies]	дежýрство [duty]	дочь [daughter]	за столóм [at table]
кричи́т [screams]	мешáет [stirs]	одéлась [got dressed]	просыпáется [wakes]
У́тром Поли́на _______ в квартúре, в котóрой она живёт вмéсте с мáтерью. Мать к э́тому врéмени ужé встáла и ______. Онá сиди́т ______ и ______ чай в стакáне. Мать спрáшивает своЮ́ ______, где онá былá всю ночь, а Поли́на ______ и говори́т мáтери, что у неё бы́ло ______. [In the morning Polina wakes up in the apartment where she lives with her mother. Her mother has already got up and got dressed. She is sitting at the table and stirring tea in a glass. The mother asks her daughter where she was all night and Polina lies and says she was on duty.]			

Note: All words are in the required form, and there is one extra item. Translations are not provided in the actual class handout.

TABLE 9.7. Sample Activity: The Characters' Relationships and Desires

______________ хóчет, чтóбы ______________ сéла за стол.
[___ wants ___ to sit down at the table.]
______________ хóчет, чтóбы ______________ её остáвила в покóе.
[___ wants ___ to leave her alone.]
______________ хóчет, чтóбы ______________ по вечерáм сидéла дóма.
[___ wants ___ to stay home at night.]
______________ хóчет, чтóбы ______________ на неё бóльше не кричáла.
[___ wants ___ not to scream at her anymore.]

Note: Translations are not provided in the actual class handout.

As learners complete the vocabulary activities, the work shifts to targeted morphology and syntax: verb conjugations, tense and aspect use, verb government, and declensions of new nouns. The activities are designed to focus the learner's attention on vocabulary acquisition before requiring them to notice new grammar forms in the input. Lexical exercises can also embed work on a grammar point. The activity excerpted in Table 9.7 recycles language input from the scene and teacher-generated narration but situates it in the context of asking students to decide—based on their evaluation of what they have seen and heard—what each character wants (or does not want) the other one to do. This activity provides structured input for using the construction čtoby with past-tense verb forms and shifts work from referential to affective activities—in SI, those requiring a learner's personal response or opinion. For many of these sentences students must infer the answers based on their understanding of the scene and characters. The format of the activity leads students to use the čtoby construction in a cognitively engaging way as they read through the sentences, and the scaffolding supports accuracy in using a construction that most students at this level still find challenging. The activity also provides input for language that students are likely to want to use in their own writing when discussing the relationship between Polina and her mother. Students read sentences aloud and decide what each character wants the other character to do, and write in the names accordingly.

While working with this scene learners also benefit from opportunities to work on verb morphology, contrasting present imperfective and past perfective verb forms for lexical items such as wake up, get up, get dressed, and put on, since consistent use of tense, aspect, and time frame is an important feature of advanced proficiency. In the next activity (see Table 9.8) the teacher asks the students to use a word bank to complete a paragraph that contrasts what is happening in the scene—things the viewer sees Polina do—with what has already happened—actions her mother has already taken that morning.

After students complete the fill-in-the-blank task they are asked to go back and mark the tense and aspect of all the verbs in the paragraph, after which they can work on building two different narratives of Polina's actions in the scene using the targeted verbs in the past or present tense.

TABLE 9.8. Sample Activity: Present Imperfective and Past Perfective Verbs

встаёт [gets up]	оделась [got dressed]	надевает [puts on]	просыпается [wakes up]

1. Зри́тель не зна́ет, во ско́лько сего́дня у́тром просну́лась мать. А Поли́на ________________, когда́ она слы́шит, как мать меша́ет чай в стака́не. [The viewer does not know at what time this morning the mother awoke. Polina wakes up when she hears her mother stirring tea.]
2. Поли́на в э́той сце́не ________________ и одева́ется, а мать уже́ вста́ла и ________________. [Polina in this scene gets up and gets dressed, but her mother had already gotten up and got dressed.]
3. Мы ви́дим, как Поли́на ________________ пла́тье. А мать до нача́ла э́той сце́ны уже́ наде́ла костю́м. [We see Polina putting on her dress. Her mother had already put on her suit before the beginning of the scene.]

Note: Translations are not provided in the actual class handout.

Film as Text: Interpretive Scaffolding

Particular strategies are required to encourage learners to read a film deeply, to engage in a close reading of selected complex or visually rich scenes. One challenging plot element of *Hipsters*, especially for learners lacking knowledge of Soviet life, is an early scene in the communal apartment in which the viewer sees the many residents' morning routines while Mels's father plays the accordion and sings «Человек и кошка» ["The man and the cat"], a 1991 hit originally performed by the rock group Nol'. The scene packs into three minutes a whirlwind of images that convey an entire set of stories: the view of the communal apartment (some features of which are rendered realistically, while others are highly stylized); flashbacks telling the story of Mels's family and World War II; and the song itself, whose lyrics constitute a separate though artistically related narrative. To comprehend the various meanings conveyed in this scene the class works on it over four days. On the first day students watch the scene without sound; they are instructed to make notes about their impressions in any language they wish and are given several minutes after the end of the clip to do so. They then share their notes, and the instructor provides Russian versions of observations by writing them on the board in Russian so that students can copy them. The students offer comments and questions in both Russian and English: «очень весело» [It is very cheerful /a lot of fun]; "the apartment is crazy"; «он живёт в общежитии?» [Does he live in a dorm?]; "Why is there a blowtorch?" (eggs are cooking on a primus stove); "It's scary." One of the instructor's roles is to eliminate initial misreadings that can mar subsequent attempts at interpretation and, as Swaffar and Arens (2005) note is vital, to teach students "to attend to one pattern of textual messages at a time instead of falling into gaps of knowledge and culture" (p. 83). In class the instructor responds to the observations with questions and comments directed at the whole class in order to guide students toward a better interpretation of what they had seen. For example, responding to the comment about the blowtorch, the instructor shows an image of a primus, offering the phrase готовили на примусе [they cooked using a primus stove]. Students are asked to consider why the family is using a primus rather than the full-size stove. Using a still shot of the kitchen the instructor guides students toward understanding the primus stove not as camping equipment, as one student had speculated, but as a way for multiple families to use the kitchen simultaneously, a necessary feature of communal apartment life.

Additional SI activities help students understand and describe other aspects of the opening scene. They provide written input to help students describe the visuals from the scene (the only audio in the scene is the song «Человек и кошка» ["The man and the cat"]) and also check comprehension of the scene's images. The true-false sentences shown in Table 9.9 review features of communal apartments and ensure that students understand where and when the action in the scene takes place.

The next step is to analyze difficulties with interpretation of artistic choices that have to do with the movie's genre and to examine the content of specific frames.

TABLE 9.9. Sample True-False Activity: Binary Options

Мэлс живёт в отде́льной кварти́ре. [Mels lives in a separate (not communal) apartment.]
Мэлс живёт в коммуна́льной кварти́ре. [Mels lives in a communal apartment.]
У ка́ждого челове́ка в э́той кварти́ре есть своя́ ко́мната. [Every person in the apartment has (his) own room.]
Де́йствие э́той сце́ны происхо́дит, наве́рное, ве́чером. [The action likely takes place in the evening.]

Note: Translations are not provided in the actual class handout.

Learners viewed 10 different frames from the opening scene in the communal apartment: the overhead shots of rooms of different residents, the residents bustling about in the corridor, the synchronized kitchen chores, teeth being brushed in rhythm, and Mels and his brother counting out the seconds for the boiled eggs on the primus stove.

Instead of pushing students straight to the output phase (i.e., asking them to narrate what they see), input-based activities help students describe the images, giving them written scaffolding that enables completion of the activity in Russian using targeted lexical and grammatical forms. One SI activity targets the construction видеть как [see how] using the phrase "in this frame we see how ___ is/are." Students work in pairs to choose a set of possible sentences that could describe each screenshot, for example: "In this frame we see how (people) are boiling eggs" or "In this frame we see how (people) are brushing their teeth in rhythm." Next a categorizing activity asks learners to consider where they saw features of Soviet communal life in the images and where they saw the more highly stylized features of a musical film. Some images or description sentences are judged to belong to both categories: for example, people brushing their teeth in rhythm is deemed both normal (for communal life) and also stylized (because the action is choreographed).

On day two students work on the flashback scenes about Mels's family. An ordering activity is used to provide written input that contains both new and familiar expressions and information (i.e., father went to the front, fought in the war, returned to Moscow, saw victory, it's 1945, he discovers his wife cheating and throws [wife] out of the apartment). Some of the previous day's vocabulary is reviewed, and the song lyrics are previewed as text. Students are assigned to watch the YouTube video of a performance of the song by Nol' and complete comprehension work on the song's lyrics. Day three features a minilecture and question-and-answer session about the concept of тоска [extreme longing, ennui], which figures prominently in the lyrics.

At this point students are ready to describe this scene by themselves. However, they need scaffolding to help them organize and express ideas in more sophisticated ways using a range of connectors. Before writing their own descriptions of and

TABLE 9.10. Sample Scaffolding Activity: From Description to Observation and Interpretation

Нам понра́вилось то, что . . .	[We liked the fact that . . .]
Мы немно́го удиви́лись тому́, что . . .	[We were a little surprised that . . .]
Нам бы́ло тру́дно поня́ть, почему́ . . .	[It was hard for us to understand why . . .]
С одно́й стороны́, в э́тих ка́драх . . .	[On the one hand, in the scene . . .]
А с друго́й стороны́ . . .	[But on the other hand . . .]
Мы согла́сны с . . . в том, что она́ пи́шет о . . .	[We agree with (the author) when she says . . .]

Note: Translations are not provided in the actual class handout.

reactions to the scene, students read a short reflection about how the song fit the scene composed by a native speaker acquainted with the learners' language level. Students do comprehension activities on this sample reflection for homework, and then in class they identify ways in which the text organizes arguments ("on the one hand," "on the other hand," "it's possible that," "for example"). Using the information shown in Table 9.10 students work in pairs to compare ideas about the reflection and share results with the class. Each phrase is allotted a "box" of a table where students can write in their answers on the right.

Following these activities students write a reflection essay on whether the song fits the scene. They are expected to give examples—describing parts of the scene and referring to song lyrics where needed—and indicate agreement or disagreement with the native speaker's reaction.

Assessing Content and Language Learning

As the course goals encompass content and language learning, assessment evaluates students' progress in both areas. Content learning is assessed using a combination of in-class quizzes and homework. Quizzes contain cloze passages that require knowledge of content information on the topics covered in the readings. Homework writing prompts for shorter essays—third-person descriptions of segments of the film—direct students to include the cultural content when framing their descriptions. For example, "At the beginning of the film Mels is a Komsomol member. He meets a young woman named Polina," would receive a lower content score than: "At the beginning of the film Mels is a Komsomol member—the Komsomol was a Soviet organization for young people older than 14. He meets a young woman, a stiljaga, who is named Polina." Assignments specify appropriate vocabulary, grammar, and

TABLE 9.11. Sample Content Rubric for Scoring a Presentation

***Content (20%): ___ / 20 points**

20–19–18: You included abundant material about the group you worked on, both biographical and professional. You answered all questions in the prep handout about the group's personnel and development. You used dates and chronology so that your audience had a clear time line of events. You explained who the important people are. There are no factual errors in your verbal presentation or your slides.

17–16.5–16: You had sufficient information but in some places you needed more detail or explication. Your chronology may not have been clear or you may not have answered all the questions. You may have had 1–2 factual errors in your talk or slides.

15.5–15–14.5: You did not give a great deal of information about your topic. The listener received only the bare minimum of what could have been said. You had a number of factual errors in your talk or slides.

14–13.5–13: You gave far too little information. It was impossible to understand much of your content. There are more errors than correct information in your talk or slides.

constructions that students need to use, including: indirect speech with appropriate tenses and constructions; a range of communication verbs (e.g., inquire, request, advise, answer, say, tell); and present-tense narration.

At the end of the semester students give oral presentations on the musical groups whose music is featured in the film. Students received a checklist of expectations for content, language use, presentation skills, and citing of sources. The assessment rubric is distributed ahead of time. Students submit their writing drafts at least a day ahead of the presentation; the instructor gives written feedback about grammar and syntax (using recasts, correction of discrete forms, and metalinguistic comments), and also checks for content errors and misspelled names. Drafts whose content and language require substantial correction receive lower scores on that portion of the assignment. This rubric considers whether content and language from the preparation checklist have been used and whether the presenters have made factual errors. Of the total score for the presentation, content comprises 20%; organization—15%; vocabulary—25%; accuracy in the written draft—10%; accuracy during presentation—15%; and presentation skills (eye contact, pronunciation, delivery)—15%.

The rubric for language use specifies the targeted forms, constructions, and functions students are expected to use. This includes grammatical accuracy in using time expressions and combining those with appropriate past-tense narration to tell the story of the group's founding.

The final exam includes images related to the course content (for example, a "music on bones" record from the film or a photo of one of the rock groups from students' presentations). Students are asked to write several sentences in Russian identifying and describing a specified number of images, with the stipulation that they can choose images that were not the subject of their own oral presentation.

CONCLUSION

The student work and student evaluations of the course material suggest that the course largely met both the content and the language learning goals. It was sometimes difficult to decide how to incorporate work on language forms and to create an instructional sequence. The most time-consuming pedagogical challenge was in tailoring input in grammar explanations and language-driven activities so that they are related to the film. However, the decision to concentrate on only one film each semester and to add readings that contain related content allowed the class to unpack cultural information embedded in the film that otherwise may have been misinterpreted or remained unnoticed. These also allowed students to work in more detail on the target language forms.

I suggest the following guidelines for instructors contemplating a similar content-driven third-year course. First, film plot and characters should offer students several opportunities for retelling and speaking from the characters' points of view. Instructors should note the historical and cultural content of the film and identify which grammatical features appropriate to the learners' level appear most frequently in the film's text. Instructors need to decide which language-driven topics match the content well in order to determine which content learning can be done productively in the TL. Instructors must set concrete language production goals for students' oral and written work: for example, "retell the action of key scenes in the film using present-tense narration" or "describe a character's emotional response to events in the film," as well as specific content-driven learning goals. The subsequent stage involves selecting the right vocabulary to accomplish the student production goals and then situating that vocabulary as comprehensible input—narration or dialogue—that engages students in describing, narrating, responding to, and evaluating film scenes. Finally, instructors need to consider whether to choose a smaller amount of authentic material to teach (i.e., fewer films) in order to do more extensive interpretive work with key scenes and increase opportunities to assess content learning.

Helping students discuss a text or film with cultural awareness requires that we pedagogically view that text as more than a way to learn new vocabulary and grammar, or even as a way to get students to talk or have something to talk about (Kern, 2003; Swaffar & Arens, 2005). Learners must have the "cognitive strategies and linguistic resources necessary to comprehend and interpret a work . . . as a complicated act of communication within a culture" (Swaffar & Arens, 2005, p. 79). By calling attention to a film's intersections with related cultural content, by prioritizing content learning, and by employing activities that deeply explore text and cultural content within the framework of focus on form, we can help learners transition confidently to more nuanced, interculturally aware, and advanced language use.

NOTES

1. For example, students may be able to communicate in Russian about their own university education but they may not have been held accountable for knowing specifics of the Russian educational system.
2. PACE stands for: Presentation of meaningful language; Attention; Coconstruct an explanation; Extension activity.
3. Examples include Soviet and post-Soviet films like «Москва слезам не верит» [*Moscow does not believe in tears*] (Boguslavskii & Menshov, 1979) and «Утомленные солнцем» [*Burnt by the sun*] (Mikhalkov et al., 1994).
4. The materials for the sixth-semester course in its first iteration were the films «Вор» [*The thief*] (Bortnikov et al., 1997) and «Чучело» [*Scarecrow*] (Vulman & Bykov, 1983), and Lyudmila Ulitskaya's short story «Дар нерукотворный» ["A gift not made with human hands"] (2001).
5. The first-year textbook was *Mezhdu nami: An Interactive Introduction to Russian* (deBenedette et al., 2015); in the second-year course students used *V puti: Russian Grammar in Context* (Kagan et al., 2006).
6. Textbooks, such as *Cinema for Russian Conversation* (Kagan et al., 2005), are helpful in providing vocabulary and discussion questions; however, since they often cover multiple films, they present a challenge for a single-topic content-driven course.
7. Examples are a one-sentence explanation of a reference in the film to the American radio broadcasts by «Голос Америки» [*Voice of America*] and a brief note about the term роддом [maternity or birthing hospital].
8. To facilitate learners' work with texts the teacher relied on the procedural model for readings as articulated by Swaffar and Arens (2005).
9. Outside of class learners may complete multiple-choice questions, checking basic comprehension of the plot before the class in which vocabulary work commences.
10. A teacher-centered version of this task would ask students to listen as the instructor reads a sentence, then decide which character performs the action.

REFERENCES

Adair-Hauck, B., & Donato, R. (2016). PACE: A story-based approach for dialogic inquiry about form and meaning. In J. Shrum & E. Glisan (Eds.), *Teacher's handbook: Contextualized language instruction* (5th ed., pp. 206–30). Boston: Cengage Learning.

Altman, R. (1989). *The video connection: Integrating video into language teaching*. Boston: Houghton Mifflin College Division.

Boguslavskii, V. (Producer), & Menshov, V. (Director). (1979). *Москва слезам не верит* [Moscow does not believe in tears] [Motion picture]. USSR: Mosfilm.

Bortnikov, I., Kozlov, S., & Tolstunov, I. (Producers), & Chukhrai, P. (Director). (1997). *Вор* [The thief] [Motion picture]. Russian Federation & France: NTV-Profit & Roissy Films.

Brinton, D., Snow, M., & Wesche, M. (1989). *Content-based language instruction*. New York: Newbury House.

Byrnes, H. (2000). Meaning and form in classroom-based SLA research: Reflections from a college foreign language perspective. In J. F. Lee & A. D. Valdman (Eds.), *Meaning and form: Multiple perspectives* (pp. 125–79). Boston: Heinle & Heinle.

Byrnes, H. (2005). Content-based foreign language instruction. In C. Sanz (Ed.), *Mind and context in adult second language acquisition: Methods, theory, and practice* (pp. 282–302). Washington, DC: Georgetown UP.

Byrnes, H. (2006). Perspectives. *Modern Language Journal, 90* (ii), 244–66.

deBenedette, L., Comer, W. J., Smyslova, A., & Perkins, J. (2015). *Mezhdu nami: An interactive introduction to Russian*. Retrieved from: https://mezhdunami.org

Doughty, C., & Williams, J. (1998). *Focus on form in classroom second language acquisition.* The Cambridge Applied Linguistics Series. Cambridge: Cambridge UP.

Glikman, E., Rodnianskii, A., & Tolstunov, I. (Producers), & Bychkova, O. (Director). (2006). *Питер FM* [Piter FM] [Motion picture]. Russian Federation: STS Protel.

Kagan, O., Kashper, M., & Morozova, Yu. (2005). *Cinema for Russian conversation*. Indianapolis, IN: Focus.

Kagan, O., Miller, F. J., & Kudyma, G. (2006). *V puti: Russian Grammar in Context*. Upper Saddle River, NJ: Prentice Hall.

Kern, R. G. (2003). Literacy as a new organizing principle for foreign language education. In P. C. Patrikis (Ed.), *Reading between the lines: Perspectives on foreign language literacy.* New Haven, CT: Yale UP.

Krashen, S. (1982). *Principles and practice in second language acquisition*. Oxford: Pergamon.

Krivonoshchenko, V. (Producer), & Daneliia, G. (Director). (1979). *Осенний марафон* [Autumn marathon] [Motion picture]. USSR: Mosfilm.

Lebedev. L., Todorovsky, V., Gorianov V., & Yarmolnik, L. (Producers), & Todorovsky, V. (Director). (2008). *Стиляги* [Hipsters] [Motion picture]. Russian Federation: Krasnaya strela.

Lee, J., & VanPatten, B. (2003). *Making communicative language teaching happen* (2nd ed.). Boston: McGraw-Hill.

Lightbown, P., & Spada, N. (2013). *How languages are learned.* Oxford: Oxford UP.

Lyster, R. (2007). *Learning and teaching languages through content: A counterbalanced approach*. Amsterdam: John Benjamins.

Met, M. (1999). *Content-based instruction: Defining terms, making decisions.* NFLC Reports. Washington, DC: National Foreign Language Center.

Mikhalkov, N., & Seydoux, M. (Producers), & Mikhalkov, N. (Director). (1994). *Утомленные солнцем* [Burnt by the sun]. [Motion picture]. Russian Federation and France: Studiia TriTe & Camera One.

Musumeci, D. (1996). Teacher-learner negotiation in content-based instruction: Communication at cross-purposes? *Applied Linguistics, 17*(3), 286–325.

Paesani, K., & Willis, H. (2012). Beyond the language-content divide: Research on advanced foreign language instruction at the postsecondary level. *Foreign Language Annals, 45*(1), s54–75.

Rodgers, D. (2006). Developing content and form: Encouraging evidence from Italian content-based instruction. *Modern Language Journal, 90*(3), 373–86.

Stempleski, S., & Tomalin, B. (1995). *Video in action: Recipes for using video in language teaching.* Upper Saddle River, NJ: Prentice Hall.

Stryker, S., & Leaver, B. L. (Eds.). (1997). *Content-based instruction in foreign language education: Models and methods.* Washington, DC: Georgetown UP.

Swaffar, J., & Arens, K. (2005). *Remapping the foreign language curriculum: An approach through multiple literacies.* New York: Modern Language Association of America.

Swain, M. (1985). Communicative competence: Some roles of comprehensible input and comprehensible output in its development. In S. Gass & C. Madden (Eds.), *Input in second language acquisition* (pp. 235–53). Rowley, MA: Newbury House.

Thompson, I. (2000). Assessing foreign language skills: Data from Russian. In O. Kagan & B. Rifkin (Eds.), *The learning and teaching of Slavic languages and cultures* (pp. 255–84). Bloomington, IN: Slavica.

Tokareva, V., & Comer, W. J. (2008). *A day without lying: A glossed edition for intermediate-level students of Russian with vocabulary, exercises, and commentaries.* Bloomington, IN: Slavica.

Ulitskaya, L. (2001). Дар нерукотворный [A gift not made with human hands]. In L. Ulitskaya, *Пиковая дама и другие рассказы* [The queen of spades and other short stories]. Moscow: Vagrius.

VanPatten, B. (Ed.). (2004). *Processing instruction: Theory, research, and commentary.* Mahwah, NJ: L. Erlbaum.

Vulman, S. (Producer), & Bykov, R. (Director). (1983). *Чучело* [Scarecrow] [Motion picture]. USSR: Mosfilm.

10

ORAL HISTORY IN THE RUSSIAN LANGUAGE CURRICULUM

A Transformative Learning Experience

Benjamin Jens, Colleen Lucey, and Benjamin Rifkin

Oral history, as defined by the Oral History Association (OHA) as "a method of gathering, preserving and interpreting the voices and memories of people, communities, and participants in past events" (OHA, 2019a), constitutes learning opportunities for students to interview native speakers about their lived experiences. Oral history projects offer opportunities for meaningful communicative interactions on both enduring and contemporary questions. In this chapter we provide a theoretical framework for the development and implementation of oral history interviews in the Russian language curriculum, connecting this framework to the World-Readiness Standards for Learning Languages (NSCB, 2015); the Proficiency Guidelines of the American Council on the Teaching of Foreign Languages (2012); Benjamin Bloom's taxonomy of cognitive processes (Bloom & Krathwohl, 1956); L. Dee Fink's theory of significant learning (2013); and the Liberal Education and America's Promise (LEAP) Program of the Association of American Colleges and Universities (AAC&U) (2013). We demonstrate how oral history interviews at different proficiency levels address all five of the World-Readiness Standards, match the liberal arts learning goals of the LEAP program, and focus on the human connection that is critical for significant learning (Fink, 2013). Next we describe a model for how such a program can be implemented in accordance with college and university rules regarding institutional review of any project that involves human subjects and how such a project can offer incentives for Russian speakers to engage with L2 learners. We describe how to help students develop appropriate questions (both initial and follow-up) and how to analyze and understand the responses. Finally we cite potential and actual language and culture learning outcomes, we share student evaluations of their experience of an oral history project, and we discuss the projects' impact on motivation for studying Russian.

ORAL HISTORY IN THE FOREIGN LANGUAGE CURRICULUM: BLOOM'S TAXONOMY AND FINK'S THEORY OF SIGNIFICANT LEARNING

Oral history assignments are learning tasks in which students interview native speakers of the target language about their life experiences and synthesize that information for some kind of reaction or report. The power of oral history in the Russian language curriculum comes from having students engage in higher-level thinking skills (Bloom) and significant learning activities (Fink).

Bloom published his *Taxonomy of Educational Objectives* as two handbooks, one focused on cognitive factors (Bloom & Krathwohl, 1956) and the other on affective factors (Bloom et al., 1965). He theorizes that there exists a taxonomy of cognitive processes in which lower-level skills that engage with knowledge (based on memorization) and comprehension (based on understanding) are acquired before higher-level skills, and focus on application (based on the usage of knowledge), analysis (in which information is examined and questioned), synthesis (in which learners use information from diverse sources to create something new and original), and evaluation (the highest-order skill by which learners make judgments about the application of external criteria to evidence brought to bear on the given question). Bloom's taxonomy has been discussed, analyzed, expanded, and revised over the years, including by Anderson and Krathwohl (2014), which resulted in a reformulation of the hierarchy of cognitive processes, as depicted in Table 10.1.

As noted in Table 10.1, Anderson and Krathwohl rephrased the processes as verbs and reversed the order of the two highest cognitive processes, shifting the creation of new knowledge to the highest place in the taxonomy from Bloom's position of it as the second highest.

To the best of our knowledge the taxonomy has rarely been applied to the learning and teaching of world languages at the postsecondary level. In efforts to engage students deeply in the study of Russian, instructors should strive to design and implement learning activities that develop our students' higher-order cognitive skills, making the Russian language curriculum a valuable part of the larger liberal arts mission.

TABLE 10.1. Bloom's Taxonomy Compared to Anderson and Krathwohl's Revision of Bloom's Taxonomy

Learning tasks (ordered from highest to lowest)	
Bloom and Krathwohl (1956)	**Anderson and Krathwohl (2014)**
evaluation	create
synthesis	evaluate
analysis	analyze
application	apply
comprehension	understand
knowledge	remember

The integration of oral history assignments into the Russian language curriculum provides learners with opportunities to remember, understand, and use important information about Russian and Soviet history relevant to the lived experiences of the native speakers they are interviewing. Students apply their knowledge of Russian to formulate initial questions, understand responses, and formulate appropriate follow-up questions. Moving up the taxonomy to higher-order thinking skills, students analyze and evaluate the responses of the interviewees to create a report to share with classmates and others, either in written or oral form in Russian or in English or perhaps as a bilingual edition that the interviewees can share with relatives who may be monolingual English speakers.

Oral history projects also correspond to the theory of significant learning articulated by Fink (2013), who argues that *significant* learning experiences are those that remain with learners for many years. He defines significant learning experiences as those that occur at the intersection of several factors:

1. Foundational knowledge (the fundamental tenets of the discipline);
2. Application (using the foundational knowledge in meaningful contexts, e.g., reading a text or interacting with a native speaker);
3. Integration (using the foundational knowledge along with knowledge from other disciplines or other spheres of life, e.g., understanding a news broadcast);
4. Learning how to learn (metacognition);
5. Caring, that is, developing new feelings, interests, and values (affective and metacognitive reflection); and
6. Human dimension, that is, learning about oneself and others (using interactions with others to expand one's world view).

In many world language courses students are assigned tasks that relate to the first four of these factors, and sometimes the fifth. Students conducting an oral history project embrace Fink's sixth factor (human dimension) *outside the classroom*.

An oral history assignment can help some students overcome psychosocial resistance to participating in a study abroad experience. Of course, for many students a study abroad opportunity is an extraordinarily transformative learning experience in which they develop new perspectives on their own cultural identity. Furthermore, an oral history project can also support students who have just returned from a study abroad experience by providing an authentic context that sustains their language skills while simultaneously deepens their understanding of the cultural perspectives of native speakers of the target language. Lastly, an oral history project is of critical significance for students who never go abroad because it may be the only opportunity for them to use the language in an authentic cultural interaction that can help them grow empathy, compassion, and understanding with target culture native speakers. Thus, we argue, oral history assignments meet Fink's fifth and sixth requirements to make a learning experience *significant* (caring, human dimension).

ORAL HISTORY IN THE RUSSIAN LANGUAGE CURRICULUM: WORLD-READINESS STANDARDS AND AAC&U'S LIBERAL EDUCATION PROGRAM

The powerful impact of the oral history project is derived, also, from these projects' relationship to (a) the World-Readiness Standards for Learning Languages, (b) the ACTFL Proficiency Guidelines, and (c) the LEAP program of the AAC&U.

The World-Readiness Standards for Learning Languages (NSCB, 2015) establish curricular goals for learners of world languages in five broad areas. Table 10.2 illustrates how those five curricular goals are met in the design of an oral history project.

Native speakers from any of the former Soviet republics can tell stories of their personal experiences of events of global, national, regional, or local significance, whether they are speaking about a childhood spent in evacuation during the Great Patriotic War, the changes associated with Khrushchev's Thaw, the economic stagnation of the Brezhnev period, the advent of perestroika, or the collapse of the Soviet Union. The personal accounts of how these events were experienced on an individual

TABLE 10.2. Meeting World-Readiness Standards/Curricular Goals through an Oral History Project

World-Readiness Standards/ Curricular Goals	Goals Met in an Oral History Project
Communication: interpersonal, interpretive, and presentational	Students interact with interviewees, read and listen to culturally relevant background materials, write reports, and make presentations.
Cultures: relate cultural practices to perspectives; relate cultural products to perspectives	Students study cultural practices, perspectives, and products relevant to the life experience of the interviewee(s).
Connections: build and reinforce knowledge of other disciplines while using language; acquire and evaluate information from diverse perspectives available through the language and its cultures	Students use background information not generally available in English about Russian history, culture, economy, geography, and so forth to create their reports.
Comparisons: compare languages and cultures	Students compare their own experiences with those of their interviewees and their own language use with that of their interviewees.
Communities: communicate and interact with cultural competence in order to participate in multilingual communities at home and around the world	Students use Russian beyond the classroom in face-to-face interactions with native speakers in their community or use social media to interact with speakers elsewhere in the world.

level constitute a remarkable opportunity for meaningful interaction as well as a unique chance for students to practice using higher-order cognitive skills in the analysis of the information they collect and in the creation of a report based on that analysis.

Oral history projects can be implemented at different stages of the development of students' proficiency; they can be structured in accordance with the ACTFL Proficiency Guidelines and our understanding of the nature of the acquisition of Russian by college-age learners (see, for example, Brecht et al., 1993; Rifkin, 2005; and Thompson, 1996). Oral history projects would likely be an inefficient use of time when students are at the Novice level, when they cannot communicate autonomously and rely on memorized utterances. However, starting with the Intermediate Mid level of oral and listening proficiency, students can begin interviewing native speakers of Russian about their life experiences. At the Intermediate level interviews are likely to consist largely of sentence-length questions and responses and chronological narratives, the kind of content that the Intermediate-level speakers and listeners may struggle with but should ultimately comprehend. Intermediate-level students will be much better prepared to understand the responses of the interviewees if they have had opportunities in class to practice listening to sample responses from interviewees from previous semesters (who have given permission for their recordings to be used for that purpose). This kind of preparatory activity helps enhance students' listening skills and readiness to pose follow-up questions in the flow of the interview.

Students at the Intermediate High or Advanced level, usually those who have had a summer immersion or semester-long study abroad experience or who may be heritage learners, can conduct interviews in which they receive answers to broader questions eliciting more complex narrations. These might include questions such as "Please tell me where you were on August 19, 1991, and how you and your friends reacted to the news of the day as it unfolded" or questions eliciting descriptions, such as "Please describe how your neighborhood in Moscow changed from the 1970s to the 1990s?" These students will benefit from preparation activities consisting of the analysis of sample responses to interview questions from previous semesters.

Students at the Superior level, for example those in the Flagship context, might ask and be able to understand answers to questions focused on hypotheses and supported opinions, such as: "How do you think Soviet history might have unfolded had Brezhnev resigned from his position prior to his death?" or "Some experts believe that the collapse of the Soviet Union was a geopolitical catastrophe, while others view it as a positive development in world history. What is your opinion and why do you feel that way?"

The greatest learning impact for oral history projects will be found in work with students at the Intermediate High/Advanced threshold, who will be able to formulate questions comfortably but who will have to work hard to process the responses of the interviewees. Students at lower levels might be able to partner with peers at higher levels to conduct interviews in which the lower-level student asks preliminary questions for which answers are more predictable and within the competence range of the lower-level students in order to understand, before the higher-level students ask more open-ended questions with more complex responses. This "team approach" has the added benefit of showing the lower-level students what they can achieve if they continue studying the language and how they can successfully interact with native speakers of the target language.

Students can be assigned to create and give oral presentations or written papers about their interviewees' life experiences, all of which can be supplemented by additional research through the Internet. One of the final projects could be a bilingual biography (delivered either in writing or as a multimedia project) to be presented to interviewees, who can share it with their non-Russian-speaking relatives.

Oral history projects are also consistent with the expectations of the larger liberal arts mission, as articulated by the LEAP program, which calls for students to study, among other things, the humanities and social sciences, and engage with big questions, both contemporary and enduring, in order to develop intellectual and practical skills, including inquiry and analysis, critical and creative thinking, written and oral communication, intercultural knowledge and competence, ethical reasoning and action, and skills for lifelong learning. By integrating oral history assignments into the Russian language curriculum, we place the study of Russian at the center of the liberal arts enterprise, similar to what Rifkin has argued elsewhere (2012).

PLANNING FOR AND IMPLEMENTING THE ORAL HISTORY PROJECT

There are two key steps when planning for the implementation of an oral history project that must precede actual student work. First, the instructor must identify and obtain the necessary approvals or written documentation of exemption through his/her institution's institutional review board. Second, the instructor must identify partners both on and beyond campus in order to establish the relationships necessary for the success of an oral history project.

Institutional Research Board Approval

There are several issues to consider when planning an oral history project. The instructor(s) must ensure that the project conforms with institutional rules regarding human subjects by consulting with the university's institutional review board (IRB), a federally-mandated administrative unit that reviews the conditions in which research projects are conducted. The IRB must approve any plan to retain or dispose of the relevant recordings in order to protect the individuals who have agreed to be interviewed.

The need for IRB approval of an oral history project depends on the definition of "research," the intent of the instructor (or "investigator," in IRB terminology), and the patterns of IRB practices of the institution where the instructor works.[1] Title 45 Part 46 of the Code of Federal Regulations (45 CFR 46, also referred to as the Common

Rule) defines research as "a systematic investigation, including research development, testing, and evaluation, designed to develop or contribute to generalizable knowledge."[2] As oral history has grown in popularity, this last phrase has led to some ambiguity as to whether such projects fall under the purview of 45 CFR 46, since the code does not provide a concrete definition of "generalizable knowledge." In addition, the type of research that falls under the Common Rule often involves standard questionnaires with large samples of anonymous participants rather than the free-form interviews with identifiable participants who have given informed consent. In some cases a decisive factor would be whether the researcher intends to publish personal information collected from interviewees; in other cases the intention to publish is not as important as the fact that human subjects are participating in an instructional project sponsored by the institution.

The federal unit that oversees the implementation of 45 CFR 46 is the Office of Human Research Protections (OHRP) of the US Department of Health and Human Services. Given the lack of clarity about whether oral history falls under the Common Rule, the OHRP, the American Historical Association (AHA) worked with the Oral History Association in seeking to clarify 45 CFR 46.[3] In 2003 the OHRP concurred with the OHA policy, that oral history interviewing projects, in general, do not fall under the Common Rule because they are designed to create a record of historical events rather than draw conclusions, inform policy, or contribute to generalized knowledge. Oral history interviews that are not intended to be scientific or lead to the development of a hypothesis in a manner that would have predictive value generally do not require an IRB review under this interpretation of 45 CFR 46 but we strongly recommend that all faculty engaging in such projects discuss their plans with their IRB. In many cases a short proposal may be submitted for IRB review and the IRB can deem the project exempt from further review because it does not involve vulnerable populations (e.g., prisoners or children), does not involve intrusive procedures (such as the collection of bodily tissues), and poses little or no risk of harm to the interviewees.

Programs that implement an oral history project will need to consider what they will do with the interviews and materials after the assignment's completion. Instructors may wish to create an archive of interviews for the purpose of providing a resource for colleagues in other disciplines. Interviews can likewise be used to create an archive of authentic language samples for subsequent classes, providing students with opportunities to practice listening skills before they head to the field to conduct their own oral history interviews. If other investigators using this archive would be conducting research as defined by 45 CFR 46, the creation of this resource would constitute research as defined by the Common Rule and would require an IRB approval or exemption.

A recurring oral history component has the potential to gather first-person accounts of Soviet and post-Soviet historical events and to create an archive of material that is valuable to a variety of disciplines connected with Russian studies (history, sociology, linguistics, etc.) and leads to publications that might arise on the basis of the interviews collected for the project. It is essential that faculty members contemplate any future use of the interviews when drafting a consent form, especially if considering posting interviews online or creating class materials that use the interviews. The faculty member(s) must remember to collect and store these consent forms and other documentation in accordance with IRB requirements.

An interdisciplinary, collaborative oral history project provides a variety of benefits. While a program may have its own curricular goals for an oral history project in terms of providing language practice in the community, partnerships with other units within the institution help create a broader base of interest in Russian and potential interdisciplinary projects. Furthermore, in many colleges and universities outreach to the greater community is considered a high priority and can help garner additional external support for language programs. Colleagues in sociology, history, and other academic departments, as well as an institution's office of intergenerational learning or service learning, have valuable experience to draw on in planning and implementing an oral history project. Working with other departments creates greater visibility for the Russian program at all levels. Students of Russian who have a second major beyond Russian find that work on an oral history project may satisfy a variety of requirements, for example, an oral history project in Russian could count as advanced-level work toward both a Russian and a history major. Oral history projects provide students with opportunities to contextualize and practice material discussed in the classroom. For all of these reasons, a well-planned, collaborative oral history project can help in generating increased awareness of one's Russian program and draw students to Russian studies.

Collaborations and Partnerships

As IRB approval is being secured, we advise Russian language faculty collaborate with colleagues within their respective institutions (e.g., faculty in history, economics, political science) given the inherently interdisciplinary nature of an oral history project (Dunaway & Baum, 1996). This interdisciplinary cooperation will create a wider base of support and help with the approval process for working with human subjects while also maximizing the potential of the project with respect to learning outcomes related to other disciplines (Rawley, 2012). Colleagues in history, economics, and the like may be able to provide references relevant for the cultural, historical, political, and economic background information necessary or useful for students to understand the context of the stories told by their interviewees. Furthermore, collaboration with other disciplines can also assist in finding community partners.

Faculty need to work with community partners who can assist in finding interviewees. This step must be undertaken with a great deal of lead time because a community organization may not have access to enough native speakers to meet the needs of a large class or may not have access to enough appropriate spaces in which interviews can be conducted. Sufficient preparation will help the faculty and community partners to identify willing interviewees and appropriate spaces to conduct the interviews. If at all possible the institution should provide a small financial incentive for the interviewees for the days of the interviews; this will require additional logistical work with the budgeting office as well as time for the interviewees to fill out the necessary paperwork.

At some institutions the campus research library may play a lead role in engagement projects; at others a service-learning or community-engaged learning center may be at the heart of such a project.[4] Faculty should learn enough about nearby Russophone communities in order to contact members of the Russian-speaking populations in their area through stores, restaurants, community centers, and events. Organizations such as Jewish centers or immigrant service centers may work with Russian speakers who can be contacted to participate. Faculty working at institutions in locations lacking significant Russophone populations must first address the question of how their students will connect with native speakers. Skype, Facebook, LiveJournal, Vkontakte, and other social media platforms can be used to create virtual connections with Russian speakers. It is useful to work with existing institutional study abroad partners, where they exist, in order to recruit oral history interviewees, perhaps among the friends and family members of colleagues at the study abroad partner institution. This collaboration has the additional potential impact of reducing psychosocial barriers to studying abroad, since the oral history interview subject becomes an acquaintance or friend in the community where the student might study. Alternatively, students who participate in the project after a study abroad experience might conduct interviews with a person whom they met during study abroad, thus extending the impact of the study abroad experience beyond the point of return to the home institution. At institutions that lack study abroad partnerships or a local Russian-speaking community, instructors will need to identify a partner in Russia who can help recruit oral history interviewees, perhaps as part of a language or cultural exchange program in which the American students provide some opportunities for the native speakers of Russian to practice speaking English or participate in an oral history project focused on the American students' lived experiences. While oral history projects conducted face-to-face in the United States tend to focus on elderly interviewees, oral history projects conducted across distance that depend on technology might need to focus on younger interviewees who are comfortable using the technology.

It is important to build trust with Russian speakers before proceeding to an oral history project, beginning with the establishment of a relationship (such as between the staff of a community center and the faculty). Transparency is essential for the community center staff(s) to be willing and able to help recruit interviewees. Next, the trust-building must expand to include the students and the interviewees themselves. For example, a holiday celebration or ESL tutoring experience could be organized by students, the community center, or a civic engagement office on campus, allowing students, faculty, and interviewees the opportunity to get acquainted prior to a formal interview. Once partnerships (student[s]–interviewee) are established, it is best to set up a not-recorded meeting to explain the interview process and the goals of the oral history project and to secure the appropriate informed consent and legal release.

One key to securing informed consent is to provide a clear explanation of each storyteller's rights and interests in the recordings and any information he or she may share in the interview. Interviewees retain copyright to their interviews until it is transferred to an institution or individual (OHA, 2019a). Any consent form that transfers copyright must be signed before an interview is recorded or transcribed. All interviewees should know the multitude of ways their interviews may be used and their right to state any restrictions on that use before the interview process begins.

While some individuals may be happy to share their time and stories for free, others may need some incentive, like a stipend, a catered meal, or a gift card. Incentives help to further build trust and ensure that the oral history project will be a successful long-term endeavor supported by the community. The students may wish (or be required) to create a bilingual biography of the interviewee that the interviewees can share with their relatives. In sum, it is important to consider a variety of ways to maximize interest on the part of the interviewees to participate in the project.

Finally, once all these issues are resolved, the faculty can begin the process of creating a detailed plan for conducting the interviews and the post-interview stage of the project. In the short term the oral history project may be designed to be part of a larger unit or theme. However, an oral history project has the potential to impact the curriculum beyond a given semester if the interviewees give permission for the use of their recordings as listening comprehension materials for subsequent classes.

In many ways the space where the interviews will occur will determine the selection of the recording technology. It is advisable to arrange as quiet a spot as possible. Extraneous noises will be picked up by the microphone and affect later use of the audio file, so it is best to create a space that is both convenient to the interviewee but also minimizes background noise and distractions. Some community centers may be large buildings with poor acoustics; other spaces may be too small to allow for a large number of concurrent interviews. It is recommended that the interviewer test the microphone and recorder before beginning the interview in order to determine the recording quality and make any necessary changes to the interview space. If possible it would be ideal to conduct a pilot interview in the space to be certain that it will meet the program's needs. Faculty members should take measures to ensure that interviews are not conducted in the homes of the interviewees, as that could be an invasion of their privacy, although in some circumstances it might be necessary.

Faculty must also prepare the students to conduct the interviews. First, students can be assigned to listen to an oral history interview conducted in English, even something as short as an interview from StoryCorps (n.d.). Next, as noted above, students should have opportunities to listen to oral history interviews from previous years conducted in Russian by peers in the program or from oral history interviews online. Students will need to practice formulating initial and follow-up questions. In many cases the questions may require vocabulary or phrases with which students are unfamiliar, such as «Каковы были впечатления у ваших знакомых, друзей и родных об этой ситуации?» [What were your acquaintances', friends', family members' thoughts about this situation?] or «Как относились ваши знакомые, друзья и родные к тому, что . . . ?» [What did your acquaintances, friends, family members think about . . . ?]. Students should practice using strategies for tactfully taking the floor when an interviewee digresses into a topic that is not relevant for the interview. However, students should be prepared to accept a digression that is inherently interesting, such as when one of our interviewees happened to mention that she was at the protests in Moscow in August 1991. If the interviewees are elderly, students should consider how their own grandparents (or the grandparents of friends) interact: how to tactfully ask for repetition or rewording when something is unclear or how to patiently listen to comments that are repetitive. Finally, students should be shown how the questions they ask—and the patience they demonstrate in listening to responses—should guide most interviewees to interesting storytelling even if the interviewees are not "natural" storytellers.

While the goal of an oral history project is to record spoken recollections, silence is also an important part of the process.[5] Interviewees may need time to collect their thoughts or think through a response. Allowing for some silence at the end of a response also creates an impulse for an interviewee to think of something else to add. Student interviewers should be encouraged to be active listeners during interviews. While they may wish to take notes or ask for clarification, student interviewers should be encouraged to nod to indicate they are listening, smile when appropriate, and in general react with the kind of neutral feedback that encourages an interviewee to provide more detail and depth to a response. Verbal responses should be discouraged, as they may drown out the interviewee's voice on the recording. Through such active listening strategies student interviewers will receive longer responses while also signaling their respect for the interview subject.[6]

The approximate length of the interview should be agreed upon by the participants in advance of the first interview meeting. In order to ease the process of archiving materials later, the beginning of the interview should contain an introduction, including the interviewee's first name and patronymic (or a pseudonymous first name and patronymic, to protect the interviewee's privacy) and the date of recording, in English. Once the interview begins it is the task of the student to balance the goals of the oral history project with the narrative flow. The interviewing student must respect the right of the interviewee to decline to discuss a subject but should work to extend any inquiry in order to both sustain discourse in Russian and obtain as rich a narrative as possible.

Oral History in the Lesson Plan: Before, During, and After

Students who participate in oral history assignments gain valuable experience using language in context. Moreover, by engaging with native speakers students have an opportunity to learn about the target culture and gain confidence in their language abilities. Here we describe a model for how to organize an oral history project into a three-stage process composed of: (1) initial preparation, (2) the interviews, and (3) evaluation and reflection.

The initial preparation for conducting oral history interviews should allow students ample opportunity to think critically about the interviews they wish to produce. Activities and assignments should be structured so that participants are engaged in the process of learning, held accountable for the material being discussed, and find meaning in what they are doing (Fink, 2013). In order to foster student engagement and a sense of autonomy, in the first phase learners can be asked to think about what information oral histories provide and their value as a resource. Instructors may provide an outside reading sample on the practice of conducting oral history so students have a context for their involvement in the project.[7] Next, participants can brainstorm in groups about what introductory questions they would ask native speakers on topics such as family, education, religion, and politics. After they have had their first interactions with their assigned interviewees, students can collaborate on questions that address the specific experiences of the interviewees. In cases where the interviewees are immigrants, students can compose questions that address the individual's preconceptions about the United States and what she or he expected to find compared to what s/he actually experienced. Groups can then report to the class the questions they formulated while the instructor writes the questions on the board and later compiles them into a master list to be distributed to all participants.

Because students' prior exposure to the target culture varies, it is important to equip them with the necessary cultural background to be able to conduct effective oral history interviews with Russian-speaking immigrants. When preparing for interviews students will gain a better understanding of the cultural context if they are familiarized beforehand with aspects of Soviet and Russian culture and history. Instructors should assign participants to conduct preliminary research on the range of cultural experiences of native speakers with whom the students will conduct interviews. Instructors can assign topics for students to research individually or in pairs and present to the class (on topics such as the Great Patriotic War, life in communal apartments, being a Pioneer or a Komsomol member, the effects of perestroika on daily life, anti-Semitism in the Soviet Union, the Soviet-Afghan War, or the collapse of the USSR). Research and presentations can be conducted in Russian, if the students' proficiency level allows, or in English, using a vocabulary list of key Russian words. In certain contexts instructors may need to present students with information about the relationship between and among various ethnic groups in the former Soviet republics, especially if the community partner works with refugees. During presentations students take notes on what they are learning and can ask follow-up questions for clarification. Students can then brainstorm what questions they would like to ask interviewees based on their newly acquired knowledge. After compiling the master list of questions the instructor can make any necessary edits before distributing the list to participants.

In order to better prepare students for interviews instructors should provide ample opportunity for participants to rehearse asking both initial and follow-up questions. To this end we suggest the instructor record him/herself asking the questions so that students can listen to and practice appropriate intonation and phonetics, since oral history interviewees may or may not have experience communicating in Russian with non-native speakers. Students can practice questions and send audio recordings to the instructor for assessment and feedback. Likewise, class time can be spent having students practice asking and answering questions, including follow-up questions such as, “How interesting. Can you please tell me more about that?” Students should feel confident that they will be able to ask enough questions to keep the interviewee engaged. In instances when the instructors have an archive of recordings of previous oral history interviews, students can practice listening to possible responses and coming up with appropriate follow-up questions.

Developing listening comprehension skills for the interviews should be a focus of instruction, as some of the interview topics may be relatively new for students in terms of linguistic, cultural, and historical information. Students’ anxiety about or fear of conversing with a native speaker may negatively affect performance and lead to a lack of understanding between interviewer and interviewee (Elkhafaifi, 2005). Instructors can help assuage student fears by offering and practicing listening comprehension strategies, such as listening for the main idea, using background knowledge to make predictions, or recognizing word-order patterns that defy English norms (such as with the verb являться). In addition, students can be assigned to listen to an interview conducted in Russian and answer accompanying comprehension questions; while in class students can check their responses with peers and identify areas of confusion or misunderstanding and then find cue words that help them answer the questions. Several oral history projects in Russian can be found online at the Центр устной истории и биографии [Center for Oral History and Biography] (n.d.). Additional practice in advanced-level listening comprehension in Russian is available online from the University of Wisconsin’s Russian Advanced Interactive Listening Series (RAILS) project (Rifkin et al., 2006). Instructors can show interviews from Russian television programs to analyze how interviews are conducted and how follow-up questions are formulated. Some or all of these practices will help instructors create a less stressful learning environment in which all participants grow more confident in their interviewing skills and in listening comprehension.

When students conduct oral history interviews they should have close at hand the general list of topics and possible questions. How interviews are conducted may differ among projects but should generally begin with introductory questions (name, birthplace, education, family, hometown); these serve as both a linguistic and cultural warm-up prior to moving on to inquiries that elicit narrations and descriptions (e.g., daily life in the Soviet Union, aspirations, work-life balance) and, for students at higher levels of proficiency, require interviewees to hypothesize and give a supported opinion (e.g., reasons behind the collapse of the Soviet Union, advantages and disadvantages of various social, political, or economic policies). Instructors overseeing oral history projects may wish to partner students with varying levels of proficiency and assign interview questions according to skill level.

Students are certain to have many impressions from their experiences, which is why the final phase of any oral history project—evaluation and reflection—is essential to the learning process. Instructors can encourage student self-reflection by creating assignments that ask participants to analyze, evaluate, and report on what they have learned. For instance, participants can write journal entries in Russian about their experiences or share their reflections with classmates to discover in what ways their interviewees' experiences were similar or different. Furthermore, students should be asked to discuss how the interviewees' stories support or are at odds with information the students had read and listened to (or watched) during the preparation phase of the project. This creates a productive opportunity to discuss the difference between "big history" recorded in books by professional historians and "little history" that is experienced by individuals who create narratives to support their feelings that may not correspond to objective "facts." Building on the interviews, instructors can ask students to give presentations and/or develop something like an online wiki page as a capstone project, within the constraints of the interviewees' consent and IRB approvals. Instructors can challenge students at higher levels to transcribe some, part, or all of an interview in Russian and/or translate the conversation into English. Such an assignment would require a significant amount of work from the students but could be organized as a team project with the goal of using interviews in the Russian language curriculum or, when possible, collaborating with representatives from other disciplines (history, sociology, anthropology, education) to incorporate oral history into their curricula. Indeed, developing partnerships with students in other disciplines could be an exciting addition to their learning and provide to students from both academic spheres a greater awareness of the contribution of each discipline to the understanding of the human experience. Students could organize a symposium of presentations and invite the faculty from the relevant disciplines (e.g., historians, economists, etc.) and/or the interviewees and community center staff. By encouraging students to evaluate their experiences and reflect on the oral history interviews, instructors foster higher-level learning and meet Fink's expectations for "significant learning" (2013) because oral history projects emphasize caring and the human dimension. In addition, students should submit anonymous evaluations regarding the project and its impact on learning. Documentation of student responses can demonstrate to administrators the value of the program and its meaning for the study of language in the undergraduate curriculum.

Following the interviews the digital recordings should immediately be transferred from the recording devices and preserved in a secure place with digital back-up.[8] It is recommended that instructors conducting oral history projects use consistent, clear file names that will be easily recognized for retrieval at a later date, such as "Subject36-2017-04-02.mp3." Cross-indexing the files with the release forms and interview subjects' information helps provide quick access. This step is especially important for an oral history project that encompasses multiple academic departments, as the various participants will need to be able to access the archive easily. In addition, pseudonymization of files may be required to protect the privacy of subjects per the IRB protocol developed for the given project.

Once the files are secured it is recommended that the recordings be transcribed to make the information easier to locate and use in the creation of any course materials (Shopes, 2012). Software that slows down the playback of the audio file can help reduce the burden of creating the transcript. Of course the process of transcription is time-consuming and labor-intensive. Should the instructor choose to hire other individuals or companies to create the transcripts—rather than assigning the students to do it—the cost must be budgeted into the project. Every transcription should accurately preserve the interviewee's word choice, slang, and speech patterns, so it is recommended that consistent transcription be used on all interviews in terms of rendering the narrative and formatting the transcription. One question to consider when transcribing is how to account for sarcasm expressed through intonation or gesture (that is, not expressed in words or phrases), laughter, and other nonverbal parts of the narrative. Leaving out such notations may mean that the interviewee's intent may be distorted or missed entirely and that his or her personality may fade from view. It is up to faculty to decide how to account for such issues.

The process of transcribing the recordings can be a productive language-learning task. Students may be assigned to transcribe the interviews in Russian as an additional step in an oral history project if their proficiency level is appropriate. Students could take a first pass at the transcription and indicate where they had problems; instructors could review the recordings and guide students in areas where they had difficulty. The transcripts can also be used for additional learning opportunities in which students read partial transcripts of one another's interviews and listen to excerpts in order to complete the gaps. To prepare future cohorts of students to conduct their own oral history interviews, teachers can use the transcripts to create activities that develop students listening and question-asking skills.

The potential learning outcomes for students conducting oral history interviews are increased speaking, writing, reading, and listening comprehension; better understanding of the target culture; acquisition of sociolinguistic aspects of Russian; and enhanced student motivation in the study of Russian language and culture. In keeping with the goals set by the World-Readiness Standards for Learning Languages, participants in oral history projects engage with a community of Russian speakers and build partnerships beyond the classroom setting. Making connections with native speakers will prove influential in incentivizing students to continue studying Russian.

ORAL HISTORY IN THE RUSSIAN CURRICULUM AT THE COLLEGE OF NEW JERSEY

At The College of New Jersey (TCNJ) the faculty in the Department of Modern Languages and the History Department collaborated on an oral history project that provided students of Russian the opportunity to interview Russian-speaking immigrants in the Philadelphia area. The course, offered in 2014 and 2015, was designed as an interdisciplinary multilevel class that students took for credit during a short summer session following completion of second- or third-year Russian in the spring semester. The course is structured so that participants first study the uses of oral history in a variety of settings. At this stage students see how oral history is relevant to diverse groups of people. Once the introduction to the course topic is complete, students prepare questions for their upcoming interviews based on the ages and cities of origin of the immigrants (provided to them in advance). At this point students work in pairs and groups to practice asking their questions. Throughout the preparation phase students are asked to think critically about how an individual's frame of reference influences his/her analysis of the past. In addition to practicing questions, students are provided with useful interview strategies, namely how to begin, sustain, and conclude conversations. In this regard participants are able to realize that the interpersonal dynamic between the interviewer and interviewee relies on mutual respect.

The instructor organized a mock interview of a Russian speaker in class, with all students taking turns asking questions. Students then traveled to a community center in Philadelphia and conducted two interviews with Russian-speaking immigrants, each lasting approximately an hour. In between the first and second interviews students and native speakers gathered informally for lunch and conversation. After the second interview students thanked the interviewees and community center staff for their participation in the project and returned to campus. Students in the course then completed follow-up assignments. In the final class meeting students presented their findings and discussed their experiences in small groups and then as a class.

The oral history project at TCNJ proved to be meaningful and transformative for the students. Based on a 5-point scale (with 5 strongly agree), student responses in the follow-up questionnaires from the 2014 cohort of eight participants were nearly unanimous (with mean scores on each question between 4 and 5). Students affirmed that participating in the oral history project: (1) helped improve their understanding of more complex aspects of Russian culture in relation to history, (2) gave them a better understanding of the impact of historical events on the lives of ordinary Russians, and (3) helped them articulate the insights they gained into cultural norms and biases. The students' responses also indicated that participation in the oral history project helped them "appreciate the challenges of immigration." Evaluations affirmed that the experience interviewing immigrants led to self-reflection and cross-cultural analysis; for the question to what degree the oral history project helped them "interpret intercultural experiences from the perspectives of more than one worldview," students' mean score was 4.5 out of 5. The overall mean scores from the evaluations indicate that the oral history project did indeed produce powerful results. We are unable to detect a measurable proficiency gain in any of the four modalities for participation in this very short-term experience but are confident that the very positive reaction of the students led most of them to continue their study of Russian. Some declared a major and some went on to study abroad, but all expressed great enthusiasm for the experience of participating in an oral history project.

Students participating in this particular project were partnered with students majoring in social studies education. The social studies education students worked with the interviews to create curricular materials to teach Russian history at the high school level. These curricular materials are available at the website Internationalizing Secondary Education (2016).

CONCLUSION

We believe that oral history in the Russian-language curriculum both encourages active student engagement in the production of knowledge and develops critical thinking skills among participants. With a well-planned project, teachers of Russian can inject new approaches into the curriculum, incentivize students to continue studying Russian, and, in some cases, attract students to the study of Russian in the first place. An oral history project can also build support for the Russian program through the development of links across disciplines and departmental units as well as to the larger community. Students participating in the oral history project at TCNJ demonstrated enthusiasm for the experience and enhanced motivation for the study of Russian. Through engagement-centered projects like oral history, a program can demonstrate the importance of Russian for the larger liberal arts mission of many institutions of higher education. As the project at TCNJ illustrates, building partnerships between institutions of higher education and community organizations demonstrates the importance of Russian language to the curriculum as a whole.

Oral history projects provide a unique opportunity for students of Russian and can be a source of pride for its participants and the program. These projects can be an integral part of a language program's mission, since they involve all five curricular foci of the World-Readiness Standards for Learning Languages and meet the criteria of "significant learning."[9]

NOTES

The Oral History Project in Russian and History was made possible in part by a generous grant from the US Department of Education Division of International Studies through the Undergraduate International Studies and Foreign Language (UISFL) Program. The authors extend their sincere thanks to Michael Marino, associate professor of history and co-principal investigator for the UISFL Grant at TCNJ (with Benjamin Rifkin), without whose help and guidance this project would not have been possible.

1. For more on the background of the IRB process and its relationship with oral history projects, see Shopes (n.d.).
2. The full text of 45 CFR 46 can be found on the US Department of Health and Human Services website (n.d.). Especially relevant for oral history projects are §46.102 (d) and (f).
3. The full text of the letter to OHRP from the AHA requesting clarification of terms can be found at American Historical Association (n.d.).

4. Paschen (2009) suggests creating an advisory committee of members who are "chosen for their expertise in the particular topic, technical knowledge, and planning skills" as well as representatives of the community from which interviewees will be selected to assist with planning the project (p. 22).
5. For more on the importance of silence and listening in doing oral history, see Farmer and Strain (2011).
6. Useful discussions of best practices for interviewing can be found in Anderson and Jack (2006), Ritchie (2003, pp. 84–109), Mould (2009), and Norkunas (2011).
7. Some valuable resources on oral history include: Coles (1997), Dunaway and Baum (1996), Grele (1987, pp. 570–78), and Perks and Thomson (1998).
8. Resources for preserving recordings can be found at website of the Society of American Archivists, Oral History Resources (n.d.).
9. The OHA offers numerous resources and guides on oral history, including a detailed list of principles and best practices for all stages of the project (OHA, 2019b). One can find a wide range of examples of agreement and record-keeping forms on the Nebraska State Historical Society website (n.d.) that can assist in structuring and running an oral history project. Also, the Oral History in a Digital Age project (see Shopes, 2012)—a collaborative project between numerous institutes, museums, libraries, and universities—offers many planning guides, essays, and discussions of best practices, resources, and technology.

REFERENCES

American Council on the Teaching of Foreign Languages (ACTFL). (2012). ACTFL Proficiency Guidelines 2012. Retrieved from http://www.actfl.org/publications/guidelines-and-manuals/actfl-proficiency-guidelines-2012

American Historical Association (AHA). (n.d.). Letter to the director of the OHRP. Retrieved from https://www.historians.org/publications-and-directories/perspectives-on-history/february-2006/letter-to-the-director-of-the-ohrp

Anderson, K., & Jack, D. C. (2006). Learning to listen: Interview techniques and analysis. In R. Perks & A. Thomson (Eds.), *Oral history reader* (2nd ed.) (pp. 129–42). London: Routledge.

Anderson, L., & Krathwohl, D. (Eds.). (2014). *A taxonomy for learning, teaching, and assessing: A revision of Bloom's taxonomy of educational objectives*. Harlow, UK: Pearson.

Association of American Colleges and Universities (AACU). (2013, August 29). *About LEAP*. Retrieved from http://www.aacu.org/leap

Bloom, B., & Krathwohl, D. (1956). *Taxonomy of educational objectives, Book 1: Cognitive domain*. New York: Longmans, Green.

Bloom, B., Krathwohl, D., & Masia, B. (1965). *Taxonomy of educational objectives, Book 2: Affective domain*. New York: Longman Schools Division.

Brecht, R. D., Davidson, D. E., & Ginsberg, R. B. (1993). *Predictors of foreign language gain during study abroad*. Washington, DC: National Foreign Language Center.

Center for Oral History and Biography. (n.d.). Collections and databases. Retrieved from https://www.memo.ru/ru-ru/collections/archives/oral-history/

Coles, R. (1997). *Doing documentary work.* New York: Oxford UP.

Dunaway, D., & Baum, W. K. (Eds.). (1996). *Oral history: An interdisciplinary anthology* (2nd ed.). Walnut Creek, CA: AltaMira.

Elkhafaifi, H. (2005). Listening comprehension and anxiety in the Arabic language classroom. *Modern Language Journal, 89*(2), 206–20.

Farmer, F., & Strain, M. (2011). A repertoire of discernments: Hearing the unsaid in oral history narratives. In C. Glenn & K. Ratcliffe (Eds.), *Silence and Listening as Rhetorical Arts* (pp. 231–49). Carbondale, IL: Southern Illinois UP.

Fink, L. D. (2013). *Creating significant learning experiences: An integrated approach to designing college courses* (2nd ed.). San Francisco: Jossey-Bass.

Grele, R. (1987). On using oral history collections: An introduction. *Journal of American History 74*, 570–78.

Internationalizing Secondary Education. (2016). Introduction by Benjamin Rifkin. Retrieved from http://coldwarlessonplans.org/

Mould, D. H. (2009). Interviewing. In D. DeBlasio, C. Ganzert, D. Mould, S. Paschen, & H. Sacks (Eds.), *Catching Stories: A Practical Guide to Oral History* (pp. 82–103). Athens, OH: Ohio UP.

National Standards Collaborative Board (NSCB). (2015). *World-readiness standards for learning languages* (4th ed.). Alexandria, VA: Author.

Nebraska State Historical Society. (n.d.). Capturing the living past: An oral history primer. Retrieved from http://www.nebraskahistory.org/lib-arch/research/audiovis/oral_history/planning.htm

Norkunas, M. (2011). Teaching to listen: Listening exercises and self-reflexive journals. *Oral History Review, 38*(1), 63–108.

Oral History Association (OHA). (2019a). Oral history: Defined. Retrieved from http://www.oralhistory.org/about/do-oral-history/

Oral History Association (OHA). (2019b). Principles and best practices. Retrieved from http://www.oralhistory.org/about/principles-and-practices/

Paschen, S. (2009). Planning an oral history project. In D. DeBlasio, C. Ganzert, D. Mould, S. Paschen, & H. Sacks (Eds.), *Catching stories: A practical guide to oral history* (pp. 20–41). Athens, OH: Ohio UP.

Perks, R., & Thomson, A. (1998). *The oral history reader.* New York: Routledge.

Rawley, L. (2012). The language program administrator and policy formation at institutions of higher learning. In M. Christison & F. Stoller (Eds.), *A handbook for language program administrators* (2nd ed.). Burlingame, CA: Alta Book Center.

Rifkin, B. (2005). A ceiling effect in traditional classroom foreign language instruction: Data from Russian. *Modern Language Journal, 89*(1), 3–18.

Rifkin, B. (2012). The world language curriculum at the center of post-secondary education. *Liberal Education, 98*(3), 47–54.

Rifkin, B., Murphy, D., Spasova, S., & Thorstensson, V. (2006). Russian Advanced Interactive Listening Series (RAILS). Retrieved from https://rails.languageinstitute.wisc.edu/lessons.html

Ritchie, D. (2003). *Doing oral history* (2nd ed.). New York: Oxford UP.

Shopes, L. (n.d.). Oral history, human subjects, and institutional review boards. Retrieved from http://www.oralhistory.org/about/do-oral-history/oral-history-and-irb-review/

Shopes, L. (2012). Transcribing oral history in the digital age. In D. Boyd, S. Cohen, B. Rakerd, & D. Rehberger (Eds.), *Oral history in the digital age.* Institute of Library and Museum Services. Retrieved from http://ohda.matrix.msu.edu/2012/06/transcribing-oral-history-in-the-digital-age/

Society of American Archivists (SAA). (n.d.). Oral history resources. Retrieved from http://www2.archivists.org/groups/oral-history-section/oral-history-resources

StoryCorps. (n.d.) Get to know StoryCorps. Retrieved from https://www.storycorps.org

Thompson, I. (1996). Assessing foreign language skills: Data from Russian. *Modern Language Journal, 80*(1), 47–65.

US Department of Health and Human Services. (n.d.). Code of federal regulations. Retrieved from https://www.hhs.gov/ohrp/regulations-and-policy/regulations/45-cfr-46/index.html

11

LANGUAGE AND CULTURAL LEARNING THROUGH SONG

Three Complementary Contexts

Karen Evans-Romaine, Stuart H. Goldberg,
Susan Kresin, and Vicki Galloway

The value of introducing song into the language and culture classroom has long been noted, both in practice and in scholarship. This value includes a range of affective, linguistic, cognitive, cultural, and intercultural benefits, which differ in essential ways from those that can be gained from other analogous media such as literature and film. Together these benefits argue for the organized and pedagogically thoughtful use of song as a regular component of a well-rounded language and culture classroom.

In this chapter we outline the current state of scholarship on song in the language and culture classroom and offer models and materials for the use of song in several contexts: the beginning and intermediate classroom, including those with heritage-language learners; the advanced classroom (spotlighting the Georgia Tech Critical Languages Song Project [CLSP]); and the mixed-level classroom. We will also provide evidence from CLSP piloting surveys, which support claims made in the literature but often only anecdotally, on the benefits of integrating song into the foreign language classroom.

RESEARCH ON THE USE OF SONG IN THE FOREIGN LANGUAGE CLASSROOM

A fairly substantial body of literature extols the merits of using song in the foreign language (FL) classroom.[1] Aquil (2012), author of the CLSP materials for Arabic, provides an overview of research on various linguistic, cultural, and affective advantages of song in second-language (L2) teaching: providing students with greater access to the target culture, including authentic materials; improving listening skills; supporting vocabulary retention; reinforcing idiom, grammatical structures, and register distinctions; and providing cognitive and even therapeutic benefits. Songs provide rich and multifaceted access to culture, so it is not surprising that some studies focus on the acquisition of culture along with language (Abrate, 1983; Aquil, 2012; Carlson,

2010; Failoni, 1993; Garza, 1994, 2009; Iudin-Nelson, 1997; Jones, 2008; Kramer, 2001; Maley, 1987; Tumanov & Tennant, 2000).

Scholars have examined the effectiveness of song in enhancing language acquisition and retention, in part through what Krashen (1983) calls the "din in the head" phenomenon. Maley (1987) notes that "fragments of poems and songs stick in our minds" (p. 93) through rhythmicality and other features, while Murphey (1990, 1992) examines this more narrowly as the "song stuck in my head" phenomenon, hypothesizing about the pedagogical implications of song in activating language. Following up on this work, Salcedo (2010) conducted an experiment to determine whether text recall, measured through a cloze test, increases when the text is encountered in the form of song and whether there is greater presence of the "din" when the learner listens to song rather than spoken text. The study reveals that while text recall depends on a variety of factors, including the linguistic complexity of the song and students' language proficiency level, in most cases students exposed to song demonstrate significant increases in recall of lyrics. Moreover, double the percentage of students report "involuntary mental rehearsal (din)" (p. 25)—a certain indicator of text recall and a possible indicator of language acquisition, according to Krashen's theory.

Ludke et al. (2014) examined the use of song for enabling L2 learners to retain new vocabulary. In this study research subjects sang short melodized phrases. Through a randomized controlled experiment comparing three groups of participants, the study finds that singing is more effective than either speaking or rhythmic speaking in enabling participants to recall and reproduce short phrases in Hungarian, both immediately and after a 20-minute delay. Their findings thus isolate the tools of melody and rhythm, as distinct from rhythm alone, for aiding L2 acquisition.

Some studies on song (Failoni, 1993; Garza, 2009; Griffiths, 2012; Iudin-Nelson, 1997; Kramer, 2001) address specific practices integrating both "bottom-up" strategies that direct students' attention toward linguistic features of a text (Omaggio Hadley, 2000) and "top-down" strategies that focus on themes and cultural context. This integrative approach is supported in research on listening strategies and vocabulary acquisition, which promotes tasks that combine and balance top-down and bottom-up strategies (e.g., Nation, 2001; Robin, 2007; Schmitt, 2008; Vandergrift, 2004).

Several scholars have addressed the use of song in teaching Russian. Iudin-Nelson's 1997 dissertation contains extensive sample lesson plans based on sequences of songs from various genres. Suggested tasks include pre- and post-listening and reading activities and follow-up writing assignments for first- through third-year level classes. She argues also that song settings of poems can make poetry more accessible.

Garza (1994, 2009) proposes a methodology using music videos as an engaging and culturally rich way to increase students' time on task, a critical element of language acquisition (2009). He and colleagues at the University of Texas at Austin have developed an online collection of music videos, called Rockin' Russian (2008), accompanied by exercises at various levels on the American Council on the Teaching of Foreign Languages (ACTFL) proficiency scale. Captions can be presented in one of three ways: as Russian language transcriptions, as subtitles in colloquial English, or as subtitles with literal English translations that convey the syntax and lexicon of the original. The website's inclusion of songs in a variety of styles and the varied captioning options enhance the value of the materials for independent learning. Jones (2008) focuses on the pedagogical benefits of teaching language and culture using the songs of Vladimir Vysotsky, which include a rich range of linguistic registers. She finds that songs are a valuable source of collocations and contextually bound word meanings.

Tumanov and Tennant (2000; see also Tumanov, 1996) describe using "song-poems," such as those by Bulat Okudzhava, as a learning tool that lowers the affective filter (Krashen, 1982; cf. Carlson, 2010), increases student motivation, and allows students to acquire "chunks of language" (Tumanov & Tennant, 2000, p. 18). They assert that systematic teaching through song can aid students' metacognitive awareness of listening strategies (Tumanov & Tennant, 2000; Garza, 2009; cf. Vandergrift, 2004). They propose a 10-step approach to developing students' aural comprehension by decoding songs, which includes listening with and without the text, exercises, and comprehension checks.

We advocate for an approach that combines elements of bottom-up and top-down strategies and focuses on the cultural grounding that songs can offer. The integration of song into the FL classroom can take a variety of approaches, depending on the students' language proficiency level, the instructor's goals, and other factors.

USING SONG IN THE NOVICE- AND INTERMEDIATE-LEVEL CLASSROOM

Students at the ACTFL Novice and Intermediate levels work most successfully with songs that have concrete and straightforward lyrics, recurring vocabulary and grammatical structures, a consistent point of view, and a simple melody and rhythmic structure (Iudin-Nelson, 1997; Kramer, 2001; Wallace, 1994; see also Maxim, 2000). At these levels songs can provide an effective medium for developing focused listening comprehension skills and strategies that are applicable to other types of listening tasks. Songs deliver an affectively positive way for teaching students to listen selectively and focus on what they can understand rather than on what they cannot. In parallel to speed-reading exercises, songs help students learn to listen deductively by focusing on core words and images. Recurring refrains and rhyming patterns in the lyrics aid comprehension, as can a song's tempo, style, and general mood; visual imagery in accompanying video clips provide further support (Garza, 2009; Lonergan, 1984). Moreover, songs can model native pronunciation and prosody, with the natural prosodic contours of the lyrics accentuated by the song's melodic line and rhythm: correct placement of stress on individual words is often reinforced through rises and falls in pitch, correspondences with downbeats, and longer note values. In following the musical contour of a song, students combine the words into meaning-based phrases rather than mechanically emphasizing each stressed word.

Identifying salient words and establishing word boundaries are two of the primary skills that students must develop in order to understand spoken or sung texts without continued support. From the earliest stages of language learning students can work on deciphering familiar chunks of language by listening for cognates in songs such as «Моя Москва» ["My Moscow"] by Лигалайз [Ligalize]. Reinforced by a music video with parallel images, this song includes Russian equivalents for basketball, gangster, video, and American, adjusted to Russian patterns of pronunciation, word formation, and declension.

Likewise, songs can be used to model intonation, an area of prosody that is especially difficult for non-native speakers to internalize. For example, the hit song of the early 1990s by ДДТ [DDT], «Что такое осень» ["What is autumn"], provides a recurring model of question-and-answer intonation through the structure Что такое осень? – Это X [What is autumn? It's X.]; for instance, Что такое осень? – Это небо [What is autumn? It's the sky.]. After listening and hearing the same phrase sung repeatedly (perhaps as a homework assignment), in class students can pronounce this phrase and variants with correct prosody that follows the melodic contour of the song:

1. The question word что [what] is stressed in the song, where it is the first downbeat of a measure;
2. такое [what is] is pronounced quickly and at a lower pitch, an effect conveyed in the song by shorter notes and lower pitches;
3. As the focus of the question the word осень [autumn], is emphasized through a rise in pitch on the stressed syllable;
4. это [it's (it is)] is pronounced relatively quickly and in passing, with shorter, unaccented notes; the answer word in each verse (небо [sky], камни [stones], ветер [wind]) is emphasized and pronounced with falling intonation; it is marked by a drop in pitch, and its stressed initial syllable falls on the first downbeat of a measure;
5. All accented syllables in the phrase fall on downbeats.

Students internalize correct intonational patterns by following the prosody of the song. The song itself is an important cultural icon of its era, with the metaphor of autumn providing a window for students to learn about the Yeltsin years of uncertainty and anxiety:

Осень, доползём ли,
Долетим ли до ответа,
Что же будет с Родиной и с нами?
[Autumn, will we crawl our way,
Will we fly our way to the answer,
What will become of our Homeland and of us?][2]

The song provides a model of easily remembered phrasing and intonational contours in an engaging and culturally grounded context.

Since songs involve both repetition and phrase variations, they can provide a vivid illustration of grammatical and lexical material. The repetition of core structures helps commit them to memory. For example, the song «Если у вас нету тёти» ["If you don't have an aunt"] from the 1975 film «Ирония судьбы» [*Irony of fate*] is the genitive case song par excellence: each verse begins with the genitive of possession and of negation (cf. Iudin-Nelson, 1997). As the repeating first line of each verse illustrates, songs can also provide an accessible context for teaching colloquial variants: here, нет and нету [there is no . . .].

Similarly, many songs provide a vivid illustration of prefixed verbs of motion, which enables students to associate the context of specific songs with the various prefixes. Valerij Leont'ev's song «Если ты уйдёшь» ["If you leave"] contextualizes the antonymous pairing of the prefixes *при-* and *у-* in a simple love song with contrasting repetition of the core phrases «если ты придёшь» [if you come] and «если ты уйдёшь» [if you leave]. In addition to this microlevel contrast, applicable to bottom-up learning, the song also provides top-down contextual reinforcement of the при-/у- contrast: the first half of the song presents the hope of the lover's arrival, while the second addresses despair at the couple's possible breakup. Similarly, the song «Просто хочешь ты знать» ["You just want to know"] by Viktor Tsoi provides a memorable illustration of идти [to go] and заходить/зайти [to drop by] and can easily be combined with the general topic of visiting (for example, in Robin et al., 2013/2014, Book 2, Chapter 10; Kagan et al., 2005, Chapter 11). At the same time this song brings to life the use of indefinite pronouns: где-то [somewhere], кто-то [someone], к кому-то [someone's place], с кем-то [with someone], and кого-то [someone].

A unit covering motion verbs can be capped by study of the famous song setting of Lermontov's poem «Выхожу один я на дорогу» ["I set out on the road alone"]. With its simultaneously concrete and metaphorized meaning of the prefix *вы-* (going "out" into an open, less confining space) this poem can help students begin to think about verbal prefixes on a more abstract level. This is a classic example of a fundamental genre in Russian culture, the art song [romans] that connects poetry and music.

A cluster of songs around a single theme can be an effective way to reinforce mastery of difficult grammatical points while presenting multiple perspectives. Three songs on the theme "born in the USSR" open students' eyes to the variety of reactions to the breakup of the Soviet Union while also providing a memorable illustration of long and short past passive participles: the DDT song «Рождённые в СССР» ["Born in the USSR"]; a hip-hop version by Ligalize; and «Это моя страна» ["It's my country"] by Oleg Gazmanov, which has the recurring refrain «Я рождён в Советском Союзе, сделан я в СССР» [I was born in the Soviet Union, made in the USSR]. These closely paired models of long and short past passive participles become fixed in students' minds as set phrases due to their repetition in the context of a specific and memorable cultural frame. These songs can be a valuable springboard for conversations about the

Russophone world and the politicization of language, as well as stereotypes about Russian and Soviet culture.

Songs can be used to develop specific discourse skills and functions, such as narration, description, and inferencing, which will challenge Intermediate-level students to venture into higher-level discourse and scaffolding this development. Abrate (1983) suggests retelling the story line of a narrative song from various perspectives or in different tenses or aspectual frames as useful activities in leading students from Intermediate to Advanced. Since song lyrics often present a metaphorically rich but understated story line, students can add narrative or descriptive details to extend the story line into the past or future, or they can create a dialogue based on the content of the song. For example, the song «Телефонный разговор» ["Phone call"] by Iurii Vizbor presents one side of a telephone conversation between a man and a woman:

> Слушаю? . . . да . . . алло?
> Что за шутки с утра?
> Я, почему удивлён? Я даже очень рад. Я даже закурю.
> Ну здравствуй. Прошло сто лет.
> Сто лет прошло, говорю.
> Я не спешу, нет . . .
> [Hello? . . . Yes . . . hello?
> You're joking, this early in the morning?
> Why should I be surprised? I'm even glad. I'm even gonna light up.
> Well, hi. It's been ages.
> Ages, I said.
> No, I'm not in any hurry, no . . .]

The woman initiating the phone call, who was once in a relationship with the speaker, is now unhappily married to someone else and has a son whom she named for the other speaker. She calls him from a pay phone, not from her home number. The song presents only the man's words and reactions, but it is easy to imagine and reenact the woman's lines. Rich in models of ellipsis, inverted word order, and colloquial idioms, this song can serve as a springboard for working with a variety of discourse types, such as dialogue, narration in the past tense, reported speech, or prediction into the future. For example, students can recreate the full conversation, hypothesize about the characters' past, or report the conversation to an imagined mutual friend.

INCORPORATING SONG INTO THE MIXED L2 AND HERITAGE-LEARNER CLASSROOM

Compared with L2 learners, heritage language learners tend to find listening activities much easier, given their language exposure and cultural grounding at home. The materials discussed in this section are highly compatible with the top-down approach that is a cornerstone of contemporary heritage language instruction (Beaudrie et al.,

2015; Carreira & Kagan, 2011; Fairclough et al., 2016; Kagan & Dillon, 2001/2002) and build on heritage speakers' primary exposure to the language at the level of connected discourse. Songs are well suited for an individualized approach: students can perform different tasks and conduct independent projects based on songs studied by the whole class.

In addition, songs can be used to create a motivating context for focusing heritage students' attention on bottom-up elements of language mastery, such as orthography, grammatical endings, and vocabulary development. Various cloze and transcription exercises can help heritage students learn to identify discrepancies between phonetic sounds and their orthographic realizations (unstressed o or e, for example, or word-final consonants that are paired for voicing), identify case endings, and develop specific vocabulary. The compactness and density of meaning in song lyrics, similar to poetry, make it especially suitable for tasks involving transcription. Griffee (1992) suggests giving students song lyrics with mistakes that require attentive listening to identify and correct. This correction task builds on the heritage students' higher-level listening skills while forcing them to focus on details that may not be part of their active knowledge.

As a class project heritage students can follow the three-fold model of captioning presented on the Rockin' Russian website, using transcription as the basis for creating Russian captions, literal translations into English, and stylistically matched translations into English (Garza, 2009; see also Kagan, 2014). The creation of captions can benefit the whole class and create a "bank" of annotated songs for future classes; moreover, this type of exercise raises heritage students' awareness of structural differences between the two languages and of stylistic registers. This window into stylistic variants can be quite enlightening for heritage students, since the language of contemporary songs is likely to differ from the colloquial language of their home life—not only for generational reasons but also due to the major societal changes and rapid language shifts that have taken place over the past 30 years.

Finally, heritage students can play a valuable role in selecting and interpreting songs. Russian songs, either written for children or popular in their parents' youth, are likely to be part of their home-based Russian language experience. An added benefit is that some students, heritage or L2, may be in contact with young people in Russia and other countries in the Russophone world who can suggest popular or newly emerging groups, which reinforces the link to popular culture among their Russian-speaking peers and creates a sense of connectedness to Russian-speaking communities (cf. Carlson, 2010).

TEACHING LANGUAGE AND CULTURE TO ADVANCED-LEVEL STUDENTS THROUGH SONG: THE CRITICAL LANGUAGES SONG PROJECT

Recognized factors for achieving advanced language and cross-cultural proficiency include the desire to acquire the target language beyond the survival level (Gardner,

1982), scaffolded learning (Gibbons, 2002; Kern, 2003), communicative practice in authentic contexts (Omaggio Hadley, 2000), cross-cultural reflection (Kramsch, 1993), and time on task (Ellis, 2003; Skehan, 1998; cf. Garza, 2009). The Georgia Tech Critical Languages Song Project (2013) engages each of these factors through the use of culturally authentic song, capitalizing on the attractiveness of the medium to boost student time on task, on the challenge of the listening experience to increase attention to linguistic detail, and on the authenticity of the culture's diverse voices to deepen examination of the complexity of the "webs of significance" (Geertz, 1973) in which song, like all cultural products, is suspended.[3]

A raft of challenges confronts us in the design of effective upper-level content-based curricula, particularly for less-commonly taught languages (LCTLs). First among these is the wide variation of skill and experience level often found in the advanced language classroom. Backgrounds can vary from minimal, classroom-only preparation to a year abroad, with speaking skills in Russian ranging from ACTFL Intermediate Mid to Advanced High. A second curricular and pedagogical challenge presented especially by the Intermediate High/Advanced learner is directing students' focus to increased linguistic precision, variation, and wordplay in a content-based classroom. A third challenge, found at every level, is the identification of authentic and engaging texts—particularly oral texts—and the development of tasks that gradually stretch students linguistically and cognitively to excavate and assimilate their linguistic and cultural richness. By far the most difficult challenge, however, is finding a learning experience with staying power, one that provokes out-of-class pondering and independent engagement. CLSP addresses these challenges through an innovative web-based multimedia program that exploits the potential of song as a focus of teaching and learning at the advanced level. CLSP is based on the following principles:

1. Songs are compact, authentic, and teeming with cultural and linguistic information. Because songs are situated in the social, cultural, economic, and political discourses of their language communities, once they are embedded in a contextualizing and interdisciplinary network of texts they have the potential to draw students into wider discourses and engage them with a variety of cultural voices.
2. Because of their "stickiness," or memorability, songs may be easily internalized and aid in building a stock of idioms and providing grammatical-syntactic models for language production (Abrate, 1983; Kramer, 2001; Salcedo, 2010; Tumanov & Tennant, 2000; see also Krashen, 1983; Maley, 1987; Murphey, 1990, 1992; and especially Ludke et al., 2014).
3. Because they are dense (like poetry) and lack visual cues (unlike film), songs are conducive to a focus on discrete language forms often missed by learners in other contexts. Gisting is less effective for songs than, for instance, a film or a live conversation, both of which tend to provide more semantic redundancy.

Thus when listening to a song, the learner is forced to turn more frequently to bottom-up strategies and to targeted, repeated listening, parsing individual phrases or chunks of text that might otherwise be ignored.

The CLSP materials comprise a semester-length fourth-year course in four languages—Arabic, Mandarin Chinese, Japanese, and Russian—presented online in a dedicated interface. The materials are structured around a carefully chosen and annotated corpus of songs supported with a full pedagogical apparatus and a broad range of content presented through various media. Computer-based delivery of a rich web of content surrounding a highly annotated main corpus of songs allows for both engagement by students at the Intermediate High and Advanced levels and guided exploration of the broader cultural context by more proficient readers and listeners, who can then come together in a group discussion.

Songs, when properly scaffolded through learning tasks and placed within "webs of significance" through rich contextualizing material (paintings, historical documents, newspaper articles, poems and literary excerpts, interview or broadcast segments, etc.), become a lens through which the target culture is viewed from many angles and in many layers. In exploring and exploiting the cultural embeddedness of song, the creators of CLSP have oriented their work to a set of Seven Cs (Galloway & Goldberg, 2010):

- A knowledge of the song's *context*: its time and place in the world, its sociohistorical backdrop or political climate;
- A sense of *condition*: some understanding of the situation(s), issues, and agendas that birthed the song within its context (nostalgia, angst, playfulness, protest);
- An identification of *chorus*: the heterogeneous voices evoked by the performance of a song in its original cultural context. These often overlapping voices include the "authorial" voices of the composer and/or lyricist, the narrative voices projected by the text, and the variegated voices of the song's original historically and culturally situated audiences (both actual and implied), all of which are subsumed into the sonorous voice(s) of the singer(s);
- A recognition of the nodes of *conflict*: through which these voices at times express themselves; that is, the culture's internal tension points where potentially competing values, perspectives, and visions clash and ultimately generate the seeds of culture change;
- An understanding of *connotation*: the impact of factors such as the aforementioned in giving in-group meaning to words, the sense of a word that cannot be found in a dictionary query. The notion of connotation includes silence as well as sound and the pause as well as the utterance, particularly in the case of high-context cultures (cf. Hall, 1959);
- An appreciation for *continuity*: the role of song in constructing and sustaining community identity and group cohesion; that is, the personal associations

and emotional content that define communities with collective knowledge and experiences within the target culture and demonstrate the diversity of overlapping identities and allegiances in society;
- The ability to make *comparison*: nonjudgmental and contextualized comparison of perspectives and practices both within and between cultures. Students should be guided to see how the views expressed in a particular song relate to the views of other eras or groups (of varying age, nationality, ethnicity, socioeconomic background, etc.).

In addition, aspects of style, such as instrumentation, vocal timbre, pitch (melody, harmony, register), rhythm, and compositional form expose cultural traditions that may have deep historical or spiritual significance (cf. *enka* in Japan or Gypsy song in the Russian context), while cultural-musical fusions illustrate the porosity of borders and the impact of itinerant and immigrant voices. The CLSP modules organize this cultural knowledge as it relates to a carefully chosen corpus of songs and scaffold student engagement through listening, reading, writing, and speaking tasks that stimulate linguistic awareness, increase communicative precision, and generate expanding, if not contiguous, tracts of dense cultural knowledge. CLSP thus employs an interdisciplinary approach that merges culture, content, and language in a stimulating, learner-centered environment of the type specifically called for in the World-Readiness Standards for Learning Languages (NSCB, 2015).

A typical unit of the Russian program (approximately three contact hours of material) is structured around one or two central songs. After unit or song introductions (with subtly indicated roll-over glosses), students proceed to the first activity, «Аудирование» [Listening], with prelistening context and vocabulary priming, cloze exercises (with a large percentage of blanks), and open-ended-answer exercises. The nature of the exercises is dictated by the character and difficulty of the song. At the end of the listening exercises a password is supplied to provide access to the next segment, «Текст-примечания-контекст» [Text-notes-context], which includes the text of the song and extensive annotation on semantic, grammatical, stylistic, and cultural planes using text, images, web links, and attached documents. A word or phrase may carry multiple types of annotation, and whole lines can be annotated while preserving glosses of individual words. Types of annotations include:

- definitions via Russian phrase, image, or, when expedient, English gloss;
- stylistic-morphological information;
- links to information on a figure, place, or phenomenon; additional clarification (e.g., a scene from Bondarchuk's film *War and Peace* to illustrate the untranslatable concept of *gusarstvo*); or a cultural artifact alluded to in a song («Песня про зайцев» ["Song about the rabbits"], an icon of the Ascension, a Yeltsin photo-op with miners, etc.);

◇ questions (in Russian): for instance, calling attention to the use of ellipsis (What words are omitted here?) or the implications of nonstandard word usage (What is surprising about this phrase? Compare the more customary . . .).

A button on the webpage yields the lyrics and accompanying notes in printable format. Below the annotated text of the song are found web links and documents with additional cultural context, targeted primarily toward more proficient students. For example, the section on Okudzhava's «Молитва Франсуа Вийона» ["Prayer of François Villon"] delves into prayer in Russian culture («Отче наш» [Our Father] and short poem-prayers or poems about prayer by Lermontov, Tiutchev, Nekrasov, and Akhmatova); the history of Soviet atheism (the cover of the first issue of «Безбожник» [*The godless one*] from 1923, photos of the destruction of the Christ the Savior Cathedral in 1931, and an excerpt from a book on scientific atheism from 1967); and poetry by Villon in Russian translation (harmonizing with the poetics of Okudzhava's song) and excerpts from Mandelstam's essay on Villon. For Timor Shaov's «Выбери меня» ["Choose me"] there are examples of Putin-era satire, including a link to one of the final episodes of the satirical television show «Куклы» [*Puppets*]) and of satire in Russian and Soviet history, as well as memorabilia of the 2011–12 elections and Bolotnaja Square protests. No individual would be expected to read or view all the material available; rather, instructors can assign or students can choose at their challenge level from the extensive "curation."

The website's following section, «Вопросы к тексту» [Questions for understanding], uses primarily open-ended questions to guide students through a close reading of the song-text and its immediate cultural context. «Темы для обсуждения и письма» [Topics for discussion and writing] takes a broader view of the cultural themes. Progressing from the concrete to the abstract, these questions engage students' analytical, integrative, and creative faculties and draw on their knowledge of the outside world and other disciplines. Writing topics are structured to allow for responses at various ACTFL levels.

«Что слушать дальше?» caps each unit with suggestions for further listening and delves into musical forms not represented in the main unit songs, e.g., folk music, mass song, songs of the criminal world, Alla Pugacheva, or ВИА [VIA] (Vocal-instrumental ensembles, officially permitted bands, in contradistinction to unofficial Soviet rock).

Songs are chosen primarily for the density of cultural information they encode, their musical or lyrical quality, and their potential to engage, incite, and elicit discussion. While reinforcement of specific language structures is not a criterion, the songs inevitably illustrate advanced grammar, syntax, stylistics, and diverse linguistic registers. They engage a broad range of themes, cultural models, and musical styles. Selections range from (Russian) Gypsy songs to popular 1930s jazz and tango, a reggae rendition of the Soviet national anthem, war songs, guitar bards (classic and contemporary), a prison camp song, popular ballads, rock, and other contemporary forms. Additional covered topics include the fate of the capable individual in Brezhnev's Russia; Soviet attitudes toward jazz and other Western musical forms as well as the subcultures that formed around them; the history of the Soviet-Russian national anthem; ironic strategies for challenging official discourse; the Soviet experience during World War II; reflections of Putin's Russia in songs of the Chechen war; the sociology and psychology of Soviet prison camps; the Soviet-era cult of the hero and its reverberations (Gagarin); glasnost-era rock music and youth alienation; complicated love for the motherland; the fate of communism and communists in a post-communist era; the "little man" in capitalist Russia; the problem of compromise or noncompromise of principles in choosing a career; and the siren of emigration.

One example of how song interacts with context is that of Boris Grebenshchikov's «Московская октябрьская» ["Moscow October song"], which, superlative in every regard, would be catchy but hardly comprehensible to an advanced language student lacking deep cultural knowledge. To one versed in the history and cultural situation of the Soviet Union and Russia in the early 1990s, aware of changing and debated attitudes toward sexuality and the West, prepared to experience allusions to such disparate texts as Bulgakov's *Master and Margarita* (the brief chapter "Azazello's Cream" is included in toto on the site) and the Soviet national anthem, the song becomes a brilliant evocation of the quixotic struggle of the post-Soviet Russian Communist Party and those who share its members' social outlook to come to terms with a society they can no longer control. The knowledge base necessary for such an understanding can be acquired by advanced students pursuing a well-delineated and directed study of engaging texts. Moreover, the holistic cultural knowledge that emerges transcends the individual topics and source texts, for the songwriter has already synthesized them into a densely compact, potent, and memorable whole.

Students at lower language proficiency levels benefit from the site's introductory material and the extensive notes to the texts of the songs as well as from the acquired knowledge that more fluent readers and viewers introduce into the class discussion. In class, a fruitful strategy has been to give the least proficient students the first opportunity to address a new question or topic. The more advanced students then fill in, refine, and expand.

The feedback from piloting the CLSP materials, collected through anonymous online surveys, both indicates success in achieving the goals of linguistic growth and development of expanding tracts of deep cultural knowledge and provides added evidence for the validity of some of the assumptions and hypotheses discussed in the literature review. The following data refer collectively to the similar results from the piloting of the Japanese and Russian materials. Although this sample was significantly larger than that of much other scholarship in this area, the survey population was small and yielded data for six instructors outside of Georgia Tech and 38 students [20 Japanese, 18 Russian] at and beyond Georgia Tech, with five of eight groups completing a full-semester pilot. We note a potential for self-selection bias among the instructors who volunteered and who presumably had a preexisting interest in the use of song in language pedagogy.[4]

Listening (cf. Aquil, 2012; Garza, 1994, 2009; Iudin-Nelson, 1997; Tumanov & Tennant, 2000; Vandergrift, 2004): four of six instructors describe the course materials as "much more effective than other courses in developing [. . .] students' overall listening ability," with instructors divided evenly between "much more effective" and "more effective" in "developing my students' ability to listen for detail." No instructor rated the materials lower than "as effective as other courses" with regard to the other modalities—speaking, reading, and writing. Students' median reaction to the prompts "This course increased my overall listening comprehension" and "This course increased my ability to listen for detail" was 4 out of 5 ("more than other courses"; averages of 4.22 and 4.08, respectively); and their own vision of their progress in other modalities was stronger than that of their instructors (median 4 in each). A total of 23 of the 38 students marked the strongest affinity for "I understand [Russian/Japanese] songs better on initial hearing than at the outset of the course" (median 5, average 4.46).

Culture (Abrate, 1983; Aquil, 2012; Carlson, 2010; Failoni, 1993; Garza, 1994, 2009; Iudin-Nelson, 1997; Jolly, 1975; Kramer, 2001): The success in teaching culture is the finest achievement of the course materials. Students gave a median of 5 ("strongly agree") to the prompt "Songs chosen reflect the target culture very well" (average 4.14); to the prompt "I learned very much about the target culture in this course" (4.55); to "The songs demonstrated the historical context and sociological conditions of their times" (4.42); and to "The notes attached to the lyrics were effective in aiding a deep understanding of the songs" (4.29); as well as a median of 4 ("agree") for "provided a solid basis for bias-free comparison between cultures," "portrayed the emotional force of the times," "echoed a broad diversity of voices," and "helped me better visualize the communities and groups that make up [the target] culture." Instructors were even more enthusiastic, with medians of 4.5 or 5 and averages of 4.5 or higher for every aspect of the cultural element of the program.

Pronunciation (Failoni, 1993; Jolly, 1975) yielded mixed results. Three instructors felt this course developed pronunciation as much or less than other classes, while another three said more or much more. Students were modestly positive that "this course improved my pronunciation" (median 4, i.e., "agree," and average 3.61).

Intrinsic interest and staying power (Abrate, 1983; Carlson, 2010; Failoni, 1993; Iudin-Nelson, 1997; Kramer, 2001): Of the 38 student respondents, 11 "agreed" and 20 "strongly agreed" with the statement "I expect to listen to more [Russian/Japanese] music in the future than I would have had I not taken this course" (median 5, average 4.29). For over half the students, then, this course promises to serve as a powerful multiplier of our pedagogical efforts.

Retention of grammatical structures and idioms (Abrate, 1983; Kramer, 2001; Salcedo, 2010; Tumanov & Tennant, 2000; see also Krashen, 1983; Maley, 1987; Murphey, 1990, 1992; and especially Ludke et al., 2014): Instructors were divided, with a 3.5 median for the prompt "This course was effective in developing my students' language accuracy." Note that the course in Russian (unlike the one in Japanese) included no explicit grammar sections. Unfortunately we lack survey data on retention of idiom, as no prompt specifically addressed this element. This is, however, an area in which experimental data exist (cf. Salcedo, 2010).

The courses got high median marks from instructors for expansion of students' vocabulary (median 4), its organization (4.5), the quality of open-ended questions about the songs (4), discussion topics that could "spur rich interactions and extended communication" (4), writing topics "effective in motivating students of various levels to challenge themselves" (4), and further listening/viewing suggestions (5).[5]

Also noteworthy is the very high quality of the student work the course inspired. The example below is by a student at approximately the Advanced Low proficiency level (cited verbatim):

> Опишите песню (слова и музыку) человеку, который никогда не слышал цыганских песен.
> [Describe the song (words and music) to a person who has never listened to a Gypsy song.]
>
> В самом начале, она показиваеться непостижимой. Она одновреммено оживленная и меланхоличная, и время от времени возникают взрыв в резултате борьбы между приглушеннией и интенсивностю чувств. Это показывается и в музыке, и в словах песни.
> [In the beginning, it seems incomprehensible. It is at once lively and melancholic, and from time to time arise an explosion as a result of the struggle between mutedness and intensity of feelings. This is felt in the music and the words of the song.]

The response's combination of errors (not strongly interfering with sense) and precise and evocative description underscores the extent to which this student has challenged herself, both linguistically and through cultural reflection. Encouraging students to take on this challenge is our ultimate goal.

TEACHING LANGUAGE THROUGH SONG IN THE MIXED-LEVEL CLASSROOM

Teaching students at mixed levels in one classroom is a common problem not only for Russian, but for LCTL teaching in general. Mixed classrooms present a special challenge; however, teaching through song can provide an effective means to reach students at a variety of levels. Although CLSP materials were designed for students at the Intermediate High and Advanced levels, these materials can be adapted and supplemented for teaching an even more diverse group.

The Russian-language dormitory floor at the University of Wisconsin–Madison, Russkii dom [Russian house], presents just such a challenge. Russkii dom is housed in the International Learning Community (ILC). ILC language floor residents pledge to use the target language as much as possible while in the dormitory and at ILC activities; they benefit from the guidance of graduate student resident coordinators, who are usually native speakers of the language. A faculty director teaches a biweekly course in the target language on some aspect of the target culture. Russkii dom students are required to take this biweekly course, as well as a Russian language class outside of the ILC, unless they are high-functioning heritage or native speakers of Russian; they are also required to participate both in Russian-language events several times a week and in biweekly ILC dinners for all residents. These students are highly motivated: they may also be Russian majors or participants in the UW–Madison Russian Flagship Program. Regardless, they share a strong common interest in Russian language and cultures of the Russophone world. As members of a living-learning community they are generally less reluctant to take linguistic risks in front of others than students in a traditional FL classroom. Russkii dom residents take first- through fifth-year Russian and speak at ACTFL Novice through Superior levels, so the challenge of creating a single course for such a linguistically disparate group can be formidable.

One of the most effective ways to meet this challenge has been through music. CLSP provides a highly effective framework that, if supplemented for students at various levels, helps guide lower-level students who might otherwise feel overwhelmed while also providing sufficiently complex material for advanced students. Background information aimed at Advanced-level students can be glossed or otherwise scaffolded for greater accessibility to students at lower levels. Moreover, CLSP gives students the opportunity to apply their own interests and skills to the study of Russian culture through song.

Russkii dom classes on Russian music are guided in part by the CLSP framework and arranged both in chronological order and, within each lesson, in order of difficulty of the songs. Some songs are from the CLSP; others are selected to supplement CLSP units. Class themes have included Russian and Soviet national anthems; World War II and the Stalinist Terror expressed in music; cosmonaut Yuri Gagarin and Cold War dreams; Russian bard music; Perestroika rock groups Akvarium and Kino; and Russian views today. Musical examples are taken from the songs themselves, as well as from documentary and feature films and music videos.

The structure of lessons adheres loosely to Rifkin's five stages of lesson planning (2003): overview; preparation or priming (i.e., input; see Krashen, 1982); practice (working with the text in pairs or as a group); check or accountability; and follow-up, which includes summaries of discussed themes, general questions, and some preparation for the next topic. The goals of the lessons follow the World-Readiness Standards. Galloway and Goldberg's Seven Cs, embedded in the planning of CLSP units, present challenges both to those ready to meet them in Russian during the class and to those not yet ready to meet them in Russian but prepared to do so in English outside the classroom; students in the latter group can inform their level-appropriate class presentations with knowledge gained from the CLSP, class discussions, consultations, and independent research.

The course often begins with a focus on the national anthem to stimulate discussion on music and context: it allows students to think about their own national anthem and about ways in which music can set a mood. For students in first-year Russian it is possible to listen to a national anthem without words and to play a word association game involving words that are either within their range or accessible as cognates: хорошо [good], патриотизм [patriotism], позитив [positivity], триумф [triumph]. It is also possible to play a word association game about the context in which Americans and Russians might hear or sing their national anthem aided with appropriate graphics: бейсбол [baseball] or футбол/американский футбол [soccer/football], спорт [sports], Олимпийские игры [Olympics], парад [parade], фейерверк [fireworks], and so forth. Intermediate- and Advanced-level students can then supply their own thoughts about when a national anthem is played, what moods it can inspire, and so forth. Given adequate comprehensible input and support, everyone can participate in the discussion.

The history of the national anthem in Russia presents a highly complex issue that not all students are prepared to discuss in Russian. Yet input and assignments can be adapted to many levels of Russian within one group of students. First-semester students can look at the list of Russian and Soviet anthems and dates and be asked to find the same name(s) in different listings. Knowing the word слово [word], they can see the expression без слов [without words] in order to begin to work with the concept of case endings, in parallel with their first-semester Russian classes. Most students will already be familiar—often to their own astonishment—with the melody of the 1815 version of «Боже царя храни» ["God save the tsar"], the same as that of the British national anthem "God Save the King" and the American patriotic hymn "My Country, Tis of Thee." They may have heard the melody of an 1833 hymn written by Alexei Lvov, since Lvov's melody, written at the request of Nicholas I, was incorporated into Tchaikovsky's 1812 Overture and is familiar to many Americans from Fourth of July celebrations and other occasions. Many may also be familiar with the melody of the Soviet national anthem.

In working with these anthems, first-semester students can be provided with input in the form of cognates and key words, accompanied by visual cues like flags as well as brief musical excerpts. They can be encouraged to answer simple either/or questions about where they have heard those melodies (Это—британский гимн [It's the British anthem] or американская песня [an American song], or Чайковский [Tchaikovsky]). Thus the music combined with students' knowledge of geography, history, and politics provides entryways for them to participate in the class.

Following the accepted guideline to change the task, not the text (Omaggio Hadley, 2000; Shrum & Glisan, 2010; see also Garza, 2009; Robin, 2007), the instructor can use the CLSP list of Russian and national anthems, assigning each anthem and its text to student pairs or small groups. Lower-level students can be asked to list words they associate with a given melody and the familiar words in the anthem's text.

Advanced-level students can be asked to complete assignments either taken directly from the CLSP corpus (cloze exercises, open-ended questions) or versions of those assignments as modified by the instructor in level-appropriate ways. Students can be asked to find word changes in the versions of the Soviet anthem, to focus on word roots, to dismantle and rebuild participles, to examine collocations, to use a search engine to find phrases and explore their contexts (e.g., дружба народов [friendship of peoples]), to restate lines from the anthem, to summarize stanzas, and so forth. Given the richness of the anthems' texts, the list is endless. Students can then be asked to share with each other what they learned.

Students at any level respond to the reggae version of the anthem by the musical group 5'nizza and can recall or find alternative versions of national anthems or other patriotic songs—in Russian, English, or other languages. Students could submit examples of alternate versions of national anthems along with level-appropriate commentary in Russian, either as homework or as a class presentation. Essay or presentation assignments could include discussion of alternative versions of a patriotic song, including versions of the Russian/Soviet national anthem; discussions inspired by questions on the CLSP site; or presentations on a patriotic song—its history, where and when it can be heard, and why it could be considered patriotic. Assignments can range from Novice to Superior levels. Students at a variety of levels share information and benefit from their diversity. For example, even a Novice-level student could introduce a singer unknown to others.

One of the most successful CLSP units for application to the multilevel Russian language classroom is on Yuri Gagarin. Space travel is a topic familiar to many Americans and often among one of the main reasons they study Russian. Not every American student knows the name Gagarin, but most are aware that the first manned spaceflight was Soviet and are curious to learn more. The Gagarin story has broad appeal, and the image of the cosmonaut as national hero is easily understandable to American students. This CLSP unit presents a perfect case for application at multiple levels, because although the basics of the Gagarin story are potentially of broad interest, the CLSP unit on Gagarin goes far beyond what a lower-level student could grasp as it moves from the basic story, through its Cold War–era treatment in a relatively easily comprehensible song, to a contemporary song loaded with a mixture of admiration and irony.

The unit begins with a brief introduction to Gagarin's first flight, which is followed by a 77-second documentary footage clip of the first launch. An instructor could adapt the opening text to students at all levels. Students at the third-year level and above could puzzle out the text on their own with the aid of the vocabulary glosses, possibly with additional glossing for third-year students. Students at the first-year level could identify familiar words and the date of the first flight and then work together in pairs or small groups with Intermediate-level students, who could provide additional information to interpret the text. Pairs could be asked to report to the group on what they have learned from the introduction.

The brief video footage of the first launch provides a gold mine of vocabulary (cosmonaut, planet, hero, spaceflight, rocket launch, and related terms) as well as easily repeatable and learnable phrases, from the introductory phrase, which seems written for the second-semester student («Юрий Гагарин стал первым космонавтом планеты» [Iurii Gagarin became the planet's first cosmonaut]) to the launch date in the genitive case, to such gems for the first-year classroom as «Доброго полёта» [Have a good flight], «Всё нормально» [Everything is okay], «Я вас понял» [Roger!], and «Вы меня слышите?» [Can you hear me?]. Students could be asked to provide their own equivalent for the phrase «Приём» [Over!] and then be shown the exam cheating scene from the «Наваждение» [Hallucination] segment of Leonid Gaidai's film «Операция „Ы"» [*Operation Y*], which plays on the same word. Students at higher levels could be set the challenging task of piecing together more parts of the audio puzzle, which is made more complex by the relatively poor quality of the video. Intermediate students could be assigned the task of figuring out the participants' code names. All students could reenact the scene or participate in a news report of their own devising. Students could then be assigned follow-up writing or presentation tasks to report on the basics of Gagarin's biography, on one of the many available films on Gagarin's life and death, or on Russian/Soviet spaceflight. The second film clip in the CLSP unit, an interview by a Finnish journalist with Gagarin while aboard a train, presents numerous possibilities for Intermediate- and Advanced-level assignments, from recasting the interview questions to finding in his answers the Russian equivalents of certain words and phrases (provided in English in the assignment), to retelling his responses as a news broadcaster. Students could be assigned similar interviews on an imaginary train trip. Tasks could culminate in group performances and discussion.

The songs in this unit are extraordinary resources for teaching. They constitute polar opposites in style: one a lyric song from the 1960s, the other a highly referential and cheekily ironic song from the Putin era, with both sharing a slow to moderate tempo, clear articulation, and mixed emotions (pride, nostalgia, fear of loss). The CLSP assignment for «Нежность» ["Tenderness"], a song whose lyrics hint at the deaths of cosmonauts, the fear of more deaths in spaceflight, and the anguish of their loved ones, and which was subsequently associated with Gagarin's death, presents the Advanced-level challenge to transcribe the entire text of the song as a dictation task. Novice- and Intermediate-level students could be presented with a more scaffolded version of the dictation assignment through cloze tasks, word searches from the word такси [taxi] to forms of the word пустой [empty], focus on motion verbs conveying flying, information-gap exercises in which partners complete parts of the text together, and so forth. Presentation assignments could include a report on the article or documentary film on the history of the song; a presentation on the Russian version of Antoine de Saint-Exupéry's *Little Prince*, referred to in the song and familiar to many students; a presentation of the 1967 film «Три тополя на Плющихе» [*Three poplars on Pliushchikha street*], in which the already popular song was performed; presentations and discussions of alternate performances of the song, some of which are listed in the CLSP unit; extended responses to some of the questions posed on the song, including reaction pieces and interpretations of the song and its historical context; discussion and comparison of the song's style with that of other Russian, European, or American music from the period, including film scores; even a group performance of the song.

The second song from this unit, «Гагарин, я вас любила» ["Gagarin, I loved you"], presents far more intellectual and linguistic challenges and yet has broad appeal for students at various levels. The introduction to the song presents rich opportunities for further classroom material, from the Любэ [Ljubè] song «Ребята нашего двора» ["Kids from our courtyard"] with its reference to Gagarin, to the sots-art movement and discussion of the concept of *стёб* (irony through identification with a suspect ideology). Listening comprehension and interpretation assignments related to the song could vary widely, along the lines discussed above; however, two opposite elements are present: a highly complex text, making the task more difficult, and the addition of a rich video, making the song both more complicated and more accessible. Novice-level students can learn the simplest elements from the lyrics' refrain, while Advanced-level students puzzle out the ellipses and complex syntax and Intermediate-level students work at the level of vocabulary and retelling of isolated lines. The video also presents a multitude of opportunities for interpretation. Novice-level students could be asked to list items in the room. Intermediate-level students could describe what people are wearing and doing or speculate on the stories behind the video; Advanced-level students could be asked to complete the same assignment in greater detail. All students could play a scavenger hunt in teams for items or words shown in the video. Intermediate- and Advanced-level students could discuss and present on aspects of its deeply layered cultural elements: from music to film, to nostalgia for things Soviet and American, to competitions in hockey and space, to contemporary treatments of the Cold War. The general discussion questions on the space race present numerous possibilities for classroom discussion and presentations, as do the songs presented in the section «Что слушать дальше?» [Suggestions for further listening]. Opportunities for discussion of official and unofficial musical culture are boundless and can be made accessible to students at various levels if songs are chosen carefully. The topics of nostalgia for the Cold War era, youth culture, and irony (стёб) could lead the class in the direction of a film that invites discussion of American culture from the Russian and Soviet point of view, «Стиляги» [*Hipsters*], which is the setting for a song in the final CLSP unit.

In sum, the principle of changing the task, not the text, can be applied to song presented in a multilayered and multifaceted cultural context, and themes can be expanded almost infinitely, depending on the interests and proficiency levels of the students and the goals of the class. The benefits of such exploration can be linguistic and cultural, cognitive and metacognitive, drawing on the principles elaborated in the World-Readiness Standards. Song has the potential to multiply the results of our efforts because of its compactness; memorability; phonetic, linguistic, and cultural authenticity; embeddedness within the matrices of meaning of the target culture; and the simultaneous immediacy of its emotional impact and its ability to reveal layers of meaning on repeated examination, once we as instructors do the intricate work of song selection, materials preparation, and scaffolding. At a minimum, song-based work can be a particularly effective modality for language and cultural study. In the best case it can help unobtrusively inspire students to make Russian language and Russophone culture a habitual and significant aspect of their lives.

NOTES

1. The authors thank Sandrine Pell, University of Wisconsin–Madison, for her assistance in locating relevant literature on L2 teaching and learning through song, as well as the anonymous reviewers for their suggestions.
2. See also Iudin-Nelson, 1997 on DDT's «Родина» ["Homeland"] and «Предчувствие гражданской войны» ["Anticipating civil war"] as prime material for discussing the mood of the early 1990s in Russia.
3. For reasons of copyright, the Georgia Tech Critical Languages Song Project materials are password protected. Access is provided at no charge to instructors and, through them, to students in a university setting. Access is also granted to independent learners with a bona fide educational need. For a review or to use the materials, please send a brief message to sgoldberg@gatech.edu.
4. Among survey respondents was one of the co-authors of this chapter. Students should not be seen as self-selecting, however, since in LCTLs they likely had few or no other choices for a fourth-year course at their institutions.
5. In their final versions the courses have benefitted from the open-ended suggestions and criticisms of students and instructors taking part in the pilot as well as from outside review by specialists in the language/culture areas and in pedagogy.

REFERENCES

Abrate, J. H. (1983). Pedagogical applications of the French popular song in the foreign language classroom. *Modern Language Journal, 67*(1), 8–12.

American Council on the Teaching of Foreign Languages (ACTFL). (2012). ACTFL Proficiency Guidelines 2012. Retrieved from http://www.actfl.org/publications/guidelines-and-manuals/actfl-proficiency-guidelines-2012

Aquil, R. (2012). Revisiting songs in language pedagogy. *Journal of the National Council of Less Commonly Taught Languages, 11*, 75–96.

Beaudrie, S., Ducat, C., & Potowski, K. (2015). *Heritage language teaching.* New York: McGraw-Hill.

Carlson, J. R. (2010). Songs that teach: Using song-poems to teach critically. *English Journal, 99*(4), 65–71.

Carreira, M., & Kagan, O. (2011). The results of the National Heritage Language Survey: Implications for teaching, curriculum design, and professional development. *Foreign Language Annals, 43*(3), 40–64.

Ellis, R. (2003). *Task-based language learning and teaching.* Oxford, UK: Oxford UP .

Failoni, J. (1993). Music as a means to enhance cultural awareness and literacy in the foreign language classroom. *Mid-Atlantic Journal of Foreign Language Pedagogy, 6* (Spring), 97–108.

Fairclough, M., Beaudrie, S., Valdés, G., & Roca, A. (Eds.). (2016). *Innovation strategies for heritage language teaching: A practical guide for the classroom.* Washington, DC: Georgetown UP.

Galloway, V., & Goldberg, S. (2010). The seven Cs. Retrieved from www.clsp.gatech.edu

Gardner, R. C. (1982). Language attitudes and language learning. In E. Bouchard Ryan & H. Giles (Eds.), *Attitudes towards language variation* (pp. 132–47). London: Edward Arnold.

Garza, T. (1994). Beyond MTV: Music videos as foreign language text. *Journal of the Imagination in Language Learning, 2,* 106–11.

Garza, T. (2009). (Un)Chained melodies: Russian music videos in web-based language and culture instruction. In R. Brecht, L. Verbitskaya, M. Lekic, & W. Rivers (Eds.), *Mnemosynon: Studies on language and culture in the Russophone world* (pp. 313–30). Moscow: Azbukovnik.

Geertz, C. (1973). *The interpretation of cultures.* New York: Basic.

Georgia Tech Critical Languages Song Project. Advanced Arabic, Chinese, Japanese and Russian. (2013). Retrieved from clsp.gatech.edu

Gibbons, P. (2002). *Scaffolding language, scaffolding learning: Teaching second language learners in the mainstream classroom.* Portsmouth, NH: Heinemann.

Griffee, D. T. (1992). *Songs in action.* New York: Prentice Hall.

Griffiths, C. (2012). Using songs in the language classroom. *Procedia—Social and Behavioral Sciences, 70,* 1136–43.

Hall, E. T. (1959). *The silent language.* Garden City, NY: Doubleday.

Iudin-Nelson, L. J. (1997). *Songs in the L2 syllabus: integrating the study of Russian language and culture* (Doctoral dissertation). Retrieved from Proquest Dissertations and Theses Global (Accession Order No. 9734824).

Jolly, Y. S. (1975). The use of songs in teaching foreign languages. *Modern Language Journal, 59*(1/2), 11–14.

Jones, R. (2008). *Echoing their lives: teaching Russian language and culture through the music of Vladimir S. Vysotsky* (Doctoral dissertation). Retrieved from Proquest Dissertations and Theses Global (Accession Order No. 3315090).

Kagan, O. (2014). Russian heritage language learners: From students' profiles to project-based curriculum. In T. Wiley, J. Peyton, D. Christian, S. Moore, & N. Liu (Eds.), *Handbook of heritage, community, and Native American languages in the United States* (pp. 177–85). New York: Routledge.

Kagan, O., & Dillon, K. (2001/2002). A new perspective on teaching Russian: Focus on the heritage learner. *Slavic and East European Journal, 45*(3), 507–18.

Kagan, O., Miller, F., & Kudyma, G. (2005). *V puti: Russian Grammar in Context* (2nd ed.). Upper Saddle River, NJ: Pearson.

Kern, R. G. (2003). Literacy and advanced foreign language learning: Rethinking the curriculum. In H. Burns, H. H. Maxim, & S. Sieloff Magnan (Eds.), *Advanced foreign language instruction* (pp. 2–18). Boston: Cengage Learning.

Kramer, D. J. (2001). A blueprint for teaching foreign languages and cultures through music in the classroom and on the web. *ADFL Bulletin, 33*(1), 29–35.

Kramsch, C. (1993). *Context and culture in language teaching.* New York: Oxford UP.

Krashen, S. (1982). *Principles and practice in second language acquisition.* Oxford: Pergamon.

Krashen, S. (1983). The din in the head, input, and the language acquisition device. *Foreign Language Annals, 16*(1), 41–44.

Lonergan, J. (1984). *Video in language teaching.* Cambridge: Cambridge UP.

Ludke, K., Ferreira, F., & Overy, K. (2014). Singing can facilitate foreign language learning. *Memory and Cognition, 42*, 41–52.

Maley, A. (1987). Poetry and song as effective language-learning activities. In W. Rivers (Ed.), *Interactive language teaching* (pp. 93–109). Cambridge: Cambridge UP.

Maxim, H. H. (2000). Integrating language learning and cultural inquiry in the beginning foreign language classroom. *ADFL Bulletin, 32*(1), 12–17.

Murphey, T. (1990). The song stuck in my head phenomenon: A melodic din in the LAD? *System, 18*(1), 53–64.

Murphey, T. (1992). The discourse of pop songs. *TESOL Quarterly, 26*(4), 770–74.

Nation, I. S. P. (2001). *Learning vocabulary in another language.* Cambridge: Cambridge UP.

National Standards Collaborative Board (NSCB). (2015). *World-readiness standards for learning languages* (4th ed.). Alexandria, VA: Author. Retrieved from http://www.actfl.org/publications/all/world-readiness-standards-learning-languages

Omaggio Hadley, A. (2000). *Teaching language in context* (3rd ed.). Boston: Thomson Heinle.

Rifkin, B. (2003). Guidelines for foreign language lesson planning. *Foreign Language Annals, 36*(2), 167–79.

Robin, R. (2007). Learner-based listening and technological authenticity. *Language Learning and Technology, 11*(1), 109–115.

Robin, R., Evans-Romaine, K., & Shatalina, G. (2013/2014). *Golosa: A basic course in Russian* (Vols.1–2) (5th ed.). Upper Saddle River, NJ: Pearson.

Rockin' Russian. (2008). Retrieved from http://coerll.utexas.edu/rr

Salcedo, C. S. (2010). The effects of songs in the foreign language classroom on text recall, delayed text recall and involuntary mental rehearsal. *Journal of College Teaching & Learning, 7*(6), 19–30.

Schmitt, N. (2008). Instructed second language vocabulary learning (review article). *Language Teaching Research, 12*(3), 329–63.

Shrum, J. L., & Glisan, E. W. (2010). *Contextualized language instruction: Teacher's handbook* (4th ed.). Boston: Heinle.

Skehan, P. (1998). *A cognitive approach to language learning.* New York: Oxford UP.

Tumanov, V. (1996). *Listening to Okudzhava: Twenty-three aural comprehension exercises in Russian.* Newburyport, MA: Focus.

Tumanov, V., & Tennant, J. (2000). Using songs to teach aural comprehension in the Intermediate-Advanced foreign language classroom. *Russian Language Journal, 54,* 13–33.

Vandergrift, L. (2004). Listening to learn or learning to listen? *Annual Review of Applied Linguistics, 24,* 3–25.

Wallace, W. T. (1994). Memory for music: effect of melody on recall of text. *Journal of Experimental Psychology: Learning, Memory, and Cognition, 20,* 1471–85.

PART IV

◇◇◇◇

CURRICULUM AND MATERIALS DEVELOPMENT

12

DEVELOPING A TEXTBOOK

A Framework and Reflections

Olga E. Kagan and Anna S. Kudyma

This chapter proposes guidelines for developing textbooks for learners of Russian as a foreign language (FL) as well as for heritage language (HL) speakers of Russian. Any textbook development must initially determine a target audience and the expected learning outcome(s) for that audience. The 1986 publication of the American Council on the Teaching of Foreign Language (ACTFL) Proficiency Guidelines led to a considerable rethinking of learning outcomes and resulted in the development of proficiency-oriented textbooks and a subsequent focus on communication competence.[1] Another document that affected foreign language teaching was the National Standards for Foreign Language Education, which was first published in 1996 (Phillips & Abbott, 2011). A recently revised edition of the national standards, titled World-Readiness Standards for Learning Languages (NSCB, 2015), has shifted the focus to communication and identified three modes of communication as the targeted areas of language teaching: interpersonal, interpretive, and presentational.

Developing a textbook combines theoretical knowledge of second language acquisition with practical experience gained in the classroom. It also requires creativity, a desire to challenge previous ideas, and a vision of what the field will need in the future. Textbook development differs from a teacher's development of instructional materials for a class. The needs of unknown students and teachers can be met only through a flexible, almost-open-ended textbook that all instructors can adapt to their personal teaching styles while accommodating the multiple learning styles and interests of students.

Here we suggest some guidelines for developing a Russian language textbook. The basis for these suggestions is our experience as authors who have produced 14 textbooks over the past 30 years, some as a collective endeavor, some individually, or with coauthors.[2] We reflect on our own approaches and experiences with textbook development and provide what in literary theory is known as «обнажение приёма» [baring the device] (Shklovsky, 1983). For our current purpose we limit our discussion to three textbooks for FL learners of Russian, all coauthored by the same three authors: *V puti* (2nd ed.) (Kagan, Miller, & Kudyma, 2006), *Beginner's Russian* (Kudyma, Miller, & Kagan, 2010), and *Russian: From Intermediate to Advanced* (Kagan, Kudyma, &

Miller, 2014). For HL speakers of Russian we review the textbook «Учимся писать по-русски» [*Learning to write in Russian*] (Kagan & Kudyma, 2012b). Lastly we compare our textbooks for FL and HL learners and suggest some guidelines for future HL textbooks.

Starting with the second edition of *V puti* (2006) we adopted the principles of backward design for textbook development (Wiggins & McTighe, 2000). These principles involve three steps: (1) setting targets in all skills (speaking, reading, writing, and listening); (2) determining a means of measuring the outcomes; and (3) selecting texts and designing activities to meet these goals.[3] Steps 1 and 3 apply to developing the content of the textbook, while Step 2 pertains to the written tests and oral prompts for instructors that are available on the websites for *Beginner's Russian* and *V puti*. Students have access to self-graded tests in all three textbooks.

We describe here the targets corresponding to Step 1 (functions, content/context, and text type). To meet the goal of Step 3 we discuss the selection of materials (vocabulary, grammar, and cultural materials) and the design of activities for the interpersonal, interpretive, and presentational modes of communication.

SELECTION OF TARGETS: PROFICIENCY LEVEL, FUNCTION, CONTENT/CONTEXT, AND TEXT TYPE

Targeted competencies for our textbooks are based on the ACTFL Proficiency Guidelines as reflected in the following proficiency ranges: Novice to Intermediate Mid (*Beginner's Russian*), Intermediate Mid to Intermediate High (*V puti*), and Intermediate High to Advanced Mid (*Russian: From Intermediate to Advanced*). In addition to the proficiency ranges we target functions and text types as well as the content and context in each textbook, which helps in selecting texts, designing activities, and making decisions about vocabulary, grammar selection, and cultural content. The level of targeted proficiency and the functions determine the context, content, and type of text(s) for each activity.

SELECTION OF VOCABULARY, GRAMMAR, AND CULTURAL CONTENT

Once we established the level of targeted proficiency and the corresponding functions, we turned to the selection of vocabulary, grammar, and cultural content.

Vocabulary

The principles followed in selecting vocabulary were the same for all our textbooks: the target proficiency levels and the functions that students should address determined the choice of lexical items.

We based the selection of lexical items used in our three textbooks for FL learners on the *Russian Federation Lexical Minimums* (Andrjušina & Kozlova, 2006a, 2006b; Andrjušina, 2011). *Minimums* uses the following criteria for lexical selection: (a) neutrality of style; (b) universality, i.e., commonality of used words and word combinations; (3) breadth of subject range; (4) potential for word formation; (5) word frequency (Andrjušina & Kozlova, 2000, p. 5). To the lexical items taken from *Minimums* we added country-specific vocabulary that allows students to discuss their own experiences in the American context (Akishina & Kagan, 2004; Kagan, 1993).

While there are no direct correlations between the *Russian Certification Levels of Competency* (Andrjušina & Vladimirova, 1999) and the ACTFL Proficiency Guidelines (2012), our previous research established some equivalencies (Kagan & Kudyma, 2012a): the Elementary/Basic levels roughly correspond to the ACTFL Novice range and the First- and Second-Certification levels (TRKI-1 and TRKI-2) correspond approximately to the ACTFL Intermediate and Advanced ranges. *Beginner's Russian,* which targets Intermediate Low proficiency, is based on the *Elementary/Basic Lexical Minimums* (Andrjušina & Kozlova, 2000), which contains 1,300 lexical items. Our textbook includes most of the vocabulary from this publication but excludes some vocabulary items based on our judgment of learners' communicative needs. We also add some words important in the American context. *Beginner's Russian* offers 1,000 lexical items, while *V puti* contains 1,300–1,400. We chose the vocabulary for *V puti* based on Andrjušina and Kozlova (2000, 2006a, 2006b) and added lexical items important for local context. For example, *Basic Level Lexical Minimum* does not include words related to natural disasters. The word *earthquake* appears in the Certification Level 1 Lexical Minimum and *fire* appears in the Certification Level 2 Lexical Minimum. Local conditions make it necessary to include some vocabulary items deemed to be infrequently used by the Russian developers of the frequency lists.

Most of the vocabulary selected for *Russian: From Intermediate to Advanced* derives from the Russian Federation Lexical Minimum for the Second Certification Level (Andrjušina, 2009). The number of new lexical items in the textbook is 1,600–1,800. We include frequently used formulaic and semiformulaic expressions from the Second Certification lexical list; for example, добро пожаловать [welcome], между прочим [by the way], чувство юмора [sense of humor], and proverbs and sayings, such as Век живи, век учись [Live and learn] and Хорошо там, где нас нет [The grass is always greener on the other side].

Grammar and Activities to Support Grammar Practice

The targeted proficiency levels and the functions that students are expected to perform determine the choice of grammar for the textbook. To reach higher levels of proficiency students need a solid grammar base (Brecht et al., 1995; Leaver et al., 2004). In all of our textbooks we are mindful of the importance of grammar and we subjugate grammar selection to function. The guiding question is what grammar is necessary to handle a certain function and meet the thematic focus of a chapter. Although the bulk of the discourse at the Novice to Novice High level is formulaic or memorized, students nevertheless must comprehend simple sentence structure and learn the case system and verb forms in order to engage in conversation. This foundation helps learners create personalized speech "islands" to express their own meaning as a memorized chunk (Shekhtman et al., 2002). At the Intermediate Low to Intermediate Mid levels students are creating with the language, acquiring an ability to understand, and asking and answering questions, all of which require developing a facility in the use of cases and tenses (past, present, and future verbs). At the Advanced level being able to understand and produce "narration and descriptions in all major time frames" (ACTFL, 2012) assumes an ability to build paragraphs using complex syntax and competency in handling verbal government. Thus at each step of the learning process grammar is of paramount importance.

Kagan and Kudyma (2012a) note that the most problematic areas of Russian grammar for learners at the Intermediate to Advanced level include: aspect, verbs of motion with prefixes, participles, verbal adverbs, and conjunctions in complex sentences (e.g., что vs. чтобы [that vs. so that]; если vs. ли [if vs. whether]; то, что [that which]; который [which], как [as], etc.). In *Russian: From Intermediate to Advanced* we offer grammar as a discourse element. For example, under the rubric "How to Tell Stories" we introduce time frames and time expressions, use of verbal aspects, tenses in reported speech, and complex syntax with cohesive devices.

Comer (2013) raises the question of what can increase the integration of form and meaning and reduce the amount of time devoted to mechanical form-practice in the classroom. While mechanical grammar practice has its place (Leaver et al., 2004), we contextualize grammar that targets interpersonal communication through micro-dialogues targeting interpersonal communication (e.g., in *Beginner's Russian*, Chapter 13, exercises 13-6 and 13-8) and in short texts for interpretive reading (e.g., *V puti*, Chapter 9, ex. 9-17). We combine grammar practice with authentic (real-life) activities that integrate form, meaning, and content.

The following examples illustrate a variety of authentic activities to teach grammar at different proficiency ranges. In *Beginner's Russian* an interpretive reading activity involves noting the use of раз [time] with numbers and time words (e.g., day, week, month, year). Students take a lifestyle test to determine whether their lifestyles are healthy. The test contains a list of activities considered either healthy or unhealthy (e.g., eating meat, eating vegetables, going for a walk). To integrate the element of time, students indicate how frequently they engage in such activities; for example, every day, three to five times a week, once a week, or etc. (Chapter 9, ex. 9-9). In *V puti* students explore time on the half hour by studying an event schedule. Next, they participate in an event-planning exercise and create an incremental schedule indicating events that start and end on the half hour (Chapter 3, ex. 3-36). This activity combines grammar practice with interpretive reading, interpersonal communication, and presentational writing. In *Russian: From Intermediate to Advanced* students use a list of statements to examine several texts on family issues and to discuss gender roles. The activity focuses not on manipulation of grammatical forms but rather on discussion. However, the statements for discussion contain accusative case constructions targeted in the chapter (Chapter 4, ex. 4-42). A second example from *Russian: From Intermediate to Advanced* concerns politics. In this example students respond to an initial survey, fill out a questionnaire, and debate the question «Каким должен быть политик 21 века?» [What should a 21st-century politician be like?]. However, the activity also focuses on verbal constructions (Chapter 10, ex. 10-48). In both cases we carefully scaffold activities to allow students to focus on meaning while using the targeted grammar forms.

Cultural Content

When selecting cultural content we include both "Big C" and "small c" culture. In the approach to Big C culture we select materials that are well known and immediately recognizable by Russian speakers and that do not go out of date rapidly. The centrally directed elementary and secondary school curriculum determines Russian society's cultural canon; thus our textbooks introduce culture as it is understood by an average educated speaker in Russia. This approach is used by Gerhart in *The Russian's World* (1974 and subsequent editions) and expanded by Boyle and Gerhart in *The Russian Context* (2002). In the introduction to *The Russian Context* Boyle and Gerhart write: "There *is* a body of information that 'everybody knows' and refers to, even if it is a little fuzzy on the edges" (p. vii). In our textbooks we adhere to a similar approach. In *V puti* Kagan and Miller (1996) introduce a section in each chapter titled "What Every Russian Knows." We use the same approach in the other textbooks as well.

Small c cultural information can rapidly become dated. For example, over the course of a year of a textbook's creation prices will most likely change and go out of date by the time of publication. Thus a more cautious approach is to direct students to find current information on the Internet, but even that requires caution because websites tend to migrate or disappear without warning. In *Russian: From Intermediate to Advanced* we provide tags to help students find information on a particular subject.

AUTHENTICITY OF TEXT: READING AND LISTENING ACTIVITIES

In our textbooks we use authentic and semiauthentic texts that conform to real-life genres of reading and listening. By "authentic" materials we mean texts created by native speakers for communicating with native speakers. An authentic activity is a response to the communicative purpose of a specific text or situation. Many authors and practitioners posit that if activities are "based around authentic texts . . . [they] can play a key role in enhancing positive attitudes to learning, in promoting the development of a wide range of skills, and in enabling students to work independently of the teacher" (McGarry, 1995, cited in Mishan, 2005, p. 9). ACTFL recommends using authentic texts because they "provide real-life examples of language used in everyday situations. The rich language found in authentic materials provides a source of input language learners need for acquisition" (n.d., para 2).

On the other hand, we find it is more useful to adhere to the authenticity of genres rather than to include unaltered authentic texts. We refer to such texts as semiauthentic; these are texts created by native and non-native speakers and based on original language materials but adapted to fit curricular needs (Center for Open Educational Resources and Language Learning, n.d.).

Mishan (2005) offers a set of guidelines on constructing authentic learning activities. She suggests developing activities that reflect the original communicative purpose of the text, elicit a response from the learners, approximate real-life tasks, activate learners' existing knowledge of the target language and culture, and encourage purposeful communication among learners. These guidelines could operate as a checklist when creating activities for a textbook.

As an example of an authentic learning activity based on a semiauthentic prompt, in *V puti* students read a letter posted to a Web-based advice column «Даша даёт советы» [Dasha's advice column]. In the letter a teenage girl describes her relationship with her boyfriend and asks for advice. Students discuss what types of advice to provide, choose the best suggestion, and write a collective response (Chapter 6, exs. 6-36 and 6-42).

In addition to the guidelines from Mishan, we keep in mind Bloom's taxonomy for creating activities that promote higher-level cognitive skills (Bloom, 1956; Anderson et al., 2001). Tomlinson (2012) notes that even learners at lower levels of proficiency can develop higher-level skills if they are unrestricted by materials that stress only linguistic decoding. In effect, textbook activities need to combine top-down and bottom-up endeavors to be successful, to activate learners' schemata and provoke their curiosity (Byram et al., 2002; Celce-Murcia, 1991, 2007; Savignon, 1991).

The questions related to copyright issues arise whenever one mentions the use of authentic materials. Access to the Internet makes finding authentic materials in Russian easy for all levels of proficiency, even the lowest. We rely on Russian language sites that allow free use of their appropriately cited published materials. A typical statement about sources used might read: «Использование любых материалов, размещённых на сайте, разрешается при условии ссылки на (название сайта или фамилия автора)» [One can use materials from this site if the reference to the site is provided (the name of the site or the author)].

DETERMINING MAJOR LEARNING EXPERIENCES IN ALL MODES OF COMMUNICATION

Setting consistent goals in all modes of communication determines what learners are able to do with the language in the interpersonal, interpretive, and presentational modes at different levels of proficiency.[4] The backward design approach of Wiggins and McTighe prompts the formulation of outcomes before developing appropriate activities. For each of our textbooks we formulate outcomes for each mode of communication and develop activities accordingly.

Interpersonal Communication

Interpersonal communication activities in our textbooks employ real-life scenarios, such as conducting interviews and surveys, participating in discussions and debates, and acting out role-play situations. These interpersonal activities are typically combined with interpretive readings or listenings and presentational writing or speaking. The targeted proficiency level determines the complexity of the activity. Below we provide examples of some authentic activities from each textbook. Each prompt uses the same genre (a survey) but the level of required and targeted proficiency determines the outcome. The activity targets different modes of communication.

Example 1: Beginner's Russian, *Chapter 4, Ex. 4-22*

An activity that targets interpersonal communication and presentational speaking follows interpretive reading: Ци́фры и фа́кты. Шко́ла № 15. г. Москва́ [Statistics and facts. School #15. Moscow]. (1) Look at the graph and discuss the students' responses in Russian, and (2) conduct a similar survey among your classmates or ask others and report the results in class. Вопро́с: Како́й твой люби́мый предме́т? [Question: What is your favorite subject at school?]

Результа́ты опро́са [Results of the Survey]

Математика [math]	30% (процентов)
Русский язык [Russian language]	9% (процентов)
Чтение/литература [reading/literature]	12% (процентов)
Иностранный язык [foreign language]	12% (процентов)
География [geography]	9% (процентов)
Труд [shop]	12% (процентов)
Музыка [music]	6% (процентов)
Физкультура [physical education]	20% (процентов)
Информатика [computer science]	13% (процентов)
История [history]	12% (процентов)

Example 2: V puti, *Chapter 2, Ex. 2-22*

Presentational writing and speaking following interpersonal communication: Опрос. Что значит «хорошо провести время»? [What does it mean to "have a good time"?]. Conduct a survey to find out what "having a good time" means for your classmates. Write down your conclusions and tell them to the rest of the class.

Example 3: Russian: From Intermediate to Advanced, *Chapter 4, Ex. 4-6*

Presentational writing and speaking following interpersonal communication: Опрос и презентация [Survey and a presentation]. Conduct a survey among your friends on the following question: «Роль женщины в современном мире» [the role of women in contemporary society] (interview at least two women and two men). Present the results of your survey to the class (1–2 minutes). Include in your presentation data about the respondents: age, where they study or work, if they are married, etc.

Survey on the Role of Women in Contemporary Society

1. Мать и жена, хранительница домашнего очага [mother and wife, keeper of the hearth]	Да [Yes	Нет No	Не знаю Not sure]
2. Бизнес-леди, т.е. надо быть наравне с мужчиной, сделать карьеру, чтобы чувствовать себя материально независимой [businesswoman, i.e., wants to make a career equal to men, be financially independent]	Да [Yes	Нет No	Не знаю Not sure]
3. Другое (что именно?) [other (specify)]			

Interpretive Mode (Reading and Listening)

Developing activities for the interpretive mode in reading requires details. We follow a similar pattern in creating activities for listening.

The 2012 ACTFL Proficiency Guidelines (and earlier editions) and works by Swaffar et al. (1991) and Nuttall (1996) guide the selection of texts and activities for reading. Recent studies by Clifford et al. (2004) and Clifford and Cox (2013) offer some valuable suggestions for the selection of reading texts. Clifford and Cox triangulate the author purpose, text type, and reader task. This alignment of purpose, type, and task can lead to a more principled selection of reading texts and accompanying activities when tied to proficiency levels.

Criteria for Text Selection at Each Level of Proficiency

Because both reading and listening comprehension are schemata-based and "draw on knowledge of linguistic code, cognitive processing skills and contextual cues both within and outside of text" (Omaggio Hadley, 2001, p. 179), text genre can serve as the cornerstone of selection.

Although Clifford and Cox (2013) suggest a triangulation of author purpose, text type, and reader task when selecting texts for teaching reading comprehension at various levels of proficiency, we add a fourth component, genre, to formulate a guide for text selection (see Figure 12.1).

Simple short texts are suitable for Novice High to Intermediate Low learners. Readers should orient themselves by focusing on dates, names, and familiar words (possibly cognates). Visual cues typically support the texts. The genre of such texts can be announcements about events, advertisements, weather reports, recipes, graphs based on public opinion polls, short informal e-mails, or Internet forums. Because these genres are familiar to learners based on their own experiences, they help schemata formation. *Beginner's Russian* employs these kinds of texts.

The proficiency target in *V puti* is from Intermediate Low to High. Simple, short texts wherein the author's purpose is to communicate information are appropriate to

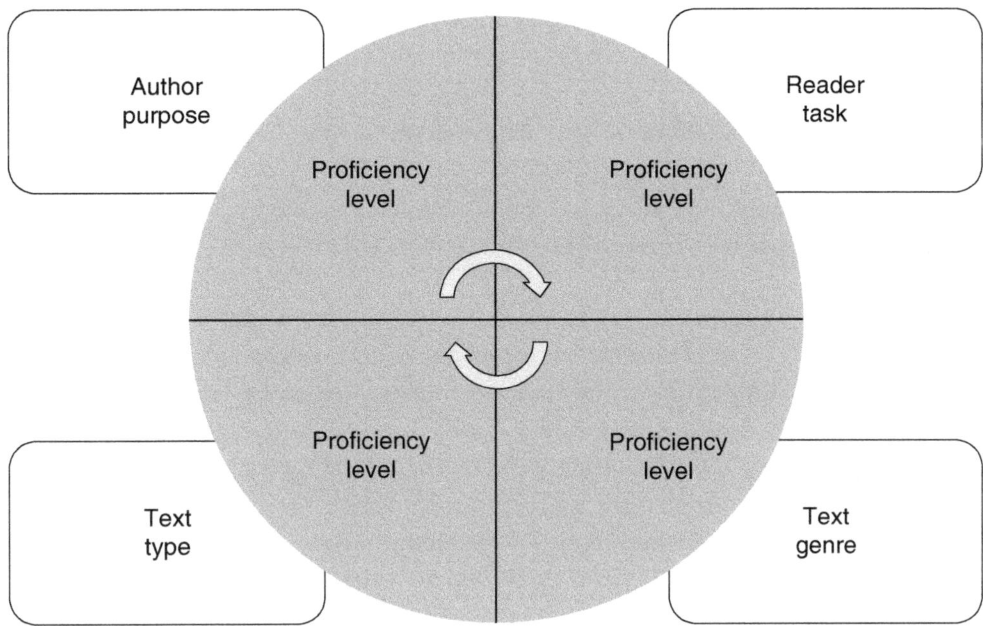

FIGURE 12.1. Criteria for Text Selection

that level of proficiency. Although such texts can be loosely organized, they follow cultural and societal norms. The reader's task is to identify the main topic and basic facts. The text genres that meet these conditions are e-mails, blog and forum postings, informal letters, and short news items on familiar topics.

Russian: From Intermediate to Advanced targets Intermediate High to Advanced Mid proficiency levels. Texts that match this level instruct or inform by communicating factual information. These texts contain connected factual discourse with compound or complex sentences. The reader's task is to understand not only central facts but also supporting details, such as temporal and causative relationships. The identity of the author is not important at this level, but since it becomes important at the Superior level we add some questions to the reading activities about the voice of the author. The genres of the texts are significantly expanded. While we use all the genres listed above, we add articles on a broad variety of topics, some of which are factual and others that express opinions. Examples below illustrate text genre and reader/listener activities.

Example 1: Beginner's Russian, *Chapter 5, Ex. 5-24*

Interpretive reading is followed by interpersonal communication and presentational speaking. Students read the results of a survey about exercise habits in Russia, they examine the pie chart, and they summarize the results, in percentages. The reader's goal is to understand the main ideas and summarize them in English. As a follow-up, students conduct a similar survey among their peers and organize their findings as a graph then present it to the class.

Example 2: V puti, *Chapter 5, Ex. 5-8*

Interpersonal communication and presentational speaking follow interpretive reading. Students read apartment classified ads and decide which apartment would meet their needs. Afterward, students explain their decision to the class.

Example 3: Russian: From Intermediate to Advanced, *Chapter 3, Ex. 3-49*

Presentational speaking follows interpretive reading. Students read a movie review and analyze the text structure by dividing it into three parts—introduction, main text, and conclusion—and summarize each part. In the follow-up activity students explain the author's reasoning, organizing their arguments with the help of во-первых, во-вторых, в-третьих [first, second, third]. Additionally they guess whether a man or a woman wrote the review and explain their choice to the class.

Example 4: Russian: From Intermediate to Advanced, *Chapter 3, Ex. 3-31*

After reading an interview with the singer Vladimir Chernov (Chapter 3, ex. 3-29), students watch a video clip about his concert in Moscow and choose the correct statements that correspond to the information presented in the video. This activity requires interpretive listening.

Presentational Mode (Speaking and Writing)

In presentational speaking activities students report the results of interviews or surveys or give oral presentations. These activities typically combine with the interpretive reading or listening activities described earlier. Presentational speaking and writing activities often require some research on the part of the students. In *Russian: From Intermediate to Advanced* (Chapter 6) students read multiple texts and watch several video clips about the problems faced by young people in Russia. Following that activity students conduct an Internet search about the problems confronting young people in their own country (Chapter 6, ex. 6-74). Presentations in class conform to the genre of a formal presentation by using an appropriate register and vocabulary as well as the sentence openers listed below:

1. Те́ма моего́ докла́да . . . [In my presentation I discuss . . .]
2. В своём выступле́нии я хочу́ останови́ться на сле́дующих основны́х моме́нтах . . . [In this talk I will discuss the following points: . . .]
3. В пе́рвую о́чередь сле́дует обрати́ть внима́ние на то, что . . . [It is of paramount importance to . . .]
4. Кро́ме того́, необходи́мо отме́тить, что . . . [In addition I should note that . . .]

5. На мой взгляд, . . . [In my opinion . . .]
6. Таки́м о́бразом, как мы ви́дим . . . [We can thus conclude that . . .]
7. В заключе́ние мо́жно сде́лать вы́вод, что . . . [To sum up . . .]
8. А тепе́рь я гото́в/а отве́тить на вопро́сы [I will be happy to answer questions].

In another example of presentational writing and speaking that follows interpersonal communication, students develop their own survey questions, conduct the survey, describe the results in writing, and make a presentation in class (*Russian: From Intermediate to Advanced,* Chapter 4, ex. 4-17*)*. For an example of one student's writing as an outcome of this activity see Appendix 1.

The three textbooks discussed here were written for learners of Russian as a foreign language. Each targets a certain level of proficiency and assumes that the learner's experience is mostly classroom-based. Even if students spend some time in a Russian-speaking country and take language classes, their exposure to the language outside the classroom remains limited. This makes them different from the students who, since the late 1990s, have been categorized as heritage language speakers (Peyton et al., 2001).

DEVELOPING A TEXTBOOK FOR HERITAGE LANGUAGE LEARNERS

This section points out the differences between the needs of FL and HL learners and explores the development of a textbook for HL learners of Russian.

Foreign Language and Heritage Language Learners: A Comparison

Heritage language learners often start at the Intermediate Low or higher in spoken proficiency even when they have no literacy (Kagan, 2005; Kagan & Dillon, 2001; Smyslova, 2009). For example, Smyslova found that all of her HL speaking respondents "including those who started the course without writing skills" (p. 102) perform at the Intermediate or higher level of oral proficiency. Conversely, FL students of Russian frequently remain in the Intermediate range of proficiency after three or four years of language study (Malone et al., 2004; Rifkin, 2005; Thompson, 2000).

For information on the typical characteristics of Russian HL speakers we rely on Carreira and Kagan (2011), Dengub (2012), Dubinina and Polinsky (2013), Geisherik (2010), Kagan (2005, 2010), Kagan and Friedman (2004), Kagan and Kudyma (2012a), Karkafi (2014), Polinsky (2006, 2008, 2011), and Polinsky and Kagan (2007). Davidson and Lekic (2013) explore the differences between FL and HL students in an intensive Flagship study abroad program.[5]

Here we compare the HL textbook «Учимся писать по-русски» [*Learning to write in Russian*] (Kagan & Kudyma, 2012b) to our beginning and advanced textbooks of Russian as a foreign language (see Table 12.1). The main differences between teaching these two groups of students are the starting point and the approach to instruction in literacy.

TABLE 12.1. Comparison of Textbooks for Foreign Language and Heritage Language Learners

Titles	***Beginner's Russian* (2010)**	***Russian: From Intermediate to Advanced* (2014)**	**«Учимся писать по-русски» (2012) [*Learning to write in Russian*]**
Targeted Proficiency Levels	Assumes no knowledge of Russian. Expected outcomes: Novice High/ Intermediate Low (ACTFL); Basic Level/general proficiency (Russian Federation).	Assumes Intermediate. Expected outcomes: Advanced (ACTFL); Second Certification Level/general proficiency (Russian Federation).	Assumes Intermediate Low/Intermediate in speaking, Intermediate High/Advanced in listening, Novice in reading and writing. Expected outcomes: Intermediate High/ Advanced Low in four skills (ACTFL); First Certification Level/ general proficiency (Russian Federation).
Teaching Literacy	Students are presented the alphabet and start to write individual words. Texts have stresses.	Students are literate. Texts have stresses.	Students are presented the alphabet and taught the differences between spoken and written Russian. Texts have stresses.

Table 12.1 summarizes the findings in Kagan (2005) and Kagan and Kudyma (2012a). The comparison shows that the aural/oral proficiency of HL students falls somewhere between beginning students and Intermediate/Advanced-level students, but both groups need instruction in literacy. The HL learner's strength in speaking and listening allows for faster progress in reading and writing. Nevertheless, the HL learner often does not have a good grasp of stresses; thus, the textbook for HL speakers needs stresses just like textbooks for FL learners. The early chapters in «Учимся писать по-русски» [*Learning to write in Russian*] target Intermediate proficiency in reading, while later chapters aim at Advanced Mid or Advanced High. For example, the reading text in Chapter 21 discusses ecology; the text in Chapter 22 is a review of the film *The 12,* directed by Nikita Mikhalkov, followed by an interview with the director. The activities accompanying these texts are at the Advanced High level of proficiency. For example, students display their understanding of a statement from the film review that queries whether moviemaking should aim to be entertainment or an art form. These high-level activities may not meet the needs of all students but they allow flexibility in a typically heterogeneous class.

A Macro Approach to Teaching Heritage Learners

A program or textbook for HL speakers should take a macro approach (Carreira, 2016; Kagan & Dillon, 2001), elsewhere referred to as a top-down approach (Celce-Murcia, 2007). The macro approach allows instructors to consider student background proficiencies from the onset of instruction. As Carreira (2016) notes, "HL teaching should make strategic use of HL learners' strengths to address gaps in their knowledge [and it can employ macro-based activities to] respond to HL learners' linguistic and affective needs" (p. 130). In developing the textbook for HL learners we adhere to an enrichment model of instruction rather than one focused on the eradication of errors (Valdés, 2016). We also rely on the "From > To" principles, which advocate the following approaches to HL instruction: (a) from aural to literacy, (b) from spoken to written, (c) from home-based register to general and academic registers, (d) from everyday real-life activities to classroom activities, and (e) from HL specific identities and motivations to content.[6]

From Aural Proficiency to Literacy

HL students' listening comprehension is typically their strongest skill (Carreira & Kagan, 2011; Montrul, 2016); therefore, they can be taught spelling by comparing spoken language to orthographic rules. Demonstrating the differences between what one can hear (and what HL speakers tend to put on paper) and the correct spelling should be a recurring activity (see Table 12.2 for an example of such activity from «Учимся писать по-русски» [*Learning to write in Russian*], Chapter 5).

In «Учимся писать по-русски» [*Learning to write in Russian*] dictations and partial dictations reinforce the correlation between spoken language and correct spelling. One example of a partial dictation activity in Chapter 5 (ex. 5-10), where students must write one letter only, for example, се_одня (сегодня [today]), Все_о хороше_о (всего хорошего [best wishes]). Other dictations are complete texts (see Chapter 8, ex. 8-13). We also include texts for listening, with an assignment to summarize the text in writing (Chapter 19, ex. 19-13).

From Speaking to Writing

To help HL learners use their speaking proficiency in order to transition to literacy, we follow the recommendations put forward by Chevalier (2004). Her model features

TABLE 12.2. Difference Between What HLs Hear and Write vs. the Correct Spelling

СЛЫШИМ и ГОВОРИМ [We hear and say]	ПИШЕМ [We write]
[што]	что
[канешна]	конечно
[щасте]	счастье

the genres of written discourse that closely approximate oral genres. In «Учимся писать по-русски» [*Learning to write in Russian*], after learning the alphabet, students explore the differences in informal and formal styles by comparing informal and formal biographies (Chapter 5, ex. 5-1). One of the two biographies uses an informal style that is typically found in oral discourse (Я родилась в небольшом городке около Москвы [I was born in a small town near Moscow]), while the other employs a formal (official) style (Я, Петров Василий Иванович, родился в . . . [I, Petrov, Vasily Ivanovich, was born in . . .]). This type of activity teaches students to recognize formal and informal genres and prepares them for reading and writing. Another activity calls for a response to a letter. The letter is in an informal style (a mother complains that her son is addicted to computer games); thus, the response can also be informal (Chapter 8, ex. 8-4).

From a Home-Based Register to General/Academic Registers

Leeman and Serafini (2016) suggest a sociolinguistic approach to teaching HL learners, noting that "the study of language variation, contact and change can provide insights on the formal features of HL students' language" (p. 56). A rudimentary example of such an approach compares different registers and identifies the features of formal and informal discourse. In «Учимся писать по-русски» [*Learning to write in Russian*] students read a letter written in a highly colloquial style and rewrite it in a neutral style (Chapter 8, ex. 8-6). They continue to read and analyze four letters written in different registers (Chapter 15, ex. 15-2). This approach can expand their home-based linguistic repertoire and aid their development of academic literacy. More important, instead of approaching home-based language as incorrect or ungrammatical, students learn that "the language varies from place to place, [. . .] exhibiting phonological, lexical, syntactic, morphological and pragmatic variation" (Leeman & Serafini, 2016). Therefore, students learn to view language as a social construct and not only a series of rules unrelated to real life.

From Everyday Activities to In-Class Activities

Even though HL speakers typically use less of their heritage language once they start school, they continue using it to a degree (Kagan, 2010). Kagan's study, conducted with second or 1.5 generation HL speakers of Russian, shows that close to 90% of the HL respondents speak Russian on the phone, 69% watch films or videos that use Russian, 75% listen to Russian music, and 14% attend community events.[7] Some examples of literacy activities that build on students' everyday life include writing a short post on an Internet forum about their hobbies (Chapter 8, ex. 8-3), compose greeting cards to family members on different occasions (Chapter 11, ex. 11-3), interview family members (Chapter 10, ex. 10-11), or describe a family holiday tradition (Chapter 11, ex. 11-12). To capitalize on HL students' aural proficiency and the fact that 69% watch Russian-language films or videos, we include a film review activity. Students watch a film, read a review, and discuss the differences between their own impressions and the reviewer's commentary. They also compose their own review (Chapter 22, exs. 22-1 and 22-4).

From Motivation and Identity to Content

Carreira and Kagan (2011) show that a primary motivation for HL speakers is a desire to communicate with their family members in the United States and to learn about their linguistic and cultural roots. «Учимся писать по-русски» [*Learning to write in Russian*] contains several family histories (e.g., Chapter 10, ex. 10-1, and Chapter 15, ex. 15-9); texts about Russian traditions (the Old New Year, Chapter 11, ex. 11-4); and biographies of famous Russians (Kapitsa, Akhmatova, and Tokareva, in Chapter 6). We select themes that connect students to their families and to the culture and history with which their families are familiar to promote intergenerational interaction.

The "From>To" principles described here can provide a framework for a textbook or a curriculum for HL speakers of Russian. However, it is important to keep in mind that the proficiencies of HL speakers correlate with their age at immigration and their use of language at home. Any new textbook for HL speakers must analyze the current wave of immigration and the linguistic and cultural needs of the intended audience.

CONCLUSIONS

We have discussed some basic principles that guided our development of textbooks for FL learners of Russian (*Beginner's Russian, V puti, Russian: From Intermediate to Advanced*) and a textbook for HL learners («Учимся писать по-русски» [*Learning to write in Russian*]). As we designed our textbooks we relied on backward design. The first step was to determine the targeted proficiency levels according to the ACTFL Proficiency Guidelines, to consider initial competencies and the desired target competencies in all skills, and to select functions, content/context, and text type. The final step involved selecting vocabulary, grammar, and cultural content. We used authentic genres of texts and activities at all levels.

Unlike instructors developing materials for a particular class or a specific lesson, as textbook authors we do not have personal knowledge of the students who will use the books. We do not know their learning styles or their instructors' teaching styles and preferences. We see our textbook as a blueprint; once construction starts many details can be expected to undergo changes. Leaving room for the flexibility and creativity of the users is thus an important element in textbook development.

By its very nature textbook development is a collaborative effort—a collaboration between coauthors with different experiences and views, a collaboration with students in class piloting and teaching, and multiple virtual collaborations following publication. We enjoyed all of these collaborations in developing textbooks for various levels of proficiency and various needs of learners and we hope to develop new textbooks in the future, which naturally leads to the question of the textbook needs of future students. The basis for new textbook construction could be a macro (top-down) approach, such as project-based or experiential learning. A macro approach is particularly well suited for HL learners and students at proficiency levels above Intermediate High. Lower-level and younger learners might also use this approach if presented with age-appropriate materials and strategies.

New textbook developers may want to include all of the post-Soviet Russian-speaking space with bilingual and bicultural traditions (rather than focusing on Russia only) as well as changes in the language that have occurred since the collapse of the Soviet Union. This could lead to a broader sociolinguistic approach to content selection and may better meet the affective needs of new HL learners, many of whom have family ties with the countries of the former Soviet Union outside of Russia.

One of the as-yet-unmet needs voiced by parents and community schoolteachers is a textbook for younger HL speakers. Although Web-based textbooks may be the wave of the future, it is not the vehicle of delivery that matters most in a textbook. Rather, it is a book's appeal to students and instructors and its ability to inspire students to continue learning.

APPENDIX A: RUSSIAN FROM INTERMEDIATE TO ADVANCED, CHAPTER 4, EX. 4-17

Опрос и презентация «Что вы считаете самым важным в семейных отношениях?» [A survey and a presentation "What do you consider most important in family relations?"]

Conduct a survey among your friends, relatives, parents, etc.: (1) Make a list of questions; (2) Present the results in class; Include background information: age, sex, and education.

- Как надо членам семьи относиться друг к другу? [How should family members treat each other?]
- Важно ли, чтобы были общие интересы у членов семьи? [Do family members need to share interests?]
- Что надо делать, чтобы иметь хорошие семейные отношения? [How can one maintain good relations in a family?]

This text is presented exactly as written by the student:

> «Респонденты опроса были моя мама (46, имеет высшее образование), мой двоюродный брат (10, учится в начальной школе), и моя подруга (19, учится на втором курсе). Отвечая на вопрос «Как надо членам семьи относиться друг к другу?», все респонденты сказали, что членам семьи надо любить и уважать друг друга, и мама добавила, что детям нельзя обманывать родителей. Отвечая на вопрос «Важно ли иметь общие интересы?», брат сказал, что обязательно, поскольку он хочет, чтобы родители играли с ним в его любимые игры. А мама и подруга ответили, что члены могут иметь разные интересы. Отвечая на вопрос «Что надо делать, чтобы иметь хорошее семейные отношения?», все сказали, что надо много разговаривать, вместе проводить свободное время, и быть честными, активными, и доброжелательными. Можно делать вывод из этих результатов, что счастье семьи тесно связано с тем, как члены относятся друг к другу. Не важно иметь много денег в семье, а важно, чтобы члены любили и берегли друг друга.» (UCLA, Fall 2014, 4th-year Russian)
>
> [The survey respondents were my mother (46, a university graduate), my cousin (10, elementary school student), and my girlfriend (19, sophomore at a university). Answering the question "How should family members treat one another?," all respondents said that family members need to love and respect each other, and my mother added that children should be truthful with parents. Answering the question "Is it important to have common interests?" my

cousin said that it was necessary because he wanted his parents to play his favorite games with him. My mother and my friend said that family members don't have to share interests. Answering the question "What should I do to have a good family relationship?" everyone said that it is necessary to talk a lot, spend free time together, and to be honest, active, and helpful to each other. It can be inferred from these results that family happiness is closely tied to how family members relate to each other. It is not important to have a lot of money in the family, but it is important that family members loved each other and took care of each other.]

NOTES

1. Many Russian language textbooks published in the last 20 years employ approaches and activities worthy of mention and analysis; however, because our goal is to reflect upon our own practices of textbook development, all our examples originate from our coauthored textbooks.
2. Our first joint project was a second-year textbook, *V puti* (1996), coauthored by Olga Kagan and Frank Miller. A second edition, with a new coauthor, Anna Kudyma, followed in 2006.
3. We use the term *activities* to refer to textbook exercises, tasks, and assignments in order to avoid any controversy that may arise from different understandings by different authors or readers.
4. For a detailed description of goals in language learning see the NCSSFL-ACTFL Can-Do Statements (National Council of State Supervisors for Languages, & American Council on the Teaching of Foreign Languages, 2015).
5. To be accepted into the Flagship program students must demonstrate oral proficiency of at least Advanced ACTFL/2 ILR level. After the program, while the nonheritage learners typically achieve Superior/3 level of proficiency, most of the HL students test at Distinguished/3+ or 4.
6. These principles were first discussed by Kagan in an ACTFL webinar (Kagan & Carreira, 2015).
7. Collection of these data took place in 2007–9, when 64% of the respondents were 1.5 generation HL born in the former Soviet Union. Because of changes in immigration patterns, the results today may be different, with less Russian spoken by U.S.-born children in immigrant families.

REFERENCES

Akishina, A. A., & Kagan, O. E. (2004). Учимся учить: для преподавателя русского языка как иностранного [Learning to teach: For teachers of Russian as a foreign language]. Moscow: Russian Language Publishers.

American Council on the Teaching of Foreign Languages (ACTFL). (n.d.). Use of authentic texts in language learning. Retrieved from https://www.actfl.org/guiding-principles/use-authentic-texts-language-learning

American Council on the Teaching of Foreign Languages (ACTFL). (1986). ACTFL Proficiency Guidelines: Speaking. Alexandria, VA: Author.

American Council on the Teaching of Foreign Languages (ACTFL). (2012). ACTFL Proficiency Guidelines 2012. Retrieved from http://www.actfl.org/publications/guidelines-and-manuals/actfl-proficiency-guidelines-2012

American Council on the Teaching of Foreign Languages (ACTFL). (2015). ACTFL Performance Descriptors for Language Learners. Retrieved from https://www.actfl.org/sites/default/files/pdfs/ACTFLPerformance-Descriptors.pdf

Anderson, L. W., Krathwohl, D. R., & Bloom, B. S. (2001). *A taxonomy for learning, teaching, and assessing: A revision of Bloom's taxonomy of educational objectives*. Boston: Allyn & Bacon.

Andrjušina, N. P. (2009). Лексический минимум по русскому языку как иностранному. Второй сертификационный уровень. Общее владение [The lexical minimum of Russian as a foreign language. Second certification level. General proficiency]. St. Petersburg: Zlatoust.

Andrjušina, N. P. (2011). Лексический минимум по русскому языку как иностранному. Первый сертификационный уровень. Общее владение [The lexical minimum of Russian as a foreign language. First certification level. General proficiency]. St. Petersburg: Zlatoust.

Andrjušina, N. P., & Kozlova, T. V. (2000). Лексический минимум по русскому языку как иностранному. Базовый уровень. Общее владение [The lexical minimum of Russian as a foreign language. Basic level. General proficiency]. St. Petersburg: Zlatoust.

Andrjušina, N. P., & Kozlova, T. V. (2006a). Лексический минимум по русскому языку как иностранному. Базовый уровень. Общее владение [The lexical minimum of Russian as a foreign language. Basic level. General proficiency]. St. Petersburg: Zlatoust.

Andrjušina, N. P., & Kozlova, T. V. (2006b). Лексический минимум по русскому языку как иностранному. Элементарный уровень. Общее владение [The lexical minimum of Russian as a foreign language. Elementary level. General proficiency]. St. Petersburg: Zlatoust.

Andrjušina, N. P., & Vladimirova, T. E. (1999). Типовые тесты по русскому языку как иностранному [Standard tests of Russian as a foreign language]. St. Petersburg: Zlatoust.

Bloom, B. S. (1956). *Taxonomy of educational objectives* (Vol. 1). New York: McKay.

Boyle, E. M., & Gerhart, G. (Eds.). (2002). *The Russian context: The culture behind the language*. Bloomington, IN: Slavica.

Brecht, R., Davidson, D., & Ginsberg, R. (1995). Predicting and measuring language gains in study abroad settings. In B. F. Freed (Ed.), *Second language acquisition in a study abroad context* (pp. 37–66). Philadelphia: John Benjamins.

Byram, M., Gribkova, B., & Starkey, H. (2002). *Developing the intercultural dimension in language teaching: A practical introduction for teachers*. Strasbourg, France: Council of Europe.

Carreira, M. (2016). Supporting heritage language learners through macro-based teaching. In M. Fairclough & S. M. Beaudrie (Eds.), *Innovative approaches in heritage language teaching: From research to practice* (pp. 123–42). Washington, DC: Georgetown UP.

Carreira, M., & Kagan, O. (2011). The results of the National Heritage Language Survey: Implications for teaching, curriculum design, and professional development. *Foreign Language Annals*, *44*(1), 40–64.

Celce-Murcia, M. (1991). Grammar pedagogy in second and foreign language teaching. *TESOL Quarterly*, *25*(3), 459–80.

Celce-Murcia, M. (2007). Rethinking the role of communicative competence in language teaching. In E. Alcon Soler, M. P. Safont Jorda, & M. Pilar (Eds.), *Intercultural language use and language learning* (pp. 41–57). Dordrecht, Netherlands: Springer Science and Business Media.

Center for Open Educational Resources and Language Learning. (n.d.). Lesson 2: Proficiency and cultural literacy. Retrieved from https://coerll.utexas.edu/methods/modules/culture/02/texts.php

Chevalier, J. (2004). Heritage language literacy: Theory and practice. *Heritage Language Journal, 2*(1), 1–19.

Comer, W. (2013). Communicative language teaching and Russian: The current state of the field. In V. Makarova (Ed.), *Russian language studies in North America: New perspectives from theoretical and applied linguistics* (pp. 133–56). London: Anthem.

Clifford, R., & Cox, T. (2013). Empirical validation of reading proficiency guidelines. *Foreign Language Annals, 46*(1), 45–61.

Clifford, R., Granoein, N., Jones, D., Shen, W., & Weinstein, C. (2004). *The effect of text difficulty on machine translation performance: A pilot study with ILR-rated texts in Spanish, Farsi, Arabic, Russian, and Korean.* Monterey, CA: Defense Language Institute.

Davidson, D., & Lekic, M. (2013). The heritage and non-heritage learner in the overseas immersion context: Comparing learning outcomes and target-language utilization in the Russian flagship. *Heritage Language Journal, 10*(2), 226–52.

Dengub, E. (2012). *Investigating syntactic and lexical complexity, accuracy, and fluency in the writing of heritage speakers of Russian* (Doctoral dissertation). Retrieved from Proquest Dissertations and Theses Global (Accession Order No. 3564142).

Dubinina, I., & Polinsky, M. (2013). Russian in the US. In M. Moser & M. Polinsky (Eds.), *Slavic languages in migration* (pp. 130–58). Vienna, Austria: University of Vienna.

Geisherik, A. (2010). *Aspects of teaching literacy to heritage learners of Russian: Linguistic and methodological aspects of accommodating heritage speakers in Russian language courses at the university level.* Saarbrücken, Germany: VDM.

Gerhart, G. (1974). *The Russian's world: Life and language.* New York: Harcourt Brace Jovanovich.

Kagan, O. (1993). Отбор словаря для американских учебников русского языка [Vocabulary selection for American textbooks of Russian]. *Russkij jazyk za rubežom,2*, 32–35.

Kagan, O. (2005). In support of a proficiency-based definition of heritage language learners: The case of Russian. *International Journal of Bilingual Education and Bilingualism, 8*, 213–21.

Kagan, O. (2010). Russian heritage language speakers in the US: A profile. *Russian Language Journal, 60*, 215–30.

Kagan, O., & Carreira, M. (2015, January 28). *Teaching heritage languages: Approaches and strategies* [ACTFL Webinar].

Kagan, O., & Dillon, K. (2001). A new perspective on teaching Russian: Focus on the heritage learner. *Slavic and East European Journal, 45*, 507–18.

Kagan, O., & Friedman, D. (2004). Using the OPI to place heritage speakers of Russian. *Foreign Language Annals, 36*, 536–45.

Kagan, O., & Kudyma, A. (2012a). Heritage language learners of Russian and L2 learners in the Flagship program: A comparison. *Russian Language Journal, 62*, 27–46.

Kagan, O. E., & Kudyma, A. S. (2012b). Учимся писать по-русски: экспресс-курс для двуязычных взрослых [Learning to write in Russian: An express course for bilingual adults]. St. Petersburg: Zlatoust.

Kagan, O. E., Kudyma, A. S., & Miller, F. J. (2014). *Russian: From intermediate to advanced.* London: Routledge.

Kagan, O., & Miller, F. J. (1996). *V puti: Russian Grammar in Context.* Upper Saddle River, NJ: Prentice Hall.

Kagan, O., Miller, F. J., & Kudyma, G. (2006). *V puti: Russian Grammar in Context* (2nd ed.). Upper Saddle River, NJ: Prentice Hall.

Karkafi, L. (2014). *Negative language transfer: A study of essays by heritage and L2 students of Russian at the Intermediate Mid level of proficiency* (Doctoral dissertation). Retrieved from Proquest Dissertations and Theses Global (Accession Order No. 3636452).

Kudyma, A., Miller, F. J., & Kagan, O. (2012). *Beginner's Russian with interactive online workbook.* New York: Hippocrene.

Leaver, B. L., Rifkin, B., & Shekhtman, B. (2004). Apples and oranges are both fruit, but they don't taste the same: A response to Wynne Wong and Bill VanPatten. *Foreign Language Annals, 37*(1), 125–32.

Leeman, J., & Serafini, E. (2016). Sociolinguistics for heritage language educators and learners: A model for critical translingual competence. In M. Fairclough & S. M. Beaudrie (Eds.), *Heritage language teaching: From research to practice* (pp. 56–79). Washington, DC: Georgetown UP.

Malone, M. E., Rifkin, B., Christian, D., & Johnson, D. E. (2004). Attaining high levels of proficiency: Challenges for language education in the United States. *Journal for Distinguished Language Studies, 2,* 67–88.

McGarry, D. (1995). *Learner autonomy 4: The role of authentic texts.* Dublin, Ireland: Authentik Language Resources.

Mishan, F. (2005). *Designing authenticity into language learning materials.* Bristol, UK: Intellect.

Montrul, S. (2016). *The acquisition of heritage languages.* Washington, DC: Georgetown UP.

National Council of State Supervisors for Languages, and American Council on the Teaching of Foreign Languages (NCSSFL/ACTFL). (2015). NCSSFL/ACTFL Can-Do Statements. Retrieved from http://www.actfl.org/sites/default/files/pdfs/Can-Do_Statements_2015.pdf

National Standards Collaborative Board (NSCB). (2015). *World-readiness standards for learning languages* (4th ed.). Alexandria, VA: Author.

Nuttall, C. (1996). *Teaching reading skills in a foreign language.* Portsmouth, NH: Heinemann.

Omaggio Hadley, A. (2001). *Teaching language in context* (3rd ed.). Boston: Heinle & Heinle.

Peyton, J. K., Ranard, D. A., & McGinnis, S. (2001). *Heritage languages in America: Preserving a national resource.* Language in Education: Theory and Practice. McHenry, IL: Delta Systems.

Phillips, J. K., & Abbott, M. (2011). A decade of foreign language standards: Impact, influence, and future directions. Retrieved from https://www.actfl.org/sites/default/files/publications/standards/NationalStandards2011.pdf

Polinsky, M. (2006). Incomplete acquisition: American Russian. *Journal of Slavic Linguistics, 14*(2), 191–262.

Polinsky, M. (2008). Gender under incomplete acquisition: Heritage speakers' knowledge of noun categorization. *Heritage Language Journal, 6*(1), 40–71.

Polinsky, M. (2011). Reanalysis in adult heritage language. *Studies in Second Language Acquisition, 33*(2), 305–28.

Polinsky, M., & Kagan, O. (2007). Heritage languages: In the wild and in the classroom. *Language and Linguistics Compass, 1*(5), 368–95.

Rifkin, B. (2003). Oral proficiency learning outcomes and curricular design. *Foreign Language Annals, 36*(4), 582–88.

Rifkin, B. (2005). A ceiling effect in traditional classroom foreign language instruction: Data from Russian. *The Modern Language Journal, 89*(1), 3–18.

Savignon, S. J. (1991). Communicative language teaching: State of the art. *TESOL Quarterly, 25*(2), 261–78.

Shekhtman, B., Leaver, B. L., Lord, N., Kuznetsova, E., & Ovtcharenko, E. (2002). Developing professional-level oral proficiency: The Shekhtman Method of Communicative Teaching. In B. L. Leaver & B. Shekhtman (Eds.), *Developing professional-level language proficiency* (pp. 119–40). Cambridge: Cambridge UP.

Shklovsky, V. B. (1983). О теории прозы [About the theory of prose]. Moscow: Soviet Writer Publishers.

Smyslova, A. A. (2009). *Developing four-skill literacy among adult heritage learners: Effects of linguistic and non-linguistic variables on the attainment of low-proficiency heritage students of Russian within a dedicated college-level bridge course* (Doctoral dissertation). Retrieved from Proquest Dissertations and Theses Global (Accession Order No. 3354849).

Swaffar, J. K., Arens, K., & Byrnes, H. (1991). *Reading for meaning: An integrated approach to language learning.* New York: Pearson.

Thompson, I. (2000). Assessing foreign language skills: Data from Russian. In O. Kagan & B. Rifkin (Eds.), *The learning and teaching of Slavic languages and cultures* (pp. 255–84). Bloomington, IN: Slavica.

Tomlinson, B. (2012). Materials development for language learning and teaching. *Language Teaching, 45*(2), 143–79.

Valdés, G. (2016). Curricularizing language: Implications for heritage language instruction. In M. Fairclough & S. M. Beaudrie (Eds.), *Innovative approaches in heritage language teaching: From research to practice* (pp. 255–69). Washington, DC: Georgetown UP.

Wiggins, G., & McTighe, J. (2000). *Understanding by design.* Upper Saddle River, NJ: Merrill Education.

13

ADDRESSING THE REPRESENTATION OF DIVERSITY IN RUSSIAN LANGUAGE TEXTBOOKS

Rachel Stauffer

Undergraduate students in the United States are more diverse in identity than ever before in the history of higher education in the United States. By 2020, 45% of undergraduate students will identify as a member of at least one non-socially-dominant race or ethnicity.[1] The number of first-generation college students and low income students has also increased significantly (NCES, 2011; Bull & Young, 2015; Jiang, Ekono, & Skinner, 2015; McMurtie, 2016).[2] In US society, perceptions of nonbinary gender, nonheterosexual orientation, and nontraditional definitions of family are also rapidly evolving. Studies of identity in foreign language (FL) teaching, applied linguistics, and second language acquisition (SLA) suggest that student identity impacts the learning experience and plays an important role, in particular, in the FL classroom (Ibrahim, 1999; Norton, 2000; Pennycook, 2001; Buzelli & Johnston, 2002; Kubota et al., 2003; Dörnyei, 2005; Byram, 2008; Kramsch, 2009; Kubota & Lin, 2009; Anya, 2011; Azimova & Johnston, 2012; Lightbown & Spada, 2013; Wight, 2015). Students whose identities are not represented or underrepresented in language course content or materials may negatively perceive the language-learning experience and discontinue study of the language (Norton, 2000; Pennycook, 2001; Shardakova & Pavlenko, 2004; Byram, 2008; Kramsch, 2009; Anya, 2011; Kim, 2012). Studies of FL textbooks have found that source culture and target culture favor socially dominant categories of race, ethnicity, socioeconomic status (SES), religion, gender, sexual orientation, and ability (Jewell, 1998; Nelson, 1999; Shardakova & Pavlenko, 2004; Grose, 2012; Kim, 2012; Azimova & Johnston, 2012; Thompson, 2013; Del Valle, 2014).[3]

Given the role that identity plays in FL learning and the changing demographics of American undergraduates, I advocate for fuller representation of non-socially-dominant source and target culture identities in Russian language (RL) textbooks. This chapter strives to provide a neutral but persuasive discussion of this important topic, informed by interdisciplinary scholarship and textbook analysis. *Diversity* signifies different things to different people. Here the goal is not to solve every possible issue of equitable representation in the field of RL instruction; rather, the goal is to consider how instructional materials in Russian are, are not, or can become inclusive, particularly at the introductory level. This article continues and extends existing research on the topic of representation and inclusivity in RL textbooks, with specific suggestions and approaches for enacting change.

The current vacancy of diverse representation in RL textbooks is a product of historically based, widespread systemic oppression of women, people of color (POC), and the working class. Systemic oppression contributes to curricular practices in the United States that feature only socially dominant categories in the source culture of FL textbooks (e.g., whiteness, heterosexuality, ability, cisgenderism, education level, and SES). To illuminate the inequity found in source and target culture in RL textbooks published in the United States, I offer an analysis of the content of popular introductory RL textbooks. The results of the analysis compel RL instructors to offer materials that are more inclusive of non-socially-dominant categories of race and ethnicity, disability, nonheteronormativity, and nontraditional family structures. In conclusion I discuss approaches to textbook content and FL instruction at the introductory level of Russian that may foster a greater sense of inclusivity and equitable representation of diverse categories of race, ethnicity, religion, gender, gender identity, sexual orientation, ability, and SES. It is impossible to fully discuss all inequity. While not an exhaustive treatment of the subject, I hope this study might foster greater consideration of such matters among RL teachers. This discussion in no way intends to accuse anyone, any textbook authors or any RL instructors of intentional bias. My intent is to highlight the ways textbooks may be improved in order to serve students for many more decades. The field's adaptation to increasing student identity diversity is crucial for the achievement of high-impact teaching and research and essential for educational equity and social justice.

Historically in the United States, Russian has been offered in elite postsecondary institutions, many of which have been less accessible to women, minorities, and students of low SES. *Brown vs. Board of Education* authorized the desegregation of schools in 1954, although desegregation was neither immediate nor beneficial to most minority students, particularly in the US South. As the civil rights movement "threatened to undermine the position of the United States in the Cold War[,] Soviet propaganda took special delight in publicizing every embarrassing incident. [. . .] The international situation was a central backdrop to the growing debate over the race question" (Karabel, 2005, p. 379). Subsequently, the Higher Education Act (HEA) of 1965 authorized Title VI funding for education, which led to greater expertise about the world (especially Russia, Eastern Europe, and Eurasia) and also introduced the Pell Grant and other need-based and merit-based financial aid, improving access to postsecondary education for underrepresented groups. For much of the 20th century the majority of students in elite postsecondary institutions were white: "Blacks were barely visible on campus, constituting just 15 of the 3,000 students who had entered Harvard, Yale, and Princeton in 1960" (Karabel, p. 379). Other higher-ed institutions that had RL programs by 1960 (e.g., Columbia, UC-Berkeley, Chicago, Cornell, among others; see Parry, 1967 for details) were similarly homogeneous. The admission and financial support of women, minorities, and students with lower SES to allow attendance at prestigious institutions did not begin until the 1960s and 1970s. Although women had access at single-sex institutions, such institutions mostly catered to white women of high SES. Increased access to education for minorities became possible through the civil rights movement and its establishment of federal laws that promised to deliver educational opportunity and equity to those for whom such opportunities had previously been restricted or entirely inaccessible.

Subsequent additions to the 1965 HEA, such as Title III, Title V, and Title IX, continue to support equity and access to postsecondary education. Title VII of the Civil Rights Act of 1964 established the principle of equal employment opportunity (EEO), which prohibits discrimination against individuals based on race, color, religion, sex, and national origin. The category of sex in EEO is more frequently interpreted not only to prevent discrimination on the basis of biological sex but also to outlaw discrimination on the basis of gender identity and sexual orientation (US Equal Employment Opportunity Commission). In the second half of the 20th century the American LGBTQ+ community, although not explicitly denied opportunities to higher education, became more intentionally visible, which contributed to greater advocacy for equality of nonheterosexual orientations and non-cis and nonbinary gender identities.[4]

Although since the 1960s higher education has become more accessible, a profound lack of minorities continues in tenured positions, administrative roles, and graduate programs (McMurtie, 2016). Russian is offered at over 185 postsecondary institutions in the United States (NCES, 2015). However, of the more than 100 historically black colleges and universities (HBCUs) in the country, only one, Howard University, offers Russian. Although there is no evidence that can provide an answer as to why HBCUs in particular are less likely to offer Russian than other institutions, one possible explanation is the glaring overall lack of minority students and scholars combined with the absence of minorities in Russian language instructional materials. Additionally, there are gaping holes in areas of research inquiry concerning the experiences and contributions of non-socially-dominant individuals and communities in Russia and the former Soviet Union. As Jennifer Wilson has observed, "Whereas imperialism and the colonial legacy (including the ramifications for race, ethnicity, and gender) are integral to many other fields, both on the level of undergraduate curriculum and advanced scholarship, those dialogues exist in our field on the fringes, as if to reveal the dirty truths that hid behind the Iron Curtain would be tantamount to treason" (2014). Wilson's observation is similarly applicable to FL instruction in Russian, as evidenced by textbook content that presumes most imagined learners as white, middle- and upper-class, and male.

Source and target culture homogeneousness has been observed in analyses of RL textbooks (Shardakova & Pavlenko, 2004; Azimova & Johnston, 2012). These studies find that imagined learners are primarily members of socially dominant categories and that in the most popular Russian textbooks most imagined learners are white. "Whiteness refers to not only skin color but also cultural knowledge constructed in Western colonial histories. [. . .] Whiteness constitutes an invisible taken-for-granted social norm" (Kubota & Lin, 2009, p. 25). Although federal legislation has cultivated admissions and financial aid policies that foster educational equity, many academic disciplines continue to approach instructional content in a uniform way, making assumptions that the life experiences that students bring with them to the classroom are all the same. As Pierre Bourdieu (1997) has asserted, "Scholastic yield from educational action depends on the cultural capital previously invested by the family. Moreover, the economic and social yield of the educational qualification depends on the social capital, again inherited, which can be used to back it up" (p. 48). Cultural capital plays a significant role in a student's ability to succeed academically, particularly at institutions of higher education that have been less accessible to non-socially-dominant groups. Because of the work of Bourdieu and others we now understand more about how caregivers' backgrounds, including education, vocation, and income level, directly contribute to students' gains in cultural capital (Winkle-Wagner, 2010).

Many other psychological and social factors—including age, motivation and aptitude, SES, gender, ethnicity, and ability—contribute to an individual's success in FL learning (Benson & Nunan, 2005). As existing studies have shown, RL textbooks presume a universally high level of cultural capital, a presumption that only benefits students whose identities are largely defined within socially dominant categories (Azimova & Johnston, 2012; Shardakova & Pavlenko, 2004). Prior to the 1960s American college students studying Russian consisted almost entirely of socially dominant races, genders, and classes. Future undergraduate students undoubtedly will identify as non-socially-dominant races, ethnicities, abilities, gender categories, sexual orientations, and social classes in comparison to the students who studied Russian in the previous century (NCES, 2011). While in RL textbooks "the choice of a protagonist as a 'typical American man' may appear random and harmless [. . .] in reality it may be a harmful choice because it preempts all other choices and allows textbook authors to portray a privileged language learner and to avoid discussing difficult encounters faced in Russia by American women, African American, Asian American, and Latinx students, and gay, lesbian, disabled, or working-class individuals" (Shardakova & Pavlenko, 2004, p. 33). For example, lexicons and texts emphasizing ballet, the opera, or museum exhibitions, as many introductory textbooks of Russian do, implicitly suggest that students come to the task with a privileged understanding of cultural capital. The source and target cultural content of FL textbooks in general persists in its characterization of imagined learners as citizens of "a world in which young, heterosexual, middle-class, well-educated people live in big houses and travel and shop incessantly" (Jewell, 1998, p. 4). Granted, this claim is dated and broad, but unfortunately is still applicable to most FL textbook content. In scholarship on FL learning and identity we find that the cultural capital presumed within a textbook has the potential to disenfranchise students from fully identifying with the target culture. The relationship between language learning and identity is key to understanding how the portrayal of source and target culture in textbooks may negatively impact the language-learning process if it is not fully representative.

STUDENT IDENTITY, TEXTBOOK BIAS, AND SUCCESS IN FL LEARNING

In FL learning experiences an important connection exists between student identity and source and target culture representation (Norton Peirce, 1995; Ibrahim, 1999; Norton, 2000; Pennycook, 2001; Kramsch, 2009). Students and instructors, regardless of background, come together with unique-to-them identities. In the FL classroom multiple cultural perspectives regularly interact consciously, subconsciously, and unconsciously. Students and instructors bring their own source cultures to the FL classroom and instructors bring knowledge of the target culture(s). Instructors, curricula, and textbooks "represent not so much timeless truths and knowledge but rather very particular ways of understanding the world" (Pennycook, 2001, p. 130). Textbooks, too, are not without their own biases. For example, in an analysis of the content of Swahili language textbooks, Thompson (2013) finds that the homogeneous and oversimplified presentation of source culture for Swahili speakers ultimately prevents students from understanding cultural diversity among the many different Swahili speech communities (p. 949). The same can be said of Russian textbooks, which generally characterize Russian speakers as ethnic Slavs who live in the Russian Federation's largest cities. FL textbooks are the primary source of target culture transmission to Novice-level students; they encode a plethora of assumptions about source and target culture that do not fully present diverse, intersectional identities of source or target language speakers (Azimova & Johnston, 2012).

In order to achieve fuller representation of target- and source-culture identities in RL textbooks we must view the textbook as a sociocultural artifact that implicitly and explicitly communicates values. Sometimes such values are associated with inflexible characterizations of identity. Language learning through textbooks, therefore, contributes to students' identity formation not only in student's' primary language(s) but also in the target language. As King (2008) argues, "When language learners speak, they are doing more than just exchanging information with target language speakers; rather, they are continually organizing and reorganizing awareness of who they are and of their connections to the social world" (p. 234). Throughout the FL learning process student identity is developing but textbooks are rarely similarly fluid. Through greater representation and inclusivity of race, ethnicity, gender fluidity, ability, sexual orientation, SES, and religious belief and practice in FL textbooks student awareness of "who they are and of their connections to the social world" may be more adequately gained and expressed in the target language.

For example, in a study that emphasizes identity, motivation, experience, and the measures of achievement among African-American students in FL classes, Anya

(2011) finds that "the acquisition of an L2 can be seen as a transformative agent in student identity through which learners first imagine themselves as target language users and then work toward the realization of this future self as their abilities, interactional possibilities, and perspectives change" (p. 443). The type of identity transformation that Anya describes relies on opportunities for students to imagine themselves as speakers of the target language. Successful learners must experience a "sense of connectedness and investment in their immediate community of learners in direct relation to their past and present ethnic, racial, and linguistic identities" and be able to envision "themselves interacting with members of a community of target language speakers who mirrored both these future/ideal L2 speakers and, sometimes, their past/present ethnoracial selves" (p. 458). Anya advocates strongly for more consistent and equitable representations of black culture (i.e., African, African-American, and African diasporic) in FL course content.

Like the systemic oppression of racial and ethnic minorities, the oppression of nonbinary and nonheterosexual identities is "extensive, pervasive, and corrosive" (Crookes, 2010, p. 340). Therefore, just as underrepresentation of students' racial and ethnic identities may negatively impact the language-learning experience, "homophobia (prejudice) and heterosexism (systematic discrimination) adversely affect learning and teaching" (Nelson, 1999, p. 372). Heterosexuality is the unmarked category implicit in language textbooks and classrooms. RL textbooks are generally cisnormative (i.e., acknowledging only the biological sex and socially constructed gender roles of individuals without consideration of gender fluidity, nontraditional gender roles, or trans individuals), heteronormative (i.e., emphasizing only heterosexual relationships and norms), and heteropatriarchical (emphasizing traditional marriage, binary gender, traditional gender roles, and heterosexual dominance in lexicon, grammar, and usage) (Rifkin, 1998; Liddicoat, 2009; Nelson, 1999; Shardakova & Pavlenko, 2004; Azimova & Johnston, 2012). Norton and Toohey (2011) find that even if students are highly motivated to learn a language, when they encounter racism, sexism, elitism, homophobia, or other forms of exclusion or discrimination in the language classroom they are less likely to fully engage with the content (p. 421). In order to provide students of all identities the opportunity to engage with the material, FL textbook content needs equitable representation of diversity, which ultimately has the potential to lead to greater motivation and achievement in the target language.

ANALYSIS OF INCLUSIVE CONTENT IN RL TEXTBOOKS

Table 13.1 shows the most popular first- and second-year textbooks, as determined by American University's Census on College and Pre-College Russian in 2013–14.[5]

The textbooks that are discussed here tend more toward the introductory level:

(1) *Beginner's Russian* by A. Kudyma, F. J. Miller, and O. E. Kagan (2010).
(2) *Golosa: A Basic Course in Russian, Book 1,* by R. Robin, K. Evans-Romaine, and G. Shatalina (2012).

(3) *Golosa: A Basic Course in Russian, Book 2,* by R. Robin, K. Evans-Romaine, and G. Shatalina (2012).
(4) *Russian Stage One: Live from Russia!, Volume 1* by M. Lekic, D. E. Davidson, and K. Gor (2008).
(5) *Russian Stage One: Live from Russia!, Volume 2* by M. Lekic, D. E. Davidson, and K. Gor (2008).
(6) *Mezhdu nami* by L. deBenedette, W. J. Comer, A. Smyslova, and J. Perkins (2015).
(7) *Troika* by M. Nummikoski (2012).[6]

Existing studies of RL textbook content that account for inclusive representation employ different qualitative methodologies for analysis (Rifkin, 1998; Shardakova & Pavlenko, 2004; Azimova & Johnston, 2012). Rifkin (1998) offers a criteria-based analysis of close to 20 different image-based or text-based qualities that, according to percentage, frequency, or ratio of occurrence were viewed to contribute to the overall impression of equitable gender representation in L2 introductory and intermediate RL textbooks.[7] Shardakova and Pavlenko (2004) conducted a text-based analysis of introductory RL textbooks and multimedia materials based on two guiding questions: (a) Which learners are targeted and which are not?, and (b) Which speakers of the target language are likely to be encountered by learners? Azimova and Johnston (2012) count the number of mentions of nonethnic Russian speakers of Russian in the text and accompanying images of nine introductory and intermediate RL textbooks.

The methodology used here loosely resembles the criteria-based models used by Rifkin (1998) and Azimova and Johnston (2012). Rifkin's model is the most straightforward and comprehensive because it relies on a count of criteria-based instances of representation in images and text, which the following analysis will also employ. For the image analysis only those depicting people are counted. The analysis includes

TABLE 13.1. The Most Popular First- and Second-Year Foreign Language Textbooks

First Year	Second Year
Golosa: Book 1	*Golosa: Book 2*
Nachalo: Book 1	*Nachalo: Book 2*
Russian Stage One: Live from Russia!	*Russian Stage Two: Welcome Back!*
Beginner's Russian	*V puti*
Troika	*Schaum's Russian Grammar*
Russian Alive!	*Making Progress in Russian*
Colloquial Russian	*Grammatika v kontekste*
Mezhdu nami	*Russian as We Speak It*

Note: Popularity as determined by American University's Census on College and Pre-College Russian, 2013–14.

both the total number of images in each textbook and the number of images depicting people from non-socially-dominant categories.

The text analysis requires more attention because the materials under examination contain varying types of texts. Three types of texts are analyzed here: dialogue, vocabulary list, and "other," the latter of which includes items such as letters, e-mails, other authentic materials, and cultural notes.[8] Speech situations are examined since they are presumed to model communicative competence in both source and target culture. Vocabulary lists offer a broad overview of both active and passive vocabulary used. It is not necessary to count all parts of speech in vocabulary lists since not all words contribute to equitable representation; only nouns, pronouns, adjectives, and verbs have been counted.

The following categories are used to analyze the content of images and texts that are representative of race, ability, LGBTQ+ identity, and nontraditional family (insofar as all of these categories can be discerned from the images only) but excludes multimedia materials such as video and audio clips, online exercises, and other printed materials like workbooks. The review does include photographs, illustrations, drawings, vocabulary lists, and other text items (e.g., cultural notes, dialogues, readings in Russian) that explicitly mention or discuss:

1. Non-socially-dominant race or ethnicity (in source or target culture);
2. Disability (physical, emotional, mental);
3. Nonheteronormative relationship and nonbinary gender;
4. Nontraditional family (same-sex couple, single parent, legal guardian, adoptive parent, step-parent, step-sibling, half-sibling).

For each category the number of occurrences is given as of the total. Tables 13.2 and 13.3 provide the overall totals for images and vocabulary lists, while Tables 13.4

TABLE 13.2. Image Analysis of All Textbooks under Examination

Textbook	Non-socially-dominant races or ethnicities	Disabilities	Nonhetero-normativities	Nontraditional families
Beginner's Russian	6 of 320	0 of 320	0 of 320	0 of 320
Golosa: Book 1	15 of 235	0 of 235	0 of 235	0 of 235
Golosa: Book 2	1 of 221	0 of 221	0 of 221	0 of 221
Russian Stage One: Live from Russia!	1 of 67	0 of 67	0 of 67	0 of 67
Russian Stage Two: Welcome Back!	0 of 83	0 of 83	0 of 83	0 of 83
Mezhdu nami	202 of 550	0 of 550	0 of 550	0 of 550
Troika	1 of 270	0 of 270	0 of 270	0 of 270

TABLE 13.3. Vocabulary Lists of All Textbooks under Examination

Textbook	Non-socially-dominant races or ethnicities	Disabilities	Nonhetero-normativities	Nontraditional families
Beginner's Russian	8 of 1,031	0 of 1,031	2 of 1,031	0 of 1,031
Golosa: Book 1	9 of 906	0 of 906	0 of 906	2 of 906
Golosa: Book 2	4 of 729	0 of 729	0 of 729	0 of 729
Russian Stage One: Live from Russia!	22 of 943	0 of 943	0 of 943	0 of 943
Russian Stage Two: Welcome Back!	0 of 465	0 of 465	1 of 465	0 of 465
Mezhdu nami	20 of 1,187	0 of 1,187	0 of 1,187	0 of 1,187
Troika	8 of 1,406	3 of 1406	3 of 1,406	5 of 1,406

TABLE 13.4. Text Types: *Beginner's Russian*

	Non-socially-dominant races or ethnicities	Disabilities	Nonhetero-normativities	Nontraditional families
Cultural notes	0 of 48	0 of 48	0 of 48	0 of 48
Conversations	0 of 59	0 of 59	0 of 59	0 of 59
Other texts	4 of 37	0 of 37	0 of 37	0 of 37

TABLE 13.5. Text Types: *Golosa: Book 1*

	Non-socially-dominant races or ethnicities	Disabilities	Nonhetero-normativities	Nontraditional families
Культура и быт [Culture and everyday life]	0 of 26	0 of 26	0 of 26	0 of 26
Dialogues	1 of 44	0 of 44	0 of 44	0 of 44
Давайте почитаем [Let's read]	4 of 44	0 of 44	0 of 44	0 of 44

through 13.10 provide totals for other text items counted in each textbook, respectively, since the types of text items used in each textbook are not uniform.[9]

As the tables indicate, the textbooks that were examined provide little to no representation of disability, nonheteronormativity, and nontraditional families in their imagery, vocabulary lists, and texts. Non-socially-dominant races and ethnicities are represented in the images and texts of all the textbooks examined, although such representations are not equal to those of socially dominant categories.

TABLE 13.6. Text Types: *Golosa: Book 2*

	Non-socially-dominant races or ethnicities	Disabilities	Nonhetero-normativities	Nontraditional families
Культура и быт [Culture and everyday life]	1 of 25	0 of 25	0 of 25	0 of 25
Dialogues	2 of 49	0 of 49	0 of 49	0 of 49
Давайте почитаем [Let's read]	0 of 56	0 of 56	1 of 56	0 of 56

TABLE 13.7. Text Types: *Russian Stage One: Live from Russia! Volume 1*

	Non-socially-dominant races or ethnicities	Disabilities	Nonhetero-normativities	Nontraditional families
Cultural footnotes	1 of 45	0 of 45	0 of 45	0 of 45
Speech situations	0 of 210	0 of 210	0 of 210	0 of 210
Readings	0 of 10	0 of 10	0 of 10	0 of 10
Other texts	2 of 17	0 of 17	0 of 17	0 of 17

TABLE 13.8. Text Types: *Russian Stage One: Live from Russia! Volume 2*

	Non-socially-dominant races or ethnicities	Disabilities	Nonhetero-normativities	Nontraditional families
Cultural footnotes	0 of 48	0 of 48	0 of 48	0 of 48
Speech situations	0 of 148	0 of 148	0 of 148	0 of 148
Readings	1 of 7	0 of 7	0 of 7	0 of 7
Other texts	0 of 8	0 of 8	0 of 8	0 of 8

TABLE 13.9. Text Types: *Mezhdu nami*

	Non-socially-dominant races or ethnicities	Disabilities	Nonhetero-normativities	Nontraditional families
Texts (includes dialogues)	15 of 305	0 of 305	0 of 305	0 of 305
Вы всё поняли? [Did you understand everything?]	3 of 56	0 of 56	0 of 56	0 of 56
Немного о языке [A bit about the language]	6 of 65	0 of 65	1 of 65	0 of 65
Читаем по-русски [Reading Russian]	0 of 5	0 of 5	0 of 5	0 of 5

TABLE 13.10. Text Types: *Troika*

	Non-socially-dominant races or ethnicities	Disabilities	Nonhetero-normativities	Nontraditional families
Cultural notes	5 of 54	0 of 54	0 of 54	2 of 54
Dialogues	0 of 31	0 of 31	0 of 31	0 of 31
Other texts	9 of 41	0 of 41	0 of 41	2 of 41

ANALYSIS

The following section discusses the findings in greater detail.

Images

Both *Beginner's Russian* and *Golosa: Book 1* have several images (drawings and/or photographs) of people of color. Based on the methodology employed, *Mezhdu nami* has the largest number of images of individuals of a non-socially-dominant race or ethnicity. The substantial quantity of such images in comparison to the other textbooks analyzed owes to the repeated imagery of two of the website's central characters, Amanda Lee, a Chinese-American graduate student from San Francisco, and Antonio "Tony" Morales, an undergraduate from El Paso who speaks Spanish at home. Another character, Caitlin Browning, is white and attends Ohio State University. Her storyline places her in Kazan with a Tatar host, who appears frequently as a non-socially-dominant representative. *Mezhdu nami* definitely creates a culture of diversity by often discussing diversity, and challenges common views on imagined learners of Russian. (Amanda and Tony are both often asked by Russians about their ethnic backgrounds, and another character is identified as Jewish.) The addition of a black student and that student's experiences, discussed as openly as those of Tony and Amanda, would be an excellent complement to the existing content.[10] In this analysis no textbook contained images or discussions of nonheteronormative romantic relationships, nontraditional families, or people with physical, emotional, or mental disabilities.

Text

Live from Russia! has the most text items reflecting geographic and ethnic diversity in Russia and Eurasia. *Mezhdu nami* has more words that refer to diversity than *Live from Russia!*, but *Live from Russia!: Volume 1* includes many Russian-speaking Central Asian countries and capitals, which not all textbooks do. *Live from Russia!: Volume 2* includes in its vocabulary the word партнёр [partner], which has been counted here as a potentially nonheteronormative item, although contextually it was intended as a translation for business partner. *Mezhdu nami* consistently portrays racial and ethnic diversity in text and in imagery, and in source and target culture. *Troika* is the only book that is inclusive across all four categories. It is the only textbook that includes lexical items for disability by including немой [person who has a communication disorder], глухой [person who is deaf], and слепой [person who is blind/visually impaired]. *Troika* also includes the words брак [marriage] and пожениться [to get married], which can be applied to traditional and nontraditional couples, unlike other expressions about marriage which require binary gender identification and are cis- and heteronormative (e.g., замужем [a married woman], женат [a married man], выйти замуж [to get married, women], or жениться [to get married, men]). It is unclear whether terms like женат [a woman married to another woman] or замужем [a man married to another man] are used in Russian speech communities.

Each textbook contains cultural notes in English but because they vary greatly in their respective definitions of culture, they are difficult to compare. *Golosa: Book 2*, for example, includes sociopragmatics (e.g., use of second-person pronouns and patronymics) as culture. *Live from Russia!: Volumes 1 and 2* offer culture notes about historical events and monuments, often located in Moscow or St. Petersburg. Text pieces designed to develop reading comprehension appear in all textbooks; in *Golosa* and *Live from Russia!* as the texts progress in complexity it becomes clear that the underlying assumption is that students take Russian to study Russian literature. In *Golosa* the authors included are predominantly canonical (e.g., Chekhov, Tolstoy, Dostoevsky, Pushkin). In *Live from Russia!* the texts are less canonical, offering a text by Dovlatov, for example, an émigré author unfamiliar to Westerners. Similarly, *Beginner's Russian* has a section on the Russian diaspora in the United States. *Mezhdu nami* does not include literary texts, but dialogues and other texts depict student life in Russia as seen through American eyes. *Troika* offers readings on social issues in Russia, such as divorce, which is not offered by other textbooks.

Overall, the analysis of textbook content reveals that there are many opportunities to improve representation in RL textbooks. The following sections will discuss these possibilities.

WAYS TO INCLUDE NON-SOCIALLY-DOMINANT RACE AND ETHNICITY

The imagery of RL textbooks could be more inclusive. Students of non-socially-dominant identities are enrolled in RL classes in postsecondary institutions all over the United States, yet people of color rarely appear in textbooks. In culture sections all textbooks could incorporate historical notes about famous nonwhite Americans who traveled to or are well known in Russia (e.g., Langston Hughes, Duke Ellington, James Baldwin, Angela Davis) or famous Russian speakers from non-ethnically-Russian backgrounds (e.g., Sergei Shoigu, Joseph Stalin, Viktor Tsoi, Zemfira Ramazanova, Timati [Timur Yunusov]). In order to show the diversity among Russian speakers within the Russian Federation and elsewhere, textbooks could feature imagery and texts about Russian-speaking individuals in the North Caucasus, Buryatia, Kalmykia, Uzbekistan, Kazakhstan, the Kyrgyz Republic, or the Russian Far East, for example. The interviews of Afro-Russians in a recent article in the *Guardian* offer another example of more representative content.[11] For instance, including a contemporary figure like Timati, a Jewish Tatar who runs a major music label and production company that specializes in Russian hip-hop, rap, and dance music and has collaborated with major musicians of color in the United States (e.g., Snoop Dogg, P. Diddy), would achieve this diversity on multiple levels for both source and target culture representation (Timati, 2016).[12] The introductory level of Russian is ideal for these conversations. Students at the introductory level are still forming their opinions about the target culture and about their own identities.

We might take a cue from US textbooks of commonly taught languages; for example, introductory Spanish textbooks include many different Spanish-speaking countries and communities. Diversity abounds in their imagery and texts. The most widely used Spanish textbooks published for US college students portray Spanish speakers from all over the world—even from Equatorial Guinea.[13] Within the first chapter or two, Novice-level textbooks present many words to describe nationality and ethnicity (e.g., *argentino/a* [Argentinian], *panameño/a* [Panamanian], *guatemalteco/a* [Guatemalan]) alongside words for minority indigenous people and languages (*maya* [Maya], *azteca* [Aztec], *quiché* [Quiché, Incan language]). In contrast, Russian textbooks are mostly uniform in their depictions of Russian speakers as white European Russians. There is a noticeable lack of ethnic terminology for non-ethnically-Russian citizens of the Russian Federation who make up the largest minority groups (e.g., чеченец/ка [Chechen], башкир/ка [Bashkir]). Just as Spanish-language textbooks offer a broad overview of the Spanish-speaking world beyond Spain, and in their discussions of Latin America and the Caribbean often include indigenous communities, so might RL textbooks offer greater visibility of non-ethnically-Russian speakers of Russian from all parts of the globe.

INCLUDING DIVERSITY OF GENDER, SEXUAL ORIENTATION, AND FAMILY OF ORIGIN

In the United States, issues of sexual orientation and gender identification recently have entered public discourse more visibly than ever before: "The western world has seen a lightning fast revolution in, first, the acceptance of gay people, and more recently, the visibility of transgender people" (G., 2015). With regard to gender and sexuality, Russia has been instituting laws since the 2000s that severely limit LGBTQ+ rights in the Russian Federation, but this does not mean that such communities are nonexistent. The reasons for Russia's anti-gay propaganda policies are disputed, and the policies themselves are influenced by legislators who espouse increasingly one-sided Orthodox or nationalistic views that reinforce the state's push for population growth (Sperling, 2015). Given the growing acceptance of these communities in the United States, there is an opportunity for more visibility of these communities in RL textbooks.

One related emergent issue for RL speakers and teachers is how to communicate nonbinary gender in Russian.[14] RL textbooks do not yet include lexical or pronoun options for nonbinary gender identities. The neuter pronoun *оно* exists, but is understood to refer to an inanimate noun, like the English "it," and therefore the word is typically not acceptable for use as a nonbinary gender pronoun for individuals who prefer a designation other than он [he] or она [she]. It is becoming more common on college campuses in the United States to have students identify a preferred gender pronoun (PGP) in the application and/or enrollment process (Moss, 2015; Bennett, 2016). Because the past tense and long- and short-form adjectives in Russian also require indicating the gender of the subject, it is important to determine which form a student prefers, and this should correspond to the student's PGP for usage of the past tense. If using the past-tense masculine ending (consonant) or the feminine (-a) is not desired, we might consider using -o; or if the PGP for a student is *they*, the plural past tense ending might be a possible alternative. We might collaborate with our colleagues who teach languages spoken in cultures where LGBTQ+ communities are similar to Russia in terms of legislation and cultural views that are less progressive. We might also collaborate with our colleagues who teach languages of more progressive regions in order to understand how PGPs are determined, assigned, and used. There is still much to consider on this topic.

For instructors who assign Russian first names to students, it would be worthwhile to have a discussion of name choice with self-identifying gender-fluid individuals or allow students to self-select their names. There are alternatives to assigning gender-specific names, such as assigning names like Саша or Женя, which may be used for either sex. There are also ways to make names less gender specific, such as changing Анна to Анно, for example. By adopting these types of inclusive practices and adding to textbooks other lexical items (e.g., гей [gay], квир [queer], лесбиянка [lesbian], трансгендер [transgender]) we do not require students to come out or to perform identity. Instead we acknowledge that student identity is diverse, intersectional, and complex; we give visibility to Russian-speaking LGBTQ+ communities; and we do both simply by providing more diverse lexical items to be used if students wish to use them.[15]

Marriage and family vocabulary in RL textbooks is fully heteronormative, (i.e., relationships depicted are solely between men and women). Students may have diverse notions of *family*. For some students, primary caregivers may include extended family, same-sex couples, single parents, legal guardians, siblings, or foster/ adoptive parents. In addition, primary caregivers may be undocumented migrants or residing in another country. Students may be emancipated minors. We can enrich existing family vocabulary with items like однополый брак [same-sex marriage], однополая пара [same-sex couple], заключить брак [to enter into marriage], among others. In the teaching of patronymics, which connects to family of origin, it may be useful to provide additional commentary in textbooks that gives students examples in which Russian speakers choose a name other than the father's name, in the event that they do not communicate with or have never known their father, or they have two fathers or two mothers, or their primary caregiver is a grandparent or other individual not related by blood. Adding the words мать-одиночка [single mother] and отец-одиночка [single father] may help. Limiting the otherwise exclusive use of родители [parents] in questions directed to students is also important. It is important to remember that not all students' parents' relationships are intact, even if that contradicts instructors' own life experiences. Even though Russian culture, as seen specifically through the lens of Russian Orthodoxy, advocates a traditional family model, families of all kinds exist in contemporary Russia (though indeed sexual orientation is more openly and publicly discussed in the United States). Sperling (2015) argues that Russian politics "relies on a clear delineation of masculinity and femininity (and on the attendant notion that properly feminine, attractive women should love and support only properly masculine, macho men)" (p. 306). Presently there is little scholarly work on language change in Russian that reflects nontraditional partnerships, nonbinary gender, or nonheterosexuality. Online discussion forums and websites that serve the Russian-speaking LGBTQ+ community may be reliable sources for supplemental information for instructors seeking to better understand and address the issue. At a minimum, perhaps, textbooks could include glossed Russian words for use in communicating nonbinary gender and sexual orientation identities and extended lexicons for many different kinds of families.

Ability

"Abled" is a socially dominant category, and "disabled" is its marginalized and often poorly accommodated equivalent in Russia. Granted, provisions for wheelchairs have been made in major cities with the addition of wheel ramps on steps in underpasses. Despite this, getting around in a Russian city with a physical disability that impedes walking on two legs remains more difficult than it is in many cities in the United States. The language, text, and imagery of RL textbooks is ableist. No textbook has a single image of a person in a wheelchair or walking with crutches or using other assistive devices.

Similarly, no Russian textbook discusses chronic mental or emotional disabilities. Taking medication for anxiety or depression, for example, is common among American undergraduates but in Russia these conditions are considered normal states of human experience and not often treated with medication. Other disabilities, both cognitive and physical, afflict both Americans and Russians (e.g., attention deficit disorder, obsessive-compulsive disorder, autism) yet are never mentioned in RL textbooks. We may want to include notes on these kinds of topics as early as the Novice level in order to prepare students to understand Russian cultural views on these issues, for Russian language students who have been diagnosed and wish to discuss these conditions and for those whose friends or family members have disabilities.

CONCLUSIONS AND FUTURE CONSIDERATIONS

Based on existing research and the findings here, there are ample opportunities for RL textbooks to be more representative of race and ethnicity, nonbinary gender, nonheteronormative sexual orientation, and nontraditional family structures. This includes providing vocabulary (e.g., афроамериканец/афроамериканка [African American]) to describe themselves and their identities. Of course, in some instances Russian may not have the exactly appropriate terminology. In order to create an inclusive classroom culture we might have to be creative or use more specific country- or region-oriented terminology (колумбиец [Colombian] or латиноамериканка [Latina] as opposed to Latinx, for example). In other situations Russian may have words but lack an individual's preferred identity term (e.g., черный [black], чернокожий [black]). Although in American English students may identify as or be referred to as *black*, the Russian word for black in this usage is pejorative. Miscommunication about racially charged terms can happen between an American English speaker and a Russian speaker simply because of the cruel legacy in the United States of some Russian words (e.g., мулат [mulatto], негр [Negro]), and the level of offense they evoke, particularly when used by a white person. Using such terms to describe race or ethnicity is offensive and inappropriate (Wilson, 2014). In one language the perceived sociocultural weight or pejorative nature of a word referring to identity or culture may not match the cognates in another language. If instructors are not already discussing these terms with students, such conversations should be encouraged.

According to the American Council on the Teaching of Foreign Languages (ACTFL) Proficiency Guidelines, students at the Novice level are able to provide basic information about themselves and their immediate surroundings. They then progress to talking about others, gradually developing the skills needed to talk about more specific topics not necessarily related to self and others (e.g., business, politics, contemporary affairs, etc.).[16] To be more inclusive we do not need to change the progression; we only need to add more identity-based language for students to be able to describe themselves and others. There are also changes that can be made to existing content to diversify the perception of the target culture, such as including the lexicon for minority Russian-speaking communities and religious identities other than Russian Orthodox.

We also could be more inclusive in lexical choices on the topics of family, social class, and SES. In textbook scenarios depicting romantic relationships, an improvement would be to include nonheteronormative relationships in images and texts. This is both more representative and offers opportunities for discussions of source and target culture perceptions of nonheteronormative relationships. To be more socioeconomically inclusive, textbooks could present professions beyond those of the educated middle and upper classes, following the example set by *Troika*, which includes many words for blue-collar professions (e.g., косметолог [cosmetologist], строитель [construction worker]) and other jobs that students themselves commonly hold while in college (e.g., бармен [bartender], лаборант [laboratory assistant]). As Rustin (2000) writes: "Social structures—classes, extended families, occupation communities, long-term employment within a firm—which formerly provided strong frames of identity, [are now] weaker" (p. 33). Such changes to social structures could be more adequately reflected in an introductory Russian vocabulary. The professions commonly listed in elementary Russian textbooks, like инженер [engineer], юрист [lawyer], врач [doctor], писатель [writer], экономист [economist], артист [artist], актер [actor], актриса [actress], историк [historian], поэт [poet], физик [physicist], биолог [biologist], ветеринар [veterinarian], психолог [psychologist], and бизнесмен [businessman] are noticeably (a) middle- and upper-class educated professions in the United States and in Russia, and (b) desirable professions among Russians since the late Soviet period, as *Troika* astutely notes. Some textbooks do include more work-related vocabulary, like продавец/продавщица [salesperson], механик [mechanic], электрик [electrician], сантехник [plumber], безработный [unemployed], and кассир [cashier], but it is uncommon to see words like дворник [custodian], маляр [painter], садовник [landscaper], водитель [driver], слесарь [locksmith], сварщик [welder], мусорщик [sanitation worker], шахтер [miner], техник [technician], or other professions that do not require postsecondary education. To create an inclusive classroom that does not alienate students of lower SES students and first-generation college students whose parents are not lawyers, economists, or physicists, textbooks could offer a range of vocabulary not solely oriented toward the college-educated middle and upper classes.

With regard to names, ethnicity, and religious identity, RL textbooks usually include names of Slavic origin, often from Russian Orthodox tradition, that are popular among ethnic Russians. Azimova and Johnston (2012) point out that in Russian textbooks, the "main characters as a rule have Slavic names, such as *Il'ia Il'ich*, *Vera Nikolaevna*, *Natal'ia Ivanovna*, *Sergei Petrovich*, *Misha*, *Nikita*, *Maksim* and others. Characters with non-Slavic names largely do not exist" (p. 344). According to Moscow ZAGS [Civil registry office] records, in 2014 one of the most popular names of newborn boys in Moscow was Timur, which has become a Russian name but etymologically comes from Tamerlane and remains a common name in Central Asia and the Caucasus regions.[17] Yet the vast majority of names in RL textbooks are Slavic, which is not reflective of the diversity of non-Slavic names and ethnicities of Russian speakers. Outside of the largely Russian urban centers of Moscow and St. Petersburg, religious and ethnic affiliations of names are more obvious, as in the Makhachkala regional government, where three officials have the patronymic Magomedovich and one has the surname Magomedov.[18] Dagestan is only one of several historically Islamic regions in the North and South Caucasus, in addition to entire countries outside of the Russian Federation, which may continue to pass down Russified Islamic names for the foreseeable future. As Muslims continue to live in large Russian cities like Moscow and St. Petersburg, where American students often study, the chances of encounters with Muslim people and names of Islamic origin are far more likely than in the past. We should more readily describe the diversity of religion and faith practices in Russian places like Dagestan, Chechnya, Buryatia, Kalmykia, Tatarstan, and Komi. Similarly, we may need to consider how we present Russia's cultural heritage. We should balance the traditional Western, Eurocentric approach to RL and culture that focuses primarily on the literary canon. We should include but also strive beyond the approach that Moscow and St. Petersburg are the only legitimate Russian cultural centers by offering equal representation of the places of origin of non-ethnically-Russian artistic figures and the locations of national landmarks. Textbooks should offer information about regions where Russian is spoken in addition to local languages such as Tatar, Bashkir, Chuvash, Chechen, Buryat, Latvian, or Uyghur. As has already been noted, we can learn much from colleagues in other languages; Spanish language textbooks teach about Spain but also incorporate a multinational approach that teaches students about Spanish-speaking communities in North, Central, and South America, the Caribbean, and Africa (Del Valle, 2014). Similarly, textbooks of French emphasize France but also discuss French-speaking communities in Africa, the Caribbean, and the Americas, championing French as an international *lingua franca* of commerce, education, and diplomacy.

Several theoretical approaches have to date not adequately been pursued in the area of RL pedagogy. Critical pedagogical works might guide our inclusivity efforts. In Paolo Freire's *Pedagogy of the Oppressed*, for example, the author suggests that learners should be allowed to make decisions about instructional content: "Instead of following predetermined plans, leaders and people, mutually identified, together create the guidelines of their action" (Freire, 1970, p. 181). Instead of requiring heavily formularized workbooks and textbooks that predetermine the vocabulary to be learned, students and teachers could work together and decide what vocabulary they want to learn, in part based on how to fully represent all students in the course. The present era of social networking and user-generated content, an environment in which students are engaged daily, could help students and instructors work together more cooperatively toward mutually agreeable and meaningful content (Dembovskaya & Klimanova, 2013).

RL textbooks and instructional materials can more effectively foster a classroom culture of inclusivity, community, and shared experience. In order to accomplish this, instructional materials should reflect the current and future diversity of target and source culture and should reject the homogeneity that has been widely accepted as the cultural norm in both Russia and the United States. More representative vocabularies in introductory-level textbooks have the potential to help students engage more personally with the target language through the description of self and others. Greater inclusivity also contributes to broader educational equity by providing all students with the language they need to describe themselves in terms of their own unique identity. RL textbooks should expand the geographic and ethnic lens through which they present the Russian-speaking world in order to be more inclusive of Russian-speaking communities in countries other than the Russian Federation and among non-Russian ethnic groups, particularly those that make up large percentages of the population of the Russian Federation (e.g., Ukrainian, Tatar, Armenian, Chechen, Chuvash, Bashkir). A more inclusive approach that represents non-socially-dominant identities has the potential to increase the enrollment of diverse learners in RL courses. We need more diverse perspectives in the Slavic field. With greater inclusivity we may concomitantly generate greater interest in the language beyond the introductory sequence. Perhaps more important, we might accomplish this goal while also offering a less biased presentation of the Russian-speaking world.

APPENDIX A: GLOSSARY OF INCLUSIVE TERMS THAT CAN BE FOUND IN AT LEAST ONE EXISTING INTRODUCTORY RUSSIAN TEXTBOOK

Азербайджан: Azerbaijan
Алма-Ата: Almaty
арабский: Arab, Arabic
Армения: Armenia
Армянин: Armenian (male)
Ашхабад: Ashkhabad
Байкал: Baikal
Баку: Baku
бармен: bartender
Беларусь: Belarus
Бишкек: Bishkek
Бразилия: Brazil
брак: marriage
бурят: buryat
глухой: unable to hear
грузинский: Georgian
Грузия: Georgia
Душанбе: Dushanbe
еврей: Jewish
Ереван: Yerevan
завод: factory
Израиль: Israel
Индия: India
Кавказ: Caucasus
Казань: Kazan
Казахстан: Kazakhstan
Камчатка: Kamchatka
Киев: Kiev
Киргизстан (Киргизская Республика): Kygryzstan (Kyrgyz Republic)
китайский: Chinese
китаянка: Chinese (female)
корейский: Korean
косметолог: cosmetologist
Крым: Crimea
лаборант: laboratory assistant
мексиканский: Mexican
механик: mechanic

мечеть: Mosque
Молдавия: Moldova
немой: unable to speak
няня: babysitter, nanny
Одесса: Odessa
официант/официантка: waiter, waitress, server
пожениться: to get married (to each other)
разведен/а/ы: divorced
рэп: rap
Саудовская аравия: Saudi Arabia
Сахалин: Sakhalin
синагога: Synagogue
слепой: unable to see
строитель: construction worker
Таджикистан: Tajikistan
татарин: Tatar (male)
татарский: Tatar
Татарстан: Tatarstan
Ташкент: Tashkent
Тбилиси: Tbilisi
Туркменистан: Turkmenistan
узбек: Uzbek
Узбекистан: Uzbekistan
Украина: Ukraine
украинец/украинка: Ukrainian
Урал: Urals
Ханука: Hanukkah
хип-хоп: hip-hop
Южная Корея: South Korea
янонец: Japanese (male)
Япония: Japan
японский: Japanese

APPENDIX B: GLOSSARY OF SUGGESTED INCLUSIVE LEXICAL ITEMS FOR INTRODUCTORY TEXTBOOKS AND RUSSIAN-LANGUAGE CLASSROOMS

агент по продаже недвижимости: real estate agent
армянин/армянка: Armenian
аутизм: autism
аутичный/аутистический человек: person with autism
афроамериканец/афроамериканка: African American
афролатиноамериканец/афролатиноамериканка: African Latino, African Latina, African Latinx
башкир/башкирка: Bashkir
Башкортостан: Bashkortostan
безработный: unemployed
бисексуал: bisexual
буддизм: Buddhism
буддийский: Buddhist
буддист/буддистка: Buddhist
водитель: driver
сантехник: plumber
врач скорой помощи (парамедик): paramedic
гей: gay
гендерквир: genderqueer
гендерная неконформность/гендерный нонконформизм: gender nonconformity
горничная: housekeeper (hotel)
дацан: Buddhist temple or school
дворник: yard keeper, street cleaner
депрессия: depression
детский дом: children's home, orphanage
единокровная/единоутробная сестра: half-sister (same father) / half-sister (same mother)
единокровный/единоутробный брат: half-brother (same father) / half-brother (same mother)
железнодорожник: railroad worker
Ид аль-Адха: Eid Al-Adha
инвалидная коляска: wheelchair
Йом-Киппур: Yom Kippur
католик/католичка: Catholic
католицизм: Catholicism
квир: queer
костыли: crutches

латиноамериканец/латиноамериканка: Latino, Latina, Latinx
ЛГБТК: LGBTQ
лесбиянка: lesbian
маляр: painter (not artist)
мачеха: stepmother
менеджер: manager
мусорщик: sanitation worker
мусульманство/ислам: Islam
мусульманин/мусульманка: Muslim
обсессивно-компульсивное расстройство: obsessive-compulsive disorder
однополая пара: same-sex couple
однополый брак: same-sex marriage
отдел обслуживания клиентов: customer service department
отчим: stepfather
охранник: security guard
пансексуал: pansexual
партнёр: partner
пожарный: firefighter
полицейский: police officer
помощник (ассистент, заместитель): assistant
посттравматический синдром: post-traumatic stress disorder (PTSD)
приёмный ребёнок: adopted/foster child
приёмный брат/приёмная сестра: adopted/foster brother, sister
приёмный отец/приёмная мать: adoptive/foster father, mother
приёмные родители: adoptive/foster parents
X-ого происхождения (например: татарского происхождения): of X origin (e.g., of Tatar origin)
протез: prosthetic (leg, foot, arm, hand)
Рамадан: Ramadan
Рош ха-Шана: Rosh Hashanah
рыбак: fisher
садовник: gardener, landscaper
санитар/санитарка: hospital attendant, orderly
сварщик: welder
сводная сестра (по маме/по папе): stepsister (on mother's side / father's side)
сводный брат (по маме/по папе): stepbrother (on mother's side / father's side)
синдром дефицита внимания: attention-deficit disorder
синдром Туретта: Tourette's syndrome
слесарь: metalworker, locksmith
спасатель: lifeguard
татарин/татарка: Tatar
техник: technician

травма: trauma
трансгендер: transgender
тревожность/тревожное расстройство: anxiety
тюрьма: jail
уборщик/уборщица: custodian
филиппинец/филиппинка: Filipino / Filipina / Filipinx
хадж: Hajj
христианин/христианка: Christian
христианство: Christianity
чеченец/чеченка: Chechen
чеченский: Chechen
Чечня: Chechnya
чуваш/чувашка: Chuvash (adj.)
Чувашия: Chuvash Republic
шахтёр: miner
электрик: electrician

NOTES

1. The terms *race* and *socially dominant category* are used here in the sense defined by Adams et al. (2007): race is a social construct created to justify socioeconomic arrangements in ways that accrue to the dominant social group (p. 82).
2. To date there are no quantitative studies that provide data on the ethnic self-identification of students in pre-college or undergraduate RL programs. In recent years a Title VI–funded National Resource Center has been established at the University of Wisconsin–Madison and at the University of Pittsburgh. These offer summer RL and culture programs for students from underrepresented groups, with an emphasis on African American and Hispanic/Latinx students, many of whom attend secondary schools with RL programs (e.g., Chicago's Noble College Prep and Pritzker College Prep).
3. Kirkgöz and Ağçam (2011) identify three types of culture that appear in English language textbooks: source culture (the culture of the place where the language is being taught), target culture (the culture of the target language), and international target culture (global culture relevant to both the source and the target cultures).
4. The acronym in use here, LGBTQ+, is an all-inclusive term for lesbian, gay, bisexual, transgender, queer, genderqueer, intersex, asexual, androgynous, polyamorous, and pansexual individuals. The acronym continues to expand, thus leading to a truncation of the full acronym to LGBTQ+ (also LGBTQIA+).
5. Omitted from this list are reports of self-generated materials and books that are not specifically language textbooks (e.g., literary texts, supplementary materials, references). For the complete list see http://www1.american.edu/research/CCPCR/. *Nachalo* is out of print and is not examined. For those who are interested, the three previous studies of Russian textbooks do provide analysis of *Nachalo*.
6. The textbooks *Russian Alive!, Colloquial Russian, Schaum's Russian Grammar, Making Progress in Russian, Russian as We Speak It,* and *Grammatika v kontekte* were all published prior to the year 2000, so although they are still in use, their content is not recent enough for the analysis of current source or target culture. *V puti* has already been analyzed by Rifkin (1998) and by Azimova and Johnston (2012).
7. For example, portrayals of all female or majority-female groups or the frequency of association of women with domesticity as opposed to professionality; see Rifkin (1998, p. 235) for a complete list.
8. In the summary tables of the analysis, the names of the sections included as "other texts" are the ones used in each textbook, respectively (e.g., in *Golosa* the cultural sections are named Культура и быт [Culture and everyday life]).
9. For a list of some of the inclusive text items counted in this analysis, see Appendix A.
10. Undergraduate enrollment trends over the last decade indicate that there are more black students than Latinx students seeking postsecondary education (NCES, 2015).
11. See https://www.theguardian.com/world/2016/feb/15/black-in-the-ussr-whats-life-like-for-a-russian-of-colour.
12. For more on Timur Ildarovich Yunusov (aka Timati), see https://en.wikipedia.org/wiki/Timati and http://black-star.ru/artists/timati/.

13. See *Puntos de partida,* 9th ed.; *Como se dice,* 9th ed.; *Unidos,* 2nd ed.
14. At least two such discussions have recently occurred on the SEELANGS email listserv (February 2015 and September 2016), both initiated by instructors of Russian at US postsecondary institutions whose students specify a nonbinary PGP. In American English the pronouns *ze* (subject) and *zir(s)* (possessive) have been created as unmarked for gender, and *they* or *their* may also be used to refer to a non-binary person. In Russian speech communities this practice is less widespread. As Kevin Moss writes in the February exchange, "The phenomenon is not unknown in Russia, but it is far from reaching the level of familiarity it has reached on our [US] college campuses" (Moss, 2015).
15. For a suggested list of lexical items, see Appendix B.
16. ACTFL standards describe the Novice and Intermediate levels in these terms in the 2012 Guidelines: https://www.actfl.org/sites/default/files/pdfs/PerformanceDescriptorsLanguageLearners.pdf.
17. See http://zags.mos.ru/stat/imena/imena_detei.php.
18. See http://www.mkala.ru/authorities/administration/okontrol/.

REFERENCES

Adams, M., Bell, L. A., & Griffin, P. (2007). *Teaching for diversity and social justice.* New York: Routledge.

Anya, U. (2011). Connecting with communities of learners and speakers: Integrative ideals, experiences, and motivations of successful black second language learners. *Foreign Language Annals, 44*(3), 441–66.

Azimova, N., & Johnston, B. (2012). Invisibility and ownership of language: Problems of representation in RL textbooks. *Modern Language Journal, 96*(iii), 337–49.

Bennett, J. (2016, 30 January). She? Ze? They? What's in a gender pronoun? *The New York Times.* Retrieved from http://www.nytimes.com/2016/01/31/fashion/pronoun-confusion-sexual-fluidity.html

Benson, P., & Nunan, D. (Eds). (2005). *Learners' stories: Difference and diversity in language learning.* Cambridge, UK: Cambridge University Press.

Bourdieu, P. (1997) The forms of capital. In J. Richardson (Ed.), *Handbook of Theory and Research for the Sociology of Education* (pp. 241–58). New York: Greenwood. Reprinted in A. H. Halsey, et al. (Eds.), *Education, Culture, Economy, Society* (pp. 46–58). Oxford: Oxford UP.

Bull, E., & Young, T. (2015). American demographics are changing rapidly: Can education and job training keep up? Brookings Institution. Retrieved from https://www.brookings.edu/blog/brookings-now/2015/03/31/american-demographics-are-shifting-rapidly-can-education-and-job-training-keep-up

Buzzelli, C., & Johnston, B. (2002). *The moral dimensions of teaching.* New York: Routledge Falmer.

Byram, M. (2008). *From foreign language education to education for intercultural citizenship.* Clevedon, UK: Multilingual Matters.

Crookes, G. (2010). The practicality and relevance of second language critical pedagogy. *Language Teaching*, *43*, 333–48.

deBenedette, L., Comer, W. J., Smyslova, A., & Perkins, J. (2015). *Mezhdu nami: An interactive introduction to Russian*. Retrieved from: https://mezhdunami.org

Del Valle, J. (2014). The politics of normativity and globalization: Which Spanish in the classroom? *The Modern Language Journal*, *98*(1), 358–72.

Dembovskaya, S., & Klimanova, L. (2013). L2 identity, discourse, and social networking in Russian. *Language Learning & Technology*, *17*(1), 69–89.

Dörnyei, Z. (2005). *The psychology of the language learner: Individual differences in second language acquisition*. Mahwah, NJ: Lawrence Erlbaum.

Freire, P. (1970). *Pedagogy of the oppressed*. New York: Bloomsbury Academic.

G., R. L. (2015, November 27). Non-binary language in a binary world. *The Economist*. Retrieved from http://www.economist.com/blogs/prospero/2015/11/johnson-gender

Grose, T. (2012). Uyghur language textbooks: Competing images of a multi-ethnic China. *Asian Studies Review*, *36*(3), 369–89.

Ibrahim, A. (1999). Becoming Black: Rap and hip-hop, race, gender, identity and the politics of ESL learning. *TESOL Quarterly*, *33*, 349–69.

Jewell, J. (1998). A transgendered ESL learner in relation to her class textbooks, heterosexist hegemony and change. *Melbourne Papers in Applied Linguistics*, *10*, 1–21.

Jiang, Y., Ekono, M., & Skinner, C. (2015). *Basic facts about low-income children*. National Center for Children in Poverty. New York: Columbia University.

Karabel, J. (2005). *The chosen: The hidden history of admission at Harvard, Princeton, and Yale*. New York: Houghton Mifflin.

Kim, H. (2012). Social and cultural issues in some EFL textbooks in Korea. *Hawaii Pacific University TESOL Working Paper Series*, *10*, 30–39.

King, B. (2008). Being gay guy, that is the advantage: Queer Korean language learning and identity construction. *Journal of Language, Identity, and Education*, *7*(3), 230–52.

Kirkgöz, Y., & Ağçam, R. (2011). Exploring culture in locally published English textbooks for primary education in Turkey. *CEPS Journal*, *1*(1), 153–67.

Kramsch, C. (2009). *The multilingual subject*. Oxford: Oxford UP.

Kubota, R., Austin, T., & Saito-Abbott, Y. (2003). Diversity and inclusion of sociopolitical issues in foreign language classrooms: An exploratory survey. *Foreign Language Annals*, *36*(1), 12–24.

Kubota, R., & Lin, A. (2009). *Race, culture, and identities in second language education*. New York: Routledge.

Kudyma, A., Miller, F. J., & Kagan, O. E. (2013). *Beginner's Russian*. New York: Hippocrene.

Lekić, M., Davidson, D., & Gor, K. (2008). *Russian stage one: Live from Russia!, Volumes 1 and 2* (2nd ed.). Dubuque, IA: Kendall/Hunt.

Liddicoat, A. J. (2009). Sexual identity as linguistic failure: Trajectories of interaction in the heteronormative language classroom. *Journal of Language, Identity and Education*, *8*(2), 191–202.

Lightbown, P., & Spada, N. (2013). *How languages are learned* (4th ed.). Oxford: Oxford UP.

McMurtie, B. (2016). How do you create a diversity agenda? *The Chronicle of Higher Education, 62*(6). Retrieved from http://www.chronicle.com/article/How-Do-You-Create-a-Diversity/236427

Moss, K. (2015, February 16). Re: Queering grammatical endings and self-identification. [Electronic mailing list message retrieved from SEELANGs].

National Center for Education Statistics (NCES). (2011). Projections of education statistics to 2020. Retrieved from https://nces.ed.gov

Nelson, C. (1999). Sexual identities in ESL: Queer theory and classroom inquiry. *TESOL Quarterly, 33*(3), 371–91.

Norton, B. (2000). *Identity and language learning*. Harlow, England: Pearson Education.

Norton, B., & Toohey, K. (2011). Identity, language learning and social change. *Language Teaching, 44*, 412–46.

Norton Peirce, B. (1995). Social identity, investment, and language learning. *TESOL quarterly*, 29(1), 9–31.

Nummikoski, M. (2012). *Troika*. Hoboken, NJ: John Wiley & Sons.

Parry, A. (1967). *America learns Russian*. Syracuse, NY: Syracuse UP.

Pennycook, A. (2001). *Critical applied linguistics: A critical introduction*. Mahwah, NJ: Lawrence Ehrlbaum.

Rifkin, B. (1998). Gender representation in foreign language textbooks: A case study of textbooks of Russian. *The Modern Language Journal, 82*(2), 217–36.

Robin, R., Evans-Romaine, K., & Shatalina, G. (2012). *Golosa: A Basic Course in Russian, Books 1 and 2* (5th ed.). Upper Saddle River, NJ: Pearson.

Rustin, M. (2000). Reflections on the biographical turn in social science. In P. Chamberlayne, J. Bornat, & T. Wengraf (Eds.), *The turn to biographical methods in social science: Comparative issues and examples* (pp. 33–52). London: Routledge.

Shardakova, M., & Pavlenko, A. (2004). Identity options in Russian textbooks. *Journal of Language, Identity, and Education, 3*(1), 25–46.

Sperling, V. (2015). *Sex, politics, and Putin*. Oxford: Oxford UP.

Thompson, K. D. (2013). Representing language, culture, and language users in textbooks: A critical approach to Swahili multiculturalism. *Modern Language Journal, 97*(4), 947–64.

Timati. (n.d.) Retrieved from https://en.wikipedia.org/wiki/Timati

US Equal Employment Opportunity Commission. Facts about discrimination in federal government employment based on marital status, political affiliation, status as a parent, sexual orientation, and gender identity. Retrieved from https://www.eeoc.gov/federal/otherprotections.cfm

Wight, M. C. (2015). Students with learning disabilities in the foreign language learning environment and the practice of exemption. *Foreign Language Annals, 48*(1), 39–55.

Wilson, J. (2014). Is Slavic ready for minorities? NYU Jordan Center. Retrieved from http://jordanrussiacenter.org/news/slavic-studies-racially-tone-deaf/

Winkle-Wagner, R. (2010). *Cultural capital: The promises and pitfalls in education research*. Hoboken, NJ: John Wiley & Sons.

14

CORPUS LINGUISTICS AND RUSSIAN LANGUAGE PEDAGOGY

Olesya Kisselev and Edie Furniss

Over the past several decades, corpus linguistics (CL) has become an established subfield in linguistics and second language acquisition (SLA). Although corpus methods have been in use for centuries, only with the advent of computers in the 1950s and 1960s have they allowed for efficient exploratory and data-driven studies of language (McCarthy & O'Keeffe, 2010). Corpus approaches are distinguished by a focus on authentic data and the use of technological tools that allow for a quick yet rigorous analysis of vast quantities of data. The research enabled by corpus methods has changed our views on language, language use, and language acquisition, as it has shed light on actual usage in real contexts across language users and text types. Corpus linguists are able to analyze and describe language more accurately and more thoroughly thanks to recent technological developments. The "corpus revolution" (Tognini Bonelli, 2012, p. 17) has had an immediate impact on the field of language teaching, albeit predominantly in the field of teaching English as a foreign or second language.

While the corpus approach has influenced research within Russian linguistics, the same cannot be said for the field of teaching and learning Russian as a second language.[1] Despite the fact that the terms *corpus studies*, *language corpus,* and *corpus approach* are frequently found in conference presentations, research articles, and professional conversations, many Russian language practitioners admit to knowing little about corpus linguistics and its potential applications to the teaching and learning of Russian. In this paper, we hope to provide Russian language teachers and learners with a better understanding of the main tenets of CL, its basic assumptions, methods, instruments, and practical applications. More importantly, we will address the advantages of corpus approaches to the study of Russian language acquisition and pedagogy, and of the Russian language itself.

This chapter is organized as follows: we first provide a general overview of the field of CL, including a short introduction to basic corpus methodologies and the impact advances in CL have had on language study in general and Russian linguistics in particular. We then provide a survey of corpus resources available for the Russian language and suggest specific examples and pedagogical implications for teachers and learners of Russian.

WHAT IS CORPUS LINGUISTICS?

Delineating the field of corpus linguistics is not an easy task. CL has been described as a theory (although this remains a contentious statement; for discussion of the issue, see Gries, 2011; McEnery & Hardie, 2012), a method, and a practice for the study of language using large machine-readable collections of authentic texts. Unlike more traditional topics or subfields in linguistics that study particular aspects of language (e.g., phonology, syntax, or semantics), the focus of CL is specifically on the "set of procedures, or methods" that can be used to analyze these domains of language (McEnery & Hardie, 2012, p. 1).

It is important to note that this set of procedures includes not only techniques for data analysis (which we will briefly review below) but also the approaches to creating the databases, or *corpora*, themselves. More specifically, compiling corpora requires the *principled* selection of *authentic* texts that *represent* a language (or a specific variety or genre) as *fully* as possible. To illustrate: to create a general-purpose corpus that aims to reflect a particular language at the current stage of its development, one begins by collecting authentic texts, that is, texts created by users of the language for real-life purposes. Adhering to this principle of authenticity allows for the examination of the language as it is used by its speakers and as it evolves over time. Authenticity alone may allow us to make conclusions about certain observable language patterns; however, in order to conclude that certain patterns hold across different speakers, different genres, and different modes of speech, corpus texts must consist of a balanced (not random) selection from a range of authors, genres (fiction, newswriting, personal communication, etc.), styles (official, neutral, colloquial), modes of delivery (written and spoken), and regional and historical varieties. A truly representative corpus must ensure that any conclusions about language use drawn from its analysis are reflective of the language as whole or of particular registers. Although each specific variety of the language may not be included to the same extent, corpora compilers strive for as balanced a representation of a language as possible. Finally, to ensure that observations about language are substantiated and apply to language in general and not only to some speakers, a general-purpose corpus needs to be large (typically, hundreds of millions of words). The principle of large quantities allows researchers to speak about general and exceptional linguistic patterns.[2]

The flagship general corpus for Russian, which embodies the properties mentioned above, is the Russian National Corpus (RNC), located at http://ruscorpora.ru/. The RNC has been available to the public since 2004 and has been funded by the Russian government and academic institutions of the Russian Federation (http://ruscorpora.ru/corpora-about.html#task).[3] As of May 2019 the RNC consists of a main corpus (76,882 texts and 209,198,275 word tokens) and 10 specialized subcorpora: deeply annotated (i.e., texts with morphological and syntactic annotation), newswriting, dialectical, educational (which contains fiction included in the Russian school curriculum), parallel, poetry, oral, word stress, multimedia, and historical corpora. The main corpus is comprised of both fiction (6,087 texts and 90,398,323 word tokens) and nonfiction (70,689 texts and 118,934,827 word tokens). Texts selected for inclusion in the corpus cover a range of genres, subjects, and eras (although 94% of the texts come from the 20th and 21st centuries).[4] In addition to its breadth and thoroughness, the RNC is notable for its intuitive, user-friendly interface—something that cannot be said for all publicly available general corpora. Furthermore, the RNC is constantly growing and expanding and therefore reflects changes in the language itself.

Not all corpora are as large and diverse as the RNC or other well-known national corpora such as the British National Corpus or the Czech National Corpus, nor do they need to be. Many corpora are created for specific purposes or are intended to investigate particular language phenomena. Thus the amount and type of annotation—that is, how elements of a text are marked up—reflect project-specific goals. For instance, the spoken Russian language corpus Рассказы о сновидениях и другие корпуса звучащей речи [Stories about dreams and other corpora of oral language] contains only spontaneous informal spoken discourse, with a few texts produced by a few authors (see http://spokencorpora.ru). This corpus is relatively small (its four subcorpora range from 5,000 to 14,000 words in volume). However, its transcription and annotation schemes are more detailed and sophisticated than would be practical for a large general corpus; its in-depth descriptions of the intricacies of speech achieve a highly nuanced analysis of spoken speech. Specialized corpora can focus on certain modes and genres of language:

- written language (e.g., Корпус русского литературного языка [Russian literary language corpus] at http://narusco.ru/)
- journalistic prose (e.g., Компьютерный корпус текстов русских газет конца XX-ого века [Computer corpus of Russian newspapers of the late 20th century] at http://www.philol.msu.ru/~lex/corpus/)
- learner language (e.g., Russian Learner Corpus at http://web-corpora.net/RussianLearnerCorpus/search/)
- dialectal and historical language varieties (e.g., Корпус диалектных текстов [Corpus of dialectal texts] at http://www.ruscorpora.ru/search-dialect.html and Исторический корпус русского языка [Historical corpus of Russian language] at http://ruscorpora.ru/search-orthlib.html)

Regardless of its specific type or purpose, a language database can be called a corpus if it is reasonably large, principally and systematically collected, and representative and balanced.

In the same way that samples of language for corpora are systematically collected, they must be systematically described. In other words, information about texts in a corpus—the name and biodata of the author(s) and speaker(s) (age, gender, region, etc.), the date of creation/occurrence, the genre, and other data (depending on the availability and/or the aim of the corpus)—should accompany the texts themselves in the form of meta-tags or special labels that describe the texts. Most contemporary corpora are also annotated with tags that label individual words to provide grammatical, semantic, and (less commonly) discoursal information about these linguistic units. The most widely used annotations are part-of-speech (POS), grammatical (person, number, gender, case, voice, tense, aspect), syntactic (sentence diagramming), and errors (classification).

Once a corpus has been compiled and annotated, a linguist, teacher, or student can conduct his or her own corpus analyses. Here are some of the most frequently conducted and best-known operations used in corpus linguistic research:

- *word lists,* i.e., sorting all the lexical items found in a corpus in the form of a "dictionary," ordered either alphabetically or by frequency. Frequency lists based on general purpose corpora may be used by curriculum designers and textbook writers to determine which words and phrases should be targeted at different proficiency levels. A frequency list generated from a specialized corpus may be used in classes focused on specific topics (e.g., a newspaper corpus in a course on current events).
- *descriptive statistics,* i.e., collecting information on the number of word tokens (the raw word count) and word types (the number of unique word forms), the number of sentences or paragraphs, the length of linguistic units, etc.[5] Statistical information about texts may be useful to materials designers and teachers in establishing the level of text difficulty (including both vocabulary diversity and syntactic complexity); the results of descriptive statistics tests may also be used in analyzing student writing.
- *concordancing,* i.e., extracting samples, or contexts, that contain a specific term (usually a word, a phrase, or a grammatical pattern). The extracted samples, known as *concordances* or *concordance lines,* can be sorted in different ways (e.g., alphabetically by the first word to the left or right of the search term) in order to highlight patterns in the data. Figures 14.1 and 14.2 are concordance lines generated for the search term глаз- [eye-] in the first five chapters of the novel *The Master and Margarita* by Mikhail Bulgakov. Figure 14.1 shows data sorted by the first word to the left of the search term; it shows which actions the eye can perform (вытаращить, выпучить [bulge]) or how the eyes are described (его [his], зеленый [green]). Figure 14.2 shows the same lines resorted by the first word to the right of the search term, then the first word to the left, then the second word to the right of the search term. This sorting highlights the structure V+глаза+на+ACC 'V+eyes+ON+ACC.' Concordancing may be pedagogically helpful in teaching students vocabulary in a variety of contexts and uses.
- *keyword analysis,* i.e., identifying particular words found in one or more texts in the corpus, whose frequency is unusually high relative to some "norm" (typically a baseline corpus). This type of analysis is helpful when examining the unique features of a particular genre, mode, or set of texts (e.g., written by a particular writer) and can be used in class, particularly when dealing with specialized topics (such as Russian politics, a survey of Dostoevsky's works, etc.)

◇ *collocation,* i.e., retrieving lists of *collocates* (lexical units or strings that co-occur with the search term more frequently than would be expected by chance), e.g., крепкий чай (but not *сильный чай), обратить внимание, принять решение, ставить на вид, etc. The term *colligation* refers to this phenomenon but with grammatical rather than lexical constructions. Examples of colligations in Russian include verb government, prepositional government, and other syntactic patterns, including the construction highlighted in Figure 14.2.

The suggested analyses listed here may be most frequently used but the number of analyses available to corpus linguists today is continuously expanding as tools and lines of inquiry rapidly develop (McEnery & Hardie, 2012).

Obviously, the types of analyses listed above require the use of special software. A corpus itself can be stored in a rather simple database (documents in .txt format stored in hierarchically organized folders) but the analysis of a corpus is typically conducted with the use of a program such as WordSmith Tools (Scott, 2016) or AntConc (Anthony, 2019). Many large corpora available online have built-in tools for conducting corpus searches and sophisticated analyses of frequencies and patterns. In addition there are web-based corpus tools available to researchers and students that provide instruments for building, annotating, and analyzing small "custom-built" corpora (e.g., IntelliText at http://corpus.leeds.ac.uk/it/ and GOLD at http://gold.gwserver1.net/).

Над вами потешаться будут». Берлиоз выпучил глаза. «За завтраком... Канту?.. Что это он плете
ми с кусками стерлядки на вилках и вытаращив глаза. Швейцар, вышедший в этот момент из де
е привык. Еще более побледнев, он вытаращил глаза и в смятении подумал: «Этого не может б
голову! Бездомный дико и злобно вытаращил глаза на развязного неизвестного, а Берлиоз сп
нчатся, голова пройдет. Секретарь вытаращил глаза на арестанта и не дописал слова. Пилат п
осил Пилат, и дьявольский огонь сверкнул в его глазах. – Очень добрый и любознательный чел
лся прокуратор не оттого, что солнце жгло ему глаза, нет! Он не хотел почему-то видеть групп
жас до того овладел Берлиозом, что он закрыл глаза. А когда он их открыл, увидел, что все кон
– хриплым голосом спросил больной и закрыл глаза. – Да, Левий Матвей, – донесся до него вь
дровича, уставив на него свои бойкие зеленые глаза, и лишь изредка икал, шепотом ругая абр
анец, обращая к Берлиозу свой левый зеленый глаз. – Нет, вы не ослышались, – учтиво ответи
енно, именно, – закричал он, и левый зеленый глаз его, обращенный к Берлиозу, засверкал, –
мный немец, тоскливо и дико блуждая зеленым глазом по Патриаршим прудам. – Как? А... где
ебнулся воздухом, краска сбежала с его лица и глаза обессмыслились. Марк одною левою рук

FIGURE 14.1. Example of Concordance Lines Sorted by First Left

нчатся, голова пройдет. Секретарь вытаращил глаза на арестанта и не дописал слова. Пилат п
голову! Бездомный дико и злобно вытаращил глаза на развязного неизвестного, а Берлиоз сп
ной голове прокуратора. Он смотрел мутными глазами на арестованного и некоторое время м
не дописал слова. Пилат поднял мученические глаза на арестанта и увидел, что солнце уже дов
нтана и вылетела на волю. Прокуратор поднял глаза на арестанта и увидел, что возле того стол

FIGURE 14.2. Example of Concordance Lines Sorted by First Right, First Left and Second Right

USES OF CORPORA

Corpora exist to facilitate linguistic research, both synchronically and diachronically. CL methods have had a revolutionary impact on the field of linguistics (Hunston, 2002; Plungjan, 2005; Kopotev & Mustajoki, 2008; Gries, 2011). Corpora allow researchers to test theories and hypotheses, retrieve persuasive supporting evidence, and fine-tune (or sometimes contradict) previously held ideas about certain linguistic notions. Studies using corpus methodologies can accurately describe the current state of a linguistic system. In fact, most modern "truly scientific" descriptions of grammars, dictionaries, and language reference materials (see RNC, http://www.ruscorpora.ru/en/corpora-intro.html) are based on corpus studies (most notably Biber et al., 2002; Carter & McCarthy, 2006; the Collins COBUILD series of dictionaries and grammars, and the Longman Dictionary of Contemporary English series).

Inroads are being made in corpus-based descriptions of the Russian language. Русская корпусная грамматика [Russian corpus grammar], at http://rusgram.ru, is an ambitious project that aims at a thorough and continually updated description of the grammar of Russian based on quantitative analyses of the RNC. Русская корпусная грамматика consists of four large sections that represent the traditional substrata in grammar description: morphology, syntax, discourse, and semantics. Various linguistic categories (e.g., verbs, conjunctions) and structures (e.g., noun phrases, indefinite personal pronoun sentences) are described based on quantitative and statistical information obtained from corpus studies, with references to how they have been categorized historically and in comparison to other languages. Русская корпусная грамматика is an invaluable resource: by providing a detailed description of the current state of Russian grammar it serves as a reference for Russian language specialists as well as nonspecialists and is a point of departure for further linguistic research.

Other resources that draw on the RNC data include Новый частотный словарь русской лексики [New frequency dictionary of the Russian lexicon] (Ljaševskaja & Šarov, 2010) at http://dict.ruslang.ru/freq.php, which utilizes frequency data; Словарь русской идиоматики: Сочетания слов со значением высокой степени [Dictionary of idioms: Collocations denoting *high degree*], (Kustova, n.d.) at http://dict.ruslang.ru/magn.php; and Словарь глагольной сочетаемости непредметных имен русского языка [Dictionary of Russian verb collocations with abstract nouns] (Biriuk et al., n.d.) at http://dict.ruslang.ru/abstr_noun.php. These resources are useful for researchers, language teachers and learners, and other language users as they provide specific information about the Russian language that is often unavailable in textbooks.

The corpora and corpus-based resources described here (and many other projects) help advance our understanding of the nature of language. With its focus on authentic language (i.e., actual contextualized usage of linguistic forms and meanings) CL has advanced the usage-based functionalist perspective on language, where "different frequencies of (co-)occurrences of formal elements [. . .] are assumed to reflect functional regularities [. . .] intended to perform a particular communicative function" (Gries,

2009, p. 4). These resources, along with pedagogical techniques and innovations ushered in by the corpus revolution, also hold great potential for improving language instruction and facilitating language acquisition.

CORPUS LINGUISTICS AND TEACHING

CL has had a significant impact on second-language pedagogy (Conrad, 1999; McCarthy et al., 2005) by offering educators new pedagogical techniques and materials based on authentic language. Increasing research in CL has paved the way for innovative materials: a great number of available grammars of English have been informed by large corpus studies and new materials have been developed for English Language Teaching (ELT). These include *Focus on Vocabulary: Mastering the Academic Word List* (Schmitt & Schmitt, 2005), the Touchstone series (McCarthy et al., 2005), *Real Grammar: A Corpus-Based Approach to English* (Conrad & Biber, 2009), and others. Coxhead (2000) and Martinez and Schmitt (2012) have made significant contributions to ELT with their Academic Word List and PHRASal Expressions List, respectively. These lists were compiled through methodical manipulation and analysis of corpus data resulting in vocabulary sets useful to both educators and learners. They ensure that pedagogical focus stays centered on words and phrases that have the most utility due to frequency across genres.

While the CL revolution has inspired a surge in ELT materials and pedagogical approaches that utilize corpus data, the materials for other languages (Russian included) have lagged behind. In the following we review the principles of corpus-informed pedagogy and the resources that are available for teaching Russian and suggest other ideas for the application of CL approaches to Russian pedagogy.

Flowerdew (2012) observes that pedagogical corpus applications generally fall into two categories: indirect and direct. Indirect applications include the use of corpus data to determine a teaching syllabus and to inform the development of references and instructional materials. Direct applications entail the hands-on use of corpora by teachers and learners to test hypotheses and make discoveries about language. Regarding the indirect applications, we have demonstrated the utility of corpus data in determining the frequency and nature of usage of the various dimensions of language: phonetic, lexical, grammatical, syntactic, discoursal, and pragmatic. Since course syllabi are often determined by textbooks and tradition, they may not reflect actual usage or developmental sequencing. Corpus data, on the other hand, claim to accurately represent a language, and this type of information is useful when making decisions of how and what to teach language learners. Insights from CL can be used to inform the development of both commercial and in-house instructional materials; teachers can also rely on corpus findings to supplement existing textbooks and references or to sequence a more pedagogically useful syllabus. For instance, frequency information on grammatical structures can help inform a more useful sequencing of grammatical topics. Frequent and salient features may need to occupy little instructional space, whereas frequent but nonsalient features may require special noticing activities;

infrequent constructions can be saved for instruction at advanced levels of proficiency. Information on frequency and the collocational behaviors of vocabulary items can help structure course dictionaries. It can guide the selection of general vocabulary for lower-level courses and of academic vocabulary and topic-specific vocabulary for upper-level topic-based courses that require precise vocabulary and even grammatical constructions (e.g., Russian politics, survey of 20th-century Russian literature).[6]

The value of corpus approaches to language pedagogy extends to instructional materials as well. Furniss (2013) evaluates commercially available ELT textbooks that utilize corpus data to some extent, arguing for their utility as models for materials in Russian. In the Touchstone series (McCarthy et al., 2005), for example, selection and sequencing of material is informed by corpus research, and notes on frequency and usage (obtained from corpus analyses) are subtly integrated into the text. In addition to serving as a source of raw data for material and analysis, corpora can be used to compare the contents of textbooks (e.g., included vocabulary) to actual usage in order to determine the accuracy of a textbook. Although no commercially available Russian language textbooks can claim to be based on corpus data, at least two recent textbooks make use of examples and texts sourced from the RNC; these are *Panorama: Intermediate Russian language textbook* (Rifkin et al., 2017) and *Rodnaya Rech': An introductory course for heritage learners of Russian* (Dubinina & Kisselev, 2019). In addition, most notably the proceedings from a conference on the RNC and education, available at http://studiorum-ruscorpora.ru/. This portal, affiliated with the RNC, contains articles and graduate theses on projects in Slavic linguistics and Russian language pedagogy that make use of RNC data, as well as lesson plans for language and literature classrooms.

Similarly, Israeli (2011) has used the Internet as a corpus to answer difficult questions about Russian grammar posed by American learners and teachers of Russian. The use of search engines, such as Google or Yandex, and Google N-gram, to conduct corpus research, is debated (since the sampling of texts cannot immediately adhere to the principles of corpus data collection we outlined at the beginning), but proponents of Web-as-corpus have nonetheless contributed significant scholarship in this area (Hundt et al., 2007).

Regarding direct corpus applications, learners and teachers of Russian have multiple resources at their disposal to conduct investigations into language, the most user-friendly of which is arguably the RNC.[7] Its potential has been explored by scholars of Russian, including Levinzon (2007), who proposes the use of the RNC as a pedagogical tool for teaching advanced Russian as a second language and Russian for professional purposes; and Janda (2007), who promotes the RNC as a platform for unguided exploration of linguistic phenomena by advanced learners. Since the RNC consists of both a general corpus and specialized subcorpora, users can select the search parameters appropriate for the questions they are asking. For example, as many a teacher and learner of Russian will agree, colloquialisms, slang, and grammatical structures characteristic of speech are normally scantily represented in textbooks and references. Thankfully, samples of these language varieties are easily found in the oral subcorpus of the RNC. The oral subcorpus (3,034 texts and 10,122,579 word tokens) consists of transcripts of recorded private and public speech samples as well as Russian-language film scripts. Teachers and learners of Russian can query words, phrases, and grammatical structures to analyze usage in authentic oral language. For instance, students might be curious about a new phrase they overheard in a conversation, such as Да ты что? [Really?]. While their bilingual or monolingual dictionary might not contain this phrase, they can query the oral subcorpus of the RNC and have immediate access to plentiful contextualized, authentic usage examples, like the following:

Даша, жен, 18: Да / а у тебя какой размер?
Алена, жен, 20: Сорок два.
Даша, жен, 18: Да ты что?
Алена, жен, 20: Да / я вообще похудела.
(Разговор во время прогулки по городу // Из материалов Ульяновского университета, 2007)[8]

[Dasha, fem, 18: Yep / and what size are you?
Alyona, fem, 20: Forty-two.
Dasha, fem, 18: Really?
Alyona, fem, 20: Yes / I lost some weight actually.
(Conversation during a walk around town // Materials of Ulyanovsk University, 2007)]

Mauranen (2004) notes that "a speech corpus can be extremely useful for checking the meaning of a puzzling expression heard in speech but not adequately described in reference materials, or in preparing a spoken presentation" (p. 95). Spoken corpora contain "frozen" instances of conversation, which learners can then examine in depth without the hindrance of the ephemeral nature of speech or the urgent need to participate in an interaction. By reading corpus excerpts a student can be exposed to many authentic uses of a phrase within a variety of contexts, which can aid in interpreting the meaning of the phrase in question. These types of investigations can be easily translated into classroom activities. For example, the worksheets provided at CALPERLEX (https://calper.la.psu.edu/publications/publication-items/calperlex-russian) demonstrate the types of inductive activities that can be created on the basis of corpus data. Learners also can be asked to create dictionary entries for conversational words or phrases based on their independent corpus inquiries (Mishan, 2004).

Instructors and students can make their own corpora for various purposes. Such corpora can guide instructors in selecting the most useful vocabulary for a given group of learners. A corpus of course readings can be easily created and analyzed using a free corpus tool like AntConc (Anthony, 2019), as long as the user has plain text files with the preferred encoding.[9] After uploading the texts, word lists can be compiled and used to inform vocabulary selection. Students can also be asked to design their own small specialized corpora after determining principles for selection based on the types of questions they hope to answer with the corpus data (Mishan, 2004).

Teachers can use corpus data in the classroom to promote inductive learning. For instance, a vocabulary unit in a Russian class may encounter two close synonyms with the same English translation. The instructor can give students a handout featuring two concordances—one for each of the two words. Using the concordances as raw data for analysis, students must identify the differences in usage. The RNC produces excerpts containing the search term as well as statistics (number of tokens, how often the search terms appears in each genre or text type, etc.). For example, тоже and также often pose difficulties for learners as both words can be translated as "also," but when concordances of each word are examined side-by-side, students can see differences in usage. Comparisons can also be made between usages in the spoken subcorpus of the RNC vs the general corpus in order to illustrate contrasts between oral and written usage in Russian.

Using corpora for linguistic analysis allows students to see beyond the meaning of individual lexical items and begin to use constructions in a more native-like manner. To illustrate, consider the Russian constructions 'много+Noun.Gen' [many.ADV+Noun.Gen] and 'многие+Noun.Nom' [many.ADJ+Noun.Nom], which learners of Russian may see as interchangeable. A teacher can show two sets of concordance lines with the two structures, each set containing 8–10 examples, as in the following:

> Многие люди, родившиеся и выросшие в городе, бежали от городской жизни и, живя среди природы, находили своё счастье.
> (Дарья Князева. На привале (2002) // «Сад своими руками», 2002.12.15)
> [Many people, having been born and raised in the city, ran from city life and, living among nature, found their happiness.
> (Daria Knjazeva. At a rest stop (2002) // "Your garden," 2002.12.15)]
>
> В то время года в Мехико было особенно много людей.
> (В. Э. Карпов, Т. В. Мещерякова. Об автоматизации нетворческих литературных процессов // «Информационные технологии», 2004)
> [At that time of year in Mexico there were especially many people.
> (Karpov & Mescheryakova. Automatization of non-creative literary processes // "Information Technologies," 2004)]

These raw data can be accompanied by a list of guiding questions: Does the construction appear in the role of a subject or object? Do the two sets of sentences have similar predicates? Does the structure appear toward the beginning or toward the end of the sentence? Learners will quickly see the difference in syntactic structure and, having considered the extended context, will likely arrive at the functional distinction, namely the difference in the informational focus that these two constructions mark.

Corpus data can also be utilized to create worksheets for the classroom. In the following exercise on the particles -то [some-] and -нибудь [any-], corpus excerpts were used to create a cloze activity in which students must choose the correct particle depending on the context:

1. Или вот сидишь за столом, что- ________ выпил или съел, и в животе как заурчит . . .
   (Евгений Гришковец. «ОдноврЕмЕнно» (2004)
   [Or you're sitting at the table, having drank or eaten something, and your stomach begins to growl . . .
   (Evgenij Griškovec. *OdnovrEmEnno* (2004)]
2. Недавно Владимира Путина спросили: есть ли что- ________ такое, за что ему больно и стыдно.
   (Магомет Яндиев. Где на Руси жить хорошо (2003) // «Время МН», 2003.07.30)
   [Not long ago Vladimir Putin was asked if there was anything that he felt shame and pain over.
   (Magomet Jandiev. "Where in Russia one lives well" (2003) // *Vremja MN*, 2003.07.30)]

Exercises like this have the advantage of containing real-life exemplars rather than invented sentences that may or may not reflect actual usage. Cloze activities can also focus on lexicon: vocabulary words can be queried in a corpus then removed from selected corpus excerpts and listed in a "word bank" from which students must choose.

Lists of collocations can also be helpful for learners as they illuminate which lexical combinations sound more native-like than others. Using the bigram search feature of the RNC, one can retrieve lists of collocates for word pairs difficult for learners to distinguish, such as, for example, жаркий [hot] and горячий [hot]. Жаркий frequently collocates with the nouns день [day], время [time], погода [weather], спор [argument], while горячий [hot] collocates with вода [water], следы [tracks], рука [hand], чай [tea], and so on. By being exposed to typical word combinations learners can expand and deepen their knowledge of lexical items and their uses in context. Such exposure can also open their eyes to the fact that knowing a word well entails knowing how it combines with other words in typical usage. Although direct examples from a general use corpus are better suited for Intermediate- and Advanced-level learners, Novice learners can benefit from corpus data too. The following example from the RNC provides an introduction that could be used in lieu of invented dialogues in order to show how people introduce themselves in real-life contexts:

Катюша: Мне мама с незнакомыми тетями разговаривать не разрешает.
Светлана: Понятно. А как тебя зовут?

Катюша: Катюша.
Светлана: А меня Светлана Ивановна. Вот и познакомились.
(Разговор о животных // Из коллекции НКРЯ, 2006)

[Katiusha: My mom doesn't allow me to talk to strangers.
Svetlana: Ah. What's your name?
Katiusha: Katiusha.
Svetlana: Mine's Svetlana Ivanovna. Now we're no longer strangers.
(Conversation about animals // From the RNC collection, 2006)]

A burgeoning area of research within CL utilizes corpus methodologies to investigate the development of language learners' pragmatic competence. Pragmatics refers to the knowledge necessary for using language in contextually appropriate ways (for example, the intricacies of using *ты* and *вы* pronouns). Apresjan (2013) uses corpus data to examine "emotional etiquette" in English and Russian, finding that the usage of emotion-expressing vocabulary varies across language; for example, Russian speakers tend to express shame, fear, and contempt more frequently than English speakers. Findings like Apresjan's have implications for learners of Russian, as pragmatic competence includes awareness of which emotions are appropriate to certain contexts.

Although corpus linguists are generally very enthusiastic about the benefits corpora provide to learners, using corpora is still uncommon in foreign language classes (Aijmer, 2009). Working with corpus data is not always a straightforward process, as "real-life language from a corpus can be messy and difficult to analyze, and generally does not lend itself to succinct usage explanations, like those found in traditional grammars" (Furniss, 2013, p. 196). A variety of issues still need to be addressed in empirical research: Who should utilize corpora—teachers, or the students themselves? How should learners use corpora—under direction or freely? At what level of proficiency can learners be reasonably expected to use corpora to answer language-related questions? Should raw corpus excerpts be manipulated for pedagogical efficacy? A number of experimental studies have attempted to gauge the effectiveness of various corpus applications among varied learners in a range of contexts (see for example Belz & Vyatkina, 2008, and Vyatkina, 2013). Still, a need for empirical research evaluating the resulting outcomes of these innovations persists and "much work still remains to be done in bridging the gap between research and practice" (Römer, 2011, p. 206).

CORPUS LINGUISTICS AND LEARNER LANGUAGE

Granger (2009) argues that the gap between CL and language pedagogy can be better bridged by conducting studies involving learner acquisition. Learner corpus linguistics—as the name suggests—is a field of inquiry that investigates corpora containing language produced by L2 language users (that is, learners in a foreign or second-language context). The main objective of this field is to gain insight into acquisition of second or additional languages.

This approach was pioneered in Granger's groundbreaking work with the International Corpus of Learner English (ICLE) and was subsequently applied in many other projects around the world (see Learner Corpora Around the World, https://uclouvain.be/en/research-institutes/ilc/cecl/learner-corpora-around-the-world.html). A survey of these projects reveals a fruitful line of future research that looks into group-specific and universal patterns of interlanguage. This research includes descriptive and comparative studies on linguistic portraits of non-native speakers of various linguistic levels, patterns of error by heritage and traditional learners of language at different levels, frequency of cohesion devices used in writing by L2 and L1 speakers, collocation usage in L1 and L2 production, the use of formulaic language in L2 speech, and the effectiveness of pedagogical intervention as demonstrated by corpus data (Dagneaux et al., 1998; Granger, 1996, 1999; Hinkel, 2001; Nesselhauf, 2005; Paquot & Granger, 2012; Vytakina, 2012, 2013; Gries & Wulff, 2013; Vyrenkova et al., 2014; Kisselev & Alsufieva, 2017).

Despite the opportunities afforded by this type of research within the fields of SLA and language pedagogy, as well as in linguistics in general, the development of learner corpora for languages other than English has been slow, which can be largely explained by the fact that the development of these databases is not a simple task. It requires not only access to a large number of learners and learner texts but abundant human and material resources as well. "Learner corpora are in some ways more complex as datasets than native speaker corpora" (Barlow, 2005, p. 335), which means that all corpus procedures—from compilation and annotation to statistical analysis and interpretation—require innovative approaches.

First of all, a researcher has to consider carefully the questions of representativeness and balanced selection: How many learners of a particular level or L1 comprise the sample representative? How many texts or words per learner are sufficient? How will the level of target language command be gauged—by the number of instruction hours, years, or using external test scores? How will learners' history of language learning, including first and other foreign languages, be measured? What about the question of the context of language acquisition? The challenge of having a large combination of factors that influence language production by L2 learners is best mitigated by using a detailed and highly descriptive system of metatags.

More challenging, however, are the technological difficulties inherent in creating automated and semiautomated annotations of learner language. Most automated taggers have been developed for standard linguistic forms and are often inapplicable to learners' many "deviations." It is not easy to develop tools and procedures for annotating "noisy" texts (i.e., language filled with nonstandard and often unpredictable forms), especially for languages like Russian, with its rich inflectional morphology. Raw text, that is, text that has not been annotated, can, of course, be used in corpus analyses, but the lack of annotation limits the extent of analytical procedures that can be undertaken. For instance, in order to look into patterns of acquisition of inflectional morphology in Russian (e.g., development of case or gender marking), a corpus must contain either morphological tags or *error tags* (i.e., special labels—usually inserted into text manually—that describe structural and, often, typological properties of errors and provide the correct or intended form). Furthermore, the search interface must allow for users to search by tag.

The potential for error-tagged learner corpora within SLA research and language teaching is substantial. Systematic errors (i.e., errors that reach a certain frequency threshold) can be grouped by structural and functional properties as well as by frequency information. Researchers can then use these data to describe interlanguage properties, to understand developmental processes of Russian language acquisition, to test hypotheses about L1 transfer, and to answer many other important questions typical in SLA research. In other words, error analysis can aid in achieving the general goal of learner corpus research—revealing, quantifying, and describing the recurrent lexical, grammatical, and discourse patterns that characterize different learner groups, different learning histories, different instructional settings and, possibly, individual learner characteristics (Barlow, 2005).

Promisingly, a large-scale Russian learner corpus is currently under construction. The Russian Learner Corpus (RLC) (at http://web-corpora.net/heritage_corpus) is envisioned as a large repository of texts (oral and written) produced by L2 and heritage speakers of Russian and representing different levels of language proficiency and a variety of dominant languages. Currently the largest part of the corpus is the Russian Learner Corpus of Academic Writing (RULEC), a longitudinal corpus of advanced-level writing by L2 and heritage students of Russian collected by Kisselev and Alsufieva.[10] RULEC contains highly detailed metatags: each contains information on the learner's *gender*, *language background* (heritage vs. second language), *level of language proficiency* (according to the ACTFL scale), *name of the course* for which the paper was written, *text type* (paragraph, essay, research paper), *function* targeted by the task (definition, narration, argumentation), and *time* restriction (timed or untimed writing). This detailed system allows researchers to compare subcorpora or at least to take into consideration these text and author characteristics. For instance, one could examine the effect of genre (function in RULEC) on the linguistic performance of the students or compare the language of Intermediate versus Advanced learners with the goal of establishing markers of development in writing or patterns of persistent errors.

The RLC is already available in raw and POS-tagged form, and the corpus will also eventually be error-tagged. The work on manual tagging and classification of errors in the RLC is currently being carried out by the team of researchers at the Heritage Russian Research Group (Higher School of Economics, Russia). Paired with a user-friendly web interface, this POS- and error-tagged corpus will become an indispensable resource in research on Russian SLA.

CL methodologies can also be used on learner data that have been collected with research-specific questions in mind. Whenever a researcher collects a large enough language sample from a large enough (i.e., representative) group of language learners, if the unit of analysis is something that can be entered into a concordance software search field, corpus techniques can aid in the analysis. Most published learner corpus research involving Russian L2 learners belongs to this category. For instance, one of the first Russian learner corpus studies, conducted by Pavlenko and Driagina (2007), focuses on the acquisition of emotion vocabulary by American speakers of Russian as an L2. The researchers collected three small corpora of oral narratives produced by American L2 speakers of Russian, using Russian monolinguals and American monolinguals as comparison groups. The authors compared the frequencies and appropriateness of emotion words (e.g., расстраивается [get upset], грустное [sad]) and their stems (расстра/о- [upset], груст- [sad]) among the three groups and found that, unlike Russian monolinguals, who show strong preference for verbs, the learners prefer adjectival constructions in Russian (similar to monolingual Americans), they generally use a smaller range of emotion words, and they often confuse or violate conceptual restrictions on the use of emotion vocabulary (e.g., by employing разозлилась [got mad] instead of расстроилась [got upset]). This research informed the development of an instructional resource for learners of Russian, *Advancing in Russian through Narration* (Pavlenko & Driagina, 2008).

Hasko (2009, 2010) conducted another study—this time focused on verbs of motion—that illustrates the application of corpus methods to the analysis of learner language. In this study, Hasko compiled an experimental corpus of spontaneous oral narratives elicited from learners of Russian and native speakers of Russian. The corpus was manually tagged for verbs of motion and patterns of grammatical representation of motion. The author finds that the learners in the study exhibit a lack of systematic conceptual structuring of unidirectional motion despite the fact that they are experienced learners of Russian. This work has resulted in a theoretical treatise on the concept of motion in Russian (Hasko, 2009, 2010) and a set of instructional materials, Motion Verbs in Narratives: Materials for Intermediate and Advanced Learners of Russian (Hasko, 2014).

Undoubtedly, teachers of Russian would benefit greatly from a diversity of full-scale corpus studies in Russian SLA. Language educators and language learners can also benefit from knowing how to conduct small-scale, targeted searches of available learner corpora or how to custom build their own corpora. Alsufieva et al. (2012) provide an example of a corpus query that addresses a very specific language issue of the type that arises in everyday practice. In this example teachers use RULEC to investigate the usage of the preposition через [through] in learner data. Through a simple concordance search the authors established a usage pattern of the preposition, identified the problematic construction—which in this case involved the mediating function of the preposition через (e.g., через анализ советской музыки Сталинского периода мы увидели . . . [through an analysis of Soviet music during Stalin's rule we saw]; Америка показала свою прогрессивность через избрание афро-американца в Белый дом [America showed its progressiveness through the election of an African

American to the White House])—and created a set of instructional activities to target the construction (for more details see Alsufieva et al., 2012).

Another fruitful direction within learner corpus linguistics involves the compilation and analysis of longitudinal data, i.e., corpora collected from the same group of learners at different points in their language learning careers. Longitudinal corpora can provide teachers with concrete and reliable data on students' linguistic progress. Even a small longitudinal corpus created for the purposes of a particular course may provide a teacher with a better assessment option than more traditional tests do, since:

> it does not require additional tests and can assess the current state of the language as well as linguistic progress of an individual student or a whole group of learners; the corpus-based assessment may be more comprehensive than a test (one can assess different language categories in different contexts) and more flexible (through the use of different base-lines such as native speech, the performance of the cohort, and the performance in previous terms. (Alsufieva et al., 2012, p. 96)

Sophisticated analyses of learner writing, for example, can be performed quickly with software designed for corpus research. WordSmith Tools 6.0 (Scott, 2016) automatically provides general statistical information on word tokens and types, sentences, and paragraphs, as well as type/token ratio (TTR) and mean length of a word, sentence, or paragraph. A documented increase in word token count or in the number of words per sentence from a corpus of student writing collected at the beginning of a course versus a corpus of writing collected two months later might indicate growing fluency in language production. Growth in the number of word types and changing TTR counts might reveal development in vocabulary skills. Word lists can also be easily compiled and compared with frequency lists from native Russian corpora in order to analyze whether students are beginning to use less common, more sophisticated vocabulary. The length of text or TTR are not likely to change dramatically at advanced levels of language proficiency; however, one can look for other markers of development. In a comparison of the performance of learners of Russian at Intermediate High and Advanced Low/Intermediate levels, Kisselev and Alsufieva (2017) observe that sentence length appears to grow slightly and paragraph length increases significantly as student proficiency increases. Interestingly, at the same time the number of sentences per 1,000 words decreases as students move to higher levels of proficiency. The authors propose that these trajectories are complementary and possibly reflect growing informational density of sentences and paragraphs, which might be a good marker of development at the advanced level.

For a more comprehensive assessment, of course, one needs to choose more detailed analyses and appropriate research questions. The focus of the Kisselev and Alsufieva study was, for instance, on the development of syntax, specifically the use of complex sentences with subordinating conjunctions. Having analyzed the concordance lines with conjunctions, the authors were able to assess the quantitative changes in the use of different conjunctions as well as the rates of accuracy in the use of different conjunctions and the types of error patterns. The researchers also found that the L1 Russian learners continue to produce errors with conjunctions that require structural manipulation with the constituents of the subordinated clause (e.g., то, что [that]; чтобы [in order to]; который [which]), while heritage learners continue to struggle with the appropriate punctuation required to separate a dependent clause. The pedagogical implications of such a study are obvious and immediately applicable.

With the exception of the aforementioned studies, corpus approaches to the assessment of writing in Russian are not thoroughly developed. In fact, even in ELT the methodologies that use corpus as an assessment tool are still being developed and debated (Taylor & Barker, 2008). However, the corpus approach to assessment allows for precise analyses of students' linguistic progress in specific areas, such as lexical item collocations, cohesive devices, and punctuation. Explicit focus on these components can raise awareness of problem areas and equip instructors and materials developers with the kinds of concrete, research-based evidence needed to formulate targeted pedagogical descriptions of usage.

Learner corpora can also be employed as a source for developing appropriate pedagogical materials. Teachers can create "lexical and grammatical exercises, as well as those that target spelling, morphology, punctuation and syntax, discourse, and register variation" in the form of a cloze activity or hands-on corpus search conducted by students (Alsufieva et al., 2012, p. 94). Learner corpora often contain language that is easier for other learners to understand and manipulate; erroneous samples may be used in correction exercises.

The applications of learner corpora and the advantages of the learner corpora to the field of SLA and pedagogy are broader than the ones described above. The scope and the nature of a corpus-based investigation is only somewhat limited by technology and depends on the needs, and often the imagination, of the researcher. When properly applied, the learner corpus approach can successfully address global issues of SLA, as well as allow an instructor to uncover issues relevant to a particular group of students and to address them in real time.

CONCLUSION

This chapter has reviewed the state of the field of corpus linguistics, with an emphasis on previous, current, and future applications for the teaching and learning of Russian. Corpus-informed pedagogy is beneficial to learners, since accurate information about language usage in various genres and in both the written and spoken modes is of critical importance to language acquisition. Boulton and Pérez-Paredes (2014), in an editorial on pedagogical applications of corpora for a special issue of *ReCALL*, state that, "rather than trying to bring corpus linguistics into the language classroom, the emphasis is increasingly placed on the L2 user and how he or she might benefit from corpus linguistic tools and techniques" (p. 122). This shift reflects the establishment of CL as an accepted and legitimate field that has become integrated into applied linguistics. However, this integration has occurred predominantly within ELT. Russian language educators and textbook authors should follow the lead of the English-language specialists and harness the benefits of corpus research.

Historically, language descriptions in pedagogical materials are predominantly based on intuition, with little to no reference to usage (O'Keefe et al., 2007). Instructors and materials developers can ensure greater accuracy by taking advantage of the insights afforded by corpus data (Biber & Conrad, 2010). Corpus data can similarly inform course designers in selecting and sequencing language topics and vocabulary in a way that is immediately useful for students. Furthermore, a variety of learner corpora that encompass different levels, genres, modes, and designs can enhance knowledge of SLA and, in turn, language pedagogy.

However, there are barriers to corpus use among teachers, including accessibility. Since corpus tools have been developed for use by programmers and for computational linguists, they are typically not user-friendly for the nonspecialist. Fortunately, the increase in web-based corpora open to public use has resulted in tools with a much lower barrier to use. In order to promote the use of corpus methodologies and corpora like the RNC and the RLC there is a need for hands-on practice with corpora in graduate courses for novice teachers of Russian and in professional development workshops for more experienced educators. If preservice and practicing teachers are given opportunities to learn the basics of CL research, they can then implement corpus tools in their teaching and in turn transfer their knowledge to their students. Corpus tools are just that: tools. They enable language instructors to do the things they already do—select and sequence materials for instruction, create language activities, and gauge student performance and progress—in a more systematic way. There is also a need for more extensive uptake in order to improve Russian language instruction and materials beyond the local level, that is, in ways that can impact the greater community of Russian learners. This can be accomplished through journal and book publications that document the development of corpus-informed resources and their role in the teaching and learning process. Russian language teachers and materials developers can now make use of the statistics and rich real-world examples made accessible by corpora and make the educational experiences of Russian language learners more meaningful, interesting, and relevant.

NOTES

1. For a compilation of corpus studies on the Russian language, refer to http://ruscorpora.ru/corpora-biblio.html.
2. In determining the size of a corpus researchers generally consider two main factors: the kind of research questions they intend to answer (translated into CL terms: the kinds of queries they anticipate to run) and the methodologies they intend to use (Sinclair, 2004). For example, a lexicographer may need more than 20 different

instances of use to unambiguously define a word or a particular meaning of a polysemous word. To put things in perspective, "For the first million-word corpus of general written American English (the Brown corpus), there was a vocabulary of different word forms of 69002, of which 35065 occurred once only" (Sinclair, 2004). In other words, the rarer the word (or phrase, or grammatical structure), the bigger the corpus must be. However, if the goal of a corpus study is more specialized (e.g., analysis of Leo Tolstoy's letters to his wife), a small corpus will suffice as long as the linguistic features under analysis appear frequently enough to benefit from statistical analyses.

3. For a detailed early history of the RNC, see the article by Sičinava at http://ruscorpora.ru/corpora-about.html.
4. More statistical information on the composition of the RNC is available at http://ruscorpora.ru/corpora-stat.html.
5. For example, a corpus may contain 100 tokens of the word type 'house.' The word type counts each unique word form once, while the token refers to the total number of occurrences of that word type.
6. For an informative example of creating a corpus-informed syllabus on business Russian, see Wilson et al., 2014.
7. Another Russian language corpus project that holds promise for Russian language classroom practice is HANCO (Хельсинский аннотированный корпус русского языка), located at http://www.ling.helsinki.fi/projects/hanco/). HANCO presents a collection of texts published in the early 2000s in the Russian-language magazine *Itogi*. The corpus is relatively small (100,000 words) but contains exact and detailed grammatical annotation accessible to instructors and students. Some ideas for the use of HANCO in teaching Russian as an L2 are discussed in Kopotev (2008).
8. In accordance with RNC's fair use requirement, all examples retrieved from the RNC corpus must be cited as such, along with a reference to the original text (http://www.ruscorpora.ru/en/corpora-usage.html).
9. For Cyrillic texts, AntConc requires UTF-8 encoding.
10. A description of this corpus is available in Alsufieva et al., 2012.

REFERENCES

Aijmer, K. (Ed.). (2009). *Corpora and language teaching*. Philadelphia: John Benjamins.

Alsufieva, A., Kisselev, O., & Freels, S. (2012). Results 2012: Using Flagship data to develop a Russian learner corpus of academic writing. *Russian Language Journal, 62*, 79–105.

Anthony, L. (2019). AntConc (Version 3.4.3) [software]. Tokyo: Waseda University. Retrieved from http://www.laurenceanthony.net/

Apresjan, V. (2013). Corpus methods in pragmatics: The case of English and Russian emotions. *Intercultural Pragmatics, 10*(4), 533–68.

Barlow, M. (2005). Computer-based analyses of learner language. In R. Ellis & G. Barkhuizen (Eds.), *Analysing learner language* (pp. 335–69). Oxford: Oxford UP.

Belz, J., & Vyatkina, N. (2008). The pedagogical mediation of a developmental learner corpus for classroom-based language instruction. *Language Learning and Technology, 12*(3), 33–52.

Biber, D., & Conrad, S. (2010). *Corpus linguistics and grammar teaching.* White Plains, NY: Pearson Education.

Biber, D., Conrad, S., & Leech, G. (2002). *The Longman student grammar of spoken and written English.* London: Longman.

Biriuk, O., Gusev, V., & Kalinina, E. (n.d.) *Словарь глагольной сочетаемости непредметных имен русского языка* [Dictionary of Russian verb collocations with abstract nouns]. Retrieved from http://dict.ruslang.ru/abstr_noun.php

Boulton, A., & Pérez-Paredes, P. (2014). Editorial: Researching uses of corpora for language teaching and learning. *ReCALL, 26*(2), 121–27.

Carter, R., & McCarthy, M. (2006). *Cambridge grammar of English.* Cambridge: Cambridge UP.

Centre for English Corpus Linguistics (2002). Learner corpora around the world. Retrieved August 26, 2016, from https://uclouvain.be/en/research-institutes/ilc/cecl/learner-corpora-around-the-world.html

Conrad, S. (1999). The importance of corpus-based research for language teachers. *System, 27*(1), 1–18.

Conrad, S., & Biber, D. (2009). *Real grammar: A corpus-based approach to English.* New York: Pearson-Longman.

Coxhead, A. (2000). A new academic word list. *TESOL Quarterly, 34*(2), 213–38.

Dagneaux, E., Denness, S., & Granger, S. (1998). Computer-aided error analysis. *System, 26*, 163–74.

Dubinina, I., & Kisselev, O. (2019). *Rodnaya Rech': An introductory course for heritage learners of Russian.* Washington, DC: Georgetown UP.

Flowerdew, L. (2012). *Corpora and language education.* Basingstoke, UK: Palgrave Macmillan.

Furniss, E. (2013). Using a corpus-based approach to Russian as a foreign language materials development. *Russian Language Journal, 63*, 195–212.

Granger, S. (1996). From CA to CIA and back: An integrated approach to computerized bilingual and learner corpora. In K. Aijmer, B. Altenberg, & M. Johansson (Eds.), *Languages in contrast. Papers from a symposium on text-based cross-linguistic studies. Lund 4–5 March 1994* (pp. 37–51). Lund, Sweden: Lund UP.

Granger, S. (1999). Use of tenses by advanced EFL learners: Evidence from an error-tagged computer corpus. In H. Hasselgard & S. Oksefjell (Eds.), *Out of corpora. Studies in honour of Stig Johansson* (pp. 191–202). Amsterdam: Rodopi.

Granger, S. (2009). The contribution of learner corpora to second language acquisition and foreign language teaching. In K. Ajmer (Ed.), *Corpora and language teaching* (pp. 13–32). Philadelphia: John Benjamins.

Gries, S. (2009). What is corpus linguistics? *Language and Linguistics Compass, 3*(5), 1225–41.

Gries, S. (2011). Methodological and interdisciplinary stance in corpus linguistics. In G. Barnbrook, V. Viana, & S. Zyngier (Eds.), *Perspectives on corpus linguistics: Connections and controversies* (pp. 81–98). Philadelphia: John Benjamins.

Gries, S., & Wulff, S. (2013). The genitive alternation in Chinese and German ESL learners: Towards a multifactorial notion of *context* in learner corpus research. *International Journal of Corpus Linguistics, 18*(3), 327–56.

Hasko, V. (2009). The locus of difficulties in the acquisition of Russian verbs of motion by highly proficient learners. *Slavic and Eastern European Journal, 53*(3), 360–85.

Hasko, V. (2010). The role of thinking for speaking in adult L2 speech: The case of (non) unidirectionality encoding by American learners of Russian. In Z. Han & T. Cadierno (Eds.), *Linguistic relativity in SLA: Thinking for speaking* (pp. 34–58). Bristol, UK: Multilingual Matters.

Hasko, V. (2014). Motion verbs in narratives: Materials for intermediate and advanced learners of Russian. University Park, PA: CALPER.

Hinkel, E. (2001). Matters of cohesion in L2 academic texts. *Applied Language Learning, 12*(2), 111–32.

Hundt, M., Nesselhauf, N., & Biewer, C. (Eds.). (2007). *Corpus linguistics and the web.* Amsterdam: Rodopi.

Hunston, S. (2002). *Corpora in applied linguistics.* Cambridge: Cambridge UP.

Israeli, A. (2011). *What you always wanted to know about Russian grammar (*but were afraid to ask).* Bloomington, IN: Slavica.

Janda, L. (2007). Студенты-пользователи Национального корпуса русского языка [Student users of the Russian National Corpus]. In N. Dobrushina (Ed.), *Proceedings from Nacionalnyj korpus russkogo jazyka i problemy gumanitarnogo obrazovanija* (pp. 60–73). Moscow: Teis.

Kisselev, O., & Alsufieva, A. (2017). The development of syntactic complexity in the writing of Russian language learners: A longitudinal corpus study. *Russian Language Journal,* 67, 27–53.

Kopotev, M. (2008). Использование электронных корпусов в преподавании русского языка [Using electronic resources in the teaching of Russian]. *SLAVICA HELSINGIENSIA, 35,* 110–18.

Kopotev, M., & Mustajoki, A. (2008). Современная корпусная русистика [Contemporary Russian corpus linguistics]. In A. Mustajoki, M. Kopotev, L. Birjulin, & Protasova, Ju. (Eds.), *Instrumentarij rusistiki: Korpusnye podxody* (pp. 7–24). Helsinki: Helsinki UP.

Kustova, G. (n.d.). Словарь русской идиоматики: Сочетание слов со значением высокой степени [Dictionary of Russian idioms: Collocations denoting *high degree*]. Retrieved from http://dict.ruslang.ru/magn.php

Levinzon, A. (2007). Использование Национального корпуса русского языка в обучении русскому языку англоязычных студентов [Using the Russian National Corpus in the teaching of Russian to English-speaking students]. *Russkij jazyk za rubežom, 4,* 64–73.

Ljaševskaja, O. N., & Šarov, S. A. (2010). Частотный словарь современного русского языка [Frequency dictionary of the contemporary Russian language]. Moscow: Azbukovnik.

Martinez, R., & Schmitt, N. (2012). A phrasal expressions list. *Applied Linguistics, 33*(3), 299–320.

Mauranen, A. (2004). Spoken corpus for an ordinary learner. In J. M. Sinclair (Ed.), *How to use corpora in language teaching* (pp. 89–105). Philadelphia: John Benjamins.

McCarthy, M., McCarten, J., & Sandiford, H. (2005). *Touchstone 1 & 2.* Cambridge: Cambridge UP.

McCarthy, M., & O'Keeffe, A. (2010). Historical perspective: What are corpora and how have they evolved? In A. O'Keeffe & M. McCarthy (Eds.), *The Routledge handbook of corpus linguistics* (pp. 3–13). London, UK: Routledge.

McEnery, T., & Hardie, A. (2012). *Corpus linguistics: Method, theory and practice.* Cambridge: Cambridge UP.

Mishan, F. (2004). Authenticating corpora for language learning: A problem and its resolution. *ELT Journal, 58*(3), 219–27.

Nesselhauf, N. (2005). *Collocations in a learner corpus.* Philadelphia: John Benjamins.

O'Keefe, A., McCarthy, M., & Carter, R. (2007). *From corpus to classroom: Language use and language teaching.* Cambridge: Cambridge UP.

Paquot, M., & Granger, S. (2012). Formulaic language in learner corpora. *Annual Review of Applied Linguistics, 32*(1), 130–49.

Pavlenko, A., & Driagina, V. (2007). Russian emotion vocabulary in American learners' narratives. *The Modern Language Journal, 91,* 213–34.

Pavlenko, A., & Hasko, V. D. (2008). *Advancing in Russian through narration.* University Park, PA: CALPER.

Plungjan, V. A. (2005). Зачем нужен Национальный корпус русского языка? Неформальное введение [Why do we need the Russian National Corpus?: An informal introduction]. In *Nacional'nyj korpus russkogo jazyka: 2003–2005* (pp. 6–20). Moscow: Indrik.

Rifkin, B., Dengub, E., & Nazarova, S. (2017). *Panorama. Intermediate Russian language textbook.* Washington, DC: Georgetown UP.

Römer, U. (2011). Corpus research applications in second language teaching. *Annual Review of Applied Linguistics, 31,* 205–25.

Schmid, H. (2000). *English abstract nouns as conceptual shells: From corpus to cognition.* New York: Mouton de Gruyter.

Schmitt, D., & Schmitt, N. (2005). *Focus on vocabulary: Mastering the Academic Word List.* White Plains, NY: Longman.

Scott, M. (2016). WordSmith Tools [software]. Oxford: Oxford UP. Retrieved from http://www.lexically.net/wordsmith/

Sinclair, J. McH. (2004). (Ed.). With R. Carter. *Trust the text: Language, corpus and discourse.* New York: Routledge.

Taylor, L., & Barker, F. (2008). Using corpora in language assessment. In E. Shohamy & N. H. Hornberger (Eds.), *Encyclopedia of language and education*, *Volume 7: Language testing and assessment* (2nd ed.) (pp. 241–54). New York: Springer.

Tognini Bonelli, E. (2012). Theoretical overview of the evolution of corpus linguistics. In A. O'Keeffe & M. McCarthy (Eds.), *The Routledge handbook of corpus linguistics* (pp. 14–27). New York: Routledge.

Vyatkina, N. (2012). The development of second language writing complexity in groups and individuals: A longitudinal learner corpus study. *Modern Language Journal, 96*(4), 572–94.

Vyatkina, N. (2013). Discovery learning and teaching with electronic corpora in an advanced German grammar course. *Die Unterrichtspraxis/Teaching German, 46*(1), 44–61.

Vyrenkova, A. S., Polinskaja, M. S., & Raxilina, E. V. (2014). Грамматика ошибок и грамматика конструкций: «Эритажный» («унаследованный») русский язык. [The grammar of mistakes and the grammar of constructions: Heritage Russian language]. *Voprosy jazykoznanija, 3*, 3–19.

Wilson, J., Sharoff, S., Stephenson, P., & Hartley, A. (2014). Innovative methods for LSP-teaching: How we use corpora to teach business Russian. In E. Bárcena, T. Read, & J. Arús (Eds.), *Languages for specific purposes in the digital era* (pp. 197–222). Switzerland: Springer.

PART V

TEACHING CULTURE

15

DEVELOPING INTERCULTURAL COMPETENCE IN A RUSSIAN LANGUAGE CLASS

Ekaterina Nemtchinova

Intercultural competence (IC) has long been recognized as an important goal of foreign language education, as evidenced by its prominent place in the World-Readiness Standards for Learning Languages (NSCB, 2015) and other professional publications (American Council on the Teaching of Foreign Languages, 2014; Modern Language Association, 2007). Successful interpersonal communication in today's globalized and culturally diverse world requires not only an effective exchange of information, it also demands people's "ability to decentre and take up the other's perspective on their own culture, anticipating and where possible resolving dysfunctions in communication and behavior" (Byram, 1997, p. 42). In practical terms, IC means that in addition to being linguistically capable of participating in personal and professional communication with speakers of a target language, students need to understand the cultural ideas, opinions, and attitudes of their interlocutors and to be able to express themselves in a culturally appropriate way.

While current research on IC focuses on integrating language and culture goals in language programs (Díaz, 2013), there exists a certain disconnect between the theoretical explanations of IC and the teaching practices used to realize it. Educators still debate the definition of culture in the context of a foreign language classroom, how intercultural competence goals translate into concrete instructional objectives, and how culture-related learning outcomes should be formally assessed. Building on recent models of IC (Díaz, 2013; Liddicoat & Scarino, 2013), this chapter attempts to advance cultural instruction by describing how IC objectives and assessment practices can be integrated into traditional language learning activities in order to promote IC development. After an examination of different models of IC, the discussion turns to teaching and assessment issues and provides practical suggestions for facilitating intercultural instruction in the foreign language curriculum.

UNDERSTANDING INTERCULTURAL COMPETENCE

Although there is no single comprehensive definition of IC, several of the descriptions developed over recent years agree that it is "a complex of abilities needed to perform effectively and appropriately when interacting with others who are linguistically and culturally different from oneself" (Fantini, 2009, p.458). These abilities could be developed by acquiring "the culture-specific and culture-general knowledge, skills, and attitudes required for effective communication and interaction with other cultures. It is a dynamic, developmental, and ongoing process which engages the learner cognitively, behaviorally, and affectively" (Paige et al., 2003, p. 177).

These and other descriptions suggest that IC is a complex, multifaceted construct; Spitzberg and Changnon (2009) list 325 interpersonal, communicative, and cultural components of IC. In addition to factual knowledge (the cognitive domain), IC includes an individual's behavior (the behavioral domain) and attitudes and beliefs (the affective domain). The behavioral and affective domains gradually develop as learners are exposed to L2 culture and expand their ability to accept a different point of view, tolerate ambiguity, and become nonjudgmental and flexible (Witte, 2014).

The concept of identity transformation is central to many interpretations of IC. Byram (1997) stresses the importance of openness and curiosity in learning about new beliefs, values, and viewpoints in order to establish and maintain the relationship of equality with the target language speaker. His inventory of factors comprising IC starts with *attitude* to one's own and others' beliefs and *knowledge* of self and others. Similarly, Deardorff (2006) names transformation of attitudes, self-awareness, and openness to new values and beliefs as critical first steps to achieving IC. A shift in personal views could present a challenge: according to Chapelle's (2010) investigation of student cross-cultural experiences in study abroad and Internet collaborations, one of the reasons for cultural misunderstandings is American students' lack of awareness of their own culture and their difficulty "in suspending their certainty and their own way of interpreting what they see and hear around them," which makes it difficult to imagine "the logic of another person" (p. 29). A monolingual and monocultural identity and a lack of the ability to perceive the world through others' languaculture is commonly seen as the main obstacle to IC development (Fonseca-Greber, 2010). Therefore, challenging preconceived notions through learning and reflection, raising awareness of self and others, and modifying one's responses, communication behaviors, and expectations should be the primary goals of instructors aiming to develop IC in their students.

Many researchers of IC underscore the recursive nature of its development. Far from being a straightforward path from none to full, true IC is a spiral progression through different stages accompanied by gradual growth (Deardorff, 2006). The process of IC development is "continuous intercultural learning through experience and critical reflection. There can be no final end-point at which the individual achieves the intercultural state, but rather to be intercultural is by its very nature an unfinishable work-in-progress of action in response to new experiences and reflection on the action" (Liddicoat & Kohler, 2012, p. 81). The process is not easy. Kramsch (1993), for example, suggests the development of IC involves *conflict* because it is "a struggle between the learner's meanings and those of the native speakers" (p. 24). She maintains that rather than simply conveying cultural information, teachers should encourage the learners to create the inner "third place" that emerges from their awareness of the interactions between their native and the target culture. Gudykunst (1998) notes that encounters with a foreign culture create feelings of anxiety and uncertainty. These feelings could be controlled by developing mindfulness, which he describes as analyzing the source of anxiety with a focus on oneself and one's reactions to the host culture. This again underscores the importance of identity transformation in IC development.

Theoretical Framework

Several models have been developed to conceptualize and assess IC in a systematic way. Bennett (1993) proposes a developmental model of intercultural sensitivity (DMIS) based on his analysis of the cultural communication problems of Western workers abroad and their reactions to cultural differences. His model includes six developmental levels of IC arranged into three ethnocentric and three ethnorelative stages (defined as the individual's culture as the center of a worldview and the individual's culture as one of many equally valid worldviews, respectively), which together represent a continuum of IC development, awareness, and sensitivity (Table 15.1). In this framework an individual first goes through the ethnocentric stages of denial, in which she or he denies the differences between cultures by creating psychological, social, or physical barriers in the form of isolation and separation from other cultures; defense, which involves a reaction against the threat of other cultures by denigrating and negatively stereotyping them while promoting the superiority of one's own culture; and minimization, in which the individual acknowledges cultural differences on the surface but considers all cultures fundamentally similar. During the first ethnorelative stage of acceptance an individual accepts and respects cultural differences, behavior, and values. S/he then goes through adaptation, in which s/he develops the ability to shift his/her frame of reference to other culturally diverse worldviews through empathy and pluralism. In the last stage of integration the individual incorporates other worldviews into his/her own worldview (Bennett, 1993).

TABLE 15.1. Bennett's Developmental Model of Intercultural Sensitivity

Ethnocentric stages			Ethnorelative stages		
Denial	**Deference**	**Minimization**	**Acceptance**	**Adaptation**	**Integration**
• isolation • separation	• denigration • superiority	• physical universalism • transcendent universalism	• respect for behavioral differences • respect for value differences	• empathy • pluralism	• contextual evaluation • constructive marginality

Despite the fact that the DMIS focuses on the development of IC among adult professionals, and not among second language learners, it enjoys popularity among language instructors and serves as a basis for several assessment tools (Sinicrope et al., 2007). At the same time it has been criticized for its neglect of the linguistic aspect of cultural practices. The model does not encompass language patterns associated with a given cultural context and ignores the linguistic content of communicative interactions that focus exclusively on cultural aspects of communication (Witte, 2014). Critics also charge that DMIS disregards the sociocultural context and authenticity of the target language and leads to an ethnocentric view of the target culture (Fantini, 2009). Another criticism points out that DMIS as a linear model in which the learner moves from one stage to the next, adding new cultural information to the existing cultural knowledge; but there is no indication of how the progression from the ethnocentric to the ethnorelative worldview evolves. By describing methods and procedures that may advance intercultural sensitivity while ignoring the question of how learners actually develop it as they progress through various stages of the model, DMIS represents the point of view of the teacher, not the learner (Witte, 2014).

A different and influential, multidimensional model of IC is suggested by Byram (1997). Based on his analysis of foreign language teaching in the European context, he identifies five key factors of IC: *attitudes*, which describe the ability to relativize one's self and value others; *knowledge* of social groups and their practices in one's own and in the target culture, as well as the rules for individual and social interaction; *skills of interpreting and relating*, which enable an individual to interpret, explain, and relate events and documents from another culture to his/her own; *skills of discovery and interaction*, related to the acquisition of new cultural knowledge and relating it to existing knowledge, attitudes, and skills to use in cross-cultural interactions; and *critical cultural awareness* that encourages learners to reflect critically on the values, beliefs, and behaviors of their own society as compared to other societies (Byram, 1997).

Byram's model underscores the inseparability of language and culture in developing *intercultural speakers*. It does not, however, offer an integrative approach to incorporating IC into teaching practices or a coherent way of addressing the *knowledge*, *skills*, and *attitude* components of IC in the teaching curriculum. The cognitive, behavioral, and affective factors remain on the list; it is not clear how they interact with one another and with the linguistic, sociolinguistic, and discourse elements of IC (Díaz, 2013). A solution is offered by Díaz (2013), who presents the concept of critical languacultural awareness as a multilevel taxonomy of awareness levels and related skills that can be developed by addressing both language and culture learning and use in communication. Díaz distinguishes between two types of reflective skills involved in critical awareness: *consciousness* (an awareness of specific perceptions, an individual's feelings about them, assessment of the efficacy of perceptions, and an awareness of value judgments about perceptions) and *critical consciousness* (analyzing verbal and nonverbal communication cues to interpret the interlocutor's behavior; comparing, challenging, and modifying native and target cultural beliefs; accepting the negotiable nature of cultural behavior; and suspending judgment). She also recognizes different levels of awareness (basic, complex, meta-cognitive, and epistemological) and matches them with corresponding skills drawn from Bloom's taxonomy (1956). Thus, at the basic level of awareness, or *noticing*, learners need to recognize their native languaculture schemata by observing, identifying, and comparing elements of their own languaculture to those of the target language and culture. This comparison leads to *analysis*, a more complex level of consciousness, at which learners are encouraged to question their languaculture schemata. Cross-cultural comparisons lead to the critical consciousness level of meta-cognitive awareness in which learners are able to challenge cultural stereotypes by appraising cultural contrasts identified earlier. The model is cyclical in that the output of observation at the basic level of awareness feeds higher levels, which in turn serve as input for new noticing and reflection.

Critical languaculture awareness involves "learners using language in interaction to interpret and construct meaning, and analyzing and reflecting upon this experience and continuing to learn from the use of language in intercultural interactions" (Díaz, 2013, p. 48). Locating culture in language and discussing such aspects of culture as, for instance, social routines or expression of feelings and emotions, allows teachers to guide their students toward exploring both native and target languacultures. To promote critical languaculture effectively, teachers need "flexible, principled pedagogical actions" to articulate the connection between instructional goals and classroom content, appropriate materials and techniques to explicitly present various aspects of linguaculture to students, and adequate assessment tools to account for IC development (pp. 118–19).

ISSUES IN TEACHING IC

How do the existing definitions of IC inform foreign language teaching? The IC models described earlier argue for a learner-centered, interactive, collaborative classroom where students are actively involved in the process of cultural exploration. They share native and target cultural experiences, make comparisons, and critically reflect on cultural values and practices (Byram et al., 2002; Moore, 1996). The process of cultural exploration is facilitated by the instructor, who guides students through analysis and reflection. Rather than simply conveying factual information, the teacher is expected to help students discover meaning through a variety of authentic materials, monitor students' progress, and provide feedback. As teachers add open-ended questions to the discussion of an artifact or a cultural event, they invite students to notice, compare, build connections, and reflect (Liddicoat & Scarino, 2013). In practice, however, IC development remains on an abstract level with little intercultural language teaching occurring in the classroom (Liddicoat & Kohler, 2012).

Despite well-documented attempts at conceptualizing IC, classroom pedagogy for implementing IC lags behind because research offers few practical suggestions on how to develop the necessary skills and behaviors for integrating the appropriate activities into the foreign language curriculum. A number of Russian language textbooks published in the United States since 2000 (e.g., *Troika, Golosa, Nachalo*) appeal predominantly to the cognitive domain of IC, a common approach to teaching culture across languages (Pennycock, 1995; Ilieva, 2001). Colored "culture boxes" and supplemental video clips present target culture as a series of isolated facts and the distinct behaviors of an average speaker, expressing to learners what people of the target culture do in a particular situation or contemporary attitudes regarding a topic the students are studying so that they can act accordingly. But the cognitive domain, although important, is only one aspect of IC (Byram, 1997; Díaz, 2013; Spitzberg & Changnon, 2009). While it could have been assumed that the systematic account of cultural data found in textbooks would eventually be able to provide students with the information they need to deal with situations in which cultural misunderstandings can occur, Kramsch (1993) suggests that such an approach to culture can lead to stereotyping and equip students with some fixed, generalized, and inaccurate accounts of the target culture. Presenting culture in isolation and with reference to some universal target population does little to develop students' understanding of cultural phenomena; it encourages students to learn *about* the culture, not how to interact with it, which is crucial for fostering IC (Ilieva, 2001).

Further complicating the challenge of IC development is the fact that the teaching and learning of culture does not enjoy the same curricular presence as the language teaching itself. Moore's (1996) analysis of high school foreign language classes confirms the low importance of culture in the language curriculum. In his survey only 26% of teachers said they regularly include culture instruction into their lesson plans; 54% of respondents indicate that reading textbook cultural notes is their preferred way of teaching culture; 46% of teachers use authentic materials while 41% rely on lecture to convey cultural information. Although Moore's information is dated and the classroom approach to teaching culture may have changed, anecdotal evidence suggests that instructors often pay little attention to cultural information and instead concentrate on grammar and vocabulary. Even when culturally appropriate behaviors are practiced in class through role-playing, such activities mainly focus on the linguistic means of expression and omit the need to develop students' perceptions of the similarities between the two cultures. It has also been noted that cultural instruction is restricted to "the four Fs: food, fairs, folklore and statistical facts" (Kramsch, 1991, p. 218) or the fine arts (Mantle-Bromley, 1997). Generally speaking, intercultural objectives are seldom included in course syllabi because of the predominance of linguistic goals and the opinion that "language and culture cannot be taught in an integrated way" (Sercu et al., 2005, p. 164).

In order to counteract the neglected status of culture in language teaching, Díaz (2013) proposes integrating IC aspects of communication into language education by striving to achieve critical languacultural awareness by first raising learners' awareness of their own culture and its linguistic, pragmatic, and sociocultural rules, which are often unnoticed by native speakers of the language. The next step is for students to observe the differences between the native and target languacultures and to reflect on the nature of differences and modify their practices to accommodate this new input. The process of noticing, reflecting, and modifying creates a continuous cycle of acquisition, which should be integrated from the beginning stages of language learning because a delay, while still possibly resulting in culture learning, may cause a prescriptive view of the target culture. Díaz calls for purposeful and systematic embedding of critical languaculture awareness processes into the curriculum from the onset of language instruction.

As applied to classroom teaching, the theoretical model of critical languacultural awareness translates into a deeper understanding of native and target cultural practices such as greetings, eating, or leisure activities through explanation, elaborations, and reflection. Students should be encouraged to participate in constructing new cultural knowledge rather than simply processing it. For example, after reading a "cultural box" in the textbook, the class can be asked to compare Russian and American practices, ideas, and attitudes. Students who have visited Russia are invited to share their insights about the reading and the instructor offers his/her perception of the issue in question. As students discuss the generalized textbook view of the culture and the personal observations of class members, they notice that differences in cultural values depend on the social position, age, location, etc. of the speaker(s) and the complexities of native and target cultural values. They make inquiries into their own as well as the target culture by drawing meaningful cross-cultural comparisons and exploring several perspectives on a cultural topic.

Finding time for cultural discussions can be difficult in an already busy class. Many teachers feel that adding an intercultural dimension to the curriculum takes time away from teaching language that must be learned for communicative competence; they also often feel guilty for devoting time to interesting but "unnecessary" cultural discussions (Díaz, 2013, p. 123). To partially alleviate this time concern, a part or all of the discussion can be moved to online platforms available through electronic course management systems. Online discussions allow students to respond at their time and pace and allows shy students to overcome their reluctance to speak in class and contribute to the discussion. Also, many students are attracted to online discussions because of their experience with social networks (O'Dowd, 2007). Additionally, for many of the activities described here, a large part of research, analysis, and reflection can happen outside of class without interrupting regular language work. Finally, some of the cultural discussion can be conducted in English so that students can express their ideas in more depth without searching for words and sacrificing the content. While instructors generally strive for maximum use of the target language within the classroom, native language is occasionally used in a foreign language classroom to clarify a point, to cross social or ethnic boundaries, to make cultural references, or to reduce anxiety (Díaz-Rico, 2013; Kraemer, 2006). Given the predominance and inevitability of target language use in the first- and second-year classes (Comer, 2013), cultural conversations should take advantage of students' mother tongue. The discussions do not have to be long; from my experience even five minutes of class exchange of experiences and opinions creates a stimulating opportunity for students to learn about the cultural context of the language.

ISSUES IN ASSESSING IC

The difficulty of assessing IC has been noted by many researchers (Díaz, 2013; Schulz, 2007; Witte, 2014). The complexity of IC and its conceptualization through highly abstract and subjective notions such as identity transformation and attitudinal changes make it difficult to define clear IC teaching and learning sequences and to translate them into observable and measurable outcomes. There also exists a paucity of assessment instruments and lack of consensus over which form of assessment to use (Díaz, 2013; Witte, 2014). How does one evaluate empathy, for example? Perhaps because of these challenges the discussion of assessment is absent from many publications describing IC activities and projects. In addition, IC assessment can also be susceptible to subjectivity on the part of both learners and the instructor (Lázár, 2007). On the one hand, students may not be used to self-evaluation and reflection and thus they lack the cognitive and affective skills needed to gauge their IC. On the other hand, instructors "cannot be neutral on cultural issues since they respond to other cultures as human beings and not just as language teachers" (Byram et al., 2002, p. 30). Factors such as age, gender, and social status can also affect one's judgment of IC.

How can teachers achieve a reliable assessment of students' IC, including their knowledge, abilities, and beliefs? Typical educational assessment distinguishes between traditional (assessment of learning) and alternative (assessment for learning) paradigms, both of which can be applied to IC. The former emphasizes the cognitive aspect of knowledge and tests students' ability to acquire, store, and recall knowledge in a test situation. Students respond to test items with no intervention from the teacher and receive feedback in the form of a grade after the evaluation is complete, i.e., when they are studying for the next test. Although traditional assessment involves some subjective interpretation and modification of attitude as seen in one's acceptance of target cultural values, it does little to provide insight into the transformation of the identity of the learner, which is expected of the more-highly-developed levels of IC. Tests of this kind measure one's familiarity with cultural information that is "only superficially internalized and has no lasting effect on emotional or attitudinal domains of the learners. Therefore, [teachers] are hardly in a position to validly and comprehensively facilitate or evaluate the development of [a] genuine third place on the part of the learners" (Witte, 2014, p. 388).

Alternative assessment is based on the social-constructivist view of learning (Vygotsky, 1978). Social-constructivism in the classroom encourages learners not so much to pick up facts from the incoming stream of information but rather to inject their personal inner selves into the learning process, which involves a change of the learners' subjective attitudes and opinions. The primary concern of alternative assessment is the dynamic progress of the personal learning process, which is believed to be driven by socially created subjective intentions, social interactions, and discourse (Brown, 2007). The alternative paradigm focuses on teaching practice and the learning process as much as on assessing them. It recognizes the active role played by learners in assessment processes and constructs outcomes representing summaries of learner competencies that are detailed, descriptive, and informative (Fox, 2008, p. 102). In view of this approach to assessment, Liddicoat and Scarino (2013) pronounce the alternative paradigm to be more suitable for assessing IC in language because it is "inherently social and cultural, and includes a process of interpretation and seeking to make sense of the learning" (p. 137). Alternative assessment incorporates both summative and formative assessment; it is an ongoing dynamic practice that allows for a variety of formats and emphasizes the product as well as the process of learning. On a classroom level, alternative assessment includes all teacher and student activities (e.g., teacher observation, classroom discussion, analysis of homework and tests) that yield information that can be used to diagnose strengths and weaknesses and change teaching and learning accordingly (Black & William, 1998).

While traditional assessments that use multiple choice, matching, fill-in-the-blanks, or complete-a-sentence tests remain an important means of measuring student progress in discrete-item terms, alternative assessments complement traditional formats by focusing on meaning rather than on form, documenting the process rather than the product of learning (including peer assessment and group tasks), and reflecting real-life conditions of language use. Alternative assessment (e.g., self-reports, dialogues between students, interviews with other students or adults) can be integrated into everyday class activities and become a natural part of the learning process. To develop criteria for assessing IC development it is useful to draw on one of the existing IC models to measure what students can do. Díaz (2013) and Liddicoat and Scarino (2013) identify some indicators of progress that can be used in formulating the learning outcomes that reflect the interconnection of the important dimensions of IC such as knowledge, skills, and attitudes. Thus students should be expected to recognize, observe, and describe Russian cultural events, norms, and values (noticing); compare, classify, and explain the differences between Russian and American cultures (analysis); assess, value, and understand Russian cultural beliefs, attitudes, and perspectives (evaluation); and question, reflect on, and explain assumptions about their own culture as well as Russian cultural norms (reflection).

To obtain a record of students' progress toward IC goals instructors can create IC performance criteria and assign numeric values to represent different levels of performance. The Intercultural Knowledge and Competence VALUE Rubric (Association of American Colleges and Universities, 2010) is a good example of an IC assessment that could be adapted for specific classroom needs. Setting assessment rubrics makes IC expectations transparent and defines success criteria in explicit terms. The score provides a quantifiable and summative measure of learning; it can also be used formatively to garner evidence of students' IC knowledge and skills, to give an insight into individual IC processes, and to serve as a guide for student improvement. The IC assessment targets should complement linguistic objectives in planning instructional activities to support instructors and students in teaching and learning language and culture.

At the same time, commercial testing materials that accompany Russian language textbooks do little to capture the many facets of IC and the complex ongoing processes of its development. The test banks in the popular Russian textbooks *Nachalo, Golosa,* and *V puti* focus predominantly on language. They reflect the cognitive approach to teaching culture usually adopted in textbooks by asking factual questions, e.g., Кто такой Мусоргский? [Who is Musorgsky?], which provide little opportunity for intercultural reflection. Unless textbook tests are supplemented with additional resources and activities to support IC learning outcomes, instructors have no effective way of monitoring IC development. And yet, given the undisputable role of culture in language learning, assessment of IC should parallel the assessment of language progress itself. Including IC assessment into instructional goals highlights its importance for students and aligns outcomes with instruction.

CONNECTING THEORY AND PRACTICE

To foster IC development the author has incorporated the activities described here into beginning and intermediate Russian classes. A concerted effort has been made to coordinate language goals with IC goals and to include both in teaching and assessment. While similar activities are often used in language learning classrooms to promote teaching culture, the present examples connect learning about Russian cultural practices with understanding and interpreting Russian and American cultural values. The activities include the goals of noticing, analyzing, evaluating, and reflecting on cultural perspectives and invite students to observe and explore the target culture, contemplate cultural similarities and differences, and begin to develop IC understanding and skills in the context of language learning while granting the instructor flexibility in monitoring and evaluating their IC growth using an alternative assessment paradigm. Although no qualitative data are available at this point, teacher observations and student comments from course evaluations suggest evidence of emerging intercultural awareness (and are quoted where appropriate).

Telecollaboration Projects

Telecollaboration is a popular way of fostering IC development. It involves "the application of global computer networks to foreign and second-language learning and teaching in institutionalized settings" (Belz, 2003, p. 2). Its use for foreign language and culture learning is supported by research that highlights such positive effects as the development of oral and written communication skills, improved motivation, promotion of student-centered learning, opportunity for equal participation, and the satisfaction students experience from learning about a target culture (Liaw, 1998; Gonglewski et al., 2001; Ware, 2005).

These benefits inspired a "key-pal" project for an Intermediate Russian class in which eight American college students were paired with Russian eleventh graders from the city of Tula for weekly e-mail exchanges with the dual purpose of building language skills and advancing IC. Students first interviewed each other to get acquainted and discuss topics of mutual interest (schoolwork, music, sports, movies), and then asked each other preselected questions about culture that had been generated in a brainstorming session based on Schenker's (2012) and Vinagre's (2007) suggestions and tied to the class topic. While Russian key-pals were proficient enough to discuss both personal and cultural topics in English, Americans used Russian for familiar everyday topics and English for cultural discussion, which considerably increased their input and understanding of cultural matters. A minimum of two e-mails per week were required. The American students were required to participate in a weekly online discussion through the Blackboard course management system to share what they had learned about and from their partners and how that experience had contributed to or changed their previous understanding of Russia and Russians. To support the intercultural goals of the activity students were asked to respond to specific questions, such as "Did the e-mail exchange provide any insights into Russia as well as your own cultural rules and biases?," "How did it affect your beliefs about Russian as well as American culture?," and "Did you discover any significant differences between Russian and American cultures?" The following excerpt from a student online discussion illustrates how the interaction with a Russian peer inspired intercultural observation, evaluation, and comparison:

> One of the things I noticed were strong family ties. When I graduated high school I was expected to move out of the house and figure things out. I learned that Marina and most of her friends over there would live with their families until marriage. Also, I learned that the older generation would live back with their children when they retired. It seemed to me that Russian families definitely have more of a say in each others' lives and would give and seek advice far more than many of my American friends.

A three-minute individual presentation at the end of the quarter afforded the American students another opportunity to make connections between the native and the target cultures and to reflect on their discoveries and how their view of Russia had changed. The key-pal project was graded on a completion/noncompletion basis as a part of the regular homework for the American students, while weekly online discussions and the final presentation allowed for dynamic ongoing assessment, feedback, and guidance. The course evaluations reveal that students appreciate the opportunities to engage in IC activities: "The best thing was that we were talking with real people, not some textbook characters" and "Learned a lot about Russians and it changed my outlook completely." These student statements indicate the beginning of the attitude transformation, an important step toward IC. Students also state that they "now have language [actual words and expressions] to talk about complex topics like cultural stereotyping in Russian."

While a key-pal exchange is probably the least technologically and logistically complicated way of fostering IC, there are many other ways in which telecollaboration can be used to achieve linguistic and intercultural goals. As modern technology affords a variety of communication platforms, many instructors use Skype, WIKI technology, Google Plus and Hangouts, audio-conferencing, discussion boards, and virtual learning environments such as Moodle to organize online exchanges between groups of students; many projects combine several communication tools for maximum student benefit (e.g., Chase & Alexander, 2007; Kourova, 2013; O'Dowd, 2007).

Proverbs and Sayings

Proverbs are often used to teach culture to foreign language students because of the significant role they play in everyday life. Many scholars believe that studying folklore can help establish cross-cultural understanding based on respect for differences and acknowledgment of similarities (Gholson & Stumpf, 2005).

The Proverbs and Sayings project in the second-year Russian class seeks to integrate intercultural awareness into language work. This activity has two goals. To meet language development objectives, students are asked to produce written texts in the target language incorporating new vocabulary items. The cultural objectives include familiarizing students with an important part of Russian culture beyond the textbook and developing appreciation for the depth of content, imagery, and folk wisdom of Russian proverbs. To make the cultural objectives explicit, the assignment specifically asks students to explore the Russian cultural values reflected in the proverbs and discuss if any of these values are shared by American people as expressed in American sayings. The project constitutes 15% of the final grade: 10% for students' original writing (regularity of posts, grammatical accuracy, vocabulary variety, and attention to culture) and 5% for commenting on classmates' posts. Points are awarded for substantial comments that address the cultural values and symbols found in the proverbs and/or provide some cross-cultural comparison.

After looking at examples of Russian and American proverbs and sayings and discussing their definitions, the difference between idioms and colloquialisms, and their cultural role, students receive a list of websites to find Russian proverbs and sayings. Alternatively, they can search for «русские народные пословицы и поговорки» [Russian folk proverbs and sayings] to find a saying that they like. Their task is to provide an English equivalent or a passable translation (asking native speakers for help or checking the Internet if necessary) and describing a situation in Russian—either real or imagined—in which a particular proverb could be used. Students are also required to read and comment on their classmates' entries. The instructor corrects grammar and vocabulary and comments on the cultural aspect of the entry by asking questions about American culture, offering insights, and noting the popularity of some proverbs (Без труда не выловишь и рыбку из пруда [No pain, no gain]) versus others (Рукам–работа, душе–праздник [When the hands work, the soul rejoices]).

The project uses the WIKI function of the Blackboard course management system because of its collaborative writing capability. A sample proverb entry is provided to clarify the expectations (see Appendix A here). Students post a new entry every week using Russian for all project-related communication. According to course evaluations, students find the assignment challenging but enjoyable and praise its benefits for both the language learning and the understanding of culture. They note the focus on spiritual rather than material aspects of the Russian person, the importance of hard work, the acceptance of responsibility, and the values of communalism, optimism, and friendship typical of the Russian culture. Many students comment on Christian images associated with Russian Orthodox tradition (бог [God], божий [God's], and Господь [Lord]). They refer to equivalent American sayings and shared cultural values of family, religion, and hard work and thereby consider their own language and cultural backgrounds. Some say that now they use Russian proverbs while they speak English, which makes them feel more Russian.

Russian Paintings

Another project that combines language and culture learning and presents sufficient assessment opportunities is devoted to Russian art. The study of the artistic expression of ideas, emotions, and opinions can be an important way of understanding the Russian cultural canon and its reflection of the national consciousness. Yet it is rarely explored in Russian language textbooks.

Once the instructor has introduced the project by inviting the class to discuss the cultural significance of art, has explained the requirements and the evaluation criteria, and has shown a sample text, students receive a list of links to Russian paintings from different periods and genres (Appendix B). The choice of paintings is determined by the clear narrative content of the pieces, i.e., it has an action, situation, or event that can be described in concrete terms. Students pair up to research a painting, the artist, and the historical context. They use Russian to present their findings in class; each pair member has three minutes to speak. Their presentations should include three grammatical tenses, be accompanied by a visual aid in the form of slides or a poster, and be spoken rather than read. In a question-and-answer session after each presentation students note intercultural similarities and contrasts (e.g., meals; attitude to wars and territory expansion in both Russian and American cultures) as well as comment on their own cultural assumptions. The teacher uses this opportunity for formative assessment, providing additional input and feedback, which complements the summative evaluation based on the rubric (Appendix C).

Course evaluations show that students see the main advantage of the project is in working with authentic materials: it allows them to gain knowledge, interpret ideas, become aware of the values behind the paintings, and expand their own cultural base.

Blogging

Blogs have become a popular and universal means of self-expression. One way of using blogging in foreign language teaching is to organize and make sense of one's cultural observations (Bartz & Vermette, 1996) during study abroad. As students write blogs they describe encounters with native speakers and places, often accompanying their stories with pictures. Remarkably, students' accounts, no matter how detailed and passionate, seldom extend from noticing cultural phenomena and patterns of communication to evaluation, analysis, and reflection associated with IC. To bring intercultural awareness to a new level, bloggers need to be reminded to write critically and to include reflective analysis in their descriptions of their experiences with the target culture. This reflection provides an opportunity for students to deal with the intercultural aspects of communication in a conscious way by considering the target language perspective and developing their own voices. The following excerpts, from recent study abroad blogs written by the author's students, capture the process of intercultural comparison (1), evaluation (2), acceptance of the Russian cultural norms (3), and adapting one's own behaviors accordingly (4). (These aspects are referenced using the corresponding numbers that appear in the texts.)

> I find the difference between the contrasting ideas of a "public persona" striking. Obviously how we look and act and speak when in public (on the street, in a grocery store, waiting for a train, etc.) varies throughout the different regions of America, but in Saint Petersburg I find the public persona to be very cold by American standards (1). People do not look at each other, smile, say greetings, or ask "How are you?" at the store. The cashier is impatient and verging on rude (2) when you forget to weigh and tag your produce. There is no obligation to make eye contact with someone you pass on the street (2). I learned to keep my gaze down or straight ahead and not to expect those verbal exchanges between myself and a stranger (4). I found this strange at first, but now it is comfortable for me (3) and even better than the American model of pretending to care (1, 2).

> I went to the greenhouse and arboretum yesterday. The attendant for tickets had the typical air of "hurry up and move along" (2) when I asked for a ticket, but once she understood it was my first time there, she carefully (and even happily) explained about the tours through the greenhouse and exactly which ticket I should buy. I love how when I engage with a Russian person beyond the most commonplace interactions, they are warm, kind, and helpful (3).

Although a study abroad blog is not a required curricular activity, many students appreciate narrating their experiences for a real-life audience and reading subsequent comments. Once the instructor receives an invitation to read a student's blog, she asks for permission to share it with her class and encourages the writer to reflect on the IC experiences abroad. Individual blogs have several uses in a Russian class. Blogs are read by the authors' US classmates, who write comments and questions to their posts in English or Russian. Reading their peers' record of cultural encounters and reactions allows students to gain valuable cultural information as well as learn about the writer's perspective on a given topic. Blog entries can spark a class discussion on culture; some intercultural exchanges presented in posts can be acted out in a role-play (e.g., the greetings and the greenhouse tour scenarios described above). More important, a blogs afford the instructor a unique glimpse of the writer's development of IC as well as ample opportunities for formative assessment, feedback, and guidance through the blog's comment function.

In addition to the project-length activities described above, IC learning and assessment opportunities can be built into everyday language work. Further activities are familiar to teachers and students as common means of facilitating and assessing aural, oral, and written skills. To strengthen the IC component, linguistic work should be supplemented by deliberate comparison, discussion, and explanation of how culture is reflected in the language use. These formats provide enough flexibility to address different aspects of linguistic and cultural knowledge; once filled with appropriate content, they can be integrated into any unit of study.

Guest Speakers

Inviting guest speakers into a language classroom is a popular means of connecting language and culture in a meaningful way. An interview with a native Russian speaker meets linguistic as well as IC objectives: as students engage in cross-cultural communication, they practice language for authentic purposes, gain firsthand insight into the life of a target language speaker, and enhance their understanding of the two cultures. To prepare for a Skype or an in-person interview, students could receive an assignment worksheet as adapted from Díaz (2013). The first student task is to draw up a list of questions, discussion points, and relevant language expressions, which is then circulated via e-mail to avoid grammatical mistakes and repetitive questions. Preparing questions in advance allows students to identify and formulate their individual interest in the target culture. Some common questions, such as "What do you think our people have in common? How could you describe a typical Russian? What should I know if I want to make Russian friends?," show students' interest in intercultural understanding. In the second assignment, completed after the interview and based on their notes and recordings, students write vocabulary notes, giving a meaning and a sample sentence for five new words they have encountered. The third task is to summarize the interview in Russian. The fourth part is a purposeful intercultural analysis in English, asking students to explore aspects of Russian culture they noticed during the interview and to reflect on how the new information modifies their previous knowledge and beliefs about Russia and their own culture (Appendix D). Programming a reflective component into the activity facilitates the development of critical intercultural awareness through students' individual reactions and interpretations and reveals the subtle matter of cultural attitudes that otherwise might have gone unnoticed.

The formative and/or summative assessment of the guest speaker interview activity (Appendix D) reflects a twofold linguistic and IC objective. The assessment criteria include

- ◇ student questions (both open-ended and cultural; sufficient number of discussion points and vocabulary expressions);
- ◇ vocabulary (correctness of structure; completeness of notes);
- ◇ summary (main points of the discussion included; correctness of vocabulary and structure);
- ◇ intercultural analysis (evidence of noticing, questioning, connecting the two cultures).

Asking Questions about Culture

Familiar language-learning activities, such as true/false and multiple-choice questions, can lead to an intercultural discussion when they accompany an audio or video document that students observe for sociolinguistic behaviors (Bartz & Vermette, 1996). First, students listen to a conversation and check their comprehension by answering true-false questions or completing a multiple-choice task. Second, the class analyzes the expressions of culture in the language of the audio/video document. For example, the form "about seven o'clock" in the sample dialogue (Appendix E) is a typical Russian way of conveying an approximate rather than exact time of meeting. It signifies Russians' somewhat relaxed attitude toward time, as compared to American punctuality (Richmond, 2003; Sergeeva, 2006). The discussion of the language-culture connection should complement language work; it can highlight other expressions used in the same function, as well as possible cultural motives behind linguistic behavior, and can suggest an appropriate reaction in case of misunderstanding. The deliberate inclusion of intercultural objectives along with linguistic ones ensures that students not only understand the text but also critically engage with native and target cultural notions such as politeness, time, social distance, etc.

Short-answer/essay-type questions can be used with textual, visual, and auditory input. By varying the type of questions (e.g., closed, open, referential) teachers can address different aspects of knowledge and access students' comprehension of and adaptability to distinct patterns of behavior in the target culture. For example, a visual example of an authentic cultural situation (Bartz & Vermette, 1996) can entail such questions as "What are the people doing/saying?," "Why do you think they are doing it?," or "What would an American do in this situation?" Students' oral or written responses can lead to a class discussion of cultural dimensions of a social situation or be used for assessment.

Scenario-Based Activities

The need to resolve conflict situations or critical incidents is one type of activity that is based on cross-cultural interactions that may cause negative assumptions about the target culture (Bartz & Vermette, 1996). For example, a Russian student asks her American friend for help with a test at a US university. When the friend refuses, she feels confused and hurt. Or a student is invited to a dinner hosted by a Russian family and feels obligated to eat large quantities of food out of fear of offending the hosts. Still another potential conflict situation arises when asking questions about money and salary, which is quite acceptable from the Russian point of view but is considered a private matter in American culture.

There are several ways to use critical incidents in a language class. When given a prompt containing a conflict situation, students can provide responses orally or in writing, describing how a situation might be resolved. They can develop the critical incident into a story or act it out in a role-play. Critical incident activities provide an opportunity for a subjective interpretation of a situation, for verbalization of an individualized reaction, and for exercising tolerance and the skill of negotiating a potential conflict situation, all in the target language. As students explain the source of misinterpretation and develop an acceptable solution to the problem, they arrive at a deeper understanding of American and Russian cultural assumptions.

Role-plays may involve conflict situations as well as the general practice of culturally appropriate conventions and situations students may encounter (e.g., requests and invitations). To facilitate intercultural awareness, the cultural aspect of the textbook or teacher-designed situation needs to be emphasized. Thus a role-play on making requests can refer to the fact that repeating one's request and continuing to talk to an employee or official even after receiving a negative answer may bring the desired result. In an activity focusing on making and responding to compliments, learners act out a Russian reaction of appearing slightly embarrassed and refuting praise with a denial of what has been said. A role-play of a host and a house guest situation should include a host insistently offering drinks or food and a guest not accepting the offer right away. A role-play followed by an analysis of the social dynamics of the situation and the cultural values expressed in it helps increase students' intercultural awareness and allows students to relate language and culture in a meaningful way.

CONCLUSION

Increasing IC is an important mandate of foreign language teaching in today's global world. A number of theoretical IC models have identified awareness of one's values and beliefs regarding the native and target culture and one's attitude transformation as crucial characteristics of interculturality. Modern approaches to IC emphasize the effect of a continuous cycle of noticing, analyzing, and reflecting on the interplay of the two cultures for IC development (Díaz, 2013; Liddicoat & Scarino, 2013). But cultural exploration and reflection processes cannot be simply appended to a language course; IC development should be purposefully integrated into language-learning activities in and out of the classroom. Language teachers need to create opportunities for students to engage with Russian and American cultures beyond the presentation of facts and objects by using students' individual perceptions, critical analysis, and interpretation. A concerted effort should be made to invite students to examine their beliefs and develop appreciation of their own culture at the same time as they gain insights into the target one and learn the language that expresses it.

The systematic inclusion of an IC dimension into the language curriculum requires a substantial investment of time and effort. However, the importance of meeting the national standard of producing interculturally competent speakers of Russian makes IC development an imperative for language educators (NSCB, 2015). This chapter has given an example of how IC can be developed and assessed in a Russian language classroom using well-known activities and projects and provided recommendations for raising Russian students' intercultural awareness by combining language work with analysis, comparison, and reflection on the native and target cultures. These activities bring into focus students' own perceptions of intercultural contexts while allowing the instructor to evaluate students' emerging IC skills within the alternative assessment paradigm. Formulating specific IC learning objectives makes intercultural goals explicit for both teachers and learners, adds transparency to the relationship between language and culture, and supports ongoing alternative assessment. It is hoped that expanding the language curriculum to include cross-cultural activities will "inform and guide the deliberate fostering of subjective IC in the L2 classroom and beyond" (Witte, 2014, p. 323).

APPENDIX A: SAMPLE PROVERB ENTRY

Мы с сестрой очень похожи, но нам нравятся абсолютно разные вещи. Я не люблю смотреть телевизор, а сестра все время смотрит сериалы. Она любит ездить на машине, а я – ходить пешком. Я люблю классическую музыку, а сестре нравится рок. Она интересуется модой, а я – театром. Только одно увлечение у нас общее – кроссворды. Мы всегда решаем их вместе, потому что одна голова хорошо, а две лучше!

APPENDIX B: RUSSIAN PAINTINGS RECOMMENDED FOR CLASS USE

Виктор Васнецов. *С квартиры на квартиру*
Илья Глазунов. *Русские идут!*
Василий Кандинский. *Всадник Святой Георгий*
Александр Лактионов. *Письмо с фронта.*
Юрий Пименов. *Лирическое новоселье*
Василий Пукирев. *Неравный брак*
Илья Репин. *Иван Грозный и его сын Иван*
Илья Репин. *Не ждали*
Илья Репин. *Запорожцы пишут письмо турецкому султану*
Федор Решетников. *Опять двойка*
Зинаида Серебрякова. *За завтраком*
Василий Суриков. *Покорение Сибири Ермаком*
Марк Шагал. *Над городом*
Татьяна Яблонская. *Утро*

APPENDIX C: EVALUATION CHECKLIST—RUSSIAN PAINTINGS

TABLE 15.2. Evaluation Checklist: Russian Paintings

Criterion	Score
1. **Developing and sequencing** Creatively developed; many details; entertaining	0 1 2 3 4 5
2. **Language structure** Consistent and accurate verb conjugations and usage of case endings and verb tenses; minor errors do not affect the ability to communicate	0 1 2 3 4 5
3. **Delivery** Effortless and smooth, no unnatural pauses; effective visual aids	0 1 2 3 4 5
4. **Pronunciation and intonation** Mostly correct with only minor flaws	0 1 2 3 4 5
5. **Vocabulary** Accurate, diverse, and creative usage; minor errors do not affect the ability to communicate	0 1 2 3 4 5
6. **Culture** Demonstrated understanding of the history, culture, values, and customs behind the chosen painting	0 1 2 3 4 5
7. **Group work** All group members participated in all components of the project, including final presentation	0 1 2 3 4 5

APPENDIX D: GUEST SPEAKER INTERVIEW WORKSHEET

We will interview a Russian guest speaker in class on [date]. The interview will be a good opportunity for you to speak Russian in a real communication with a native speaker and to learn about Russian culture. To make the most of the visit please do the following:

1. BEFORE THE INTERVIEW: Make a list of at least five questions, three discussion points, and five to eight relevant language expressions you would like to use during the interview. Your questions should be in Russian; include both open-ended (What is your opinion on . . .) and culture questions. E-mail your list to others in the class to avoid repetitive questions and topics.
2. DURING THE INTERVIEW: Record the interview and take notes to complete parts 3–5 of the worksheet.
3. AFTER THE INTERVIEW: Recall whether you encountered any unknown words in the interview. Choose five new words that you would like to learn. For each of them:
   - Write the Russian word and its part of speech (you might also include gender for nouns and I or II conjugation for verbs);
   - Write the most concise definition for the word;
   - Write a sample sentence using this word.
4. AFTER THE INTERVIEW: Write a summary of the interview in Russian.
5. AFTER THE INTERVIEW: Reflect (in English) on your interactions with the guest speaker. Some questions to consider are:
   - What did you find interesting?
   - Did you observe any behaviors, communication patterns, or perspectives specific to Russian culture?
   - What were your feelings and reactions to those?
   - How does Russian culture compare with American culture?
   - What did you learn today about Russian culture?
   - What aspects of American culture became more visible for you in your interactions with the guest speaker?
   - How does what you've learned change or add to what you already know about Russians?
   - What else would you like to learn about Russian culture?
   - How are you going to apply what you learned today outside the classroom?

APPENDIX E: SAMPLE DIALOGUE AND TRUE-FALSE QUESTIONS

(Phone rings)
А: Алло?
[Hello?]
Б: Привет, это Наташа. Ты мне звонил?
[Hi, this is Natasha. Did you call me?]
А: Да, я хотел пригласить тебя на концерт нашей группы.
[Yes, I would like to invite you to our rock band's concert.]
Б: Спасибо, с удовольствием. А когда?
[Thank you, I'd love to (attend). And when?]
А: В четверг. Давай встретимся часов в семь у метро.
[On Thursday. Let's meet at the metro station at about seven.]
Б: Договорились.
[Agreed.]

1. Правда или неправда? Эти два человека знакомы.
   [True or false? These two people know each other.]
2. Правда или неправда? Павел приглашает Наташу в театр.
   [True or false? Pavel invites Natasha to a theater.]
3. Правда или неправда? Концерт начинается в семь часов.
   [True or false? The concert begins at 7 o'clock.]

REFERENCES

American Council on the Teaching of Foreign Languages (ACTFL). (2014). ACTFL global competence position statement. Retrieved from www.actfl.org/news/position-statements/global-competence-position-statement

Association of American Colleges and Universities (AACU). 2010. Intercultural Knowledge and Competence VALUE Rubric. Retrieved from https://www.aacu.org/value/rubrics/intercultural-knowledge

Bartz, W., & Vermette, R. (1996). Testing cultural competence. In A. J. Singerman (Ed.), *Acquiring cross-cultural competence: Four stages for students of French* (pp. 75–84). Lincolnwood, IL: National Textbook.

Belz, J. A. (2003). From the special issue editor. *Language Learning and Technology*, 7(2). Retrieved from llt.msu.edu/vol7num2/speced.html

Bennett, J. (1993). Towards ethnorelativism: A developmental model of intercultural sensibility. In R. M. Paige (Ed.), *Education for the intercultural experience* (pp. 21–71). Yarmouth, ME: Intercultural.

Black, P., & William, D. (1998). Inside the black box: Raising standards through classroom assessment. *Phi Delta Kappa, 80*(2), 139–48.

Bloom, B. S. (1956). *Taxonomy of educational objectives: The classification of educational goals.* New York: Longmans, Green.

Brown, H. D. (2007). *Principles of language learning and teaching* (5th ed.). New York: Pearson Education.

Byram, M. (1997). *Teaching and assessing intercultural communicative competence.* London, UK: Multilingual Matters.

Byram, M. (2009). Intercultural competence in foreign languages: The intercultural speaker and the pedagogy of foreign language education. In D. Deardorff (Ed.), *The SAGE Handbook of Intercultural Competence* (pp. 321–32). Thousand Oaks, CA: SAGE.

Byram, M., Gribkova, B., & Starkey, H. (2002). *Developing the intercultural dimension in language teaching: A practical introduction for teachers.* Strasbourg, France: Council of Europe.

Chapelle, C. A. (2010). If intercultural competence is the goal, what are the materials? *Proceedings of Intercultural Competence Conference, August 2010, 1,* 27–50. Retrieved from cercll.arizona.edu/_media/development/conferences/2010_icc/chapelle.pdf

Chase, C., & Alexander, P. (2007). The Japan-Korea culture exchange project. In R. O'Dowd (Ed.), *Online intercultural exchange: An introduction for foreign language teachers* (pp. 259–64). Clevedon, UK: Multilingual Matters.

Comer, W. (2013). Thinking through teacher talk: Increasing target language use in the beginning Russian classroom. *Russian Language Journal, 63,* 91–112.

Deardorff, D. (2006). Identification and assessment of intercultural competence as a student outcome of internalization. *Journal of Studies in International Education, 10*(3), 241–66.

Díaz, A. (2013). *Developing critical languaculture pedagogies in higher education.* London: Multilingual Matters.

Díaz-Rico, L. (2013). *Strategies for teaching English learners.* Upper Saddle River, NJ: Pearson.

Fantini, A. (2009). Assessing intercultural competence: Issues and tools. In D. Deardorff (Ed.), *The SAGE handbook of intercultural competence* (pp. 456–76). Thousand Oaks, CA: SAGE.

Fonseca-Greber, B. (2010). Social obstacles to intercultural competence in America's language classrooms. *Proceedings of Intercultural Competence Conference, August 2010, 1,* 102–23. Retrieved from http://cercll.arizona.edu/_media/development/conferences/2010_icc/fonseca_greber.pdf

Fox, J. (2008). Alternative assessment. In E. Shohamy & N. H. Hornberger (Eds.), *Encyclopedia of language and education*, Vol. 7, *Language testing and assessment* (pp. 97–109). New York: Springer and Business Media.

Gholson, R., & Stumpf, C. A. (2005). Folklore, literature, ethnography, and second language acquisition: Teaching culture in the ESL classroom. *TESL Canada Journal, 22*(2), 75–91.

Gonglewski, M., Meloni, C., & Brant, J. (2001). Using e-mail in foreign language teaching: Rationale and suggestions. *Internet TESL Journal,* 7(3), 1–12.

Gudykunst, W. B. (1998). Applying the anxiety/uncertainty management (AUM) theory to intercultural adjustment training. *International Journal of Intercultural Relations, 22*(2), 227–50.

Ilieva, R. (2001). Living with ambiguity: Toward culture exploration in adult second-language classrooms. *TESL Canada Journal, 19*(1), 1–16.

Kagan, O., Miller, F., & Kudyma, G. (2005). *V puti: Russian Grammar in Context.* Upper Saddle River, NJ: Pearson.

Kourova, A. (2013). Connecting classrooms: Russian language teaching project at UCF. *Russian Language Journal, 63,* 79–91.

Kraemer, A. (2006). Teachers' use of English in communicative German language classrooms: A qualitative analysis. *Foreign Language Annals, 39*(3), 435–50.

Kramsch, C. (1991). Culture in language learning: A view from the States. In K. DeBot, R. B. Ginsberg, & C. Kramsch (Eds.), *Foreign language research in crosscultural perspective* (pp. 217–40). Amsterdam: J. Benjamins.

Kramsch, C. (1993). *Context and culture in language teaching.* Oxford: Oxford UP.

Lázár, I. (2007). Developing and assessing intercultural communicative competence. *Babylonia, 3,* 9–13.

Liaw, M.-L. (1998). Using electronic mail for English as a foreign language instruction. *System, 26*(3), 335–51.

Liddicoat, A. J., & Kohler, M. (2012). Teaching Asian languages from an intercultural perspective: Building bridges for and with students of Indonesia. In X. Song & K. Cadman (Eds.), *Another pedagogy is possible: Bridging transcultural divides through Asian studies and languages* (pp. 73–100). Adelaide, Australia: University of Adelaide Press.

Liddicoat, A. J., & Scarino, A. (2013). *Intercultural language teaching and learning.* Oxford, UK: Wiley-Blackwell.

Lubensky, S. (2000). *Nachalo.* New York: McGraw-Hill.

Mantle-Bromley, C. (1997). Preparing students for meaningful culture learning. In P. R. Heusinkveld (Ed.), *Pathways to culture* (pp. 437–60). Yarmouth, ME: Intercultural.

Modern Language Association (MLA). (2007). Foreign languages and higher education: New structures for a changed world. Retrieved from www.mla.org/pdf/forlang_news_pdf

Moore, Z. (1996). Culture: How do teachers teach it? In Z. Moore (Ed.), *Foreign language teacher education: Multiple perspectives* (pp. 269–88). Lanham, MD: University Press of America.

National Standards Collaborative Board (NSCB). (2015). *World-readiness standards for learning languages* (4th ed.). Alexandria, VA: Author.

Nummikoski, M. (2011). *Troika: A communicative approach to Russian language, life, and culture*. Hoboken, NJ: Wiley.

O'Dowd, R. (2007). Online intercultural exchange: An introduction for foreign language teachers. Clevedon, UK: Multilingual Matters.

Paige, R. M., Jorstad, H. L., Siaya, L., Klein, F., & Colby, J. (2003). Culture learning in language education: A review of the literature. In D. L. Lange & R. M. Paige (Eds.), *Culture as the core: Perspectives on culture in second language learning* (pp. 173–236). Greenwich, CT: Information Age.

Pennycock, A. (1995). English in the world/The world in English. In J. W. Tollefson (Ed.), *Power and inequality in language education* (pp. 34–58). Cambridge: Cambridge UP.

Richmond, Y. (2003). *From Nyet to Da: Understanding the Russians*. Yarmouth, ME: Intercultural.

Robin, R., Evans-Romaine, K., Shatalina, G. (2011). *Golosa: A basic course in Russian*. Upper Saddle River, NJ: Pearson / Prentice Hall.

Schenker, T. (2012). Intercultural competence and cultural learning through telecollaboration. *Calico Journal, 29*(3), 449–70.

Schulz, R. (2007). The challenge of assessing cultural understanding in the context of foreign language instruction. *Foreign Language Annals, 40*(1), 9–26.

Sercu, L. E., Bandura, P., Castro, L., Davcheva, C., Laskaridou, U., Lundgren, M. C., Méndez García, D., & Ryan, P. (2005). *Foreign language teachers and intercultural competence: An international investigation*. London: Multilingual Matters.

Sergeeva, A. V. (2006). *Какие мы, русские*? [What are we Russians like?] Moscow: Russkij Jazyk.

Sinicrope, C., Norris, J., & Watanabe, Y. (2007). Understanding and assessing intercultural competence: A summary of theory, research, and practice. *Second Language Studies, 26*(1), 1–58.

Spitzberg, B. H., & Changnon, G. (2009). Conceptualizing intercultural competence. In D. Deardorff (Ed.), *The SAGE handbook of intercultural competence* (pp. 2–53). Thousand Oaks, CA: SAGE.

Vinagre, M. (2007). Integrating tandem learning in higher education. In R. O'Dowd (Ed.), *Online intercultural exchange: An introduction for foreign language teachers* (pp. 240–50). Clevedon, UK: Multilingual Matters.

Vygotsky, L. S. (1978). *Mind in society: The development of higher psychological processes.* M. Cole, V. John-Steiner, S. Scribner, & E. Souberman (Eds.). Cambridge, MA: Oxford UP.

Ware, P. (2005). "Missed" communication in online communication: Tensions in a German-American collaboration. *Language Learning and Technology, 9*(2), 64–89.

Witte, A. (2014). *Blending spaces.* Boston: Walter de Gruyter.

16
THE LITERARY CANON AND PRECEDENT TEXTS IN TEACHING RUSSIAN LANGUAGE AND CULTURE AT THE INTERMEDIATE LEVEL

Tatiana Smorodinska

THE PLACE OF LITERARY TEXTS IN THE RUSSIAN CURRICULUM

The *Report to the Teagle Foundation on the Undergraduate Major in Language and Literature* (MLA, 2009) underlines the close connection between language and literature: "Without language there is no communication, speculative thought, or community; without literature, there is no in-depth understanding of narratives that lead to the discovery of other cultures in their specificities and diversity and to the understanding of other human beings in their similarities and differences." Indeed, if the goal of foreign language (FL) instruction in the 21st century is to achieve "translingual and transcultural competence" (Geisler et al., 2007) and students are expected to meet the World-Readiness Standards for Learning Languages (Communication, Cultures, Connections, Comparisons, and Communities), literature study plays a crucial role in the process (NSCB, 2015). However, according to the 2007 MLA report (Geisler et al.), the present structure of most university foreign language curricula, in which a two- or three-year language sequence is followed by a set of courses on literature, usually in translation, is not sufficient to achieve the desired level of competence.

According to Bernhardt (2011), "after the Second World War, when the oral approach to language learning was seen to be of a value, reading then became a subset of the language learning curriculum, a supporting character in the project" (p. 1). In the 1960s, when establishment of the ACTFL led to professionalization of FL teachers (Kramsch & Kramsch, 2000), the divide between literary scholarship and language teaching was created, which later contributed to "a faith-based conflict" in which "literature-oriented academics argue that communicative approaches encroaching on the curriculum have led to ignorance of the *belle lettres* while language-oriented academics question the privileged status afforded to literary texts as appropriate vehicles for learning" (Bernhardt, 2011, p. 97). In the 1980s and 1990s literary texts moved to the periphery of the language curriculum, and literature was used mostly for "providing an 'authentic' experience in the target culture" or a cultural commentary (Kramsch & Kramsch, 2000, p. 568). "The language-literature split," which has curricular, professional, and political implications in the field (Kern, 2002, p. 21), actually has existed for a long time and in FL instruction it affects primarily the place of literary texts at the beginning and intermediate levels (the first two years of college or university study in the United States). "The gap that all too often separates introductory communicative language teaching and advanced literary teaching" (Kern, 2002, p. 24) can still be observed despite the MLA's call for curriculum reform and appeal for the development of a unified language-and-literature curriculum throughout the course of FL study (Giesler et al., 2007).[1]

Regarded often as secondary to everyday communicative needs, a literary text serves in most beginning and intermediate language textbooks as a thematic illustration of a particular topic but not as a core text of the instructional unit. This function today is fulfilled by dialogues or monologues (texts such as letters, blogs, e-mails). Literature and literary analysis are the focus of study only in Advanced-level courses.[2] Since according to the ACTFL Guidelines (2012) Novice-level readers should be able "to understand key words and cognates, as well as formulaic phrases that are highly contextualized" (p. 24), texts typically included as reading exercises in beginning textbooks consist of schedules, menus, simple advertisements, and informational texts of practical value that feature topically controlled vocabulary and simple syntax. Literary texts, if included, are usually restricted to short adapted excerpts or easy-to-interpret poems. Major criteria for literary text selection in a course for beginners include predictably level-appropriate syntax and vocabulary and/or thematic relevance. For example, the textbook *Golosa: Books 1 and 2* (Robin et al., 2012) features a section called Reading for Pleasure in which Pushkin's poem «Осень» ["Fall"] complements the theme of the lesson Weather and Travel and an adapted version of Chekhov's story «Ванька» ["Van'ka"] is an illustration for Means of Communication.

The second-year curriculum typically follows the same structure: it is organized thematically and the themes repeat those at the Novice level, in line with ACTFL Guidelines and Intermediate-level students' ability to speak on familiar topics related to their daily life. Intermediate-level readers should be able to understand information conveyed in simple, predictable, loosely connected texts such as weather reports, social announcements, notices, and forums. Therefore informational and expository texts tend to dominate the curriculum, whereas literary texts continue to play a supportive role. For example, the popular intermediate Russian language textbook *V puti* (Kagan et al., 2006) offers literary texts (usually poems) at the end of each unit plus excerpts from classical Russian literary works in the accompanying *Student Activities Manual*, but both are treated as supplemental material.

Systematic and comprehensive study of a literary text is usually postponed until the third- and fourth-year curriculum or delegated to Russian literature courses taught in translation. A major in Russian traditionally requires literature courses in translation to ensure that students acquire the *symbolic cultural capital* or *knowledge capital* contained in literature.[3] A language curriculum, on the other hand, is concerned mostly with "linguistic capital" seasoned with "small c" culture; only occasionally does it incorporate excerpts from the works of Russian literature to bridge the gap between "Big C" and "small c" cultures.

However, as Rosengrant (2000) notes, if Intermediate-level students are to become Advanced-level readers, they must learn to read literary works while still at the Intermediate level. The desire to include literature early on in language instruction is shared by many Russian language instructors, and they often incorporate literary texts into their intermediate courses and assign works from various anthologies and collections to complement the textbook. Literary works presented as linear narratives are useful for analyzing complex syntactic constructions (such as subordinate clauses, which are introduced and analyzed at the Intermediate level). Texts that are organized according to a "story" format (i.e., those that have an introduction, plot development, conflict resolution, and ending) improve readers' ability to recall the text (Shrum & Glisan, 2010) and facilitate comprehension because of their predictable structure. Studies demonstrate that narrative texts in general help readers to generate more inferential questions than expository texts (DuBravac & Dalle, 2002). Literary texts, outside of the familiar everyday experience, can provoke more sophisticated and culturally substantial discussion and increase motivation, which is particularly important at the Intermediate level, which has the highest attrition rate. At the Intermediate level students often feel a disheartening futility of their efforts to master Russian quickly and the discrepancy between their limited linguistic means and desire to express complex ideas. Incorporation of a literary text into an Intermediate-level language course may stimulate the interest and build confidence.

Another important factor that drives Russian language teachers to search for a literary text to complement the curriculum is students' own explicit desire to read works of the celebrated Russian literary canon. It is well known that one of the "main recruiters" for Russian language study are the 19th-century classical writers: Tolstoy, Dostoyevsky, and Chekhov.[4] However, students' engagement with Russian literature in the original is often delayed until the Intermediate High or Advanced levels (i.e., in graduate school, mostly) because of text difficulty combined with students' lack of background knowledge and their inability to comprehend cultural references. Such concerns are shared by learners and instructors; however, if the goal of FL instruction in the 21st century is "translingual and transcultural competence" (Geisler et al., 2007), students should be exposed to literary texts at a much earlier stage. One way of making original literature accessible to lower-level learners is to adapt the text; however, many SLA researchers would argue for using only authentic materials. According to Shrum and Glisan, the instructor should edit the task, not the text (2010, p. 196). The discussion on the instructional values of original versus adapted texts in teaching foreign languages is ongoing, and there are research findings to advocate for both approaches.[5] In my view, at the Intermediate level reading a number of abridged and adapted works of fiction is more effective at improving learners' language proficiency than reading a few longer and unadapted original texts. Regardless of whether original or adapted versions are chosen, the role of literary texts in the Intermediate language classroom should be emphasized. Furthermore, it should not be regarded as a supplemental activity but should become a core element of instruction.

A narrative literary text placed in the center of the curriculum may be better than dialogues or informational texts in preparing students for sophisticated and syntactically complex oral and written productions.[6] Nevertheless, the communicative goals of the curriculum should by no means be lowered. New vocabulary and grammar in a core narrative text can be recycled within the same instructional unit as a variety of communicative assignments and texts, which may include dialogues and informational or expository texts related to the communicative goals of the lesson. A good example of a literary text as the core of a four-skill approach to teaching Russian is Comer's 2008 textbook, *День без вранья* [*A day without lying*], a glossed edition of Viktoria Tokareva's story, which is designed to ease the transition from reading novice informational texts to reading a longer literary text in Russian. The author selected Tokareva's story because her prose is linguistically accessible to students, the language of the text reflects contemporary conversational Russian, it introduces readers to Russian urban life in the 1960s and the main concept of the story and the situations described are familiar to readers. In addition, the longer text (6,700 words) helps students practice strategies for doing extensive reading. The story is not an adapted version and therefore is a "great confidence builder for students" (Tokareva & Comer, 2008, pp. 2–3). This text, however, is not familiar to a majority of native speakers and due to its length will take up a significant part of the curriculum. I propose additional text selection criteria: a text's place as required reading in the Russian school curriculum and the extent of native speakers' familiarity with it. In the course of language study limited to a maximum of four years of instruction, this may be a more effective approach.

RUSSIAN LITERARY CANONS

The cultural component in the language curriculum is expected to build "a culturally compatible knowledge base" (Bernhardt, 2011, p. 47) and help students access a cultural reference system. Teaching students the target culture's customs, traditions, and values is important, but not sufficient. Literature plays a significant role in the formation of national ideologies, intellectual traditions, and cultural history in general (Kramsch & Kramsch, 2000). This role is particularly large in Russia, which traditionally projects its culture as literature-centric.[7] Being culturally competent implies being familiar with the major literary works and authors of the target culture, i.e., the national literary canon. Familiarity with the national literary canon and its plots, characters, and famous quotes is highly beneficial in being able to access the unifying common cultural and ideological national narrative.

A national literary canon, that is, a predetermined set of authors and their works, reflects political and social agendas and serves to form a cultural identity and unify the nation. Cultural paternalism is implemented first and foremost through education, and the national canon is formed by the academy (Gorak, 1997). In modern industrial societies mass education plays a major homogenizing role, of which a literary canon, or "a literate codified culture, which permits context-free communication" (Gellner & Smith, 1996, pp. 367–68), is an important component. In the United States a prescribed group of literary works for compulsory reading at schools ceased to exist as a result of the "canon wars" of the 1980s (Freese, 2008). The classic literary canon was determined to be stagnant, exclusive, patriarchal, and dictatorial and was replaced by an open list of diverse works, including ones by women and authors from a variety of backgrounds. The debate resulted in the democratization and diversification of the national curriculum, which now differs significantly from state to state and from school to school. In Russia, however, one can claim that a certain set of literary works is familiar to the entire population because Russia has: (1) a single mandatory countrywide school curriculum, which has existed for over a century, (2) required secondary education, and (3) literary-centric traditions that are historically rooted in the national culture.

Rigorous ideological control over education in the USSR produced a compulsory uniform curriculum for all Soviet schools (there were some minor deviations in the Soviet republics, and insignificant modifications over time).[8] As a result, all Soviet schools used the same textbooks in all subjects, including literature. In addition to the fact that all students were expected to use the same reading list, literature in Soviet society played the role of cultural marker, where knowledge of the Russian literary canon was "a fundamental tool for achieving *kul'turnost'*, for imposing social skills and binding Soviet society together" (Mjør, 2009, p. 89). The Soviet educational literary canon served political goals and excluded, for example, writings by dissidents and émigré writers.

After the breakup of the Soviet Union the canon was substantially reworked and enhanced to reflect previously suppressed authors and their works, but the 19th-century classical literary canon remained practically unchanged. In the 1990s a variety of textbooks and manuals appeared on the market to replace the universal Soviet textbook and challenge the mandatory reading list. However, in 2009 the introduction of a standardized test in literature, the *ЕГЭ по литературе* [Unified State Exam in Literature], ensured the return of a prescribed educational canon even for the twentieth century (Loria, 2016).[9] In 2014 the Russian State Duma proposed to reintroduce one universal literature textbook in all public schools throughout the country in an attempt to enhance ideological control over the school curriculum (Iarovaia, 2014).[10] The initiative caused rather heated debates (Gorbovskaia, 2014), but critics who argue against the introduction of a universal textbook for the most part do not object to having a prescribed list of literary works, which demonstrates a general consensus in Russian society regarding the benefits of an educational canon in teaching literature. School curriculum and mass education are instrumental in the nation-building process and conducive to creating a shared national narrative, which unites people around common values, myths, images, symbols, and texts. This task is politically urgent in contemporary post-Soviet Russia, a large multiethnic and multiconfessional state in search of a new identity. Furthermore, it helps to bridge the gap between generations schooled in the Soviet Union and in post-Soviet Russia and to form a shared collective memory and a common cultural paradigm.

It is important to note that there also exists a western Russian literature canon, which was established by scholars in western Europe and the United States in the 20th century. It was molded by various factors, including political agendas, particularly during the Cold War, and excluded some of Soviet writers who belonged to the national canon in the home country (for example, Sergei Simonov, Aleksandr Tvardovsky, and Nikolai Ostrovsky). At present, literature courses taught in translation in the United States in general follow the Western canon and implement the historical-philological approach, as opposed to the canon-oriented one, by selecting only works of undisputed artistic value.[11] Texts from the Russian mandatory school canon, if they do not exemplify the most noteworthy or representational works of a canonized author, are unlikely to be taught in Western universities or selected for translation into English. The choice of works taught in literature courses in the United States is also driven by the availability of translations.

In recent years many PhD programs in Russian literature in the United States have revised their reading lists in order to diversify the Western canon by incorporating contemporary Russian writers and to give students more freedom in selecting the works they might find useful for their own research agendas. Princeton University, for example, now allows graduate students to compile their own reading lists. Columbia University warns students that the PhD reading list is intended as a study tool, not a definitive canon. At Stanford University in 2014 the reading list was completely redesigned in order to find a balance between "a canon, that was identified in the past" and "the needs of the present and the future, to demonstrate the required expertise and to be able to produce creative or scholarly writing to satisfy current and future audiences" (Safran, 2014). According to Safran, Russian faculty at Stanford added three *byliny* [epic poem], three fairy tales, texts by Korney Chukovsky, Samuil Marshak, Bulat Okudzhava, and works by women writers, including Lyudmila Petrushevskaya, Lyudmila Ulitskaya, Viktoriya Tokareva, and Tatyana Tolstaya. They also made the previously required texts by Valentin Kataev and Mikhail Sholokhov optional. Reading lists will shape the future of the field because current PhD students will be teaching from them, and those lists create their notion of a canon and shape the Western pedagogical canon for Russian literature. Table 16.1 demonstrates that even when revised the PhD reading lists do not include many works from the Russian school canon.

At the same time, some works from the Western canon of Russian literature, such as «Цемент» [*Cement*] by Gladkov and «Зависть» [*Envy*] by Olesha are on the graduate-level reading list at most US universities, even though in Russia they are known only to experts or a small group of avid readers. An examination of PhD reading lists confirms that literature courses offered to American undergraduate students in translation do not include many texts from the Russian school canon, such as Turgenev's «Муму» [*Mumu*] or Nekrasov's «Дед Мазай и зайцы» [*Grandpa Mazai and the hares*], which are read by all Russian school children in the fifth or sixth grades. The content gap between the Russian primary school canon and Russian literature courses taught at American universities creates a real problem: texts that are well known to an average Russian are often missing from both literature and language curricula in the United States. Language instructors delegate systematic study of Russian literature to courses in translation, and courses in translation typically follow the Western pedagogical canon. As a result students, even upon returning from Russia with a relatively high level of linguistic competence, often think that Mumu is just the name of a restaurant in Moscow and are puzzled by numerous political cartoons or jokes alluding to the Golden Fish. Including more precedent texts in language classes at the intermediate level will help address this problem.

PRECEDENT TEXTS

Most works of the Russian school canon have become *прецедентные тексты* [precedent texts], as they are known in Russian scholarship. A precedent text is a popular, frequently quoted and referenced text, allusions to which provide a context-free shorthand used in communication among native speakers. The term *precedent text* was coined by Karaulov in his 1987 book «Русский язык и языковая личность» [*Russian language and language identity*]. According to Karaulov, a precedent text is общеизвестный [well known], хрестоматийный [belongs to a national canon], and possesses эмоциональная и познавательная ценность [emotional and cognitive value]. It can be reinterpreted and reproduced in other texts, discourses, and various artistic media, formats, and genres; hence a precedent text transforms into a *fact of culture* that is recognizable in many guises. When Karaulov talks about хрестоматийность [belonging to the national canon] he primarily means texts included in the school curriculum along with the texts that are known to the speakers one way or another, such as folklore, fairy tales, jokes, myths, and so on (2007).[12]

In Russia the notion of a precedent text has become a popular topic in foreign language pedagogy research. Hundreds of articles, dissertations, and conference papers all over the country have been devoted to classifications, interpretations, and analysis of precedent texts in teaching Russian as a foreign language (Petrova, 2010). Russian scholars have explored *precedent names* (usually names of characters from the school canon, such as Oblomov or Taras Bulba), *precedent expressions* (which in essence are famous quotes), and *precedent situations* (archetypal situations) (Gudkov, 1999). Under the umbrella of precedent text some researchers actually deal with intertextuality (Bazhenova, 2006) and others examine nonverbal precedent texts: famous works of art, architecture, film, and music (Krasnykh, 1998). The notion of precedent is analyzed on several levels: personal, social, national, and universal. The national level seems to be the most relevant to teaching Russian language and culture to foreign students and is

TABLE 16.1. Comparison of the Russian Literary Canon and Selected PhD Reading Lists

	Columbia University	University of Toronto	Yale University	University of Pittsburgh	Harvard University	University of Southern California	UCLA	Required for the Unified State Exam
Крылов. «Ворона и лисица» [Krylov, "The crow and the fox"]	No	Yes / No	No	No	Yes / No	Yes	Yes	Yes
Пушкин. «Сказка о рыбаке и рыбке» [Pushkin, *The tale of the fisherman and the fish*]	No	Yes	Yes/No	No	No	Yes	Yes	Yes
Гоголь. «Тарас Бульба» [Gogol, *Taras Bulba*]	No	No	Yes / No	No	Yes / No	No	Yes	Yes
Тургенев. «Муму» [Turgenev, *Mumu*]	No	No	No	No	No	No	No	Yes
Некрасов. «Дедушка Мазай и зайцы» [Nekrasov, *Grandpa Mazai and the hares*]	No	No	No	No	No	No	Yes	Yes
Салтыков-Щедрин. «Сказки» [Saltykov-Shchedrin, *Tales*]	No	No	No	No	No	No	No	Yes

Толстой. «Кавказский пленник» [Tolstoy, *The prisoner of the Caucases*]	No	No	No	No	No	No	No	Yes
Чехов. «Хамелеон» [Chekhov, "The chameleon"]	No	No	No	No	No	No	No	Yes
Горький. «Старуха Изергиль» [Gorky, *Old Izergil*]	No	No	No	No	No	No	No	Yes
Шолохов. «Судьба человека» [Sholokhov, *The fate of a man*]	No	No	No	No	No	No	No	Yes
Есенин. «Письмо матери» [Esenin, "A letter to mother"]	Yes / No	Yes / No	No	Yes	Yes	Yes / No	No	Yes
Твардовский. «Василий Теркин» [Tvardovsky, *Vasily Terkin*]	Yes	No	No	No	No	No	Yes	Yes

Note: Yes = included; No = not included; Yes/No = recommended or unspecified particular works (selected poems, selected fables, etc.).

characterized by phenomena that are familiar to «любому среднему представителю того или иного лингвокультурного сообщества и входят в когнитивную базу этого сообщества» [the average representative of this or that linguocultural community and are included in the cognitive basis of that community] (Prokhorov, 2004, p. 149). In other words, to speak the same language as Russians students need to be familiar not only with customs, traditions, songs, and folklore but also with the texts known to the majority of natives, including those in the school canon.

The concept of precedent text appears to be unique to Russian national scholarly discourse. In Western scholarship such a term does not exist; instead one can find discussions on concepts such as culturally relevant materials, intercultural competence, and intertextuality. Those concepts imply an infinite cultural paradigm that is so diverse that it is virtually impossible to devise a static list of texts that are known to the majority of native speakers. However, Russian culture is a different case. There are particular historical reasons that the notion of precedent text is relevant to the Russian cultural context. The obligatory universal education curriculum is a set of texts familiar to every member of the society who has attended secondary school (and secondary education has been compulsory for several generations). As far as mass culture is concerned, century-long ideological restrictions, financial constraints, and totally controlled and therefore meager channels of cultural distribution have resulted in minimal yet effectively promulgated mass cultural production. For example, state radio broadcasts, imposed on every citizen through radio receivers installed in every Soviet kitchen, included the same song playlist over and over again for years.

A parallel situation can be found in Soviet-era film production and distribution. Soviet film studios produced a relatively small number of films and cultural authorities, burdened with censorship, reduced the number of films released for distribution even further.[13] Due to the limited number of national "blockbusters" and no access to foreign production, one can compile a list of popular Soviet films that are not only familiar to the majority of Soviets but are also quoted and referenced on a daily basis even today. Even though most popular films belong to the Soviet cultural experience, they continue to be shown repeatedly on television in post-Soviet Russia and other former republics. In addition, numerous remakes of old Soviet blockbusters or their sequels have been released recently with significant box office success.

Today, popular films, songs, descriptions of national customs, traditions, and values are consistently included in Russian language curricula in the United States, whereas precedent texts are often overlooked. Most anthologies and collections are compiled according to genre, time period, or authorship but do not use a canon-oriented approach. One can find some precedent texts from the more stable 19th-century classical literature canon in various collections. For example, in Rosengrant and Lifschitz's *The Golden Age* eight of 12 texts are taken from the Russian school canon. The authors selected works in the original that are "both linguistically accessible to students with limited reading skills (Intermediate Mid) and that also occupy a prominent position in the nineteenth-century literary canon" (Rosengrant & Lifschitz, 1996, pp. iv–v). Precedent texts from the school canon are sometimes included in various series, for example the Russian Texts series (Bristol Classical Press). Produced as separate books, the original texts are accompanied by notes, introductions, and glossaries.

It seems rather ambitious to include in an Intermediate language course more than one or two texts in the original per semester, due to both linguistic complexity and the length of the works. A curriculum at the Novice level does not prepare students to deal with literary works, especially ones from the 19th century. The transition from reading simple dialogues and expository texts at the Novice and Intermediate levels to reading authentic literary texts at the Advanced level requires extensive scaffolding. Students need to "have time and opportunity to acquire automaticity in reading before moving on to challenging material" (Birch, 2002, p. 147). One solution is the use of graded readers (books adapted for learners of foreign languages with simplified vocabulary and syntax that are used to support the extensive reading approach to teaching foreign languages), which were very popular in the past. Now it is rather difficult to find Russian graded readers on the US market, which reflects a shift in pedagogical views on the benefits of reading literature in the original.[14] However, in Russia the recent substantial academic discussions of precedent texts in teaching Russian as a foreign language (RFL) has led to a noticeable growth in publications of literary texts from the school canon, adapted or retold to fit different levels of linguistic competence.

St. Petersburg publisher Zlatoust produces numerous graded readers, most of which belong to the corpus of precedent texts. The series «КЛАСС!ное чтение» [Class! Reading] offers simplified masterplots of major Russian classical novels. For example, Dostoyevsky's novel *Crime and Punishment* is retold in 62 pages, and Tolstoy's *Anna Karenina* is reduced to one plot line, three characters, and 32 pages. The educational series «Золотые имена России» [Golden names of Russia] employs a different approach to precedent texts: each book presents a prominent author and consists of a brief biography, an abridged and adapted version of a major work, and a documentary film about the author on an accompanying disk. According to the introduction, all texts in the book are composed using the active vocabulary of the B-1 (Intermediate Low) level, which means they were not adapted or abridged but are basically rewritten for educational purposes (Potapurchenko, 2013). One can always ask if a literary text retold by an instructor has any cultural value. Will a text that was simplified, restructured, and deprived of its poetic aspects during the process of adaptation still reflect the greatness of Russian literature? Perhaps not, but in contemporary Russia adapting or retelling precedent literary texts is a popular approach to teaching RFL, and such readers are widely used. In my opinion text adaptation profoundly differs from retelling, and incorporation of adapted precedent texts into intermediate curricula adds cultural content and is suitable as a transition toward reading in the original.

ONE PRACTICAL APPROACH

Precedent texts (literary texts, films, songs, and famous works of art) comprise the common cultural vernacular of Russian native speakers. Textbooks based on popular films and cartoons have proved to be a valuable resource for Russian language teachers (for example, Kashper et al., 2005; Merrill et al., 2009). However, literary precedent texts still require additional attention and consideration. Of course no curriculum can guarantee familiarity with every literary text read by the average Russian, but an effort should be made to include as many precedent texts as possible. The choice of readings at the Intermediate level is controlled by the instructor, and the selection should be made wisely.

The reintroduction of a mandatory list of literary works for all schools in Russia makes the task of compiling a manageable catalog of texts familiar to the overwhelming majority of the Russian adult population somewhat feasible. In the age of digital humanities the concept of a published anthology should be reassessed. It is unlikely that a perfect anthology can be compiled, but open access online resources, produced as a collaborative effort of educators, could be an answer. Middlebury College has launched a web-based anthology of literary texts from the Russian school canon. Every text is presented in three versions: abridged (or, in some cases, adapted) for the Novice level, abridged for the Intermediate level, and an original version for Advanced students.[15] Each precedent text is available to students as a text for reading and as an audio recording for listening comprehension. There are separate sections on poetry and links to screen adaptations, songs, relevant websites, and scholarly articles. The anthology is a resource for both teachers and students and could serve as a key or an access code to the world of contemporary Russian discourse. The Middlebury web anthology covers only a small number of precedent texts (20 prose texts and 34 poetic texts as of January 2017) but it is an ongoing project.

I would like to present an example of how a precedent text from the school canon can be used as a core text of an educational unit at the Intermediate level.[16] The text is an adapted and abridged version of Tolstoy's story «Кавказский пленник» [*A prisoner of the Caucasus*]. The story is included in the Russian school program in the fifth or sixth grade. *A Prisoner of the Caucasus* uses an archetypal plot in the Russian literary tradition from Pushkin to Makanin and is also frequently referenced in film and media. There are several film adaptations of the story and numerous texts and films based on the same archetypal plot, including Gaidai's famous comedy «Кавказская пленница» [*Female prisoner of the Caucasus*]. Incorporation of this text into the curriculum will help build students' common background knowledge and introduce important social, cultural, and historical dimensions, all of which are vital to the Russian society at present.

The teaching goals of the unit are: prefixed verbs of motion, talking about travel (narration in the past), asking for help and directions, and description of people and places. According to the ACTFL Proficiency Guidelines, readers at the Intermediate Mid level "may get some meaning from short connected texts featuring description and narration, dealing with familiar topics" (2012). The plot of the story is a typical adventure sequence involving captivity, friendship, and escape; it is a predictable one for students. The story includes several descriptions of people and places, and many dialogues in the text contain examples of making requests. The narrative model of the text can serve as a blueprint for narration of a trip in the past tense, as the plot is driven primarily by verbs of motion presented in contextualized situations.

The story provides input of the grammatical structures under acquisition. One approach to teaching how to read a literary text consists of prereading questions, commentaries, introductory notes, vocabulary lists, comprehension questions (embedded in the text or immediately following the text), postreading writing vocabulary activities, looking for key words, and listening to the recording of the text. Input is followed by analysis, which consists of various activities aimed at identifying and examining the grammar material in focus. Structured output (or exercises following the analysis) may range from pattern drills monitored by the instructor to translation tasks. One example of the structured output is recall protocol procedure (устный пересказ или письменное изложение) or readers' reconstruction of the text.

In a communicative classroom the core text should be used as a basis for more personalized learning activities. Working with this text will help to collect the necessary vocabulary to handle situations and transactions related to travel and examine the grammar necessary to reach the lesson's communicative goals. Additional texts, such as dialogues, blogs, expository, and informational texts concerning travel will help to bridge reading and communication. Guided practice in all four skills may include various communicative assignments, such as asking for directions, buying tickets, booking hotel rooms, or getting information from various travel ads online. Extension activities are devoted to students' oral and written independent speech production, such as planning a trip, working on an itinerary, choosing a country to visit, writing a letter home, requesting help, and writing short posts; longer narratives in the past could describe a trip in which active vocabulary and grammar is used creatively. The recommended discussions at the end of the unit on the symbolic nature of Tolstoy's story, the concept of us versus them, and other social and historical dimensions of the text give students a sense of intellectual accomplishment in addition to linguistic progress and help to integrate communicative goals and cultural enrichment.

CONCLUSION

In 2013 Merrill conducted a survey in an attempt to discover students' major reasons and goals for studying Russian. Students ranked information about everyday life, prose literature, and history as the three most desired outcomes of language learning. Merrill concludes that "students of Russian do not reject literature as cultural content and consistently place it near the top of desired subjects" (p. 74). Merrill also points out that Russians increasingly use social media, and students need to be prepared to function in the realm of global media. However, Russian discourse in all spheres of life is saturated with frequent allusions to precedent texts, especially from the literary school canon. References, in the form of direct and indirect quotes, populate media, pop culture, political commentaries, and interpersonal communication are found everywhere, from Russian Facebook posts to Putin's speeches.[17]

Exposing students to a number of precedent texts at the Intermediate level combined with doing the consistent work to accomplish goals in oral proficiency intensifies the learning process and offers multifaceted linguistic and cultural benefits to students. Placing literary precedent texts in the center of the curriculum will prepare students for reading literature at the Advanced level, give them access to a common cultural reference system, and become an important step toward the development of a unified language-and-literature curriculum throughout the course of foreign language study.

NOTES

1. Kern (2002) proposes reconciling the language-literature split by focusing on literacy, which could bridge the gap between introductory communicative language teaching and advanced literary teaching.
2. The word "literature" is not mentioned in the ACTFL Proficiency Guidelines (2012), and the term "literary (readings)" appears only in the description of reading skills at the Advanced High and Superior levels.
3. Guillory (1993) distinguishes between *linguistic capital,* the language, and *symbolic capital,* which is "a kind of knowledge capital whose possession can be displayed upon request and which thereby entitles its possessor to the cultural and material rewards of the well-educated person" (p. ix). Both terms are revisions of Bourdieu's (1986) terminology in his works on cultural capital.
4. Merrill's 2013 survey results show that desire to read Russian authors in the original is one of the top three reasons students choose to study Russian.
5. See Bernhardt (2011) and Shrum (2010) for discussion on the contradictory research findings.
6. For a description of teaching grammar using a story-based approach see *Teacher's Handbook: Contextualized Language Instruction* (Shrum & Glisan, 2010).
7. The literature on Russian culture being literature-centric is abundant: from works by Belinskii to Boym (Boym, 2009). In their book «Родная речь: Уроки изящной словесности» [*Mother tongue: Lessons in refined literature*] (1991), Vail and Genis state that literature for Russia is the symbol of faith and an ideological and moral foundation.
8. For example, the works of Dostoevsky were banned in the Soviet Union in the 1930s–1950s, and only in the 1970s was his novel *Crime and Punishment* included in the school program (Zolotukhina, n.d.).
9. The comprehensive list of literary works included in the required school program may be found online (at http://www.schoollib.h1.ru/school.htm or http://www.uroki.net/docrus/docrus10.htm), or in publications distributed by the Russian Ministry of Education, such as at http://www.edu.ru/db/portal/obschee/index.htm. Another

resource is official documentation pertaining to the Unified State Exam in Literature: http://ege.edu.ru; http://www.fipi.ru/content/otkrytyy-bank-zadaniy-ege. Also one can refer to the published Russian literature textbooks (grades 5–11) approved by the Ministry of Education and Sciences of the Russian Federation (http://fpu.edu.ru/fpu/).

10. A universal literature textbook is currently being planned and will be ready by 2018 ("Концепцию единого учебника по литературе подготовят к 2018 году," 2015).
11. The historical-philological approach differs from the canon-oriented one: "The former thematizes temporal distance, the latter ignores it and aims instead at identification and application in the present" (Mjør, 2009, p. 94).
12. Another group of precedent texts are literary works in translation included in the school canon, such as «Маленький принц» [*The little prince*] by Antoine de Saint-Exupéry and «Малыш и Карлсон» [*Karlsson-on-the-roof*] by Astrid Lindgren, which also greatly contribute to the system of cultural references in Russian discourse.
13. For example, in 1940 the number of films released in the United States was 529, compared to 36 in the USSR. In 1986 the numbers were 625 in the United States and 182 in the USSR (www.imdb.com\year\1986). In 1986 the production capacity of Mosfilm, the largest film studio in the Soviet Union, was 55 films per year (Mosfilm, 1986).
14. Occasionally Western publishers produce graded readers, but very few include works from the Russian school canon. For example, in 2015 Routledge published *Graded Modern Russian Reader* (compiled by L. Buranova), which contains adaptations of mass media articles and stories by popular contemporary authors such as Grishkovets and Shishkin but nothing from the school canon.
15 At present the project includes only 19th-century works, due to copyright laws and because the 19th century is a more stable canon (http://sites.middlebury.edu/russianshortstories/).
16. This example comes from an online textbook "MiddRussian," which uses a text-centric approach for teaching Russian at the Intermediate level and gives preference to a large number of adapted and/or abridged versions of literary texts from the Russian school canon or precedent texts.
17. Examples of Putin's literary and culture quotes and references in his speeches include a quote from Lermontov's poem «Бородино» ["Borodino"] (http://www.svoboda.org/content/article/24493226.html); a reference to Ilf and Petrov's novel «Двенадцать стульев» [*The twelve chairs*] (https://www.newsru.com/russia/23may2005/otmertvogoslaushi.html); and a direct quote from the Govorukhin's film «Место встречи изменить нельзя» [*The meeting place cannot be changed*] (http://inosmi.ru/politic/20101216/164983704.html).

REFERENCES

American Council on the Teaching of Foreign Languages (ACTFL). (2012). Proficiency Guidelines 2012. Retrieved from http://www.actfl.org/publications/guidelines-and-manuals/actfl-proficiency-guidelines-2012

Bazhenova, E. A. (2006). Интертекстуальность [Intertextuality]. In *Стилистический энциклопедический словарь русского языка* [Stylistic encyclopedia of Russian] (pp. 104–8). Moscow: Flinta.

Bernhardt, E. (2011). *Understanding advanced second-language reading*. New York: Routledge.

Birch, B. (2002). *English L2 reading: Getting to the bottom*. Mahwah, NJ: Lawrence Erlbaum.

Bourdieu, P. (1986). The forms of capital. In J. Richardson (Ed.), *Handbook of theory and research for the sociology of education* (pp. 241–58). New York: Greenwood.

Boym, S. (2009). *Common places: Mythologies of everyday life in Russia*. Cambridge: Harvard UP.

DuBravac, S., & Dalle, M. (2002). Reader question formation as a tool for measuring comprehension: Narrative and expository textual interferences in a second language. *Journal of Research in Reading*, *25*(2), 217–31.

Freese, P. (2008). American national identity in a globalized world as a topic in the advanced EFL Classroom. *American Studies Journal*, *51*. Retrieved from: http://www.asjournal.org/51-2008/american-national-identity-in-a-globalized-world/#sdfootnote17sym

Geisler, M., Kramsch, C., McGinnis, S., Patrikis, P., Pratt, M. L., Ryding, K., & Saussy, H. (2007). Foreign languages and higher education: New structures for a changed world: MLA ad hoc committee on foreign languages profession. *Profession*, *12*, 234–45.

Gellner, E., & Smith, A. (1996). The nation: Real or imagined?: The Warwick Debates on Nationalism. *Nations and Nationalism*, *3*, 357–70.

Gorak, J. (1997). Canons and canon formation. In G. A. Kennedy (Ed.), *The Cambridge history of literary criticism* (pp. 560–84). Cambridge: Cambridge UP.

Gorbovskaia, E. (2014). Единый учебник литературы [A unified literature textbook]. Retrieved from http://megabook.ru/article/Единый%20учебник%20литературы

Gudkov, D. B. (1999). *Прецедентное имя и проблемы прецедентности* [The precedent name and the problem of precedence]. Moscow: Moscow State University.

Guillory, J. (1993). *Cultural capital: The problem of literary canon formation*. Chicago: University of Chicago Press.

Iarovaia, I. (2014, July 2). Вариативность учебников создает опасность дискриминации детей [Variations in textbooks create the danger of discrimination among children]. RIA novosti. Retrieved from https://ria.ru/society/20140702/1014428690.html

Karaulov, Y. N. (2007). *Русский язык и языковая личность* [The Russian language and language identity]. Moscow: LKI.

Kashper, M., Kagan, O., & Morozova, Y. (2005). *Cinema for Russian conversation*. Newburyport, MA: Focus/R. Pullins.

Kern, R. (2002). Reconciling the language-literature split through literacy. *ADFL Bulletin*, *33*(3), 20–24.

Концепцию единого учебника по литературе подготовят к 2018 году [The concept of a unified literature textbook is being prepared for 2018]. (2015, June 15). Parlamentskaja gazeta. Retrieved from https://www.pnp.ru/social/2015/06/15/koncepciyu-edinogo-uchebnika-politerature-podgotovyat-k-2018-godu.html

Kramsch, C., & Kramsch, O. (2000). The avatars of literature in language study. *The Modern Language Journal*, *84*(4), 553–73.

Krasnykh, V. V. (1998). Виртуальная реальность или реальная виртуальность [Virtual reality or real virtuality]. In *Человек. Сознание. Коммуникация* [Person. Consciousness. Communication]. Moscow: Dialog.

Loria, E. (2016, May 31). Список литературы внесет некую вменяемость в существующее зло ЕГЭ [The literature list will bring some sense to the existing evil of the EGE]. Izvestija. Retrieved from http://izvestia.ru/news/616061

Merrill, J. (2013). Our Russian classrooms and students: Who is choosing Russian, why, and what cultural content should we offer them? *Russian Language Journal*, *63*, 51–78.

Merrill, J., Mikhailova, Y., & Alley, M. (2009). *Animation for Russian conversation*. Newburyport, MA: Focus/R. Pullins.

Mjør, K. J. (2009). The online library and the classic literary canon in post-Soviet Russia: Some observations on "The Fundamental Electronic Library of Russian Literature and Folklore." *Digital Icons: Studies in Russian, Eurasian and Central European New Media*, *1*(2), 83–99.

Modern Language Association (MLA). (2009, February). Report to the Teagle Foundation on the undergraduate major in language and literature. In Modern Language Association (Web publication, p. 143).

Mosfilm. (1986). In *Кино. Энциклопедический словарь* [Cinema. Encyclopedic dictionary]. Moscow: Sovetskaja entsiklopedija.

National Standards Collaborative Board (NSCB). (2015). *World-readiness standards for learning languages* (4th ed.). Alexandria, VA: Author.

Petrova, N. V. (2010). Эволюция понятия прецедентный текст [Evolution of the concept of precedent texts]. *Вестник Иркутского государственного университета* [Newsletter of Irkutsk state university], *2*(10), 176–81.

Potapurchenko, Z. (2013). *Федор Достоевский* [Fedor Dostoevsky]. Moscow: Russkij jazyk.

Prokhorov, Y. E. (2004). *Действительность. Текст. Дискурс* [Reality. Text. Discourse]. Moscow: Flinta.

Rosengrant, S. (2000). Teaching literature at the Intermediate level of proficiency: An interactive approach. In O. Kagan & B. Rifkin (Eds.), *The learning and teaching of Slavic literatures and cultures* (pp. 81–89). Bloomington, IN: Slavica.

Rosengrant, S., & Lifschitz, E. (1994). *The golden age: Readings in Russian literature of the nineteenth century*. New York: John Wiley & Sons.

Safran, G. (2014). Stanford Slavic department revises its reading list. *NewsNet*, *54*(5), 1–3.

Shrum, J., & Glisan, E. (2010). *Teacher's handbook: Contextualized language instruction*. Boston: Heinle, Cengage Learning.

Tokareva, V., & Comer, W. J. (2008). *A day without lying: A glossed edition for intermediate-level students of Russian*. Bloomington, IN: Slavica.

Vail, P., & Genis, A. (1991). *Родная речь:Уроки изящной словесности* [Mother tongue: Lessons in refined literature]. Moscow: Nezavisimaja gazeta.

Zolotukhina, O. (n.d.) Изучение русской литературы в советской школе [The study of Russian literature in Soviet schools]. In *Трансформации русской классики* [Transformations of the Russian classics]. Retrieved from http://transformations.russianliterature.com/metodologicheskie-osnovy-izuchenija-russkoj-literatury-v-shkole-sov-period

17

EXTRACURRICULAR ACTIVITIES IN RUSSIAN LANGUAGE AND CULTURE PROGRAMS

Challenges and Perspectives

Alla Epsteyn and Maia Solovieva

Russian language programs are constantly looking for ways to teach Russian more effectively and to maintain and increase enrollments, even as they respond to various external pressures, including geopolitical events and conceptual changes in higher education. The 2006 Modern Language Association (MLA) report, "Foreign Languages and Higher Education: New Structures for a Changed World," argues that foreign language departments "must transform their programs and structure" (Geisler et al., 2007, p. 237) to keep up with changes that have already taken place in the profession. Extracurricular activities (ECAs) are widely recognized as a valuable part of any successful language program. While teachers routinely discuss ways to be more effective in the classroom, much less attention has been given to the role of ECAs as part of a well-rounded language program.

The nature of ECAs on our campuses is evolving, and a reevaluation of ECAs is already under way in Russian studies, as evidenced by the roundtable organized at the 2015 Conference of the American Association of Teachers of Slavic and East European Languages entitled "Beyond Russian Table: Building Blocks of a Strong Russian Program." We argue that ECAs should no longer be considered merely supplemental but instead an important—indeed, integral—component of an effective language education. Our purpose here is to reexamine the concept of ECAs, highlight the challenges and successes of their use, and provide practical recommendations for innovative approaches to ECAs.

ECAS IN RUSSIAN AND FOREIGN LANGUAGE STUDIES

The word "extracurricular" in the name "extracurricular activities" implies that out-of-classroom activities are not essential for faculty who organize such events and that they are optional for students who participate in them. Nonetheless, we use the term ECAs because it is the one most widely accepted in our professional community.

The definition of an ECA has evolved over the past several decades, from the notion of "any educational activity which supplements the regular course of classroom instruction" (Campbell, 1973, p. 1) to the more complex definition in *The Encyclopedia of Education* (Guthrie, 2003), which links ECAs explicitly to a broad educational mission that combines specific institutional goals with the development of learners as well-rounded individuals. ECAs "positively impact students' emotional, intellectual, social, and interpersonal development. By working together with other individuals, students learn to negotiate, communicate, manage conflict, and lead others" (Tenhouse, 2003, p. 374).

Research on language- and culture-related ECAs in Russian studies at the college level is sparse. Tumanov (1983) uses the Department of Slavic Languages and Literatures at the University of Toronto as a case study and analyzes the role of ECAs and their potential shortcomings, such as ineffective planning, "excessive supervision by the instructors," and a tendency to underestimate "the creative potential of the students" (p. 837). He concludes that "the most negative and weak part of the program [was] that we failed to incorporate extracurricular activities of the students with our in-class program" (pp. 837–38).

More recent publications do not always use the term extracurricular activity but nonetheless consider research on different aspects of language learning environments as inseparable from what happens inside and outside the classroom. This is the case, for instance, in Romanov's survey (2000) of students' motivations for learning Russian. The survey addresses various kinds of ECAs, such as film screenings, interactions with native speakers outside of class, and language club activities such as field trips to plays, exhibitions, and performances. Based on the survey data, the author draws conclusions about the factors that motivate undergraduates to study Russian, which can be linked to a desire to socialize with peers and suggests conducting regular surveys among them.

Merrill (2013) claims that "the more we know about our students, the better we can prepare our language classes and keep them relevant for the realities of today's students and the challenges they face" (p. 53). Responses collected from 607 Russian language learners who studied at Middlebury College between 1991 and 2011 show that they started taking Russian for a variety of reasons and that they have not necessarily become more job oriented. Merrill's findings suggest that learners are "attracted to Russian by Russian literature and culture, much like students 15–20 years ago" (p. 59). Learning how students are using Russian today and how they would like to use it in their future professional careers gives language educators valuable information and clear opportunities to support their own professional goals. Merrill concludes that we need "to be ready for the changing types of jobs our students might be finding and for the new technologies in which they will be using Russian" (p. 59). ECAs can be utilized to identify and support these career goals; for instance, by inviting guest speakers who have pursued careers that entail the use of Russian or by organizing informal public discussions on how language skills can be used after graduation.

Rifkin (2005) also explores the nonexplicit use of ECAs. He compares the traditional classroom setting with an immersion setting and promotes the study of a foreign language in an immersion setting in order to break the "ceiling effect." Rifkin acknowledges that students benefit from immersion learning environments not only in the classroom but also through participation in ECAs. While Rifkin does not use the term ECA, he does discuss the impact on learning of activities that take place outside the classroom: "students in the immersion program converse in Russian with one another, their teachers, and other native speakers in the dining hall at meals, in the dormitory corridors, at social events (such as karaoke evenings, films, or dance parties), and at formally organized clubs and activities (e.g., newspaper club, volleyball team)" (p. 11). Although Rifkin describes a total immersion setting in an already existing program where only Russian is spoken, we argue that organizing ECAs at home institutions can to some extent replicate the effect of that kind of immersion environment by offering more opportunities to interact with the target language and culture.

In response to Rifkin's call to overcome the "ceiling effect," language professionals have developed innovations in curricular design, such as by teaching an advanced language course through global debate (Brown et al., 2015) or by exploring in the classroom the power of learners' own narratives (Kearney, 2010). We agree with the conclusion of Brown et al. (2015), that "while time in the target language certainly plays a valuable and needed role, this research suggests that innovative curricular design and instruction in the university foreign language classroom combined with appropriate scaffolding can equal, if not exceed, uptake that occurs in extended immersion environments" (p. 83). At the same time we argue that we need to explore the full potential of what ECAs can bring to our campuses. For instance, both of the approaches that Brown and Kearney mention (global debates and students' narrative reflections) could lead to exciting ECAs that work synergistically with classroom activities.

Research on on-campus foreign language houses (FLHs) suggests that home-immersion has many benefits (e.g., Wolf, 2002; Martinsen et al., 2010, 2011; Bown et al., 2011). Martinsen et al. (2011) compare findings regarding students' gains across study abroad, domestic immersion, and classroom-only language study. The authors conclude that "the learning setting plays an important role in language learning, although no one setting appears to be uniformly better than another" (p. 275). The authors' findings confirm that an FLH provides "an environment in which the students were able to explore and feel comfortable using the L2 in a variety of situations. Moreover, it demonstrates that the students can in fact simulate an immersion experience with each other" (p. 284–85). The profession needs more information about the design and function of language houses as well as more research on how language houses might fit into a broader system of ECAs on our campuses.

In addition to FLHs, some universities approach ECAs as a core component of their language programs. Prager and Kramer (2014) argue that "extracurricular activities in foreign language programs are often treated as an afterthought, as an appendix to the curriculum, or as simply an opportunity for students to boost their grades with a few extra-credit points" (p. 43). To provide an example of a successful system of ECAs they analyze the Kulturevent series in the German and Russian Department at Washington and Lee University. As part of this series the faculty created a student *Kulturpass* as a "physical, symbolic object that would actually remain in the students' possession and function both to remind them of the cultural events program and to forge a sense of belonging" (p. 45). The authors also highlight the challenges that even a successful ECAs program faces and that are common to almost any language program regardless of the language.

Makarova and Reva's (2017) survey-based report investigates the perceived effect of ECAs on students' language learning at universities in Canada and Russia. The authors' findings show "a positive effect of ECAs on the overall language proficiency as well as on all language skills" (p. 57) and on the personality development of the ECA participants. We agree with Makarova and Reva's conclusion that ECAs are "not integrated into foreign/second language curricular at university levels" and we support their suggestion "to conduct a future study of the teacher's opinions on the value of ECA[s] and potential ways of accounting for them in curriculum planning" (p. 58).

There is no good answer on how to integrate language and culture activities successfully under the umbrella of ECAs and how to connect them to the academic curriculum. We still know very little about our students' motivation for language study, including their expectations and desires regarding ECAs. Therefore many questions remain that require additional research. By taking a closer look at the existing practice of ECAs at the college level we hope to initiate a broader discussion on this subject in our profession.

To this end we conducted a survey of 48 programs that offer ECAs with the following questions in mind:

1. What are the experiences of faculty with Russian language and culture ECAs at the undergraduate level at institutions of higher education in the United States? Which components of their ECAs are perceived as successful?
2. What are the major differences in the organization and structure of ECAs at different types of institutions of higher education?
3. What are the major challenges in organizing and running ECAs effectively?

METHODOLOGY: PROCEDURES AND PARTICIPANTS

The survey consisted of six sections. The first part collected demographic information about the respondents, their teaching positions and teaching experience, their program or department structure, and their type of institution. The second part focused on how Russian language is connected with other academic disciplines at their institution. The third part asked about students, including course enrollments, number of majors and minors, and postgraduation career trends. Part 4 contained questions about ECAs held on and off campus and their connections with the academic curriculum. Part 5 dealt with ECA logistics, planning, and organization. The final section of the survey offered reflective questions about faculty satisfaction with the state of ECAs and their role in creating a vibrant cultural environment on campus.

A mixed-method design was used to examine the current state of ECAs on US campuses. Quantitative and qualitative data were collected by means of questionnaire surveys that contained Likert-style items and open-ended questions. In addition we conducted semi structured follow-up interviews with nine volunteer survey participants.

Mean scores were calculated for the four learning outcomes that were scored on Likert scales in the original survey (i.e., students' attitudes toward learning, their learning motivation[s], cultural knowledge, and language learning). Qualitative data obtained from the instructors' free responses to questions in the questionnaire relating to key challenges of running ECAs were analyzed by manually coding the data into themes based on key words and terms; these themes encompassed such categories as lack of student participation, difficulty scheduling, insufficient funding, shortage of faculty, and students' low motivation. Once the responses were organized within each category they were counted and factored according to how frequently each was cited. A one-way ANOVA test ($\alpha=0.05$) was used to compare mean responses to particular survey questions.

The survey was disseminated through: SEELANGS (the Slavic and East European Languages and Literature listserv), the Language Educators' community group at the American Council of Teachers of Foreign Languages (ACTFL); and the Committee on College and Pre-College Russian (CCPCR).

The total sample of the survey consisted of 48 faculty from various academic institutions including 20 from state universities (41.67%), 13 from private universities (27.08%), 13 from liberal arts colleges (27.08%), and two from military colleges (4.17%). Faculty respondents represent a variety of age groups: under 25 (2.08%), 25–34 (6.25%), 34–45 (35.42%), and 45–54 (25%), over 55 (27.08%), and prefer not to say (4.17%). We collected responses from all faculty ranks: full professor (12.5%), associate professor (33.33%), assistant professor (16.67%), and instructor/lecturer (10.42%). Our sampling also includes responses from adjuncts (14.58%) and visiting professors (12.5%).

After the survey 12 faculty expressed their willingness to participate in a follow-up interview, nine of whom agreed to be interviewed by telephone or to respond in writing to follow-up questions. These nine represent faculty from various types of institutions: three from state universities, four from private universities, one from a liberal arts college, and one from a US military academy. Five of these nine volunteers preferred to give written answers to the follow-up questions; the other four participated in 20-minute telephone interviews, which were recorded (with the interviewees' permission) and subsequently transcribed by the authors.

ANALYSIS OF SURVEY RESULTS

Respondents at 22 institutions (45.83%) report an increase in enrollments over the last 10 years, faculty at 15 institutions (31.25%) report a decrease, and faculty at nine institutions (18.75%) see no change in the number of students. There is no clear enrollment trend at two institutions (4.17%). There is no major difference in the enrollment trends among the four types of institutions of higher education.[1]

Our data do not reveal a clear up or down enrollment trend. At institutions where enrollments rose, respondents cite the following reasons for the increase in numbers: relevance of global politics (37.50%), study abroad incentives (12.5%), program improvements (6.25%), outstanding faculty (6.25%), and increased recruitment efforts (6.25%). Interview responses reveal a variety of factors that affect enrollments, including both external (geopolitical changes and campus improvements) and internal factors (faculty recruitment efforts, curriculum changes): "Russia was out of the public sphere until rather recently. . . . Recent political events have brought it to the fore and sparked better enrollments of late [the last few years]." Survey respondents at institutions that have seen declining enrollments cite the perceived lack of practicality of the Russian language (62.5%) among a variety of other contributing factors: "Russian is not a popular language right now. Students are being pressured to turn away from languages and humanities to focus on business and STEM." Participating language faculty feel enrollments can be influenced by students' and parents' negative perceptions of Russia: "Students are opting to take Arabic and Chinese over Russian, thinking that there are more opportunities that knowledge of those languages provides. Russian is hard and not all students want to work hard. There is a sense that Russia, somehow, is not important."

There is also no uniform trend in the number of Russian majors and minors. Responses indicate no change in the number of graduates at 15 of the surveyed institutions (31.25%), an increase in the number of majors at 14 of the institutions (29.17%), and a decrease at 13 institutions (27.08%). Meanwhile, over the last 10 years there has been no clear major/minor trend at six of the institutions (12.5%) (see Figure 17.1).

Reasons cited for these trends are similar to the factors impacting enrollment numbers. The relevance of global politics (37.5%) and the increasing number of study abroad programs (12.5%) are among the major factors for the increase in the number of majoring/minoring students. Faculty also cite the following factors as contributing to an increase in the number of students majoring or minoring in Russian: "Strong motivation to work for the government or nonprofit organizations, and to travel and live in Russia." A perceived lack of the practicality of a Russian-related degree (62.5%) might explain the decrease in the number of graduates with a major or minor in Russian. Other factors identified as negatively impacting the number of majors include program redesign (16.67%), coursework difficulty (12.50%), recruitment efforts (4.16%), and scheduling conflicts (4.16%).

Our respondents emphasize the correlation between a Russian major or minor and potential employment after college and cite the perception that there are meager job opportunities for graduates with a Russian major. Respondents note a recent trend among undergraduates to double major in Russian in combination with another subject. The survey did not ask about any trends in double majoring, but some of our

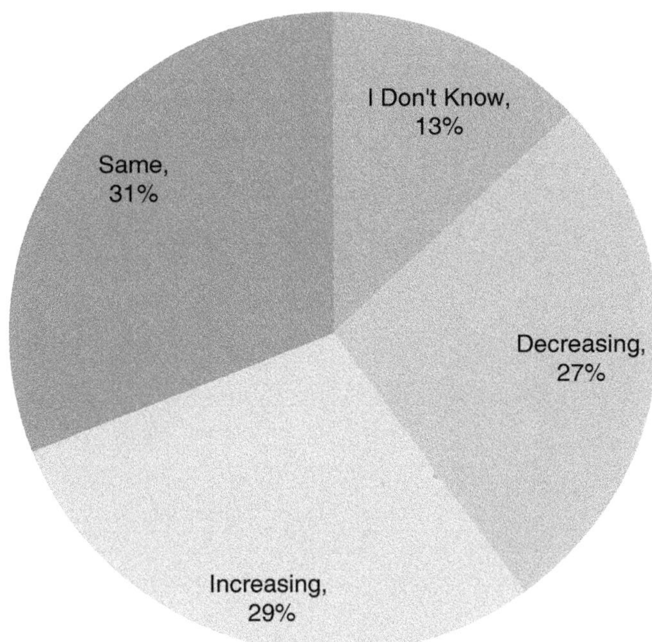

FIGURE 17.1. Perceived Trends Concerning Majors and Minors in Russian

respondents see the combination as a way to increase enrollment in language courses. Offering ECAs that pair their various interests can draw in students that would otherwise give lower priority to their interest in Russian to their major in STEM, business, political science, etc.: "We would like to see other departments do more with Russia and coordinate with us from art, music, and theater to environmental science to political science to religion and philosophy." These kinds of responses suggest that exploring new forms of engagement between Russian language programs and other academic disciplines on campus might be helpful for language enrollments.

Current State of Extracurricular Activities: On-Campus ECAs

Faculty respondents to our survey have a robust selection of on-campus ECAs at their institutions. The most popular are language-related activities, such as Russian Table (81.25%); cultural events sponsored by the Russian program, such as lectures and panel discussions (79.17%); cultural events open to the entire college community—music recitals, film showings, Maslenitsa festivals—(70.83%); events sponsored by student organizations (68.75%) or by various college-wide international organizations (47.92%); a living-and-learning community in the form of a Russian House or Corridor (25%); and on-campus residencies by musicians and artists (10.42%) (see Figure 17.2).

These on-campus events are offered at all four types of institutions. The only significant difference found across institutions is the living-and-learning community in the form of a Russian house or Russian corridor. Significantly more liberal arts colleges

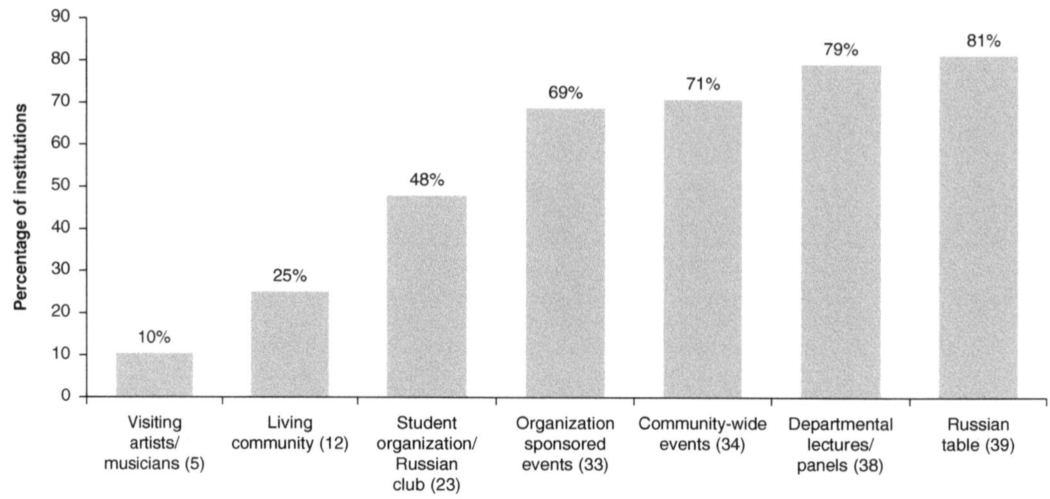

FIGURE 17.2. On-Campus ECA Offerings

offered Russian corridors/houses (61.54%) than private (7.69%) or state (5.0%) universities: $F(3,44) = 6.558$, $p < 0.001$. Other than this one exception, each type of institution offers a relatively similar variety of ECAs.

The survey grouped on-campus events either by the type of activity (language-related Russian Table, culture-related lectures, panel discussions, film nights) or by their sponsors (Russian Department or program, a student organization such as Russian Club, or an institution's international student center). These events are frequently organized and led by one or several individual(s), including permanent faculty members (82.98%), students (61.70%), teaching assistants (27.66%), resident faculty members (25.53%), or by no one (4.26%). Both Russian faculty and student organizations engage in collaboration and advising for ECAs. However, 30.77% of liberal arts colleges held events organized by a faculty-in-residence, which is significantly greater than private and state universities, none of which report having a faculty-in-residence program: $F(3,44) = 4.75$, $p < 0.01$.[2] Military institutions do not offer a faculty-in-residence program either, but the low sample size precludes statistical analysis.

Many responses bring to the fore the issue of learners' active engagement in on-campus events, which gives faculty "a partner in event organization and provides a vehicle for student initiative." Many faculty members reflect on such initiatives by stating they "recently learned that some students did organize their own 'Russian movie night' as an informal social activity for a small circle of Russian-interested students." Respondents emphasize the success of ECAs that are organized by students: "Events organized by the Russian Club are attended very well, as students decide on the nature of events and bring their friends, etc." Finally, faculty responses suggest that campus-wide cultural activities are a positive factor for enrollment as they increase the visibility of Russian programs.

Current State of Extracurricular Activities: Off-Campus ECAs

The respondents' institutions organize off-campus ECAs such as trips to films, restaurants, and museums (37.5%); trips to operas, ballet, and theater (31.25%); engagement with local Russian communities (20.83%); and intercollegiate events with other nearby institutions (12.5%). However, some institutions do not offer any off-campus extracurricular activities or events (18.75 %) (see Figure 17.3).

Many responders describe off-campus events as "very occasional" because there is "no Russian community" or "no budget for fieldtrips" or because "theater/ballet/opera are usually prohibitively expensive." Our data indicate that the variety of off-campus ECA offerings depends on the location of the institution. For instance, institutions located in metropolitan areas with a local Russian community tend to offer a higher level of off-campus ECAs. In contrast, institutions situated in areas lacking a Russian community have comparatively limited opportunities for off-campus ECAs (see Figure 17.4).

Faculty responses reveal that liberal arts colleges have significantly more off-campus ECA offerings than both private and state universities: $F(3,44) = 6.726$, $p < 0.001$. Since many faculty members do not know their annual ECA budget, this result cannot easily be explained through institutional variation in funding. Nevertheless, it may stem from the fact that different types of institutions face different challenges. Public universities often have state-related funding issues whereas many private colleges and universities, due to their remote location and lack of a local Russian community, tend to be more self-reliant and creative in finding ways to enhance their students' ECA experiences.

Some respondents speak about participation in regional events that bring together undergraduates from institutions across a state or region: "The one thing we do annually

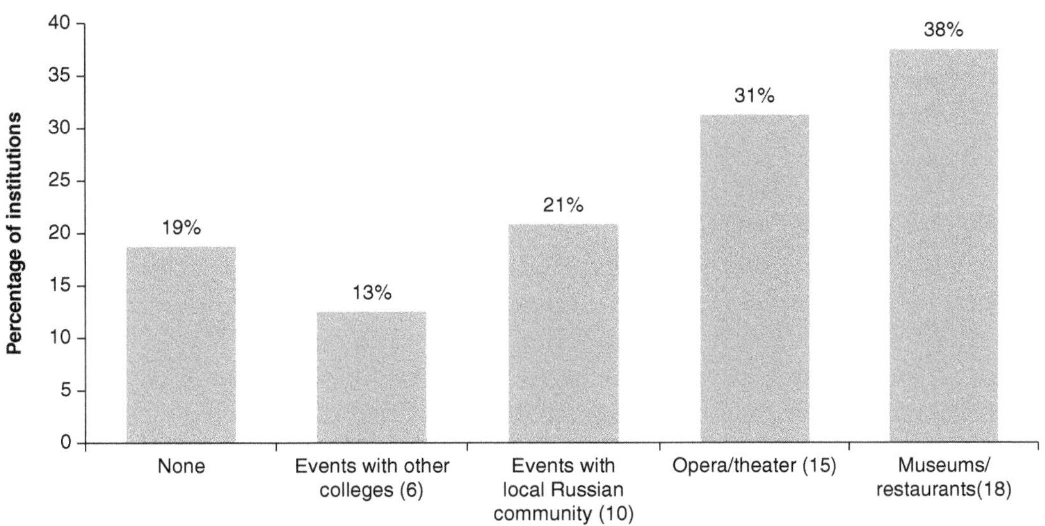

FIGURE 17.3. Off-Campus ECA Offerings

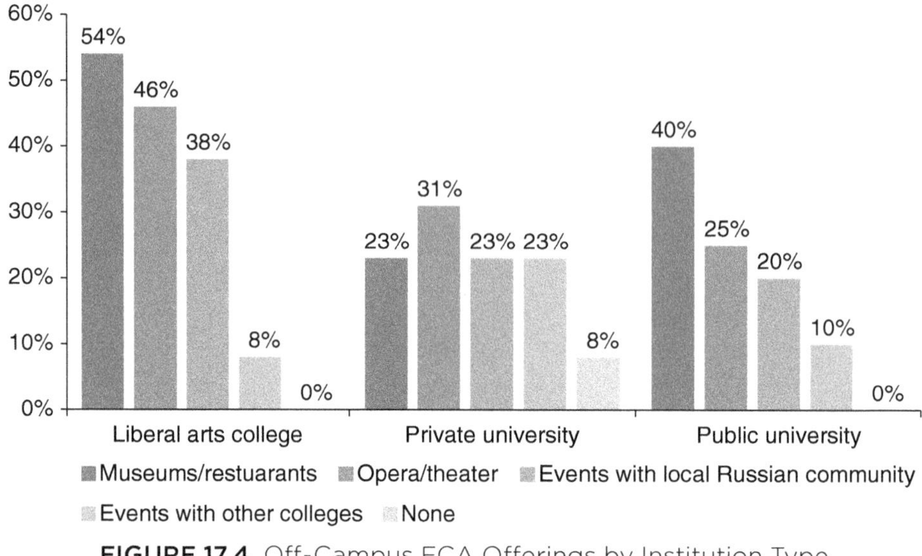

FIGURE 17.4. Off-Campus ECA Offerings by Institution Type

is participate in a regional Russian-language competition that involves five to eight postsecondary institutions from our state. It's a one-day event, but it does give our students a sense that they are not the only people in the state studying Russian."

We were interested to see if a connection exists between institutions that are experiencing an increase in enrollment in Russian-language courses and institutions that are implementing a robust cocurricular program in Russian. Correlation tests of linear regression do not reveal any significant correlation between enrollment and richness of ECA offerings, with one exception in which the correlation between enrollment and off-campus ECA offerings approaches significance. There is a significant difference observed in enrollments between Russian programs offering off-campus field trips to opera, ballet, or theater productions and those that do not: $F(1, 44) = 4.624$, $p < 0.05$. No other significant differences are found for individual ECA events.

Cooperation with Other Departments

Typical campus-wide events include international culture shows, food festivals, and study abroad fairs coordinated by international centers or offices. Only one respondent spoke about a joint event with another foreign language programs: "This spring semester, together with the German program (and including participation from our Chinese, Japanese, and Arabic programs), we hosted a scholarship workshop oriented toward students interested in critical language/study abroad–related fellowships (e.g., Critical Languages Scholarship program (CLS), Boren, Fulbright)."

Under half (47.92%) of all faculty report being satisfied with the degree of interdepartmental partnerships, specifically with the ECAs organized in conjunction with other foreign languages, humanities, and science departments. The majority of the rest report being dissatisfied with the degree of interdepartmental partnerships at their current institutions. One instructor chose not to reply. This lack of interdepartmental partnerships and the resulting burden on individual faculty to create initiatives may explain why so many respondents are dissatisfied: "Cross-departmental collaboration depends a lot on individual faculty members and what they are teaching in a given semester. Our college offers opportunities to team teach and to bring in guests for short courses, and there is funding to organize conferences and collaborative projects for students and faculty. But it is all at the initiative of individual faculty members, so it varies a lot from year to year."

The almost 50-50 distribution of faculty satisfaction suggests that the current level of cooperation among foreign language departments is insufficient and that there is room for improvement in this area. In order to foster connections between the faculties of Russian and other departments on campus, our responders recommend "Advocacy from faculty beyond those with courses directly connected with Russian, such as criminology, business, . . . and advocacy from the dean and higher administration on behalf of less commonly taught languages."

Student Participation in ECAs

The survey asked faculty members whether or not they require participation in language and culture ECAs as a part of their courses. A total of 56.25% of faculty responders state that participation in at least one event is required, while 43.75% say that participation is not required (see Figure 17.5).

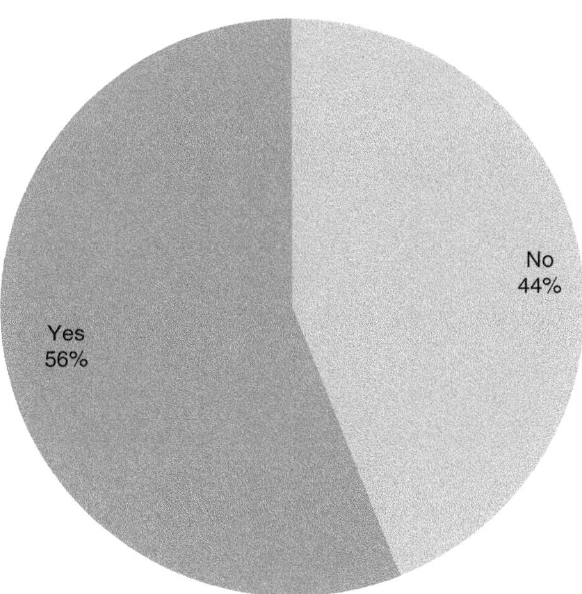

FIGURE 17.5. Is ECA Participation Required?

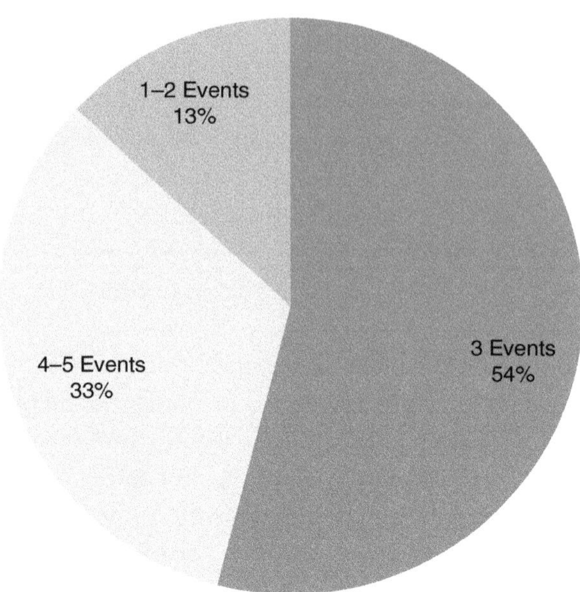

FIGURE 17.6. Degree of ECA Attendance Required by Faculty

Twenty-four faculty report that their program requires ECA participation. Where participation is mandatory, each semester programs require: one event (12.5%); two events (16.67%); three events (37.50%); four events (4.16%); or five events (29.16%) (see Figure 17.6).

Faculty attitudes on requiring participation is not homogeneous. The survey shows that one third (33.33%) view ECAs as an important part of learners' education. Some respondents strongly disagree with making ECAs mandatory for students but others (8.89%) believe that participation in ECAs should be somehow required.

A small number of faculty (8.33%) support an incentivized approach, using extra credit, prizes, and other forms of reward to encourage attendance: "Better carrot than stick. And anyway, if the events are attractive, students will participate. If they are an integrated part of the curriculum and done in lieu of classwork, then, certainly, they should be mandatory."

Faculty that support some kind of attendance enforcement cite several methods of confirming attendance at events, including the use of signed attendance sheets or requiring participants to submit a summary report of the event.[3] The survey respondents indicate that they are well aware of the dilemma of requiring ECA attendance: "I do not give extra credit. I do not believe students should be bribed to attend events. Some students (as was the case when I was a student) have no time for this: they are too busy working to pay for tuition, etc. However, clearly many of these events would benefit the students."

Faculty have different expectations regarding attendance, and it depends on a learner's language level: "In our lower-level courses most of us require students to attend any five cultural, cocurricular events in the course of the semester as part of their learning. By the time they are in third year it becomes commonplace for them to attend and for them to enjoy the small, tight community around the department."

A number of faculty express their concerns about laying out expectations on event attendance, citing scheduling conflicts, competing requirements of other courses, and the financial burden that leads students to work during the school year or expedite their time to degree. The majority of faculty tend to give their classes flexibility in ECA participation.

Faculty Expectations of ECA Impact on Student Learning

Ninety-eight percent of respondents believe that ECAs have a significant impact on three essential categories: cultural knowledge, interest in the language, and motivation toward studying Russian language and culture. Respondents generally believe that ECAs have some impact on students' learning motivation (81.25%) and none think that extracurricular events have no impact. The majority of respondents also believe that there is some impact on students' cultural knowledge (70.83%) and none feel that ECAs have no significant impact (see Figure 17.7).

Faculty demonstrate a range of beliefs concerning the impact of ECAs on students' language learning. While some believe ECAs have a very significant (18.75%) or some impact (35.42%), a small minority (4.17%) report that, in their opinions, ECAs do not significantly influence language development. Faculty feel that ECAs play a lesser role in developing language proficiency than in cultivating cultural understanding or improving motivation.

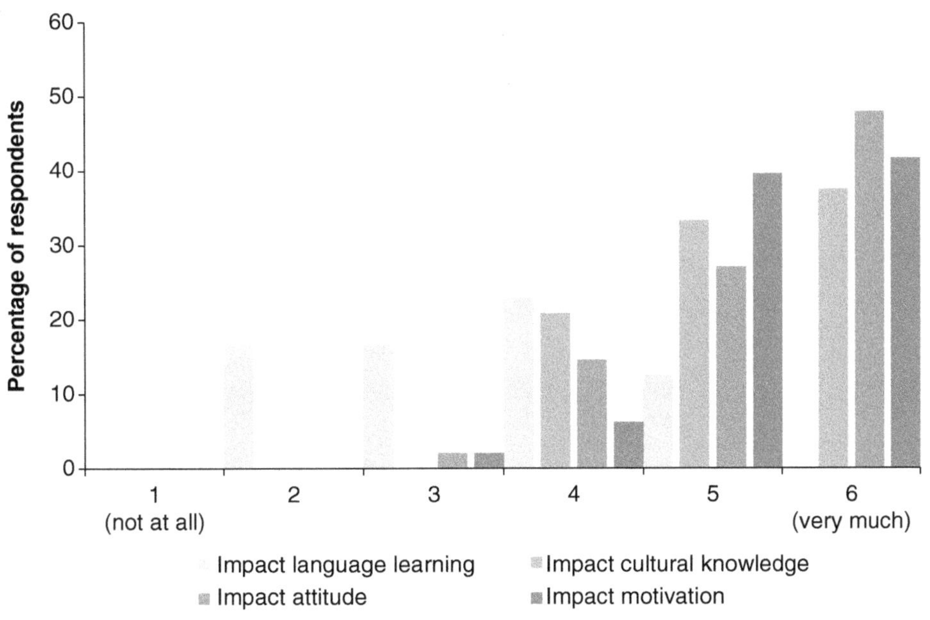

FIGURE 17.7. Impact of ECAs on Student Learning

Our survey split various forms of ECAs into the two categories of language-related and cultural activities. The Russian Table is the most widely used language activity offered outside of the classroom: 81.3% of respondents reported that their program sponsored a Russian Table. Despite the ubiquity of the Russian Table among ECA programs in Russian departments, faculty members have remarkably low expectations regarding the effect of ECAs on students' language proficiency: 43.8% do not believe the impact is significant.

ECA Success and Challenges

Over half of the surveyed faculty (56.25%) report being satisfied with their department's extracurricular offerings, while 41% reported being dissatisfied. One respondent chose not to reply (see Figure 17.8).

Among the major challenges hindering the development of ECAs, faculty cite factors such as low participation rates (56.25%), difficulty scheduling events (21.88%), and lack of funding (18.75%) (see Figure 17.9).

When asked to supply other reasons, faculty also cite personality conflicts and poor communication (18.75%), busy schedules (10.42%), a lack of structural support for interdisciplinary programming (6.25%), and low visibility of Russian program on campus and high enrollment pressure (2.85%). If examined across institutions rather than across faculty, student participation is most commonly cited as a key challenge for ECA implementation (see Figure 17.10). While not an issue for liberal arts and private universities, funding is the second most important issue facing public universities. Scheduling is a less common problem but is more frequently seen as an obstacle that affects both public and private institutions.

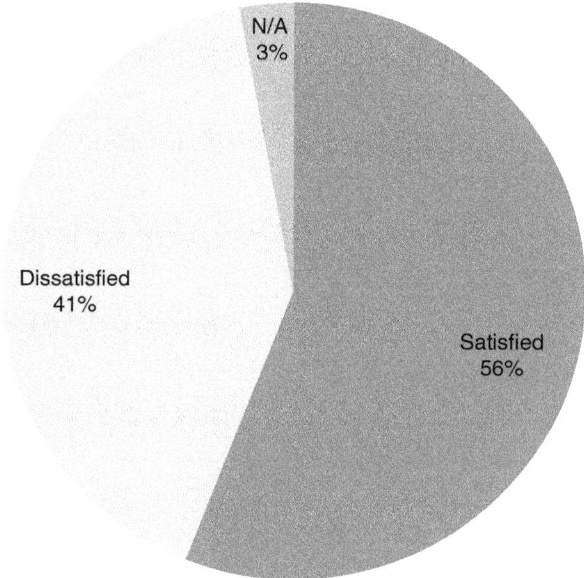

FIGURE 17.8. Faculty Satisfaction with Department ECA Offerings

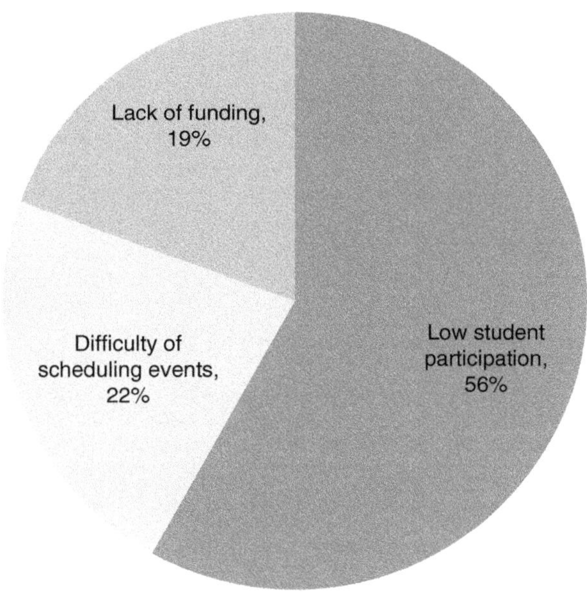

FIGURE 17.9. Key ECA Challenges across Faculty

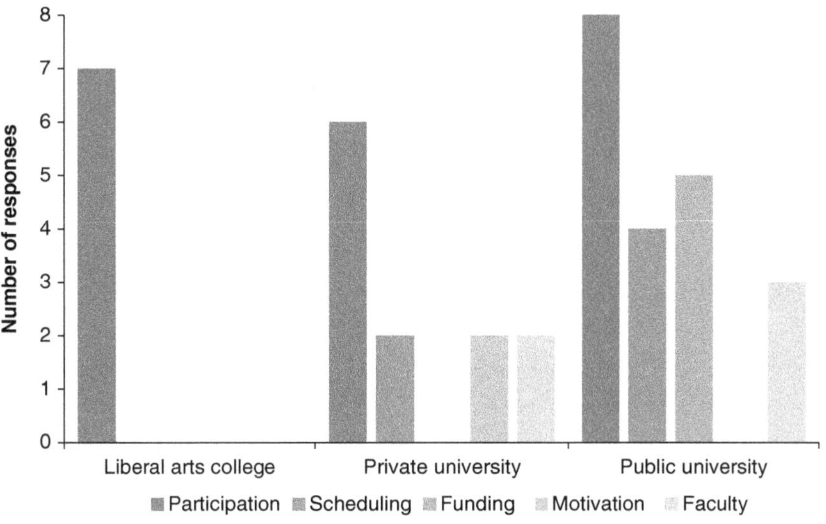

FIGURE 17.10. Key ECA Challenges across Institutions

The most common suggestions for improvement correspond directly to the most common challenges facing ECAs: increasing overall attendance at events (43.24%), expanding ECA funding allocations (16.22%), improving faculty involvement (10.81%), providing better announcements of ECA programming (8.11%), and strengthening interdepartmental collaboration (8.11%) (see Figure 17.11).

Although our study clearly shows that ECAs play an important role among language departments, many responders feel that ECAs are to some extent an underappreciated resource that could be used more effectively. Faculty responses to the

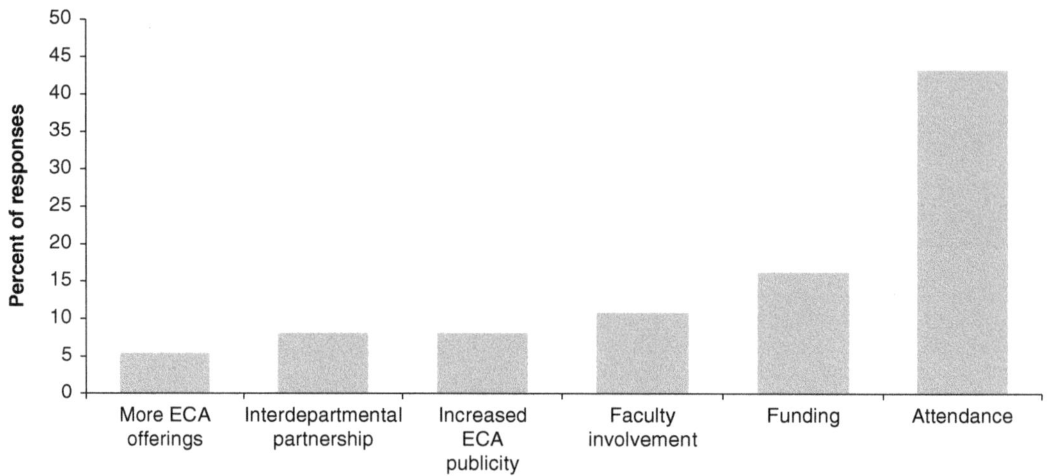

FIGURE 17.11. Commonly Cited Suggestions for ECAs' Improvements

survey's open-ended questions provide a wealth of suggestions for ECA improvement. Their recommendations address some of the previously mentioned challenges to ECAs. Improvements in participation and event scheduling include the following specific ideas:

- "Better attendance and more students living in the Russian House."
- "Development of Russian Club [is] one possibility (increase student investment in ECA). Or a large all-campus event."
- "More careful scheduling of events and better outreach to other units whose offerings may produce students in our program, or at least attendance at some of our events. More concerted planning farther in advance to organize and advertise events better. Better contact with majors about what events THEY would be most likely to come to, and help from them with publicizing and involving other students in the process. More varied types of events, not just lectures or tea / socializing."

Faculty propose inviting high-profile speakers to campus and expanding off-campus offerings, including more interaction with community members and events with other institutions: "'Bigger' names invited to campus and more fieldtrips to theater productions, ballets, operas, museums—events that involve interaction with community members—more intercollegiate events."

Many faculty see potential benefits in establishing interdisciplinary partnerships across campus:

- "We would like to see other departments do more with Russia and coordinate with us, from art, music, and theater to environmental science and political science, to religion and philosophy."

- "More involvement on the part of other program faculty; a Russian-related (or even more broadly critical language–related) "FIG" (freshman interest group) would be excellent. Having a dedicated (=paid) graduate student responsible for scouting out Russian-related events on campus and in the community would be great—again, decentralization of campus makes it difficult to stay on top of happenings."

Many faculty express their frustration with lack of funding and institutional support: "We need more money and support from the university. Everything is done on a shoestring budget and run by a lecturer."

When asked to share experiences demonstrating the impact of ECAs on students' learning outcomes, respondents describe compelling cases in which, through regular participation in ECAs, students are able to accelerate their language learning and improve their proficiency level. Many respondents also note that active participation in ECAs increases learners' confidence, boosts their morale, and helps them overcome their shyness in speaking the language. ECAs give students more opportunities to make new friends with similar interests, which builds a sense of community and later translates into both higher retention rates at the upper levels and higher enrollment numbers at the beginning: "One first-year student actively sought out ECAs and got hooked on Russian language and culture right away. After her freshman year she studied at Middlebury, returned and matriculated into third-year Russian, went on a study abroad the following summer, returned, and matriculated into fourth-year Russian and then went on the Moscow Internship Program the following summer. By the end of the Moscow program she was rated Superior on the ACTFL Oral Proficiency Interview (OPI)." Stories like this should be shared with prospective majors to make a compelling case for continuing to study Russian.

Summary of Survey Results

Our first research question probed the current state of ECAs by examining trends in Russian language enrollment, the various types of ECAs offered, and the opinions of faculty members on their efficacy. Attitudes on enrollment are evenly split: although no clear enrollment trends were established by the survey, faculty members agree that innovative approaches have become necessary to maintain students' interest in Russian language studies. However, instructor responses reveal a relatively homogenous distribution of ECA types, demonstrating that new approaches to ECAs are rare.

Our second research question asked whether different types of institutions utilize institution-specific ECA models. The results indicate an absence of institution-specific ECA models and that there is no single ECA model ideally suited to all types of institutions. The following quote summarizes the overall faculty opinion of ECAs: "It is important that the department must value ECAs strongly, but not insist on a lockstep approach to those activities and the academic program. Often ECAs offer participants opportunities to learn about culture material not covered academically.

Ideally, ECAs should know and include cultural touchstones that are part of the departmental program but [faculty] should have the freedom to devise creative programming of their own (based on the interests of those directing ECAs and student interests)."

Our third research question addressed the challenges of ECAs. We observed a pattern among all respondents, that all types of institutions have three major challenges in conducting ECAs: participation, scheduling, and funding. Many respondents feel there is a need to rethink the traditional approach to ECA organization, in which faculty organize events for students: "The combination of student-run and teacher-supported [events] makes the events very well attended."

DISCUSSION OF FOLLOW-UP INTERVIEWS

Given the lack of robust statistical trends in faculty perception of ECA vis-à-vis enrollment, it is evident that there is no one ECA model that is universally effective. Nevertheless, faculty suggestions for event development provide a number of recommendations and real insight into what makes a particular ECA program effective. After participating in the initial survey, nine faculty members agreed to a follow-up in-depth interview on the changing role of ECAs in the Russian language curriculum and redefining the profession's approach to ECAs.

Our survey results demonstrate that the perception of ECAs as a series of out-of-classroom activities that supplement an academic curriculum has evolved, and interviewees deliberate on the changing role of ECAs in their programs: "On the one hand, I'd love there to be more 'connectivity' between our curriculum and ECAs. But given how few faculty members there are on campus who do things Russian (and the difficulty of overcoming the forces of decentralization), that's really not possible. On the other, I'm as interested in ECAs that are not specifically connected to our curriculum (which, given our size, is fairly narrow), because (1) it broadens student exposure to the different ways in which one can approach Russian culture, and (2) it draws in a greater number of students than anything tied directly to our curriculum would be."

Because of the changing nature of ECAs and the challenge of student participation, we asked the nine interview participants to comment further on these important issues. Participants' opinions reflect the notion that the perception of ECAs has shifted: "I don't like to call it extracurricular. I think it's more cocurricular because it is accompanying a particular class. I think cocurricular activity is a more appropriate term for it." This shift in understanding supports our proposal to redefine these events from extracurricular to cocurricular.

Many interviewees indicate that events planned by various Russian programs are tied in with specific course offerings: "Coordinating the activities we offer with the content of courses usually makes students' engagement more meaningful." Respondents also affirm that "ECAs are tightly connected to the role of the program." Interviewees emphasize that coordination between ECAs and course material results in better ECA attendance, especially when connected with a particular course: "The screenings were not always well attended sometimes, but when incorporated [into the course] there is a motivation for the screening, and then we could hope to get more people to attend." Even when faculty speak about ECAs as supplemental, the underlying motif is that ECAs complement the existing course offerings because they can tap into topics that are otherwise unavailable: "Extracurricular activities allow us to connect to more contemporary stuff because in many cases . . . speakers, or films that we're showing, or lectures that we're organizing have to do with what's happening in Russia now, which is not necessarily reflected in our courses."

By broadening the students' exposure, in this case to contemporary Russia, ECAs fuel their interest in language and culture study, as many interviewees agree. One respondent summarized the role of ECAs as "on-campus immersion opportunities . . . that are connected with coursework. [ECAs are] Simply enhancing and broadening [students'] exposure to Russian culture in general."

Reflecting on the relationship between ECAs and the academic curriculum, one respondent emphasized their potential for student recruitment: it is ECA that first captures students' attention and generates interest in Russian studies, which then draws learners into the Russian program: "There are so many demands on students' time, and at the same time we have so many students who start studying Russian who are not going to major in Russian studies, they just take it out of general interest. That ties the ECAs to the curriculum and our hope is that it will capture their interest and entice them to come to the events even if they were not planning to."

There is also a sense among Russian educators that ECAs need to be better connected with the academic curriculum and with specific goals for Russian majors. One respondent stated: "I don't think we've spent a lot of time carefully articulating what we're doing in any one area of extracurricular activity to any stated goals for Russian majors or for foreign language majors in general."

Our interviewees spoke overwhelmingly in favor of making students play a more active role in organizing and running the events, thus "making students a part of the activities (rather than recipients of information)." Faculty suggest the key aspects to engaging students are: "quality, variety of events (including Russian Radio, language nights at a local café), and creating community when singing classes are welcoming of all levels of language and are conducted by our senior lecturer in Russian and a professor of music who specializes in Russian vocal diction."

Student-run organizations like the Russian Club help language departments by getting undergraduates more involved in ECAs. Interviewees give examples of such collaboration in the form of student ambassadors or undergraduate departmental representatives: "We usually have two students per year, and involving them and figuring out how to spread the word is the key for us because they know how students prefer to get information and they know the ins and outs of the system, so they spread the flyers and they create Facebook events."

One interviewee suggested that a designated Russian space be created on campus and online. "Even more important is to have a designated space if it's a Russia-themed party or even for a lecture . . . if you have Russian teas, conversation tables, lunch tables, it's good to have a designated online space where you post not only advertisements about what the next Russian tea will be about but also post pictures from the previous tea. It's not just advertising for an event, it's [spreading information] after the event."

Faculty-student collaboration is essential for creating a dynamic cultural environment on campus. Interviewees believe that from the students' perspective, ECAs play an important social role by building a community of learners through which they can socialize with each other and their instructors. One respondent stated: "Students are looking for a social stimulation and, in other words, opportunities to actually socialize with real-life human beings."

The students consider their participation in ECAs from perspectives meaningful to them (socializing with friends, building an impressive resume for a potential employer, practicing language in a less stressful environment, etc.).[4] Faculty respondents state that language education should be "a longer-term, gradual process of students immersing in Russian culture" and that we should prioritize "not the language study first but the cultural interest, then the language study starts to become more serious." The survey results clearly shows that many faculty view ECAs not in terms of the immediate learning outcomes in linguistic proficiency but as "direct contact with the culture with real tactile, direct, experiential nature," as "enhancing and broadening their exposure to Russian culture in general," and as "subliminal learning." We need to promote this "subliminal" perspective among the students and likely their parents as well. The process of individual learner exploration of language and culture in the context of ECA settings is incredibly promising. It will help us find new ways of involving students in ECAs and in creating forms of faculty-student collaborations on campus.

DIRECTIONS FOR FUTURE RESEARCH AND PRACTICAL RECOMMENDATIONS

We view ECAs as an increasingly vital component of language learners' development and of a successful language-learning experience. This study shows that ECAs can exist in a variety of forms and can potentially focus on different educational goals depending on the needs of the language departments and the particular culture of a given campus. Effective ECAs are not just a series of events that support an academic curriculum or classroom learning goal, but a dynamic, flexible, open environment designed to expand opportunities to study the target language and culture with collective input from both faculty and students. Thus faculty perceptions of these activities has shifted from being extracurricular to being cocurricular.

As far as we know, the present survey-based study is the first attempt to analyze successful and challenging aspects of ECAs from the perspective of the Russian language faculties. The rich data and detailed responses to open questions suggest that this is an important issue that deserves wider discussion in our professional community. Our research demonstrates that students' out-of-classroom engagement with Russian language and culture enhances their motivation and language proficiency, based on the feedback of the participating Russian faculty. In order to make a stronger and more comprehensive case, a similar measure of the impressions of students with ECAs is also needed. As we embarked on this study, we intended to survey both faculty and students and thus created two surveys—one for faculty and one for students. The student surveys were distributed at Wellesley College and Oberlin College. Due to IRB restrictions we were unable to survey students from other institutions. As a result, the sample size is too insignificant to include in the collected data of the current study. As a direction for further research we propose that more data be collected from students in order to provide stronger evidence that Russian ECAs enhance students' motivation and proficiency in language and culture. A larger sample size would also facilitate an in-depth statistical analysis that could define how particular ECA offerings impact enrollments. The present study observed a significant increase in Russian program enrollment when language courses were complemented by off-campus ECA offerings such as trips to the opera, the theater, and ballet. A more detailed study would be able to confirm this positive effect of ECAs on enrollments.

Another important question for future research is the degree to which participation in ECAs enhances students' motivation and language proficiency. A comparison between two groups of learners with differing degrees of ECA engagement may shed light on this issue. In order to facilitate data collection from a large number of participants, such a study would require coordination among either Russian language faculty from various institutions or cooperation among foreign language faculty within the same institution. This study could survey students in order to have a more accurate and detailed picture of their interests, expectations, and needs, and might increase their ECA participation. We recommend a variety of survey formats for undergraduates within one Russian department, for students in various foreign language departments across one campus, or among learners in various Russian programs across multiple institutions. These extensive surveys would not only increase the sample size of the collected data but would potentially offer useful information for future collaboration in ECA programming across a wide range of departments, institutions, and regions.

Our study shows a disparity in faculty expectations regarding language-related and culture-related activities: faculty expect ECAs to have a significant cultural impact on students but an insignificant linguistic impact on them. We need more research on effective cocurricular language activities that will develop their proficiency as well as more creative ways of encouraging student engagement in language-related activities. To this end, we have assembled a compilation of the most outstanding events shared with us by the survey participants (see Appendix).

Based on feedback from faculty we put forward the following practical recommendations for innovative approaches to ECAs that address the aforementioned findings and challenges:

- *Design a successful ECA environment.* Our data strongly support a shift from a faculty-run to a student-run or cooperative ECA model. We should empower learners in a way that encourages such a transition and supports student-led events that reflect their interests. Students may be more actively engaged in events when they have a chance to share their success stories about study abroad or summer internships. Allowing successful alums to lead panels on future careers in Russian-related fields may also help stimulate student engagement. In addition to student-led events on campus, we need to encourage them to participate in off-campus events like the ACTR National Postsecondary Russian Essay Contest or undergraduate Olympiad of Spoken Russian organized by various universities. Such events bring together students across campuses and allow them to experience a sense of belonging to a wider community of Russian learners.

Our study also shows that effective ECAs foster creation of a "mini-immersion" environment on campus. In addition to the ubiquitous Russian Table we propose to experiment with a wider variety of language-related activities that fit the specific campus culture. For instance, offering a language pledge in a Russian living community (Russian house or Russian corridor), planning a Russian coffee break with faculty for more advanced speakers, or creating a new Russian activity out of an existing one by incorporating a Russian ECA into a popular existing event with consistently high participation (e.g., Russian referees for sports, Russian music festivals).

- *Increase the visibility of Russian on campus through ECAs.* Bringing high-profile guests for campus-wide events that connect Russia with other disciplines or regions requires long-term planning that involves the college's administrators as well as cooperation with other departments. For instance, the focus of such events may shift from Russia as a country to Eurasia as a region and thus invite cooperation with Asian language programs. Lectures on Russian space exploration or the history of Russian math and science may bring together learners across humanities and STEM disciplines. These efforts would foster a spirit of interdepartmental partnerships and campus collaborations.
- *Connect existing ECAs through technology and social media.* We acknowledge that technology can play a significant role in engaging students in ECAs and can connect learners across campuses in the United States and with peers in Russia. It can be as simple as asking your students to switch the settings on their computers and smart phones to Russian in order to take a step toward an imitation of an immersion environment. In addition, the emergence of Russian social networking groups within student communities is indicative of their developing Russian identities. The impact of educational technology on curricular changes in Russian teaching suggests it has an equally valid role to play in ECAs and should be considered in future research.

We propose putting these discussions in the context of the changing goals of language education and the innovative approaches to the language instruction applicable within extracurricular settings.

APPENDIX: OUTSTANDING RUSSIAN EVENTS SHARED BY SURVEY PARTICIPANTS

- Our Russian singing club concerts are a standout event in our program. Students work with our Russian language lecturer and a professor of music who specializes in Russian vocal diction to learn classical folk and contemporary songs in Russian. They perform at the end of each semester to a large audience of supporters.
- The introduction of a separate conversational coffee klatch limited to advanced students has been an excellent innovation, helping to create stronger bonds between students and faculty.
- Last year's Russian Week was especially successful, with a wide variety of events and high levels of student turnout. The activities included a cooking demonstration at a faculty member's home, lectures on popular culture, and a roundtable on the Ukraine Crisis.
- Several years ago we had a very active Russian Club presidency that organized an annual fundraiser for an orphanage in Russia. Students, faculty, and community members alike contributed to the musical evening and raised a considerable sum of money that benefited the orphanage.
- For Lermontov's 200th birthday the students reenacted his duel with Martynov and recited/read poetry and Martynov's memoir about the duel, which the students translated.
- The Year of Russia: Reimagining Russia's Realms, funded by the College of Arts & Sciences. Featured 88 events that included guest speakers, a Russian dinner, a Maslenitsa celebration, a film festival, craft workshops, etc.
- Diversity Day, which included food, dancing, music, videos, and representatives from foreign countries.
- With Asia Center funding we ran a Siberian film festival. Participation wasn't great but it did draw people from other areas, which was nice cross-fertilization.
- Annual celebration of Maslenitsa, complete with a blini-making workshop.
- Food, cooking events, trips: cooking night, trip to a nearby town that had a large Russian Orthodox community and that was hosting a Russian festival.
- Residencies of artists, poets, musicians, filmmakers: performance-art event by Psoi Korolenko; visit by Russian poet Vera Pavlova; screening of Alina Rudnitskaya's documentary film *Blood* and Q&A with the director; performance by Grenada music group; Moscow Nights émigré song and dance performance from Cleveland, Ohio; visit of Sayan and Erzhena Zhambalov from Buryatia for a week-long residency to teach throat singing and Buryatian folk music.
- Panels, presentations by faculty.
- Music, poetry, dance, crafts: annual Student Talent Show; Cheburashka making party; Easter egg painting; annual music/poetry recital; a watch party for the opening ceremonies of the Winter Olympics in Sochi.

NOTES

1. The MLA's "Survey of Enrollments in Languages Other than English" (Goldberg et al. 2015) reports that "Russian enrollments decreased nationally by 17.9% since 2009, but 48.7% of all Russian programs reported either stability or growth in 2013." The MLA's 2016 preliminary report confirms the decline in overall foreign language enrollments and suggests that "the results for 2013 are the beginning of a trend rather than a blip; the decline between 2009 and 2016 is 15.3%" (Looney & Lusin, 2018, p. 2). Retrieved from https://www.mla.org/content/download/83540/2197676/2016-Enrollments-Short-Report.pdf.
2. Humboldt State University describes this position this way: "The Faculty/Staff-in-Residence reside on campus. They sponsor and participate in educational programs and provide informal mentoring for students. They are also responsible for engaging students in activities that integrate curricular and co-curricular education." Retrieved from https://housing.humboldt.edu/residence-life-employment.
3. For an example of such a report, see Prager and Kramer (2014).
4. For more on students' motivation, see Merrill (2013).

REFERENCES

Bown, J., Dewey, D. P., Martinsen, R. A., & Baker, W. (2011). Foreign language houses: Identities in transition. *Critical Inquiry in Language Studies*, *8*(3), 203–35.

Brown, T., Bown, J., & Eggett, D. L. (2015). Advanced foreign language study through global debate. In T. Brown & J. Bown (Eds.), *To advanced proficiency and beyond: Theory and methods for developing superior second language ability* (pp. 73–83). Washington, DC: Georgetown UP.

Campbell, H. (1973). *Extracurricular foreign language activities.* ERIC Focus Reports on the Teaching of Foreign Languages No. 29. New York: American Council on the Teaching of Foreign Languages.

Geisler, M., Kramsch, C., McGinnis, S., Patrikis, P., Pratt, M. L., Ryding, K., & Haun, Saussy (2007). Foreign languages and higher education: New structures for a changed world. Modern Language Association Ad Hoc Committee on Foreign Languages. *Profession*, 234–45.

Goldberg, D., Looney, D., & Lusin, N. (2015). Enrollments in Languages Other than English in US Institutions of Higher Education, Fall 2013. Modern Language Association of America. Retrieved from https://apps.mla.org/pdf/2013_enrollment_survey.pdf

Guthrie, J. W. (Ed.). (2003). *Encyclopedia of education.* New York: Macmillan Reference.

Kearney, E. (2010). Cultural immersion in the foreign language classroom: Some narrative possibilities. *Modern Language Journal*, *94*(2), 332–36.

Looney, D., & Lusin, N. (2018). Enrollments in Languages Other than English in US Institutions of Higher Education, Summer 2016 and Fall 2016: Preliminary Report. Modern Language Association of America. Retrieved from https://www.mla.org/content/download/83540/2197676/2016-Enrollments-Short-Report.pdf

Makarova, V., & Reva, A. (2017). Perceived impact of extra-curricular activities on foreign language learning in Canadian and Russian university context. *Apples—Journal of Applied Language Studies, 11*(1), 43–65.

Martinsen, R., Baker, W., Dewey, D. P., Bown, J., & Johnson, G. (2010). Exploring diverse settings for language acquisition and use: Comparing study abroad, service learning abroad and foreign language housing. *Applied Language Learning, 20*(1&2), 45–69.

Martinsen, R., Baker, W., Bown, J., & Johnson, G. (2011). The benefits of living in foreign language housing: The effect of language use and second-language type on oral proficiency gains. *Modern Language Journal, 95*(2), 274–90.

Merrill, J. (2013). Our Russian classrooms and students: Who is choosing Russian, why, and what cultural content should we offer them? *Russian Language Journal, 63*, 51–78.

Prager, D., & Kramer, J. (2014). The *Kulturpass*: Strategies for enhancing cultural engagement outside the German-language classroom. *Die Unterrichitspraxis/Teaching German, 47*(1), 42–48.

Rifkin B. (2005). A ceiling effect in traditional classroom foreign language instruction: Data from Russian. *Modern Language Journal, 89*(1), 3–18.

Romanov, A. (2000). Student motivation for studying Russian: Survey and analysis. In O. Kagan & B. Rifkin (Eds.), *The learning and teaching of Slavic languages and cultures* (pp. 145–66). Bloomington, IN: Slavica.

Tenhouse, A. (2003). College extracurricular activities. In J. W. Guthrie (Ed.), *Encyclopedia of education* (pp. 373–76). New York: Macmillan Reference.

Tumanov, A. (1983). Extra-curricular activities in second-language teaching in a university setting: Experience of a Russian program. *Canadian Modern Language Review, 39*(4), 827–39.

Wolf, G. (2002). A reevaluation of the language house: Foreign language curriculum, advocacy, articulation, and outreach. *ADFL Bulletin, 33*(2), 81–85.

PART VI

◇◇◇◇

TEACHING AND LEARNING RUSSIAN WITH TECHNOLOGY

18
MIXING IT UP WITH BLENDED LEARNING

Shannon Spasova and Kristen Welsh

This chapter offers a guide to blended learning as the authors have used it to teach Russian in two different institutional contexts.[1] Blended learning expands the contact hours available for active learning in class by using technology to present traditional lecture content and certain other activities outside of class. Both authors have found positive, even transformative results from introducing blended learning: it has permitted us to cover more concepts than in the past, to increase active learning in face-to-face classroom settings, and even to begin rethinking methodology. We are enthusiastic advocates for this approach yet acknowledge that there is no universal road map for blended learning and that our own journeys include false starts and wrong turns. This chapter, therefore, is designed to streamline the process for instructors who wish to try blended learning and to encourage those who feel they are working in isolation.

There are multiple and important differences between our two projects and contexts, which aptly demonstrate the versatility and broad applicability of blended learning even within the relatively small realm of postsecondary Russian language teaching. Some of these differences are obvious: Shannon Spasova teaches at Michigan State University, a large public research university located in a metro area of nearly 500,000; Kristen Welsh teaches at Hobart and William Smith Colleges, a small, private liberal arts college in a city with just over 13,000. Shannon has focused her project on intermediate Russian courses, while Kristen has created materials for beginners. Shannon's project is institutionally driven and part of her formal job description. Kristen's project is instructor-driven: although she received institutional support to launch her project, it is not part of a departmental or institutional blended-learning initiative.

We begin with primary concepts from second-language acquisition (SLA) theory that underpin our pedagogical practices but this chapter does not provide an exhaustive theoretical treatment of blended learning, not least because the practice itself is still new. We then address the goals, benefits, and challenges of blended learning. Our focus is practical, and we offer case studies that describe how we created our projects. We conclude with lessons learned and by offering recommendations for colleagues who wish to embark on blended-learning projects, whatever their own training, teaching responsibilities, and institutional affiliation.

This chapter illustrates the effectiveness and the transformative potential of digital pedagogies. Using digital tools does not mean simply putting already-available materials online; rather, it means asking what effective practices digital tools make possible that previously could not have been implemented or even imagined. It gives instructors the opportunity to revisit and even challenge the how, what, and why of our teaching, creating the desire for innovative and renewed teaching and the space in which to achieve it.

BLENDED LEARNING AND SLA THEORY

Although a thorough discussion of SLA concepts and their relevance for blended learning is beyond the scope here, we will highlight several ways in which blended learning addresses three of the most critical elements in the language-acquisition process: input, output, and feedback. While there is disagreement about the exact mechanisms by which input contributes to acquisition, all major theories of SLA give input a central role. As we will argue, blended learning allows for more, and more varied, opportunities to engage with input. Input by itself is, of course, not sufficient for language acquisition; learners must be given the chance to negotiate meaning through output (Swain, 1985) and blended learning can offer more chances to engage in output, with more opportunities for producing utterances. SLA researchers have long noted the role that negative evidence or feedback (such as recasts) plays in acquisition (Gass, 1997). Blended learning can improve acquisition by reducing a learner's wait time for feedback on independent work. Both automatic grading, which can be targeted for specific incorrect answers, and adaptive tools are beginning to provide more of the feedback that is so crucial for learning a second language. We discuss some of the ways our projects harness the potential of blended learning to increase input, output, and feedback. The field needs more classroom-based research to investigate whether blended environments are contributing to a faster rate of acquisition, but some of our observations hint that they may be doing so.

GOALS OF BLENDED LEARNING

Blended/hybrid and flipped learning share the common goal of making class time more active and student-centered and of making the entire learning experience more flexible, regardless of where instruction occurs and how much of it is delivered digitally. In some of the scholarly literature on teaching and learning the terms *hybrid learning* and *blended learning* are used interchangeably.[2] The *flipped classroom* is a distinct term, though it is often associated with blended learning.[3] In flipped classrooms the basic course content, especially lectures on static concepts such as conjugation and declension patterns, is delivered outside of class, usually via digital video; this feature is central to our blended-learning projects. In the past the main roadblock to implementing video lectures was the actual delivery mechanism, but digital technologies have become more available, less expensive, and easier to use. They have also become more varied. The live lecture format is no longer the only option: digital whiteboarding, voice and visual annotation, simulation, storytelling, and animation apps are some new technologies that we have used to create video content in blended-learning projects.

One essential question is whether there is a difference between language acquisition in a traditional classroom as opposed to acquisition when part of the course material is given online, particularly in cases where classroom contact hours are reduced as part of a blended course. The results of current research, as summarized in Blake (2007) and Goertler and Winke (2008), are encouraging so far: in most cases there does not seem to be a significant difference in language gains when comparing the skills of students who learn the language in a blended setting versus in a traditional classroom. Studies in which the main finding was "no significant difference" are the most prevalent, while some studies document a greater gain in writing by students in blended courses (Chenoweth et al., 2006; Thoms, 2012; Young & Pettigrew, 2012). Meta-analyses in the language learning field find similar results (Goertler, 2012).

In many ways blended learning parallels what language teachers have done for a long time: we ask students to read pages in a textbook to prepare for class then use class time to concentrate on interactive parts of the course, including group work and speaking exercises. In Russian, however, formal instruction in grammar has remained a staple of many programs, with teachers striving to find the balance between grammar and other activities that foster communicative competency, as highlighted by Rifkin's (2003) statement, "If foreign language teachers teach only grammar, students will never learn to communicate; however, they will not be able to communicate without learning some grammar" (p. 168). Particularly in our field, then, blended learning can help instructors achieve this balance: enhancing acquisition by putting students in the center of the course, maximizing active learning, and creating space for new approaches to teaching.

BENEFITS AND CHALLENGES OF BLENDED LEARNING

To identify the major benefits and challenges of blended learning for Russian language programs we discuss two broad categories: structures and materials. By structures we mean issues relating to the creation and delivery of the learning experience; this category includes the *when*, *where*, and *who* of teaching and learning. Materials include the *what* and, methodologically speaking, *how* of learning, or what we might think of as the content of our courses. Our own experiences inform the discussion but initially we describe the practice of blended learning in general, not the practices at our institutions.

Structures

Changes in structure represent the most obvious, and usually the most immediate, shifts that occur with blended learning. Benefits include greater scheduling flexibility, more active learning during class time, and increased potential for using metadata to further enhance the student learning experience. Conversely these changes can lead instructors to sense a loss of control, and implementing them is costly in both money and time.

Scheduling

Foreign language courses typically have more contact hours per week than courses in many disciplines, especially at the beginning levels. Blended learning changes scheduling in a way that positively affects language courses: either the amount of formal instruction increases while classroom contact hours remain the same, or in-person contact hours are reduced while the overall amount of formal instruction is maintained. The former scheduling model may appeal to institutions where foreign language contact hours are lower than the national average. Using blended learning to achieve a de facto increase in contact hours without changing either the credit load of a course or increasing an instructor's time in the classroom (Ducate et al., 2012) could be especially helpful for Russian language classes by addressing the conundrum that it takes more contact hours to reach the Advanced level in Russian than is typically seen in undergraduate curricula (Rifkin, 2005).

Reducing in-person contact hours while maintaining the same overall amount of instruction may allow more students to fit language learning into their schedules, especially full-time students who work at outside jobs more than 20 hours per week.[4] The question of access is also one of social justice: if language learning is restricted to students who have the luxury of scheduling one to three additional classroom hours per week, then as a profession we risk making real the perception that studying languages is a pursuit for the moneyed elite. Thus blended learning can help create equity. It can also help to sustain or grow enrollments through scheduling that creates access for as many students as possible.

Flexibility, Autonomy, and Motivation

Researchers argue that giving students more freedom over when, where, and how they do their coursework can increase autonomy and motivation, and this increased flexibility helps improve completion and retention rates, especially as compared with fully online courses, which tend to have higher rates of attrition (Harker & Koutsantoni, 2005). Online materials allow students to better control their learning experiences because they are always available; students can pause when necessary or watch videos and complete exercises as many times as they want for reinforcement or when a gap in skill has been identified. This repetition can be especially helpful to students who find language learning challenging (Blake, 2012), as well as allow particularly motivated students to revisit assignments in pursuit of mastery. Positive effects on motivation may be especially evident when the online portion of a course allows students to choose activities that meet their own needs.[5]

Though the additional freedom provided by blended learning can inspire some students, it can overwhelm others. Students who have a strong preference for learning in a face-to-face environment may lose motivation when a portion of direct instruction is moved online. Strambi and Bouvet (2003) have demonstrated that in distance learning a variety of factors (seemingly modest gains in proficiency, a low amount of interaction with instructors and classmates, inadequate feedback, lack of clear instructions, technical glitches) can decrease the motivation and engagement of some blended learners, so it is important for instructors to address these issues in the planning stages of their blended-learning projects. However, as instructors and students become more comfortable with online learning, this problem may diminish (Pichette, 2009). Increasing accountability requires conscious decision-making and set-up time on the part of the instructor, but a number of options are available to ensure that students come to class prepared, such as brief multiple-choice comprehension quizzes paired with videos or readings and taken online. As Carrasco and Johnson (2015) note, online work that does not have a point value assigned to it is often disregarded by students (see also Kraemer, 2008), so linking even a modest amount of credit to each assignment is essential. Blended learning also permits the incorporation of direct homework guidance from the instructor. Students who are expected to learn a new topic outside of class may lack the skills to convert passive reading or viewing into active mastery. Making independent study more active and adding the instructor's voice (literally) to work done outside of class increases the effectiveness of student preparation and leaves more class time for student-centered communicative activities.

Another major benefit of blended learning is that online activities can be configured so that students find out immediately whether their responses are correct; such feedback plays an essential role in language acquisition. In many cases immediate feedback eliminates instances in which students repeat an error multiple times. Naturally this kind of response is limited to discrete points with clear answers, but allowing the computer to grade what it can frees time for the instructor to provide the more detailed, personalized feedback demanded by other types of assignments. Murphy and Hurd (2011) find feedback to be linked positively with motivation and Cerezo (2012) argues that explicit feedback delivers a significant advantage for learning. However, if students become frustrated when they are not given enough information about the reasons for their errors, or receive no feedback at all, this potential benefit of blended learning can become a drawback.

Data Availability, Differentiation, Adaptive Tools

Having students do work online provides instructors with the opportunity to understand more about what they are doing and how they are learning. Course management systems automatically log a tremendous amount of information about the material being accessed by students, when they access it, and how long they spend working on it. Data can help us respond more efficiently to the needs of students by pinpointing concepts on which they spend more viewing or quiz time or that they do not appear to understand. This information can open new research avenues. If instructors learn more about how to teach students most effectively they can maximize the resources available, enhance outcomes, and better communicate their successes to their institutions.

The flexibility of blended learning also allows for differentiation. Learners can make choices about fulfilling course requirements in accordance with their own needs or interests. Goertler (2012) suggests that "in the online portion of the course, students can be encouraged to move through the materials in an individualized fashion" (p. 39), whether that means doing assignments at their own pace or undertaking different assignments within the online part of the course (Kraemer, 2008). Differentiation might alleviate one challenge faced by smaller Russian programs, where a single course includes students of very different proficiency levels. Finally, adaptive tools that automatically adjust exercises and assessments to students' levels may be out of the reach of allowed budgets, but blended-learning courses provide a ready structure for implementing such tools. In some instances adaptive tools may allow consideration of a competency-based model that lets students move at their own pace, according to their achievements, rather than in lockstep with their classmates or on a time line determined by the materials.[6] These innovations can lead to higher levels of interest from students and allow instructors to better meet their individualized needs.

Shifting Roles

Blended learning is an extension of the student-centered pedagogy commonly found in language classrooms, but it goes further by taking an intentional additional step toward shifting the role of the instructor during class time. Materials that students use outside of class may still deliver information in teacher-centered ways such as lectures. When in class, however, students will be asked to be more engaged in activities and more responsible for their own learning. As Long (1996) expresses in his interaction hypothesis, "negotiation for meaning, and especially negotiation work that triggers interactional adjustments by the NS [native speaker] or more competent interlocutor, facilitates acquisition" (p. 451). Blended learning fosters classroom conditions that lead to increased interaction, but a shift in roles can cause both students and teachers to feel unmoored. Many students have been socialized to feel most comfortable being passive in the classroom. When forced to become more active participants, students may react negatively: they may perceive instructors as not doing their job (Bergmann & Sams, 2012) and thus resist adapting to blended learning (Murphy & Hurd, 2011); they may believe that blended courses are easier and not approach them with the necessary discipline; or they may feel threatened, especially if they are anxious about speaking in front of their peers. Instructors, similarly, may feel that they have lost control of their teaching because they are not present to witness students' reaction to instruction that occurs outside class meetings. Although these responses may be subjective, they create a disincentive for engagement and must be addressed generally by providing students with a clear introduction to the reasons for and potential benefits of blended learning. Teachers and students alike may need time to adjust to the changes (Bergmann & Sams, 2012; Murphy & Hurd, 2011) as a teacher-centered approach is replaced by student-centered activation.

Cost

Discerning the true cost of moving from traditional to blended learning is a complex task. Blended learning may create long-term savings but start-up and maintenance costs are high. Programs should consider the obvious monetary expenses (software, hardware, training, infrastructure) alongside less-visible costs, including the time required to create courses and other opportunity costs.[7] For institutions facing budgetary constraints the decision to move courses online may arise less from the pursuit of pedagogical innovation than from the hope that such courses will save money. Although savings is often a motivation, there is no consensus about the budgetary implications of blended courses and expenditures can exceed what even the most careful planning predicts.[8] Instructors and institutions can be caught off guard by hidden costs and by the time, money, and training required to launch even modest blended-learning projects. Goertler et al. (2012) provide a thoughtful overview of this topic, noting that budgetary uncertainty results in part from the variability of blended learning—both its scope and its tools—and from the difficulty of accurately calculating the costs. They also point out that many set-up costs are not factored into project estimates. These costs are difficult to measure and track in a complex institutional context but they cannot be forgotten when planning for such programs, especially if a program that is initially grant-funded is slated to become institutionally funded at some future point.

What appears to be time savings in blended learning often proves to be more of a trade-off. For example, class time is replaced with evaluation time, since the extra work done online needs to be tracked and graded. In other cases instructors may find themselves recreating a course twice: the first time by transforming in-class lessons into asynchronous learning objects and the second time by reworking lesson plans and developing new activities to fill the class time previously taken up by traditional instruction. Each re-creation phase requires multiple time-intensive tasks such as embedding automatic feedback in new online materials (Amoraga-Piqueras at al., 2011), so blended learning projects can make demanding claims on instructor time even after the initial stages are complete. This instructor time, as well as the time necessary for instructors to give feedback on assignments that cannot be automatically graded by computer software, must be included in an accounting of an instructor's workload.

Genuine time savings, especially at the institutional level, may materialize in the long run, but the initial time investment is large and is cited as a deterrent to adopting a blended program.[9] Rubio and Thoms (2012) argue that "implementing and maintaining an effective FL hybrid program can be challenging if LPDs [language program directors] are not allowed the necessary time and resources for this endeavor" (p. 2; also see Goertler et al., 2012). Some data from the field of instructional design and e-learning can be illuminating here. In 2000 the Web-based Education Commission estimated that online-only courses can take from 66% to 500% more time than traditional courses to create (quoted in Kraemer, 2008). An extensive study undertaken by the Chapman Alliance shows that creating even the most basic e-learning materials takes an average of 79 hours per one hour of instruction (Chapman, 2010). While some Spanish- and French-language textbook publishers are increasingly offering digital ancillaries to their textbooks, the practice is still uncommon for Russian textbook publishers and significant investment by publishers of less-commonly taught languages is unlikely (Rubio & Thoms, 2012).

Additionally, copyright concerns make searching for and logging the use of materials time-intensive. In-class use of materials created by others has rarely been strictly monitored; creators of online resources, however, must be vigilant about operating within the bounds of fair use. Creative Commons licenses, which are increasingly being used for pedagogical materials from English-language websites, facilitate legal and ethical reuse. Few websites on the Russian-language Internet tag their materials as available for reuse, which results in a dearth of certain culturally authentic resources for instructors of Russian.[10] Placing materials beyond the passwords of a course-management system can mitigate the risk of copyright infringement, but this practice inhibits the sharing of materials across the profession that could help instructors save time. Making materials accessible can also increase the time cost of a blended-learning project.[11] A key to any significant time or cost savings through blended learning lies in archiving new materials and streamlining their sharing so that instructors do not need to develop materials independently for every topic. Sharing may already be an established practice in programs that teach multiple sections of a single course. Indeed, to date most blended foreign-language courses are in the commonly taught languages (Goertler et al., 2012), which usually have multiple sections. Russian language instructors, however, often have to cross institutional boundaries to realize savings. One way to do so is to use open educational resources (OERs), which can be more flexible and modular than textbooks as well as cheaper for students. As Blyth (2012) argues, OERs can help to avoid curriculum-development duplication.

Another crucial and potentially costly element of making the shift to blended learning is the training required for teachers and students. Creating online materials is generally not included in most instructors' graduate training, and they may feel ill-equipped to take on the development of digital materials or to adjust to a new way of teaching. They also may fear that technical problems will undermine their authority or drain away time. The technological backgrounds of the instructors involved, as well as their attitudes toward technology, can make a big difference in how well blended and flipped courses will work (Kraemer, 2008). Blake (2007) reports that teachers' lack of experience with technology is often the most serious barrier to successful technology integration. Additionally, despite claims that students are "digital natives," teachers should anticipate student challenges with technology (Winke et al., 2010; Rubio, 2012). Bergmann and Sams (2012) point out that even for students who have grown up with digital tools, flipped or blended learning will probably require a paradigm shift because a significant number of their courses still follow the more traditional model; students may require direct instruction in how to use the videos and in the importance of actively controlling these learning tools. Winke et al. (2010) reiterate the need for specific training and find that students of less-commonly taught languages or those that have non-Roman alphabets, as Russian does, are often unprepared to engage in online or hybrid learning and less inclined to consider choosing a hybrid course. They suggest that helping students get comfortable with technologies, such as typing in Cyrillic, must serve as a bridge before blended programs can be maximally successful.

Materials

Changes in materials, although not an obvious outcome, are one of the most exciting and potentially transformative results of blended learning projects. By materials we mean the content of courses—what is taught and how it is taught. Such changes come about because, as noted earlier, blended learning means more than simply using new technologies to teach in the same way. In the short term blended learning enhances the student experience by increasing the types and amount of input students receive. In the long term it creates space to enrich courses with new materials and pedagogies. Providing materials online allows for more—and more varied—input (Goertler, 2012; Murphy & Hurd, 2011). Teachers can integrate many more forms of media into lessons, and one outcome can be that this variety captures the interest of a broader swath of students. More time, whether in class or online, may also be found for topics that usually receive short shrift in traditional teaching, such as pragmatics, intercultural competence, or greater use of authentic materials.

Increasing the amount of work that we expect our students to complete online contributes to the development of their 21st-century skills, which include conducting research online and collaborating asynchronously with other students or colleagues (Partnership for 21st Century Skills, 2011). In many cases we are the sole source of education on 21st-century skills that use the target language and culture. In the future, as the pedagogy moves from a blended model that focuses mostly on providing teacher-to-student instruction online to one that will likely require students to use web tools to interact with each other, with their instructor, and possibly even with a target language community, instructors have an opportunity to help students develop digital literacy in the target language. By doing so we may even facilitate an involvement in the target language community that could lead to lifelong learning. Indeed, the American Council of Teachers of Foreign Languages (ACTFL) outlines making connections, engaging in global communities, and lifelong learning as part of the World-Readiness Standards toward which we as language educators should guide our students (NSFLEP, 2015).

BLENDED LEARNING IN PRACTICE: OUR EXPERIENCES

Both authors have similar graduate training, but our current positions, our home institutions, and the approaches we have taken for incorporating blended learning are different. Kristen Welsh uses blended learning at the introductory level at a small private liberal arts college; Shannon Spasova is at a large public research university and worked first with blended learning at the Intermediate level. In the context of these differences, our case studies demonstrate the flexibility of blended learning.

Overview: First-Year Russian at a Small Liberal Arts College

The project described in this section implements blended learning in Kristen Welsh's introductory Russian sequence classes (Russian 101 and 102) at Hobart and William Smith Colleges (HWS).[12] The discussion here addresses four topics: motivation, planning and production, implementation, and outcomes. The case study covers the first two years of the project: a calendar year of planning and object creation followed by a spring-semester pilot course, a summer assessment, and a full-year blended-learning course. During this period I created and implemented 122 learning objects (65 digital videos, totaling 6.25 hours, and 57 digital quizzes). More important than this quantitative outcome was the transformation in how introductory Russian was taught.

Motivation for Change

HWS's introductory Russian sequence provides only three to four contact hours per week, for a total of 90–120 hours per academic year. This small number of contact hours presents an obvious challenge: how does the instructor give students active learning opportunities while maintaining the attention to grammar that research shows (Rifkin, 2003) is necessary for acquiring proficiency in Russian? Using significant class time to present detailed lectures on grammar meant I often lacked time for in-class exercises that activate grammatical and lexical concepts and improve communicative skills. I needed to become a more efficient instructor by changing how, when, and where I lectured.

Planning

I was fortunate to secure a grant that included funds for equipment, software, and a student assistant. During the first semester of the project I was on sabbatical, but the remainder of the project has been done while maintaining a full teaching load. I planned to create video lessons on grammar for students to watch outside the classroom. Instead of filming myself delivering a traditional lecture, I determined that digital whiteboarding presented a smart alternative. In the planning phase, I researched equipment and apps, as well as which grammar topics to cover using the blended approach.[13] In addition to testing functionality, instructors should carefully review the end-use license agreement (EULA) for any software or app they consider. Concerns about intellectual property rights, durability (continuing availability) of the objects, and potential limitations on dissemination of learning objects may sway the instructor's decision. The app I initially preferred gave ownership of my work to the developer; the Explain Everything iPad app that I eventually chose had a EULA that raised no red flags.

Because the project would be piloted while I was teaching Russian 102, I selected five topics from the second half of the assigned textbook, including some that were conceptually and grammatically simple and others that were more complex.[14] I discovered that a seemingly small grammar topic can require from 15 to 30 minutes of explication. Experts on blended learning believe students can easily process short segmented video lessons, so I often divided a grammatical topic into separate video lessons on function, morphology, and application.[15] For example, when introducing the dative case, a series of five lessons was appropriate. Breaking a topic into smaller segments not only fosters comprehension; it maximizes the potential for using video lessons in multiple settings (e.g., intermediate students who remember the dative endings but make mistakes in usage can be assigned to review only the material they need).

Production and Implementation

During the pilot semester I revised individual video lessons, changing the production process to make it more efficient. I ceased experimenting with a different format for each new lesson and instead aimed for consistent formatting across lessons.[16] Upon completing a video lesson it was uploaded to the school's course management system and assigned as homework, along with the relevant explanations in the textbook and the accompanying written workbook exercises. I continued assigning the textbook explanations with which the students were familiar from their first semester of Russian in order to ease them into learning grammar via digital lectures. The goal was to reinforce the knowledge that they had multiple tools at their disposal that addressed multiple learning styles or preferences.

As the pilot semester progressed, I discovered that most students were not watching the video lessons. Two factors contributed to this lack of engagement: the students' established language-learning habits, which did not include asynchronous lectures, and a lack of integrated assessment features in the lessons themselves. The former is a complex topic, and it took almost a year of reflection to realize the extent to which students must be trained to successfully work within the blended model. Integrated assessment, on the other hand, was an omission that could be addressed immediately. When the project began I believed that asynchronous learning was a tool students would embrace readily: they could watch videos outside of class, control the pace of the lecture to suit their own learning styles, and spend more time in class speaking, reading, writing, and listening to Russian. Because the students were not familiar with this model of learning, however, they considered watching the videos to be extra work, even when other homework was reduced. Therefore, the next stage of the project involved developing online quizzes to follow each video, which gave the students and me rapid feedback about comprehension and furnished a graded, low-stakes outcome as an incentive.

During the summer following the pilot semester, I created quizzes and question banks in the school's Canvas platform and tested them with help from a student assistant. His feedback led to the addition of a password key to the quizzes. To do this I edited the audio track in Explain Everything in order to embed a spoken password at a random point in the video. Because students hear but do not see the password they cannot skip straight to the password by scrubbing through the video to find a visual cue. This step was taken not to prevent cheating but to make sure the students would watch the video lessons before they launched the quizzes. Each quiz consists of five multiple-choice questions pulled from a larger question bank; students receive a different set of questions each time they take the quiz and the order of the multiple-choice answers is shuffled each time a question is used. The questions were as simple as possible, testing basic comprehension of the material in the video lessons. As often as time permitted, explanations and corrections for wrong answers, or congratulations and conceptual reinforcement for correct ones, were added, thus providing feedback to facilitate acquisition. Students can submit a quiz and immediately see their score, which answers are right and wrong, and any additional commentary created.

Outcomes, Assessment, and Future Plans

As already noted, students in the pilot semester resisted the blended approach. They had no prior experience with blended learning in any subject and had already studied Russian for a full semester using the traditional approach. Their failure to embrace blended learning helped me realize the significant shift the blended approach requires, both in how instructors teach and how students learn. My experience bears out the findings discussed in the section on the benefits and challenges of blended learning: that students require direct training in new approaches to learning if they are to make the transition successfully and enthusiastically. Therefore, in my next blended courses (Russian 101, 102), I explained early in the semester why the courses were structured this way and emphasized the benefits of using a variety of learning resources outside of class. Direct instruction in using the video lessons and quizzes, along with an explanation of the motivation for using a blended approach, helped enormously. An additional factor in this second group's acceptance of blended learning is that these students had never formally studied Russian any other way. They were much more engaged with the asynchronous learning activities than the students in the pilot semester had been. The second group's data showed that students who were engaged in class and completed the written homework assignments were also completing the video lessons and online quizzes. When in-class engagement, attendance, or completion of written work suffered, so did completion of the asynchronous work.

In the first full year using the blended approach for Russian 101 and Russian 102, the students completed the entire textbook. In previous years they would usually complete only 80% of the book. In addition, students did more speaking, reading, and listening activities in class than had been possible in the past, and the amount of English used in the classroom was reduced. At the end of the year students had learned more grammatical material and they had activated more grammar, vocabulary, and constructions. Proceeding more quickly through the textbook did require me to develop activities to make use of the newfound time, which added to the initial time cost of the project.

A second clear measure of progress came when oral midterms were administered in the first blended Russian 101 course. The exam had the same format as those from previous years but also included structures that, prior to the blended-learning project, had not even been introduced at the same point in prior semesters. The mean score in the blended course differed by less than one percentage point from previous semesters. Maintaining the same level of performance, as measured by grades but on a more challenging exam, provided evidence that the blended approach was having a positive effect on student learning.

The most unexpected outcome was realizing that the textbook that had been used for years was no longer the best option for the Russian language program. The class time freed up by having students view grammar lessons online needed to be filled with more communicative activities, so I switched to a book that offers a greater variety of speaking, listening, and reading exercises. Finally, the project led to a fundamental shift in my methodology, allowing me to introduce more elements of processing instruction and creating a more effective and engaging classroom experience.

Overview: Second-Year Russian at a Large Public University

The Center for Language Teaching Advancement (CeLTA) at Michigan State University (MSU) initiated a program that involved faculty members from several languages with a goal of developing materials for online or blended courses. The goals of the project were to pool resources and provide a collaborative environment for faculty to create more flexibility in student schedules while at the same time maintaining high-quality language programs. Faculty members involved in the project, each with expertise in instructional technology, have a certain percentage of their appointment dedicated to the development of online or blended materials. This type of larger-scale project may interest instructors at institutions involved in course sharing or consortia arrangements.

Program Goals

One goal of the Russian program was to have both first- and second-year Russian offered as blended courses. The plan consisted of reducing in-class time from four 50-minute class hours per week to three. The additional hour was to be replaced by online work. This reduction was presumed to eventually allow the courses to be scheduled as Monday-Wednesday-Friday courses, giving students more flexibility in their schedules and potentially increasing enrollments by eliminating the conflict between the fourth hour of Russian and other courses in the Tuesday-Thursday time slot. A second goal in implementing a blended approach was to create materials that could be reused and shared among instructors in the Russian program.

The materials I have developed focus mostly on grammar and some on vocabulary in order to reduce as much as possible the time spent in the classroom on these topics and to minimize the in-class use of English. Students must watch a presentation and be prepared to participate in related communicative activities in class. Generally the modules consist of a video that incorporates visual presentation of the material using images or animation and audio, a short explanation of the concept, and interactive self-check exercises that give feedback to students on whether they have understood the concepts and to ensure that they have engaged with the material.

Project Pilot

I created one set of lessons as a pilot program during the spring semester, making nine video screencasts that ranged in length from two to six-and-a-half minutes, using mostly Google slides with a voiceover through a screencast. The videos included a series of quiz questions that students had to complete in order to receive credit.

Student feedback from an informal survey, in addition to what I learned, was used to tweak how the structure of the course for the following year. The survey indicated that students:

- ◇ prefer automatic feedback on the interactive parts of the lessons;
- ◇ find a mix of handwritten and typed work ideal;
- ◇ consider the videos useful, not just for an introduction to the topic but also as review.

Probably the most significant issue that came out of the preparatory period was planning properly for the time required to create quality materials. The learning curve, development process, and maintenance of these types of materials are time-consuming (Amoraga-Piqueras et al., 2011; Carrasco & Johnson, 2015). As noted in the discussion of the benefits and challenges of blended learning, e-learning materials require substantial preparation and development time; they often require time and money for the additional training of instructors; and they may also require instructors to start from scratch to avoid copyright infringement.

Implementation: Year 1

After the pilot lesson, I committed to using the blended approach for the whole next academic year. Because of the time required to create materials, I prioritized grammar topics to make sure the most difficult or most important topics were covered. At the beginning of the fall semester students were informed of the plan to alter the schedule and have some of their work done online. One day each week was identified as a study day, when they would be responsible for completing the class preparation activities by their due date. I explained the rationale and let them know they would be asked for feedback on their experience later.

Once the semester began, I realized that student results were not being consistently sent by the platform being used. After searching in vain for the source of the problem, a change was made to the way the videos were made. To maximize the opportunity for reuse of materials, I made them more modular: most topics had a video that could be housed on YouTube and then embedded into another application to provide interactive activities.[17] This shift meant that even if the technology that is mediating between video and interactive activities becomes obsolete, the core of the video remains available and can be delivered to students via a different program or application. This modularity is one of the major lessons learned from the initial stages of the course's implementation.

To date I have created several hundred activities (for first- and second-year courses) that I call class-preparation activities and which mostly replace in-class grammar and some vocabulary presentations. I used a variety of tools to create these activities, the majority using Google slides with a voiceover/screencast through Camtasia and extensive use of images and animation. These videos are then uploaded to YouTube and embedded into H5P, which houses a small number of interactive self-check exercises for each video. The interactive activities provide students the opportunity to check their understanding. Online assessments for speaking, listening, and grammar activities were subsequently created utilizing the school's course management system as well as apps such as Flipgrid, which allows students to submit speaking assignments via asynchronous conversations or as responses to prompts.

Outcomes

As outlined earlier, research shows that blended courses do as well as face-to-face courses, so it is reasonable to assume that the students would be grateful for the extra day of study time and increased flexibility and therefore would put extra effort into being prepared for class and participating in the group activities. However, students in the blended course were no more nor less willing to participate than my former students had been. There is no one solution that ensures students will be completely prepared after completing the modules. Adjustments are needed on both sides.

The project succeeded in reducing time spent on grammar and vocabulary in class and in increasing the amount of time spent on group and interactive activities, but it was not always easy to go into the classroom and not teach in the traditional sense. The loss of control over how students spent their time can also feel uncomfortable: if they were given all these ways to spend time on Russian but they choose not to, with whom does the responsibility lie? On the one hand, we do want our students to become self-motivated and independent in their learning and we cannot micromanage their lives, but on the other hand we want to make sure that we are keeping them accountable. This accountability is something we do automatically in face-to-face courses but takes more strategizing to implement in a blended course.

Blending the class also brought some unexpected benefits. Naturally, when we are teaching students basic Russian we want to make sure that they master the building blocks of the language in order to function. In teaching beginning and intermediate students I feel the need to cover everything. Providing students with grammar explanations online freed up from this pressure, allowing me more choice in how to use class time. As a result, I have integrated more games, more mingle activities, and more practice exercises that include online reading and listening, as well as modules that focus on digital literacy and preparation for study abroad and simulated real-life scenarios. Putting part of the assignments online also appears to have succeeded in catering to a variety of student needs and preferences, because some students clearly preferred doing the homework online while others wanted to stay with the paper workbook. In the end I felt that my decisions about which exercises to put online and which to keep handwritten remained largely justified, though in the future I may do as much as I can to ensure that students can complete the homework in the medium of their choice as often as possible.[18]

Lessons Learned

A survey of the students showed that two-thirds prefer the hybrid course format to the traditional format.[19] A strong majority (92%) said that the greater flexibility in schedule was beneficial, and 85% expressed the opinion that being able to watch the videos to review was helpful. Being provided with various types of video (videos with animation, visuals, audio, text, grammar explanation, examples, and videos in which they could see their instructor), the students found those with grammar explanation and examples the most helpful.

While some students watched the videos on average only once, a relatively large number sometimes watched them more than once, and up to three times. The learners' tendency to review material may help increase the number of overall contact hours. Interestingly, one student wrote in the survey: "I don't think its [*sic*] about the course as much as it is about the individual taking the course. As it is set up right now, with the various changes you've made to the traditional model, the course is well designed to teach the language. But if a student doesn't take advantage of the opportunities it offers, then they obviously won't get as much out of it."

The survey also asked students to comment on online homework assignments and online speaking assignments (oral tests). More than 50% preferred completing both tasks online, although it was clear from the numbers and student comments that having a mixture was beneficial.

Future Plans

As I continue to teach using the blended approach, I continue to make a number of adjustments. First, I am becoming more comfortable with the apparent loss of control of the classroom as the class becomes less teacher-centered and continue to increase the percentage of meaningful interactive activities in class. Second, while self-check exercises are included for almost every class preparation activity, I would like to add more targeted feedback to align with research showing that providing specific information about the source of errors is particularly useful.[20] Third, I would like to take better advantage of the data collected by online applications. These data will allow me to learn more about how students are using the materials, how to best provide work that will be useful and engaging to them, and how to explore ways to document their learning in the class. I also continue to tweak according to the needs of my colleagues, who also use the materials. This revision time also needs to be accounted for in the development and maintenance of these kinds of materials.

TIPS, OPPORTUNITIES, AND LOOKING AHEAD

For instructors considering using blended learning in their classrooms, we have the following recommendations.

Experience Online Language Materials Yourself

As Winke et al. (2010) suggest, experiencing what it is like to do online coursework from the student's perspective benefits instructors. If you have colleagues who teach with technology, consider auditing their classes. There are also professional development programs that offer opportunities, such as through the national foreign language centers and professional organizations.

Start Small

If you are like most faculty and do not have time designated in your schedule for developing materials, you should start small. Pick one topic from each chapter and create an activity that students will do in advance of the lesson. If you like the approach you can add a few more topics each semester. Related to this point, do not be too ambitious about the tools you use. Choose one and give yourself time to experiment and become comfortable with it.[21] Limiting the number of tools will save you time and will reduce the amount of adjustment your students must do, meanwhile increasing the likelihood of their successful adaptation to blended learning.

Give Yourself Time

Even after limiting the topics and tools, give yourself more time than you think you will need. Developing materials tends to take much longer than expected. Also, in our experience materials development is difficult to get done in short stints. Course release time that can be taken in larger chunks is conducive to the task but not always available; for many of us materials development happens during the summer. We also recommend budgeting time each year for maintenance: inevitably some update of an app or your school's course management system will force you to reorganize. Keeping good notes during the year of what should be done to improve the course is essential to efficiency in updating and revising materials.

Advocate for Support

Educate your colleagues and administrators about blended learning. We encourage faculty to seek out grants for course development and teacher training, especially if home institutions do not provide this support internally. We hope that others in the profession, perhaps using the information here and in the studies we cite, will advocate with chairs, administrators, and trustees or governors for the support necessary to embark on blended-learning projects. This support should include stipends, equipment funds, release time, and training. Such advocacy is especially important in scenarios where decision-makers focus on blended learning as a cost-saving measure without understanding the start-up and maintenance costs. Additionally, advocate that your institution provide resources and training to help assess these approaches. As institutions become more interested in using learning analytics for assessment, language instructors should be prepared to ask departments, divisions, or institutions for the support necessary to apply these data to their work in blended learning.

Plan Ahead for Sharing and Reusing

We find that modularity is crucial to reusing materials. The system being used may not last, or you may switch to a new textbook. Archive the raw materials of each lesson so that you can easily adjust them to future changes in sequencing, structure, or platform. Planning for sharing of materials is also essential. If you are not the only one who teaches the course, or if you have to coordinate across multiple sections or with teaching assistants, you may want to work with your IT department or language center to determine the best way to store and share materials. Consistent organization of course materials is important, for both your colleagues and your students. Consistency helps students easily locate course materials on your website and establishes a routine that keeps them on track. We also recommend including estimates of how much time each activity will take so that students can better structure their time.

Ensure Audio Quality

Make sure you have access to a microphone that is of better quality than the one preinstalled on your laptop. Even a small investment makes a big difference in how clear and professional your material sound.[22] Clear, crisp audio is, of course, especially important in language teaching.

Include Self-Check Exercises or Low-Stakes Quizzes

One of the main benefits of having students do work online is the availability of immediate feedback. Students can discover much sooner which topics they need to review and seek immediate help directly from the instructor or online. Students who have taken part in our projects cite regular, immediate feedback as a substantial benefit. If you can, provide focused feedback in self-check exercises that pinpoint the source(s) of the most common errors.

Plan Technical Support for Students

Provide students with the support they need to use the tools you require. Before your course begins you should meet with the instructional technology staff at your university, at the very least to give them advance warning that your students may approach them for help. Head off problems by providing exceptionally clear instructions that walk students through each online task, step-by-step, and include screenshots or explanatory videos when possible. Be thoroughly familiar with the tools yourself, including from the perspective of the student. Be aware that your help materials will need to adjust as the tools and interfaces are updated.

Shape Student Expectations

Students need careful introduction to the blended learning model in order to understand its power and efficiency. Be transparent about why you are asking them to do the work in this format and how it may benefit them. Give them strategies for how to get the most out of the materials you are providing. Point out that they can watch the videos more than once, they can pause the videos when necessary, and they can access some of the materials that you used to create the videos (presuming you make them available).

Hold Students Accountable

Keep students accountable by assigning an assessment value to online exercises and by establishing deadlines. To make the blended model work optimally students must complete assignments before the class period in which a given topic will be used; we have found that strict time deadlines combined with point values for each assignment are essential for motivating students to complete these class-preparation activities. However, taking into consideration the relatively low weight of the credit given for these activities, as well as how limited the technology tools are in interpreting students' work, we cannot put a high premium on scoring. We often use these activities as the very first contact with a new concept because we do not want students to feel deflated by a low score.

Gather Feedback and Evaluate Your Work

Ask for student feedback on the structure of the course and your materials. We surveyed our students, the results of which led us to adjust both the content of and the approach to our courses. Informing students about the rationale behind the choices we made and their classmates' varied reactions to the materials helped with student buy-in.

Leverage Meta-Data

Because today's students are working online more often, usually within structures like course management systems that keep detailed records of their actions, we have new opportunities to understand how they learn Russian. However, few of us are trained in the analysis of such data. We as a profession should dedicate resources to learning more about using data to improve student learning, improve retention and outcomes, and help direct funding.

Mobile Learning

As students spend much of their online time on mobile devices such as smartphones and tablets, we will have to consider how to offer materials in a mobile format. Availability of materials on mobile devices increases student engagement, but creating online materials that behave equally well in mobile and traditional online formats is a technological challenge.

Interaction and Collaboration

In our case studies we leveraged the strengths of blended learning by moving some of the less interactive course elements to the online context while keeping intact the elements that require direct student-instructor and student-student interaction. As web-based tools improve we should consider how the online environment can offer students additional ways to interact, with class members and with target language communities.[23]

Real-World and 21st-Century Skills

We have a responsibility to acquaint our students with the tools that are important in the target culture. Learning cursive handwriting and typing and how to negotiate the Russian-speaking World Wide Web help students develop the technological skills that allow them to live and work using the target language. Early on we can teach students keyboarding and to use search engines, social networking, news media, and other sites available to Russian speakers, helping them develop their target-language digital literacy.

Professional Advocacy

Current research does not show that blended learning saves time and money, but the idea that it does remains appealing to some decision-makers. As a profession we must be adamant that blended learning should not be a means of cutting instructional staff. Instead it should be used to improve outcomes, to help faculty save time in the long term that can be devoted to other professional tasks, and to do more without substantially increasing expenditures. "Only when *pedagogy* drives the implementation of technology can it be a successful endeavor" (Goertler et al., 2012, p. 301, emphasis added).

As pressure on instructors to provide more content online increases, we must also provide technical training for faculty members and graduate students.[24] While we can avail ourselves of needed services, such as consultations with instructional designers, we want to make sure that control of content remains with the faculty. As a profession we need to consider how we value work on pedagogical and technological innovation. The time involved in creating these kinds of materials should be acknowledged and compensated, the projects themselves should be evaluated as part of tenure and promotion files, and the professional risk and opportunity costs inherent in trying new pedagogies must be recognized.

Moving Forward

We have presented the blends that we have created for our own courses and we can imagine more possibilities for the future, especially if we cross our institutional divides and work together. Moving forward, we as a profession can:

- team teach courses from afar to capitalize on the strengths of a colleague in another part of the country or world and thereby enrich content while keeping the essential vibrancy of face-to-face discussion and individualized feedback;
- provide courses for diverse populations of students (working professionals, heritage learners) who might complete the face-to-face portion of the course using alternative means, such as video conferencing, or in larger chunks of time that accommodate differences in location or time;[25]
- combine online work with a short intensive residency requirement to help learners at higher levels maintain their language proficiency (Blake, 2012);
- utilize e-tutors in combination with quality open educational resources (Cerezo, 2012);
- consider a competency-based model or even some form of self-paced course;
- do more sharing among institutions that teach Russian;
- learn from instructors who use blended learning in other fields;
- find a way to collectively employ someone to coordinate the development of quality instructional materials that benefits everyone or to use an existing model such as that of open educational resources (OER) to share materials;[26]
- conduct joint research to better understand the data that our students' online behavior generates.

Call to Action

As an extension of this discussion we would like to issue a call to action to examine how we as a profession can take advantage of the possibilities mentioned above. We propose three concrete steps:

1. Hold an annual conversation, via a roundtable discussion at a professional conference such as AATSEEL, that addresses blended learning and connected topics that emerge as technology and pedagogy change.
2. Establish a community of practice, possibly through social media venues, made up of people interested in blended learning or the implementation of technology in the teaching of Russian and other Slavic languages in general.
3. Establish a digital commons, that is, a learning objects repository of open educational resources that could be shared among the community of practice to avoid duplication of efforts and to promote high-quality materials.[27]

Through these efforts, we hope to continue the conversation about blended learning and foster the successful, pedagogically driven integration of technology into the teaching of Russian.

NOTES

1. Thanks to Amanda Ewington (Davidson College), Susan Hess (Hobart and William Smith Colleges), and the volume editors and reviewers for their support and feedback on this chapter.
2. Blake (2012) suggests a distinction, defining blended learning as "using technology as a supplement to classroom instruction" and hybrid learning as "providing instruction both in class and online" (p. 13).
3. Jonathan Bergmann and Aaron Sams are credited with developing the flipped classroom (Bergmann & Sams, 2012).
4. In 2012, 25% of full-time college students were employed for 20 or more hours per week (Kena, et al., 2014). See also Perna (2010).
5. As Goertler (2012) notes, outcomes depend on what learners do with that input.
6. Bergmann and Sams (2012) demonstrate the benefits of and give practical advice for implementing what they term the "flipped-mastery classroom" (pp. 51–93). Analyzing the potential for using learning analytics to improve outcomes, Brown (2015) notes that "students who are metacognitively participatory in their learning achieve higher success rates than students who are not. Analytics for teaching and learning seeks to promote learner success by providing near real-time information to instructors and advisors, helping them build and sustain positive learner momentum" (para. 28.) See also Murphy and Hurd (2011).
7. For example, Goertler et al. (2012) describe a hypothetical situation in which tenure-track professors might spend more time on a blended course than they would have spent on a traditional course, impeding progress toward tenure (p. 302). This problem is a particular concern where institutional or departmental review committees lacking firsthand experience of blended-course development might have difficulty recognizing the challenges this type of work brings.
8. Rubio and Thoms (2012) point out that "the few cost/benefit analyses [. . .] have shown that using technology only marginally saves money" (p. 18).
9. Indeed, some programs have begun to ask TAs to teach more sections as a result of the reduction in contact hours for each section of the blended courses (Young & Pettigrew, 2012).
10. Repositories of culturally authentic objects that are designated for reuse for educational purposes are beginning to be available; in addition, general-use image repositories increasingly include Russian content.
11. Some institutions mandate that all online videos automatically provide captions, which is particularly problematic for language courses: captioning programs or services may not be available for the target language and in some cases having captions available would defeat the purpose of the exercise for students who are not hearing impaired.
12. This project was supported in part by an Innovative Digital Pedagogies grant from The Andrew W. Mellon Foundation.
13. During the initial stage I worked closely with Juliet Habjan Boisselle, the specialist from HWS's Digital Learning Center who had been paired with me for the first year

of the grant. During the summer assessment phase Hobart College undergraduate James Prowse worked as my assistant.

14. Developing digital video lessons for all the grammar topics I teach is a multiyear endeavor. When starting a blended learning project instructors should convert the material incrementally, allowing for tinkering, testing, and revision.
15. Doolittle et al. (2015) demonstrate that "segmentation facilitates recall and application, and that more segmentation leads to greater time engagement with the tutorial and more learning" (p. 1340), linking their findings to the cognitive load theory. They also connect their results to "research concerning instructional tutorial length [that] suggests that shorter tutorials promote engagement [. . .] (Guo, Kim, & Rubin, 2014; Kim *et al.*, 2014)" (p. 1340).
16. Although consistency was the goal, it was surprising to discover that the student assistant had a strong positive reaction to the most spontaneous and least polished of all the provided videos. It is possible that student users perceive highly edited videos as less human and less immediate, so spending the time to perfect videos that are a little rough may not always be desirable.
17. H5P, a lesson-authoring software (https://h5p.org/) was used.
18. While typing is gaining in importance and the need for handwriting is decreasing, we still need to make sure that students can understand and produce both typed and handwritten texts, and some activities benefit from automatic feedback more than others. Likewise, some activities, like practicing a new lexicon, might work best as a handwritten assignment.
19. Twenty-six of 33 students completed the survey.
20. Green et al. (2011) claim that "research has shown that learners are less likely to engage in self-study activities that involve open-ended writing tasks and therefore have no clear solutions, and some learners may omit them altogether. Even when model answers are provided, they are often not seen as helpful" (p. 175).
21. As of this writing, Camtasia or Explain Everything would be recommended to start with, but technology changes quickly. The profession can make a difference in this area by offering easy-to-find and up-to-date information on which apps people are using the most. One such source is the FLTMAG (https://fltmag.com).
22. The importance of audio quality is often cited in instructional design literature, as in, for example, Kuhlmann's (2009) blog post that gives tips for recording better audio.
23. See Ducate et al. (2012) about using social media as a meaningful context for interaction in a language class.
24. See Gallardo et al. (2011) for a discussion of teacher development in blended learning.
25. See Peters and Shi (2011) for a discussion on teaching community languages in a blended format. This approach could be an option for communities that have sizeable Russian populations.
26. See Blyth (2012) for a discussion of some of the challenges of OERs.
27. Some of these efforts are already underway. Teach Russian (http://teachrussian.org) and the LLC Commons through the University of Arizona (http://llccommons.arizona.edu) seek to allow institutions to share materials online.

REFERENCES

Amoraga-Piqueras, M.-R., Comas-Quinn, A., & Southgate, M. (2011). Teaching through assessment. In M. Nicolson, L. Murphy, & M. Southgate (Eds.), *Language teaching in blended contexts* (pp. 75–94). Edinburgh, Scotland: Dunedin Academic.

Bergmann, J., & Sams, A. (2012). *Flip your classroom: Reach every student in every class every day*. Eugene, OR: International Society for Technology in Education and ASCD.

Blake, R. (2007). New trends in using technology in the language curriculum. *Annual Review of Applied Linguistics, 27*, 76–97.

Blake, R. (2012). Best practices in online learning: Is it for everyone? In F. Rubio & J. Thoms (Eds.), *AAUSC 2012 Volume—Issues in language program direction: Hybrid language teaching and learning: Exploring theoretical, pedagogical and curricular issues* (pp. 10–26). Boston: Heinle.

Blyth, C. S. (2012). Opening up foreign language education with Open Educational Resources: The case of Francais interactif. In F. Rubio & J. Thoms (Eds.), *AAUSC 2012 Volume—Issues in language program direction: Hybrid language teaching and learning: Exploring theoretical, pedagogical and curricular issues* (pp. 196–218). Boston: Heinle.

Brown, M. (2015, June 22). Six trajectories for digital technology in higher education. Retrieved from http://er.educause.edu/articles/2015/6/six-trajectories-for-digital-technology-in-higher-education

Carrasco, B., & Johnson, S. M. (2015). *Hybrid language teaching in practice: Perceptions, reactions, and results*. Dordrecht, Netherlands: Springer.

Cerezo, L. (2012). Beyond hybrid learning: A synthesis of research on e-tutors under the lens of second language acquisition theory. In F. Rubio & J. Thoms (Eds.), *AAUSC 2012 Volume—Issues in language program direction: Hybrid language teaching and learning: Exploring theoretical, pedagogical and curricular issues* (pp. 50–66). Boston: Heinle.

Chapman, B. (2010). How long does it take to create learning? [newsletter]. Retrieved from http://www.cedma-europe.org/newsletter%20articles/misc/How%20long%20does%20it%20take%20to%20develop%20training%20by%20Brian%20Chapman%20(Sep%2010).pdf

Chenoweth, N., Ushida, E., & Murday, K. (2006). Student learning in hybrid French and Spanish courses: An overview of language online. *CALICO Journal, 24*(1), 115–46.

Doolittle, P., Bryant, L., & Chittum, J. (2015). Effects of degree of segmentation and learner disposition on multimedia learning. *British Journal of Education Technology, 46*(1), 1333–43.

Ducate, L., Lomicka, L., & Lord, G. (2012). Hybrid learning spaces: Re-envisioning language learning. In F. Rubio & J. Thoms (Eds.), *AAUSC 2012 Volume—Issues in language program direction: Hybrid language teaching and learning: Exploring theoretical, pedagogical and curricular issues* (pp. 67–91). Boston: Heinle.

Gallardo, M., Heiser, S., & Nicolson, M. (2011). Teacher development for blended contexts. In M. Nicolson, L. Murphy, & M. Southgate (Eds.), *Language teaching in blended contexts* (pp. 219–31). Edinburgh, Scotland: Dunedin Academic.

Gass, S. (1997). *Input, interaction, and the second language learner*. Mahwah, NJ: Lawrence Erlbaum.

Goertler, S. (2012). Theoretical and empirical foundations for blended language learning. In F. Rubio & J. Thoms (Eds.), *AAUSC 2012 Volume—Issues in language program direction: Hybrid language teaching and learning: Exploring theoretical, pedagogical and curricular issues* (p. 27–49). Boston: Heinle.

Goertler, S., Bollen, M., & Gaff Jr., J. (2012). Students' readiness for and attitudes toward hybrid FL instruction. *CALICO Journal, 29*(2), 297–320.

Goertler, S., & Winke, P. M. (Eds.). (2008). *Opening doors through distance language education: Principles, perspectives and practices.* Computer Assisted Language Instruction Consortium.

Green, H., St. John, E., Warnecke, S., & Atkinson, V. (2011). Asynchronous online teaching. In M. Nicolson, L. Murphy, & M. Southgate (Eds.), *Language teaching in blended contexts* (pp. 169–86). Edinburgh, Scotland: Dunedin.

Harker, M., & Koutsantoni, D. (2005). Can it be as effective? Distance versus blended learning in a web-based EAP programme. *ReCALL, 17*(2), 197–216.

Kena, G., Aud, S., Johnson, F., Wang, X., Zhang, J., Rathbun, A., Wilkinson-Flicker, S., & Kristapovich, P. (2014). The condition of education 2014 (NCES 2014-083). US Department of Education, National Center for Education Statistics, Washington, DC. Retrieved from http://nces.ed.gov/pubsearch

Kraemer, A. (2008). *Engaging the foreign language learner: Using hybrid instruction to bridge the language-literature gap* (Unpublished doctoral dissertation). Michigan State University, East Lansing, MI.

Kuhlmann, T. (2009, June 2). 4 simple tips for recording high-quality audio. Retrieved from http://blogs.articulate.com/rapid-elearning/4-simple-tips-for-recording-high-quality-audio/

Long, M. (1996). The role of the linguistic environment in second language acquisition. In W. Ritchie & T. Bahtia (Eds.), *Handbook of second language acquisition* (pp. 413–68). San Diego: Academic Press.

Murphy, L., & Hurd, S. (2011). Fostering learner autonomy and motivation in blended teaching. In M. Nicolson, L. Murphy, & M. Southgate (Eds.), *Language teaching in blended contexts* (pp. 43–58). Edinburgh, Scotland: Dunedin Academic.

National Standards Collaborative Board (NSCB). (2015). Two-page summary of World-readiness standards for learning languages. ACTFL, Inc. Retrieved from http://www.actfl.org/sites/default/files/pdfs/World-ReadinessStandardsforLearningLanguages.pdf

National Standards in Foreign Language Education Project (NSFLEP). (2015).

Partnership for 21st Century Skills. (2011). 21st century skills map. Retrieved from https://www.actfl.org/sites/default/files/pdfs/21stCenturySkillsMap/p21_worldlanguagesmap.pdf

Perna, L. W. (2010). Understanding the working college student. *Academe 96*(4), 30–32. Retrieved from https://www.aaup.org/article/understanding-working-college-student#.WFiY3_krI2x

Peters, H. & Shi, L. (2011). Teaching community languages in blended contexts. In M. Nicolson, L. Murphy, & M. Southgate (Eds.), *Language teaching in blended contexts* (pp. 187–202). Edinburgh, Scotland: Dunedin Academic.

Pichette, F. (2009). Second language anxiety and distance language learning. *Foreign Language Annals, 42*(1), 77–93.

Rifkin, B. (2003). Guidelines for foreign language lesson planning. *Foreign Language Annals, 36*(2), 167–79.

Rifkin, B. (2005). A ceiling effect in traditional classroom foreign language instruction: Data from Russian. *Modern Language Journal, 89*(1), 3–18.

Rubio, F. (2012). The effects of blended learning on second language fluency and proficiency. In F. Rubio & J. Thoms (Eds.), *AAUSC 2012 Volume—Issues in language program direction: Hybrid language teaching and learning: Exploring theoretical, pedagogical and curricular issues* (pp. 137–59). Boston: Heinle.

Rubio, F., & Thoms, J. J. (2012). Hybrid language teaching and learning: Looking forward. In F. Rubio & J. Thoms (Eds.), *AAUSC 2012 Volume—Issues in language program direction: Hybrid language teaching and learning: Exploring theoretical, pedagogical and curricular issues* (pp. 1–9). Boston: Heinle.

Strambi, A., & Bouvet, E. (2003). Flexibility and interaction at a distance: A mixed-mode environment for language learning. *Language, Learning & Technology, 7*(3), 81–102.

Swain, M. (1985). Communicative competence: Some roles of comprehensible input and comprehensible output in its development. In S. Gass & C. Madden (Eds.), *Input in second language acquisition* (pp. 235–53). Rowley, MA: Newbury House.

Thoms, J. J. (2012). Analyzing linguistic outcomes of second language learners: Hybrid versus traditional course contexts. In F. Rubio & J. Thoms (Eds.), *AAUSC 2012 Volume—Issues in language program direction: Hybrid language teaching and learning: Exploring theoretical, pedagogical and curricular issues* (pp. 177–95). Boston: Heinle.

Winke, P., Goertler, S., & Amuzie, G. L. (2010). Commonly taught and less commonly taught language learners: Are they equally prepared for CALL and online language learning? *Computer Assisted Language Learning, 23*(3), 199–219.

Young, D. J., & Pettigrew, J. L. (2012). Blended learning in large multisection foreign language programs: An opportunity for reflecting on course content, pedagogy, learning outcomes, and assessment issues. In F. Rubio & J. Thoms (Eds.), *AAUSC 2012 Volume—Issues in language program direction: Hybrid language teaching and learning: Exploring theoretical, pedagogical and curricular issues* (pp. 92–136). Boston: Heinle.

19

RESEARCH-BASED INTERNET WRITING PROJECTS IN THE RUSSIAN CURRICULUM

Cori Anderson and Irina Walsh

Writing assignments in the foreign language curriculum often function as a means of evaluating student progress in the acquisition of vocabulary and grammar structures rather than as an authentic task aimed at developing learners' proficiency. At lower levels of instruction (first- and second-year) and student proficiency (Novice Mid to Intermediate Mid), topics for such writing assignments generally are limited to a student's personal information (e.g., family, living accommodations) and practical needs (e.g., making plans via text messages). However, students at the university level often do not find such assignments intellectually stimulating. To increase student interest and to support the development of learners' writing proficiency, we propose research-based Internet writing projects on Russian culture, current events, and topics of students' academic and personal interest, which can be implemented as early as the first year of language study.[1]

We present two models of such projects, which allow students to learn through writing rather than write for assessment alone: a class blog, in which students write entries and comment on other students' entries; and a wiki project, in which students individually or collaboratively produce a single website on a particular topic. Depending on their level of proficiency, students conduct research for the projects in the native language (L1) or in the target language (TL), relying on Russian and non-Russian sources. They use the Internet, both to find information and to publish their final products.

The proposed models have several advantages. One is their adaptability, because students can choose any topic within the realm of Russian culture. We have found that these projects, when implemented throughout the Russian language curriculum, provide students with opportunities to acquire a deep understanding of Russian culture and contemporary issues and increase continuity between courses since students may write on the same topic across several semesters. From the students' perspective, having a choice of topics for research is also important because it allows them to individualize their study of Russian culture. Students develop a sense of ownership in the project and become invested in improving their language skills so that they can access more Russian-language sources and learn even more about their chosen topic in the future.

A second advantage is that these projects are scalable to all levels of instruction. The same model, whether a blog or a wiki, can be repeated with increasing complexity each year, which allows students to notice their progress in the language. The project topics can vary from semester to semester. The type of text students are asked to produce varies depending on their proficiency levels.[2] For instance, first-year students, who are typically at the Novice level, can produce a English-language blog on an aspect of Russian culture but can insert 10 to 15 Russian words and phrases in the text. Second-year students who have crossed the Intermediate level threshold can write their blog posts in Russian using loosely connected sentences on concrete topics, with perhaps one additional paragraph in English for abstract topics. In the third and fourth years, as students move toward the Advanced level of proficiency, they will write entirely in Russian and are encouraged to produce paragraph-length discourse using appropriate connecting devices. Increasing the complexity and length of text produced in Russian requires greater use of original sources as students' proficiency increases.

An additional advantage of project-based writing is that it engages multiple skills, which allows students to improve more than just their writing proficiency. Students read and listen to authentic materials as they conduct research and engage with the final products of their classmates. An oral component can be added to give students an opportunity to practice presentational speaking skills, and discussions or question and answer sessions about students' final products in the TL can enhance students' interpersonal speaking skills. By reading and contributing to each other's blogs and wiki pages, students use the TL for meaningful communication.

Our proposed projects meet the American Council of Teachers of Foreign Languages (ACTFL) World-Readiness Standards for Learning Languages—the Five Cs of Communication, Culture, Connections, Comparisons, and Communities—and they help prepare students to engage with a multilingual and multicultural world (NCSB, 2015).[3] More specifically, students are expected to *communicate* effectively in the TL in a variety of settings and in all three modes—interpersonal, presentational, and interpretive—and to use knowledge of the target *culture* in their interactions. Students are given opportunities to use these skills to make *connections* between the TL and the target culture (TC) and other fields of study or personal interest. They should be able to make *comparisons* between the L1 and the TL and between their native and target cultures, thereby gaining insights into the nature of language and the importance of cultural perspective. Finally, they should use their communicative skills and cultural competence to participate in *communities* of speakers "at home and around the world" (NSCB, 2015).

Communication is a natural component of any writing assignment, as students use the TL to express ideas to a reader, and research-based projects incorporate multiple modes of communication. Our writing projects also require students to engage with various elements of the TC (e.g., current events, historical figures, and authentic source materials). Students make connections to other disciplines while using the TL as they work with Russian sources on a variety of topics during the process of conducting research and evaluating different perspectives. The projects also provide students with excellent opportunities to make comparisons between the TL and their L1 and between cultural products and practices that are relevant to the topic of a given project. For instance, in a project on Russian geography our students have compared the historical expansion of borders in Russia and the United States and for a current events project students have noted the differing perspectives of mass media in Russia and the West. Projects allow students to communicate outside the classroom through writing and engage with the Russian-speaking community on the Internet.

The proposed writing projects also lend intellectual complexity to a Russian course at any level. Students conduct research about their chosen topics and must think critically as they present sometimes disparate points of view from Russian and non-Russian sources and develop analytical skills by evaluating the form and content of what their classmates have written through peer evaluation and in-class presentations and discussions.

Finally, there are important benefits of the blog and wiki models that reach beyond developing language abilities. By participating in such writing projects students learn to conduct independent research both in L1 and in the TL. In first-year projects students use a finite set of Internet sources provided by the instructor, the majority of which are in English. In subsequent courses students are better prepared to find new sources on their own, including through Russian-language search engines and reference websites, and to take responsibility for their study of Russian culture.

While working on these projects students gain experience with technology as they use blogging sites or wiki platforms to share and exchange information and store various multimedia elements (such as pictures, video clips, links, and glossaries).[4] In addition, these projects aid in the development of skills necessary for effective presentations because students must consider both the logical and visual organization of information. Working with Internet-based platforms prepares them better for the demands of today's workforce.

In the next section we discuss how we prepare students to engage in research and writing. We then describe two models of research-based Internet writing projects, that is, blogs and wikis, followed by three sample topics: a biography wiki project, a current events blogging project, and a geography wiki project. We conclude with recommendations for successful implementation of the projects.

PREPARING STUDENTS FOR THE WRITING PROCESS: PREWRITING ACTIVITIES, INSTRUCTOR FEEDBACK, AND PEER- AND SELF-EDITING

When working with research-based Internet writing projects we implement both product- and process-oriented approaches to writing.[5] Students who follow the product-oriented approach read an appropriate model of a wiki article or a blog post to become familiar with the characteristics of the genre. With the instructor's guidance, students analyze the model's various linguistic components: first- and second-year students focus on vocabulary and syntax while third- and fourth-year students concentrate on connecting devices and paragraph structure. Students are given a variety of prewriting assignments, including rephrasing, sentence combination, summarizing, and sentence completion activities.

In accordance with the process-oriented approach to TL writing, instructors should dedicate class time to brainstorming topics, drafting sample outlines, and making lists of relevant vocabulary. For instance, when preparing to write about Russian geography, students should brainstorm what information to include in their articles, in what order to present that information, and what vocabulary to use for discussing the topic. Next they should read a sample essay about the geography of Moscow and create an outline of the reading, comparing it to the topics from the brainstorming activity. Finally, students should answer comprehension questions in Russian and analyze the text for grammatical constructions and the vocabulary they may need for their own essays. Students can create semantic maps from the lexical items referring to location, history, topographical features, and climate.

In addition to prewriting activities, feedback and revision are important components of the writing process regardless of the approach. Corrective feedback from the instructor has shown to have beneficial results on learner writing (Fathman & Whalley, 1990; Ricken, 1991; Frantzen, 1995; Ferris, 1997). Students can receive this feedback as written commentary or orally during teacher-student conferencing. Feedback should involve more than error identification at the word or sentence level (e.g. agreement errors, or spelling or word choices); it should also bring attention to issues at the global level, such as organization, syntax, and the use of connectors to create a cohesive text. For feedback to be effective students need to know how to interpret it. For instance, instructors can mark errors with a code; afterward, during an in-class self-correction workshop, students can work with the codes to edit their essays (Lalande, 1982; Ferris, 2001).

Other means of feedback, such as peer- and self-editing, engage students in the evaluation process (Roebuck, 2001; Brown et al., 2009). The goal of self-editing is not for learners to develop perfect accuracy in the TL but rather to become independent writers: "Self-editing allows learners to review their compositions in a detailed manner, focusing on content and organization, in addition to grammar" (Roebuck, 2001, p. 210). Self-editing is an effective tool in the writing process, even at the Novice level, because it creates a greater sense of ownership as learners become more aware of their writing and gain a deeper understanding of the TL grammar. Self-editing also allows students to see writing as a process, which can make them more comfortable with writing in the TL outside of the classroom. Before students can participate in meaningful self-editing they need instruction on how to recognize typical errors, such as those related to case and agreement, in order to be able to identify and avoid them in the future.

Peer-editing can be another useful approach to providing feedback on TL writing, either as an in-class activity or as an assignment outside of class. One immediate advantage of peer-editing is higher motivation to write a "respectable first draft" because work will be scrutinized by peers and, moreover, "the skills gained through peer-editing will ultimately assist students in editing their own compositions" (Roebuck, 2001, p. 210). As with self-editing, students benefit from direct instruction and the setting of clear guidelines, such as when the instructor explains the purpose of the task and provides a rubric for students to complete while editing. The peer-editing task may be used for checking accuracy, organization, and content (Brown et al., 2009).

However, peer-editing presents a number of potential challenges. For instance, stronger students may not receive valuable feedback, while weaker students may struggle to participate in the peer-editing process. One way to overcome this inequality is to use groups of three or four rather than pairs. Assigning each student two essays to peer-edit can create more opportunities for meaningful feedback and reduce the risk of stronger students not receiving helpful comments. Stronger students will still benefit from the peer-editing process, as they will learn how to explain their feedback. An additional issue is that students may not feel comfortable sharing their work with a classmate or with giving critical feedback to a classmate. Maintaining anonymity during the peer-editing process can alleviate some of this anxiety. In our experience attitudes toward peer-editing vary from cohort to cohort. Asking students to comment on whether they found the process useful can help instructors decide whether to continue it in subsequent semesters.

In summary, when implementing research-based Internet projects it is important for instructors to incorporate both product- and process-oriented steps: to provide models of TL writing on a similar topic, to instruct students on the process of writing, to give meaningful feedback, and to include students in the editing process. In the following section we present detailed descriptions of the writing projects that we implement in our respective classrooms.

SAMPLE RESEARCH-BASED INTERNET WRITING PROJECTS

Students can engage in research-based Internet writing alongside traditional compositions, starting as early as the first year of study. Table 19.1 summarizes how we implement a range of writing projects throughout our curricula.

Through the wiki and blogging projects we encourage students to learn about the TC and make connections between their study of Russian and other areas of academic or personal interest. Furthermore, the scaffolding in the curriculum helps students conduct research in the TL and introduces best practices for creating engaging articles with images and hyperlinks on Internet-based platforms.

Many of the projects and topics can be repeated, with increasing linguistic challenges, that is, incorporating more Russian and less English, as students move through the curriculum. For example, the first-year blogging project requires students to mostly

TABLE 19.1. Sample Three-Year Writing Curriculum

Course/Level	Writing Assignment
1st semester	• Culture paper, in English (optional)
2nd semester	• Composition, in Russian (100–150 words) • Current events blog or wiki, in English *OR* Biography of Russian figure, half in Russian, half in English
3rd semester	• Composition, in Russian (150–200 words) • Pen Pal email exchange, in Russian
4th semester	• Composition, in Russian (250 words) • Current events blog or wiki, half in Russian, half in English *OR* Geography wiki project, in Russian
5th semester	• Composition, in Russian (300–400 words), geared toward practicing advanced skills (narration, description, summation) • Current events blog or wiki, in Russian
6th semester	• Composition, in Russian (400–500 words) • Literature or film wiki, in Russian

Note: The first semester optional culture paper (for extra credit) is not part of the writing curriculum per se, but it does allow students to begin personalizing their study of Russian culture immediately. The second semester composition assignment (an offline writing project) and the third semester Pen Pal project (which is not based on research) are outside the scope of the present discussion.

write in English using only a few words in the TL (nouns, proper nouns, dates), but the biography project allows students of the same level to write half of the article in Russian even though their sources are still primarily in English. In the second year students are expected to produce texts using a mix of Russian- and English-language sources, with a greater percentage of Russian, depending on the topic of research. In the third year students write their entire texts in Russian and use exclusively Russian-language sources. This linguistic scaffolding gives students an opportunity to track their own progress from semester to semester, both in their writing proficiency and in their reading and listening comprehension (e.g., from audiovisual sources), as they use more Russian-language sources for their research.

The Wiki Model and the Blogging Model

A wiki project involves publishing articles on a particular topic on a website that can be edited and viewed by anyone in the course.[6] On the wiki website students create subpages for their articles and thus can make digressions from their original themes or delve deeper into certain aspects of their topic. Students supplement their articles with pictures, citations, hyperlinks, and a glossary of new words. Depending on the size of the class, students can work on their wiki articles either individually or as a group. Wiki projects are inherently student centered: students are responsible for their individual final products on the group website. However, when students work in groups they collaborate on the layout of their group's subpage, which somewhat blurs the boundaries of individual authorship. The wiki page featuring student-produced output becomes input for other students in the class. Thus students are both the authors and the audience of the project (Thorne & Payne, 2005).

Like wikis, blogs allow students to write posts of varying length and sophistication on topics of students' interest, with images, citations, hyperlinks, and a glossary.[7] Unlike a wiki, however, which requires a single article, a blog is updated on a regular basis with multiple short blog posts. For instance, students may write one post per week over the course of a month, or less frequently over the course of an academic term. As part of the project students read their classmates' posts and leave comments, because as in the wiki project, students are both the authors and audience of the project. Blogs allow for a high level of asynchronous interaction between the writer and the readers (via the comments feature), which gives students an opportunity for rethinking, revising, and negotiating meaning (Ducate & Lonicka, 2005). Unlike a wiki project, in which writing can be collaborative and authorship is blurred, the blogging model accentuates authorship (Thorne & Payne, 2005) because posts are written by single authors.

In the following subsections we present one project for each of the three years of language curriculum outlined in Table 19.1. Two of the projects are based on the wiki model and one project demonstrates the blogging model.

Biography Wiki Project for First-Year Russian

Given the content of many first-year Russian textbooks and the proficiency outcomes for these courses, most students can write autobiographies or biographies toward the end of a first-year sequence. To build on that and to make a connection between the course material and Russian culture, the second-semester students find English-language information online about prominent Russians (authors, scientists, politicians, artists, etc.), then write a 500-word biography, half in Russian and half in English, and then either post it on the course website as a wiki article or present their findings orally in class, or both. Students choose a figure based on their academic and personal interests. They use Russian to provide basic information about the person, such as date and place of birth and death, and the figure's field, location of university study, and perhaps family background, utilizing vocabulary that is introduced in first-year textbooks. Students use English to explain why their chosen individual is of interest and provide more detailed information about the significance of the figure to Russian culture. (See Appendix A for the project's specific instructions.)

In order to guide students in organizing the information in their projects we first read several sample biographies in class. Students write a first draft of the biography, engage in self- or peer-editing of their writing, receive instructor feedback on it, and revise the work into a final draft. Next students post edited articles to the course wiki site, adding images and links to source materials. Students are responsible for making the wiki page clear and easy to navigate.[8] Students make oral presentations as the final stage of the project. During the presentation the rest of the class takes notes and then participates in a question-and-answer session. The note-taking and question sessions may be conducted in English or Russian.

One advantage of creating a group wiki site and making oral presentations is that all students become familiar with a greater number of important figures from Russian history and culture. Instructors can hold students accountable for the information from the course wiki site by requiring them to ask questions during a question-and-answer session at the end of presentations, by incorporating this information into unit tests, or by using some other assessment of cultural literacy.

This project can be completed in a variety of ways: over the course of a semester, with only one component assigned outside of class each week; over the course of a month, with more work due each week; or over the course of a single week that is dedicated entirely to the project. The final grade for the wiki article is based on several components: timely submission of all drafts, evidence of self-editing, fulfillment of length and language requirements, accuracy of Russian (e.g., spelling, grammar, syntax, vocabulary), accuracy of English, evidence of research, organization of information, layout of wiki page, and citation of all sources. (The full rubric is given in Appendix A.) Our goal is to both assess the students' ability to communicate through writing in Russian and also ensure that students fully participate in the process of researching, editing, and publishing their articles. As with any research paper, the information must be accurate and sources must be cited, including for all images used. The rubric also includes a peer evaluation component; students read two of their classmates' articles and evaluate them according to the following criteria: is the Russian section easy to understand, is the English section easy to understand, is the information clearly organized, is the wiki page easy to navigate, and are all sources cited. The oral presentation is assessed for content, pronunciation and intonation, comprehensibility (including grammatical accuracy), and use of visual aids.[9]

Russian Geography Project for Second-Year Russian

The geography of Russia is an important component of cultural knowledge, yet students often learn little about it, especially what lies beyond the major cities. Therefore we designed the project to present students with an opportunity to explore various regions of Russia and to learn vocabulary related to both rural and urban features.

Students work individually or in groups (depending on the size of the class) to create a wiki site on the physical and social geographies of various parts of Russia.[10] They select a region of interest in Russia outside Moscow and Saint Petersburg to expand their knowledge of the country as a whole. Before students write their own wiki articles the instructor presents a sample project that fulfills requirements as they pertain both to form (i.e., vocabulary, syntax, connecting devices, layout) and content (i.e., accuracy of information). After analyzing the sample project students conduct Internet research on their chosen regions, using Wikipedia, encyclopedias, and other websites in the TL. Students write several texts of various lengths: a 300- to 400-word article about the physical geography of the region, a 200- to 300-word article about the history and social geography of a major city in the region, and finally a 100- to 150-word biography of a local prominent figure. In larger classes students may work in pairs or small groups to write about the physical geography of a region and work independently on the city and biography articles. In smaller classes students may need to work individually on all of the articles in order to allow for a greater number of regions being represented on the class wiki, in which case the length of the articles can be adjusted. As with the biography project, students write a first draft of each article, which receives either self- or peer-editing and instructor feedback. The second draft is reviewed by the instructor only before students post their articles on the wiki page. Students are required to create a page for each region on the wiki and may choose to put all articles on one page or arrange their essays on several pages. Students also evaluate the wiki pages of their classmates. Next, students give oral presentations in class using visual aids such as PowerPoint presentations and videos, while other students take notes and ask questions. They also reread their classmates' articles to prepare for in-class discussions, in which students determine the best region for a particular investment project, such as a chocolate factory, a stadium for the World Cup, or a new study abroad location for their university. Finally, students write a 200-word summary of the discussion, in Russian, which ensures that they pay close attention to and take notes during their classmates' contributions.

As with the biography project, students are evaluated on all components of the project, including their full participation in all stages of research, writing, editing, and creating the wiki page. Instructors evaluate student articles for the accuracy of grammar and vocabulary in Russian, the organization and accuracy of information, and the evidence of research and citations for all sources. Instructors may choose to require a certain number of references overall or of Russian-language references. When a group of students works on the same wiki page, each student's final grade includes evaluations from their teammates on the amount of effort s/he put into the project as well as a self-evaluation. These evaluations are part of the individual student's grade in order to prevent one strong student from carrying the whole group without recognition. A preproject contract, in which students explicitly state which members of the team are responsible for which aspects, signals to students that their work will be graded fairly and commensurate with effort. (A detailed grading rubric is given in Appendix B.)

Current Events Blog for Third-Year Russian

For this project students utilize a broad range of Internet news sources, such as websites of major newspapers, magazines, and radio stations that are available in Russian only, and also examine non-Russian sources for comparison.[11] Given the current nature of Russian-language media, with government and nongovernment outlets often publishing divergent information, a student may be asked to compare how different sources represent the same event (e.g., the government-supported newspaper «Аргументы и факты» vs. the independent «Новая газета», vs. Western media such as *The New York*

Times). For instance, students who focus on political issues may find more criticism of the Russian government in the American media than in the Russian media.

Students select from a set of topics that can be found in the news (domestic politics, foreign policy, business and economics, ecology and the environment, social issues, culture and the arts) and choose a particular issue/subtopic within that topic. Instructors approve students' choices to ensure that the blog covers a variety of topics. Before making their selections students are asked to spend time outside of class reading the recommended newspapers online to find a broad subtopic, such as the Russian oil industry.

Once students have selected their topics and subtopics, they read Internet newspaper articles and then share their findings with classmates in class. Outside of class students write weekly posts, without drafts, and post them to the course blog. In addition, students are required to read the blog posts of their classmates and leave comments on one or two that include questions or opinions. Reading and commenting allow for additional interactions between students outside the classroom. Alternatively, students can engage in an informational scavenger hunt, looking for answers to instructor-provided questions about the week's blog posts, as a way to interact with the writing of their classmates, for example, "find 10 things we learned this week."

Each blog post is evaluated by the instructor per the following categories: fulfillment of all process expectations, fulfillment of all product expectations, evidence of research, depth of analysis, organization of information, accuracy of writing, and citation of sources. Comments are evaluated for grammar, spelling, and content. (For a complete grading rubric see Appendix C.)

CONSIDERATIONS FOR IMPLEMENTING RESEARCH-BASED INTERNET WRITING PROJECTS

Research-based Internet writing projects have many advantages, as we have shown. However, implementing them takes careful planning, as there are multiple components and the technological aspect requires some training for instructors and students. Two factors should be considered before assigning research-based Internet writing projects: preparing students to conduct online research in Russian and choosing the appropriate online platform for publication of student work. Even though today's undergraduate students are comfortable finding information on the Internet, they are not necessarily able to apply research methods and analyses to Internet sources (or properly identify keywords to put into search engines). We ask our students to verify information by using more than one source, if that is possible. Students may also be required to provide a weekly annotated bibliography that explains why they found a particular source interesting or useful. Their explanations may be presented in English or in Russian, depending on the proficiency level.

Students may also be unfamiliar with particular wiki or blogging platforms. Library and information technology departments often can provide training sessions or make documentation available to students on how to create wiki pages or blog posts and how to edit their texts and layouts on a given platform. Instructors should ensure that all students possess the skills necessary to complete the project and dedicate time in class to reviewing and reinforcing these skills.[12]

Another issue to consider is whether to use a publicly available tool or a university-hosted site for posting the projects. Many publicly available tools, such as Wordpress and Blogger, are easily accessible and commonly used outside the university context. However, many public tools require students to create an account and raise concerns about online privacy. While it is possible to limit the ability of a website that can be found through search engines or limit access through password protection, some students may not be comfortable with posting their work on public sites.

Cost is another consideration: while many publicly available platforms are free to use, they display advertisements.[13] Alternatively, using tools and platforms integrated into an institution's Course Management System (CMS), such as Blackboard or Canvas, guarantees that students will already have an account, ensures the privacy of students, and will come at no cost and be free of advertisements.[14] Most major universities offer some means of creating simple websites or blogs, whether as part of the CMS or as a separate tool. One such tool is Confluence, which allows for both simple HTML commands and rich-text editing.[15] The disadvantages of university-hosted CMS tools are that these platforms may not be used beyond the university and thus do not provide transferable skills, plus they may be more difficult to use. However, if research-based Internet writing projects are used throughout the curriculum, students have the opportunity to master the technical side of the project during their first years of study, when more writing is done in English.

While there are clear advantages to using blogs and wikis for the purpose of engaging students with the work of their peers, the overall pedagogical design of the project should drive the choice of the specific platform rather than the reverse. For instance, a blogging project should involve students not only writing blog posts but also reading the posts of their classmates and engaging with these posts through comments (a form of peer-editing through conversation and a form of semiformal interpersonal communication). Creating a website for student-produced content should go beyond the text through the addition of images and hyperlinks to the sources used therein, thus requiring students to support their arguments with reliable sources. Requiring student interaction with the final product, through commenting or peer evaluation, is also a crucial element to these projects. Without this interaction the use of an Internet platform is equivalent to the traditional writing assignment but with the extra and unnecessary step of posting them online.

Plagiarism and machine translation are considerations for any writing assignment, and for these writing projects in particular, given the temptation for students to simply copy and paste from their online sources. Our guidelines (see Appendixes A, B, and C) clearly state that any project with plagiarized material will receive a score of zero. We also explain to students that we can recognize a suspiciously error-free usage of advanced grammatical constructions. In order to teach students to avoid plagiarism, we practice rephrasing texts during prewriting activities. We also discuss how to properly use an English-Russian dictionary and how to avoid word-for-word translations from English, which often result in awkward Russian constructions.

CONCLUSION

The research-based Internet writing projects presented here provide an alternative to traditional writing assignments. Our projects utilize both product- and process-oriented approaches to writing by incorporating prewriting activities and multiple stages of editing before producing a final article to be posted online. Traditional writing assignments, however, are often only product-oriented and are used as an evaluation of what students have learned in a unit.

By publishing their work on a class wiki or blog, students are able to interact with their classmates either as a group to create a collaborative wiki project or prepare for the next assignment of the project or asynchronously by commenting on each other's blog posts. Traditional writing assignments typically involve only the student and the instructor, or perhaps a peer editor. In our way students are both authors and audience, while only the instructor is the audience for a composition. The Internet component of these projects provides opportunities to gain technological literacy, information literacy, global perspectives, and research skills and experience in the TL.

We have designed our projects to allow students to choose a topic that relates to their individual interests, in connection to a particular aspect of Russian culture or history. In line with the World-Readiness Standards (NCSB, 2015), students use Russian to learn about other disciplines and see how continuing their study of Russian will benefit them in their other areas of interest. Students can bring their expertise in other fields to the writing projects and then take the information gained through these projects to other classes. Additionally, these projects provide a means for introducing new topics of Russian culture beyond the textbook and easily incorporating them into the curriculum.

Finally, by relying on a process-oriented approach to writing, with prewriting activities, multiple stages of editing, and peer evaluation, students have more opportunities to improve their proficiency in writing and reading. By adding oral components to these projects we also provide speaking and listening practice. These projects can be easily adapted to any topic and allow for meaningful writing assignments at all levels of TL proficiency. As the sample writing curriculum discussed here shows, such projects become increasingly complex as students progress in their study of Russian.

Our sample projects can be made appropriate for all levels of language learners by adjusting the language requirements to meet student proficiency. Furthermore, in upper-level and heritage-language classes, project-based learning provides structure to a curriculum that may not center around a textbook, as do many first- and second-year classes. Thus a writing project can serve as the backbone for such a course. For example, a current events blog can be a major component for a course focused on reading Russian newspapers, or a wiki page of Russian movies and directors can assist a course on cinema. These projects are truly flexible in their topics, length, complexity, and TL level, and they provide more meaningful opportunities for student writing than traditional writing assignments do.

APPENDIX A: BIOGRAPHY PROJECT DESCRIPTION AND GRADING RUBRIC

Russian Biography Wiki Project (First-Year Russian)

This term you will be creating a class wiki about a prominent Russian figure from history or today. You may choose any figure of interest to you. Here are some ideas to get you started:

Юрий Гагарин, cosmonaut
Александр Герцен, philosopher
Сергей Прокофьев, composer
Ольга Книппер, actress
Фёдор Достоевский, author
Александра Коллонтай, communist revolutionary
Виктор Пелевин, author
Вера Панова, author
Дмитрий Менделеев, scientist
Майя Плисецкая, ballerina
Александр Овечкин, hockey player
Александр Пушкин, author
Мария Шарапова, tennis player
Валентина Терешкова, cosmonaut
Владимир Маяковский, painter, poet
Лев Толстой, author
Казимир Малевич, painter
Пётр Чайковский, composer
Михаил Горбачёв, first (and last) president of USSR
Антон Чехов, author
Борис Ельцин, first president of Russian Federation
Дмитрий Шостакович, composer
Иван Павлов, physiologist
Михаил Барышников, ballet dancer, choreographer

You will do the primary research for and write a 500-word biography about the Russian figure you choose, half of which must be in Russian. Specifically, you will write in Russian about the basic facts of the person's life, such as when and where they were born, where they lived, what kind of family they had, basic information about their education and profession, and briefly why they are considered noteworthy. The English text should go into more detail about importance of this person to Russian history, culture, or society. This prepares you for writing projects in second-year Russian when *all* of your work will be in Russian.

You may use online sources as the basis of the biography. All websites and images should be cited in your blog entries, with a hyperlink to every source. The use of Wikipedia, whether in English or in Russian, is allowed (and encouraged!), although plagiarism will result in a grade of zero for the essay.

After you write your final draft you will post your work to a class wiki, which should include images, with citations, and links to any websites you consulted. You must also provide translations for any Russian words you have looked up outside of the class textbook. The class wiki site will be organized thematically and each group can choose to organize its site as they choose. Your web page(s) will be evaluated by classmates from other groups.

Finally, you will give a 2–3 minute oral presentation, in Russian, about your selected Russian figure. You must use visual aids, such as PowerPoint panels or Prezi slides, and you may only use one 3 × 5 notecard during your presentation. *NB*: you should be taking detailed notes on all the presentations. Also, questions about the great Russians presented by your classmates will be included on the final exam. The project will count as 10% of your final grade in the course.

Possible sources for your research include

- Encyclopedia Britannica: http://www.britannica.com
- Russian Wikipedia: http://ru.wikipedia.org/wiki/Заглавная_страница
- Русская виртуальная библиотека: http://www.rvb.ru/indices/author_index.htm

A note on dates: The Julian calendar was used in Russia until the October Revolution of 1917 (according to the Julian calendar). Thereafter the Gregorian calendar was adopted, and dates were shifted, e.g. "Old New Year" is now January 14. Consult the following site to accurately determine the Gregorian dates relevant for the life of the Russian figure you have chosen: http://en.wikipedia.org/wiki/Conversion_between_Julian_and_Gregorian_calendars.

Project Assessment

Online essay 60% (60 points)

- Timely submission, evidence of self-editing: 10 points
- Fulfillment of length and language requirements: 5 points
- Mechanics of Russian (grammar, syntax, vocabulary): 15 points
- Mechanics of English: 10 points
- Accuracy of information, evidence of research: 5 points
- Organization, coherence: 5 points
- Online layout: 5 points
- Citations: 5 points

Oral presentation 25% (25 points)

- Fulfillment and preparation: 5 points

- ◇ Pace: 5 points
- ◇ Pronunciation: 5 points
- ◇ Comprehensibility (grammar, vocabulary): 5 points
- ◇ Visual aids, notes: 5 points

Online evaluation 15% (15 points)

- ◇ Participation: 5 points
- ◇ Peer evaluation 1: 5 points
- ◇ Peer evaluation 2: 5 points

APPENDIX B: GEOGRAPHY PROJECT DESCRIPTION AND GRADING RUBRIC

Russian Geography Wiki Project (Second-Year Russian)

What are the 10 largest cities in Russia? What are the demographics of Siberia? These are questions that few Americans can answer, but for you as a student of the Russian language it is helpful to have the context of where the language is spoken.

For this project you will work in teams of two to three students to learn about a region. Please note that you cannot choose to work on Moscow or St. Petersburg, as the goal of the project is to introduce you to places that are less well-known to westerners.

Possible choices include (but are not limited to) the following:

- The Golden Ring (cities of Vladimir, Suzdal, Yaroslavl, Kostroma, Ivanovo)
- The Volga Region (cities of Nizhny Novgorod, Kazan, Ulyanovsk, Samara, Saratov, Volgograd, Astrakhan, Perm, Penza)
- The Urals (cities of Ufa, Yekaterinburg, Chelyabinsk, Magnitogorsk, Orenburg, Tyumen)
- Russia's Far East (cities of Vladivostok, Khabarovsk, Yakutsk, Nakhodka, Petropavlovsk-Kamchatsky, Blagoveshchensk)
- Northwest Russia (cities of Arkhangelsk, Murmansk, Smolensk, Novgorod Veliky, Tver, Vologda, Petrozavodsk, Tula)
- Northern Caucasus (cities of Grozny, Vladikavkaz, Novorossiysk, Sochi, Makhachkala, Pyatigorsk)
- Siberia (cities of Irkutsk, Novosibirsk, Omsk, Tomsk, Tyumen, Krasnoyarsk, Kemerovo, Novokuznetsk)
- The Black Sea Region (cities of Rostov-on-Don, Krasnodar, Novorossiysk, and the Crimean cities of Yalta, Sevastopol, Simferopol)

Teams will write collaboratively about the physical geography of their selected region, and students will write individually about the social geography and history of one city in the region. Teams will then work collaboratively to post their essays, along with images and links, to a class wiki, and prepare an oral presentation. Each student will also read two wiki pages on other regions created by their peers and evaluate their form and content. Finally, the class will participate in a group discussion to determine which city or region is best suited for future economic investment.

During the first several weeks of the semester you should read up on the region, using Russian and English websites. We will also read materials in class. Be sure to save the links you use as you will need to give proper citation of information and any images you take from it/them. You may use Wikipedia in English or in Russian, but plagiarism will result in a grade of zero.

Possible sources:

- Encyclopedia Britannica: http://www.britannica.com/
- Russian Wikipedia: http://ru.wikipedia.org/wiki/Заглавная_страница

Written assignment: This project will have several components: two essays written in Russian, two oral components, and the creation of a wiki page. These will be completed over the course of the semester.

- Essay 1 (team work): Где? (physical geography). Where is the region located? What is the terrain like? What is the weather like? What are the major cities? What are the major bodies of water, mountain ranges, etc.? 300–400 words.
- Essay 2 (individual work): Что? Кто? (social geography). What is the history of the region? What is the region/city known for today? What are the demographics of the region (age, ethnicity, religion, education, income, etc.)? What are the major industries and/or natural resources? 200–300 words.
- A mini-essay (100–150 words) on a prominent local figure (e.g., the city's mayor, a famous Russian from the region, etc.).

Web assignment (team work): Each team will create a wiki page for their selected region, including the essays for the cities. The page, built on the CMS, should include images (with citations) along with links to all websites consulted. Your page will be evaluated by members of other groups in the week following the posting of the project.

Oral presentation (team work): Based on what you learned, give a brief oral presentation on your region (~5 minutes), including visual aids (in the form of a PowerPoint or Prezi presentation, which should include any vocabulary you had to look up). During the presentation you may use one 3 × 5 notecard with notes.

Discussion: Investors are considering various regions in Russia for several new projects, such as a potential host city for the Olympics, location for an international film festival, or a Russian-language school for foreigners. You will discuss the pros and cons of each region and, based on what you have learned from the oral presentations, will determine which region is best suited for each project.

Summary of discussion: Summarize the class discussion and give your own point of view on the proposed location of potential host city for the Olympics, location for an international film festival, or a Russian-language school for foreigners. These should consist of two paragraphs, about 200 words total.

Project Assessment

Online essay 50% (50 points)

- Timely submission, evidence of self-editing: 10 points
- Fulfillment of length and language requirements: 5 points
- Mechanics of Russian (grammar, syntax, vocabulary): 15 points

- Accuracy of information, evidence of research: 5 points
- Organization, coherence: 5 points
- Online layout: 5 points
- Citations: 5 points

Oral presentation 25% (25 points)

- Fulfillment and preparation: 5 points
- Pace: 5 points
- Pronunciation: 5 points
- Comprehensibility (grammar, vocabulary): 5 points
- Visual aids, notes: 5 points

Discussion 10% (10 points)

- Active participation: 2 points
- Quality of content of contribution: 3 points
- Comprehensibility of contribution: 3 points
- Written summary of discussion: 2 points

Online evaluation 15% (15 points)

- Participation: 5 points
- Peer evaluation 1: 5 points
- Peer evaluation 2: 5 points

APPENDIX C: CURRENT EVENTS PROJECT DESCRIPTION AND GRADING RUBRIC (FIRST-YEAR RUSSIAN)

Current Events Blog

This term you will be following the current events in Russia by reading online news sources from both Russia and the West. In order to maximize benefits from this project you will choose the type of news to follow:

- ◇ Russian domestic politics and policy (ethnic conflict in Chechnya or the Caucasus, party politics, regional elections, federal appointments, major legislation, politics in any of the major cities, etc.)
- ◇ Russian foreign policy (Russia and: Ukraine, Turkey, Belarus, Baltic States, Central Asian States, the United States, Western European countries, China, Iran, North Korea, Africa, India, Pakistan, the Middle East, NATO, etc.)
- ◇ Russian business and the Russian economy (significant indicators on un/employment, savings and investment, gross national product, family income, consumer confidence, manufacturing, trends in individual business sectors [such as mining, timber, gas and oil], legislation related to business or trade, etc.)
- ◇ Russian environment, natural resources, and ecology (deforestation, urban sprawl, traffic, air pollution, water pollution, water and desalinization, extinction of species, gas and oil, gold, uranium, nickel, recycling or lack thereof, etc.)
- ◇ Russian culture and the arts (literature, film, theater, music, opera, ballet, fine art, architecture, popular music [including bands, concerts, performances], etc.)
- ◇ Russian social issues (alcoholism, tobacco use, declining life spans, declining birth rates, health care, migration, religious holidays, trends in attendance at churches, mosques, or synagogues, conscription, hazing in the military, birth centers, emergency assistance, funeral practices, etc.)

In January you will choose a topic, and a subtopic, in order to ensure that there is not a significant amount of overlap between entries to the class blog.

During February you and your classmates will write entries on your topics for a class blog. This site will be open only to students enrolled in this course. You will write four weekly blog entries (250–300 words each) and you will be required to write thoughtful comments/responses on two of your classmates' posts, roughly 25–50 words each. These comments must be on posts about a topic that is different than yours. New vocabulary (words that you have to look up or that are not in the active vocabulary of the class) must be given in translation.

You will be using a variety of online sources as the basis for your blog posts. All websites and images that you use should be cited in your blog entries, with a hyperlink to every source. Furthermore, you are required to cite at least one Russian-language website per entry. You must also cite one non-Russian website, such as *The New York*

Times, *The Guardian*, BBC, etc. The use of Wikipedia for background information, whether in English or Russian, is allowed (and encouraged!), but plagiarism will result in a grade of zero for the given post. Machine translation will also result in a grade of zero for the given post.

Possible Russian-language sources:

- Российская газета: http://rg.ru/
- *Russia today*: http://russian.rt.com/
- A popular Russian news site: http://lenta.ru/
- Russian BBC service: http://www.bbc.co.uk/russian/
- RIA Novosti (a government news agency): http://ria.ru/
- *Novaya Gazeta* (an independent newspaper): http://www.novayagazeta.ru/
- Popular Russian search engine: http://www.yandex.ru/

Possible English-language newspapers based in Russia:

- http://www.sptimes.ru/
- http://www.themoscowtimes.com/

Summary of Project:

—Four blog posts total, one per week (200–250 words each)
—Eight comments total, two per week (25–50 words each)
The project will have a total score of 100 points.

Blog Entries: 80% (20 points each)

- Completion: 3 points
- Grammar/syntax: 5 points
- Vocabulary: 4 points
- Organization (paragraph structure, connective devices, online layout): 3 points
- Originality/creativity (variation of sentence type, interesting to read, etc.): 3 points
- Proper citation of all sources and images: 2 points

Comments: 20% (2.5 points per comment)

- Completion: 0.5
- Grammar/syntax: 1
- Vocabulary: 0.5
- Comment is on topic, thoughtful: 0.5

NOTES

1. We thank Benjamin Rifkin for the original design of the wiki project model described here. We also extend our gratitude to Katherine Duda, Emily Ewers, Erin Franklin, Zachary King, Benjamin Jens, Colleen Lucey, Esther Peters, Antje Postema, Matthew Sutton, and Ted Trotman for their assistance in implementing writing projects, and thank the students at our current and previous institutions for providing feedback on earlier versions of the projects.
2. All references to proficiency levels in this article are based on the ACTFL Proficiency Guidelines (2012).
3. Written communication skills and information literacy are both part of the essential learning outcomes of the liberal education and America's Promise Initiative of the American Association of Colleges and Universities (2007). These learning outcomes take into consideration the skills that should be developed in a liberal arts education in the 21st century and that will provide students with tools that future employers will seek in today's college graduate. See Rifkin (2012) for a discussion of how the foreign language curriculum as a whole is compatible with many other learning outcomes.
4. A blog is a website that contains multiple postings over time, posted by one or more authors. Posts are not edited after publication but the website is updated with the addition of each posting. A wiki page is one website that has multiple authors or can be edited by multiple authors; the final product may have inaccuracies but is a quick and simple way to compile information to share with others via the Internet. It can be quickly updated and edited over time.
5. A product-oriented approach to writing asks students to follow a model text (Hyland, 2003; Matsuda, 2003; Llach, 2011) whereas a process-oriented approach views writing as consisting of multiple actions: brainstorming, planning, outlining, drafting, revising, reviewing, analyzing, and synthesizing (Scott, 1996; Hyland, 2003).
6. By "article" we mean a self-contained summary of independent research that is shorter in length than a traditional research paper. The style of the article should not be conversational but is not necessarily held to the standards of academic writing.
7. A blog post is a discrete entry onto a website that is updated on a regular basis. The style of the post is not entirely informal but also is not held to academic or journalistic standards.
8. Students receive in-class training from instructors on organizing their wiki pages before the start of the project, as well as on detailed description of potential issues, such as how to use headings for sections or how to insert hyperlinks.
9. The presentation should be comprehensible to listeners accustomed to dealing with non-native speech, in line with the ACTFL Proficiency Guidelines (2012) for learners at the Novice and Intermediate levels.
10. This topic is particularly appropriate in the second year of study, as many students go abroad after this year.

11. The inclusion of both Russian and non-Russian sources allows students to consider differences in media coverage. The ACTFL World-Readiness Standard for Comparisons specifically states that students should be able to compare the target culture with the native culture, so examining both Russian and non-Russian perspectives is an important component of the project (NCSB, 2015).
12. In our experience it often takes just a few minutes in class to direct students to resources before they begin and to answer any questions as they arise.
13. The cost primarily occurs at the institutional level rather than for individuals. Most institutions have support for instructional technologies that can offer guidance on what options are available locally.
14. Wiki sites and blogging capabilities are typically included in most course management software platforms, such as Blackboard or Canvas. Some universities may also offer additional platforms, such as Confluence.
15. Rich-text editing allows the text to appear on the editing screen as it will appear on the published site.

REFERENCES

American Council on the Teaching of Foreign Languages (ACTFL). (2012). ACTFL Proficiency Guidelines. Retrieved from http://www.actfl.org/publications/guidelines-and-manuals/actfl-proficiency-guidelines-2012

Association of American Colleges and Universities. (2007). *College learning for the new global century: A report from the National Leadership Council for Liberal Education and America's Promise.* Washington, DC: Association of American Colleges and Universities.

Brown, A., Bown, J., & Eggett, D. (2009). Making rapid gains in second language writing: A case study of a third year Russian language course. *Foreign Language Annals, 42*(3), 424–52.

Ducate, L., & Lonicka, L. (2005). Exploring the blogosphere: Use of web logs in the foreign language classroom. *Foreign Language Annals, 38*(3), 410–21.

Fathman, A., & Whalley, E. (1990). Teacher response to student writing: Focus on form versus on content. In B. Kroll (Ed.), *Second language writing: Research insights for the classroom* (pp. 178–90). Cambridge: Cambridge UP.

Ferris, D. (1997). The influence of teacher commentary on student revision. *TESOL Quarterly, 31*(ii), 315–39.

Ferris, D. (2001). Error feedback in L2 writing classes: How explicit does it need to be? *Journal of Second Language Writing, 10*(3), 161–84.

Frantzen, D. (1995). The effect of grammar supplementation on written accuracy in an intermediate Spanish content course. *The Modern Language Journal, 79*(3), 329–55.

Hyland, K. (2003). *Second language writing.* Cambridge: Cambridge UP.

Lalande, J. (1982). Reducing composition errors: An experiment. *The Modern Language Journal, 66*, 140–49.

Llach, M. P. A. (2011). *Lexical errors and accuracy in foreign language writing.* Bristol, UK: Multilingual Matters.

Matsuda, P. K. (2003). Second language writing in the twentieth century: A situated historical perspective. In B. Kroll (Ed.), *Exploring the dynamics of second language writing* (pp. 15–34). New York: Cambridge UP.

National Standards Collaborative Board (NSCB). (2015). *World-readiness standards for learning languages* (4th ed.). Alexandria, VA: Author. Retrieved from http://www.actfl.org/publications/all/world-readiness-standards-learning-languages

Ricken, E. (1991). *The effect of feedback on the frequency and accuracy of use of the passé compose by field-independent and field-dependent students of beginning French* (Doctoral dissertation). University of Illinois at Urbana-Champaign.

Rifkin, B. (2012). The world language curriculum at the center of postsecondary education. *Liberal Education, 98*(3). Retrieved from http://www.aacu.org/liberaleducation/le-su12/rifkin.cfm

Roebuck, R. (2001). Teaching composition in the college level foreign language class: Insights and activities from sociocultural theory. *Foreign Language Annals, 34*(5), 206–15.

Scott, V. M. (1996). *Rethinking foreign language writing.* Boston: Heinle & Heinle.

Thorne, S., & Payne, S. (2005). Evolutionary trajectories, Internet-mediated expression, and language education. *CALICO Journal*, *22*, 371–97.

EDITORS

Evgeny Dengub is a senior lecturer at the University of Massachusetts–Amherst. He holds a PhD in Russian and second language acquisition from Bryn Mawr College. He teaches Russian at all levels and is an ACTFL certified oral proficiency and writing proficiency tester. He is the coauthor of *Panorama: Intermediate Russian Language and Culture* (Georgetown UP, 2017), the winner of the Best Contribution to Language Pedagogy prize from AATSEEL in 2019. He is the founder and director of TeachRussian.org, an online resource center for Russian teachers.

Irina Dubinina is an associate professor and the director of the Russian language program at Brandeis University. She teaches Russian at all levels, including introductory and advanced courses for heritage speakers, and is the recipient of two prizes for excellence in teaching. She is the coauthor of a textbook for Russian heritage learners, *Rodnaya Rech'* (Georgetown UP, 2019). Her research interests focus on pragmatics in heritage Russian and heritage language pedagogy, which are the topics of many articles written and coauthored by her.

Jason Merrill is a professor of Russian at Michigan State University. He is the coauthor of *Animation for Russian Conversation* (2008) and *Russian Folktales: A Reader for Students of Russian* (2016) and the author of articles on the works of the symbolist Fedor Sologub, on Russian cinema, and on Russian pedagogy. Since 2010 he has served as the director of the Middlebury College Kathryn Wasserman Davis School of Russian.

CONTRIBUTORS

Cori Anderson, PhD, is the Russian language program coordinator in the Department of Germanic, Russian and East European Languages and Literatures at Rutgers University. She holds a PhD in Slavic and theoretical linguistics from Princeton University. She has taught Russian at all levels, methods of teaching Slavic languages, and linguistics. Her research interests include foreign language writing development, teacher training, heritage language learning, and Baltic morphosyntax.

Christine Campbell, the president of Campbell Language Consultants (PhD in foreign language education, Purdue University, 1986) has worked in language education for over 30 years, managing language and assessment programs and teaching world languages—Spanish, French, and ESL. Associate provost of the Defense Language Institute Foreign Language Center for nine years, she has most recently published in the areas of achieving higher levels of proficiency and technology applied to language learning. She is a member of the editorial boards of *Applied Language Learning* and *Dialog on Language Instruction*. In 2015 she joined the editorial board of the *New Horizons Report: Innovating Language Education*. She has served as president of the American Association of the Teachers of Spanish and Portuguese and as a member of the board of governors, UC Consortium for Language Learning and Teaching. She was named Distinguished Alumna by Purdue University in 1994.

William J. Comer, PhD, is a professor of Russian and director of the Russian Flagship Program at Portland State University. His main research interests include input processing and structured input approaches for teaching Russian grammar and the pedagogy of reading in Russian as a foreign language. His edition of Viktoria Tokareva's short story *A Day without Lying* (Slavica, 2008) makes the story accessible to Intermediate-level students of Russian, and it won the American Association of Teachers of Slavic and East European Languages (AATSEEL) prize for Best Book in Language Pedagogy in 2010. He is coauthor of *Mezhdu nami*, an online, open-access textbook for elementary Russian, which implements an input-rich approach to teaching Russian.

Lynne deBenedette is a senior lecturer in Russian at Brown University. She is the coauthor, with William J. Comer, Alla Smyslova, and Jonathan Perkins, of the first-year Russian language textbook *Mezhdu nami*. At Brown she coordinates the Russian language program and teaches Russian and (occasionally) Czech.

Alla Epsteyn is a senior lecturer at Wellesley College, where she acts as director of the winter Session-in-Moscow program for the Russian Department. A graduate of Moscow State University, she holds a PhD from the Academy of Sciences Institute of World History. Her research interest in language pedagogy stems naturally from her teaching experience and is reflected in her recent publications in Russia.

Karen Evans-Romaine is a professor of Russian at the University of Wisconsin–Madison and director of the UW–Madison Russian Flagship Program. Her research focuses on both Russian Modernist poetry, with particular reference to intersections between poetry and music, and Russian language pedagogy. She is coauthor, with Richard Robin and Galina Shatalina, of the two-volume introductory Russian textbook *Golosa*, now in its fifth edition (Pearson, 2012/2014); coeditor, with Dianna Murphy, of the collection *Exploring the US Language Flagship Program: Professional Competence in a Second Language by Graduation* (Multilingual Matters, 2017); and coeditor, with Tatiana Smorodinska and Helena Goscilo, of the Routledge *Encyclopedia of Contemporary Russian Culture* (2007).

Edie Furniss is a digital learning content developer in Helsinki, Finland. She has taught Russian in intensive summer programs across the United States for almost a decade and has coauthored a beginning Russian textbook, *Russian Full Circle* (Yale UP, 2013). Her research interests include interlanguage pragmatics, corpus linguistics, foreign language materials development, and computer-assisted language learning.

Vicki Galloway is a professor of Spanish and associate chair of the research and graduate programs in the School of Modern Languages at Georgia Institute of Technology, where she also serves as director of the Language for Business and Technology overseas programs in Mexico, Ecuador, and Peru. She teaches a wide variety of courses in language, literature, business, film, and culture studies, focusing on themes of sustainable development, immigration, indigenous issues and perspectives, and intercultural communication. She has authored eight textbooks, has published extensively in nationally prominent journals and professional volumes on second-language acquisition and intercultural communication, and has been editor of three volumes on content-based education and intercultural pedagogy and assessment.

Thomas J. Garza is a Distinguished Teaching Associate Professor in the Department of Slavic and Eurasian Studies and director of the Texas Language Center at the University of Texas at Austin. He teaches courses on the Russian language, language pedagogy, and contemporary Russian culture. He has received numerous prizes for undergraduate and graduate teaching. He has published numerous language textbooks, book chapters, and articles on Russian language and culture and online resources on language and culture. His current research is on reverse design and intensive language instruction and on comparative portraits of machismo in contemporary Russian and Latino popular cultures.

Aline Germain-Rutherford, PhD, is the vice provost of academic affairs at the University of Ottawa. Prior to her tenure at the University of Ottawa she was associate vice president of the language schools and graduate programs of Middlebury College and the director of the Middlebury College French School. She has received a doctorat de didactologie/didactique des langues et des cultures at La Sorbonne Nouvelle and is the author of numerous publications on faculty development, second language pedagogy, speech technology, and the integration of innovative pedagogy in e-learning practices. She has been a visiting professor and keynote speaker in Europe, North America, Asia, Africa, and the Middle East. She is a recipient of the 3M National Teaching Fellow Award, a Canadian award that recognizes excellence in teaching and leadership in higher education.

Stuart H. Goldberg is an associate professor of Russian at the Georgia Institute of Technology. He is the author of *Mandelstam, Blok and the Boundaries of Mythopoetic Symbolism* (Ohio State UP, 2011; authorized translation NLO, 2020), and articles on Russian poetry and Polish Romantic drama. He was initiator and director of the Georgia Tech Critical Languages Song Project and author of the Russian materials for it. His current project is *An Indwelling Voice: Sincerities and Authenticities in Russian Poetry, 1782–2006*, for which he was awarded an American Council of Learned Societies Fellowship (2017).

Benjamin Jens received his PhD in Slavic languages and literature from the University of Wisconsin–Madison. He is currently an assistant professor in the Department of Russian and Slavic Studies at the University of Arizona and has previously taught Russian language, literature, and culture courses at The College of New Jersey and the University of Vermont. Jens's main area of research is the use of silence as a mode of communication in 19th-century Russian literature; he also has research interests in Russian and East European cinema, Eastern Orthodoxy, and cultural ties between the western Balkans and Russia.

Olga E. Kagan was a professor in the UCLA Department of Slavic, East European and Eurasian Languages and Cultures and director of the Title VI National Heritage Language Resource Center (NHLRC). She coedited three volumes of research papers and 10 textbooks of Russian, both as a foreign language and as a heritage language. Her textbook of Russian as a heritage language, *Russian for Russians*, received a book award from the American Association of Teachers of Russian and Eastern European Languages (AATSEEL). Her main research interest was heritage language studies. In 2015 she received an MLA award for distinguished service to the profession. Dr. Kagan died in April 2018.

Olesya Kisselev is an assistant professor in the Department of Bicultural-Bilingual Studies, College of Education and Human Development at the University of Texas at San Antonio. She completed her PhD (2018) at the Pennsylvania State University in the Department of Applied Linguistics. Her dissertation, titled "Word Order and Information Structure in the Writing of Heritage and Second Language Learners of Russian," won the prestigious Dissertation Award Grant from the National Federation of Modern Language Teachers Association. Olesya's primary research interests include corpus linguistics and discourse analysis, especially as they apply to the study of various aspects of second language and heritage language acquisition. Her contributions to the field include published research as well as the textbook *Родная Речь: An Introductory Course for Heritage Learners of Russian*.

Angelika Kraemer is the director of the Language Resource Center at Cornell University. Prior to starting at Cornell in July 2018, she worked in the Center for Language Teaching Advancement (CeLTA) at Michigan State University for 10 years. Her research interests include online and blended learning, early language learning, program administration, and second language acquisition, and she has published and presented widely in these areas. She currently serves as coeditor of the journal *Die Unterrichtspraxis/Teaching German* published by the American Association of Teachers of German (AATG) and president-elect of the International Association for Language Learning Technology (IALLT).

Susan Kresin is a senior lecturer in the Department of Slavic, East European and Eurasian Languages and Cultures at UCLA, where she teaches Russian, Czech, and Slavic linguistics. She is the student coordinator of the UCLA Russian Flagship Program. Her research focuses on contemporary Russian and Czech, bridging the fields of linguistics and language pedagogy. She is a former vice president of the American Association of Teachers of Slavic and East European Languages and co-president of the International Association of Teachers of Czech, and a coauthor of the introductory Czech textbook *Čeština hrou*.

Anna S. Kudyma is a senior lecturer and teaching assistants supervisor in the UCLA Department of Slavic, East European and Eurasian Languages and Cultures. She holds an MA in Russian language pedagogy and a PhD in linguistics. Her primary interests are language pedagogy and computer-assisted language learning. She is the coauthor of textbooks, including a second-year Russian textbook, *V puti* (Prentice Hall, 2005), a first-year textbook, *Beginner's Russian* (Hippocrene, 2010), *Учимся писать по-русски: экспресс-курс для двуязычных взрослых* [*Learning to write in Russian: An express-course for bilingual adults*] (Zlatoust, 2011), a third- and fourth-year Russian textbook, *From Intermediate to Advanced* (Routledge, 2014), and *Russian Through Art* (Routledge, 2019).

Betty Lou Leaver (PhD, Pushkin Institute), recently retired as provost at the Defense Language Institute and is executive editor at MSI Press LLC. Previous positions have included chief academic officer/academic dean at New York Institute of Technology in Jordan; language supervisor at NASA; president of the American Global Studies Institute; and Russian language training supervisor at the Foreign Service Institute, along with 10 years of international educational consulting through American Councils for International Education, the US State Department, and ministries of education in 24 countries. During her career she has founded three centers (CelCAR at Indiana University, ADLP Center at San Diego State University, and the Coalition of Distinguished Language Studies) and published dozens of articles and books in the areas of foreign language acquisition, specific teaching methods, and learner differences in the United States, the United Kingdom, Russia, and Latin America.

Colleen Lucey is an assistant professor of Russian and Slavic Studies at the University of Arizona. She holds a PhD in Slavic Languages and Literature from the University of Wisconsin–Madison. Prior to joining the faculty at the University of Arizona, she taught at the Middlebury College Kathryn Wasserman Davis School of Russian and The College of New Jersey. Her research interests include the portrayal of prostitution in Russian literature, with particular focus on works of the late imperial period, as well as Russian language instruction. She has published widely on the politicization of commercial sex in nineteenth-century Russian culture and is the coauthor of *About That, Which Did Not Happen: An Annotated Russian Reader* (2015) and *Russian Folktales: A Reader for Students of Russian* (2016).

Sally Sieloff Magnan is a professor emerita of French at the University of Wisconsin–Madison. She had a 14-year tenure as editor of the *Modern Language Journal* and also served as series editor for the AAUSC publication Issues in Language Program Direction. Among her numerous publications she is the coauthor of the elementary French textbook *Paroles* (Wiley, 2006) and coauthor of the 2014 *Modern Language Journa*l monograph, *Goals of Collegiate Learners and the Standards for Foreign Language Learning*. Her main research has included proficiency testing, standards-based research and teaching, learner variables, and study abroad. While at UW–Madison she was founding director of the Language Institute and the doctoral program in second language acquisition.

Cynthia L. Martin (PhD in Slavic languages and literatures, University of Pennsylvania) is an associate professor of Russian at the University of Maryland, College Park. Martin's scholarly interests include second language acquisition and assessment (theory and practice), as well as contemporary Russian culture and art. She is the author of numerous publications and translations, including an intermediate-level Russian textbook, *Russian Stage II: Welcome Back!* (ACTR/Kendall Hunt, 2001, 2010).

She is an active ACTFL OPI certified tester and trainer and is currently involved in a number of national assessment initiatives for academia as well as commercial and government sectors.

Jason Merrill is a professor of Russian at Michigan State University. He is the co-author of *Animation for Russian Conversation* (2008) and *Russian Folktales: A Reader for Students of Russian* (2016) and the author of articles on the works of the symbolist Fedor Sologub, on Russian cinema, and on Russian pedagogy. Since 2010 he has served as the director of the Middlebury College Kathryn Wasserman Davis School of Russian.

Julia Mikhailova is an associate professor (teaching stream) in the Department of Slavic Languages and Literatures at the University of Toronto. She holds an MA in linguistics from Syracuse University and a PhD in Slavic linguistics from the Ohio State University. She coordinates the Russian language program, supervises teaching assistants, teaches a course on methods of teaching Slavic languages, and provides Russian instruction at all levels, including Russian for heritage speakers. She is a co-author of *Animation for Russian Conversation* (2008), and serves as the division head of the Pedagogy and Second Language Acquisition at AATSEEL Program Committee.

Dianna Murphy is the director of the Language Institute at the University of Wisconsin–Madison, where she also serves as associate director of the Russian Flagship, executive director of the Korean Flagship, and co-director of the Wisconsin Language Roadmap Initiative. She is also a core member of the UW–Madison doctoral program in second language acquisition. Her recent scholarship includes the 2017 edited volume (with Karen Evans-Romaine), *Exploring the U.S. Language Flagship Program: Professional Competence in a Second Language by Graduation*, the 2014 Modern Language Journal monograph (with Sally Sieloff Magnan and Narek Sahakyan), *Goals of Collegiate Learners and the Standards for Foreign Language Learning*, and the 2019 article in the ADFL Bulletin on the gender and race or ethnicity of US undergraduate majors in foreign languages, literatures, and linguistics.

Ekaterina Nemtchinova is a professor of TESOL and Russian at Seattle Pacific University, where she teaches courses in linguistics, methodology of foreign language teaching, and Russian language, literature, and culture. She holds an MA from Moscow State Linguistic University and a PhD in Applied Linguistics from SUNY Stony Brook. Her research interests include teacher education, particularly the issues of nonnative English speaking professionals in TESOL, and technology in language teaching. She was named Professor of the Year at Seattle Pacific University in 2018. In addition to articles, she published a Russian language textbook, *Listen Up!* (University Press of the South, 2011) and *Teaching Listening* (TESOL, 2020).

David Prestel is a professor emeritus of Slavic Languages and Literatures at Michigan State University. He served as senior associate dean for research and administration in the MSU College of Arts and Letters, codirector of the Center for Language Teaching Advancement (CeLTA), and chairperson of the Department of Linguistics and Germanic, Slavic, Asian and African Languages. His research and teaching interests include foreign language education, philology, and Early Slavic studies. He has published across these areas in addition to pursuing a sponsored research agenda.

Benjamin Rifkin received his PhD in Slavic languages and literatures from the University of Michigan. He is currently the dean of Hofstra University's College of Liberal Arts and Sciences. Rifkin has taught Russian at all levels, from first-year through graduate-level courses at UW–Madison, Temple University, The College of New Jersey, and the Middlebury College School of Russian. His primary research interests are foreign language education, especially performance-based learning outcomes assessment, applied linguistics, second language acquisition, and contemporary Russian film. In his work in university leadership, Rifkin has focused on reducing impediments to student participation in high-impact/transformative learning experiences such as study abroad, internships, community-engaged learning, and undergraduate research.

Narek Sahakyan is an associate researcher at the WIDA (World-Class Instructional Design and Assessment) Consortium at the Wisconsin Center for Education Research. His degree in agricultural and applied economics is from the University of Wisconsin–Madison, for his research in the field of economic corruption. Sahakyan's current research interests include time-series and panel data analysis, value-added models, and economics of ELL (English language learner) education.

Tatiana Smorodinska received a PhD in Russian literature from the Ohio State University and an MA in philology from Moscow State University. She teaches Russian language, culture, and literature courses at Middlebury College. Smorodinska published a book on the poetry of Konstantin Sluchevsky, several articles on Russian poetry, film, and language pedagogy, and was one of the editors of *Encyclopedia of Contemporary Russian Culture* (Routledge, 2007). She has authored Russian language textbooks, various teaching materials, and a digital anthology of literary texts used for language instruction.

Maia Solovieva is a faculty in residence and lecturer in the Department of Russian Language, Literature, and Culture at Oberlin College. She specializes in upper-level Russian instruction with emphasis on developing reading and writing skills. Her research interests include Chekhov's life and prose in the language classroom as well as various aspects of second language acquisition theory.

Shannon Spasova (PhD, Slavic languages and literature, University of Wisconsin–Madison; MEd, instructional design, University of Massachusetts–Boston) is an assistant professor of Russian in the Department of Linguistics and Germanic, Slavic, Asian and African Languages and technology specialist at the Center for Language Teaching Advancement at Michigan State University. She has taught Russian language and literature face-to-face, in an immersion setting, in a blended format, using interactive television, and online. She has participated in the award-winning curriculum development projects RAILS (Russian Advanced Interactive Listening Series) and "Real Life in Russia."

Rachel Stauffer holds a PhD in Slavic Languages and Literatures from the University of Virginia and is currently pursuing a Master's of Education in Equity and Cultural Diversity at James Madison University, where she teaches courses in Russian and Spanish. She has taught Russian language, literature, folklore, cinema, and culture in Virginia schools, colleges, and universities since the early 2000s. Her areas of expertise include theoretical and applied linguistics, Russian phonology, foreign language teaching methodology, and Russian literature and cinema. Her current projects are focused on integrating best practices in multicultural education and instruction in Russian language and culture courses.

Anna Tumarkin is the director of the Russian language program and the assistant director of the Russian Flagship Program in the Department of German, Nordic, and Slavic at University of Wisconsin–Madison. She holds a PhD in Russian Literature from UW–Madison. She teaches Russian at all levels and is an ACTFL certified oral proficiency tester. Her research interests include language teaching methodology, instructional technology, 19th- and 20th-century Russian literature and culture and Russian satire.

Irina Walsh is a lecturer in the Department of Russian at Bryn Mawr College, where she also completed a PhD in Russian and second language acquisition. She is codirector of the Russian Language Flagship Program and the Russian Language Institute. She teaches Russian language, film, and culture classes. Aside from L2 learner writing, she is interested in teaching through film, project-based learning, methods in language teaching, and Slavic morphology and etymology.

Kristen Welsh (PhD, Slavic languages and literatures, Yale University) is an associate professor of Russian area studies at Hobart and William Smith Colleges. She teaches Russian language, literature, culture, and film in a highly interdisciplinary program. In addition to the practice of language teaching she works on contemporary and 20th-century Russian-American writers, with publications and papers on Vladimir Nabokov, Vladislav Khodasevich, Olga Grushin, and Gary Shteyngart.

INDEX

Figures, notes, and tables are indicated by f, n, and t following the page number.

CPSIA information can be obtained
at www.ICGtesting.com
Printed in the USA
BVHW021108290721
613054BV00004B/50

9 781647 120016